Hermeneia
—A Critical
and Historical
Commentary
on the Bible

Acts of the Apostles

A Commentary on
the Acts of the Apostles

by Hans Conzelmann

Translated by
James Limburg, A. Thomas Kraabel, and
Donald H. Juel

Edited by
Eldon Jay Epp
with
Christopher R. Matthews

Fortress
Press

Philadelphia

Translated from the German *Die Apostelgeschichte* by
Hans Conzelmann; 2., verbesserte Auflage, 1972.
Handbuch zum Neuen Testament begründet von
Hans Lietzmann in Verbindung mit Fachgenossen,
herausgegeben von Günther Bornkamm, 7. © 1963
J. C. B. Mohr (Paul Siebeck), Tübingen. Biblical
quotations, unless otherwise noted, are from the
Revised Standard Version of the Bible, copyright
1946, 1952, © 1971, 1973 by the Division of Christian
Education of the National Council of the Churches of
Christ in the U.S.A., and are used by permission. The
fragment on the front endpaper is courtesy of the State
Museum in Berlin, capital of East Germany, Papyrus
Collection, Inventory Number P.11765, Photo of the
State Museum.

Library of Congress Catalog Card Number 86–45203
ISBN 0–8006–6018–8

Printed in the United States of America
Design by Kenneth Hiebert
Type set on an Ibycus System at Polebridge Press
2522A87   20–6018

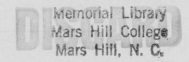
TO THE HIGHLY ESTEEMED
THEOLOGICAL FACULTY OF THE
RUPRECHT-KARLS-UNIVERSITY
AT HEIDELBERG
AS A TOKEN OF GRATITUDE
FOR THE HONOR BESTOWED
IN GRANTING A DEGREE OF
DOCTOR OF THEOLOGY

[1st edition, 1963]

Hans Conzelmann, born in 1915, served on the theological faculties at Tübingen, Heidelberg, and Zürich before assuming a position on the theological faculty at Göttingen. He is well known in English for *The Theology of St. Luke* (1960), *An Outline of the Theology of the New Testament* (1969), and *Jesus* (1973). He has also contributed to Kittel's *Theological Dictionary of the New Testament, Religion in Geschichte und Gegenwart, Das Neue Testament Deutsch,* the *Handbuch zum Neuen Testament,* and the *Meyer Kommentar.* His thorough revision of Martin Dibelius's *The Pastoral Epistles* and his commentary on *1 Corinthians* have already appeared in *Hermeneia.*

Contents
Acts of the Apostles

Commentary

The name *Hermeneia*, Greek ἑρμηνεία, has been chosen as the title of the commentary series to which this volume belongs. The word *Hermeneia* has a rich background in the history of biblical interpretation as a term used in the ancient Greek-speaking world for the detailed, systematic exposition of a scriptural work. It is hoped that the series, like its name, will carry forward this old and venerable tradition. A second entirely practical reason for selecting the name lies in the desire to avoid a long descriptive title and its inevitable acronym, or worse, an unpronounceable abbreviation.

The series is designed to be a critical and historical commentary to the Bible without arbitrary limits in size or scope. It will utilize the full range of philological and historical tools, including textual criticism (often slighted in modern commentaries), the methods of the history of tradition (including genre and prosodic analysis), and the history of religion.

Hermeneia is designed for the serious student of the Bible. It will make full use of ancient Semitic and classical languages; at the same time, English translations of all comparative materials—Greek, Latin, Canaanite, or Akkadian—will be supplied alongside the citation of the source in its original language. Insofar as possible, the aim is to provide the student or scholar with full critical discussion of each problem of interpretation and with the primary data upon which the discussion is based.

Hermeneia is designed to be international and interconfessional in the selection of authors; its editorial boards were formed with this end in view. Occasionally the series will offer translations of distinguished commentaries which originally appeared in languages other than English. Published volumes of the series will be revised continually, and eventually, new commentaries will replace older works in order to preserve the currency of the series. Commentaries are also being assigned for important literary works in the categories of apocryphal and pseudepigraphical works relating to the Old and New Testaments, including some of Essene or Gnostic authorship.

The editors of *Hermeneia* impose no systematic-theological perspective upon the series (directly, or indirectly by selection of authors). It is expected that authors will struggle to lay bare the ancient meaning of a biblical work or pericope. In this way the text's human relevance should become transparent, as is always the case in competent historical discourse. However, the series eschews for itself homiletical translation of the Bible.

The editors are heavily indebted to Fortress Press for its energy and courage in taking up an expensive, long-term project, the rewards of which will accrue chiefly to the field of biblical scholarship.

The translation of this volume began many years ago and a number of translators have contributed to its completion. James Limburg, in consultation with A. Thomas Kraabel, produced a first draft, which was then utilized by Donald H. Juel as the basis for a further, refined stage of the translation. When the volume editor took over the project, one task among many was the provision of the English translations for a number of Greek and Latin texts; these were provided largely by two Harvard doctoral students, Gregory Riley for the remaining Greek texts and Kelly Del Tredici for the Latin. In addition, numerous bibliographical entries, the Reference Codes, the Short Titles list, and the indices awaited completion, and countless other details required attention. Christopher R. Matthews, also a doctoral student at Harvard University, undertook the arduous task of preparing the entire volume for publication, and he did so with patience, competence, and meticulous care. The series editors, the volume editor, and the readers are heavily in his debt.

The editor responsible for this volume is Eldon Jay Epp of Case Western Reserve University.

December 1986   *Frank Moore Cross*   *Helmut Koester*
                For the Old Testament   For the New Testament
                Editorial Board   Editorial Board

The exegesis of the Acts of the Apostles presented here retains the seasoned style of the *Handbuch* series. This type of exegesis appears to me even today to have maintained its value not only for academic instruction and for the information of non-theologians, but also for the work of the clergy and of religious teachers. It provides resources so that students need not adopt readymade solutions and enables them instead to do their own work on the text. I have endeavored so to select the particulars of the literature that with their help all the essential materials can be found.

I wish to express thanks first of all to Ernst Haenchen. Although each of us reached our initial understandings of the Lukan writings independently, the collaboration that developed subsequently has been a constant source of enrichment.

I thank also my distinguished colleague at Göttingen, F. Wieacker, for translating and commenting on a difficult juristic text (Appendix 11). My former assistant, Miss Susi Hausammann, has aided me untiringly in producing the manuscript. Her contribution extends far beyond merely technical assistance. Later, two others joined in the work, my present assistant, Mr. Heinz-Dieter Knigge, who also undertook the final checking, and then Wolfgang Hinze, a student of theology and philosophy.

The publishing house of Vandenhoeck and Ruprecht made possible the provision of a map.

Geismar bei
Göttingen
23 May 1963

Hans Conzelmann

This new edition has been corrected and expanded. I am indebted to the publisher, Dr. *honoris causa* Hans Georg Siebeck, and his staff, as well as to my assistant, Mr. Wolfgang Hinze, for the painstaking effort that they have given to the production of the new version.

The first edition was dedicated to the Theological Faculty at the University of Heidelberg as a token of gratitude for the honor bestowed in granting a Doctor of Theology degree. My gratitude with respect to the Faculty of that time remains undiminished.

Geismar bei
Göttingen
2 May 1972

Hans Conzelmann

1. Sources and Abbreviations

Acts John	Acts of John
Acts Pet.	Acts of Peter
Acts Pil.	Acts of Pilate
Acts Thom.	Acts of Thomas
ad loc.	ad locum
Aelian	
Var. hist.	Varia historia
Aeschylus	
Agam.	Agamemnon
Eum.	Eumenides
Pers.	Persae
AGG	Abhandlungen der (königlichen) Gesellschaft der Wissenschaften zu Göttingen. Philologisch-historische Klasse
AGJU	Arbeiten zur Geschichte des antiken Judentums und des Urchristentums
AJT	American Journal of Theology
Angelos	Angelos: Archiv für neutestamentliche Zeitgeschichte und Kulturkunde
Ante-Nicene Fathers	The Ante-Nicene Fathers: Translations of the Writings of the Fathers down to A.D. 325 (10 vols.; ed. Alexander Roberts and James Donaldson; rev. and chronologically arranged by A. C. Coxe; American reprint of Edinburgh ed.; Grand Rapids: Eerdmans, 1952–53)
Antike	Die Antike: Zeitschrift für Kunst und Kultur des klassischen Altertums
ANTT	Arbeiten zur neutestamentlichen Textforschung
Ap. Jas.	Apocryphon of James
Apollonius Rhod.	Apollonius Rhodius
Arg.	Argonautica
Appian	
Bell. civ.	Bella civilia
Apuleius	
Met.	Metamorphoses
Aristeas	Letter of Aristeas
Aristophanes	
Eq.	Equites
Aristotle	
Eth. Nic.	Nicomachean Ethics
Arrian	
Anab.	Anabasis
ARW	Archiv für Religionswissenschaft
Asc. Is.	Ascension of Isaiah
ASNU	Acta seminarii neotestamentici upsaliensis
ASTI	Annual of the Swedish Theological Institute
AThANT	Abhandlungen zur Theologie des Alten und Neuen Testaments
Athenagoras	
Supplication	Supplication for the Christians
ATR	Anglican Theological Review
b.	Babylonian Talmud
BAG	W. Bauer, W. F. Arndt, and F. W. Gingrich, A Greek-English Lexicon of the New Testament
Barn.	Epistle of Barnabas
B.C.E.	Before the Common Era
BCH	Bulletin de Correspondance Hellénique
BDF	F. Blass, A. Debrunner, and R. W. Funk, A Greek Grammar of the New Testament
BETL	Bibliotheca ephemeridum theologicarum lovaniensium
BEvTh	Beiträge zur evangelischen Theologie
BFCTh	Beiträge zur Förderung christlicher Theologie
BGBE	Beiträge zur Geschichte der biblischen Exegese
BGU	Ägyptische Urkunden aus den Kgl. Museen zu Berlin
BHK	R. Kittel, Biblia hebraica
BHTh	Beiträge zur historischen Theologie
Bib	Biblica
BLE	Bulletin de littérature ecclésiastique
ByzZ	Byzantinische Zeitschrift
BZ	Biblische Zeitschrift
BZAW	Beihefte zur ZAW

BZNW	Beihefte zur *ZNW*	Dionysius Halic.	Dionysius of
ca.	*circa*, approximately		Halicarnassus
CAH	*Cambridge Ancient History*	*Ant. Roma*	*Roman Antiquities*
CBQ	*Catholic Biblical Quarterly*	Diss.	Dissertation
CD	Cairo (Genizah text of the) Damascus Document	ed(s).	editor(s), edited by, edition(s)
C.E.	The Common Era	e.g.	for example
cf.	compare with	*1 Enoch*	*Ethiopic Enoch*
chap(s).	chapter(s)	*Ep.*	*Epistle(s)*
Chrysostom		*Ep. ad. Jas.*	*Epistle of Clement to James* (Ps.- Clem.)
Hom. on Acts	*Homilies on the Acts of the Apostles*		
		Ep. Apost.	*Epistula Apostolorum*
Cicero		*Ep. Petri*	*Epistle of Peter to James* (Ps.-Clem.)
De leg.	*De legibus*		
Fam.	*Epistulae ad familiares*	*EThL*	*Ephemerides theologicae lovanienses*
Fin.	*De finibus*		
Nat. deor.	*De natura deorum*	Epiphanius	
Off.	*De officiis*	*Adv. haer.*	*Adversus haereses (Panarion)*
Philipp.	*Philippics*		
Rab. post.	*Pro rabirio postumo*	esp.	especially
Tusc. disp.	*Tusculanae disputationes*	Euripides	
Verr.	*In verrem*	*Bacc.*	*Bacchae*
CIG	*Corpus inscriptionum graecarum*	*Herc. fur.*	*Hercules furens*
		Iph. Taur.	*Iphigenia Taurica*
CII	*Corpus inscriptionum iudaicarum*	Eusebius	
		Chron.	*Chronica*
CIL	*Corpus inscriptionum latinarum*	*Hist. eccl.*	*Historia ecclesiastica*
		Praep. ev.	*Praeparatio evangelica*
CIS	*Corpus inscriptionum semiticarum*	*EvTh*	*Evangelische Theologie*
		ExpTim	*Expository Times*
1–2 Clem.	*1–2 Clement*	fasc.	fascicle
Clement Alex.	Clement of Alexandria	ff	(and the) following (pages)
Strom.	*Stromata*		
ClR	*Classical Review*	*FGH*	F. Jacoby (ed.), *Die Fragmente der griechischen Historiker*
col(s).	column(s)		
ConNT	*Coniectanea-neotestamentica*		
Constantine		fig(s).	figure(s)
Cod. Theod.	*Codex Theodosianus*	frg(s).	fragment(s)
Const. Ap.	*Apostolic Constitutions*	FRLANT	Forschungen zur Religion und Literatur des Alten und Neuen Testaments
Corp. Herm.	*Corpus Hermeticum*		
CSEL	Corpus scriptorum ecclesiasticorum latinorum		
		Frontinus	
DACL	*Dictionnaire d'archéologie chrétienne et de liturgie*	*Aq.*	*De aquaeductu urbis Romae*
DB	*Dictionnaire de la Bible*	GCS	Die Griechischen christlichen Schriftsteller der ersten drei Jahrhunderte
DBSup	*—Supplément*		
Demosthenes			
Orat.	*Orationes*		
Did.	*Didache*	*Gos. Heb.*	*Gospel of the Hebrews*
Dig.	*Digesta*	*Gos. Pet.*	*Gospel of Peter*
Dio Cass.	Dio Cassius Cocceianus	*Gos. Thom.*	*Gospel of Thomas*
Dio Chrys.	Dio Chrysostom	HAT	Handbuch zum Alten Testament
Or.	*Orations*		
Diodorus Sic.	Diodorus of Sicily	Heliodorus	Heliodorus of Emesa
Diogenes L.	Diogenes Laertius	*Aeth.*	*Aethiopica*
Diogn.	*Epistle to Diognetus*		

Herm.	*Hermas*	*Jos. Asen.*	*Joseph and Asenath*
Sim.	*Similitudes*	Josephus	
Vis.	*Visions*	*Ant.*	*Jewish Antiquities*
Hermeneia	Hermeneia—A Critical and Historical Commentary on the Bible	*Bell.*	*The Jewish War*
		C. Apion.	*Against Apion*
		Vita	*The Life*
Hermes	*Hermes: Zeitschrift für klassische Philologie*	*JQR*	*Jewish Quarterly Review*
		JR	*Journal of Religion*
Hippolytus		*JRomS*	*Journal of Roman Studies*
Ref.	*Refutatio omnium haeresium*	*JTS*	*Journal of Theological Studies*
HKAT	Handkommentar zum Alten Testament	*Jub.*	*Jubilees*
		Julian	
HNT	Handbuch zum Neuen Testament	*Or.*	*Orationes*
		Justin	Justin Martyr
Homer		*Apol.*	*Apology*
Il.	*Iliad*	*Dial.*	*Dialogue with Trypho*
Od.	*Odyssey*	Juvenal	
Horace		*Sat.*	*Satires*
Sat.	*Satires*	KEK	Kritisch-exegetischer Kommentar über das Neue Testament (Meyer)
HSCP	*Harvard Studies in Classical Philology*		
HTR	*Harvard Theological Review*	*Kg. Pet.*	*Kerygma Petri*
		KlT	Kleine Texte
HTS	Harvard Theological Studies	KNT	Kommentar zum Neuen Testament
Iamblichus		Lactantius	
Myst.	*De mysteriis*	*Inst.*	*Divinae institutiones*
Vita Pyth.	*De vita Pythagorica*	LCL	Loeb Classical Library
idem	the same (author)	LD	Lectio divina
i.e.	that is	Lucian	Lucian of Samosata
IG	*Inscriptiones graecae*	*Abdic.*	*Abdicatus*
Ignatius		*Alex.*	*Alexander*
Eph.	*Letter to the Ephesians*	*Bis acc.*	*Bis accusatus*
Magn.	*Letter to the Magnesians*	*Demon.*	*Demonax*
Phld.	*Letter to the Philadelphians*	*Dial. deor.*	*Dialogi deorum*
		Hermot.	*Hermotimus*
Pol.	*Letter to Polycarp*	*Hist. conscr.*	*Quomodo historia conscribenda sit*
Smyrn.	*Letter to the Smyrnaeans*	*Jup. trag.*	*Juppiter tragicus*
Trall.	*Letter to the Trallians*	*Merc. cond.*	*De mercede conductis*
IGR	R. Cagnat (ed.), *Inscriptiones graecae ad res romanas pertinentes*	*Navig.*	*Navigium*
		Pergr. mort.	*De morte Peregrini*
		Philops.	*Philopseudes*
ILS	"*Inscriptiones latinae selectae*	*Sacr.*	*De sacrificiis*
Irenaeus		*Salt.*	*De saltatione*
Adv. haer.	*Adversus haereses*	*Syr. dea*	*De Syria dea*
JAC	Jahrbuch für Antike und Christentum	*Tox.*	*Toxaris*
		Ver. hist.	*Verae historiae*
JBL	*Journal of Biblical Literature*	LXX	Septuagint
		4 Macc.	*4 Maccabees*
JEH	*Journal of Ecclesiastical History*	Marcellinus	
		Vita Thuc.	*Life of Thucydides*
Jerome		*Mart. Carpi*	*Martyrdom of Saints Carpus, Papylus, and Agathonice*
Chron.	*Chronicon*		
Comm. in Tit.	*Commentarius in epistulam ad Titum*		
Ep.	*Epistulae*	*Mart. Isa.*	*Martyrdom of Isaiah*

Mart. Justin	*The Martyrdom of Saints Justin, Chariton, Charito, Evelpistus, Hierax, Paeon, Liberian, and Their Community*	Ovid	
		Am.	Amores
		Ep.	Epistulae
		Metam.	Metamorphoses
		Tr.	Tristia
Mart. Pionii	*Martyrdom of Pionius*	p(p).	page(s)
Mart. Pol.	*Martyrdom of Polycarp*	Pap.	Papyrus
Meg.	*Megilla*	Pap. Oxy.	Oxyrhynchus Papyri
MGWJ	*Monatsschrift für Geschichte und Wissenschaft des Judentums*	par(s).	parallel(s)
		Pass. Perp.	Passio Perpetuae
		passim	in various places
Mid.	*Middot*	*Paul and Thecla*	*Acts of Paul and Thecla*
Moulton-Milligan	J. H. Moulton and G. Milligan, *The Vocabulary of the Greek Testament*	Paulus	Julius Paulus
		Sent.	Sententiae
		PEQ	Palestine Exploration Quarterly
ms(s).	manuscript(s)		
MT	Masoretic Text (Hebrew)	*Peripl. Erythr.*	Periplus of the Erythraean Sea
MThS	Münchener theologische Studien		
		PG	J. Migne, Patrologia graeca
MThZ	*Münchener theologische Zeitschrift*	PGM	K. Preisendanz (ed.), *Papyri graecae magicae*
n(n).	note(s)	Philo	Philo of Alexandria
NedThT	Nederlands theologisch tijdschrift	Abr.	De Abrahamo
		Cher.	De cherubim
NGG	Nachrichten von der königlichen Gesellschaft der Wissenschaften zu Göttingen. Philologisch-historische Klasse	Decal.	De decalogo
		Det.	Quod deterius potiori insidiari soleat
		Deus imm.	Quod deus sit immutabilis
		Ebr.	De ebrietate
NHC	Nag Hammadi Codices	Exsecr.	De exsecrationibus
NJKlA	Neue Jahrbücher des Klassischen Altertums	Flacc.	In Flaccum
		Jos.	De Josepho
NKZ	*Neue kirchliche Zeitschrift*	Leg. all.	Legum allegoriarum libri
no(s).	number(s)	Leg. Gai.	De legatione ad Gaium
NovT	*Novum Testamentum*	Migr. Abr.	De migratione Abrahami
NovTSup	—Supplements	Mut. nom.	De mutatione nominum
n.p.	no place (of publication)	Op. mundi	De opificio mundi
n.s.	new series	Prob.	Quod omnis probus liber sit
NT	New Testament		
NTAbh	Neutestamentliche Abhandlungen	Prov.	De providentia
		Rer. div. her.	Quis rerum divinarum heres sit
NTAbhSup	—Supplements		
NTApoc	Hennecke-Schneemelcher, *New Testament Apocrypha*	Spec. leg.	De specialibus legibus
		Vita Mos.	De vita Mosis
		Philostratus	
NTD	Das Neue Testament Deutsch	Vita Apoll.	Vita Apollonii
		Pindar	
NTS	*New Testament Studies*	Isthm.	Isthmia
NTTS	New Testament Tools and Studies	*PJ*	Palästina-Jahrbuch
		pl(s).	plate(s)
Odes Sol.	*Odes of Solomon*	Plato	
OGIS	W. Dittenberger (ed.), *Orientis Graeci Inscriptiones Selectae*	Apol.	Apologia
		Criti.	Critias
		Gorg.	Gorgias
OLZ	Orientalistische Literaturzeitung	Phaedr.	Phaedrus
		Rep.	Respublica
Origen		Soph.	Sophista
Cels.	*Contra Celsum*	Symp.	Symposium
OT	Old Testament	Tim.	Timaeus

Pliny	Pliny (the elder)	4QFlor	*Floriegium* (or *Eschatological Midrashim*) from
Nat. hist.	*Naturalis historia*		Qumran Cave 4
Pliny	Pliny (the younger)	4QTestim	*Testimonia* text from
Ep.	*Epistulae*		Qumran Cave 4
Plutarch		Quintilian	
Aem. Paulus	*Aemilius Paulus*	*Inst. orat.*	*Institutio oratoria*
Alex.	*Alexander*	RAC	*Reallexikon für Antike und*
Caes.	*Caesar* [*Vitae parallelae*]		*Christentum*
Cic.	*Cicero* [*Vitae parallelae*]	RB	*Revue biblique*
Cleom.	*Cleomenes*	RBén	*Revue bénédictine*
Defect. orac.	*De defectu oraculorum*	RE	*Realencyklopädie für*
Demetr.	*De Demetrio*		*protestantische Theologie*
Is. et Osir.	*De Iside et Osiride*		*und Kirche*
Mor.	*Moralia*	RechSR	*Recherches de science*
Pomp.	*De pompeio*		*religieuse*
Vita.	*Vitae parallelae*	rev.	revised (by)
Polycarp		*RevQ*	*Revue de Qumran*
Phil.	*Letter to the Philippians*	RGG	*Religion in Geschichte und*
Porphyry			*Gegenwart*
Vita Pyth.	*Vita Pythagorae*	*RHPhR*	*Revue d'histoire et de*
Procopius			*philosophie religieuses*
Arc.	*Historia arcana*	RhM	*Rheinisches Museum für*
Ps.-Callisth.	Pseudo-Callisthenes		*Philologie*
Ps.-Clem.	Pseudo-Clementine	RQ	*Römische Quartalschrift für*
Hom.	*Homilies*		*christliche Altertumskunde*
Recog.	*Recognitions*		*und Kirchengeschichte*
Ps.-Philo	Pseudo-Philo	RSV	*Revised Standard Version*
Ant.	*Biblical Antiquities*	RVV	Religionsgeschichtliche
Ps.-Scylax	Pseudo-Scylax		Versuche und
Pss. Sol.	*Psalms of Solomon*		Vorarbeiten
PSTJ	*Perkins (School of Theology)*	SAB	Sitzungsberichte der
	Journal		Preussischen Akademie
PTMS	Pittsburgh Theological		der Wissenschaften zu
	Monograph Series		Berlin. Philologisch-
pub.	published		historische Klasse
PW	Pauly-Wissowa, *Real-*		
	Encyclopädie der classischen	Sallust	
	Altertumswissenschaft	*Cat.*	*Bellum Catilinae*
PWSup	Supplement to PW	SAH	Sitzungsberichte der
Q	Qumran documents		Heidelberger Akademie
1QapGen	*Genesis Apocryphon* from		der Wissenschaft, phil.-
	Qumran Cave 1		hist. Klasse
1QH	*Hodayot (Thanksgiving*	*Sanh.*	*Sanhedrin*
	Hymns) from Qumran	SANT	Studien zum Alten und
	Cave 1		Neuen Testament
1QM	*Milhamah (War Scroll)*	SBT	Studies in Biblical
1QpHab	*Pesher on Habbakuk*		Theology
	from Qumran Cave 1	*SEÅ*	*Svensk exegetisk årsbok*
1QS	*Serek hayyahad (Rule of*	*Šeb.*	*Šebi'it*
	the Community, Manual	SEG	*Supplementum epigraphic*
	of Discipline)		*graecum*
1QSa	Appendix A *(Rule of the*	Seneca	
	Congregation) to 1QS	*Ep.*	*Epistulae*
1Q29	*Liturgy of Three Tongues*	*Herc. oet.*	*Hercules oetaeus*
	of Fire	*Nat. quaest.*	*Naturales quaestiones*
4QExod[a]	Fragment = Exod	ser.	series
	1:1–5 from Qumran	SHT	Studies in Historical
	Cave 4		Theology

SHVU	Skrifter utgivna av k. humanistika vetenskapssamfundet i Uppsala. Acta societatis litterorum humaniorum r. Upsaliensis. Uppsala 1, 1890ff	Hist.	Histories
		TAPA	Transactions of the American Philological Association
Sib. Or.	Sibylline Oracles	TDNT	G. Kittel and G. Friedrich (eds.), Theological Dictionary of the New Testament
SIG	W. Dittenberger (ed.), Sylloge Inscriptionem Graecorum		
SNTSMS	Society for New Testament Studies Monograph Series	Tertullian	
		Adv. Marc.	Adversus Marcionem
SO	Symbolae osloenses	Apol.	Apologia
SOSup	—Supplements	Bapt.	De baptismo
Sophocles		Nat.	Ad nationes
Ant.	Antigone	Praescr. haer.	De praescriptione haereticorum
Oed. col.	Oedipus coloneus		
Phil.	Philoctetes	Res.	De resurrectione carnis liber
SPAW	= SAB		
SPB	Studia post-biblica	Test. Sol.	Testament of Solomon
Stad.	Stadiasmus Maris Magni	Tg.	Targum
StEv	Studia Evangelica	Neof.	Neofiti I
StJud	Studia Judaica	Ps.-J.	Pseudo-Jonathan
STK	Svensk teologisk kvartalskrift	Th	Theodotion (Greek version of OT)
StNT	Studien zum Neuen Testament		
Str-B	[H. Strack and] P. Billerbeck, Kommentar zum Neuen Testament	Theophilus	
		Autol.	Ad Autolycum
StTh	Studia theologica	ThExH	Theologische Existenz heute
Stud. Cath.	Studia catholica		
Suetonius		ThHKNT	Theologischer Handkommentar zum Neuen Testament
Aug.	Augustus (De vita Caesarum)		
		ThLZ	Theologische Literaturzeitung
Claud.	Claudius (De vita Caesarum)	ThQ	Theologische Quartalschrift
		ThR	Theologische Rundschau
SUNT	Studien zur Umwelt des Neuen Testaments	ThStK	Theologische Studien und Kritiken
s.v(v).	under the word(s) (entry[ies])	ThViat	Theologia Viatorum
		ThZ	Theologische Zeitschrift
SVF	von Arnim (ed.), Stoicorum Veterum Fragmenta	trans.	translation, translated by
		TS	Theological Studies
Symm	Symmachus (Greek version of OT)	TThSt	Trierer Theologische Studien
t.	Tosepta	TThZ	Trierer theologische Zeitschrift
T. Mos.	Testament of Moses (= Assumption of Moses)	TToday	Theology Today
		TU	Texte und Untersuchungen
T. 12 Patr.	Testaments of the Twelve Patriarchs	UUÅ	Uppsala universitets årsskrift
T. Jos.	Testament of Joseph	UNT	Untersuchungen zum Neuen Testament
T. Jud.	Testament of Judah	VC	Vigiliae christianae
T. Levi	Testament of Levi	Vegetius	Vegetius Renatus
T. Naph.	Testament of Naphtali	Epit. rei mil.	Epitoma rei militaris
Tacitus		Vg	Vulgate
Agr.	Agricola	Virgil	
Ann.	Annals	Aen.	Aeneid
		Georg.	Georgics

v.l.	*variae lectiones*, variant reading(s)
vol(s).	volume(s)
Vopiscus	Flavius Vopiscus
Div. Aur.	*Divus Aurelianus (Scriptores historiae Augustae)*
vs(s)	verse(s)
VT	*Vetus Testamentum*
WMANT	Wissenschaftliche Monographien zum Alten und Neuen Testament
WUNT	Wissenschaftliche Untersuchungen zum Neuen Testament
Xenophon	
Mem.	*Memorabilia*
Xenophon Eph.	Xenophon Ephesius
Eph.	*Ephegiaca*
y.	Jerusalem Talmud
ZAW	*Zeitschrift für die alttestamentliche Wissenschaft*
ZKG	*Zeitschrift für Kirchengeschichte*
ZKTh	*Zeitschrift für katholische Theologie*
ZNW	*Zeitschrift für die neutestamentliche Wissenschaft*
ZRGG	*Zeitschrift für Religions- und Geistesgeschichte*
ZSTh	*Zeitschrift für systematische Theologie*
ZThK	*Zeitschrift für Theologie und Kirche*

2. Short Titles of Commentaries, Studies, and Articles Often Cited

Commentaries on Acts as well as a few basic reference works are cited by author's name only. Page numbers have been provided, however, for Haenchen, *The Acts of the Apostles,* inasmuch as references are not always easy to locate. Additional short titles are used within a specific sequence of footnotes for works cited only with reference to a single passage; full bibliographical information accompanies the first citation.

Apophoreta
> *Apophoreta: Festschrift für Ernst Haenchen* (ed. W. Eltester and F. H. Kettler; BZNW 30; Berlin: Töpelmann, 1964).

Aux sources de la tradition
> *Aux sources de la tradition chrétienne: Mélanges offerts à M. Maurice Goguel* (Bibliothèque théologique; Neuchâtel/Paris: Delachaux & Niestlé, 1950).

Bauer, *Orthodoxy and Heresy*
> Walter Bauer, *Orthodoxy and Heresy in Earliest Christianity* (ed. Robert A. Kraft and Gerhard Krodel; Philadelphia: Fortress, 1971).

Bauernfeind
> Otto Bauernfeind, *Die Apostelgeschichte* (ThHKNT 5; Leipzig: Deichert, 1939), reprinted in his *Kommentar und Studien zur Apostelgeschichte* (WUNT 22; Tübingen: Mohr [Siebeck], 1980).

Beginnings
> F. J. Foakes Jackson and Kirsopp Lake, *The Beginnings of Christianity. Part I: The Acts of the Apostles* (5 vols.; London: Macmillan, 1920–33; reprinted Grand Rapids: Baker, 1979).

Bell, *Jews and Christians*
> H. Idris Bell, *Jews and Christians in Egypt: The Jewish Troubles in Alexandria and the Athanasian Controversy* (Oxford: Oxford University, 1924; reprinted Milan: Cisalpino, 1977).

Benoit, *Jesus and the Gospel*
> Pierre Benoit, *Jesus and the Gospel* (2 vols.; New York: Herder, 1973–74).

Betz, *Lukian*
> Hans Dieter Betz, *Lukian von Samosata und das Neue Testament* (TU 76; Berlin: Akademie-Verlag, 1961).

Bieler, *Theios Aner*
> Ludwig Bieler, Θεῖος ἀνήρ: *Das Bild des "göttlichen Menschen" in Spätantike und Frühchristentum* (2 vols.; Vienna: Hofels, 1935–36; reprinted Darmstadt: Wissenschaftliche Buchgesellschaft, 1967).

Bihler, "Der Stephanusbericht"
> Johann Bihler, "Der Stephanusbericht (Apg 6,8–15 und 7,54—8,2)," *BZ* n.s. 3 (1959) 252–70.

Björck, ῾Ην διδάσκων
> Gudmond Björck, ῾Ην διδάσκων: *Die periphrasten Konstruktionem im Griechischen* (SHVU 32:2; Uppsala: Almqvist & Wiksell, 1940).

Braun, *Gesammelte Studien*
> Herbert Braun, *Gesammelte Studien zum Neuen Testament und seiner Umwelt* (2d ed.; Tübingen: Mohr [Siebeck], 1967).

Braun, *Qumran*
> Herbert Braun, *Qumran und das Neue Testament* (2 vols.; Tübingen: Mohr [Siebeck], 1966).

Brox, *Zeuge und Märtyrer*
> Norbert Brox, *Zeuge und Märtyrer: Untersuchungen zur frühchristlichen Zeugnis-Terminològie* (SANT 5; Munich: Kösel, 1961).

Bultmann, *Exegetica*
> Rudolf Bultmann, *Exegetica: Aufsätze zur Erforschung des Neuen Testaments* (ed. Erich Dinkler; Tübingen: Mohr [Siebeck], 1967).

Bultmann, "Quellen"
> Rudolf Bultmann, "Zur Frage nach den Quellen der Apostelgeschichte," *New Testament Essays: Studies in Memory of Thomas Walter Manson 1893–1958* (ed. A. J. B. Higgins; Manchester: Manchester University, 1959) 68–80, reprinted in his *Exegetica*, 412–23.

Burchard, *Der dreizehnte Zeuge*
> Christoph Burchard, *Der dreizehnte Zeuge* (FRLANT 103; Göttingen: Vandenhoeck & Ruprecht, 1970).

Cadbury, *Acts in History*
> Henry J. Cadbury, *The Book of Acts in History* (New York: Harper, 1955).

Cadbury, "'We' and 'I' Passages"
> Henry J. Cadbury, "'We' and 'I' Passages in Luke-Acts," *NTS* 3 (1956–57) 128–32.

von Campenhausen, *Ecclesiastical Authority*
> Hans von Campenhausen, *Ecclesiastical Authority and Spiritual Power in the Church of the First Three Centuries* (London: Black; Stanford, CA: Stanford University, 1969).

Casson, "Speed Under Sail"
> Lionel Casson, "Speed Under Sail of Ancient Ships," *TAPA* 82 (1951) 136–48.

Cerfaux, "Citations"
> Lucien Cerfaux, "Citations scripturaires et tradition textuelle dans le Livre des Actes," *Aux sources de la tradition,* 43–51, reprinted in *Recueil Cerfaux* 2.93–103.

Cerfaux, "La composition"
> Lucien Cerfaux, "La composition de la première partie du Livre des Actes," *EThL* 13 (1936) 667–91, reprinted in *Recueil Cerfaux* 2.63–91.

Recueil Cerfaux
> *Recueil Lucien Cerfaux: Études d'exégèse et d'histoire religieuse de Monseigneur Cerfaux* (3 vols.; BETL 6, 7, 18; Gembloux: Duculot, 1954–62).

Conzelmann, *Theology*
> Hans Conzelmann, *The Theology of St. Luke* (London: Faber & Faber; New York: Harper, 1960; reprinted Philadelphia: Fortress, 1982).

Corinth
> *Corinth: Results of Excavations Conducted by the*

American School of Classical Studies at Athens (vols. 1–; Princeton, NJ: American School of Classical Studies at Athens, 1929–).

Deissmann, *Light from the Ancient East*
Adolf Deissmann, *Light from the Ancient East: The New Testament Illustrated by Recently Discovered Texts of the Graeco-Roman World* (rev. ed.; trans. L. R. M. Strachey; Garden City, NY: Doubleday Doran, 1927).

Deissmann, *Paul*
Adolf Deissmann, *Paul: A Study in Social and Religious History* (2d ed.; London: Hodder & Stoughton, 1926).

Dibelius-Conzelmann, *Pastoral Epistles*
Martin Dibelius and Hans Conzelmann, *A Commentary on the Pastoral Epistles* (trans. Philip Buttolph and Adela Yarbro; ed. Helmut Koester; Hermeneia; Philadelphia: Fortress, 1972).

Dibelius, *Studies*
Martin Dibelius, *Studies in the Acts of the Apostles* (ed. Heinrich Greeven; London: SCM, 1956).

Dodd, *Scriptures*
C. H. Dodd, *According to the Scriptures: The Sub-Structure of New Testament Theology* (London: Nisbet; New York: Scribner's, 1953).

Dupont, *Études*
Jacques Dupont, *Études sur les Actes des Apôtres* (LD 45; Paris: Cerf, 1967).

Dupont, "La famine"
Jacques Dupont, "Notes sur les Actes des Apôtres: IV. La famine sous Claude (Actes XI,28)," *RB* 62 (1955) 52–55, reprinted in his *Études*, 163–71.

Dupont, *Sources*
Jacques Dupont, *The Sources of Acts: The Present Position* (London: Darton, Longman & Todd, 1964).

Eger, *Rechtsgeschichtliches*
Otto Eger, *Rechtsgeschichtliches zum Neuen Testament* (Basel: Reinhardt, 1919).

Ephesos
Forschungen in Ephesos (vols. 1–; Vienna: Österreichischen Akademie der Wissenschaften, 1906–).

Epp, *Theological Tendency*
Eldon Jay Epp, *The Theological Tendency of Codex Bezae Cantabrigiensis in Acts* (SNTSMS 3; Cambridge/New York: Cambridge University, 1966).

Frisk, *Le Périple*
Hjalmar Frisk, *Le Périple de la mer Érythrée: Suivi d'une étude sur la tradition et la langue* (Göteborgs Högskolas Årsskrift 33:1; Göteborg: Elanders, 1927).

Gärtner, *Areopagus Speech*
Bertil Gärtner, *The Areopagus Speech and Natural Revelation* (ASNU 21; Lund: Gleerup; Copenhagen: Munksgaard, 1955).

Gerhardsson, *Memory and Manuscript*
Birger Gerhardsson, *Memory and Manuscript: Oral Tradition and Written Transmission in Rabbinic Judaism and Early Christianity* (ASNU 22; Lund: Gleerup; Copenhagen: Munksgaard, 1961).

Haenchen
Ernst Haenchen, *The Acts of the Apostles* (ed. R. McL. Wilson; Philadelphia: Westminster, 1971).

Haenchen, *Gott und Mensch*
Ernst Haenchen, *Gott und Mensch: Gesammelte Aufsätze* (Tübingen: Mohr [Siebeck], 1965).

Haenchen, "Quellenanalyse"
Ernst Haenchen, "Quellenanalyse und Kompositionsanalyse in Act 15," *Judentum, Urchristentum, Kirche: Festschrift für Joachim Jeremias* (ed. Walther Eltester; BZNW 26; Berlin: Töpelmann, 1960) 153–64.

Haenchen, "Schriftzitate"
Ernst Haenchen, "Schriftzitate und Textüberlieferung in der Apostelgeschichte," *ZThK* 51 (1954) 153–67, reprinted in his *Gott und Mensch*, 157–71.

Haenchen, "Text"
Ernst Haenchen, "Zum Text der Apostelgeschichte," *ZThK* 54 (1957) 22–55, reprinted in his *Gott und Mensch*, 172–205.

Harnack, *Acts*
Adolf Harnack, *The Acts of the Apostles* (New Testament Studies 3; Crown Theological Library 27; London: Williams & Norgate, 1909).

Hengel, *Die Zeloten*
Martin Hengel, *Die Zeloten: Untersuchungen zur jüdische Freiheitsbewegung in der Zeit von Herodes I. bis 70 n. Chr.* (2d ed.; AGJU 1; Leiden: Brill, 1976).

Holtz, *Zitate*
Traugott Holtz, *Untersuchungen über die alttestamentliche Zitate bei Lukas* (TU 104; Berlin: Akademie-Verlag, 1968).

Hommel, "Areopagrede"
Hildebrecht Hommel, "Neue Forschungen zur Areopagrede Acta 17," *ZNW* 46 (1955) 147–78.

Hommel, "Platonisches bei Lukas"
Hildebrecht Hommel, "Platonisches bei Lukas: Zu Act 17:28a (Leben—Bewegung—Sein)," *ZNW* 48 (1957) 193–200.

Jeremias, *Abba*
Joachim Jeremias, *Abba: Studien zur neutestamentlichen Theologie und Zeitgeschichte* (Göttingen: Vandenhoeck & Ruprecht, 1966).

Jeremias, *Jerusalem*
Joachim Jeremias, *Jerusalem in the Time of Jesus: An Investigation into Economic and Social Conditions during the New Testament Period* (Philadelphia: Fortress, 1969).

Jeremias, "Quellenproblem"
Joachim Jeremias, "Untersuchungen zum Quellenproblem der Apostelgeschichte," *ZNW* 36 (1937) 205–21, reprinted in his *Abba*, 238–55.

Juster, *Les Juifs*
Jean Juster, *Les Juifs dans l'Empire romain: Leur condition juridique, économique et sociale* (2 vols.; Paris: Guenther, 1914).

Käsemann, "Disciples of John"
Ernst Käsemann, "The Disciples of John the
Baptist in Ephesus," *Essays on New Testament
Themes* (SBT 41; London: SCM, 1964) 136–48.

Kilpatrick, "Eclectic Study"
George D. Kilpatrick, "An Eclectic Study of the
Text of Acts," *Biblical and Patristic Studies in
Memory of Robert Pierce Casey* (ed. J. Neville Birdsall
and Robert W. Thomson; Freiburg/Basel/New
York: Herder, 1963) 64–77.

Kirsten and Kraiker, *Griechenlandkunde*
Ernst Kirsten and Wilhelm Kraiker, *Griechenland-
kunde: Ein Führer zu klassischen Stätten* (5th ed.;
Heidelberg: Winter, 1967).

Klein, *Rekonstruktion*
Günter Klein, *Rekonstruktion und Interpretation:
Gesammelte Aufsätze zum Neuen Testament* (BEvTh
50; Munich: Kaiser, 1969).

Klein, "Synkretismus"
Günter Klein, "Der Synkretismus als theologisches
Problem in der ältesten christlichen Apologetik,"
ZThK 64 (1967) 40–82, reprinted in his *Rekon-
struktion*, 262–301.

Klein, *Die zwölf Apostel*
Günter Klein, *Die zwölf Apostel: Ursprung und
Gehalt einer Idee* (FRLANT 77; Göttingen:
Vandenhoeck & Ruprecht, 1961).

Klijn, *Survey*
A. F. J. Klijn, *A Survey of the Researches into the
Western Text of the Gospels and Acts* (Utrecht:
Kemink, 1949).

Kümmel, "Urchristentum"
Werner Georg Kümmel, "Das Urchristentum,"
ThR n.s. 14 (1942) 81–95, 155–73.

Kümmel, "Urchristentum III"
Werner Georg Kümmel, "Das Urchristentum: III:
Die Geschichte der Urkirche," *ThR* n.s. 17 (1948–
49) 3–50, 103–42.

Larrañaga, *L'Ascension*
Victorien Larrañaga, *L'Ascension de Notre-Seigneur
dans le Nouveau Testament* (Rome: Pontifical
Biblical Institute, 1938).

Linton, "Third Aspect"
Olaf Linton, "The Third Aspect: A Neglected
Point of View: A Study in Gal. i–ii and Acts ix and
xv," *StTh* 3 (1949) 79–95.

Lösch, *Dietas Jesu*
Stephan Lösch, *Dietas Jesu und Antike Apotheose:
Ein Beitrag zur Exegese und Religionsgeschichte*
(Rottenberg a.N. [Württ.]: Bader, 1933).

Magie, *Roman Rule*
David Magie, *Roman Rule in Asia Minor to the End
of the Third Century after Christ* (2 vols.; Princeton:
Princeton University, 1950; reprinted New York:
Arno, 1975).

Menoud, "Forty Days"
Philippe H. Menoud, "'During Forty Days' (Acts
1. 3)," *Jesus Christ and the Faith*, 167–79.

Menoud, *Jesus Christ and the Faith*
Philippe H. Menoud, *Jesus Christ and the Faith: A
Collection of Studies* (PTMS 18; Pittsburgh: Pick-
wick, 1978).

Milik, *Ten Years*
J. T. Milik, *Ten Years of Discovery in the Wilderness of
Judaea* (trans. John Strugnell; SBT 26; London:
SCM, 1959).

Mommsen, "Rechtsverhältnisse"
Theodor Mommsen, "Die Rechtsverhältnisse des
Apostels Paulus," *ZNW* 2 (1901) 81–96.

Munck, *Paul*
Johannes Munck, *Paul and the Salvation of Mankind*
(Richmond: John Knox, 1959).

Mussner, "Die Idee der Apokatastasis"
Franz Mussner, "Die Idee der Apokatastasis in der
Apostelgeschichte," *Lux tua veritas: Festschrift für
Hubert Junker* (Trier: Paulinus, 1961) 293–306,
reprinted in his *Praesentia salutis*, 223–34.

Mussner, *Praesentia salutis*
Franz Mussner, *Praesentia salutis: Gesammelte
Studien zu Fragen und Themen des Neuen Testaments*
(Düsseldorf: Patmos-Verlag, 1967).

Musurillo, *Acta Alexandrinorum*
Herbert A. Musurillo, *Acta Alexandrinorum: De
mortibus Alexandriae nobilium fragmenta papyracea
graeca* (Leipzig: Teubner, 1961).

Musurillo, *Acts of the Pagan Martyrs*
Herbert A. Musurillo, *The Acts of the Pagan
Martyrs: Acta Alexandrinorum* (Oxford: Clarendon,
1954).

Neutestamentliche Studien für Rudolf Bultmann
Neutestamentliche Studien für Rudolf Bultmann (ed.
Walther Eltester; BZNW 21; Berlin: Töpelmann,
1954).

Newton, *Inscriptions*
C. T. Newton, ed., *The Collection of Ancient
Inscriptions in the British Museum*. Part 3, *Priene,
Iasos and Ephesos*, ed. E. L. Hicks (Oxford: Claren-
don, 1886), 67–291.

Nilsson, *Geschichte*
Martin P. Nilsson, *Geschichte der griechischen
Religion*, vol. 2: *Die hellenistische und römische Zeit*
(HKAW 5:2.2; Munich: Beck, 1950; 2d ed.,
1961).

Nilsson, *Zauberpapyri*
Martin P. Nilsson, *Die Religion der griechischen
Zauberpapyri* (Lund: Gleerup, 1948).

Nock, "Book of Acts"
Arthur Darby Nock, *Gnomon* 25 (1953) 497–506,
review of Dibelius, *Studies,* reprinted as "The Book
of Acts," in his *Essays on Religion and the Ancient
World* (ed. Zeph Stewart; 2 vols.; Cambridge:
Harvard University, 1972) 2.821–32.

Norden, *Agnostos Theos*
Eduard Norden, *Agnostos Theos: Untersuchungen zur
Formengeschichte religiöser Rede* (Leipzig/Berlin:
Teubner, 1913; reprinted Stuttgart: Teubner,

1923; Darmstadt: Wissenschaftliche Buchgesellschaft, 1956).

O'Neill, *Theology*
J. C. O'Neill, *The Theology of Acts in Its Historical
Setting* (2d ed.; London: SPCK, 1970).

Plümacher, *Schriftsteller*
Eckhard Plümacher, *Lukas als hellenistischer
Schriftsteller: Studien zur Apostelgeschichte* (SUNT 9;
Göttingen: Vandenhoeck & Ruprecht, 1972).

Pohlenz, "Paulus"
Max Pohlenz, "Paulus und die Stoa," *ZNW* 42
(1949) 69–104.

von Premerstein, "Edikte des Augustus"
Anton von Premerstein, "Die fünf neugefundenen
Edikte des Augustus von Kyrene," *Zeitschrift für
Savigny-Stiftung*, Rom Abt (1928).

Preuschen
Erwin Preuschen, *Die Apostelgeschichte* (HNT 4:1;
Tübingen: Mohr [Siebeck], 1912).

Prümm, *Handbuch*
Karl Prümm, *Religionsgeschichtliches Handbuch für
den Raum der altchristlichen Umwelt* (Freiburg:
Herder, 1943).

Radermacher, *Grammatik*
Ludwig Radermacher, *Neutestamentliche Grammatik: Das Griechisch des Neuen Testaments im
Zusammenhang mit der Volkssprache* (2d ed.; HNT
1; Tübingen: Mohr [Siebeck], 1925).

Ramsay, *St. Paul*
William M. Ramsay, *St. Paul the Traveler and the
Roman Citizen* (7th ed.; London: Hodder &
Stoughton, 1898; reprinted Grand Rapids: Baker,
1949).

Ramsay, *Social Basis*
William M. Ramsay, *The Social Basis of Roman
Power in Asia Minor* (Aberdeen: University Press,
1941).

Rese, *Alttestamentliche Motive*
Martin Rese, *Alttestamentliche Motive in der Christologie des Lukas* (StNT 1; Gütersloh: Mohn, 1969).

Schoeps, *Theologie*
Hans-Joachim Schoeps, *Theologie und Geschichte des
Judenchristentums* (Tübingen: Mohr [Siebeck],
1949).

Schultze, *Altchristliche Städte*
Victor Schultze, *Altchristliche Städte und Landschaften* (3 vols.; Gütersloh: Bertelsmann, 1913–
30).

Schürer, *History*
Emil Schürer, *The History of the Jewish People in the
Age of Jesus Christ (175 B.C.—A.D. 135)* (3 vols. [3.2
forthcoming]; rev. and ed. Geza Vermes and
Fergus Millar; Edinburgh: T. & T. Clark, 1973–
86).

Schwartz, "Chronologie"
Eduard Schwartz, "Zur Chronologie des Paulus"
(NGG; Berlin: Weidmannsche Buchhandlung,
1907).

Simon, *St Stephen*
Marcel Simon, *St Stephen and the Hellenists in the
Primitive Church* (London/New York/Toronto:
Longmans, Green, 1958).

Simon, *Verus Israel*
Marcel Simon, *Verus Israel: A Study of the Relations
between Christians and Jews in the Roman Empire (A.D.
135–425)* (trans. H. McKeating; Littman Library
of Jewish Civilization; Oxford/London/New
York: Oxford University, 1986).

Söder, *Die apokryphen Apostelgeschichten*
Rosa Söder, *Die apokryphen Apostelgeschichten und
die romanhafte Literatur der Antike* (Würzburger
Studien zur Altertumswissenschaft 3; Stuttgart:
Kohlhammer, 1932; reprinted Darmstadt:
Wissenschaftliche Buchgesellschaft, 1969).

Strecker, *Judenchristentum*
Georg Strecker, *Das Judenchristentum in den
Pseudoklementinen* (2d ed.; TU 70; Berlin: Akade-
mie-Verlag, 1981).

Studies in Luke-Acts
Leander E. Keck and J. Louis Martyn, eds., *Studies
in Luke-Acts: Essays Presented in Honor of Paul
Schubert* (2d ed.; Philadelphia: Fortress, 1980).

Surkau, *Martyrien*
Hans Werner Surkau, *Martyrien in jüdischer und
frühchristlicher Zeit* (FRLANT 54; Göttingen:
Vandenhoeck & Ruprecht, 1938).

Tabachovitz, "In Palladii"
D. Tabachovitz, "In Palladii Historiam Lausiacam
observationes quaedam," *Eranos* 30 (1932) 97–
109.

Trocmé, *Livre des Actes*
Etienne Trocmé, *Le "Livre des Actes" et l'histoire*
(Études d'histoire et de Philosophie Religieuses
45; Paris: Presses Universitaires de France, 1957).

Vögeli, "Lukas und Euripides"
Alfred Vögeli, "Lukas und Euripides," *ThZ* 9
(1953) 415–38.

Wendt
Hans Hinrich Wendt, *Die Apostelgeschichte* (9th ed.;
KEK 3; Göttingen: Vandenhoeck & Ruprecht,
1913).

Wikenhauser, *Apostelgeschichte*
Alfred Wikenhauser, *Die Apostelgeschichte und ihr
Geschichtswert* (NTAbh 8:3–5; Münster: Aschen-
dorf, 1921).

Wilckens, *Missionsreden*
Ulrich Wilckens, *Die Missionsreden der Apostelgeschichte: Form- und traditionsgeschichtliche Untersuchung* (2d ed.; WMANT 5; Neukirchen-Vluyn:
Neukirchener, 1963).

Zahn
Theodor Zahn, *Die Apostelgeschichte des Lucas* (2
vols.; 3d and 4th eds.; KNT 5; Leipzig and
Erlangen: Deichert, 1922–27).

The English translation of the Acts of the Apostles printed in this Commentary is from the *Revised Standard Version,* modified in accordance with the exegetical decisions of the commentator. The author's German translation was consulted throughout. Whenever possible, all other biblical translations follow the *RSV.*

Translations of ancient Greek and Latin texts are taken from the Loeb Classical Library in all instances in which no particular source for the translation is identified. Other translations of ancient literature follow standard editions whenever possible, such as the *Ante-Nicene Fathers.* Occasionally the translators or editors have rendered short texts into English.

Modern scholarly literature is cited according to published English translations whenever these are available. Translations of quotations from literature not available in English have been provided by the translators or editors.

Select bibliographies of modern commentaries and of modern works on Acts have been provided, and each has been supplemented by a few additional studies that have appeared since 1972.

The front endpaper in this book is the reverse side of uncial manuscript 0189, containing Acts 5:12–21. Not only is this the oldest manuscript of Acts, but it is the oldest parchment manuscript of the New Testament, dating in the 2d/3d century. It is found in Berlin at the State Museum (number P 11765), and is reproduced by permission. The back endpaper is a map from the endpaper in *The Rise of Christianity* by W. H. C. Frend (Philadelphia: Fortress Press, 1984).

Introduction

1. External Testimony to Acts[1]

It is doubtful that the Pastoral Epistles show knowledge of Acts. There is indeed a certain theological and historical similarity: both operate with a similar conception of tradition, both refer to the laying on of hands and to ordination, and both associate the institution of presbyters with Paul, contrary to historical fact. But there are also considerable differences, and literary dependence of the Pastorals upon Acts cannot be demonstrated with certainty. 2 Tim 3:11 alludes to experiences of Paul in Pisidian Antioch, Iconium, and Lystra, but there may have been traditions concerning these events outside of Acts.[2] The names of Timothy's grandmother and mother as given in 2 Tim 1:5 are not taken from Acts. The mention of Luke in 2 Tim 4:11 does not prove anything.[3]

There are reminiscences of Acts in the Apostolic Fathers, but some of these are merely phrases or expressions common to the language of early Christianity. For example:

1 Clem. 2.2

πλήρης πνεύματος ἁγίου ἔκχυσις ἐπὶ πάντας ἐγίνετο
The Holy Spirit was poured out in abundance on you all

and Acts 2:17

ἐκχεῶ ἀπὸ τοῦ πνεύματός μου ἐπὶ πᾶσαν σάρκα
I will pour out my Spirit upon all flesh

1 Clem. 5.4, 7

Πέτρον . . . μαρτυρήσας ἐπορεύθη εἰς τὸν ὀφειλόμενον τόπον τῆς δόξης . . . . ἐπὶ τὸ τέρμα τῆς δύσεως ἐλθὼν καὶ μαρτυρήσας ἐπὶ τῶν ἡγουμένων, οὕτως ἀπηλλάγη τοῦ κόσμου καὶ εἰς τὸν ἅγιον τόπον ἀνελήμφθη
Peter . . . having given his testimony went to the glorious place which was his due. . . . When he [Paul] had reached the limits of the West he gave his testimony

before the rulers, and thus passed from the world and was taken up into the Holy Place

and Acts 1:25[4]

λαβεῖν τὸν τόπον τῆς διακονίας ταύτης καὶ ἀποστολῆς ἀφ᾽ ἧς παρέβη Ἰούδας πορευθῆναι εἰς τὸν τόπον τὸν ἴδιον
to take the place in this ministry and apostleship from which Judas turned aside, to go to his own place

Polycarp *Phil.* 2.3

μνημονεύοντες δὲ ὧν εἶπεν ὁ κύριος διδάσκων
but remembering what the Lord taught when he said . . .

and Acts 20:35[5]

μνημονεύειν τε τῶν λόγων τοῦ κυρίου Ἰησοῦ ὅτι αὐτὸς εἶπεν
remembering the words of the Lord Jesus, how he said . . .

Polycarp *Phil.* 6.3

καὶ οἱ προφῆται, οἱ προκηρύξαντες τὴν ἔλευσιν τοῦ κυρίου ἡμῶν
and the prophets who foretold the coming of our Lord

and Acts 7:52[6]

τίνα τῶν προφητῶν οὐκ ἐδίωξαν οἱ πατέρες ὑμῶν; καὶ ἀπέκτειναν τοὺς προκαταγγείλαντας περὶ τῆς ἐλεύσεως τοῦ δικαίου
Which of the prophets did not your fathers persecute? And they killed those who announced beforehand the coming of the Righteous One

Polycarp *Phil.* 12.2

Deus autem et pater domini nostri Iesu Christi, et ipse sempiternus pontifex, dei filius Iesus Christus, aedificet vos . . . et det vobis sortem et partem inter sanctos suos et nobis vobiscum et omnibus, qui sunt sub caelo, qui credituri sunt in dominum nostrum et deum Iesum Christum et in ipsius patrem, qui resuscitavit eum a mortuis
Now may God and the Father of our Lord Jesus Christ, and the "eternal

---

1   Literature:
Donatien de Bruyne, "Les plus anciens prologues latins des Evangiles," *RBén* 40 (1928) 193–214.
Richard Glover, "'Luke the Antiochene' and Acts," *NTS* 11 (1964–65) 97–106.
Adolf Harnack, "Die ältesten Evangelienprologe und die Bildung des Neuen Testaments," SAB (1928) 322–41.
Richard G. Heard, "The Old Gospel Prologues," *JTS* n.s. 6 (1955) 1–16.
August Strobel, "Lukas der Antiochener (Bemerkungen zu Act 11:28 D)," *ZNW* 49 (1958)

131–34.
Alfred Wikenhauser, "Die altkirchliche Überlieferung über die Abfassungszeit der Apostelgeschichte," *BZ* 23 (1935–36) 365–71.
2   Note the role of this district in *Paul and Thecla.*
3   Cf. Phlm 24; Col 4:14.
4   Cf. Ignatius *Magn.* 5.1; Polycarp *Phil.* 9.2; *Herm. Sim.* 9.27.3.
5   Cf. *1 Clem.* 13.1–2; see Helmut Koester, *Synoptische Überlieferung bei den apostolischen Vätern* (Berlin: Akademie-Verlag, 1957) 5–6.
6   *1 Clem.* 17.1; Justin *Dial.* 16.

Priest" himself, Jesus Christ, the Son of God, build you up . . . and may he give you lot and part with his saints, and to us with you, and to all under heaven who shall believe in our Lord and God Jesus Christ and in his Father who raised him from the dead

and Acts 2:5
Ἦσαν δὲ εἰς Ἰερουσαλὴμ κατοικοῦντες Ἰουδαῖοι, ἄνδρες εὐλαβεῖς ἀπὸ παντὸς ἔθνους τῶν ὑπὸ τὸν οὐρανόν
Now there were dwelling in Jerusalem Jews, devout men from every nation under heaven

and 4:12[7]
καὶ οὐκ ἔστιν ἐν ἄλλῳ οὐδενὶ ἡ σωτηρία, οὐδὲ γὰρ ὄνομά ἐστιν ἕτερον ὑπὸ τὸν οὐρανὸν τὸ δεδομένον ἐν ἀνθρώποις ἐν ᾧ δεῖ σωθῆναι ἡμᾶς
And there is salvation in no one else, for there is no other name under heaven given among men by which we must be saved

This passage, Polycarp *Phil.* 12.2, also alludes to:

Acts 8:21[8]
οὐκ ἔστιν σοι μερὶς οὐδὲ κλῆρος ἐν τῷ λόγῳ τούτῳ
You have neither part nor lot in this matter

and 20:32
καὶ τὰ νῦν παρατίθεμαι ὑμᾶς τῷ θεῷ καὶ τῷ λόγῳ τῆς χάριτος αὐτοῦ, τῷ δυναμένῳ οἰκοδομῆσαι
And now I commend you to God and to the word of his grace, which is able to build you up

2 Clem. 20.5
τῷ μόνῳ θεῷ ἀοράτῳ, πατρὶ τῆς ἀληθείας, τῷ ἐξαποστείλαντι ἡμῖν τὸν σωτῆρα καὶ ἀρχηγὸν τῆς ἀφθαρσίας
To the only invisible God, the father of truth, who sent forth to us the Savior and prince of immortality

and Acts 3:15
τὸν δὲ ἀρχηγὸν τῆς ζωῆς ἀπεκτείνατε ὃν ὁ θεὸς ἤγειρεν ἐκ νεκρῶν
and killed the Author of life, whom God raised from the dead

and 5:31[9]
τοῦτον ὁ θεὸς ἀρχηγὸν καὶ σωτῆρα ὕψωσεν τῇ δεξιᾷ αὐτοῦ
God exalted him at his right hand as Leader and Savior

2 Clem. 4.4
καὶ οὐ δεῖ ἡμᾶς φοβεῖσθαι τοὺς ἀνθρώπους μᾶλλον, ἀλλὰ τὸν θεόν
And we must not fear men rather than God

and Acts 4:19[10]
εἰ δίκαιόν ἐστιν ἐνώπιον τοῦ θεοῦ ὑμῶν ἀκούειν μᾶλλον ἢ τοῦ θεοῦ, κρίνατε
Whether it is right in the sight of God to listen to you rather than to God, you must judge

Herm. Sim. 9.28.2
οἱ παθόντες ὑπὲρ τοῦ ὀνόματος τοῦ υἱοῦ τοῦ θεοῦ
They who have suffered for the name of the Son of God

and Acts 5:41
οἱ μὲν οὖν ἐπορεύοντο χαίροντες ἀπὸ προσώπου τοῦ συνεδρίου, ὅτι κατηξιώθησαν ὑπὲρ τοῦ ὀνόματος ἀτιμασθῆναι
Then they left the presence of the council, rejoicing that they were counted worthy to suffer dishonor for the name

and 9:16
ἐγὼ γὰρ ὑποδείξω αὐτῷ ὅσα δεῖ αὐτὸν ὑπὲρ τοῦ ὀνόματός μου παθεῖν
For I will show him how much he must suffer for the sake of my name

and 15:26
ἀνθρώποις παραδεδωκόσι τὰς ψυχὰς αὐτῶν ὑπὲρ τοῦ ὀνόματος τοῦ κυρίου ἡμῶν Ἰησοῦ Χριστοῦ
people who have risked their lives for the sake of our Lord Jesus Christ

The situation is similar where there are allusions to fixed formal material:

1 Clem. 59.2
Ἰησοῦ Χριστοῦ, δι᾽ οὗ ἐκάλεσεν ἡμᾶς ἀπὸ σκότους εἰς φῶς, ἀπὸ ἀγνωσίας εἰς ἐπίγνωσιν δόξης ὀνόματος αὐτοῦ
Jesus Christ, through whom he called us from darkness to light, from ignorance to the full knowledge of the glory of his name

and Acts 26:18
ἀνοῖξαι ὀφθαλμοὺς αὐτῶν, τοῦ ἐπιστρέψαι ἀπὸ σκότους εἰς φῶς καὶ τῆς ἐξουσίας τοῦ σατανᾶ ἐπὶ τὸν θεόν
To open their eyes, that they may turn from darkness to light and from the power of Satan to God

Barn. 7.2
εἰ οὖν ὁ υἱὸς τοῦ θεοῦ, ὢν κύριος καὶ μέλλων κρίνειν ζῶντας καὶ νεκρούς, ἔπαθεν
If then the Son of God, though he was the Lord and was destined to judge the living and the dead, suffered . . .

and Acts 10:42[11]
καὶ παρήγγειλεν ἡμῖν κηρύξαι τῷ λαῷ καὶ διαμαρτύρασθαι ὅτι οὗτός ἐστιν ὁ ὡρισμένος

---

7 Cf. Col 1:23; Eccl 1:13; 3:1.
8 Cf. Col 1:12.
9 Cf. Heb 2:10.

10 Cf. Matt 10:28; *1 Clem.* 14.1; *2 Clem.* 5.4; see the commentary on Acts 4:19.

ὑπὸ τοῦ θεοῦ κριτὴς ζώντων καὶ νεκρῶν
And he commanded us to preach to the people, and to testify that he is the one ordained by God to be judge of the living and the dead

Polycarp *Phil.* 1.2

Ἰησοῦν Χριστόν . . . ὃν ἤγειρεν ὁ θεός, λύσας τὰς ὠδῖνας τοῦ ἅδου
Jesus Christ . . . whom God raised up, having loosed the pangs of Hades

and Acts 2:24

ὃν ὁ θεὸς ἀνέστησεν λύσας τὰς ὠδῖνας τοῦ θανάτου, καθότι οὐκ ἦν δυνατὸν κρατεῖσθαι αὐτὸν ὑπ᾽ αὐτοῦ
But God raised him up, having loosed the pangs of death

Barn. 19.8 and *Did.* 4.8 call to mind Acts 4:32, but these passages derive from the *Two Ways Catechism;* the form in Acts is more Hellenistic:

Barn. 19.8

κοινωνήσεις ἐν πᾶσιν τῷ πλησίον σου καὶ οὐκ ἐρεῖς ἴδια εἶναι· εἰ γὰρ ἐν τῷ ἀφθάρτῳ κοινωνοί ἐστε, πόσῳ μᾶλλον ἐν τοῖς φθαρτοῖς;
Thou shalt share all things with thy neighbor and shall not say that they are thy own property; for if you are sharers in that which is incorruptible, how much more in that which is corruptible?

Did. 4.8

οὐκ ἀποστραφήσῃ τὸν ἐνδεόμενον, συγκοι-νωνήσεις δὲ πάντα τῷ ἀδελφῷ σου καὶ οὐκ ἐρεῖς ἴδια εἶναι· εἰ γὰρ ἐν τῷ ἀθανάτῳ κοινωνοί ἐστε, πόσῳ μᾶλλον ἐν τοῖς θνητοῖς;
Thou shalt not turn away the needy, but shalt share everything with thy brother, and shalt not say that it is thine own, for if you are sharers in the imperishable, how much more in the things which perish?

Acts 4:32

τοῦ δὲ πλήθους τῶν πιστευσάντων ἦν καρδία καὶ ψυχὴ μία, καὶ οὐδὲ εἷς τι τῶν ὑπαρχόντων αὐτῷ ἔλεγεν ἴδιον εἶναι ἀλλ᾽ ἦν αὐτοῖς ἅπαντα κοινά
Now the company of those who believed were of one heart and soul, and no one said that any of the things which he possessed was his own, but they had everything in common

Three passages remain to be considered. The relation between *1 Clem.* 18.1 and Acts 13:22 arises from dependence upon the same exegetical tradition:

1 Clem. 18.1

τί δὲ εἴπωμεν ἐπὶ τῷ μεμαρτυρημένῳ Δαυείδ; ἐφ᾽ οὗ εἶπεν ὁ θεός· εὗρον ἄνδρα κατὰ τὴν καρδίαν μου, Δαυεὶδ τὸν τοῦ Ἰεσσαί, ἐν ἐλέει αἰωνίῳ ἔχρισα αὐτόν
But what shall we say of the famous David? Of him said God, "I have found a man after my own heart, David the son of Jesse, I have anointed him with eternal mercy"

Acts 13:22

καὶ μεταστήσας αὐτὸν ἤγειρεν τὸν Δαυὶδ αὐτοῖς εἰς βασιλέα ᾧ καὶ εἶπεν μαρτυρήσας· εὗρον Δαυὶδ τὸν τοῦ Ἰεσσαί, ἄνδρα κατὰ τὴν καρδίαν μου, ὃς ποιήσει πάντα τὰ θελήματά μου
And when he had removed him, he raised up David to be their king; of whom he testified and said, "I have found in David the son of Jesse a man after my heart, who will do all my will"

The saying in Acts 20:35 is also found in *1 Clem.* 2.1 and *Did.* 1.5:

1 Clem. 2.1

πάντες τε ἐταπεινοφρονεῖτε μηδὲν ἀλαζο-νευόμενοι, ὑποτασσόμενοι μᾶλλον ἢ ὑποτάσσοντες, ἥδιον διδόντες ἢ λαμβά-νοντες
And you were all humble-minded and in no wise arrogant, yielding subjection rather than demanding it, giving more gladly than receiving

Did. 1.5

παντὶ τῷ αἰτοῦντί σε δίδου καὶ μὴ ἀπαίτει· πᾶσι γὰρ θέλει δίδοσθαι ὁ πατὴρ ἐκ τῶν ἰδίων χαρισμάτων. μακάριος ὁ διδοὺς κατὰ τὴν ἐντολήν· ἀθῷος γάρ ἐστιν. οὐαὶ τῷ λαμβάνοντι
Give to everyone that asks thee, and do not refuse, for the Father's will is that we give to all from the gifts we have received. Blessed is he that gives according to the mandate; for he is innocent. Woe to him who receives

Acts 20:35

πάντα ὑπέδειξα ὑμῖν ὅτι οὕτως κοπιῶντας δεῖ ἀντιλαμβάνεσθαι τῶν ἀσθενούντων, μνημονεύειν τε τῶν λόγων τοῦ κυρίου Ἰησοῦ ὅτι αὐτὸς εἶπεν· μακάριόν ἐστιν μᾶλλον διδόναι ἢ λαμβάνειν
In all things I have shown you that by so

11   Cf. Polycarp *Phil.* 2.1; *2 Clem.* 1.1; 2 Tim 4:1; 1 Pet 4:5; *Ep. Apost.* 16 (27).

toiling one must help the weak, remembering the words of the Lord Jesus, how he said, "It is more blessed to give than to receive"

Since in *1 Clement* and the *Didache* the saying is not designated as a word of the Lord, any dependence upon Acts is ruled out.[12]

Finally, the similarity between *Barn.* 5.8–9 and Acts 1:2 D(!) is not sufficient to prove literary dependence:

Barn. 5.8–9	πέρας γέ τοι διδάσκων τὸν Ἰσραὴλ καὶ τηλικαῦτα τέρατα καὶ σημεῖα ποιῶν ἐκήρυσσεν, καὶ ὑπερηγάπησεν αὐτόν. 9/ὅτε δὲ τοὺς ἰδίους ἀποστόλους τοὺς μέλλοντας κηρύσσειν τὸ εὐαγγέλιον αὐτοῦ ἐξελέξατο Furthermore, while teaching Israel and doing such great signs and wonders he preached to them and loved them greatly; but when he chose out his own apostles who were to preach his Gospel . . .
Acts 1:2 (D)	ἄχρι ἧς ἡμέρας ἀνελήμφθη ἐντειλάμενος τοῖς ἀποστόλοις διὰ πνεύματος ἁγίου οὓς ἐξελέξατο καὶ ἐκέλευσε κηρύσσειν τὸ εὐαγγέλιον Until the day when he was taken up, after he had given commandment through the Holy Spirit to the apostles whom he had chosen, and he commanded them to preach the Gospel

As far as Ignatius is concerned, one can hardly imagine that he knew Acts 20:17–38 when he wrote the *Letter to the Ephesians*.[13] Nothing can be concluded from *Diogn.* 3.4;[14] reminiscences of this kind are also found in the *Gospel of Truth*.[15]

Of the reminiscences in Justin[16] the most important are of Luke 23:49; 24:25, 44–45; and Acts 1:8 in *Apol.* 1.50.12:[17]

Justin *Apol.* 1.50.12

μετὰ οὖν τὸ σταυρωθῆναι αὐτὸν καὶ οἱ γνώριμοι αὐτοῦ πάντες ἀπέστησαν, ἀρνησάμενοι αὐτόν· ὕστερον δέ, ἐκ νεκρῶν ἀναστάντος καὶ ὀφθέντος αὐτοῖς καὶ ταῖς προφητείαις ἐντυχεῖν, ἐν αἷς πάντα ταῦτα προείρητο γενησόμενα, διδάξαντος, καὶ εἰς οὐρανὸν ἀνερχόμενον ἰδόντες καὶ πιστεύσαντες καὶ δύναμιν ἐκεῖθεν αὐτοῖς πεμφθεῖσαν παρ' αὐτοῦ λαβόντες καὶ εἰς πᾶν γένος ἀνθρώπων ἐλθόντες, ταῦτα ἐδίδαξαν καὶ ἀπόστολοι προσηγορεύθησαν

For after he was crucified even all his acquaintances deserted him, denying him. But later, when he rose from the dead and appeared to them, and taught them to consult the prophecies, in which it was predicted that all these things would happen; and when they had seen him ascending into heaven, and believed on him, and received the power which he sent them from there, and went into every race of men, they taught these things and were known as apostles

Luke 23:49

εἱστήκεισαν δὲ πάντες οἱ γνωστοὶ αὐτῷ ἀπὸ μακρόθεν καὶ γυναῖκες αἱ συνακολουθοῦσαι αὐτῷ ἀπὸ τῆς Γαλιλαίας ὁρῶσαι ταῦτα

And all his acquaintances and the women who had followed him from Galilee stood at a distance and saw these things

24:25

καὶ αὐτὸς εἶπεν πρὸς αὐτούς· ὦ ἀνόητοι καὶ βραδεῖς τῇ καρδίᾳ τοῦ πιστεύειν ἐπὶ πᾶσιν οἷς ἐλάλησαν οἱ προφῆται

And he said to them, "O foolish men, and slow of heart to believe all that the prophets have spoken!"

24:44–45

εἶπεν δὲ πρὸς αὐτούς· οὗτοι οἱ λόγοι μου οὓς ἐλάλησα πρὸς ὑμᾶς ἔτι ὢν σὺν ὑμῖν, ὅτι δεῖ πληρωθῆναι πάντα τὰ γεγραμμένα ἐν τῷ νόμῳ Μωϋσέως καὶ τοῖς προφήταις καὶ ψαλμοῖς περὶ ἐμοῦ. τότε διήνοιξεν αὐτῶν τὸν νοῦν τοῦ συνιέναι τὰς γραφάς

Then he said to them, "These are my

12 Helmut Koester, *Synoptische Überlieferung bei den apostolischen Vätern* (Berlin: Akademie-Verlag, 1957) 233–34.

13 Walter Bauer, *Orthodoxy and Heresy in Earliest Christianity* (ed. Robert A. Kraft and Gerhard Krodel; Philadelphia: Fortress, 1971) 83.

14 Cf. Acts 14:15; 17:24b.

15 [NHC 1] 17,4ff; 18,24; 18,33–38; 19,7–10; 19,15.

16 Theodor Zahn, *Geschichte des neutestamentlichen Kanons* (2 vols. each in 2 parts; Erlangen/Leipzig: Deichert, 1888–92) 1.508–9, 580–81. Skeptical is Adolf Harnack, *Das Neue Testament um das Jahr 200* (Freiburg: Mohr [Siebeck], 1889) 51–54. J. C. O'Neill, *The Theology of Acts in Its Historical Setting* (2d ed.; London: SPCK, 1970) 29–44, disputes that Justin knew Luke's Gospel. At the same time, he emphasizes the structural similarity between the theology of both authors. On his explanation, see below.

17 The translations of Justin's *First Apology* are from Cyril C. Richardson, ed., *Early Christian Fathers* (New York: Macmillan, 1970); the translation of the *Second Apology* is from *Ante-Nicene Fathers* 1.191.

words which I spoke to you, while I was
still with you, that everything written
about me in the law of Moses and the
prophets and the psalms must be
fulfilled." 45/ Then he opened their
minds to understand the scriptures

Acts 1:8
ἀλλὰ λήμψεσθε δύναμιν ἐπελθόντος τοῦ
ἁγίου πνεύματος ἐφ᾽ ὑμᾶς καὶ ἔσεσθέ μου
μάρτυρες ἔν τε Ἰερουσαλὴμ καὶ [ἐν] πάσῃ
τῇ Ἰουδαίᾳ καὶ Σαμαρείᾳ καὶ ἕως ἐσχάτου
τῆς γῆς
"But you shall receive power when the
Holy Spirit has come upon you; and you
shall be my witnesses in Jerusalem and in
all Judea and Samaria and to the end of
the earth"

Other reminiscences in Justin include:

Apol. 1.39.3
ἀπὸ γὰρ Ἰερουσαλὴμ ἄνδρες δεκαδύο τὸν
ἀριθμὸν ἐξῆλθον εἰς τὸν κόσμον, καὶ οὗτοι
ἰδιῶται, λαλεῖν μὴ δυνάμενοι
For a band of twelve men went forth
from Jerusalem, and they were common
men, not trained in speaking

and Acts 4:13
θεωροῦντες δὲ τὴν τοῦ Πέτρου παρρησίαν
καὶ Ἰωάννου καὶ καταλαβόμενοι ὅτι
ἄνθρωποι ἀγράμματοί εἰσιν καὶ ἰδιῶται,
ἐθαύμαζον
Now when they saw the boldness of Peter
and John, and perceived that they were
uneducated, common men, they wondered

Apol. 1.49.5
οἱ δὲ ἀπὸ τῶν ἐθνῶν μηδέποτε μηδὲν
ἀκούσαντες περὶ τοῦ χριστοῦ, μέχρις οὗ οἱ
ἀπὸ Ἰερουσαλὴμ ἐξελθόντες ἀπόστολοι
αὐτοῦ ἐμήνυσαν τὰ περὶ αὐτοῦ καὶ τὰς
προφητείας παρέδωκαν, πληρωθέντες χαρᾶς
καὶ πίστεως τοῖς εἰδώλοις ἀπετάξαντο καὶ
τῷ ἀγεννήτῳ θεῷ διὰ τοῦ χριστοῦ ἑαυτοὺς
ἀνέθηκαν
But people of the Gentiles, who had
never even heard about Christ until his
apostles who came forth from Jerusalem
testified to the things about him and gave
them the prophecies, were filled with joy
and faith, turned away from their idols,

and dedicated themselves to the unbe-
gotten God through Christ

and Acts 13:48
ἀκούοντα δὲ τὰ ἔθνη ἔχαιρον καὶ ἐδόξαζον
τὸν λόγον τοῦ κυρίου καὶ ἐπίστευσαν ὅσοι
ἦσαν τεταγμένοι εἰς ζωὴν αἰώνιον
And when the Gentiles heard this, they
were glad and glorified the word of God;
and as many as were ordained to eternal
life believed

Apol. 2.10.6
ὁ δὲ δαίμονας μὲν τοὺς φαύλους καὶ τοὺς
πράξαντας ἃ ἔφασαν οἱ ποιηταί, ἐκβαλὼν
τῆς πολιτείας καὶ Ὅμηρον καὶ τοὺς ἄλλους
ποιητάς, παραιτεῖσθαι τοὺς ἀνθρώπους
ἐδίδαξε, πρὸς θεοῦ δὲ τοῦ ἀγνώστου αὐτοῖς
διὰ λόγου ζητήσεως ἐπίγνωσιν προὔ-
τρέπετο
But he cast out from the state both
Homer and the rest of the poets, and
taught people to reject the wicked
demons and those who did the things
which the poets related; and he exhorted
them to become acquainted with the God
who was to them unknown, by means of
the investigation of reason

and Acts 17:23
διερχόμενος γὰρ καὶ ἀναθεωρῶν τὰ σεβάσματα ὑμῶν εὗρον καὶ βωμὸν ἐν ᾧ ἐπεγέγ-
ραπτο· Ἀγνώστῳ θεῷ. ὃ οὖν ἀγνοοῦντες
εὐσεβεῖτε, τοῦτο ἐγὼ καταγγέλλω ὑμῖν
For as I passed along, and observed the
objects of your worship, I found also an
altar with this inscription, "To an
unknown god." What therefore you
worship as unknown, this I proclaim to
you

For evidence from Marcion, see Tertullian *Adv. Marc.*
5.1–2 and *Praescr. haer.* 22. The *Epistula Apostolorum*
makes extensive use of Acts.[18]

We are on firm ground around the year 180 C.E. Acts
7:60 is cited in the account of the Martyrs of Lyons,[19]
without reference, however, to the source used. The *Acts
of Peter*, written about 190, assumes the existence of
Acts.[20] The author of the *Acts of Paul*, writing before
197, may have been acquainted with Acts.[21] Both the

---

18 The writing should be dated in the second century;
see H. Duensing in *NTApoc* 1.190–91.

19 In Eusebius *Hist. eccl.* 5.2.5.

20 This document was written before the *Acts of Paul*,
see *NTApoc* 2.275.

21 On the date, see Tertullian *Bapt.* 17; on the connection with Acts, see Wilhelm Schneemelcher, "Die
Apostelgeschichte des Lukas und die Acta Pauli,"

Apophoreta: Festschrift für Ernst Haenchen (ed. W.
Eltester and F. H. Kettler; BZNW 30; Berlin: Töpelmann, 1964) 250.

Muratorian Canon and Irenaeus explicitly identify Acts as a work of Luke. The *Muratorian Canon* states:

> But the acts of all the apostles are written in one book. For the "most excellent Theophilus" Luke summarizes the several things that in his own presence have come to pass, as also by the omission of the passion of Peter he makes quite clear, and equally by (the omission) of the journey of Paul, who from the city (of Rome) proceeded to Spain (Acta autem omnium apostolorum sub uno libro scripta sunt. Lucas optimo Theophilo comprehendit, quae sub praesentia eius singula gerebantur, sicuti et semota passione Petri evidenter declarat, sed et profectioni Pauli ab urbe ad Spaniam proficiscentis).[22]

In regard to Luke, it says the following:

> The third Gospel book, that according to Luke. This physician Luke after Christ's ascension (resurrection?), since Paul had taken him as an expert in the way (of the teaching) [iuris studiosum], composed it in his own name according to (his) thinking. Yet neither did he himself see the Lord in the flesh . . . (Tertium evangelii librum secundum Lucam. Lucas iste medicus post ascensum Christi, cum eum Paulus quasi ut iuris studiosum secum adsumpsisset, nomine suo ex opinione conscripsit, dominum tamen nec ipse vidit in carne . . .).[23]

Irenaeus calls Luke a "follower and disciple of the apostles" (sector et discipulus apostolorum *Adv. haer.* 3.10.1), "the follower of Paul" (ὁ ἀκόλουθος Παύλου *Adv. haer.* 3.1.1), and he says, "he was always with Paul and collaborated with him in (the work of) the gospel" (inseparabilis fuit a Paulo et cooperarius eius in evangelio *Adv. haer.* 3.14.1; a reference to Acts follows [15:39], particularly to the "we" in 16:10–11, 13; 20:6).

The "anti-Marcionite" prologue to Luke says:

> Luke is a Syrian of Antioch, a doctor by profession, who was a disciple of apostles, and later followed Paul until his martyrdom. He served the Lord without distraction, unmarried, childless, and fell asleep at the age of eighty-four [Latin—seventy-four] in Boeotia, full of the Holy Spirit (Ἔστιν ὁ Λουκᾶς Ἀντιοχεὺς Σύρος ἰατρὸς τῇ τέχνῃ, μαθητὴς ἀποστόλων γενόμενος καὶ ὕστερον Παύλῳ παρακολουθήσας μέχρις τοῦ μαρτυρίου αὐτοῦ, δουλεύσας τῷ κυρίῳ ἀπερισπάστως, ἀγύναιος, ἄτεκνος ἐτῶν ὀγδοήκοντα τεσσάρων [cf. Latin—septuaginta quattuor] ἐκοιμήθη ἐν τῇ Βοιωτίᾳ πλήρης πνεύματος ἁγίου).[24]

Following this is a lengthy discussion of the composition of Luke's Gospel, which concludes: "And afterward the same Luke wrote the Acts of the Apostles" (καὶ δὴ μετέπειτα ἔγραψεν ὁ αὐτὸς Λουκᾶς Πράξεις Ἀποστόλων).

According to Donatien de Bruyne and Adolf Harnack,[25] the prologue, with its anti-Marcionite force, would have been written before Irenaeus. But this cannot be demonstrated with certainty, and the dependence of Irenaeus upon the prologue cannot be proved.[26] Thus

---

22 *Muratorian Canon* lines 34–39; the translation is from *NTApoc* 1.43–44. On this passage, see Theodor Zahn, *Geschichte des neutestamentlichen Kanons* (2 vols. each in 2 parts; Erlangen/Leipzig: Deichert, 1888–92) 1.52–53. A reconstruction of the text may be found in Hans Lietzmann, *Das Muratorische Fragment und die monarchianischen Prologe zu den Evangelien* (2d ed.; KlT 1; Berlin: de Gruyter, 1933) 7.

23 *Muratorian Canon* lines 2–7; the translation is from *NTApoc* 1.43. See the preceding note on the reconstructed text. Various conjectures are offered for *iuris studiosum*; see *Das Muratorische Fragment und die monarchianischen Prologe zu den Evangelien* (ed. Hans Leitzmann; KlT 1; Bonn: Marcus & Weber, 1902) 5; Erich Klostermann, "Zum Muratorischen Fragment," *ZNW* 22 (1923) 308–9; Ernst Haenchen, *The Acts of the Apostles* (ed. R. McL. Wilson; Philadelphia:

Westminster, 1971) 12. None of the conjectures is sufficiently grounded.

24 The text may be found in Albert Huck, *Synopsis of the First Three Gospels* (13th ed.; fundamentally rev. by Heinrich Greeven; Tübingen: Mohr [Siebeck], 1981) p. x; the trans. is from R. G. Heard, "The Old Gospel Prologues," *JTS* n.s. 6 (1955) 7, where the text is also available.

25 See "Literature" above for references.

26 See Hans von Campenhausen, *The Formation of the Christian Bible* (Philadelphia: Fortress, 1972) 201–9, on Irenaeus's usage of Acts; also Haenchen, pp. 10–12.

the date of the tradition about "Luke the Antiochene" remains uncertain. The earliest subsequent attestation is found in Eusebius *Hist. eccl.* 3.4.6.

2. Date of Composition

Opinions on the date of composition vary a good deal and are naturally bound up with one's judgment about the author of the book. If the author is really Luke the physician, the companion of Paul, then a date somewhere between 60 and 100 C.E. is possible. Arguments for the earliest dating depend on the absence of any account of Paul's death. From this absence one could conclude that the book was composed prior to Paul's death.[27] A further argument for an early dating is the absence of any allusions to the letters of Paul and Luke's failure to use Paul's letters for the account of his life. The individual points of contact between Acts and the letters rest upon traditions in the Pauline churches.[28] Was Acts written before the letters were widely known in the churches? It is almost inconceivable, however, that the author of Acts knew nothing at all about the letters. Did he purposely ignore them?[29] Whatever the case, we are simply unable to fix a precise date.

If it could be shown that Luke made use of Josephus's *Antiquities*,[30] the earliest possible date for the composition of Acts would be 93 C.E. The passages in question are Acts 5:36 and *Ant.* 20.97–98; Acts 12:21–23 and *Ant.* 19.343–50; Acts 21:38 and *Bell.* 2.261–63/*Ant.* 20.169–72. But here again a literary dependence cannot be proved.[31]

Only some general observations are possible. Acts assumes a knowledge of Luke's Gospel, which was composed after the destruction of Jerusalem in 70 C.E. Occasionally, of course, someone argues that Acts is older than Luke's Gospel.[32] Such opinions are contradicted both by observations on individual passages and by the relationship between the two books as a whole. J. C. O'Neill argues for a late date for the composition of Acts, placing Luke close to the time of Justin and dating Acts somewhere between 115 and 130.[33] Luke's theology, however, is of a much earlier type than that of Justin. Dating the composition of Acts somewhere between 80 and 100 best fits all of the evidence.[34]

3. The Text[35]

At present we know of twelve papyri which contain the

---

27 For a critique of this view, see the excursus after Acts 28:31.

28 Acts 9:21, cf. Gal 1:13, 23; Acts 9:25, cf. 2 Cor 11:33; see the commentary on these passages.

29 Günter Klein, *Die zwölf Apostel: Ursprung und Gehalt einer Idee* (FRLANT 77; Göttingen: Vandenhoeck & Ruprecht, 1961) 189–92; John Knox, "Acts and the Pauline Letter Corpus," *Studies in Luke-Acts* (ed. Leander E. Keck and J. Louis Martyn; Nashville: Abingdon, 1966; reprinted Philadelphia: Fortress, 1980) 279–87.

30 Max Krenkel, *Josephus und Lucas: Der schriftstellerische Einfluss des jüdischen Geschichtschreibers auf den christlichen Nachgewiesen* (Leipzig: Haessel, 1894).

31 Maurice Goguel, *Introduction au Nouveau Testament* (4 vols. in 5; Paris: Leroux, 1922–26) 3.117–29; F. J. Foakes Jackson and Kirsopp Lake, *The Beginnings of Christianity. Part I: The Acts of the Apostles* (5 vols.; London: Macmillan, 1922–33; reprinted Grand Rapids: Baker, 1979) 2.355–59; Martin Dibelius, *Studies in the Acts of the Apostles* (ed. Heinrich Greeven; London: SCM, 1956) 186–87.

32 Pierson Parker, "The 'Former Treatise' and the Date of Acts," *JBL* 84 (1965) 52–58.

33 O'Neill, *Theology*, 1–58.

34 Hans Conzelmann, "Luke's Place in the Development of Early Christianity," *Studies in Luke-Acts,*
298–316.

35 Literature:
Jean Duplacy, "Bulletin de critique textuelle du Nouveau Testament II," *RechSR* 54 (1966) 426–76.
Idem, *Où en est la critique textuelle du Nouveau Testament?* (Paris: Gabalda, 1959).
Ernst Haenchen, "Zum Text der Apostelgeschichte," *ZThK* 54 (1957) 22–55, reprinted in his *Gott und Mensch: Gesammelte Aufsätze* (Tübingen: Mohr [Siebeck], 1965) 172–205; see on the editions of Blass, Zahn, Ropes, and Clark.
Frederick George Kenyon, "The Western Text in the Gospels and Acts," *Proceedings of the British Academy* 24 (1938) 287–315, also available as *The Western Text in the Gospels and Acts* (From the Proceedings of the British Academy 24; London: Humphrey Milford, [1938]; Oxford: Oxford University, 1939).
George D. Kilpatrick, "An Eclectic Study of the Text of Acts," *Biblical and Patristic Studies in Memory of Robert Pierce Casey* (ed. J. Neville Birdsall and Robert W. Thomson; Freiburg/Basel/New York: Herder, 1963) 64–77.
A. F. J. Klijn, "In Search of the Original Text of Acts," *Studies in Luke-Acts,* 103–10.
Idem, *A Survey of the Researches into the Western Text of*

text of Acts, among them P[45] (third century) and P[74] (Bodmer Papyrus XVII, seventh century).[36] The Greek-Sahidic bilingual P[41] also belongs to the "Egyptian" witnesses in a qualified sense.[37]

In Acts the "Egyptian" and "Western" text-types may be distinguished more clearly than in the rest of the New Testament. The Western text is represented by Codex D along with its Latin translation, in part by Codex E with its Latin translation, P[38] (ca. 300 C.E.), P[48] (third century), the Old Latin texts—in addition to the two already named—gig, h, p and others,[38] the critical notes and marginal notes of sy[h], a Coptic manuscript,[39] and quotations by the church fathers.[40]

The problem is further complicated in that the Western text has taken on additions and alterations; this text-type has no representative as pure as does the Egyptian. Moreover, D possesses marked peculiarities which are not characteristic of the text-type as a whole. Typically the Western text offers a paraphrase when compared to the Egyptian (5:15, 39; 6:10–11; 10:25; 11:2, 26, 28; 14:2, 7, 10, 19; 15 passim; 16:39–40; etc.). D intensifies the special features of the Western text so that definite tendencies appear. They include: the expansion of christological titles (1:21; 2:38; 6:7–8; 13:33; etc.)[41] and an inclination toward a more reverential way of speaking (14:10; 18:4, 8; 20:3).[42] There are specific theological shifts: the attitude toward the Jews is sharper (3:13–14; 13:28–29 the Jews and Jesus; 13:45, 50; 18:12–13 Jews and Christians); universalism is emphasized (2:17, 47) as is the importance of the church (4:32; 11:27; in the face of Judaizing tendencies, 15).[43]

Three hypotheses have been proposed to explain this situation: (1) Luke himself composed two editions of Acts, offered by the two text-types;[44] the question remains as to which edition is the earlier; (2) the Western text is a secondary paraphrase; (3) the reconstructed Western text is the original text. In order to make a judgment the results of the investigation of Luke's

the *Gospels and Acts* (Utrecht: Kemink, 1949). Idem, "A Survey of the Researches into the Western Text of the Gospels and Acts (1949–59)," *NovT* 3 (1959) 1–27, "Part II," 161–73. Idem, *A Survey of the Researches into the Western Text of the Gospels and Acts: Part Two 1949–1969* (NovTSup 21; Leiden: Brill, 1969). Bruce Manning Metzger, *The Text of the New Testament: Its Transmission, Corruption and Restoration* (2d ed.; New York: Oxford University, 1968). Walter Thiele, "Ausgewählte Beispiele zur Charakterisierung des 'westlichen' Textes der Apostelgeschichte," *ZNW* 56 (1965) 51–63. C. S. C. Williams, *Alterations to the Text of the Synoptic Gospels and Acts* (Oxford: Blackwell, 1951).

36   On the condition of the text, see Kurt Aland, "Das Neue Testament auf Papyrus," *Studien zur Überlieferung des Neuen Testaments und seines Textes* (ANTT 2; Berlin: de Gruyter, 1967) 91–136.

37   Peter Weigandt, "Zwei griechisch-sahidische Acta-Handschriften: P[41] und 0236," *Materialien zur neutestamentlichen Handschriftenkunde I.* (ed. Kurt Aland; ANTT 3; Berlin: de Gruyter, 1969) 54–95.

38   Heinrich Joseph Vogels, *Handbuch der Textkritik des Neuen Testaments* (2d ed.; Bonn: Hanstein, 1955) 94–97.

39   Theodore C. Petersen, "An Early Coptic Manuscript of Acts: An Unrevised Version of the Ancient So-called Western Text," *CBQ* 26 (1964) 225–41; Ernst Haenchen and Peter Weigandt, "The Original Text of Acts?" *NTS* 14 (1967–68) 469–81.

40   For more information about the "Caesarean" text-type, see Klijn, *Survey*, 110–46, and Haenchen, "Text," 22 n. 2, reprinted in his *Gott und Mensch*, 172 n. 2.

41   Jacques Dupont, "Notes sur les Actes des Apôtres," *RB* 62 (1955) 47–49, reprinted in his *Études sur les Actes des Apôtres* (LD 45; Paris: Cerf, 1967) 523–25.

42   C. S. C. Williams, *Alterations to the Text of the Synoptic Gospels and Acts* (Oxford: Blackwell, 1951) 56–58.

43   Eldon Jay Epp, *The Theological Tendency of Codex Bezae Cantabrigiensis in Acts* (SNTSMS 3; Cambridge/New York: Cambridge University, 1966).

44   Friedrich Blass, "Die zweifache Textüberlieferung in der Apostelgeschichte," *ThStK* 67 (1894) 86–119; idem, *Acta Apostolorum sive Lucae ad Theophilum liber alter: Editio philologica* (Göttingen: Vandenhoeck & Ruprecht, 1895); idem, *Acta Apostolorum sive Lucae ad Theophilum liber: Secundum formam quae videtur romanam* (Leipzig: Teubner, 1896); idem, *Philology of the Gospels* (London: Macmillan, 1898) 96–137; Theodor Zahn, *Die Urausgabe der Apostelgeschichte des Lucas* (Forschungen zur Geschichte des neutestamentlichen Kanons und der altkirchlichen Literatur 9; Leipzig: Deichert, 1916) 1–10.

Gospel must also be taken into account. The great number of harmonizing Western readings found there indicates that the particular intention of Luke was no longer understood; thus the Western text cannot go back to Luke himself. In Acts the Western text tends to smooth over literary seams (3:11; 14:2, 6, 20)[45] and to make "improvements" (15:20, 29; 16:30, 39). The account of the apostolic decree (15:20, 29) and the quotations of Scripture provide test cases.[46]

The alleged Semitisms of Codex D have been brought into the discussion as an argument for the originality of Western readings.[47] But aside from the fact that the relation between D and the Western text remains unexplained, these "Semitisms" are difficult to verify.[48] Some of them may be explained on the basis of paleographical discoveries, others as the influence of Latin or Greek. Besides, literary Greek cannot be taken as the standard for the classification of a word or expression as a Semitism. The movement of Koine toward Byzantine Greek

must be taken into account.[49] It is true that there are papyri which evidence "Western" readings from an early period in the East; these were circulating in Egypt (P[38], P[48]). On the whole, however, the papyri support the superiority of the "Egyptian" text.[50]

In many passages the text is clearly corrupt and must be restored through conjecture.[51]

4. The Language[52]

Luke writes Koine. Elements of literary Greek are more pronounced in his work than elsewhere in the New Testament (with the exception of Hebrews), but one still cannot describe the language as literary.[53] The vocabulary is considerable and exhibits points of contact with Josephus,[54] Plutarch, Lucian,[55] and most of all with the

---

45   Dibelius, *Studies*, 84–87.

46   See the commentary on these passages. Lucien Cerfaux, "Citations scripturaires et tradition textuelle dans le Livre des Actes," *Aux sources de la tradition chrétienne: Mélanges offerts à M. Maurice Goguel* (Bibliothèque théologique; Neuchâtel/Paris: Delachaux & Niestlé, 1950) 43–51, reprinted in *Recueil Lucien Cerfaux: Études d'exégèse et d'histoire religieuse de Monseigneur Cerfaux* (3 vols.; BETL 6, 7, 18; Gembloux: Duculot, 1954–62) 2.93–103. For a contrary opinion, see Ernst Haenchen, "Schriftzitate und Textüberlieferung in der Apostelgeschichte," *ZThK* 51 (1954) 153–67, reprinted in his *Gott und Mensch*, 157–71, and "Text," reprinted in *Gott und Mensch*, 172–205.

47   Matthew Black, *An Aramaic Approach to the Gospels and Acts* (3d ed.; Oxford: Clarendon, 1967).

48   Haenchen, pp. 54–55; idem, "Text," 49–51.

49   An example would be the construction participle + καί + finite verb; see David Tabachovitz, *Die Septuaginta und das Neue Testament* (Skrifter utg. av Svenska Institutet i Athen 8:4; Lund: Gleerup, 1956) 41–54. A. Werner, "Die Syntax des einfachen Satzes bei Genesios," *ByzZ* 31 (1931) 258–323.

50   Cf. also the Lukan text of P[75], see Haenchen, pp. 56–59.

51   See the commentary on 3:16; 4:25; 10:36–41; 19:40.

52   Literature:
     Gudmond Björck, ῞Ην διδάσκων: *Die periphrastischen Konstruktionen im Griechischen* (SHVU 32:2; Uppsala: Almqvist & Wiksell, 1940).
     Henry J. Cadbury, "Four Features of Lucan Style,"

Studies in Luke-Acts, 87–102.
     Idem, *The Style and Literary Method of Luke* (HTS 6; Cambridge: Harvard University, 1920).
     Idem, *Beginnings* 2.30–105.
     Herman Ljungvik, *Beiträge zur Syntax der spätgriechischen Volkssprache* (SHVU 27:3; Uppsala: Almqvist & Wiksell, 1932).
     Eduard Norden, *Die antike Kunstprosa vom VI. Jahrhundert v. Chr. bis in die Zeit der Renaissance* (2d ed.; Leipzig: Teubner, 1909) 480–92.
     Jonas Palm, *Über Sprache und Stil des Diodoros von Sizilien: Ein Beitrag zur Beleuchtung der hellenistischen Prosa* (Lund: Gleerup, 1955).
     H. F. D. Sparks, "The Semitisms of the Acts," *JTS* n.s. 1 (1950) 16–28.
     David Tabachovitz, *Die Septuaginta und das Neue Testament* (Skrifter utg. av Svenska Institutet i Athen 8:4; Lund: Gleerup, 1956).
     Nigel Turner, "The Relation of Luke I and II to Hebraic Sources and to the Rest of Luke-Acts," *NTS* 2 (1955–56) 100–109.
     Albert Wifstrand, "Lukas och den grekiska klassicismen," *SEÅ* 5 (1940) 139–51.
     Idem, "Lukas och Septuaginta," *STK* 16 (1940) 243–62.

53   Ludwig Radermacher, *Neutestamentliche Grammatik: Das Griechisch des Neuen Testaments im Zusammenhang mit der Volkssprache* (2d ed.; HNT 1; Tübingen: Mohr [Siebeck], 1925) 25, describes the language as "slightly polished vernacular."

54   B. Brüne, *Flavius Josephus und seine Schriften in ihrem Verhältnis zum Judentume, zur griechisch-römischen Welt*

LXX. The last is not by chance—Luke makes a conscious effort to write in a devotional and biblical style.[56]

The following elements characteristic of literary Greek may be observed. First there is the use of the optative, rare in the New Testament: (1) potential optative in an independent clause (26:29); (2) in a direct question (8:31; 17:18); (3) in an indirect question (5:24; 10:17); (4) after εἰ, "whether" (17:27); (5) in a hypothetical protasis (20:16); and (6) without ἄν for the subjunctive of the direct discourse with ἄν (25:16).[57] Next is the use of the future infinitive with μέλλειν (11:28; 27:10), and the future participle to indicate purpose (8:27; 10:22).[58] Rhetorical devices may be observed, especially in the speeches: litotes (12:18 and often), paronomasia (17:30; 21:28; 24:3), and parechesis (17:25; 18:18). Only Luke continues to use indirect discourse to any considerable degree. Words are repeated (5:2, 3; 5:5, 10; 19:35–36), but also may be varied: κτῆμα (5:2), χωρίον (5:3, 8). Further, their forms may be altered: ζήτησις and ζήτημα (15:2); τῆς θεᾶς (19:27), τὴν θεόν (19:37); ἡ ἐπαρχία (23:34), ἡ ἐπάρχειος (25:1).

On the other side of the ledger Hellenistic forms may be noted: first-aorist endings on second-aorist verbs such as ἀνεῖλαν (10:39; etc.); ἐδίδουν, ἐτίθουν (4:33, 35); ἤμην (10:30); ἤμεθα (27:37). The Attic ἴσασι in 26:4 is unusual. The distinction between comparative and superlative is disappearing; note ἀκριβέστερον (24:22) and κάλλιον (25:10). The genitive is replaced with a κατά construction in 17:28 and 26:3. Of the prepositions the Hellenistic ἐνώπιον, among others, is prominent (cf. LXX). The

distinction between ἐν and εἰς is blurred (8:40; 19:22). ἐάν is used with the indicative in 8:31, as is ἵνα in 21:24. The use of periphrastic constructions is characteristic of the times.[59] The genitive of the articular infinitive is used with much more than normal frequency.[60] The typical Hellenistic loosening up of sentence structure is evident in the increased use of the genitive absolute (cf. 21:34; 22:17) and the infinitive with subjective accusative; also where the subject of the main verb and of the infinitive are identical (25:4; 5:36).[61] Solecisms are found in 23:20; 27:10; and 26:20. A disregard for congruence occurs alongside carefully worded statements (cf. 26:2ff). The following are a few Lukan peculiarities: μὲν οὖν; γίνεσθαι with the infinitive; καί after a relative pronoun; relative clauses which are really main clauses.[62]

The extent and character of "Semitisms" has been particularly debated. Many see these as an indication of Aramaic sources.[63] But they are also found in sections which are clearly redactional, and upon closer examination prove to be LXX Greek; for example: the pleonastic ἀνιστάναι (8:26–27; 22:10); ἐν μέσῳ (1:15; 17:22); ἐπὶ τὸ αὐτό (2:1); periphrasis with πρόσωπον (3:20); χείρ (7:35). These are consciously chosen stylistic devices.[64]

The fondness for double expressions[65] is also a characteristic of many parts of the LXX, particularly 2 Maccabees. Note also the style of inscriptions,[66] of Dionysius Halic. (*Ant. Roma.* 2.23.3; 2.24.2ff), and finally of the Latin of ancient Roman prayers (Livy 29.27.1–4).

5. Sources[67]

Luke gives us no information about his sources. In order

und zum Christentume (Gütersloh: Bertelsmann, 1913).

55 Henry J. Cadbury, *The Style and Literary Method of Luke* (HTS 6; Cambridge: Harvard University, 1920).

56 Albert Wifstrand, "Lukas och den grekiska klassicismen," *SEÅ* 5 (1940) 139–51, and "Lukas och Septuaginta," *STK* 16 (1940) 243–62.

57 BDF §§ 385–86; Radermacher, *Grammatik,* 160–65.

58 On the infinitive construction after verbs of saying and perceiving, see BDF § 397.

59 Björck, Ἦν διδάσκων.

60 BDF § 400; Radermacher, *Grammatik,* 189–90.

61 BDF §§ 406, 423.

62 A. Debrunner, *Gnomon* 28 (1956) 588, review of Jonas Palm, *Über Sprach und Stil des Diodoros von Sizilien* (see above n. 52), explains these as "Latinismen"; but see Haenchen, p. 139 n. 7; D. Tabachovitz, "In Palladii Historiam Lausiacam observa-

tiones quaedam," *Eranos* 30 (1932) 97–109; A. Werner, "Die Syntax des einfachen Satzes bei Genesios," *ByzZ* 31 (1931) 258–323.

63 Charles Cutler Torrey, *The Composition and Date of Acts* (HTS 1; Cambridge: Harvard University, 1916); *Beginnings* 2.44–63.

64 Max Wilcox, *The Semitisms of Acts* (Oxford: Clarendon, 1965); see the review by Ernst Haenchen, *ThLZ* 91 (1966) cols. 355–57; see also R. A. Martin, "Syntactical Evidence of Aramaic Sources in Acts I–XV," *NTS* 11 (1964–65) 38–59.

65 See the tables in Robert Morgenthaler, *Die lukanische Geschichtsschreibung als Zeugnis: Gestalt und Gehalt der Kunst des Lukas* (2 vols.; AThANT 14–15; Zurich: Zwingli, 1948) 1.22–30.

66 *OGIS* 233.49–50; 234.14–15, 19; 244.19–20; 306.15; 319.22.

to detect them we are dependent upon indirect criteria such as style (for example, traces of an underlying report in a language other than Greek), variations in conceptuality and point of view (judgments on persons and events), contradictions, doublets, and the like. In the second half of the book the question clearly focuses on those sections which are written in the first-person plural. The problem is more complicated in the first fifteen chapters.[68]

One approach to the source analysis of Acts is to assume that a historically accurate Lukan account has been reworked and reshaped.[69] Others think in terms of one source to which Luke has added materials, such as the miraculous gift of tongues in chapter 2 and the reports about Paul and Antioch.[70]

The hypothesis of two parallel sources, proposed on the basis of alleged doublets in the early chapters (especially 4 and 5), is best known in the form developed by Harnack.[71] He takes the scenes of action as his criterion and distinguishes: (1) a Jerusalem-Caesarea source "A" including 3:1—5:16; 8:5–40; 9:31—11:18; 12:1–23; (2) a legendary composition "B" running parallel to this, including chapters 2 and 5:17–42; and (3) an Antioch-Jerusalem source which begins with 6:1 and includes 6:1—8:4; 11:19–30; 12:25—15:35. Sources A and B run parallel; A and the third source supplement one another.

Of course there are many modifications of the two-source hypothesis. Hermann Wolfgang Beyer assumes two sources for the Pentecost story.[72] Kirsopp Lake finds two sources for the martyrdom of Stephen, the founding of the church in Caesarea (Peter, Philip), and for the visit of Paul and Barnabas to Jerusalem (11:19–30 and 15:1–35).[73] The more recent development of the hypothesis occasionally tends in the direction of form-critical analysis.[74]

The hypothesis of an Antiochene source is advocated by Hans Hinrich Wendt, Joachim Jeremias, and Rudolf Bultmann.[75] According to Jeremias it includes 6:1—8:4 (so also Harnack); 9:1–30 (Harnack differs); 11:19–30; 12:25—14:28; 15:35ff (Harnack includes 15:1–34).[76] P. Benoit separates 9:1–30 and takes this section together with chapters 13 and 14; he believes this material is based upon an independent piece. In order to incorporate it, Luke has constructed the redactional connectives found in 12:25 and 15:1–2. Thus in the Antiochene

---

67 Literature:
Rudolf Bultmann, "Zur Frage nach den Quellen der Apostelgeschichte," *New Testament Essays: Studies in Memory of Thomas Walter Manson 1893–1958* (ed. A. J. B. Higgins; Manchester: Manchester University, 1959) 68–80, reprinted in his *Exegetica: Aufsätze zur Erforschung des Neuen Testaments* (ed. Erich Dinkler; Tübingen: Mohr [Siebeck], 1967) 412–23.
Jacques Dupont, *The Sources of Acts: The Present Position* (London: Darton, Longman & Todd, 1964).
Haenchen, pp. 81–90, 117–21.
Adolf Harnack, *The Acts of the Apostles* (New Testament Studies 3; Crown Theological Library 27; London: Williams & Norgate, 1909).
Massey Hamilton Shepherd, "A Venture in the Source Analysis of Acts," *Munera Studiosa: Studies Presented to W. H. P. Hatch* (ed. Massey Hamilton Shepherd and Sherman Elbridge Johnson; Cambridge, MA: Episcopal Theological School, 1946) 91–105.
Etienne Trocmé, *Le "Livre des Actes" et l'histoire* (Études d'Histoire et de Philosophie Religieuses 45; Paris: Presses Universitaires de France, 1957).
68 See the references in Haenchen, pp. 14–50, 81–90, 116–21; Trocmé, *Livre des Actes;* Dupont, *Sources.*

69 Martin Sorof, *Die Entstehung der Apostelgeschichte: Eine kritische Studie* (Berlin: Nicolai [R. Stricker], 1890); Alfred Loisy, *Les Actes des Apôtres: Traduction nouvelle avec introduction et notes* (Christianisme; Paris: F. Rieder, 1925) 9–67, 104–21.
70 Bernhard Weiss, *Lehrbuch der Einleitung in das Neue Testament* (Berlin: Hertz, 1886) 569–84.
71 Harnack, *Acts,* 162–202.
72 Hermann Wolfgang Beyer, *Die Apostelgeschichte* (8th ed.; NTD 5; Göttingen: Vandenhoeck & Ruprecht, 1957) 15–16, 28–29.
73 *Beginnings* 2.148–55.
74 Lucien Cerfaux, "La composition de la première partie du Livre des Actes," *EThL* 13 (1936) 667–91, reprinted in *Recueil Cerfaux,* 2.63–91; Trocmé, *Livre des Actes;* Dupont, *Sources,* 59.
75 Hans Hinrich Wendt, *Die Apostelgeschichte* (9th ed.; KEK 3; Göttingen: Vandenhoeck & Ruprecht, 1913) 21–40; idem, "Die Hauptquelle der Apostelgeschichte," *ZNW* 24 (1925) 293–305; Joachim Jeremias, "Untersuchungen zum Quellenproblem der Apostelgeschichte," *ZNW* 36 (1937) 205–21, reprinted in his *Abba: Studien zur neutestamentlichen Theologie und Zeitgeschichte* (Göttingen: Vandenhoeck & Ruprecht, 1966) 238–55; Bultmann, "Quellen."
76 Harnack, *Acts,* 186–88 (on 6:1—8:4), 174 (on 9:1–30), 199 (on 15:1–35).

source 15:3 was joined to 11:27–30, according to Benoit, meaning that the alleged two journeys of Paul to Jerusalem in Acts turn out to be the same journey.[77]

A turning point in the source analysis of Acts can already be seen in the work of Julius Wellhausen and Paul Wendland.[78] Martin Dibelius introduced the form-critical viewpoint in a programmatic manner (see below). There remain, however, questions regarding written sources which existed in the stage between the oral tradition and Luke's adaptation of the materials.

We may summarize the results of source analysis to this point as follows. A separation of sources on the basis of linguistic indices (such as an Aramaic substratum) has not succeeded. But the relative unity of style does not prove that no sources have been used. In the Gospel of Luke we may observe in a controlled setting the way in which the author reworks the language of his sources.

The question is: Did Luke use rather extensive sources which offered a connected historical account (beginning in Jerusalem, etc.) or did he use only individual traditions, whose original form can be reconstructed only by conjecture? Such individual traditions could have been available to him in written form. In any case he did not invent his individual stories, he merely put them into narrative form and connected them. This judgment is based on the following evidence: (1) The narrative technique. The story of Peter's deliverance in 12:3–19 exhibits stylistic peculiarities. Should one therefore conclude that Luke has worked from an earlier written account of this incident? Stylistic criteria alone are not sufficient to prove the existence of such a written account. (2) The naming of persons and locations. But this also offers only uncertain clues. For example, someone will point out that at first Barnabas ranks before Paul, tracing this back to a particular source. But this may be a result of Luke's own work. Luke has two traditions about the founding of the congregation in Caesarea; the attempt to divide up the material into two sources, however, simply does not succeed. Source

analysis on the basis of doublets is not convincing either.

There is always the possibility of a historical explanation (that chaps. 4 and 5, for example, have to do with different events) or a form-critical explanation which would suggest that individual stories were used, rather than longer continuous sources. But the assumption that there were longer sources running through the first part of Acts is precarious, since no pre-Lukan connecting pieces can be discerned between the various episodes. Moreover, it can be demonstrated in individual instances that the connection is from the hand of Luke; an example is the link between the miracle in chapter 3 and the persecution in chapter 4. Written source material is most clearly evident: (1) where lists are given (6:5; 13:1–3); (2) where a Lukan connective has been inserted into a narrative (18:19–20); (3) where there are contradictions; (4) where events are viewed from a non-Lukan perspective (such as at Antioch!); (5) where style betrays the existence of an underlying source document (12:3–19; see above); or (6) where a narrative has been mutilated by its insertion into its context (19:13–16). Thus it is certain that sources have been used. Whether their reconstruction is still possible is another question, a question which must be answered in the negative.

What written source documents, then, may have existed? There probably was a collection of stories from Jerusalem, focused on the twelve disciples. Hints for the existence of such a written collection include reports that do not fit with the general picture Luke sketches (4:36–37) as well as Lukan insertions into a connected narrative.[79] A "Hellenistic" collection appears to have connected Jerusalem and Antioch. Passages like 6:1–6, as well as the martyrdom of Stephen, indicate that this material was in written form. Furthermore, in the legends about the conversion of Saul there are tensions between the original wording and the Lukan picture. The whole complex of traditions about "Saul and Jerusalem" has a number of peculiarities.[80]

The problem of sources in the second part of Acts

77   Pierre Benoit, "La deuxième visite de saint Paul à Jérusalem," *Bib* 40 (1959) 778–92, reprinted in his *Exégèse et théologie* (4 vols.; Paris: Cerf, 1961–82) 3.285–99.

78   Julius Wellhausen, *Kritische Analyse der Apostelgeschichte* (AGG n.s. 15:2; Berlin, 1914) 1–56; Paul Wendland, *Die urchristlichen Literaturformen* (HNT 1:2–3; 2d ed.; Tübingen: Mohr [Siebeck], 1912)

332–35.

79   See the commentary on 5:4.

80   See the commentary on 22:3. On the consequences for the reconstruction of the events, see Ernst Haenchen, "The Book of Acts as Source Material for the History of Early Christianity," *Studies in Luke-Acts*, 258–78; Hans Conzelmann, *History of Primitive Christianity* (Nashville/New York: Abingdon, 1973)

focuses on the presence of "we" at various points in the narrative and Luke's use of an alleged "itinerary." If certain sections are narrated in the first-person plural, one's immediate conclusion is that the narrator is an eyewitness. Then the question is whether the author of Acts ("Luke") was with Paul for a time, or whether he has incorporated into his work the account of an eyewitness (Luke?). The abrupt manner in which the "we" appears speaks for the latter, while the uniformity of style argues for the former.[81] This argument from style is certainly not compelling, however, as the above indicates. In fact it only increases the difficulty, because one must then conclude that the author occasionally eliminates the "we" or extends its use into adjacent sections.

Dibelius sets out in a new direction. Since the "we" passages provide no certain guide for source analysis, he proceeds by means of style criticism, where "style" is understood in the comprehensive sense of form criticism. Dibelius notes that routine reports about routes, stations, stopping places, and hosts at these places can be separated from edifying stories. Thus he distinguishes between these edifying stories and the framework in which they are embedded. He calls the framework an "itinerary" and understands it as a source which runs through this second part of Acts. As support for his thesis, he notes that places are mentioned at which nothing really occurs; thus their inclusion is unrelated to the goal of the book. The author of Acts must have had access to this "itinerary." He inserted individual stories at appropriate places and the seams marking these insertions are still evident (14:6, 20). Perhaps Luke created the we-form "in order to make it clear that he himself took part in Paul's journeys."[82] This hypothesis has been widely accepted. Ernst Haenchen accepts the hypothesis and then asks the redaction-critical question: Of whom

would the reader think upon encountering this "we"? Haenchen's answer: Timothy and Silas.[83] That seems unlikely, however, because the two were already with Paul before the appearance of the "we." In addition, we would have to assume that not even the first reader of the book knew the author—meaning that the dedication of Luke's Gospel and Acts would be artifices.[84]

Doubts have been raised about the assumption of an itinerary or a travel diary.[85] If there had been a travel diary, it presumably would have been destroyed in the shipwreck at Malta.[86] The contents might have been recalled, but the hypothesis of a written source would have to be surrendered. More important, such an assumed diary would have had no uniformity. Notes about travels by land are distinct from those about travels on the sea (only in the latter does the "we" predominate), and the report about the journey to Rome stands out as distinct from both of these, as Dibelius rightly observed. He concluded that at this point the author made use of a ready-made written account of a journey. This source would have provided the only real description of Paul's experiences on his travels (9:1–30 is wholly another matter), such descriptions being absent from the presumed itinerary. But could data about Paul's experiences have been totally lacking in an "itinerary"? One may think, for example, of the intimations of such experiences during Paul's travels given in 2 Cor 11:23–27. And would there have been no references to relationships with other Christian congregations? We find nothing at all about the active communications between Ephesus and Corinth which we know from the Corinthian letters. Such an itinerary would appear to be as unilinear and schematic as Luke's own structuring of Paul's travels.[87] Therefore one must ask whether the situation was not just the reverse, that is, the author took

22–24.

81 Adolf Harnack, *Luke the Physician: The Author of the Third Gospel and the Acts of the Apostles* (Crown Theological Library 19; London: Williams & Norgate, 1907) 8–11.

82 Dibelius, *Studies*, 105.

83 Haenchen, pp. 490–91.

84 On the relation between the dedication and the "we," see Henry J. Cadbury, "'We' and 'I' Passages in Luke-Acts," *NTS* 3 (1956–57) 128–32.

85 Trocmé, *Livre des Actes*, 128–38; Gottfried Schille, "Die Fragwürdigkeit eines Itinerars der Paulus-

reisen," *ThLZ* 84 (1959) cols. 165–74.

86 A. D. Nock in a review of Dibelius, *Studies*, in *Gnomon* 25 (1953) 499, reprinted as "The Book of Acts," in his *Essays on Religion and the Ancient World* (ed. Zeph Stewart; 2 vols.; Cambridge: Harvard University, 1972) 2.823.

87 Schille, "Die Fragwürdigkeit eines Itinerars der Paulusreisen"; see also Dupont, *Sources*, 147–57.

reports of occurrences in various locations and from these fashioned the travel narrative as a whole. The addition of unimportant stopping places along the way can be explained on purely literary grounds.[88]

The problem of the "we" cannot be solved without attention to the geography involved. These passages do not portray the reporter as a co-worker of Paul, but rather as a companion in his travels from Troas or Philippi to Jerusalem, and from Caesarea to Rome. Thus the reporter appears more as an authority on Paul's imprisonment than on his missionary work. The geographical horizon consists of the coastal areas. The "itinerary" hypothesis does not account for these observations; thus the riddle of the "we" passages remains unsolved. The only certainty is that by using "we" the author attempts to convey the impression of an eyewitness account.[89] Haenchen comments on the relationship between the "we" and the literary form and purpose of Luke:

On one occasion (chapter 16) the "we" serves to provide historical certification for a decisive moment in the Pauline mission; on another, it allows the reader to feel that he is directly involved in the events of Paul's life (20—21; 27—28). But because Luke (leaving out of account a few statements) does not connect the "we" with the portrayal of the Pauline

actions and words, and because Paul is really the center of attention in the second half of Acts, the "we" is used in this second sense only in sections which report no special acts of Paul.[90]

6. The Author

A) The Form of the Whole[91]

The prologue and dedication are indications that Luke intends to write "literature."[92] He demonstrates technical knowledge (8:27) and portrays Christian witnesses as adept in their appearances before representatives of the political and intellectual world, thus giving evidence of the cultured nature of his own narrative. He can write in an archaic-biblical style when portraying the earliest period in the history of the church (with which we may compare—on another literary level—the archaic tone at the beginning of Livy's history), or in a modern style, as when describing Paul in Athens or before Agrippa II.[93] The best way to characterize the book as a whole is with the common designation "historical monograph." There are prototypes for this genre in Greco-Roman as well as in Jewish literature (1, 2, 3 Maccabees).[94] The tendency to divide histories into monographs had penetrated even the writing of universal history (e.g., in the works of Diodorus). Literary genres, of course, overlap. Historical

---

88 Cf., e.g., the extended description in Xenophon Eph. 1.11–12. (The passage belongs to the non-epitomized portions of Xenophon Eph. [!]). On the employment of the diary style by a historian, cf. Lucian *Hist. conscr.* 16 (also 24). Regarding the reliability of geographical data, see Hans Dieter Betz, *Lukian von Samosata und das Neue Testament* (TU 76; Berlin: Akademie-Verlag, 1961) 90 n. 5.

89 Cf. the persiflage in Lucian *Ver. hist.* (Appendix 3; cf. further Appendices 1 and 2); see the commentary on 16:10.

90 Ernst Haenchen, "Das 'Wir' in der Apostelgeschichte und das Itinerar," *ZThK* 58 (1961) 366, reprinted in his *Gott und Mensch*, 264.

91 Literature:
Bertil Gärtner, *The Areopagus Speech and Natural Revelation* (ASNU 21; Lund: Gleerup; Copenhagen: Munksgaard, 1955) 18–36.
Ernst Howald, *Vom Geist antiker Geschichtsschreibung* (Munich/Berlin: Oldenbourg, 1944).
Felix Jacoby, "Griechische Geschichtsschreibung," *Antike* 2 (1926) 1–29.

Idem, "Über die Entwicklung der griechischen Historiographie und den Plan einer neuen Sammlung der griechischen Historikerfragmente," *Klio* 9 (1909) 80–123.
Paul Scheller, "De hellenistica historiae conscribendae arte" (Diss., Leipzig, 1911).
Eduard Schwartz, *Griechische Geschichtschreiber* (Leipzig: Koehler & Amelang, 1957).
Otto Seeck, *Die Entwicklung der antiken Geschichtsschreibung und andere populäre Schriften* (Berlin: Siemenroth & Troschel, 1898).
Alfred Wikenhauser, *Die Apostelgeschichte und ihr Geschichtswert* (NTAbh 8:3–5; Münster: Aschendorff, 1921) 69–76.

92 See the commentary on 1:1.

93 Eckhard Plümacher, *Lukas als hellenistischer Schriftsteller: Studien zur Apostelgeschichte* (SUNT 9; Göttingen: Vandenhoeck & Ruprecht, 1972).

94 On the special genre of *Praxeis,* see the comments on the proem.

writings may contain features of the novelle as well as novel-like traits;[95] in the same way historiography and biography overlap.[96]

On this general level, comparison with other literary genres is relatively unproductive. Only single points of contact are evident. The form of Acts as a whole is stamped with the specific historical and theological views of the author, as is the case with the Gospel of Luke. Thus the speeches are composed in line with the author's theological intention, rather than in line with the patterns common to Greek historiography (whether according to classical or Hellenistic rhetoric; e.g., Dionysius Halic.).[97] Luke does not set out to provide complete biographical data. He does not describe the personality, the individual features, the appearance, virtues, or even the death of his characters. With the exception of the mission history, the biography of Paul is limited to a few schematized hints. Unlike the novel, Acts lacks the description of adventures (e.g., encounters with bandits along the way, etc.), even though Paul's travels include the scenery expected in such writings. This cannot be explained solely by a paucity of materials—since, for example, Luke is acquainted with the escape from Damascus.

Here comparison with the apocryphal acts of the apostles, where this kind of material flourishes, is instructive.[98] We tend to view Luke's failure to provide information about his sources as a flaw. But such silence is permissible for the ancient historian as is illustrated by the way Josephus proceeds in the *Jewish War*. There is a noticeable absence of chronological data, though Luke does recognize the importance of such data (Luke 3:1–2).

But over against these shortcomings are marks of true literary ability. If Luke does not write artistic literary prose (see above), he understands how to impose on his book a unity of style and meaning. He has command of a style characterized by "dramatic episodes"[99] which we find in contemporary historical works (Curtius Rufus) and in the novel. His writing is extraordinarily condensed, but he is capable of variety. He furnishes scenes with local color (Lystra, Philippi, Ephesus) and evokes atmosphere: in Athens, at the farewell in Miletus, in the great trial scenes of the final portion of the book, and in the report of the journey by sea. He is less inclined to include colorful details; thus the exception in 12:3–19 is so striking! The miracle stories are more polished in comparison with the Synoptics.[100] This means the stories have been shaped in a more literary fashion. The categories of form criticism are thus applicable to individual story units in Luke's writings only to a limited extent. In Acts we can no longer delineate precisely even the shape of his sources; in 1:15–26, for example, he weaves together two traditions and forms them into one dra-

---

95 Cf. the way Josephus reworks biblical stories; Martin Braun, *Griechischer Roman und hellenistische Geschichtschreibung* (Frankfurter Studien zur Religion und Kultur der Antike 6; Frankfurt: Klostermann, 1934).

96 Despite the views of Friedrich Leo, *Die griechisch-römische Biographie nach ihrer litterarischen Form* (Leipzig: Teubner, 1901; reprinted Hildesheim: Olms, 1965). For a correction, see Wolf Steidle, *Sueton und die antike Biographie* (2d ed.; Zetemata: Monographien zur klassischen Altertumswissenschaft 1; Munich: Beck, 1963); Albrecht Dihle, *Studien zur griechischen Biographie* (2d ed.; AGG 3:37; Göttingen: Vandenhoeck & Ruprecht, 1970); cf., e.g., the procedure of Cicero (on Lucceius in *Fam.* 5.12) and Tacitus in *Agr.* (along with its central portion).

97 Dibelius, *Studies*, 138–45.

98 Rosa Söder, *Die apokryphen Apostelgeschichten und die romanhafte Literatur der Antike* (Würzburger Studien zur Altertumswissenschaft 3; Stuttgart: Kohlhammer, 1932; reprinted Darmstadt: Wissenschaftliche Buchgesellschaft, 1969); Martin Blumenthal, *Formen und Motive in den apokryphen Apostelgeschichten*

(TU 48:1; Leipzig: Hinrichs, 1933); Günther Bornkamm, *Mythos und Legende in den apokryphen Thomas-Akten: Beiträge zur Geschichte der Gnosis und zur Vorgeschichte des Manichäismus* (FRLANT 49; Göttingen: Vandenhoeck & Ruprecht, 1933); cf. the description of outward appearance in *Paul and Thecla* 3, as well as the motivation for travel and the erotic motivation.

99 Haenchen, p. 107 n. 1; cf. 105–10.

100 This observation may be substantiated by a comparison between Luke's Gospel and Mark. See Luke 4:35; 14:1–6; and see the commentary on 3:1–11 and 9:32–35, 36–42.

matic incident. The Lukan passion narrative provides an analogy in its reshaping of the Markan account of Peter's denial and the trial of Jesus. The narrative style is not so much colorful as dramatic, leading toward a denouement which makes a programmatic or didactic point to the reader. Livy provides an instructive analogy. In many passages he takes the steady narrative of Polybius and condenses it into episodes, thereby breaking up the narrative. The episodes are understandable in themselves, but at the same time shed light on the course of the narrative as a whole.[101]

We can also sense the high literary level of Luke's writing by comparison with some of the apocryphal "acts." These are characterized by: (1) a dissolution or lack of fixed forms (in addition to the apocryphal acts, cf. also the *Gos. Pet.*); (2) the primitive character of the scenes (the childhood stories in the *Gos. Thom.*); and (3) inclinations toward the fantastic (see also the *Protevangelium of James*). The *Acts of Paul* is, of course, of special interest.[102]

Specific examples are helpful. Compare the Ananias and Sapphira story in Acts 5:1–11 with the Rufina story in the *Acts of Peter with Simon* 2 and note the embellishments in the scenes involving Simon Magus. Compare also the deliverance of Eutychus in Acts 20:7–12 with the raising of Patroklos in the *Martyrdom of Paul* 1–2. Note in addition in the *Acts of Peter with Simon:* (1) the exorcism in 11; (2) the style of miracle working in 13.20–21, 25–29 (a rather mechanical multiplication of healing stories); (3) a miracle involving punishment in 32. Further compare a miracle involving repentance and restoration in the *Acts of Paul.*[103] The absence of form corresponds both to the content and the tendency in this material: the senseless miracle flourishes no less than the edifying—such as a miracle that results in conversion.

The author who writes to Theophilus has succeeded in putting individual events together into a meaningful sequence. The reader can understand the sense of the whole, because he is caught up in it. Luke makes the intention of the individual events clear.[104] The most important means Luke employs are: (1) the manner of ordering and connecting the events; (2) summaries, which interrupt the flow of the narrative in order to abstract from it an image and thereby to indicate its meaning; and (3) the insertion of speeches.

B) The Structure

The structure of the book is clear. Two major sections portray the two epochs into which the history of the church is divided: the time of the earliest church, and the time of Paul's mission to the world; the latter forms the bridge to the present. In the first part the church remains bound to the Law; in the second Gentile Christians—through a decision of the earliest church—are freed from the Law. In this way the continuity between the church and Israel in terms of salvation history is maintained (the promises to Israel linking the two), and the continuity within the church itself is shown as a historical process. These views are further clarified by the artistic interweaving of the two parts. The first part anticipates the theme of the second as it portrays first the mission to the Samaritans, and then—as a kind of model—to the Gentiles (chaps. 10—11). Just at this point the bearer of the mission to the world takes up his task and, through the "model" first missionary journey (chaps. 13—14), prepares the church for the decision reached in chapter 15.

This pattern of linear movement from Jews through the Samaritans to the Gentiles is the author's way of indicating the divine guidance over this history. But, of course, it implies a certain schematizing and also the exclusion of historical materials which would be invaluable to us today. Whole territories are passed over, even though the author knows something about the congregations located there (Syria, Cilicia).

In the first portion of Acts the scenes of action shift back and forth: Jerusalem and Samaria, Jerusalem and Caesarea. This is necessitated by Luke's purpose: Jeru-

---

101 See Plümacher, *Schriftsteller.*

102 On the *Acts of Paul*, see *NTApoc* 2.322–90; also see 2.259–322 on the *Acts Pet.*, which include the *Acts of Peter with Simon.*

103 *NTApoc* 2.366–67.

104 Dibelius, *Studies,* 1–25; Hildebrecht Hommel, "Neue Forschungen zur Areopagrede Acta 17," *ZNW* 46 (1955) 147.

salem must remain the starting point, but at the same time the message must find new paths. The linking of Paul with the earliest congregation serves the same purpose. In the second part the action moves in only one direction: we follow Paul from place to place with only hints of other scenes of action (Ephesus/Corinth, 18:24–28). Thus during the stay in Ephesus which lasted for years we hear nothing of events in other congregations, though things were happening in places like Corinth. In general, the picture of the church is reduced to a few strokes of a sketchy nature. We hear nothing at all about the variety of trends within the church, such as the formation of the Gnostic movement. Nothing is said about the inner development of the church, with the exception of the great transition described in chapter 15, not even about its polity! The most important stylistic means used to achieve this picture of unilinear development is the schematization of Paul's work into missionary journeys. This has dominated the historical picture to the present day.

For Luke history is identical with salvation history, and that means the history of Israel, Jesus, and the church. Luke does not provide us with a description of the historical situation in the larger world as a framework or background for this salvation history. References to contemporary events are sparse and are limited to those which touch upon the destiny of the church. The Roman Empire is of interest only insofar as it impinges on the mission of the church; thus we have sections offering a political apologetic.[105]

C) The Summaries[106]

Summaries offered Luke a crucial means of interpretation. The Gospel of Mark furnished Luke with the most immediate example of such employment of sum-maries. In Acts there are short summarizing statements, easily recognizable as redactional constructions (1:14; 6:7; 9:31–32), as well as longer summaries (2:42–47; 4:32–35; 5:12–16). These passages introduce no new material but merely summarize. The three longer summaries pose a problem in that they do not appear to be logically constructed. Thus it is often concluded that we encounter here two separate layers. Either Luke himself has reworked a source[107] or a later hand has expanded the Lukan text through interpolation.[108] This second hypothesis certainly cannot be proved with linguistic arguments. The lack of structural organization may be explained by the function of the summaries in the total work. They pick up a whole assortment of themes and then seek to describe the situation of the church as perceived from within and without. Observation of Luke's procedure in his Gospel is of critical significance in this regard. In Luke 4:14, for example, he has picked up the summary found in Mark 1:14 and expanded it by inserting material from Mark 1:21–28. Thus he has created a pattern: (1) description of the setting; (2) comment about spreading fame; and (3) account of activity (even though the second ought logically to form the conclusion of these three). Compare further Mark 1:32 with Luke 4:40–44 (expanded with material from Mark 3:11–12). These examples reflect the structure of his understanding of history. Luke does not think in terms of causal connections, but rather finds the meaning of the whole in individual events.

D) The Speeches[109]

Luke follows the general example of ancient historiography by inserting "speeches" into his narrative. These serve to instruct, but also seek to please the reader; the

---

105 O'Neill, *Theology*, 59–76, 172–85.
106 Literature:
   Beginnings 5.392–402.
   Pierre Benoit, "Some notes on the 'Summaries' in Acts 2, 4 and 5," in his *Jesus and the Gospel* (2 vols.; New York: Herder, 1973–74) 2.95–103.
   Cerfaux, "La composition," reprinted in *Recueil Cerfaux.*
   Idem, "La première communauté chrétienne à Jérusalem (Act., II, 41–V, 42)," *EThL* 16 (1939) 5–31, reprinted in *Recueil Cerfaux* 2.125–56.
   Jeremias, "Quellenproblem," 206–8, reprinted in his

   Abba, 240–41.
   Heinrich Zimmermann, "Die Sammelberichte der Apostelgeschichte," *BZ* n.s. 5 (1961) 71–82.
   See the comment on 2:47.
107 Cerfaux, "La composition," reprinted in *Recueil Cerfaux.*
108 Pierre Benoit, "Some notes on the 'Summaries' in Acts 2, 4 and 5," *Jesus and the Gospel* 2.95–103.
109 Literature:
   F. F. Bruce, *The Speeches in the Acts of the Apostles* (London: Tyndale, 1943).
   Dibelius, *Studies*, 138–91.

latter is a conscious goal of historiography.[110] Luke shapes his speeches in a completely independent manner, corresponding to his conception of his work as a whole.[111] In so doing, impressions from the Old Testament and Jewish literature clearly play a part (compare the farewell speech in Acts 20:18–35 with Joshua 23 and 1 Samuel 12).[112] These are not abbreviated versions of actual speeches but are literary creations; the same practice was followed in other literature of the time.

The speeches fall into several categories. Missionary speeches to the Jews (and to the God-fearing Cornelius and his associates) dominate the first portion of the book. At first they are delivered by Peter; then, toward the end of the first section, he is replaced by Paul (13:15–41). Luke gives the conclusion of this last speech a mildly Pauline touch (13:38–39). Nevertheless, the speeches do not attempt to reflect the individual style of the speaker, but rather the substantial unity of early Christian (i.e., normative) preaching; note that Luke has Peter speak in the same Pauline manner a bit later in 15:6–11. In any case, the speeches are not presented as exemplary sermons (against the view of Dibelius). They do reiterate the apostolic kerygma, but are not intended to serve as examples of homiletical style. This is clear first of all in that they are designed specifically as sermons directed to Jews (at the time of Luke the Jewish mission was no longer current) and thus represent Luke's historical

reflections on the difference between the time of the earliest church and the time when he writes. In addition, they are not constructed according to any homiletical pattern, but rather according to a literary schema, albeit a primitive one.[113] Thus we can recognize in the speeches the specifically Lukan theology with its understanding of Christology, Scripture, promise and fulfillment, and the pattern of salvation—repentance—baptism.

The persistent elements in the structure of the speeches are as follows. The speech may begin with an appeal for a hearing. This motif has parallels in the appeal of the Old Testament prophets as well as in Hellenistic trial (defense) speeches.[114] The connection between the situation and the speech follows, at times employing the technique of a misunderstanding. The situation can also be reflected in the course of the speech itself; it does not, however, determine the content of the speech. The actual body of the speech frequently begins with a scriptural quotation. The christological kerygma follows, then the scriptural proof. The offer of salvation comes at the end, with repentance as the condition for salvation. Occasionally Luke allows the speaker to be interrupted. This is, of course, a literary device. The interruption takes place after everything essential has been said.

The outline of salvation history as found in Stephen's

O'Neill, *Theology*, 77–99.

Paul Schubert, "The Final Cycle of Speeches in the Book of Acts," *JBL* 87 (1968) 1–16.

Eduard Schweizer, "Concerning the Speeches in Acts," *Studies in Luke-Acts*, 208–16.

John T. Townsend, "The Speeches in Acts," *ATR* 42 (1960) 150–59.

Ulrich Wilckens, *Die Missionsreden der Apostelgeschichte: Form- und traditionsgeschichtliche Untersuchung* (2d ed.; WMANT 5; Neukirchen-Vluyn: Neukirchener, 1963).

Wilckens, O'Neill, and Schubert see a close connection, on the one hand, between speeches and scenes, and, on the other, between the individual speeches. The latter move along with the course of the action and in turn determine and supplement it as to its content. Now, of course, there are relationships: the speeches are connected to the scenes and produce effects in them. The series of speeches to Jews, Gentiles, and Christians, and defensive speeches correspond to the sequence of the story. On the other hand, there are deliberate repetitions. The
speeches express a message which is not determined by the scenes which frame them or by their position in the totality of Acts. Therein lies one distinction (brought into prominence by Dibelius) between the speeches of Acts and those of Greco-Roman historiography.

110 Dibelius, *Studies*, 142 n. 11; Hommel, "Areopagrede," 152–53; cf. from Judaism 2 Macc 2:25; 15:39.

111 Dibelius, *Studies*, 138–85.

112 For the review of salvation history, see the commentary on Acts 7.

113 C. F. Evans, "The Kerygma," *JTS* n.s. 7 (1956) 25–41; for another opinion, see J. A. T. Robinson, "The Most Primitive Christology of All?" *JTS* n.s. 7 (1956) 177–89.

114 For examples from the *Acts of the Pagan Martyrs*, see the commentary on 2:14.

speech (Acts 7) is in a class by itself. It follows Old Testament prototypes (and possibly a source). Luke has used this particular style in Paul's speech found in 13:15–41 and has blended it with the form of the speeches attributed to Peter. Of addresses to Gentiles, only Paul's address on the Areopagus is formed into a "speech." The farewell speech in Miletus is unique. Finally, we have Paul's great defense speeches (and the accusation delivered by Tertullus), which are wholly determined by the situation and Luke's apologetic aim.

7. Major Themes—View of History

Fundamental to Acts is a picture of the whole of salvation history divided up into three epochs: the time of Israel, the time of Jesus (as the center), and the time of the church. This picture emerges most clearly from Luke's Gospel. In Acts it is not so much developed as it is presupposed. The schema determines the ordering of the subject matter in both volumes. The continuation of the Gospel by Acts is neither accidental nor is it motivated by purely literary considerations. The presupposition is that the church is a historical entity which has its own particular time; in other words, that the imminent end of history has been transformed into a portrait of history.

The three epochs are closely connected. Each ties up with the preceding and carries it further, while also possessing its own additional characteristics. The first is the time of the Law and prophecy, the middle the time of the preaching of the kingdom of God (Luke 16:16) and its representation in the acts of Jesus, and the third epoch is the time of the church, to which the Spirit has been given and with it the power for the mission to the world. In the middle epoch only Jesus possessed the Spirit, in a manner distinct from believers in the third epoch (cf. Luke 3:22 with Mark 1:10 and Acts 2:3). In the Old Testament era the Spirit only came to individuals, and then only sporadically in the form of momentary inspiration.

Luke's division within the third epoch indicates that he conceives of the church as an entity with its own historical dimensions. The time of the earliest church is a unique epoch which stands out from the "present" form of the church. It possesses its own peculiar, nonrepeat-able structure. This is because in that community lived the eyewitnesses to Jesus' ministry and to his resurrection. The institution appropriate to that period is the apostolate with twelve members.[115] But the polity of the earliest Christian community cannot be retained. To be sure, Luke carries the office of the elders over into the later church, but only incidentally; it does not fit in with his programmatic portrayal of continuity. Given this view of history, there can be no apostolic succession (on this basis Luke denies the apostolic title even to Paul).[116] The earliest church, in contrast to that of Luke's time, was bound to the Law and in this way the continuity with Israel was preserved. The sharing of possessions tends to depict the earliest church as a model. This style of life, however, is not intended to serve as a timeless ideal by which future churches are to be measured. It certainly provides no such model in the establishment of the Pauline congregations. Luke knows neither a theology of the church's fall from its pristine love nor a theology of progressive degeneration, even though with such notions of history he could have utilized a favorite theme of Hellenistic historiography.[117]

The connection between the two periods of church history is established through the Apostolic Council. In practice the connection is made by the acceptance of the "apostolic decree," which thus has its own particular historical significance. The most important factor in providing continuity is the enduring teaching of the church, that is, in Luke's view, the picture of Jesus and his teachings as found in the tradition (for Luke there is no development of doctrine!). Continuity is also established by the Spirit as the abiding possession of the church. It is striking that continuity in the history of the church is not located in institutions. Even the position of Paul, who establishes the connection between the two periods, is not defined according to an office, but rather in a purely soteriological fashion: he is the "chosen instrument."

This conception of the whole also shapes the picture of Paul. Of course Luke does not simply invent his por-

---

115 Günter Klein, *Die zwölf Apostel;* see Haenchen, pp. 122–29, for a discussion of Klein's book.

116 In regard to the exception in 14:4, 14, see the commentary.

117 Hartmut Erbse, "Zur Entstehung des polybianischen Geschichtswerkes," *RhM* 94 (1951) 163.

trayal of Paul. He stands in a Pauline tradition.[118] But in this tradition the image of Paul had already undergone considerable transformation.[119] Furthermore, Luke introduces his own conceptions into the picture. For example, because of Luke's historical schematization, Paul has to appear subject to the Law. He cannot establish the freedom of Gentile Christians; only the earliest church can do that. Thus, this freedom is given a historical and ecclesiastical foundation, rather than one that is primarily theological, growing out of the Pauline doctrine of justification.

Luke's view of history also determines his conception of Scripture, as is evident from his use of Scripture proof. Here the continuity of salvation history is assumed. Scripture proof still focuses almost exclusively on Christology. Broader usage of such proof comes only later, in the writings of Justin, Irenaeus, and others.[120] The horizon of scriptural proof extends to the inbreaking of the kingdom of God, corresponding to Luke's schema of salvation history. The resurrected Christ provides insight into the meaning of the Scriptures (Luke 24:25–27), that is to say, Scripture is interpreted from the standpoint of the Easter faith.[121]

The Christology and the christological titles in Acts are the same as in Luke's Gospel. Variations may be explained by the differences in subject matter in each book.[122] Of course, the title $\kappa\acute{u}\rho\iota\sigma$, "Lord," plays a more

important role in Acts. The statistical difference is less significant than the fact that Luke used this title also in his Gospel. Only in Acts does Luke freely develop, in line with his biblicism, the term $\chi\rho\iota\sigma\tau\acute{o}s$ as a title.

In the Christology of Acts the notion of preexistence is absent. A strict subordinationism dominates the entire book. The view of Christ's death as atoning occurs just once, in an expression which Luke has simply taken over from the tradition (20:28) without developing it. *The salvation event is rather the resurrection.* It is expressed in three ways: (1) The direct christological declaration concerning the resurrection (or exaltation) of Christ assures the believer both of the divine guidance of the church's history and of future salvation. (2) This view is rendered concrete by interpreting Christ's resurrection as the prototype of the general resurrection from the dead. We may observe in Luke's eschatology a shift from the cosmic conception of the resurrection toward an individual expectation. (3) Christ's resurrection signifies the great turning point in the history of the world. The times of "ignorance" are past. Since God has offered the resurrection as "proof" (17:31), there is no longer any excuse for rejecting the preached message.

World history as such comes into view only at this turning point, because the whole relationship to the world is understood in the light of a theology of salvation history. The church's relationship to Israel is clear: it

118 Jacob Jervell, *Luke and the People of God: A New Look at Luke-Acts* (Minneapolis: Augsburg, 1972) 19–39; Peder Borgen, "From Paul to Luke: Observations toward clarification of the theology of Luke-Acts," *CBQ* 31 (1969) 168–82, reprinted in his *Paul Preaches Circumcision and Pleases Men and Other Essays on Christian Origins* (Relieff 8; Trondheim, Norway: Tapir, 1983) 43–57.

119 See, e.g., the commentary on 22:3.

120 Justin *Apol.* 1.31.48; Irenaeus *Adv. haer.* 4.33.11–15; Tertullian *Adv. Marc.* 4; Origen *Cels.* 1.50; etc.

121 Jacques Dupont, "L'utilisation apologétique de l'Ancien Testament dans les discours des Actes," *EThL* 29 (1953) 289–327, reprinted in his *Études*, 245–82, calls attention to the fact that the birth of Jesus is lacking in the scriptural evidence in Acts. On the topic in general, see Hans Conzelmann, *The Theology of St. Luke* (New York: Harper, 1960; reprinted Philadelphia: Fortress, 1982) 157–62; Martin Rese, *Alttestamentliche Motive in der Christologie des Lukas* (StNT 1; Gütersloh: Mohn, 1969).

In regard to the formal characteristics of scriptural

use, see Traugott Holtz, *Untersuchungen über die alttestamentliche Zitate bei Lukas* (TU 104; Berlin: Akademie-Verlag, 1968). His thesis is that the citations, which follow the wording of the LXX, were quoted by Luke directly from the LXX, that is, where Luke consults the writer himself, he follows the LXX. That is the case with the quotations from the Twelve Minor Prophets, Isaiah, and Psalms. Luke quoted the remaining citations, which diverge strongly from the LXX, from sources, perhaps "testimonies" (which also were based upon the LXX). Semitic sources for the citations have not been established.

122 C. F. D. Moule, "The Christology of Acts," *Studies in Luke-Acts*, 159–85.

stands in continuity with the ancient people of God. At the same time the church encounters unbelief among the "Jews" and now turns toward the Gentiles. The nations of the world are also seen exclusively from the perspective of mission. This great turning point which marks the end of the time of God's patience is not evident in the events of world history. It cannot be derived from the developments within the historical process (say with the help of the contemporary notion of "origin and degeneration"),[123] though this seems to be suggested by the Areopagus speech. Rather, this turning point in time is evident exclusively in the preaching of the resurrection. The understanding of the world as creation is also found only within the framework of preaching in Acts. It is not developed via a concept of nature. Finally, there is no theoretical anthropology, no reflection on fate and free will, thus also no fundamental problem with the notion of miracles. There is only the apologetic distinction between miracle and magic, which runs through the book and appears in paradigmatic scenes (8:6–24; 13:6–12; 19:11–20).[124]

Finally, limitation to the ecclesiastical perspective makes possible the peculiarly rational form of political apologetic.[125] This is not based on a concept of the state, law, or history. Luke does not argue on the basis of "principles." He does not deal with the Roman conceptions of the state as such, or with the theme of monotheism—state—church in general, but is content with the demonstration that Christian preaching does not impinge upon the power of the empire. Christian proclamation is primarily preaching of the resurrection, and

that is a matter with which Roman law does not concern itself. There is no basis in the texts for the common view that Luke wants to demonstrate to the Romans that Christianity is the true Judaism in order to claim for Christians the privileges accorded Jews. Luke does not appeal to specific Roman laws, but to imperial justice. It would not have occurred to him to present Christianity as a *religio licita*, "legal religion," because no such concept really existed. Tertullian occasionally formulated it ad hoc and the formulation shows that he is not using it as a technical term:

Since we have declared that this religion of ours depends upon very ancient Jewish records—although most people know it only as something of a novelty which came to birth during the reign of Tiberius (a fact which we ourselves acknowledge)—perhaps on this ground there should be further treatment of its status, as if, under the protecting name of a very well-known religion (and one that is, at any rate, lawful), it were concealing some claims of its own.[126]

The expression is used in connection with the concept of the *collegia* (illicit at the time of Luke) and by no means corresponds with what modern scholarship labels *religio licita*.[127] In reality, one must distinguish between two perspectives. On the one hand is the perspective of salvation history, which stresses the continuity between Israel and the church. But there is also the practical-apologetic perspective from which vantage point Luke vigorously distinguishes the Christians from the "Jews"

---

123 Cf. Karl Reinhardt, *Poseidonios über Ursprung und Entartung: Interpretation zweier kulturgeschichtlicher Fragmente* (Orient und Antike 6; Heidelberg: Winter, 1928).

124 Of another opinion is Günter Klein, "Der Synkretismus als theologisches Problem in der ältesten christlichen Apologetik," *ZThK* 64 (1967) 40–82, reprinted in his *Rekonstruktion und Interpretation: Gesammelte Aufsätze zum Neuen Testament* (BEvTh 50; Munich: Kaiser, 1969) 262–301.

125 See Conzelmann, *Theology,* 138–44.

126 Sed quoniam edidimus antiquissimis Judaeorum instrumentis sectam istam esse suffultam, quam aliquanto novellam, ut Tiberiani temporis, plerique sciunt, profitentibus nobis quoque, fortasse an hoc nomine de statu eius retractetur, quasi sub umbraculo insignissimae religionis, certe(!) licitae,

aliquid propriae praesumptionis abscondat (*Apol.* 21.1; the translation is from *The Fathers of the Church: A New Translation*, vol. 10, *Tertullian: Apologetic Works and Minucius Felix: Octavius,* trans. Rudolph Arbesmann, Emily Joseph Daly, and Edwin A. Quain [New York: Fathers of the Church, 1950] 61).

127 For the latest comprehensive treatment (but one which employs unjustifiably the concept *religio licita*), see Simeon L. Guterman, *Religious Toleration and Persecution in Ancient Rome* (London: Aiglon, 1951). Also see Conzelmann, *Theology,* 138–44, on this subject.

and appeals to the judgment of the empire. This duality is characteristic of Luke and is understandable within the context of his overall theology of salvation history.

One's opinion about the much discussed "tendencies" should be formed on the basis of Luke's positive, theological conceptions. This is because Luke's history is aimed primarily at teaching and preaching, and at establishing a foundation for both; he is not polemically motivated.[128] This applies in the presence of two fronts: (1) Against the Jews. Luke reproaches Jews for their intrigues against Christians, even during his own time. But he never denies the connection between the church and Israel in terms of salvation history; indeed, he develops this theme. The debate with the Jews is primarily concerned with basic theology and arises only secondarily out of actual controversy in which Luke is a participant.[129] (2) Against Gnosticism. The theology of Luke is wholly un-Gnostic. He stresses the corporeality of the risen Jesus (Luke 24:38–39), presents a future, cosmic eschatology, has an un-Gnostic view of the world and of history, and so forth. Because of these features many find an anti-Gnostic tendency in his work.[130] But Luke does not polemicize expressly against a Gnostic heresy. We simply do not know what role this heresy played in his environment. If it was a problem for him, he fought it through silence. In any case, conclusions about Luke and Gnosticism continue to be based on an argument from silence.

8. Chronology

The sole firm date in the New Testament, the synchronism of Luke 3:1–2, provides only an approximate clue for chronology. It places the appearance of John the Baptist in the fifteenth year of Tiberius, that is 28/29 C.E.[131] We do not know, however, where Luke got this date, whether from a source or by his own calculation. Also, Luke does not indicate the duration of the ministries of John the Baptist or Jesus.

The mention of various persons provides the fuller chronological framework: Pilate was governor from ca. 26 to 36; Claudius (11:28; 18:2) ruled from 41 to 54. The dates for the governorships of Felix and Festus are uncertain. Felix was in office from about 52 (53) to 55 or 60, and Festus from 55 or 60 to 62.[132] Agrippa I (12:1–2, 20–23) ruled over all of Palestine from 41 to 44.[133] Caiaphus was high priest from ca. 18 to 37.[134]

The fixed point for an absolute chronology is the Gallio inscription.[135] Based on that inscription, Paul's stay in Corinth is to be set at ca. 49/51. If the Apostolic Council took place in the period around 48/49,[136] then the date for Paul's call (ca. thirteen to sixteen years earlier according to Gal 1:18—2:1) would be around 32/35. The dating of events after Paul's stay in Corinth is completely uncertain. Paul's visit to Ephesus (or the "third missionary journey") should be dated between 52 and 56.[137] After this came the journey to Jerusalem, two years of imprisonment in Caesarea until 57/58,[138] the journey to Rome, and a two-year imprisonment there. Paul may have been executed around 60, in any case not as late as the Neronian persecution of 64. Haenchen's chronology differs from the above as follows. He holds that the imprisonment in Caesarea was of short duration; Paul was then taken from Caesarea in the fall of 55, arriving in Rome early in 56, where he died in 58.[139]

---

128 Willem Cornelis van Unnik, "Die Apostelgeschichte und die Häresien," *ZNW* 58 (1967) 240–46.

129 Jervell, *Luke and the People of God*, 41–74.

130 Charles H. Talbert, *Luke and the Gnostics: An Examination of the Lucan Purpose* (Nashville/New York: Abingdon, 1966); Klein, *Die zwölf Apostel;* opposed to Klein is Haenchen, pp. 122–29.

131 Regarding the uncertainty of calculation, see Jack Finegan, *Handbook of Biblical Chronology: Principles of Time Reckoning in the Ancient World and Problems of Chronology in the Bible* (Princeton: Princeton University, 1964) 259–85.

132 See the excursus after 23:24.

133 See the excursus after 12:1.

134 For Ananias, see the commentary on 23:2; for Agrippa II, see the excursus after 25:13.

135 See the excursus after 18:12.

136 See the excursus after 15:29.

137 Haenchen (p. 67) dates Paul's departure from Ephesus in 54; Werner Georg Kümmel (*Introduction to the New Testament* [trans. Howard Clark Kee; Nashville: Abingdon, 1975] 255) places the date at 55/56.

138 Differently in Haenchen, p. 661.

139 See Haenchen, pp. 60–71.

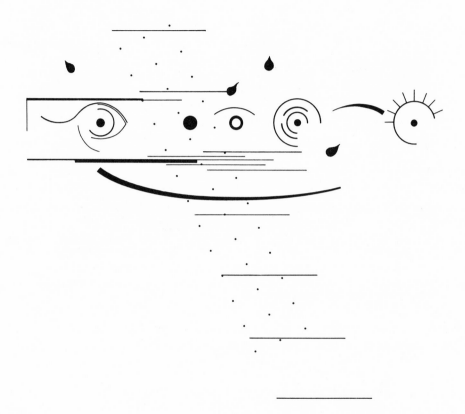

1

Dedication, Proem

1   In the first book, O Theophilus, I have dealt
with all that Jesus began to do and
teach, 2/ until the day when he was
taken up, after he had given command-
ment through the Holy Spirit to the
apostles whom he had chosen.

The title πράξεις + ἀποστόλων, "acts" + "of apostles," as
given in B is hardly original[1] (D has πρᾶξις, to be understood as an itacism). Even in the Hellenistic period, a title
is superfluous for a Greek book.[2]

■ 1 Since the opening includes at least the suggestion of a
proem,[3] Luke is making literary claims and introducing
his book as a monograph. The dedication is also in
accord with literary custom.[4] The address is shorter than
in Luke's Gospel.[5] λόγος has the sense "book" as in Philo
Prob. 1. πρῶτος, "first," with the sense of πρότερος,
"former," is Hellenistic;[6] thus it is not necessary to conclude that Luke was planning to write a third book.[7] For
πᾶς, "all," with the relative pronoun attracted to its case,
compare Luke 2:20; 3:19; 9:43 (redactional!); Acts 3:21;
10:39; 13:38.[8] ἄρχεσθαι, "to begin," is weakened to a
kind of helping verb.[9] In addition to the influence of
Aramaic (the way in which ענה, "answer," is used),
developments within the Greek language itself should be
considered,[10] as well as the unaccented Latin *coepi*, "to

begin."[11] Nevertheless, it should be noted that Luke likes
to refer to the "beginning" of Jesus' ministry (Luke 3:23;
23:5; Acts 1:22; 10:37), and that ἤρξατο has a counterpart in the proem of Luke's Gospel (ἄνωθεν, "from the
beginning"). Of course the meaning is not that the first
book tells the *beginning* of his ministry and the second its
continuation (after the exaltation), but that his ministry is
narrated from the very beginning.[12] The birth story is
skipped over since it plays no role in Luke's economy of
salvation. ποιεῖν καὶ διδάσκειν, "to do and to teach" (Mark
6:30; Matt 5:19) denotes the entire range of Jesus'
ministry.

■ 2 διὰ πνεύματος ἁγίου, "through the Holy Spirit," fits
neither with ἐντειλάμενος, "after he had given command-
ment," nor with ἐξελέξατο, "he had chosen."[13] If it is
retained, it is better to take it with ἐντειλάμενος.[14] The
witnesses of the "Western" text-type have tried to
remedy this defect in various ways. Their readings are all
secondary and are related to the Western reading of

---

1   Christian Maurer, "πρᾶξις," *TDNT* 6 (1964) 644.
2   Ernst Nachmanson, "Der griech Buchtitel: Einige
    Beobachtungen," (Göteborgs Högskolas Årsskrift
    47:19; Göteborg: Wettergren & Kerbers, 1941) 31.
    For πράξεις as a genre and book title, compare
    Callisthenes *FGH* 124, T 26; frg. 14 (with Jacoby's
    commentary); Sallust *Cat.* 4.2: "and write a history of
    the Roman people, selecting such portions as seemed
    to me worthy of record" (. . . statui res gestas populi
    Romani carptim, ut quaeque memoria digna
    videbantur, perscribere . . .); Wikenhauser, *Apostel-
    geschichte*, 94–104; PW 10.1686.
3   See the commentaries on Luke 1:1–4.
4   Rudolf Graefenhain, "De more libros dedicandi apud
    scriptores Graecos et Romanos obvio" (Diss.,
    Marburg, 1892); J. Ruppert, "Quaestiones ad
    historiam dedicationis librorum pertinentes" (Diss.,
    Leipzig, 1911); Wikenhauser, *Apostelgeschichte*, 133–
    36; J. Kroymann, "Widmung," *Lexikon der Alten Welt*
    (1965) 3272.
5   Cf. Josephus *C. Apion.* 1.1 with 2.1.
6   See the commentaries on John 1:15.
7   Theodor Zahn, *Die Apostelgeschichte des Lucas* (3d &
    4th eds.; 2 vols.; KNT 5; Leipzig/Erlangen:
    Deichert, 1922–27) 1.16–18; idem, "Das dritte Buch
    des Lukas," *NKZ* 28 (1917) 373–95.
8   BDF § 294.
9   See the commentaries on Mark 1:45.
10   David Tabachovitz, *Die Septuaginta und das Neue
    Testament* (Skrifter utg. av Svenska Institutet i Athen
    8:4; Lund: Gleerup, 1956) 24–29.
11   W. Süss, *Gnomon* 23 (1951) 314, a review of Enzo V.
    Marmorale, *La questione Petroniana* (Bari: Laterza,
    1948).
12   *Beginnings* 4.3.
13   Dibelius deletes the phrase, see *Studies*, 90.
14   Against Haenchen, p. 139.

Luke 24:50–51 (here ἀνελήμφθη, "he was taken up," is omitted; in Luke 24:51 ἀνεφέρετο εἰς οὐρανόν, "he was carried up into heaven," is omitted).[15] ἐντειλάμενος is explained by Luke 24:44–49. ἄχρι ἧς ἡμέρας, "until the day when," is a fixed expression meaning "until."[16] For ἐξελέξατο, "he chose," see Luke 6:12–13. For ἀνελήμφθη, see 2 Kgs 2:9–11; 1 Macc 2:58 (Elijah); Sir 48:9 (Elijah), 49:14 (Enoch); Luke 9:51; *Gos. Pet.* 5.19; Philo *Vita Mos.* 2.291. On the whole passage, see also *Kg. Pet.* frg. 3.[17]

Excursus: Proems[18]

Proems originally belong to the epideictic genre (cf. Philo *Prob.* 1). Their penetration into Hellenistic historiography is indicative that such literary products are thought of as monographs (Diodorus). Thus the presence of the Lukan proem argues against the thesis that Luke's Gospel and Acts originally formed a single work, separated only for "technical and canonical" reasons. Whether the proem is intact or has been altered by interpolation and thus abridged cannot be settled on stylistic grounds alone.[19] It is true that after the recapitulation of the earlier book we expect a summary of the new one (as in Josephus *C. Apion.* 2.1–2), but this element may be absent (Josephus *Ant.* 8.1–2; 13:1). Eduard Norden bases his case for an interpolation on the lack of a δέ after the μέν. In addition, the following sentences are difficult to understand, and the reference to forty days clashes with Luke 24:50–53. Of course, there is also the possibility of an interpolation in Luke.[20] The solitary μέν is found elsewhere (3:21; 4:16; 27:21; 28:22), though certainly not in such a crass form as we have here. The absence could be explained as carelessness, since the use of μέν is a matter of style. A number of facts speak against the interpolation thesis. No tendency can be discerned in the alleged interpolation, and the passage is Lukan in both style and content.[21] The difficulties with the passage are reduced when we recognize its programmatic nature—the Lukan form of the "kerygma" shines through. Philippe H. Menoud's hypothesis that the whole of 1:1–5 (along with Luke 24:50–53) was interpolated when the Lukan work was divided into two parts does not explain any of the stylistic difficulties. It must also be rejected because vs 6 does not connect smoothly with Luke 24:49.[22] In any case, Menoud has retracted his hypothesis.[23]

15   On the textual tradition, see *Beginnings* 3.256–61; J. M. Creed, "The Text and Interpretation of Acts i 1–2," *JTS* 35 (1934) 176–82.

16   BDF § 294.2, 5.

17   See Klein, *Die zwölf Apostel,* 109–10. P. A. van Stempvoort ("The Interpretation of the Ascension in Luke and Acts," *NTS* 5 [1958–59] 30–42) understands ἀνελήμφθη in Luke 9:51 as "to die," "to go away" in the sense of "passing away," essentially as the mark of a "doxological" interpretation of the ascension, though not yet with the realism of Acts 1:9–11; to the contrary, Jacques Dupont, " ᾽ΑΝΕΛΗΜΦΘΗ (Actes 1,2)," *NTS* 8 (1961–62) 154–57, reprinted in his *Études,* 477–80.

18   Literature:
      Gert Avenarius, *Lukians Schrift zur Geschichts- schreibung* (Meisenheim/Glan: Hain, 1956) 113–18.
      Dupont, *Sources,* 24 n. 3; 107 n. 2.
      G. Engel, "De antiquorum epicorum didacticorum historicorum prooemiis" (Diss., Marburg, 1910).
      Marg Kunz, "Zur Beurteilung der Proömien in Diodors historischer Bibliothek" (Diss., Zurich, 1935).
      R. Laquer, "Ephoros," *Hermes* 46 (1911) 161–206, 321–54.
      Victorien Larrañaga, *L'Ascension de Notre-Seigneur dans le Nouveau Testament* (Rome: Pontifical Biblical Institute, 1938) 270–333.
      PW 21.1543–44.
      Paul Scheller, "De hellenistica historiae con- scribendae arte" (Diss., Leipzig, 1911).

19   Eduard Norden, *Agnostos Theos: Untersuchungen zur Formengeschichte religiöser Rede* (Leipzig/Berlin: Teubner, 1913; reprinted Stuttgart: Teubner, 1923; Darmstadt: Wissenschaftliche Buchgesellschaft, 1956) 311–27.

20   Conzelmann, *Theology,* 15 n. 1; 94.

21   Larrañaga, *L'Ascension,* 223–57.

22   Philippe Henri Menoud, "Observations on the Ascension in Luke-Acts," *Jesus Christ and the Faith: A Collection of Studies* (PTMS; Pittsburgh: Pickwick, 1978) 107–20.

23   Menoud, "'During Forty Days' (Acts 1.3)," *Jesus Christ and the Faith,* 167–79.

1	Jesus' Farewell Speech and the Ascension

3 To them he presented himself alive after his passion by many proofs, appearing to them during forty days, and speaking of the kingdom of God. 4/ And while staying (or: eating) with them he charged them not to depart from Jerusalem, but to wait for the promise of the Father, which, he said, "you heard from me, 5/ for John baptized with water, but before many days you shall be baptized with the Holy Spirit."

6 So when they had come together they asked him (or: those assembled asked him now), "Lord, will you at this time restore the kingdom to Israel?" 7/ He said to them, "It is not for you to know times or seasons which the Father has fixed by his own authority. 8/ But you shall receive power when the Holy Spirit has come upon you; and you shall be my witnesses in Jerusalem and in all Judea and Samaria and to the end of the earth." 9/ And when he had said this, as they were looking on, he was lifted up, and a cloud took him out of their sight. 10/ And while they were gazing into heaven as he went, behold, two men stood by them in white robes, 11/ and said, "Men of Galilee, why do you stand looking into heaven? This Jesus, who was taken up from you into heaven, will come in the same way as you saw him go into heaven."

■ **3** Connection by means of the relative pronoun,[1] and καί, "and," following the relative are typical Lukan constructions. The sentence structure is out of joint, as is the case in other "kerygmatic" passages (3:13–15; 4:10; 10:34–35; 13:31). Also typical of Luke is the use of πάσχειν, "to suffer," for the whole of the "passion" (Luke 22:15; 24:26, 46; Acts 3:18; 17:3; 26:23),[2] and the stereotyped summary of Jesus' teaching.[3] According to this verse Jesus seems to appear only to the apostles (for Luke, the Twelve), while the parallel in 13:31 says he appeared to all who went with him on the journey from Galilee to Jerusalem. The contradiction is not a serious one, however, nor is there any real difference between the forty days mentioned in this text and the ἡμέρας πλείους, "many days," of 13:31. We do not know where the number forty comes from. It plays a role in the Old Testament and in other texts as well.[4] The number is found at Qumran, though it is not a typical expression.[5] It makes its way into church tradition slowly, not appearing again until Tertullian *Apol.* 21.29.[6] The date of the

---

1 This is very common in Byzantine Greek; see Tabachovitz, "In Palladii," 99–102, and Haenchen, p. 139 n. 7.

2 Wilhelm Michaelis, "πάσχω κτλ.," *TDNT* 5 (1967) 912–16; Wilckens, *Missionsreden,* 117.

3 Conzelmann, *Theology,* 218; Alfred Wikenhauser, "Die Belehrung der Apostel durch den Auferstandenen nach Apg 1,3," *Vom Wort des Lebens: Festschrift*

für Max Meinertz (ed. Nikolaus Adler; NTAbhSup 1; Münster: Aschendorff, 1951) 105–13.

4 See BAG, *s.v.* τεσσαράκοντα; Juda Bergmann, "Die runden und hyperbolischen Zahlen in der Agada," *MGWJ* 82 (1938) 361–76.

5 Herbert Braun, *Qumran und das Neue Testament* (2 vols.; Tübingen: Mohr [Siebeck], 1966) 1.139.

6 Urban Holzmeister, "Der Tag der Himmelfahrt des

ascension is different in Luke 24:50–53 and *Barn.* 15.9 (occurring on Sunday, the day of the resurrection); *Asc. Is.* 9.16 has an interval of 545 days and *Ap. Jas.* one of 550.[7]

Luke's reference to forty days implies a fundamental separation between the period of the appearances and the era of the church. This distinction is important, for example, in the interpretation of Paul's Damascus vision. Menoud emphasizes the symbolic character of the number forty—it has its origins in Luke's own reflection.[8]

ὀπτάνεσθαι, "to appear," is a Hellenistic present form (cf. 1 Kgs 8:8 LXX). For belief in the appearances (and miraculous acts) of the dead θεῖος ἀνήρ, "divine man," together with the founding of a cult and proof from prophecy, compare Lucian *Pergr. mort.* 22–42, especially 38–41.[9]

■ **4** For the manner of transition to direct address here, compare 23:22; Luke 5:14; Josephus *Bell.* 1.76; *Ant.* 1.100; Arrian *Anab.* 5.11.4. For the use of ἀπό instead of ἐκ, see 1:9 and 16:39.[10] The setting for the incident described here is not clear,[11] nor is the sense of the verb συναλίζεσθαι. Does it mean "assemble" (this is the sense of the active in Josephus), or "eat (salt) together" (cf. 10:41!)?[12] The command to remain in Jerusalem (Luke 24:47, 49) sets forth Luke's idea of the church: Jerusalem represents the continuity between Israel and the church.[13] According to *Kg. Pet.* 2, the apostles remained in the city for twelve years.

■ **5** The ὅτι, "for," which begins this verse should not be understood as indicating direct discourse (ὅτι *recitativum*), despite 11:16. A saying of John the Baptist (Luke 3:16) is attributed to Jesus. The Spirit is the characteristic of the new epoch in salvation history and the expectation of an immediate Parousia is replaced by the promise of the Spirit. 1QS 4.20–21:

> Then, too, God will purge all the acts of man in the crucible of His truth, and refine for Himself all the fabric of man, destroying every spirit of perversity from within his flesh and cleansing him by the holy spirit from all the effects of wickedness. Like waters of purification He will sprinkle upon him the spirit of truth. . . .

The litotes οὐ μετά, "not after" = "before," is not a Latinism.[14]

■ **6-7** μὲν οὖν, "so when," is a transitional device characteristic of Acts. Here the preceding scene is continued, or a new one is opened, depending on whether one translates "those who had come together then asked him" (cf. 8:4), or "when they had come together, they asked him."[15] The problem raised here had already been discussed in Luke's Gospel (Luke 17:20–21; 19:11; 21:5–36).[16] Luke allows the disciples to formulate their question on the basis of Jewish assumptions in order to correct them and to refuse absolutely any information about the date of the Parousia. The Spirit makes it possible for the church to exist in the world for an indefinite period of time. It is assumed, however, that Jesus knows the appointed date (cf. Luke 21:32–33 with Mark 13:30–32). 1 Thess 5:1 suggests that the double expression χρόνοι καὶ καιροί, "times and occasions"[17] (in itself an innocent enough

---

Herrn," *ZKTh* 55 (1931) 44–82; Larrañaga, *L'Ascension,* 492–531.

7 *NTApoc* 1.337. On the eighteen months of the Gnostics (Irenaeus *Adv. haer.* 1.3.2; 1.30.14), see H.-Ch. Puech and G. Quispel, "Les écrits gnostiques du Codex Jung," *VC* 8 (1954) 7–22, esp. 21.

8 Menoud, "Forty Days."

9 Betz, *Lukian,* 125–26.

10 BDF § 209.

11 Do vss 4–12 form a unified scene in Luke's mind? Thus Dibelius, *Studies,* 175 n. 66; see Pierre Benoit, "L'Ascension," *RB* 56 (1949) 191–92, for another opinion.

12 Cf. on the latter meaning Ps.-Clem. *Hom.* 13.4.3 (on the Lord's Supper!); similarly Charles C. Torrey, "Studies in the Aramaic of the First Century A.D. (New Testament Writings)," *ZAW* 65 (1953–54)

239–40, with reference to the Syriac מתמלח (Ezra 4:14; Ps 141 [140]:4 syᴾ).

13 Birger Gerhardsson, *Memory and Manuscript: Oral Tradition and Written Transmission in Rabbinic Judaism and Early Christianity* (ASNU 22; Lund: Gleerup; Copenhagen: Munksgaard, 1961) 214–20.

14 Cf. BDF § 213 on the equivalent πρό; on the position of the negative and the preposition, cf. § 433.3.

15 BDF § 251.

16 Conzelmann, *Theology,* 120–32.

17 Cf., in reverse order, Wis 8:8; also on secular usage, see James Barr, *Biblical Words for Time* (2d ed.; Naperville, IL: Allenson, 1962) 34–39, 47–49.

expression), became a topic in elementary Christian instruction. Franz Mussner argues that the disciples' apocalyptic expectation as such is not corrected (3:21), only the expectation that the end would come immediately.[18] The question about the "restoration" (cf. 3:21) of the kingdom to "Israel" provides the foil for both the promise of the Spirit and the universalism announced in vs 8.

■ **8** ἀλλά, "but": the Spirit is no longer the power of the end time but its substitute. Verse 8a appears to be a doublet to vs 5, but the repetition makes sense here in light of Luke's understanding of history.[19] Verse 8b indicates the plan of the book: Jerusalem/Judea (chaps. 1—7), Samaria (chaps. 8—9) linked to the mission to the world (chaps. 10—28) by 9:1–10. Things are not changed essentially if the movement is understood as twofold—first in Palestine, then beyond;[20] the arrangement is flexible. By means of this outline the delay of the Parousia is transformed into something positive in the course of salvation history. The mission is here presented as proceeding in direct fashion, for in this way God's guidance is to be recognized. For μάρτυρες, "witnesses," and the genitive μου, compare vss 21–22 and 13:31. For (ἕως) ἐσχάτου τῆς γῆς, "(to) the end of the earth," compare 13:47 (Isa 49:6) and *Pss. Sol.* 8.15 (Rome!). According to W. C. van Unnik, the expression always means the ends of the earth. For Paul this would point to Spain.[21] In the context of Luke's history, and in light of *Pss. Sol.* 8.15, it is unlikely. Apocryphal descriptions of the mission to the world may be found in *1 Clem.* 42.1–4 and Justin *Apol.* 1.39.3, etc.[22]

■ **9-11** These verses are based upon a piece of tradition which assumes no time period between the ascension and Easter. Its original form can no longer be established, because Luke has impressed upon it his episodic style.[23] On his procedure, compare Luke 24:1–12 with Mark 16:1–8, and for his descriptive style, see Luke 24:36–42. Particular manners of expression also reveal the hand of Luke: the temporal ὡς, "while"; ἀτενίζειν, "look intently at"; periphrastic conjugation;[24] καὶ ἰδού, "and behold," and καί, "and," after a relative pronoun. With respect to substantive matters we may ask if the location on the mount called Olivet was present in the material as Luke found it. We cannot be sure, but it could well have originated with Luke (vs 12 is redactional). Nevertheless, Luke may be depending on traditional data (cf. the reference to "a Sabbath day's journey" in vs 12). These verses cannot be excised as an interpolation because of the tension with Luke 24:50–53.[25]

■ **9** One should not press the text to mean that Jesus was first taken up and then later enveloped in the cloud. The event is not divided into separate acts, and the cloud is simply a vehicle (definitely in D sa), as in *Ep. Apost.* 51 (62).[26]

■ **10** For the angelic interpreters, compare Luke 24:4. They warn against the expectation of an immediate return (Haenchen)![27]

■ **11** "Galileans" is explained in 13:31. The reference to the Parousia is redactional. One should not read into this verse that the Mount of Olives is to be the site of the Parousia.[28]

---

18 Franz Mussner, "Die Idee der Apokatastasis in der Apostelgeschichte," *Lux tua veritas: Festschrift für Hubert Junker* (Trier: Paulinus, 1961) 296–98, reprinted in his *Praesentia salutis: Gesammelte Studien zu Fragen und Themen des Neuen Testaments* (Düsseldorf: Patmos, 1967) 225–27.

19 On this expression and expectation, cf. Isa 32:15 LXX.

20 Christoph Burchard, *Der dreizehnte Zeuge* (FRLANT 103; Göttingen: Vandenhoeck & Ruprecht, 1970) passim.

21 W. C. van Unnik, "Der Ausdruck ῾ΕΩΣ ᾿ΕΣΧΑΤΟΥ ΤΗΣ ΓΗΣ (Apostelgeschichte 1:8) und sein alttestamentlicher Hintergrund," *Studia Biblica et Semitica: Theodoro Christiano Vriezen* (Wageningen: Veenman & Zonen, 1966) 335–49.

22 See Walter Bauer in *NTApoc* 2.43–44.

23 Plümacher, *Apostelgeschichte*, 106–7.

24 On this, see Björck, ῏Ην διδάσκων.

25 Just the opposite of Conzelmann, *Theology*, 94.

26 Cf. Rev 11:12 and *1 Enoch* 39.3. Heracles went up in a cloud (Friedrich Pfister, "Herakles und Christus," *ARW* 34 [1937] 42–60), as did Ganymedes (Dosiadas in *FGH* 458, frg. 5); cf. further Dionysius Halic. 1.77.2, also Livy 1.16.1–2 (Romulus), Dio Cass. 56.46.2 (Augustus), Josephus *Ant.* 4.326 (Moses), Philostratus *Vita Apoll.* 8.30. See also Hermann Diels, "Die Anfänge der Philologie bei den Griechen," *Neue Jahrbücher für das klassische Altertum* 25 (1910) 1–25; Richard Holland, "Zur Typik der Himmelfahrt," *ARW* 23 (1925) 207–20; G. Strecker, "Entrückung," *RAC* 5:461–76.

27 Haenchen, pp. 149–52.

28 On the topic of the ascension see: Benoit, "The

Ascension," *Jesus and the Gospel* 1.209–53; Larrañaga, *L'Ascension;* Menoud, "Observations on the Ascension in Luke-Acts," *Jesus Christ and the Faith,* 107–20; Georg Kretschmar, "Himmelfahrt und Pfingsten," *ZKG* 66 (1954–55) 209–53; P. A. van Stempvoort, "The Interpretation of the Ascension in Luke and Acts," *NTS* 5 (1958–59) 30–42; Helmut Flender, *St Luke: Theologian of Redemptive History* (trans. Reginald H. Fuller and Ilse Fuller; Philadelphia: Fortress, 1967) 11–13; Gottfried Schille, "Die Himmelfahrt," *ZNW* 57 (1966) 183–99; S. G. Wilson, "The Ascension: A Critique and an Interpretation," *ZNW* 59 (1968) 269–81. On the development of the legend, see Walter Bauer, *Das Leben Jesu im Zeitalter der neutestamentlichen Apokryphen* (Tübingen: Mohr [Siebeck], 1909) 275–79; *Ap. Jas.* p. 14.29–15.37 (*NTApoc* 1.336–37).

1   The Earliest Congregation

12 Then they returned to Jerusalem from the mount called Olivet, which is near Jerusalem, a Sabbath day's journey away; 13/ and when they had entered, they went up to the upper room, where they were staying, Peter and John and James and Andrew, Philip and Thomas, Bartholomew and Matthew, James the son of Alphaeus and Simon the Zealot and Judas the son of James. 14/ All these with one accord devoted themselves to prayer, together with the women and Mary the mother of Jesus, and with his brothers.

■ **12** Contrary to widespread opinion (based especially on Zech 14:4), there is no evidence for a Jewish view that the Messiah would reveal himself on the Mount of Olives.[1] ἔχον, "being," with the sense of ἀπέχον, "being distant," is also found in *Peripl. Erythr.* 4.37.51.[2] A Sabbath day's journey is 2000 ells, which equals 960 yards.[3] Josephus agrees, giving the distance as 5 stadia.[4]

■ **13–14** The first summary follows. A local tradition about the meeting place can still be detected. The upper room is the place for prayer and conversation (20:8; cf. Dan 6:11), and for seclusion (*Mart. Pol.* 7.1). The list of names agrees with Luke 6:13–16.[5] The picture of the "Spirit-less" interval which consists entirely of waiting is an imaginary one. That it lasts for ten days is of no importance. In the series of salvation events the ascension does not have the same rank as Easter and Pentecost.[6] The language here is Lukan: προσκαρτερεῖν, "to be devoted to"; ὁμοθυμαδόν, "with one accord" = יַחַד, יַחְדָּיו, "together." The women are mentioned in Luke 8:1–3 and 23:49. When D adds καὶ τέκνοις, "and children," it shows that it no longer understands that Luke portrays those who are present as witnesses. The relatives of Jesus (except for James) do not appear later; Luke knew nothing concrete about them.[7]

1   W. Foerster, "ὄρος," *TDNT* 5 (1967) 484 n. 102.

2   For the text, see Hjalmar Frisk, *Le Périple de la mer Érythrée: Suivi d'une étude sur la tradition et la langue* (Göteborgs Högskolas Årsskrift 33:1; Göteborg: Elanders, 1927).

3   Str-B 2.590–94.

4   *Ant.* 20.169; *Bell.* 5.70 gives the distance not of the mount, but of the Roman encampment.

5   For the order, see the commentaries on Mark 3:16; on "Simon the Zealot," see Martin Hengel, *Die Zeloten: Untersuchungen zur jüdische Freiheitsbewegung in der Zeit von Herodes I. bis 70n. Chr.* (2d ed.; AGJU 1; Leiden: Brill, 1976) 61–150.

6   Menoud, "Forty Days."

7   On the origin of the apostolate, see Klein, *Die zwölf Apostel;* Walter Schmithals, *The Office of the Apostle in the Early Church* (Nashville: Abingdon, 1969).

1

Choice of a Replacement for Judas

15 **In those days Peter stood up among the brethren (the company of persons was in all about a hundred and twenty), and said, 16/ "Brethren, the scripture had to be fulfilled, which the Holy Spirit spoke beforehand by the mouth of David, concerning Judas who was guide to those who arrested Jesus. 17/ For he was numbered among us, and was allotted his share in this ministry. 18/ (Now this man bought a field with the reward of his wickedness; and falling headlong he burst open in the middle and all his bowels gushed out. 19/ And it became known to all the inhabitants of Jerusalem, so that the field was called in their language Akeldama, that is, Field of Blood.) 20/ For it is written in the book of Psalms,**

**'Let his habitation become desolate,
and let there be no one to live in it';**
and
'His office let another take.'

21 **So one of the men who have accompanied us during all the time that the Lord Jesus went in and out among us, 22/ beginning from the baptism of John until the day when he was taken up from us—one of these men must become with us a witness to his resurrection." 23/ And they put forward two, Joseph called Barsabbas, who was surnamed Justus, and Matthias. 24/ And they prayed and said, "Lord, who knowest the hearts of all men, show which one of these two thou hast chosen 25/ to take the place in this ministry and apostleship from which Judas turned aside, to go to his own place." 26/ And they cast lots for them, and the lot fell on Matthias; and he was enrolled with the eleven apostles.**

In this section Luke has skillfully woven together a legendary tradition about the death of Judas and some completely different material concerning the completion of the circle of the Twelve, assigning this combination to the time between the ascension and Pentecost.[1]

■ **15** The entire section is permeated with Luke's biblicistic language: "in these days"; pleonastic ἀναστάς, "he stood up," ἐν μέσῳ, "among" (Luke 2:46; 24:36; 1QS 6.22, etc.); ἐπὶ τὸ αὐτό, "in all," ὄνομα, "name," with the sense "person" (Num 1:18, etc.). One hundred and twenty men are necessary to constitute a local sanhedrin

(*Sanh.* 1.6). Luke does not have this requirement in mind, however, since women are also included in the group.[2]

■ **16** Directing the speech only to "ἄνδρες" ἀδελφοί ("men," brethren; cf. *4 Macc.* 8.19) betrays Luke's dependence on the Greek form of address (cf. 2:14). Luke has composed this speech. The motif of scriptural fulfillment (δεῖ, "it is necessary") is important here as elsewhere.[3] The use of the present tense (δεῖ) by the Western text means the scribes misunderstood the passage and related the necessity to the selection of a replacement rather than to the

---

1   Trocmé, *Livre des Actes*, 199.

2   Karl Heinrich Rengstorff, "Die Zuwahl des Matthias (Apg 1,15ff)," *StTh* 15 (1961) 35–67. On Peter, see

D. Gewalt, "Petrus: Studien zur Geschichte und Tradition des frühen Christentums" (Diss., Heidelberg, 1966).

destiny of the traitor. γραφή, "Scripture," refers to the individual passage of Scripture. Which passage Luke has in mind is debatable: (1) both passages cited in vs 20; the objection to this is that the second is not yet fulfilled (from the standpoint of the speaker); (2) the second; this thesis assumes the removal of vss 18–19 on literary grounds;[4] (3) the first; the ἔδει, "it was necessary," of vs 16 corresponds to the δεῖ, "it is necessary," of vs 21;[5] (4) neither of these passages, but rather Ps 41:10; but this cannot be. In fact the whole debate is unnecessary. Luke does not deal with the Scriptures in an isolated manner (cf. 3:21). The Spirit was already at work in Old Testament times, though only in individuals and at individual moments. The prophet, the subject of the speech, was only an instrument. On David as a prophet, compare 2:25–35. The manner in which the Judas legend is narrated assumes that the reader knows the contents of the passion story.

■ **17** The terminology of this verse has analogies in the Qumran texts.[6] κλῆρος, "share," (Deut 10:9 LXX; Ps 125 [124]:3, etc.; 1QS 1.10; CD 13.12; 20.4) is virtually synonymous with τόπος, "place," of vs 25 (1QS 2.23). διακονία, "ministry," is not yet a technical term for the office of "deacon." The term has nothing to do with the עבודה, "service," of the Qumran texts (1QSa 1.13, 16; cf. 1QS 3.26).[7] For κατηριθμημένος κτλ., "numbered, etc.," compare Luke 22:3.

■ **18** The fate of the evildoer was indirectly brought about by the blood money.

■ **19-20** These verses should not be eliminated as a later insertion. They are tied in with the context and the

language is Lukan.[8] At first reading they appear to be isolated, but this is because of the nature of the traditional material. Luke does not have Peter speak for the hearer of his own time, but for the reader of the Gospel and Acts: "in their language"! χωρίον, "field" (cf. ἔπαυλις, "habitation," vs 20; *Mart. Pol.* 7.1), differs from the "Field of Blood" as in Matt 27:7–8. For μισθὸς τῆς ἀδικίας, "reward of wickedness," compare Luke 16:8–9 and 18:6. There is no reason to alter the text, or to postulate a special meaning for πρηνής, "falling headlong" (Papias πρησθείς). The meaning is apparently that Judas fell from a roof or a cliff (cf. Wis 4:19; [2 Sam 20:10]).[9]

Excursus:
The Legend about the Death of Judas

The legend about the death of Judas is not developed into a narrative. It is not the late stage of an often-told legend about a person, but only a partially elaborated composition which Luke has constructed around a well-known motif: the death of the opponent of God. It is a "name etiology" which explains the name of the field called "Field of Blood"[10] (compare the other version in Matt 27:3–10). With Papias the legend has undergone unrestrained development (frg. 3); here even the context of the two passages cited from the Psalms (69 [68]:26 and 109 [108]:8) has had an impact on the narrative, together with Num 5:21–22, 27 (cf. also 2 Macc 9:7–10).[11] The account is naive in the way in which it connects sin and punishment; there is no possibility of forgiveness for Judas (he has not repented, in contrast to the account in Matthew).[12]

■ **20** The quotation comes from Pss 69 (68):26 and 109

3   See Conzelmann, *Theology*, 153–54.
4   Cf. Otto Bauernfeind, *Die Apostelgeschichte* (ThHKNT 5; Leipzig: Deichert, 1938) 27–28, reprinted in his *Kommentar und Studien zur Apostelgeschichte* (WUNT 22; Tübingen: Mohr [Siebeck], 1980); Trocmé, *Livre des Actes;* see below.
5   Jacques Dupont, "La destinée de Judas prophétisée par David (Actes 1, 16–20)," *CBQ* 23 (1961) 41–51, reprinted in his *Études*, 309–20.
6   Braun, *Qumran* 2.197–200.
7   Ibid., 1.140; 2.333.
8   J. Renié, "L'élection de Mathias (Act. 1, 15–26): Authenticité du récit," *RB* 55 (1948) 43–53.
9   Str-B 2.595.
10   חֲקַל דְּמָא, see Hans Peter Rüger, "Zum Problem der Sprach Jesu," *ZNW* 59 (1968) 116–18.
11   See Eduard Schweizer, "Zu Apg. 1,16–22," *ThZ* 14

(1958) 46, reprinted in his *Neotestamentica: Deutsche und Englische Aufsätz 1951–63. German and English Essays 1951–63* (Zurich: Zwingli, 1963) 416–17.
12   On the motif of the "death of the opponent of God," see Wilhelm Nestle, "Legenden vom Tod der Gottesverächter," *ARW* 33 (1936) 246–69. On the Judas legend, see: *Beginnings* 5.22–30; Benoit, "The Death of Judas," *Jesus and the Gospel* 1.189–207; Kurt Lüthi, "Das Problem des Judas Iskariot—neu untersucht," *EvTh* 16 (1956) 98–114; Ernst Haenchen, "Judentum und Christentum in der Apostelgeschichte," *ZNW* 54 (1963) 155–87.

(108):8.[13] It apparently had been related to Judas before Luke; compare Papias's independent version of the story cited above. The first part explains the fate of Judas, the second deals with his place among the Twelve. Originally these were two curses which the pious sufferer delivered against his tormentor. Here they are made into a disposition from God (note the change of the LXX optative, λάβοι, "may he take," into the imperative, "let [another] take").[14]

■ **21–22** These verses draw the conclusion. The meaning is not that the apostolate should be a permanent institution. Not *every* apostle is to be replaced, but only this *one* who has now been lost, so that the necessary number of twelve can again be filled out.[15] The apostles are considered to be representatives of the eschatological Israel. Pre-Lukan tradition is apparent here (cf. Luke 22:30).[16] The condition for eligibility reveals Luke's secondary concept of an apostle. The formulation is striking: he must be an eyewitness of Jesus' entire ministry, and as such he becomes a witness to the resurrection. Such qualifications may be explained with reference to the primary content of the apostolic message.[17] For ἀρξά-μενος, "beginning," compare 10:37, Luke 23:5 and

24:47.[18] This account should not be used in an attempt to reconstruct the polity of the earliest church, not even with the help of the Qumran texts. The reminiscences are only formal—the circle of Twelve has nothing to do with 1QS 8.1.[19]

■ **23** The subject of the verb here is unspecified. The Western text makes Peter the subject (the singular verb, ἔστησεν, "he put forward"; cf. 11:2 D; 15:1ff D).[20] Joseph Barsabbas, like many Jews, had a Latin name (others might have a Greek name) which was reminiscent of his Jewish name.[21] Papias recounts a brief legend about him (Eusebius *Hist. eccl.* 3.39.9).

■ **24** In this case the aorist participle does not indicate action prior to that of the main verb.[22] The κύριος, "Lord," is God. The grammatical relationship of ἐκ τούτων τῶν δύο, "of these two," to the rest of the sentence is not clear.

■ **25** ἴδιος τόπος, "his own place," is a euphemism for (the journey to) hell (cf. Ignatius *Magn.* 5).

■ **26** The casting of lots was a widespread practice (in Judaism 1QS 5.3). The lots were shaken in a cloth bag (Prov 16:33) or in a vessel (Livy 23.3.7) until one fell out.[23]

---

13 For the introductory formula, cf. CD 11.20; see Joseph A. Fitzmyer, "Jewish Christianity in Acts in Light of the Qumran Scrolls," *Studies in Luke-Acts*, 233–57.

14 C. H. Dodd, *According to the Scriptures: The Sub-Structure of New Testament Theology* (London: Nisbet; New York: Scribner's, 1953) 58 n. 1.

15 Menoud, "The Additions to the Twelve Apostles according to the Book of Acts," *Jesus Christ and the Faith*, 133–48.

16 Roloff Jürgen, *Apostolat—Verkündigung—Kirche: Ursprung, Inhalt und Funktion des kirchlichen Apostelamtes nach Paulus, Lukas und den Pastoralbriefen* (Gütersloh: Mohn, 1965) 196ff.

17 Klein, *Die zwölf Apostel*, passim, esp. 204–9; Norbert Brox (*Zeuge und Märtyrer: Untersuchungen zur frühchristlichen Zeugnis-Terminologie* [SANT 5; Munich: Kösel, 1961] 43–46) would restrict qualification as a "witness" to the Twelve, and explains the mode of expression on this basis: whoever meets the specified prerequisite is thereby not yet a witness in the official sense; for a similar view, see Ernst Günther, Μάρτυς: *Die Geschichte eines Wortes* (Gütersloh: Bertelsmann, 1941) 103. Acts 13:31 speaks against this restriction.

18 Wilckens, *Missionsreden*, 101–9.

19 In agreement with Herbert Braun, *Spätjüdisch-häretischer und frühchristlicher Radikalismus* (2 vols.;

BHTh 24; Tübingen: Mohr [Siebeck], 1957) 1.96 n. 1. On the place of Peter in Acts, see Jacques Dupont, "Pierre et Paul dans les Actes," *RB* (1957) 35–47, reprinted in his *Études*, 173–84; in the early church: H. Strathmann, "Die Stellung des Petrus in der Urkirche," *ZSTh* 20 (1943) 223–82; Oscar Cullmann, "Πέτρος, Κηφᾶς," *TDNT* 6 (1968) 100–112; idem, *Peter, Disciple—Apostle—Martyr: A Historical and Theological Study* (2d ed.; trans. Floyd V. Filson; Philadelphia: Westminster, 1962).

20 Joseph Crehan, "Peter according to the D-Text of Acts," *TS* 18 (1957) 596–603.

21 Cf. Jesus Justus, Col 4:11; Str-B 2.712–13; Martin Hengel, *Judaism and Hellenism: Studies in Their Encounter in Palestine during the Early Hellenistic Period* (2 vols.; Philadelphia: Fortress, 1974) 1.61–65.

22 BDF § 339.1.

23 PW 13.1451–1504, on the procedure 1484–90; William A. Beardslee, "The Casting of Lots at Qumran and in the Book of Acts," *NovT* 4 (1960–61) 245–52.

2

The Miracle at Pentecost

Prefatory Note to Acts 2

Now for the first time we encounter the Lukan composition of a scene (the miracle: vss 1–13) and a missionary speech joined to it (vss 14–40), rounded off with a conclusion to the scene (vs 41). To this is added a summary (vss 42–47).

1 When the day of Pentecost had come, they were all together in one place. 2/ And suddenly a sound came from heaven like the rush of a mighty wind, and it filled all the house where they were sitting. 3/ And there appeared to them tongues as of fire, distributed and resting on each one of them. 4/ And they were all filled with the Holy Spirit and began to speak in other tongues, as the Spirit gave them utterance.

5 Now there were dwelling in Jerusalem Jews, devout men from every nation under heaven. 6/ And at this sound the multitude came together, and they were bewildered, because each one heard them speaking in his own language. 7/ And they were amazed and wondered, saying, "Are not all these who are speaking Galileans? 8/ And how is it that we hear, each of us in his own native language? 9/ Parthians and Medes and Elamites and residents of Mesopotamia, Judea and Cappadocia, Pontus and Asia, 10/ Phrygia and Pamphylia, Egypt and the parts of Libya belonging to Cyrene, and visitors from Rome, both Jews and proselytes, 11/ Cretans and Arabians, we hear them telling in our own tongues the mighty works of God." 12/ And all were amazed and perplexed, saying to one another, "What does this mean?" 13/ But others mocking said, "They are filled with new wine."

■ **1** The expression ἐν τῷ συμπληροῦσθαι, "when [the day of Pentecost] had come" (cf. Luke 9:51), denotes—though not exactly—the arrival of a date (not the completion of a period of time). It is dependent upon biblical language (Jer 25:12; Gen 25:24; Lev 8:33). The dating of "Pentecost" (πεντηκοστή—thus Hellenistic Judaism; the Jewish festival is known as חַג שָׁבוּעֹת [Lev 23:15–21])[1] is connected with the forty days of 1:3, and thus does not necessarily belong to the substance of the story.[2] This has implications for one's judgment about the story in the context of the history of religions.

■ **2** On the transition from πνοή, "wind," to πνεῦμα, "wind, spirit," compare Prov 1:23 (cited in *1 Clem.* 57.3) and *1 Clem.* 21.9. To be sure, this passage is only making a comparison.[3]

■ **3** On tongues of fire, compare Isa 5:24 (not the LXX); *1 Enoch* 14.8–16; 71.5; 1Q29 1.3; 2.3. Fire is part of the apparatus of theophany (2 Thess 1:8). Storm and fire are associated with judgment: *4 Ezra* 13.10; at Sinai: Philo *Decal.* 46.[4] K. G. Kuhn eliminates vs 3a as an interpo-

1   Eduard Lohse, "πεντηκοστή," *TDNT* 6 (1968) 44–53.
2   Bauernfeind; differently Bent Noack, "The Day of Pentecost in Jubilees, Qumran, and Acts," *ASTI* 1 (1962) 73–95.
3   On the description, cf. Philo *Decal.* 33 (cited below in the excursus: "The Pentecost Narrative").
4   See the excursus; also Friedrich Lang, "πῦρ," *TDNT* 6 (1968) 935–48.

lation, since it occasions some unclarity about the subject of ἐκάθισεν, "resting" (in ℵ* and D the verb is plural!).[5] διαμεριζόμεναι, "divided," does not mean "divided tongues," but indicates that the tongues were distributed to each individual. The tongues entered into them (the sense is not that they formed a halo above them). This manner of the "pouring out" of the Spirit (cf. vs 33), as Luke describes it, is qualitatively different from the manner in which the Spirit came to Jesus (Luke 3:22).

■ 4 ἑτέραις γλώσσαις, "other tongues," is explained in vss 6, 8, and 11 in the sense of miraculous speaking in different languages. For ἐπλήσθησαν, "they were filled," compare Prov 15:4, Sir 48:12, and Dio Chrys. 55.12.

■ 5 The change in scene to a public place is not made clearly. For ἀπὸ παντὸς ἔθνους κτλ., "from every nation, etc.," compare Deut 2:25. In Hellenistic Greek εἰς, "into," can substitute for ἐν, "in." In accord with Luke's view of history, the message for the time being will reach only Jews.

■ 6 This verse expands upon vs 4 from the standpoint of the hearers. Even so, the exact nature of the miracle is by no means clear. φωνή, "sound," equals ἦχος, "sound," in vs 2. Compare Philo Spec. leg. 2.189: "For then the sound of the trumpet pealed [φωνὴ σάλπιγγος ἐξήχησεν] from heaven and reached, we may suppose, the ends of the universe." The author does not have in mind here the apocalyptic expectation that in the end time there would be only *one* language.[6]

■ 7 From this point on nothing new is narrated, but impressions and interpretations are conveyed to the reader. Luke has formed these into a conversation among those who are amazed. Thus we need not ask how they knew that all(!) the inspired were Galileans (1:11; 13:31).

■ 9–11 These verses illustrate the phrase, ἀπὸ παντὸς ἔθνους, "from every nation."

Excursus:
The List of Nations

Here Luke is dependent upon a list of nations which reflects the political situation of an earlier time (there is no mention of Macedonia/Achaia). It describes the constituency of the twelve kingdoms, excluding Europe. Such lists come from the geographers and the historians of Alexander and of the twelve kingdoms. In these we discover the same interchange of names of districts and of peoples, for which the astrological lists (see below) provide no example. Consider, for example, Curtius Rufus 6.3.3: "We have made ourselves masters of Caria, Lydia, Cappadocia, Phrygia, Paphlagonia, Pamphylia, the Pisidians, Cilicia, Syria, Phoenicia, Armenia, Persia, the Medes, and Parthiene."[7] Note that the Medes, who had long since disappeared from history, are mentioned in Curtius Rufus.[8] They occupy an established place in the picture of world history viewed as a sequence of (four) world empires.[9] The Elamites are also known from the literature.[10] The form Ἐλαμῖται, however, is dependent upon the Bible (cf. Isa 21:2 LXX). The mention of Judea in the list seems strange. There have, therefore, been various conjectures about this since the time of the ancient church. Dibelius suggests reading Γαλατίαν or Γαλλίαν, "Galatia."[11] Others believe that "Judea" is a post-Lukan interpolation.[12] If we remove the word, the similarity with the astrological lists (discussed below) is especially striking. Luke has overlooked the fact that the language spoken in Judea was not "foreign." Romans have been added to the list (note the difference in style; with mention of those from Rome, the twelve-kingdom pattern is broken and made to fit Luke's purposes), although in a similar astrological list (see below) Italy appears as westernmost. ἐπιδημοῦντες, "visitors," means Jews originally from Rome, now living in Jerusalem.[13] Cretans and Arabians are no longer found in real lists of nations, but are used as representative groups: "Jews and proselytes, those who live on islands and those who live on the mainland" (or "westerners and easterners"?).[14]

---

5   Karl Georg Kuhn, "Jesus in Gethsemane," *EvTh* 12 (1952–53) 269–70.

6   Cf. Isa 66:18; *T. Jud.* 25.3; Plutarch *Is. et Osir.* 370b, drawing upon Persian eschatology.

7   "Cariam Lydiam Cappadociam Phrygiam Paphlagoniam Pamphyliam Pisidas Ciliciam Syriam Phoenicen Armeniam Persiden Medos Parthienen habemus in potestate." Cf. further Arrian in *FGH* 156, frg. 1.5, where one observes the origin of the material; Ps.-Callisth. 2.4.9; 2.11.2; Ps.-Scylax 81ff; *Sib. Or.* 3.207–9; Philo *Flacc.* 45–46; *Leg. Gai.* 281–83; Lucian *Syr. dea* 32.

8   Cf. the enumeration in Tacitus *Ann.* 2.60.

9   Diodorus Sic. 2.32.5; Dionysius Halic. 1.2.2; Strabo 15.735; 16.737.

10   Appian *Bell civ.* 9.32; Plutarch *Pomp.* 36, etc.; Livy 30.48.6 (alongside the Medes), 36.4.9 (as soldiers in the Hellenistic era). See PW 5.2458–67.

11   Dibelius, *Studies,* 91.

12   Haenchen, p. 170.

13   BAG *s.v.* ἐπιδημέω.

14   Otto Eissfeldt, "Kreter und Araber," *ThLZ* 72 (1947) cols. 207–12. Cf. the end of the list in Philo *Leg. Gai.* 283: "whether in Europe or in Asia or in Libya,

By eliminating additions (Rome or Judea, in which case one must still reckon with the possibility that Judea has displaced another name), we can produce a list of twelve names. Stefan Weinstock surmises from this that Luke used an astrological catalogue of nations, in which the nations are arranged according to the zodiac.[15] An example is the list of Paul of Alexandria from the end of the fourth century, which reaches far back into earlier times, as is evident from its geographical and political horizon. It enumerates the following: Aries = Persia, Taurus = Babylon, Gemini = Cappadocia, Cancer = Armenia, Leo = Asia, Virgo = Hellas and Ionia, Libra = Libya and Cyrene, Scorpio = Italy, Sagittarius = Cilicia and Crete, Capricorn = Syria, Aquarius = Egypt, Pisces = Red Sea and India. Luke, in any case, would not have been aware of the astrological character of the list. And besides, the lists of the astrologers were taken from the lists of the historians and geographers, and appropriately modified.[16]

The expression $\tau \grave{a} \ \mu \epsilon \gamma a \lambda \epsilon \hat{\imath} a \ \tau o \hat{v} \ \theta \epsilon o \hat{v}$, "the mighty works of God," is found in the LXX and also in 1QS 1.21. Luke does not give any more precise information about the contents of their speeches—he is saving that for Peter's speech.

■ **12–13** These verses are a variant of vs 7. In similar style the narrative moves into an account of the effect upon the audience (cf. 17:32; *Corp. Herm.* 1.29). The crowd must remain ambivalent, because conversion may come only as a result of the sermon. The relationship between $\pi \acute{a} \nu \tau \epsilon s$, "all," and $\acute{\epsilon} \tau \epsilon \rho o \iota$, "others," cannot be determined in a quantitative way. The scene is purely redactional, not historical.

■ **13** The objection that there would not yet be any "new wine" at Pentecost is ridiculous. There was, in fact, a process for the preservation of unfermented wine.[17] The Qumran sect drank תירוש (new wine? wine?) at their meals (1QS 6.4–5; 1QSa 2.17–20). The phenomena of enthusiasm and intoxication are related.[18]

Excursus: The Pentecost Narrative

The Pentecost narrative alternates between an account of an outbreak of glossolalia and miraculous speech in many languages. Luke has fashioned it into its present form as an episode with a burlesque impact, a mixture of themes which lead to reflection. In addition to the meaningful event as such, the episode contains instructive material in the description of the scene itself.[19] It moves to a climax which is introduced by the appearance of Peter. What traditions did Luke have at hand? The possibilities include the following: (1) He has combined two sources; a reconstruction of these does not succeed, however, and too little material would remain for each source. (2) He had the report about mass ecstasy and interpreted it in the sense of miraculous speech in many languages; in so doing, he imported his own universalism (E. Lohse). (3) The original substratum is precisely the miraculous speech in many languages.[20] As evidence, we may note that the basis for this account is clearly not a naive legend. Already at this earliest level there are strong elements of reflection. In this case, the substratum would not then have offered a symbolic portrayal of the spread of the gospel worldwide, but an account of the gospel's spread as actually accomplished by a miraculous, eschatological act of God.

Whether these overtones of "glossolalia" were already in Luke's sources or were added by Luke is difficult to say. It should be noted that Luke himself no longer has any exact conception of the original glossolalia. He identifies it with prophesy (10:46; 19:6), making the synthesis with the language miracle easier. According to Günther Bornkamm, the combination of

---

whether in the mainlands or on the islands, whether it be seaboard or inland" ($\tau \grave{o} \ E \grave{v} \rho \omega \pi a \hat{\imath} o \nu$, $\tau \grave{o} \ ' A \sigma \iota a \nu \acute{o} \nu$, $\tau \grave{o} \ \Lambda \iota \beta \upsilon \kappa \acute{o} \nu$, $\tau \grave{o} \ \grave{\epsilon} \nu \ \mathring{\eta} \pi \epsilon \acute{\iota} \rho o \iota s$, $\tau \grave{o} \ \grave{\epsilon} \nu \ \nu \acute{\eta} \sigma o \iota s \ \pi \acute{a} \rho a \lambda \acute{o} \nu \ \tau \epsilon \ \kappa a \grave{\iota} \ \mu \epsilon \sigma \acute{o} \gamma \epsilon \iota o \nu$). Judaism utilized such lists to describe the spread of the Diaspora. Cf. in addition Str-B 2.606–14. Similar is Philo *Flacc.* 46; Ps.-Philo *Ant.* 4.3.

15 Stefan Weinstock, "The Geographical Catalogue in Acts II,9–11," *JRomS* 38 (1948) 43–46.

16 John A. Brinkman, "The Literary Background of the 'Catalogue of the Nations' (Acts 2,9–11)," *CBQ* 25 (1963) 418–27.

17 Peter Remark, *Der Weinbau im Römerreiche* (Munich:

Heimeran, 1927).

18 Philo *Ebr.* 145–48; Hans Lewy, *Sobria Ebrietas: Untersuchungen zur Geschichte der antiken Mystik* (BZNW 9; Giessen: Töpelmann, 1929); Hermann M. Kleinknecht, "$\pi \nu \epsilon \hat{v} \mu a$," *TDNT* 6 (1968) 343–52; the spirit which rushed into the body of the Pythia acted like wine (Plutarch *Defect. orac.* p. 437 cd); see *TDNT* 6 (1968) 350.

19 Plümacher, *Apostelgeschichte*, 107–8.

20 Bauernfeind; Eduard Schweizer, "$\pi \nu \epsilon \hat{v} \mu a$," *TDNT* 6 (1968) 411 n. 516.

the two phenomena stems from popular pre-Pauline Christianity.[21] By way of comparison with Acts, we may note the alternation between intelligible and unintelligible speech in Lucian *Alex.* 13; one cannot, however, speak of a language miracle in this case.[22] The degree of influence of the Jewish Sinai Haggada is debatable.[23] This question depends upon another: From what time was Pentecost interpreted as a festival celebrating the making of the covenant? In Philo this is not yet the case. This is evident from his description of the Sinai epiphany:

I should suppose that God wrought on this occasion a miracle of a truly holy kind by bidding an invisible sound to be created in the air more marvelous than all instruments and fitted with perfect harmonies, not soulless, nor yet composed of body and soul like a living creature, but a rational soul full of clearness and distinctness, which, giving shape and tension to the air and changing it to flaming fire, sounded forth like the breath through a trumpet an articulate voice so loud that it appeared to be equally audible to the farthest as well as the nearest. ... Then from the midst of the fire that streamed from heaven there sounded forth to their utter amazement a voice, for the flame became articulate speech in the language familiar to the audience, and so clearly and distinctly were the words formed by it that they seemed to see rather than hear them (ἀλλά γέ μοι δοκεῖ κατ᾽ ἐκεῖνον τὸν χρόνον ἱεροπρεπέστατόν τι θαυματουργῆσαι κελεύσας ἦχον ἀόρατον ἐν ἀέρι δημιουργηθῆναι, πάντων ὀργάνων θαυμασιώτερον, ἁρμονίαις τελείαις ἡρμοσμένον, οὐκ ἄψυχον, ἀλλ᾽ οὐδ᾽ ἐκ σώματος καὶ ψυχῆς τρόπον ζῴου συνεστηκότα, ἀλλὰ ψυχὴν λογικὴν ἀνάπλεων σαφηνείας καὶ τρανότητος, ἢ τὸν ἀέρα σχηματίσασα καὶ ἐπιτείνασα καὶ πρὸς πῦρ φλογοειδὲς μεταβαλοῦσα καθάπερ πνεῦμα διὰ σάλπιγγος φωνὴν τοσαύτην ἔναρθρον ἐξήχησεν, ὡς τοῖς ἔγγιστα τοὺς πορρωτάτω κατ᾽ ἴσον ἀκροᾶσθαι δοκεῖν ... φωνὴ δ᾽ ἐκ μέσου τοῦ ῥυέντος ἀπ᾽ οὐρανοῦ πυρὸς ἐξήχει καταπληκτικωτάτη, τῆς φλογὸς εἰς διάλεκτον ἀρθρουμένης τὴν συνήθη τοῖς ἀκρωομένοις, ᾗ

τὰ λεγόμενα οὕτως ἐναργῶς ἐτρανοῦτο, ὡς ὁρᾶν αὐτὰ μᾶλλον ἢ ἀκούειν δοκεῖν).[24]

For the rabbis Pentecost is the festival celebrating the giving of the Law. They were familiar with a story of how God's voice was divided into the seventy languages of the world on Sinai. This legend, however, is not connected with Pentecost. The discussion has taken on new life because of the Qumran texts.[25] Did the sect celebrate Pentecost as a covenant festival?[26] It cannot be proved that the festival involved a covenant renewal, and in view of the order of festivals in 1QS 1, the argument from silence is convincing. Luke does not make any connection between Pentecost and the covenant. The day of the week—Friday—also has no meaning in this connection. According to the calendar of the sect, Pentecost always fell on a Friday.[27] For a parallel which is not "Sinaitic" (but rather eschatological), compare Isa 66:15, 18 LXX: "For behold the Lord will come as a fire . . . with a flame of fire . . . I am coming to gather all nations and tongues. . . ." (Ἰδοὺ γὰρ κύριος ὡς πῦρ ἥξει . . . ἐν φλογὶ πυρός . . . ἔρχομαι συναγαγεῖν πάντα τὰ ἔθνη καὶ τὰς γλώσσας). The common features are typical elements of a theophany.

The question about the historical event which lay behind this report can be asked only on the basis of the ever problematic literary-critical and motif analysis. The assumption that the Pentecost experience was identical with the appearance of the resurrected Christ to more than five hundred brethren (1 Cor 15:6) is improbable.[28] The development from a christophany to this theophany is really not conceivable, because in the older version of the Easter christophany the Spirit is not mentioned. The only thing that can be established for certain on the basis of the Lukan shaping of the material and the Hellenistic-Jewish tradition is that there were appearances of the Spirit in the Jerusalem congregation; note, for example, the emergence of prophets like Agabus and the daughters of Philip (a hint at the Hellenistic line of tradition).[29]

---

21 Günther Bornkamm, "Faith and Reason in Paul," *Early Christian Experience* (New York: Harper, 1969) 38–39; cf. Origen *Cels.* 7.8–9.

22 Against Betz, *Lukian,* 141.

23 Str-B 2.604–6.

24 *Decal.* 33, 46.

25 *Jubilees* 6 should be considered in this connection; here, however, Pentecost is not a Sinai Covenant festival, but a harvest festival and as such a sign of the covenant.

26 J. T. Milik, *Ten Years of Discovery in the Wilderness of Judaea* (trans. John Strugnell; SBT 26; London:

SCM, 1959) 107–13.

27 A. Jaubert, "Le calendrier des Jubilés et de la secte de Qumrân: Ses origines bibliques," *VT* 3 (1953) 250–64; Milik, *Ten Years,* 107–13.

28 Thus Ernst von Dobschütz, *Ostern und Pfingsten: Eine Studie zu 1 Korinther 15* (Leipzig: Hinrichs, 1903); S. MacLean Gilmour, "The Christophany to more than Five Hundred Brethren," *JBL* 80 (1961) 248–52; idem, "Easter and Pentecost," *JBL* 81 (1962) 62–66. Against this position is C. Freeman Sleeper, "Pentecost and Resurrection," *JBL* 84 (1965) 389–99.

29 On the topic as a whole, see the following: Nikolaus

Adler, *Das erste christliche Pfingstfest: Sinn und Bedeutung des Pfingstberichtes Apg 2,1–13* (NTAbh 18:1; Münster: Aschendorff, 1938); Eduard Lohse, "Die Bedeutung des Pfingstberichtes im Rahmen des lukanischen Geschichtswerkes," *EvTh* 13 (1953) 422–36; idem, "πεντηκοστή," *TDNT* 6 (1968) 44–53, and the literature cited there; Georg Kretschmar, "Himmelfahrt und Pfingsten," *ZKG* 66 (1954–55) 209–53 with 4 pls.; Trocmé, *Livre des Actes*, 201–6; Menoud, "The Lukan Version of Pentecost and History," *Jesus Christ and the Faith*, 180–91; Walter Grundmann, "Der Pfingstbericht der Apostel-

geschichte in seinem theologischen Sinn," *Studia Evangelica, Vol. II: Part I: The New Testament Scriptures* (TU 87; Berlin: Akademie-Verlag, 1964) 584–94; Otto Betz, "The Eschatological Interpretation of the Sinai-Tradition in Qumran and in the NT," *RQ* 6 (1967) 89ff.

2

The Pentecost Sermon

14 But Peter, standing with the eleven, lifted up his voice and addressed them, "Men of Judea and all who dwell in Jerusalem, let this be known to you, and give ear to my words. 15/ For these men are not drunk, as you suppose, since it is only the third hour of the day; 16/ but this is what was spoken by the prophet Joel:

> 17/ 'And in the last days it shall be, God declares, that I will pour out my Spirit upon all flesh, and your sons and your daughters shall prophesy, and your young men shall see visions, and your old men shall dream dreams;
> 18/ yea, and on my menservants and my maidservants in those days I will pour out my Spirit; and they shall prophesy.
> 19/ And I will show wonders in the heaven above and signs on the earth beneath, blood, and fire, and vapor of smoke;
> 20/ the sun shall be turned into darkness and the moon into blood, before the day of the Lord comes, the great and manifest day.
> 21/ And it shall be that whoever calls on the name of the Lord shall be saved.'

22 "Men of Israel, hear these words: Jesus of Nazareth, a man attested to you by God with mighty works and wonders and signs which God did through him in your midst, as you yourselves know— 23/ this Jesus, delivered up according to the definite plan and foreknowledge of God, you crucified and killed by the hands of lawless men. 24/ But God raised him up, having loosed the pangs of death, because it was not possible for him to be held by it. 25/ For David says concerning him,

> 'I saw the Lord always before me, for he is at my right hand that I may not be shaken;
> 26/ therefore my heart was glad, and my tongue rejoiced; moreover my flesh will dwell in hope.
> 27/ For thou wilt not abandon my soul to [or: leave my soul in] Hades, nor let thy Holy One see corruption.
> 28/ Thou hast made known to me the ways of life; thou wilt make me full of gladness with thy presence.'

29 "Brethren, I may say to you confidently of the patriarch David that he both died and was buried, and his tomb is with us to this day. 30/ Being therefore a prophet, and knowing that God had sworn with an oath to him that he would set one of his descendants upon his throne, 31/ he foresaw and spoke of the resurrection of

the Christ, that he was not abandoned to
[or: left in] Hades, nor did his flesh see
corruption. 32/ This Jesus God raised up,
and of that we all are witnesses. 33/
Being therefore exalted at the right hand
of God, and having received from the
Father the promise of the Holy Spirit, he
has poured out this which you see and
hear. 34/ For David did not ascend into
the heavens; but he himself says,
　　'The Lord said to my Lord, Sit at my
　　right hand,
　　35/ till I make thy enemies a stool for
　　thy feet.'
36/ Let all the house of Israel therefore
know assuredly that God has made him
both Lord and Christ, this Jesus whom
you crucified."

■ **14** σύν in the phrase "standing *with* the eleven" has the sense of μετά, "with."[1] The request for attention has prototypes in the Old Testament (Gen 4:23; Job 32:10–11; the prophets) and in the speech of the accused at a trial.[2]

■ **15** The first topic is the connection with the situation (in the course of which Luke plays on a misunderstanding; cf. 3:12; 14:15). On the reason given here, compare Cicero *Philipp.* 2.41.104: "But how many days did you most disgracefully carouse in that villa! From the third hour there was drinking, gaming, vomiting" (at quam multos dies in ea villa turpissime es perbacchatus. ab hora tertia bibebatur, ludebatur, vomebatur).

■ **16** τοῦτό ἐστιν, "this is," is an interpretation formula and says nothing about whether the phenomenon is still going on. For the understanding of the present as the time of fulfilled prophecy, compare 1QpHab. On the manner in which the quotation from Scripture is introduced, see CD 10.16.

■ **17** The second topic is the introduction of the speech by means of a passage of Scripture, Joel 3:1–5 LXX. The proof in vs 21 depends on the LXX translation, thus the speech was composed in Greek from the beginning. Furthermore, it never existed without the quotations.[3] The quotation has been transmitted in two recensions, B and D.[4] At the beginning of the quotation, B and sa have (with the LXX) μετὰ ταῦτα, "after these things," instead of ἐν ταῖς ἐσχάταις ἡμέραις, "in the last days." Haenchen and Traugott Holtz believe that the former (B sa) is original because it accords better with Luke's eschatology (that is, there is no expectation of an immediate end of history). But the formula ἐν ταῖς ἐσχάταις ἡμέραις has become a stereotyped expression (cf. 1 Tim 4:1; 2 Tim 3:1) and no longer expresses an expectation of an immediate end.[5] By changing πᾶσα σάρξ, "all flesh," to the plural, D appears to be stressing universalism (cf. also vs 47 and the change of the possessive pronoun in the Western text! Whereas LXX and B read, "And your

1　BDF § 221; cf. also § 480.1.
2　See the *Acta Isidori* in *Griechische Papyri* (2d ed.; ed. Hans Lietzmann; KIT 14; Bonn: Marcus & Weber, 1910) 21; for an example in parody, see Lucian *Bis acc.* 16. For the structure of Peter's speeches, see the Introduction (pp. xliii–xlv); on the relation of scene and speech, see Wilckens, *Missionsreden*, 56–59. On the Western text of vs 14, see Epp, *Theological Tendency*, 158.
3　A. W. Argyle, "The Theory of an Aramaic Source in Acts 2:14–40," *JTS* 4 n.s. (1953) 213–14.
4　On the use of Scripture by Luke, see Jacques Dupont, "Apologetic Use of the Old Testament in the Speeches of Acts," *The Salvation of the Gentiles: Studies in the Acts of the Apostles* (New York: Paulist, 1979) 129–59; Gerhardsson, *Memory and Manuscript*, 225–34; Barnabas Lindars, *New Testament Apologetic:*

The Doctrinal Significance of the Old Testament Quotations (Philadelphia: Westminster, 1961) 36–59; Rese, *Alttestamentliche Motive*, 45–110. On the text of vss 17–21, see Kilpatrick, "Eclectic Study," 65–66; A. F. J. Klijn, "In Search of the Original Text of Acts," *Studies in Luke-Acts*, 103–10; in a wider connection (Luke and the LXX), see Haenchen, "Schriftzitate," 161–62, reprinted in his *Gott und Mensch*, 165–66 (in dialogue with Lucian Cerfaux, "Citations scripturaires et tradition textuelle dans le Livre des Actes," *Aux sources de la tradition*, 47, 50–51, reprinted in *Recueil Cerfaux* 2.93–103); see Holtz (*Zitate*, 5–14) on the relation of the Lukan form of the text to the LXX text of Codex Alexandrinus.
5　For the originality of this reading, see Franz Mussner, "In den letzten Tagen (Apg 2,17a)," *BZ* n.s. 5 (1961) 263–65 (who, however, applies the formula

[ὑμῶν] sons and your [ὑμῶν] daughters [i.e., of the Jews] shall prophesy," D has "their [αὐτῶν] sons and their [αὐτῶν] daughters [i.e., of "all flesh*es*" or Gentiles]"). Here one can see that Luke identifies glossolalia and prophecy (in contrast to Paul in 1 Corinthians 14).[6]

■ **18** Joel speaks of the menservants and maidservants of the Jews (as an additional group). These become religious designations when μου ("*my* menservants and maidservants") is inserted. The Western text abbreviates here by omitting "in those days" as well as "and they shall prophesy."

■ **19** Here again, the Western text abbreviates by omitting "blood, and fire, and vapor of smoke." In so doing, Luke's intended meaning has been blurred. He means to say that the transition from the present (that is, the time of the church) to the apocalyptic future is taking place right here. This corresponds with the picture in Luke 21. The combination of σημεῖα, "signs," and τέρατα, "wonders," is found since Polybius.[7]

■ **20** ἐπιφανής, "manifest," is a mistranslation of the LXX; it has derived נוֹרָא, "terrible," from רָאָה, "to see." Luke 17:24 shows what the author has in mind.

■ **21** "Who call on the name of the Lord" was used as a technical expression as early as Paul (Rom 10:13, cf. vs 14; 1 Cor 1:2; Acts 9:14, 21; 22:16). The interpretation of κύριος, "Lord," as Jesus is possible only on the basis of the LXX, not the MT. The continuation of the passage from Joel is found in vs 39.

■ **22** The repetition of these words of address, "Men of Israel," indicates to the reader that now Peter's own words begin.[8] The third topic is introduced here: the

christological kerygma (name—works—death—resurrection). The derivation of Ναζωραῖος, "Nazarene," is disputed.[9] ἄνδρα, "man" (cf. Luke 24:19; Acts 17:31), is not meant in the sense of an "Ebionite" Christology.[10] The proof from miracles is constitutive for Lukan Christology (Luke 4:16–19; Acts 10:37–38). The subordination of Jesus is stressed in that the miracles are characterized as acts of God *through* Jesus.[11]

■ **23** The notion of the divine plan is also typically Lukan (Luke 22:22, etc.).[12] The death of Jesus is not interpreted as a positive saving act.[13] That with this death the plan of salvation was fulfilled does not mean that the guilt of the Jews is diminished.[14] For ἔκδοτος, "delivered up," see Polybius 26.2.13 and Josephus *Ant.* 6.316. διὰ χειρὸς ἀνόμων, "by the hands of lawless men," is explained by 4:26–28 and Luke's passion narrative.

■ **24** Note the "kerygmatic" style using the relative pronoun, literally, "*whom* God raised up" (cf. 3:15; 4:10; 5:30; 10:38–39; 13:31). As with the miracles, in the case of the "resurrection" God is the one who acts.[15] ὠδῖνες, "pangs" (Pss 18 [17]:5–6; 116 [114]:3; 2 Sam 22:6), is an incorrect translation of חֶבְלִי; the LXX derives its translations from חֵבֶל, "birth-pangs," instead of from חֶבֶל, "cord." On λύειν, "to loose," see Job 39:2 LXX and Polycarp *Phil.* 1.2. One should not import into this expression the concept "death throes."

■ **25–28** The fourth topic is scriptural proof from Ps 16 (15):8–11. Again only the Greek text fits the argument, particularly with its translation of לָבֶטַח by ἐπ' ἐλπίδι, "in hope."[16] τὸν κύριον, "the Lord," is misunderstood by א D and syᵖ as referring to Jesus. εἰς ᾅδην by itself means

---

    to the time of the promise, since the Spirit had not yet been poured out. Of the promise, the outpouring of the Spirit and the cosmic signs are already fulfilled, according to him; only the Parousia has not yet arrived).

6   See the excursus immediately preceding.

7   Karl Heinrich Rengstorf, "σημεῖον," *TDNT* 7 (1971) 206–7, 239–43.

8   Haenchen, p. 179.

9   Hans Heinrich Schaeder, "Ναζαρηνός, Ναζωραῖος," *TDNT* 4 (1967) 874–79; Bertil Gärtner, *Die rätselhaften Termini Nazoräer und Iskariot* (Horae Soederblomianae 4; Uppsala: Gleerup, 1957); Kurt Rudolph, *Die Mandäer* (2 vols.; Göttingen: Vandenhoeck & Ruprecht, 1960–61) 1.115–18.

10 See the commentary on vs 36.

11 Conzelmann, *Theology*, 173–84.

12 Ibid., 151–54.

13 *Beginnings* 5.366.

14 On the later development of this topic, see Carl Schneider, *Geistesgeschichte des antiken Christentums* (2 vols.; Munich: Beck, 1954) 1.588.

15 Herbert Braun, "Zur Terminologie der Acta von der Auferstehung Jesu," *ThLZ* 77 (1952) cols. 533–36, reprinted in his *Gesammelte Studien zum Neuen Testament und seiner Umwelt* (2d ed.; Tübingen: Mohr [Siebeck], 1967) 173–77.

16 Against Jan Willem Doeve, *Jewish Hermeneutics in the Synoptic Gospels and Acts* (Assen: Van Gorcum, 1953) 168–76.

"abandon to Hades" (cf. *Pss. Sol.* 2.7). But Luke means "leave in Hades," that is, in death. The text cannot be understood as referring to a journey to Hades. Luke is unfamiliar with such a notion and we should not infer a pre-Lukan meaning.[17]

■ **29** The meaning of the quotation must be determined more exactly because David appears to be speaking of himself. By speaking of David as πατριάρχης, "patriarch," Peter identifies himself with his hearers. David's grave[18] serves as proof that David has decomposed, thus the quotation cannot refer to him.

■ **30** The positive proof follows, with the help of Ps 132 (131):11.[19]

■ **32** οὗ can be understood as masculine, "of whom" (1:8), or as neuter, "of that" (5:32).

■ **33** Despite Ps 118 (117):16 and *Odes Sol.* 25.9, τῇ δεξιᾷ should be understood as local ("to the right hand") rather than instrumental (cf. vss 30–36; 5:31; *Odes Sol.* 8.21).[20] Although Luke distinguishes the ascension from the resurrection in his narrative, in the kerygma here the resurrection appears to be identical with the exaltation. But this impression is merely the result of an attempt to give a concise summary along with the use of traditional expressions.[21] The subordination of Christ is once again clearly indicated (cf. 5:31). The present tenses (βλέπετε, "you see"; ἀκούετε, "you hear") should not be pressed to mean that (according to Luke) the rest of the Christians are still in a state of ecstacy.

■ **34a** Here reference is made to a Jewish motif (on not ascending, see Bar 3:29; *4 Ezra* 4.8) which is used by Christians for apologetic purposes (Rom 10:6–7). The scriptural proof from Ps 110 (109):1[22] again makes sense only according to the LXX translation—only on this basis is the distinction possible between κύριος, "Lord" = God, and κύριός μου, "my Lord" = Christ.

■ **36** This has an adoptionist ring, as if Jesus were made κύριος, "Lord," and χριστός, "Christ," only through his resurrection. For Luke Jesus was certainly Messiah during his lifetime (10:38; Luke 4:18), and he makes no essential distinction between κύριος and χριστός.[23] Is a pre-Lukan statement of an adoptionist type reproduced here? Hardly; the formulation may come from Luke himself. Luke derives the combination of the two titles from the scriptural proof, the results of which he summarizes here; he obtains the Messiah title (vs 31) from Psalm 16 and the κύριος title from Psalm 110.[24] Luke is not reflecting on the time of installation at all but simply sets forth God's action in opposition to the behavior of the Jews.[25]

17 Emil Freistedt (*Altchristliche Totengedächtnistage und ihre Beziehung zum Jenseitsglauben und Totenkultus der Antike* [Liturgiegeschichtliche Quellen und Forschungen 24; Münster: Aschendorff, 1928] 63) sees in the background the Jewish conception that decomposition sets in after three days; Christ is resurrected earlier. See also Dupont, "Messianic Interpretation of the Psalms in the Acts of the Apostles," *Salvation*, 103–28, esp. 106–11.

18 Josephus *Bell.* 1.61; cf. *Ant.* 13.249; 7.392–94. Joachim Jeremias, *Heiligengräber in Jesu Umwelt (Mt. 23,29; Lk. 11,47): Eine Untersuchung zur Volksreligion der Zeit Jesu* (Göttingen: Vandenhoeck & Ruprecht, 1958) 56–60, 129.

19 Eduard Schweizer, "The Concept of the Davidic 'Son of God' in Acts and Its Old Testament Background," *Studies in Luke-Acts*, 186–93.

20 Against G. Voss, *Die Christologie der lukanischen Schriften in Grundzügen* (Studia Neotestamentica 2; Paris/Bruges: Desclée de Brouwer, 1965) 133.

21 Wilckens, *Missionsreden*, 150–51; see Eph 1:20 and Col 3:1.

22 Cf. Mark 12:35–37 pars.; 14:62 par.; 1 Cor 15:25; Heb 1:13; Justin *Apol.* 1.45.1–2; *Asc. Is.* 11.32.

23 Conzelmann, *Theology*, 170–84.

24 Rese, *Alttestamentliche Motive*, 65–66.

25 Wilckens, *Missionsreden*, 170–75. Also against an adoptionist interpretation is Erik Sjöberg, *Der verborgene Menschensohn in den Evangelien* (Skrifter utgivna av Kungl. Humanistiska Vetenskapssamfundet 1 Lund 53; Lund: Gleerup, 1955) 36–37. Basic to his position is a belief in the hiddenness of the messiahship of Jesus during his earthly life. This is untenable in view of the Lukan character of the passage.

2

The Effects of the Speech

37 Now when they heard this they were cut to the heart, and said to Peter and the rest of the apostles, "Brethren, what shall we do?" 38/ And Peter said to them, "Repent, and be baptized every one of you in the name of Jesus Christ for the forgiveness of your sins; and you shall receive the gift of the Holy Spirit. 39/ For the promise is to you and to your children and to all that are far off, every one whom the Lord our God calls to him." 40/ And he testified with many other words and exhorted them, saying, "Save yourselves from this crooked generation." 41/ So those who received his word were baptized, and there were added that day about three thousand souls.

■ **37** The interruption represented by this verse is a literary device (cf. 10:44). τί ποιήσωμεν, "what shall we do," is catechetical style (cf. Mark 10:17). With little success D has attempted to describe the scene in a more realistic manner; it reads, τότε πάντες οἱ συνελθόντες καὶ ἀκαύσαντες κατενύγησαν τῇ καρδίᾳ, καὶ τινες ἐξ αὐτῶν εἶπαν πρὸς τὸν Πέτρον καὶ τοὺς ἀποστόλους· Τί οὖν ποιήσομεν, ἄνδρες ἀδελφοί; ὑποδείξατε ἡμεῖν, "Then all those who were present and heard this were cut to the heart, and some of them said to Peter and to the apostles, 'Brethren, what then shall we do? Show us.'" For κατενύγησαν, "they were cut," see Ps 109 (108):16.

■ **38** Peter concludes with the announcement of the meaning of the Christ-event for salvation, with the condition: μετάνοια, "repentance."[1] "ἐπὶ" τῷ ὀνόματι has the same meaning as "ἐν" (so B D): "in the name" (10:48).[2] The choice of the preposition here (ἐπί) is coherent with the ἐπικαλεῖν, "name by which you are called," of Jas 2:7, where the sense is to pronounce someone's name over

someone else. A baptismal formula of a single sentence is presupposed. Baptism and receiving the Spirit belong together.[3]

■ **39** This verse indicates that the accent is on the promise. καὶ τοῖς τέκνοις ὑμῶν, "and to your children," should not be taken literally,[4] but looks toward future generations. εἰς μακράν should be taken as referring to distance, "to (all that are) far off" (22:21; Sir 24:32; cf. Isa 57:19). Luke is once again referring back to Joel 3:4 LXX.

■ **40** The reference to the "many words" is a Lukan device.[5]

■ **41** Is οἱ μὲν οὖν, "so those," used here to continue the narrative without a corresponding οἱ δέ?[6] ψυχή means "person" here as in the LXX and the papyri. Of course the number cannot be historically verified (not even if it is reduced to a fraction).

1   Hans Conzelmann, *Die Mitte der Zeit* (4th ed.; BHT 17; Tübingen: Mohr [Siebeck], 1962) 213 n. 1; Rudolf Schnackenburg, "Typen der Metanoia—Predigt im Neuen Testament," *MThZ* 1:4 (1950) 1–13; Otto Glombitza, "Der Schluss der Petrusrede Acta 2:36–40: Ein Beitrag zum Problem der Predigten in Acta," *ZNW* 52 (1961) 115–16.

2   For another opinion, see Gerhard Delling, *Die Zueignung des Heils in der Taufe: Eine Untersuchung zum neutestamentlichen "taufen auf den Namen"* (Berlin: Evangelische Verlagsanstalt, 1961) 91–92.

3   See the commentary on 8:16.

4   Nor should it be used to estimate the age of infant baptism; for discussion, see Kurt Aland, *Did the Early Church Baptize Infants?* (trans. G. R. Beasley-Murray, with new material by the author; Library of History and Doctrine; London: SCM, 1963) 84–86.

5   Dibelius, *Studies,* 178.

6   BDF § 251.

2

Summary:
The Unity of
the Earliest Community

42 And they devoted themselves to the apostles' teaching and fellowship, to the breaking of bread and the prayers.
43 And fear came upon every soul; and many wonders and signs were done through the apostles. 44/ And all who believed were together and had all things in common; 45/ and they sold their possessions and goods and distributed them to all, as any had need. 46/ And day by day, attending the temple together and breaking bread in their homes, they partook of food with glad and generous hearts, 47/ praising God and having favor with all the people. And the Lord added to their number day by day those who were being saved.

■ 42 The summary interrupts the progress of the account and gives the reader some information about the nature of the earliest church.[1] The mention of the "apostles' teaching" puts the stress on the content (the "tradition" which Luke himself hands on in his books), not on the formal aspect (the mode of handing on the tradition). κοινωνία, "fellowship," is explained by 4:32. For the meals, compare 2:46.[2]

Excursus:
The Breaking of Bread

When Luke speaks of the breaking of bread he does not mean only the rite at the beginning of the meal, but rather the meal itself (cf. 20:7).[3] Do we have evidence here for a second type of Lord's Supper which is pre-Pauline (Lietzmann)? In considering this question it should be noted that Luke is thinking of the ordinary daily meal here, but he does not make a distinction between it and the Eucharist. The unity of the two is part of the ideal picture of the earliest church.

It has been suggested that the four concepts here (teaching, fellowship, breaking of bread, and prayers) describe the liturgical course of a worship service.[4] But the character of the summary, the concepts themselves, and their sequence all argue against this interpretation.[5]

■ 43 Compare 3:10 and 5:5, 11 with this verse. On the topic of fear in the presence of the holy congregation, see 1QH 4.26.

■ 44 The κοινωνία, "fellowship," is depicted as the sharing of property. A proverbial Greek expression says: κοινὰ τὰ φίλων, "the belongings of friends are held in common."[6]

■ 45 The distinction between real estate and goods is not stressed. D has again attempted to tell the story in a more realistic manner; instead of "they sold their possessions and goods," it reads "as many as had possessions or goods sold them."

1 On vs 41, cf. 4:4; 5:14; 11:24; on vs 42, cf. 1:14; on vs 43, cf. 5:5, 11, 12a; on vss 44–45, cf. 4:32, 34–35; on vs 46, cf. 1:14; 5:12b; on vs 47, cf. 5:13–14. See the Introduction (p. xliii); Haenchen, p. 195.

2 Franz Mussner, "Die UNA SANCTA nach Apg 2,42," *Praesentia salutis*, 212–22.

3 Which is different from Judaism; see Joachim Jeremias, *The Eucharistic Words of Jesus* (trans. Norman Perrin from the German 3d ed. with the author's revisions; New York: Scribner's, 1966) 118–21.

4 Ibid.

5 Similarly Heinrich Zimmermann, "Die Sammelberichte der Apostelgeschichte," *BZ* n.s. 5 (1961) 71–82.

6 Plato *Rep.* 4.424a; 5.449c; Aristotle *Eth. Nic.* 8.9, 1159b 31; Philo *Abr.* 235; Cicero *Off.* 1.16.51; Ps.-Clem. *Recog.* 10.5; strongly modified, *Barn.* 19.8.

Excursus:
The Sharing of Property

This picture of sharing property is idealized. The material was furnished by: (1) information handed on by tradition, such as 4:36–37 or 5:1–11; (2) knowledge about communistic groups, whether real (Essenes and the Qumran community: Josephus *Bell.* 2.122–23; *Ant.* 18.18–22; Philo *Prob.* 75–87; 1QS 1.11–12 and 6.2–3)[7] or ideal (for example the original "community of Pythagoreans").[8] Idealized communal portraits are associated with utopian dreams or accounts of primeval times.[9] In *Pergr. mort.* 13 Lucian reports of the Christians: "Therefore they despise all things indiscriminately and consider them common property" (κατα-φρονοῦσιν οὖν ἁπάντων ἐξ ἴσης καὶ κοινὰ ἡγοῦνται). Some of the characteristic ancient catchwords are missing in Luke: ἰσότης, "equality," and the designation of the community as φίλοι, "friends." Despite the existence of communistic groups in the vicinity of Jerusalem, Luke's portrayal should not be taken as historical (some sort of organized means of support would have been necessary, as in those groups). Thus we cannot speak of a "failure of the experiment," nor can we draw conclusions for a primitive Christian communistic ideal. Furthermore, Luke does not present this way of life as a norm for the organization of the church in his own time. It is meant as an illustration of the uniqueness of the ideal earliest days of the movement.[10]

■ **46** The attendance at the temple represents the Christians' claim to the temple (see Luke 19:45–48 along with Luke 2:49),[11] and thereby their claim to be the true Israel. With τροφῆς μεταλαμβάνειν, "to partake of food," compare Ps.-Clem. *Hom.* 1.22.3 and *Recog.* 1.19.3.[12] Is the unusual expression ἐν ἀφελότητι καρδίας, "with generous heart" (rather than ἐν ἁπλότητι καρδίας, "with a sincere heart"), used because it sounds more sonorous?

■ **47** The "favor" mentioned here balances the fear motif of vs 43. D has a universalistic emphasis, reading "all the world" for "all the people" (ὅλον τὸν κόσμον) / (ὅλον τὸν λαόν);[13] it no longer understands the biblical expression, ἐπὶ τὸ αὐτό, "to their number" (יַחְדָּו "together," especially in the Psalms; 1QS 10.17). The summary does not appear to be constructed logically.[14] This impression results from the repetition of the relationship between the Christian community and the broader public (vss 43, 47). But the repetition serves on the one hand to summarize the results of Pentecost day, and on the other to begin the story of the community in the world.

7   Braun, *Qumran* 1.77–95, 139–68.

8   Josephus compares the Essenes to the Pythagoreans in *Ant.* 15.371.

9   See Plato's view of primeval Athens: *Critias*. See further, for example, Porphyry *Vita Pyth.* 20: "They held their property in common" (τὰς οὐσίας κοινὰς ἔθεντο); Iamblichus *Vita Pyth.* 30.168: "For all things were common and the same to all, and no one possessed anything privately" (κοινὰ γὰρ πᾶσι πάντα καὶ ταὐτὰ ἦν· ἴδιον δὲ οὐδεὶς οὐδὲν ἐκέκτητο); 30.167: "Accordingly, the first principle of righteousness is commonality and equality, and that everyone experience the nearest thing to one body and one soul, and call the same thing mine and another's" (ἀρχὴ τοίνυν ἐστὶ δικαιοσύνης μὲν τὸ κοινὸν καὶ ἴσον καὶ τὸ ἐγγυτάτω ἑνὸς σώματος καὶ μιᾶς ψυχῆς ὁμοπαθεῖν πάντας καὶ ἐπὶ τὸ αὐτὸ τὸ ἐμὸν φθέγγεσθαι καὶ τὸ ἀλλότριον); cf. Plato *Rep.* 5.462c.

10 *Beginnings* 5.140–51; Hans von Schubert, *Der Kommunismus der Wiedertäufer in Münster und seine Quellen* (SAH 1919:11; Heidelberg: Winter, 1919) 27–40; Friedrich Hauck, "κοινός, κτλ.," *TDNT* 3 (1965) 789–809; cf. Friedrich Hauck and Wilhelm Kasch, "πλοῦτος, κτλ.," *TDNT* (1968) 318–32; Robert von Pöhlmann, *Geschichte der sozialen Frage und des sozialismus in der antiken Welt* (3d ed.; 2 vols.; Munich: Beck, 1925); Sherman E. Johnson, "The Dead Sea Manual of Discipline and the Jerusalem Church of Acts," *The Scrolls and the New Testament* (ed. Krister Stendahl; New York: Harper, 1957) 129–42; Jacques Dupont, "Community of Goods in the Early Church," *The Salvation of the Gentiles: Essays on the Acts of the Apostles* (New York/Ramsey, NJ/Toronto: Paulist, 1979) 85–102.

11 Conzelmann, *Theology,* 75–78.

12 Georg Strecker, *Das Judenchristentum in den Pseudoklementinen* (2d ed.; TU 70; Berlin: Akademie-Verlag, 1981) 210. On ἀγαλλίασις, "gladness," see A. B. du Toit, *Der Aspekt der Freude im urchristlichen Abendmahl* (Winterthur: Keller, 1965) 103–39.

13 See the comments on vss 17–18; cf. also vs 39; Epp, *Theological Tendency,* 75–79.

14 See the Introduction, pp. xliii.

3   Peter Heals a Lame Man

1 Now Peter and John were going up to the temple at the hour of prayer, the ninth hour. 2/ And a man lame from birth was being carried, whom they laid daily at that gate of the temple which is called Beautiful to ask alms of those who entered the temple. 3/ Seeing Peter and John about to go into the temple, he asked for alms. 4/ And Peter directed his gaze at him, with John, and said, "Look at us." 5/ And he fixed his attention upon them, expecting to receive something from them. 6/ But Peter said, "I have no silver and gold, but I give you what I have; in the name of Jesus Christ of Nazareth, walk." 7/ And he took him by the right hand and raised him up; and immediately his feet and ankles were made strong. 8/ And leaping up he stood and walked and entered the temple with them, walking and leaping and praising God. 9/ And all the people saw him walking and praising God, 10/ and recognized him as the one who sat for alms at the Beautiful Gate of the temple; and they were filled with wonder and amazement at what had happened to him.

The miracle stories of Acts no longer exhibit the strict structure of those found in the Synoptics. Nevertheless, the typical stylistic characteristics can still be recognized: the scene, exposition, the healing (word and gesture), result and demonstration, effect on the observers.[1] The healing story was originally independent: there is no connective at the beginning. The Lukan additions indicate that Luke had the story already in written form. The healing now appears as an effect of the pouring out of the Spirit.

■ **1** Originally it appears that only Peter was named.[2]

ἀναβαίνειν, "to go up," is the customary expression for going up to the temple, even if it is not uphill.[3] The imperfect is used as the tense for a narrative.[4] τὸ ἱερόν, "the temple," means the whole temple area. One of the usual times for prayer was the hour of the evening sacrifice.[5]

■ **2–3** These verses offer the exposition.[6]

1 Dibelius, *Studies*, 14–15.
2 See the commentary on vs 4.
3 Cf. also ἀνέρχεσθαι, *Pap. Oxy.* 1089 col. 2, line 27; the text may be found in Herbert Musurillo, *The Acts of the Pagan Martyrs: Acta Alexandrinorum* (Oxford: Clarendon, 1954) 4, and idem, *Acta Alexandrinorum: De mortibus Alexandriae nobilium fragmenta papyracea graeca* (Leipzig: Teubner, 1961) 3.
4 Radermacher, *Grammatik*, 153.
5 Dan 9:21; Jdt 9:1; Josephus *Ant.* 14.65; Str-B 2.696–702.
6 On begging at the temple, see Hendrik Bolkestein,

Wohltätigkeit und Armenpflege im vorchristlichen Altertum: Ein Beitrag zum Problem "Moral und Gesellschaft" (Utrecht: Oosthoek, 1939; reprinted New York: Arno, 1979) 413.

Excursus:
The "Beautiful Gate"[7]

The designation "Beautiful Gate" is not found in Jewish descriptions of the temple, either in Josephus or in the Mishnah.[8] Unfortunately both descriptions are inexact and unclear. The later Christian identification with the Susa Gate (on the east side) is impossible. Josephus mentions a "Corinthian" (or "bronze") gate, which is clearly the same as the Nicanor Gate of Jewish tradition following the Mishnah. Whether this was at the east entrance to the women's court[9] or to the men's court[10] is debated. The uncertainty is due partly to the fact that the Mishnah knows of only *one* gate on the east.[11] The sources, however, argue for the second possibility (Stauffer). The matter is made all the more difficult by the fact that Luke himself has no personal knowledge of the place. He does not distinguish between the various areas in the inner part of the temple and conceives of the "Beautiful Gate" as located in the outer enclosure. After passing through it one arrives at Solomon's Portico. The Western text of vs 11 does not really have a better knowledge of the place.[12]

■ **4** For ἀτενίζειν, "to look intently at," see 13:9 and 14:9; D and h switch the verbs of seeing and use ἀτενίζειν (not in good style) in connection with the beggar. σὺν τῷ Ἰωάννῃ, "with John," appears to be an addition. Haenchen believes that in this way Luke prepares for the appearance of *two* witnesses before the Sanhedrin (4:19–20).[13] He sees vss 4–5 and 6 together as redactional additions (by Luke). But if one excludes them, the source becomes too scanty.

■ **6** Only 6a is stylistically foreign and to be attributed to Luke. It points toward 4:32–37 (and at the same time prepares for the summary in 5:12–16). To point out that Peter must have had money for the poor (according to 4:35) really misses the point. The *name* (τὸ ὄνομα) as the effective representation of Jesus is prominent in Acts. The speech in vss 12–26 connects up with it, as does the account in chapters 4 and 5.

■ **7** A result which occurs "immediately" is typical in Luke (Luke 4:39; Acts 5:10; 13:11).[14]

■ **8** The "demonstration" is reminiscent of Isa 35:6 LXX.[15] Verse 8b seems overloaded and prepares for the redactional vs 11; thus vs 8b itself is redactional.

■ **9–10** The original narrative is brought to a close by reporting the effect upon the observers, which fits the style of the miracle story.[16]

7   Literature:
     Beginnings 5.479–86.
     Gottlob Schrenk, "τὸ ἱερόν," *TDNT* 3 (1965) 236.
     L.-H. Vincent, "Le Temple Hérodien d'après la Misnah," *RB* 61 (1954) 5–35, 398–418.
     L.-H. Vincent and M.-A. Steve, *Jérusalem de l'Ancient Testament: Recherches d'archéologie et d'histoire* (2 vols.; Paris: Gabalda, 1954–56).
     André Parrot, *The Temple of Jerusalem* (Studies in Biblical Archaeology 5; London: SCM, 1957) 78–92.
     Ethelbert Stauffer, "Das Tor des Nikanor," *ZNW* 44 (1952–53) 44–66.
     Spencer Corbett, "Some Observations on the Gateways to the Herodian Temple in Jerusalem," *PEQ* 84 (1952) 7–14 + 5 pls.
     Abraham Schalit, *König Herodes: Der Mann und sein Werk* (StJud 4; Berlin: de Gruyter, 1969) 372–97.
8   Josephus *Bell.* 2.411; 5.190–206; *Ant.* 15.410–20; *Middot;* Str-B 2.620–25.
9   André Parrot, *The Temple of Jerusalem* (Studies in Biblical Archaeology 5; London: SCM, 1957) 88–89.
10   L.-H. Vincent and M.-A. Steve, *Jérusalem de l'Ancient Testament: Recherches d'archéologie et d'histoire* (2 vols.; Paris: Gabalda, 1954–56) 2.432–70, 520–25, and pl. 52.
11   Ibid., pl. 55!
12   Against Jean Duplacy ("A propos d'une variante 'occidentale' des *Actes des Apôtres* [III, 12]," *Revue des études augustiniennes* 2 [1956] 231–42), who considers it as original and trustworthy. See below on 3:11.
13   Haenchen, p. 201.
14   Betz, *Lukian,* 157 n. 3.
15   On demonstration in the healing of someone lame, see Mark 2:11; Lucian *Philops.* 2; *SIG* 3 no. 1168.110–12.
16   Dibelius, *Studies,* 85.

3 Peter's Speech

11 While he clung to Peter and John, all the people ran together to them, in the portico called Solomon's, astounded. 12/ And when Peter saw it he addressed the people, "Men of Israel, why do you wonder at this, or why do you stare at us, as though by our own power or piety we had made him walk? 13/ The God of Abraham and of Isaac and of Jacob, the God of our fathers, glorified his servant Jesus, whom you delivered up and denied in the presence of Pilate, when he had decided to release him. 14/ But you denied the Holy and Righteous One, and asked for a murderer to be granted to you, 15/ and killed the Author of life, whom God raised from the dead. To this we are witnesses. 16/ And his name, by faith in his name, has made this man strong whom you see and know; and the faith which is through Jesus has given the man this perfect health in the presence of you all.

17 "And now, brethren, I know that you acted in ignorance, as did also your rulers. 18/ But what God foretold by the mouth of all the prophets, that his Christ should suffer, he thus fulfilled. 19/ Repent therefore, and turn again, that your sins may be blotted out, that times of refreshing may come from the presence of the Lord, 20/ and that he may send the Christ appointed for you, Jesus, 21/ whom heaven must receive until the time for establishing all that God spoke by the mouth of his holy prophets from of old. 22/ Moses said, 'The Lord God will raise up for you a prophet from your brethren as he raised me up. You shall listen to him in whatever he tells you. 23/ And it shall be that every soul that does not listen to that prophet shall be destroyed from the people.' 24/ And all the prophets who have spoken, from Samuel and those who came afterwards, also proclaimed these days. 25/ You are the sons of the prophets and of the covenant which God gave to your fathers, saying to Abraham, 'And in your posterity shall all the families of the earth be blessed.' 26/ God, having raised up his servant, sent him to you first, to bless you in turning every one of you from your wickedness."

The usual structure of the speeches is varied as the proof from Scripture is pushed into the background. Luke supplements the Pentecost speech by setting forth the situation of Israel in detail. With this he provides a foil for chapters 4 and 5. The style is archaizing.

■ 11 The connection here is artificial. The Western text

attempts to hide the seam[1] and in so doing indicates that it no longer understands the Lukan picture of the temple and is therefore secondary. With Luke it mistakenly locates Solomon's Portico in the space within the "Beautiful Gate" (5:12 D;[2] actually this portico was in the eastern outer wall, in the court of the Gentiles, Josephus *Bell.* 5.185; *Ant.* 20.221). ἔκθαμβοι, "astounded,": θάμβος, "astonishment," and φόβος, "fear," etc., are typical reactions to a miracle.[3]

■ **12** Luke again uses the technique of a misunderstanding. In so doing he differentiates the miracle from a magical thaumaturgy.[4] Note Ps.-Clem. *Recog.* 10.70: "As you see me to be a man like to yourselves, do not suppose that you can recover your health from me, but through him who, coming down from heaven, has shown to those who believe in him a perfect medicine for body and soul" (Similem vobis hominem me esse videntes nolite putare quod a me possitis recuperare salutem vestram, sed per eum, qui de caelo descendens ostendit credentibus sibi integram animi et corporis medicinam).[5] ποιεῖν, "to make," with the genitive of the articular infinitive follows the pattern of the LXX.[6]

■ **13** The introductory quotation of Scripture[7] comes from Exod 3:6, 15 (cf. Luke 20:37; Acts 7:32). It establishes the continuity between the church and Israel. Despite the reminiscence of Isa 52:13, the concept παῖς, "servant," does not imply atonement through suffering, but expresses Luke's exaltation Christology. It is an honorific title from a liturgical setting:[8] *Did.* 9.2–3; *1 Clem.* 59.2–4; (*Barn.* 6.1; 9.2); *Mart. Pol.* 14.1; 20.2.[9]

The kerygma is contained in vss 13b–15 (note the relative clauses!). παραδιδόναι, "to deliver up," and ἀρνεῖσθαι, "to deny," are thematic words. The construction is broken up (μέν without a correlative!) to stress the guilt of the Jews in a direct confrontation. The emphasis here corresponds to that of Luke's passion account.

■ **14** This verse alludes to the Barabbas episode (Luke 23:18–23). For δίκαιος, "righteous," compare 7:52; for ἅγιος, "holy," compare 4:27–30. Luke has given these messianic terms a moral sense. For the stress on the innocence of Jesus, compare Luke 23:47.[10]

■ **15** Compare this verse with 2:32. ἀρχηγός, "author" (cf. 5:31), is paraphrased in 26:23: πρῶτος ἐξ ἀναστάσεως, "first to rise from the dead." Jesus' resurrection is not causally connected with ours.[11] God is again expressly identified as the actor (cf. 4:10; 5:30; 10:40; 13:30, 37).

■ **16** The style is awkward. H. W. Moule considers the possibility that Luke left two unrevised copies of the same passage, both of which were eventually copied (perhaps true in other passages as well).[12] Two parallel clauses state that faith and healing have come about through the name of Jesus, and that this name is the object of faith. πίστις, "faith": here the faith of the sick man is meant (cf. 14:9); we have here a missionary appeal. On the phrase ἡ πίστις ἡ δι᾽ αὐτοῦ, "the faith which is through him," compare Ignatius *Phld.* 8.2.

■ **17** For καὶ νῦν, "and now," compare the Old Testament וְעַתָּה, "and now."[13] ἄγνοια, "ignorance," means a relative pardon for the one who has committed a wrong.[14]

■ **18** The prophetic witness is considered as a unity (cf. vss 21, 24; *b. Ber.* 34b).[15] Behind the formulation παθεῖν τὸν χριστὸν αὐτοῦ, "for his Christ to suffer," is a Lukan

---

1 Dibelius, *Studies,* 85.
2 Against *Beginnings* 4.32.
3 Betz, *Lukian,* 159.
4 See the commentary on 14:15.
5 *Ante-Nicene Fathers* 8.210.
6 BDF § 400.7.
7 See the commentary on 2:17.
8 See the commentary on 4:26–27; Josef Gewiess, *Die urapostolische Heilsverkündigung nach der Apostelgeschichte* (Breslau: Müller & Seiffert, 1939) 46.
9 Wilckens, *Missionsreden,* 127–31, 163–70; M. Duchaine, "Pais theou in the Acts of the Apostles" (Diss., Louvain, 1963).
10 Differently Albert Descamps, *Les justes et la justice dans les évangiles et le christianisme primitif hormis la doctrine proprement paulinienne* (Universitas Catholica Lovaniensis 2:43; Louvain: Publications

Universitaires de Louvain, 1950) 59–84.
11 See the commentary on 17:31.
12 C. F. D. Moule, "H. W. Moule on Acts iv.25," *ExpTim* 65 (1953–54) 220.
13 Joachim Jeremias, "Beobachtungen zu neutestamentlichen Stellen an Hand des neugefundenen griechischen Henoch-Textes," *ZNW* 38 (1939) 119–20.
14 See Martin Dibelius and Hans Conzelmann, *A Commentary on the Pastoral Epistles* (trans. Philip Buttolph and Adela Yarbro; ed. Helmut Koester; Hermeneia; Philadelphia: Fortress, 1972) 27, on 1 Tim 1:13; compare Luke 23:34; *T. Jud.* 19.3; *Const. Ap.* 7.36.5 (but Acts 13:27 has a different view!). Cf., however, Ernst Bammel, "Judenverfolgung und Naherwartung: Zur Eschatologie des ersten Thessalonicherbriefs," *ZThK* 56 (1959) 305 n. 8; Epp, *Theological Tendency,* 42–46, cf. 51–56; Albrecht Dihle, *Die*

schema: first a scriptural conception of the Messiah is
established, then that this conception fits Jesus (cf. 17:3;
Luke 24:26, 44–48; see also Acts 26:23).[16]

■ **19** The combination of μετανοεῖν καὶ ἐπιστρέφειν,
"repent and turn again," shows that μετανοεῖν, "repent,"
no longer signifies the conversion event as complete and
indivisible; it is now divided into a change of mind and a
change of conduct.[17]

■ **20** The parallelism between the two halves of the verse
shows that the καιροὶ ἀναψύξεως, "times of refreshing,"
are not intervals of respite in the eschatological distress,[18] but rather the final time of salvation (like the
χρόνοι ἀποκαταστάσεως, "times for restoration," vs 21).
ἀνάψυξις, "refreshing," is the subjective counterpart to
ἀποκατάστασις, "restoration." If one takes ὅπως ἄν, "in
order that," as introducing a strict purpose clause, then
the time of salvation is brought about through conversion (2 Pet 3:12). But Luke only means that conversion
properly prepares for the Parousia, not that it brings it
about! Luke has perhaps understood the προ-, "before,"
in προχειρίζειν, "to appoint," in a temporal rather than a
spatial sense. This would be in line with his use elsewhere
of other compounds with προ-.[19]

In what follows the difficulties multiply. The transition
from the historical Jesus to the Parousia is abrupt, all the
more since vs 22 immediately focuses again on the past.
The sequence of thought would be smoother if vss 20–
21 were absent. The awkwardness apparently arises from
Luke's desire to connect into an overarching schema of
salvation-history statements about the passion and resurrection present in the kerygmatic formulations available

to him (which are still barely connected) with statements
about the Parousia, combining both with proof from
Scripture. Verses 20 and 21 work out the positive side of
what vs 23 and 13:40–41 say in the negative. Otto
Bauernfeind suspects that there is a Jewish prophecy
about Elijah in the background here (the taking up into
heaven and ἀποκατάστασις, "restoration," cf. Mal 3:23;
Sir 48:10) which was later applied to Christ. He traces
this tradition back to the disciples of John the Baptist.[20]
But such a source cannot be reconstructed. Luke is following the example of apocalyptic formulations, and the
statement is essentially Lukan.[21] In christological passages Luke uses an archaizing style. This verse envisions
a lengthy interval between the resurrection and the
Parousia. Verse 21a says something about the christological character of this interval, while vss 19–20 say
something about its ecclesiological character.[22]

■ **21** Luke does not apply ἀποκατάστασις, "restoration," to
an ideal set of circumstances which will "again" be established.[23] Furthermore, the word does not refer to the
preparation, but to the time of salvation itself. The
relative after πάντων refers back to πάντων ("all that God
spoke"). For ἐλάλησεν κτλ., "he spoke, etc.," compare
Luke 1:70. For ἀπ᾽ αἰῶνος, "from of old," compare 15:7
ἀφ᾽ ἡμερῶν ἀρχαίων, "in the early days."[24]

■ **22-23** Here scriptural proof is presented from Deut
18:15, 18–19 and Lev 23:29.[25] C. H. Dodd believes that

*Goldene Regel: Eine Einführung in die Geschichte der
antiken und frühchristlichen Vulgärethik* (Studienhefte
zur Altertumswissenschaft 7; Göttingen: Vandenhoeck & Ruprecht, 1962) 17 n. 1.

15 Str-B 1.602–3; yet note the context!
16 Conzelmann, *Theology*, 171 n. 2.
17 Ibid., 99–101; Jacques Dupont, "Repentir et conversion d'après les Actes des Apôtres," *Sciences Ecclésiastiques* 12 (1960) 137–73, reprinted in his *Études*,
   421–57. On ἐξαλείφειν, "to blot out," see Martin
   Dibelius, *An Die Kolosser Epheser an Philemon* (3d ed.;
   ed. Heinrich Greeven; HNT 12; Tübingen: Mohr
   [Siebeck], 1953) 31–32 on Col 2:14.
18 Bauernfeind; Exod 8:11 LXX.
19 For another opinion, see Wilhelm Michaelis, "προχειρίζω," *TDNT* 6 (1968) 863–64; cf. 22:14; 26:16.
20 Otto Bauernfeind, "Tradition und Komposition in

dem Apokatastasisspruch Apostelgeschichte 3,20f,"
*Abraham unser Vater: Juden und Christen im Gespräch
über die Bibel: Festschrift für Otto Michel zum 60. Geburtstag* (ed. Otto Betz, Martin Hengel, and Peter
Schmidt; Leiden/Cologne: Brill, 1963) 13–23.
21 Gerhard Lohfink, "Christologie und Geschichtsbild
   in Apg 3,19–21," *BZ* n.s. 13 (1969) 223–41.
22 Mussner, "Die Idee der Apokatastasis"; Ernst Ludwig
   Dietrich, שוב שבות: *Die endzeitliche Wiederherstellung
   bei den Propheten* (BZAW 40; Giessen: Töpelmann,
   1925).
23 A. Méhat, "'Apocatastase,' Origène, Clément d'Alex-
   andrie, *Act.* 3,21," *VC* 10 (1956) 196–214.
24 On the scriptural proof, see Hans Conzelmann, *Die
   Mitte der Zeit* (4th ed.; BHTh 17; Tübingen: Mohr
   [Siebeck], 1962) 151 n. 1.
25 For the Moses typology, see the commentary on

a collection of *testimonia* has been used here.[26] The Deuteronomy passage is found in a *florilegium* from Qumran (4QTestim).[27] According to Origen, Dositheus made claims to the Samaritans that he had fulfilled this prophecy (*Cels.* 1.57).[28]

■ **24** Two expressions are combined here: (1) all prophets from Samuel onward; (2) Samuel and the prophets following him.[29] "These days" designates (despite vss 20–21) the present as the time of the preaching of salvation. The speech ends emphasizing a note of encouragement (in the following verse).

■ **25** For υἱοὶ τῆς διαθήκης, "sons of the covenant," compare Ezek 30:5; *Pss. Sol.* 17.15. For ἧς ὁ θεὸς κτλ., "which God etc.," compare Jer 11:10. The quotation (cf. Gal 3:8) comes from Gen 22:18 (cf. 12:3; 18:18). However, Luke changes ἔθνη, "nation," to πατριαί, "families," out of regard for his audience (cf. Psalm 22 = 21:28 LXX). In Gen 22:18 ἐνευλογηθήσονται is reflexive, "bless themselves," but here Luke understands it as a passive. σπέρμα, "posterity," is not collective, but refers to the *one* descendant, Jesus (cf. Gal 3:16).

■ **26** πρῶτον, "first," is explained by 13:46. The meaning of ἀναστήσας, "having raised up," follows from the OT quotation in vs 22. ἀποστρέφειν, "to turn," appears to be used intransitively.

7:35–43; Joachim Jeremias, "Μωϋσῆς," *TDNT* 4 (1967) 848–73; Marcel Simon, *St Stephen and the Hellenists in the Primitive Church* (London/New York/Toronto: Longmans, Green, 1958) 44–49; Robert McL. Wilson, "Simon, Dositheus and the Dead Sea Scrolls," *ZRGG* 9 (1957) 21–30; R. Schnackenburg, "Die Erwartung des 'Propheten' nach dem Neuen Testament und den Qumran-Texten," *StEv* I (1959) 622–39; Howard Merle Teeple, *The Mosaic Eschatological Prophet* (JBL Monograph Series 10; Philadelphia: Society of Biblical Literature, 1957).

26 Dodd, *Scriptures*, 53–57.
27 J. M. Allegro, "Further Messianic References in Qumran Literature," *JBL* 75 (1956) 183; on the relation to the Samaritan text, see Raymond Brown, "The Messianism of Qumran," *CBQ* 19 (1957) 82.
28 Cf. also Ps.-Clem. *Recog.* 1.36–40.
29 On Samuel, cf. Heb 11:32. On this general subject, cf. 26:22–23.

4

**The Arrest of Peter and John
and the Examination
before the Council**

1 And as they were speaking to the people, the priests and the captain of the temple and the Sadducees came upon them, 2/ annoyed because they were teaching the people and proclaiming in Jesus the resurrection from the dead. 3/ And they arrested them and put them in custody until the morrow, for it was already evening. 4/ But many of those who heard the word believed; and the number of the men came to about five thousand.

5 On the morrow their rulers and elders and scribes were gathered together in Jerusalem, 6/ with Annas the high priest and Caiaphas and John and Alexander, and all who were of the high-priestly family. 7/ And when they had set them in the midst, they inquired, "By what power or by what name did you do this?" 8/ Then Peter, filled with the Holy Spirit, said to them, "Rulers of the people and elders, 9/ if we are being examined today concerning a good deed done to a cripple, by what means this man has been healed, 10/ be it known to you all, and to all the people of Israel, that by the name of Jesus Christ of Nazareth, whom you crucified, whom God raised from the dead, by him this man is standing before you well. 11/ This is the stone which was rejected by you builders, but which has become the head of the corner. 12/ And there is salvation in no one else, for there is no other name under heaven given among men by which we must be saved."

13 Now when they saw the boldness of Peter and John, and perceived that they were uneducated, common men, they wondered; and they recognized that they had been with Jesus. 14/ But seeing the man that had been healed standing beside them, they had nothing to say in opposition. 15/ But when they had commanded them to go aside out of the council, they conferred with one another, 16/ saying, "What shall we do with these men? For that a notable sign has been performed through them is manifest to all the inhabitants of Jerusalem, and we cannot deny it. 17/ But in order that it may spread no further among the people, let us warn them to speak no more to any one in this name." 18/ So they called them and charged them not to speak or teach at all in the name of Jesus. 19/ But Peter and John answered them, "Whether it is right in the sight of God to listen to you rather than to God, you must judge; 20/ for we cannot but speak of what we have seen and heard." 21/ And

31

when they had further threatened them, they let them go, finding no way to punish them, because of the people; for all men praised God for what had happened. 22/ For the man on whom this sign of healing was performed was more than forty years old.

There are difficulties with this account if it is taken as a historically accurate report. Those problems disappear if we recognize it as a redactional revision of an account which can no longer be reconstructed in its original form.

■ 1 Here the literary device of an interruption is utilized after the speech has been finished![1] Luke sets up a contrast: the arrest of the apostles occurs at precisely the moment when they announce salvation to Israel. Here ἱερεῖς, "priests," is used whereas Luke usually speaks of the ἀρχιερεῖς, "chief priests" (cf. vs 6; 5:24; and B and C in 4:1). The στρατηγὸς τοῦ ἱεροῦ is the captain of the temple police (סֶגֶן, "prefect"), ranking just below the chief priest (Luke 22:4, 52 plural!).[2] The Sadducees (5:17)[3] in Acts are the stereotyped opponents of the Christians, because they deny the resurrection (23:6–8). This indicates that they are not true Israelites (26:5) and that there is a division within Judaism. In view of the redactional nature of this statement one need not ask whether hope in the resurrection really could have been used as the legal basis for an arrest. The motivation plays no further role in the book.

■ 2 ἐν τῷ Ἰησοῦ, "in Jesus," belongs with τὴν ἀνάστασιν τὴν ἐκ νεκρῶν, "the resurrection from the dead," and is placed before that expression for emphasis (for the meaning, cf. 26:23).

■ 3 For ἐπέβαλον, "lay hands on, arrest," compare 5:18; 12:1. τήρησις means custody (Josephus *Ant.* 16.321) or the prison.[4] The same ambiguity is found in Josephus *Ant.* 18.235. By postponing the hearing until the next day, Luke is able to describe the impression the speech makes on the people, thereby anticipating the failure of the proceedings (4:21).

■ 4 Compare 2:41: "And there were added that day about three thousand souls."

■ 5–6 The sentence structure is confused. On the makeup of the Sanhedrin, compare Luke 22:66 and Matt 27:1.[5] The ἄρχοντες, "rulers," are usually identified with the ἀρχιερεῖς, "chief priests," who appear elsewhere. Yet the rulers are named *alongside* the chief priests in Luke 23:13 and 24:20. Luke does not define the group precisely. The plural ἀρχιερεῖς which appears in vs 23 is explained here:[6] they are members of the high-priestly families.[7] Luke has mistakenly taken Annas (who held the office from 6 to 15 C.E.) as the ruling high priest. Wellhausen explains the correct name (Caiaphas) as an interpolation.[8] John (D: Jonathan; cf. Josephus *Ant.* 18.95) and Alexander are unknown. The conspicuous "in Jerusalem" indicates the fundamental importance of the trial (cf. vs 27, ἐν τῇ πόλει ταύτῃ, "in this city").[9]

■ 7 The question addressed here to the apostles is formulated to suit the purpose of the author. The earlier motivation for the arrest is set aside for the sake of the theological explanation of the ὄνομα, "name."

1   On the interruption as a literary technique, see the commentary on 2:37.

2   Emil Schürer, *The History of the Jewish People in the Age of Jesus Christ (175 B.C.—A.D. 135)* (3 vols. [vol. 3.2 forthcoming]; rev. and ed. Geza Vermes and Fergus Millar; Edinburgh: T. & T. Clark, 1973–86) 2.277–79; Joachim Jeremias, *Jerusalem in the Time of Jesus: An Investigation into Economic and Social Conditions during the New Testament Period* (Philadelphia: Fortress, 1969) 160–63.

3   Jeremias, *Jerusalem*, 228–32.

4   See the commentary on 5:18.

5   Gottlob Schrenk, "ἀρχιερεύς," *TDNT* 3 (1965) 270–71.

6   γένος ἀρχιερατικόν, "high-priestly family," Josephus *Ant.* 15.40; cf. 12.387.

7   Differently Jeremias, *Jerusalem*, 176–81: the holders of the highest temple offices; but it is doubtful which conception *Luke* has!

8   See the commentaries on Luke 3:1–2.

9   On the meeting place of the Sanhedrin, see Joseph Blinzler, *The Trial of Jesus: The Jewish and Roman Proceedings against Jesus Christ Described and Assessed from the Oldest Accounts* (Westminster, MD: Newman, 1959) 157–63; Paul Winter, *On the Trial of Jesus* (2d ed.; rev. and ed. T. A. Burkill and Geza Vermes; StJud 1; Berlin: de Gruyter, 1974) 27–43.

■ **8** For πλησθεὶς κτλ., "filled, etc.," compare Luke 12:11–12 and 21:14–15.

■ **9-10** Peter's answer is an abbreviated speech with kerygma (the relative clause style), proof from Scripture, and an indication of the meaning of salvation (already hinted at in σέσωσται, "he has been healed"; cf. σωτηρία, "salvation," in vs 12). ἐν τίνι, "by what," and ἐν τούτῳ, "by this," are to be understood as neuters (supply ὀνόματι, "name"). οὗτος, "this man," emphasizes that the one who had been healed is present as corpus delicti.

■ **11** The scriptural quotation from Ps 118:22 is not given according to the LXX (in contrast to Mark 12:10 and Luke 20:17).[10] κεφαλὴ γωνίας, "head of the corner," is found only here and in passages dependent on Ps 118:22. In *Test. Sol.* 22.7—23.4 and Tertullian *Adv. Marc.* 3.7, etc., the expression is understood as referring to the keystone.[11] In 1 Pet 2:7 it means the cornerstone, and so also apparently in Luke (cf. 20:17).[12] The passage is given a messianic interpretation in the Targum.[13]

■ **12** ἄλλος and ἕτερος are synonymous—they mean "other."[14]

■ **13** Note Lucilius 649:[15] "Why not? Besides, you again would say I was unlettered and a common fellow" (quid ni et tu idem inlitteratum me atque idiotam diceres). The apostles are described as uneducated also by Justin *Apol.* 1.39.3; Origen *Cels.* 1.62; Ps.-Clem. *Recog.* 1.62.[16] The astonishment here is not historical, but literary; it provides a foil: in place of a rhetorical production appears a speech which is due to the work of the Spirit (cf. the speeches of Tertullus and Paul in chap. 24).

■ **17** μὴ ἐπὶ πλεῖον, "no further," should be understood as temporal (24:4) rather than spatial (cf. 5:28).

■ **18** If the article (τό) is to be read before καθόλου, "at all" (against B ℵ*), it should be taken with this word, not with the infinitive ("to speak or [to] teach").[17]

■ **19-20** On the response of Peter and John, compare 2 Macc 7:2, *4 Macc.* 5.16–38, and Josephus *Ant.* 17.158–59.[18]

■ **21-22** The use of the article with an indirect question (literally, ". . . not finding *the* how to punish them") is Lukan.[19] For γίνεσθαι ἐπί τινα, "happen to someone," compare 5:5, 11, and 8:1.

---

10 For οὗτός ἐστιν, "this is," see the commentary on 7:35–38.

11 Joachim Jeremias, "Κεφαλὴ γωνίας—Ἀκρογωνιαῖος," *ZNW* 29 (1930) 264–80; idem, "κεφαλὴ γωνίας," *TDNT* 1 (1964) 792–93.

12 For another opinion, see Joachim Jeremias, "λίθος," *TDNT* 4 (1967) 275.

13 Bertil Gärtner, "The Habakkuk Commentary (DSH) and the Gospel of Matthew," *StTh* 8 (1955) 23–24.

14 On the construction utilizing the articular participle instead of a relative clause, see BDF § 412.4.

15 *Remains of Old Latin* (LCL) 3.217.

16 See Walter Bauer in *NTApoc.* 2.39–40.

17 BDF § 399.3; cf. Ezek 13:3, 22; 17:14; Dan 3:50 (Th).

18 For this sentence (4:19–20), see the commentary on 5:29; cf. Sophocles *Ant.* 450–60.

19 BDF § 267.

4

The Prayer of the Congregation

23 When they were released they went to
their friends and reported what the chief
priests and the elders had said to them.
24/ And when they heard it, they lifted
their voices together to God and said,
"Sovereign Lord, who didst make the
heaven and the earth and the sea and
everything in them, 25/ who by the
mouth of our father David, thy servant,
didst say by the Holy Spirit,
    'Why did the Gentiles rage,
    and the peoples imagine vain things?
    26/ The kings of the earth set them-
    selves in array,
    and the rulers were gathered together,
    against the Lord and against his
    Anointed'—
27/ for truly in this city there were
gathered together against thy holy son
Jesus, whom thou didst anoint, both
Herod and Pontius Pilate, with the Gentiles and the peoples of Israel, 28/ to do
whatever thy hand and thy plan had pre-
destined to take place. 29/ And now,
Lord, look upon their threats, and grant to
thy servants to speak thy word with all
boldness, 30/ while thou stretchest out
thy hand to heal, and signs and wonders
are performed through the name of thy
holy son Jesus." 31/ And when they had
prayed, the place in which they were
gathered together was shaken; and they
were all filled with the Holy Spirit and
spoke the word of God with boldness.

■ **23** The number of those assembled is of course not to be inferred from vs 4. When Luke speaks of the congregation as *doing* something, it is portrayed as a distinct group. The apparent tension between the occasion and the content of the prayer which follows is a result of Luke's partial dependence on a liturgical style of prayer. The closest prototype is Isa 37:16–20 (2 Kgs 19:15–19).

■ **24** The Hellenistic form of address in prayer, δέσποτα, "Sovereign Lord,"[1] is also found in Luke 2:29 and *1 Clem.* 59.4; 61.1–2. The counterpart to δέσποτα is not παῖς, "child, servant," but δοῦλος, "slave." The addition of further predications is stylistically appropriate.[2] On God as the Creator of heaven and earth, compare 14:15; Ps 146 (145):6; Josephus *Ant.* 4.40.

■ **25** The text is corrupt. The difficulty concerns: (1) τοῦ πατρὸς ἡμῶν, "of our father"; (2) πνεύματος ἁγίου, "Holy Spirit"; and (3) στόματος Δαυίδ, "mouth of David."[3] One must conjecture, and perhaps (with the Koine text) reconstruct as follows: ὁ διὰ στόματος Δαυίδ τοῦ παιδός σου εἰπών, "who by the mouth of David thy servant didst say." The quotation is from Ps 2:1 LXX. ἱνατί, "why," is elliptical for ἵνα τί γένηται, "for what reason does it

---

1   Cf. LXX; Josephus; see A. Schlatter, *Die Theologie des Judentums nach dem Bericht des Josefus* (Gütersloh: Bertelsmann, 1932) 25; Karl Heinrich Rengstorf, "δεσπότης," *TDNT* 2 (1964) 46–49.

2   On the (oriental) style (σύ, "you," and the articular participle [literally, "Thou who didst make . . ."]), see Norden, *Agnostos Theos,* 201–7.

3   C. F. D. Moule, "H. W. Moule on Acts iv.25," *ExpTim* 65 (1953–54) 220; Haenchen, "Schriftzitate," 156–57, reprinted in his *Gott und Mensch,* 160–61.

happen that . . . ?"[4]

■ **27** Exegetical style dominates here, rather than the style of prayer. This interpretation of Psalm 2 is apparently pre-Lukan.[5] The cooperation of Herod (vs 26: οἱ βασιλεῖς, "the kings") and Pilate (vs 26: οἱ ἄρχοντες, "the rulers") is illustrated by Luke 23:6–12 (cf. *Gos. Pet.* 1–2; Ignatius *Smyrn.* 1.2; Justin *Apol.* 1.40). However, the general tone here is different from that of Luke's passion narrative. There Pilate is exonerated in an apologetic manner whereas here, in line with Luke's fundamental view of salvation history, Pilate's guilt is stressed. The sense of παῖς, "son," is determined by the reference in vs 26 and the anointing at baptism (cf. Luke 3:22 with 4:18).[6]

■ **29** καὶ τὰ νῦν, "and now" (corresponding to וְעַתָּה, LXX καὶ νῦν,[7] introduces the request (cf. the prayer of petition in the OT: Isa 37:20 and 2 Chr 20:10, 11 LXX; 2 Macc 14:36; 15:23). The expression is also a regular component of the oriental letter.[8] On μετὰ πάσης παρρησίας, "with all boldness," compare 5:23.[9] Such expressions are customary in ceremonial inscriptions,[10] and they also find their way into rhetorical historiography.[11] λαλεῖν τὸν λόγον, "to speak the word," has become part of the technical vocabulary of preaching.[12]

■ **30** God's governance again stands out clearly.[13]

■ **31** Such signs that prayer has been heard are not found in the Old Testament, but are present in Greek and Roman antiquity. Compare Virgil *Aen.* 3.89–90: "'Grant, father, an omen, and inspire our hearts!' Scarcely had I thus spoken, when suddenly it seemed all things trembled" (Da pater augurium, atque animis inlabere nostris. Vix ea fatus eram: tremere omnia visa repente).[14] This detail is not a variant of the Pentecost story,[15] though καὶ ἐλάλουν, "and they spoke," suggests an original continuation with γλώσσαις, "in tongues." Rather, Luke is indicating how Pentecost becomes a present reality. καὶ ἐλάλουν does not mean that just at that time they began to speak; the sense is rather that they were speaking openly, in public. The passage forms a transition to the summary which follows (cf. 2:42–47).

4 BDF § 123.
5 Martin Dibelius, *Botschaft und Geschichte: Gesammelte Aufsätze* (2 vols.; Tübingen: Mohr [Siebeck], 1953–56) 1.289–92.
6 See the comments on 3:13.
7 See the comments on 3:17.
8 K. Galling, "Brief und Buch im Altertum," *RGG* 1.1411.
9 See the commentary on 17:11; cf. 2 Macc 3:22 and Josephus *Bell.* 3.398.
10 *SIG* 1 no. 532.7; 2 no. 547.30.
11 Eiliv Skard, "Epigraphische Formeln bei Dionys von Halikarnass," SO 11 (1932) 55–60.
12 Conzelmann, *Theology,* 218–25; Gerhardsson, *Memory and Manuscript,* 220–25.
13 On παῖς, "son," see the commentary on 3:13a.
14 Cf. Ovid *Metam.* 9.782ff; 15.669ff.
15 Against Harnack, *Acts,* 179–89.

4

Summary:
The Life of the Congregation

32 Now the company of those who believed
were of one heart and soul, and no one
said that any of the things which he possessed was his own, but they had everything in common. 33/ And with great
power the apostles gave their testimony
to the resurrection of the Lord Jesus, and
great grace was upon them all. 34/ There
was not a needy person among them, for
as many as were possessors of lands or
houses sold them, and brought the proceeds of what was sold 35/ and laid it at
the apostles' feet; and distribution was
made to each as any had need. 36/ Thus
Joseph who was surnamed by the apostles Barnabas (which means "son of
encouragement"), a Levite, a native of
Cyprus, 37/ sold a field which belonged
to him, and brought the money and laid it
at the apostles' feet.

■ **32–37** Here again the inner life and the outer situation
of the congregation are portrayed at the same time. For
this reason one gets the impression that a secondary
insertion has been made in the middle of this section (vs
33).[1] Verses 34–35 offer an explanation of vs 32b; in the
present context, vss 36–37 are an illustration. For "heart
and soul," see Deut 6:5, etc.[2] Also note Aristotle (*Eth.
Nic.* 9.8, 1168b 6ff): "Moreover, all the proverbs agree
with this; for example, 'Friends have one soul between
them,' and 'Friends' goods are common property'" (αἱ
παροιμίαι δὲ πᾶσαι ὁμογνωμονοῦσιν οἷον τὸ "μία ψυχή" καὶ
"κοινὰ τὰ φίλων"). πλῆθος, "company," can mean either an
unspecified crowd or a specific group. Note, for example, the synagogue inscription: ΕΙΡΗΝΗ ΚΑΙ ΕΛΕΟΣ ΕΠΙ
ΠΑΝ ΤΟ ΗΓΙΑΣΜΕΝΟΝ ΥΜΩΝ ΠΛΗΘΟΣ, "Peace and
mercy upon your congregation of saints [lit. "your sanctified company"]."[3] Note also the use of רב or רבים,
"multitude, multitudes," at Qumran.[4]
■ **33** See the preceding discussion of vss 32–37. The word
order is unusual; the apparent reason is to emphasize
ἀνάστασις, "resurrection." The genitive τοῦ κυρίου, "of
the Lord," is dependent upon ἀναστάσεως, "resurrection." Dependence upon ἀπόστολοι, that is, "apostles of

the Lord," would be contrary to typical Lukan usage.
■ **34** Compare Deut 15:4. The earlier summary is supplemented by information about the use of alms. Votive
offerings were laid "at the feet" of the divinity (Lucian
Philops. 20). Philo *Hypothetica* (Eusebius *Praep. ev.*
8.11.10) reports concerning the Essenes that the admin-
istrator receives the wages which each hands over: "He
takes it and at once buys what is necessary and provides
food in abundance and anything else which human life
requires" (λαβὼν δ᾽ ἐκεῖνος αὐτίκα τἀπιτήδεια ὠνεῖται καὶ
παρέχει τροφὰς ἀφθόνους καὶ τἄλλα ὧν ὁ ἀνθρώπινος βίος
χρειώδης).
■ **36–37** The name Barnabas means "son of Nebo."[5] The
meaning "son of encouragement" is incorrect. This
would fit Manaen (Menachem) in 13:1. Eduard Schwartz
assumes that a comment about Manaen has been incorrectly transferred to Barnabas.[6] τῷ γένει, "a native of,"
does not mean nationality, but denotes the place of birth
(cf. 18:2; Josephus *Ant.* 20.142). These two verses present the concrete information out of which the ideal picture of communal sharing was developed. The following
episode, however, does not fit well with the ideal.

1   See the Introduction, p. xliii.
2   *PGM* 2.22 (VII 472); for ψυχὴ μία, "one soul," see the
    excursus after 2:45.
3   *CII* 2 no. 804 (Synagogue in Apamea, Syria).
4   Hanswalter Huppenbauer, "רב, רוב, רבים in der
    Sektenregel (1QS)," *ThZ* 13 (1957) 136–37.
5   Henry J. Cadbury, "Some Semitic Personal Names in
    Luke-Acts," *Amicitiae Corolla: A Volume of Essays*

Presented to James Rendel Harris (ed. H. G. Wood;
London: University of London, 1933) 47–48.
6   Eduard Schwartz, "Zur Chronologie des Paulus"
    (NGG; Berlin: Weidmannsche Buchhandlung, 1907)
    282 n. 1.

5   Ananias and Sapphira

1   But a man named Ananias with his wife Sapphira sold a piece of property, 2/ and with his wife's knowledge he kept back some of the proceeds, and brought only a part and laid it at the apostles' feet. 3/ But Peter said, "Ananias, why has Satan filled your heart to lie to the Holy Spirit and to keep back part of the proceeds of the land? 4/ While it remained unsold, did it not remain your own? And after it was sold, was it not at your disposal? How is it that you have contrived this deed in your heart? You have not lied to men but to God." 5/ When Ananias heard these words, he fell down and died. And great fear came upon all who heard of it. 6/ The young men rose and wrapped him up and carried him out and buried him.

7   After an interval of about three hours his wife came in, not knowing what had happened. 8/ And Peter said to her, "Tell me whether you sold the land for so much." And she said, "Yes, for so much." 9/ But Peter said to her, "How is it that you have agreed together to tempt the Spirit of the Lord? Hark, the feet of those that have buried your husband are at the door, and they will carry you out." 10/ Immediately she fell down at his feet and died. When the young men came in they found her dead, and they carried her out and buried her beside her husband. 11/ And great fear came upon the whole church, and upon all who heard of these things.

The miraculous punishment assumes a greater role here than it does in the Synoptics. For parallels from the Old Testament, compare 1 Kgs 14:1–18; also see Lucian *Philops.* 19–20.[1] Luke received the material already in written form, as is evident from his insertions. The piece is not in pure narrative style, but it is interspersed with Luke's reflections. No historical kernel can be extracted.[2]

■ **1–2** $\kappa\tau\hat{\eta}\mu\alpha$, "piece of property," is equivalent to $\chi\omega\rho\acute{\iota}o\nu$, "land," vss 3, 8. For $\nu o\sigma\phi\acute{\iota}\zeta\epsilon\sigma\theta\alpha\iota$, "to keep back," compare Josh 7:1 LXX and the following context.[3] Note 1QS

6.24–25: "If there be found in the community a man who consciously lies in the matter of (his) wealth, he is to be regarded as outside the state of purity entailed by membership, and he is to be mulcted of one fourth of his food ration." At Qumran, where the surrender of property was regulated, we are dealing with a structured form of discipline; in Acts, we encounter a pneumatic judgment delivered on the spur of the moment. Of course, the Qumran community also had sacral judgments (through blessing and curse): 1QS 2.4–18; CD 19.13.[4]

■ **3** Two ideas are combined: "Why have you done this?"

---

1   Lyder Brun, *Segen und Fluch im Urchristentum* (Skrifter utgitt av det Norske Videnskaps-Akademi i Oslo 2, hist.-filos. Klasse 1; Oslo: Jacob Dybwad, 1932).

2   Philippe H. Menoud, "La mort d'Ananias et de Saphira (Actes 5, 1–11)," *Aux sources de la tradition,* 146–54; on the names, see BAG *s.vv.*

3   See *Beginnings* 4.50.

4   Manfred Weise, *Kultzeiten und kultischer Bundesschluss*

in der "Ordensregel" vom Toten Meer (SPB 3; Leiden: Brill, 1961) 94–110.

and "Satan has filled your heart."[5] That Satan is acting within someone does not serve as an excuse: remember Judas Iscariot! The wonderworker knows the secrets of the heart—a θεῖος ἀνήρ, "divine man," motif! The Spirit referred to here is not the general endowment of believers, but a metaphysical power which occasionally bursts forth. The apostles and the congregation are the means through which the Spirit works.

■ **4** This verse is a Lukan explanation. It does appear to contradict the description of the sharing of property as given above, and if it did it would be pre-Lukan. But this is a description from the standpoint of conduct (sharing in love) rather than results (the sharing of "property"). Sharing within the community and a stress on the voluntary nature of this sharing result in a tension in Luke's narrative. F. Scheidweiler would remove this tension through a conjecture, replacing οὐχί, "not," with οὐχ ὅ to be translated as follows: "In no way does that which when unsold remained at your disposal still fall under your disposition once it has been sold."[6] *If* one sold property, he would be expected to hand over the whole selling price. τί ὅτι, "how is it that" (= τί γέγονεν ὅτι, Luke 2:49), and τίθεσθαι ἐν καρδίᾳ, "to contrive in [one's] heart," are biblical expressions (cf. Luke 1:66).

■ **5** Peter does not utter any explicit pronouncement of punishment (contrast 13:11), thus the death appears as God's judgment, as in 1 Kings 14. Compare Jerome *Ep.* 130.14.5–6: "In fact the apostle Peter by no means called down death upon them as Porphyry foolishly says. He merely announced God's judgment by the spirit of prophecy, that the doom of two persons might be a les- son to many" (Apostolus Petrus nequaquam est imprecatur mortem, ut stultus Prophyrius calumniatur, sed Dei iudicium prophetico spiritu adnuntiat ut poena duorum hominum sit doctrina multorum). The notions of repentance and forgiveness are distant here. The story derives from conceptions of corporate and magical power. Thus there is no reflection about the eternal destiny of Ananias. With the statement of the impact on the audience, the story could be brought to its conclusion. The second part is a duplication, typical of popular and legendary stories.

■ **6** This notice of the young men taking out the body of Ananias serves as the demonstration and (later) to heighten the dramatic nature of the story. The position of the νεώτεροι, "young men," should not be defined as an "office."[7] The style is not realistic: there is no consideration of the actual situation of a burial. All the action occurs in a moment. Does συστέλλειν mean "wrap up" (Ps.-Callisth. 2.22.3 τῇ . . . χλαμύδι συστείλας, "wrapped in a cloak")? Or should it be understood in light of 8:2 (συγκομίζειν, "bury")? The Vulgate has *amoverunt*, "they took away."

■ **7** The congregation seems to be always in session.[8]

■ **8** Again in this second scene the goal is not to lead the woman to understanding and repentance. We cannot conclude from τοσούτου, "so much," that the money was still lying there.

■ **9** The question is abbreviated: they did not set out to tempt the Spirit but to lie, and in so doing they have tempted the Spirit.

■ **11** The resulting φόβος, "fear," is a typical motif.[9]

5   Haenchen, p. 237.
6   Felix Scheidweiler, "Zu Act 5:4," *ZNW* 49 (1958) 136–37.
7   *CII* 2 no. 755 (Hypaepa, to the south of Sardis): ΙΟΥΔΑ[Ι]ΩΝ ΝΕΩΤΕΡΩΝ.
8   See BDF § 144 on the construction here: ἐγένετο δὲ . . . καί, "and there was . . . and," with asyndetic designation of time in the nominative in between.
9   See the commentary on 3:11.

5 Summary: Signs and Wonders

12 Now many signs and wonders were done among the people by the hands of the apostles. And they were all together in Solomon's Portico. 13/ None of the rest dared join them, but the people held them in high honor. 14/ And more than ever believers were added to the Lord [or: believers in the Lord were added], multitudes both of men and women, 15/ so that they even carried out the sick into the streets, and laid them on beds and pallets, that as Peter came by at least his shadow might fall on some of them. 16/ The people also gathered from the towns around Jerusalem, bringing the sick and those afflicted with unclean spirits, and they were all healed.

This third summary supplements earlier ones (cf. 2:43) with the more detailed account of miracles, thus showing that the prayer of 4:30 has been answered. A comparison of Philostratus *Vita Apoll.* 4.45 (Philostratus reports—with reserve—how Apollonius raised from the dead a young woman on her way to be buried) with Vopiscus *Div. Aur.* 24.8 ("He [Apollonius] brought back the dead to life" [Ille mortuis reddidit vitam]) illustrates the movement from a single case to a generalization.[1]

■ **12** "All" = all Christians.[2]

■ **13** The apparent contradiction between vss 13 and 14 is mere clumsiness on the part of the narrator. The community's complex position in the world results in honor as well as fear. οἱ λοιποί, "the rest," refers to non-Christians, in contrast to the Christians mentioned in vs 12;

compare Mark 4:11 (οἱ ἔξω, "those outside") with Luke 8:10 (οἱ λοιποί, "others").

■ **14** It is not clear whether τῷ κυρίῳ should be connected with πιστεύοντες, "believers" ("believers in the Lord"; 16:15, 34)[3] or with προσετίθεντο, "were added" ("believers were added to the Lord").[4]

■ **15** The difficulty in the connection of thought continues into this verse. ὥστε καί, "so that [they] even," is frequently connected with vs 13 or vs 12, understanding vs 14 as an insertion. But what we have here is simply an awkward accumulation of various motifs.[5] The verse is reminiscent of Mark 6:56. On the power of the shadow, compare 19:12.[6]

■ **16** The information provided here (cf. Luke 6:17) provides the background for the action which follows.

---

1 Ludwig Bieler, Θεῖος ἀνήρ: *Das Bild des "göttlichen Menschen" in Spätantike und Frühchristentum* (2 vols.; Vienna: Hofels, 1935–36; reprinted Darmstadt: Wissenschaftliche Buchgesellschaft, 1967) 1.84 n. 33.

2 For Solomon's Portico, see the commentary on 3:11.

3 Bauernfeind.

4 Haenchen, p. 243, and *RSV*.

5 With Haenchen, pp. 243–45.

6 On the analogous tendency in Josephus to treat the miracle worker independently, see Bieler, *Theios Aner* 2.28.

5

The Apostles' Arrest, Miraculous Release, and Examination before the Council, including the Advice of Gamaliel

17 But the high priest rose up and all who were with him, that is, the party of the Sadducees, and filled with jealousy 18/ they arrested the apostles and put them in the common prison. 19/ But at night an angel of the Lord opened the prison doors and brought them out and said, 20/ "Go and stand in the temple and speak to the people all the words of this Life." 21/ And when they heard this, they entered the temple at daybreak and taught.

Now the high priest came and those who were with him and called together the council and all the senate of Israel, and sent to the prison to have them brought. 22/ But when the officers came, they did not find them in the prison, and they returned and reported, 23/ "We found the prison securely locked and the sentries standing at the doors, but when we opened it we found no one inside." 24/ Now when the captain of the temple and the chief priests heard these words, they were much perplexed about them, wondering what this would come to. 25/ And some one came and told them, "The men whom you put in prison stand in the temple and teach the people." 26/ Then the captain with the officers went and brought them, but without violence, for they were afraid of being stoned by the people.

27 And when they had brought them, they set them before the council. And the high priest questioned them, 28/ saying, "We strictly charged you not to teach in this name, yet here you have filled Jerusalem with your teaching and you intend to bring this man's blood upon us." 29/ But Peter and the apostles answered, "We must obey God rather than men. 30/ The God of our fathers raised Jesus whom you killed by hanging him on a tree. 31/ God exalted him at his right hand as Leader and Savior, to give repentance to Israel and forgiveness of sins. 32/ And we are witnesses to these things, and so is the Holy Spirit whom God has given to those who obey him."

33 When they heard this they were enraged and wanted to kill them. 34/ But a Pharisee in the council named Gamaliel, a teacher of the law, held in honor by all the people, stood up and ordered the men to be put outside for a while. 35/ And he said to them, "Men of Israel, take care what you do with these men. 36/ For before these days Theudas arose, giving himself out to be somebody, and a number of men, about four hundred, joined him; but he was slain and all who fol-

lowed him were dispersed and came to nothing. 37/ After him Judas the Galilean arose in the days of the census and drew away some of the people after him; he also perished, and all who followed him were scattered. 38/ So in the present case I tell you, keep away from these men and let them alone; for if this plan or this undertaking should be of men, it will fail; 39/ but if it is of God, you will not be able to overthrow them. You might even be found opposing God!"

40   So they took his advice, and when they had called in the apostles, they beat them and charged them not to speak in the name of Jesus, and let them go. 41/ Then they left the presence of the council, rejoicing that they were counted worthy to suffer dishonor for the name. 42/ And every day in the temple and at home they did not cease teaching and preaching Jesus as the Christ.

This section has been composed from various accounts which have not been completely unified. We sense a heightening of the miraculous in comparison with chapter 4, but in comparison with 12:3–19 the details are somewhat pallid.[1] The miraculous release does not affect the conduct of the hearing; the account of the hearing here is a doublet of the version in chapter 4.

Jeremias is of a different opinion;[2] he views the account as historically accurate. It corresponds, he argues, to regulations for criminal trials, according to which a warning must be issued before punishment can be handed out. Quite apart from the fact that the legal procedures laid down in the Mishnah (*Sanh.*) are quite late, the narrative indicates no relation to such regulations. Further, the movement from 5:28 to 5:38 would be unintelligible. Jeremias must identify blasphemy as the object of the trial, and of that there is no evidence here (Luke reserves the charge of blasphemy for Stephen). To maintain the hypothesis one must assume that Luke no longer understood his source,[3] whereby the hypothesis eliminates itself.

■ **17** ἡ οὖσα (ὁ ὤν), "that is," *RSV*, literally "the one at hand" (13:1; 14:13), is the language of officialdom.[4]

αἵρεσις, "party" (Josephus *Ant.* 13.171), went through a development from the neutral meaning which we find here to a more specific meaning, just as did the Hebrew מין, "party."

■ **18** Compare 4:3. δημοσίᾳ can be used as an adverb, "publicly" (16:37; 18:28; 20:20), but can also be connected with τήρησις, "prison": *custodia publica*, "public custody" (*RSV*, "common prison").

■ **19** ἄγγελος κυρίου, "angel of the Lord" (according to the LXX), is always the angel of *God* for Luke. He never speaks of an angel of Christ. The miraculous opening of the gate is artificial.[5]

■ **20** On the expression here, compare 13:26.

■ **21** Does Luke understand the Sanhedrin to be a committee of the γερουσία, "senate," or is the καί epexegetical? The expression is dependent upon Exod 12:21. γερουσία denotes the Sanhedrin in 1 Macc 12:6 (= 1 Macc 14:20 πρεσβύτεροι, "elders," *RSV*; cf. Luke 22:66), 2 Macc 1:10, and Josephus *Ant.* 13.166.[6]

■ **24** Compare 4:1. On the expression τί ἂν γένοιτο τοῦτο, "what this would come to," compare 10:17.[7]

■ **25** εἰσίν, "are," is independent;[8] the Greek, using a common periphrasis, reads literally: "*are* standing in the

---

1   See the commentary on 12:3–19.

2   Jeremias, "Quellenproblem," 205–21, reprinted in his *Abba*, pp. 238–55, following K. Bornhäuser.

3   Trocmé, *Livre des Actes*, 103.

4   Edwin Mayser, *Grammatik der griechischen Papyri aus Ptolemäerzeit* (2 vols. [vol. 2 in 3 parts]; Berlin/Leipzig: de Gruyter, 1906–34) 2:1.347–48.

5   See the commentary on 12:7–10.

6   Note the inscription: τῷ σεμνοτάτῳ συνεδρίῳ γερουσίας ("to the august council of elders"), found in R. Cagnat, ed., *Inscriptiones Graecae ad res Romanas* (4 vols. [vol. 2 never pub.]; Paris: Leroux, 1911–27; reprinted Rome: "L'Erma" di Bretschneider, 1964) 4 no. 836.6–7.

7   BDF § 386.1.

8   Björck, *Ἦν διδάσκων*, 51; cf. BDF § 353.

temple and teaching the people."

■ **26** λιθάζειν, "to stone": we ought not to ask whether the people would really have stoned the soldiers. According to Philostratus *Vita Apoll.* 1.16, the Ephesians wanted to stone the ἄρχων, "ruler," because he did not allow the baths to be sufficiently heated.

■ **28** In solemn biblical language the high priest reminds the prisoners of the earlier hearing; as in 4:17, the name of Jesus is avoided.[9] On the idea of bringing someone's blood on someone else, see Judg 9:24 and Matt 27:25.

■ **29** The wording here is closer to Plato *Apol.* 29d (πείσομαι δὲ μᾶλλον τῷ θεῷ ἢ ὑμῖν, "I shall obey the god rather than you") than to 4:19.[10]

■ **30-31** Once again the words of Peter comprise an abbreviated sermon. On κρεμάσαντες κτλ., "by hanging, etc.," compare 10:39. Does Deut 21:22–23 belong to traditional Christian apologetic tradition (Gal 3:13)? On ἀρχηγὸς (3:15) καὶ σωτήρ, "Leader and Savior," compare *2 Clem.* 20.5 (cf. also the titles given Moses in Acts 7:35).[11] On ὑψοῦν, "to exalt," compare 2:33. Instead of δεξιᾷ, "right hand," D*, gig, sa, Ir^lat have δόξῃ, "glory" (cf. Isa 62:8). δοῦναι μετάνοιαν, "to give repentance":[12] despite the wording, Luke means the *opportunity* for repentance. He does not mean that repentance as such is a gift of God, but that God gives μετάνοια in the sense of an opportunity to repent.[13] Compare Josephus *Bell.* 3.127: "and giving time for reconsideration" (καὶ μετανοίας καιρὸν διδούς, used of Vespasian)—note Acts 17:30; Philo *Leg. all.* 3.106: δίδωσι χρόνον εἰς μετάνοιαν, "gives time for repentance"; Plutarch *Alex.* 11.4. Hope for the eschatological redemption of Israel dominates the whole Jewish expectation of the end. Cleansing from sins belongs to this eschatological picture (*Pss. Sol.* 17.22–23; *Jub.* 4.26; 50.5; *1 Enoch* 10.22; *T. Levi* 18.9; *T. Jud.* 24.1).

■ **32** The juxtaposition of the testimony of the apostles

and of the Spirit is explained by 2:32–39 and Luke 24:48–49.

■ **33** Compare 7:54. The reading ἐβούλοντο, "they wanted" (B A), may be original, rather than ἐβουλεύοντο, "they decided" (ℵ D). The verse describes the mood of the council, not yet a firm plan (yet cf. Achilles Tatius 7.1.1: "he felt grief, anger, and the need of taking further counsel" (ἤχθετο, ὠργίζετο, ἐβουλεύετο).

■ **34** In his portrayal of the Pharisees Luke presents them especially as advocates of belief in the resurrection. Thus they are close to the Christians, and ought to understand that (23:6–10). Luke thereby involves himself in a contradiction when he portrays Paul, Gamaliel's student (22:3), as the chief of persecutors. We know little about Gam(a)liel I (the "elder," in distinction from his grandson of the same name).[14]

■ **36-37** For the citing of historical examples as arguments in speeches, compare Jer 26:17–23; Sallust *Cat.* 51.5–6; Josephus *Bell.* 5.376–98; etc. According to Josephus *Ant.* 20.97–104, Theudas appeared at the time of the procurator Cuspius Fadus (44 C.E.?), thus long after this "speech" of Gamaliel.[15] On the other hand, the date of Judas (the "Galilean," Josephus *Ant.* 18.23; *Bell.* 2.433)[16] is correct, although Luke has a wrong conception of the time of the census (6 C.E.).[17] Josephus says nothing about the death of Judas (but he does tell how his sons were killed, *Ant.* 20.102). Judas's movement did not die out quickly, as Luke thinks. The incorrect order Theudas—Judas leads one to ask whether this is an error based on Josephus *Ant.* 20.97–104, where both are also named in this order (though Josephus does have their chronological relationship correct!). However, it is not likely that this error resulted from the text of Josephus, and literary dependence of Acts upon the *Antiquities* cannot be demonstrated.[18]

---

9   On the dative παραγγελία, "strictly" (23:14), see BDF § 198.6.

10   See the commentary on 4:19; Friedrich August Strobel, "Schriftverständnis und Obrigkeitsdenken in der ältesten Kirche" (Diss., Erlangen, 1956); see *ThLZ* 82 (1957) cols. 69–71, for a review of Strobel.

11   On σωτήρ, "Savior," see the excursus following 2 Tim 1:10 in Dibelius-Conzelmann, *Pastoral Epistles,* 100–103.

12   See the comments on 2 Tim 2:25 in ibid., 113–14.

13   Against Jacques Dupont, "Repentir et conversion d'après les Actes des Apôtres," *Sciences Ecclésiastiques*

12 (1960) 137–73, reprinted in his *Études,* 421–57.

14   Str-B 2.636–39.

15   Paul Winter, "Miszellen zur Apostelgeschichte," *EvTh* 17 (1957) 398–406.

16   William R. Farmer, "Judas, Simon and Athronges," *NTS* 4 (1957–58) 150; Martin Hengel, *Die Zeloten: Untersuchungen zur jüdische Freiheitsbewegung in der Zeit von Herodes I. bis 70n. Chr.* (2d ed.; AGJU 1; Leiden: Brill, 1976) 79–150.

17   See the excursus after Luke 2:3 in Erich Klostermann, *Das Lukasevangelium* (3d ed.; HNT; Tübingen: Mohr [Siebeck], 1975) 32–34.

On εἶναί τι ἑαυτόν, "[giving] himself [out] to be somebody," compare 8:9; Gal 2:6; 6:3. ἀπέστησεν κτλ., "drew away, etc.": Luke combines the Greek expression "lead the people to revolt" with the biblical "lead the people after one."[19]

■ **38–39** With the change from the subjunctive ("if this plan should be of men . . .") to the indicative ("but if it is of God . . ."), Luke indicates that the "advice" really is from God; God has spoken his own judgment through the mouth of Gamaliel. Only with this understanding of the text does the consequence (μήποτε, "You might even be found") make sense. The use of conditional sentences to indicate possibility and reality here is not absolutely contrary to classical grammar.[20] To be sure, the classical εἰ, "if," with the indicative indicates the reality of the condition ("If, as these people maintain . . ."), as Haenchen correctly explains, and the classical ἐάν, "if," with the subjunctive expresses that which the speaker or writer himself believes is probable.[21] It should be observed, however, that the *reality* of that which is expressed in the εἰ-clause can also be indicated, so that εἰ is "often closely bordering on causal 'since.'"[22]

On καταλύειν, "overthrow," with personal object, see Ignatius *Trall.* 4.2. The classical meaning would be "to put down, destroy." For Gamaliel's principle, compare *Pirqe Aboth* 4.11: "Any assembling together that is for the sake of heaven shall in the end be established; but any that is not for the sake of heaven shall not in the end be established." θεομάχος/θεομαχεῖν, "opposing God/to oppose God," is used in Euripides *Bacc.* to denote the battle against the new god. There is, however, no literary dependence (cf. 2 Macc 7:19; Philostratus *Vita Apoll.* 4.44).[23] What Gamaliel proposes is the apologetic plan of Luke.

■ **40** δέρειν, "to beat," indicates the Jewish punishment of forty less one (2 Cor 11:24).

■ **41** Compare Luke 6:22–23.[24] On ὑπὲρ τοῦ ὀνόματος, "for the name," compare 9:16; 15:26; 21:13.

18 Dibelius, *Studies,* 186–87.
19 Haenchen, p. 252.
20 Against Haenchen, p. 253.
21 See Raphael Kühner and Bernhard Gerth, *Ausführliche Grammatik der griechischen Sprache* (3d ed.; 2 vols.; Hannover: Hahnsche Buchhandlung, 1890–1904) 2:2.464ff.
22 BDF § 372.1; cf. Johann Matthias Stahl, *Kritisch-historische Syntax des griechischen Verbums der klassischen Zeit* (Heidelberg: Winter, 1907) 382–83; cf. further Radermacher, *Grammatik,* 176 (for this advice I am indebted to M. Leumann).

23 Alfred Vögeli, "Lukas und Euripides," *ThZ* 9 (1953) 429–38.
24 Wolfgang Nauck, "Freude im Leiden: Zum Problem einer urchristlichen Verfolgungstradition," *ZNW* 46 (1955) 68–80.

6

The Installation of the
Seven Congregational Leaders

1 Now in these days when the disciples were increasing in number, the Hellenists murmured against the Hebrews because their widows were neglected in the daily distribution. 2/ And the twelve summoned the body of the disciples and said, "It is not right that we should give up preaching the word of God to serve tables. 3/ Therefore, brethren, pick out from among you seven men of good repute, full of the Spirit and of wisdom, whom we may appoint to this duty. 4/ But we will devote ourselves to prayer and to the ministry of the word." 5/ And what they said pleased the whole multitude, and they chose Stephen, a man full of faith and of the Holy Spirit, and Philip, and Prochorus, and Nicanor, and Timon, and Parmenas, and Nicolaus, a proselyte of Antioch. 6/ These they set before the apostles, and they prayed and laid their hands upon them.

7 And the word of God increased; and the number of the disciples multiplied greatly in Jerusalem, and a great many of the priests were obedient to the faith.

Behind this account lies a piece of tradition which Luke must have had in written form; note the manner in which the "Hellenists" and "Hebrews" are introduced. Up to this point there have been no indications of the coexistence of two groups. Observe also the list in vs 5, which no longer fits with the material as Luke has revised it.[1]

Excursus:
The Choice of the Seven

The actual events which lie behind this account of the selection of the seven can be perceived only vaguely, because Luke has radically reworked the material in order to avoid the impression of an internal crisis during the time of the apostles. The neglect of precisely this group, namely the Hellenist widows, is incomprehensible on the basis of what Luke reports. The conflict gives the impression of being artificially constructed. The role assigned to the "seven" does not fit with vss 8–14, neither with Stephen's activity nor the fact that the attack was aimed precisely at him. Nor does this role accord with the designation of Philip as "evangelist" (21:8) nor with the activity of the Hellenists after their expulsion. Apparently there was a twofold organization, and this must have been recognizable even to outsiders; otherwise the persecution could not have been limited to the Hellenists. Alongside the circle around the Twelve there was a group around the seven. The "seven" originally had nothing to do with "deacons." The continuation of the narrative indicates that there was nothing like this in Jerusalem. Luke has revised his sources in line with his conception of the church. For this reason the tension arises between vss 1–6 and 6:8—7:53. In these latter verses Stephen must appear as preacher, in order to provide a motivation for his martyrdom.

■ 1 οἱ μαθηταί, "the disciples," does not occur between Luke 22:45 and Acts 6:1. It must be a Palestinian self-designation which Luke found in a source. Use of this expression is not sufficient evidence for reconstruction of the source, since Luke himself also uses the word[2] (e.g.,

1 On the peculiarities of language, see Cerfaux, "La composition," 681–82, reprinted in *Recueil Cerfaux* 2.79–81.

2 Karl Heinrich Rengstorf, "μαθητής," *TDNT* 4 (1967) 457–59.

vs 7; 11:26).[3]

■ **2** οἱ δώδεκα, "the twelve," means the "apostles" only here in Acts.[4] The organization reflected in vss 1–2 compares with that of Jewish and other ancient relief organizations.[5]

**Excursus:
The Hellenists**

The "Hellenists" are Jews. Luke sees them as such, and this fits his view of history (no Gentile can be converted yet) and the actual historical facts. In Jerusalem at this time there was not yet a Gentile Christian group. The Hellenists are Jews whose mother tongue is Greek.[6] We can make an inference about their conduct since they were the first to be attacked. They must have come into conflict with observance of the law in Judaism, that is, they may have continued Jesus' line more clearly than the Twelve did.[7]

■ **3–4** "Seven" is an established designation (21:8). Local officials of the Jewish community[8] and also ancient councils[9] consisted of seven members. The expression διακονία τοῦ λόγου, "ministry of the word," is not a technical term, but is formulated ad hoc. The description of the installation (proposal, choice by the congregation, and ordination under the direction of the congregation) reflects the custom of the church at the time of Luke and is not to be used for the reconstruction of the polity of the early church.

■ **5–6** On ἤρεσεν, "pleased," compare 2 Sam 3:36 LXX. πλήρης, "full," is indeclinable here.[10] All the names in the list are Greek, which means that all the appointed "deacons" (Luke does not actually use the title) are Hellenists. However, with Luke they do not appear as such. The majority of the seven are unfamiliar. Philip is mentioned in 21:8. He is confused or identified by later writers with the member of the Twelve who has the same name. Legend associates Nicolaus with the Nicolaitans (Rev 2:6,

---

3   Anselm Schulz, *Nachfolgen und Nachnahmen: Studien über das Verhältnis der neutestamentlichen Jüngerschaft zur urchristlichen Vorbildethik* (SANT 6; Munich: Kösel, 1962) 144–55.

4   Béda Rigaux ("Die 'Zwölf' in Geschichte und Kerygma," *Der historische Jesus und der kerygmatische Christus: Beiträge zum Christusverständnis in Forschung und Verkündigung* [ed. Helmut Ristow and Karl Matthiae; Berlin: Evangelische Verlagsanstalt, 1964] 468–86) defends the account's historicity.

5   For Jewish evidence, see Str-B 2.643–47; Jeremias, *Jerusalem*, 128–34; Bo Reicke, *Diakonie, Festfreude und Zelos in Verbindung mit der altchristlichen Agapenfeier* (UUÅ 1951:5; Uppsala: Lundequistska; Wiesbaden: Harrassowitz, 1951) 167–85; for Hellenistic evidence, see Hendrik Bolkestein, *Wohltätigkeit und Armenpflage im vorchristlichen Altertum: Ein Beitrag zum Problem "Moral und Gesellschaft"* (Utrecht: Oosthoek, 1939; reprinted New York: Arno, 1979); PW 4.440; 7.172–82; on charity among the Essenes, see Herbert Braun, *Spätjüdisch-häretischer und frühchristlicher Radikalismus* (2 vols. in 1; BHTh 24; Tübingen: Mohr [Siebeck], 1957) 1.78.

6   Contrary to *Beginnings* 5.59–60.

7   Literature:
      Oscar Cullmann, "The Significance of the Qumran Texts for Research into the Beginnings of Christianity," *JBL* 74 (1955) 213–26, reprinted in *The Scrolls and the New Testament* (ed. Krister Stendahl; New York: Harper, 1957) 18–32. He argues that converted members of the Qumran community were among the Hellenists.

      Nils Alstrup Dahl, *Das Volk Gottes: Eine Untersuchung zum Kirchenbewusstsein des Urchristentums* (Skrifter utgitt av det Norse Videnskaps-Akademi i Oslo, 2 hist.-filos. Klasse 1941:2; Oslo: Dybwad, 1941; reprinted Darmstadt: Wissenschaftliche Buchgesellschaft, 1963) 193–98.

      Werner Georg Kümmel, "Das Urchristentum," *ThR* n.s. 14 (1942) 91.

      Idem, "Das Urchristentum: III: Die Geschichte der Urkirche," *ThR* n.s. 17 (1948–49) 23–26.

      Johannes Munck, *Paul and the Salvation of Mankind* (Richmond: John Knox, 1959) 218–28. He has a completely different conception.

      C. F. D. Moule, "Once More, Who Were the Hellenists?" *ExpTim* 70 (1958–59) 100–102.

      Albrecht Oepke, *Das Neue Gottesvolk in Schrifttum, Schauspiel, bildender Kunst und Weltgestaltung* (Gütersloh: Bertelsmann, 1950) 188–90.

      Simon, *St Stephen.*

      Ceslas Spicq, "L'Épître aux Hébreux, Apollos, Jean-Baptiste, les Hellénistes et Qumran," *RevQ* 1 (1958–59) 365–90.

      Hans Windisch, "Ἕλλην," *TDNT* 2 (1964) 511–12.

8   Str-B 2.641.

9   *septemviri*; οἱ ἑπτά, *SIG* 1 no. 495.2.

10   BDF § 137.1.

15; Irenaeus *Adv. haer.* 1.26.3; cf. Clement Alex. *Strom.* 2.20, 118.3ff; 3.4.25–26).[11]

■ **7** Contrary to the situation at Qumran, the priests who join the community have no significance for the structure of the community.[12]

---

11 For information about laying on of hands, see the excursus to 1 Tim 4:14 in Dibelius-Conzelmann, *Pastoral Epistles,* 70–71. On the difference between "leaning one's hands on someone" (סָמַךְ יָדַיִם) and "laying one's hands on someone" (שָׂם יָדַיִם), see David Daube, *The New Testament and Rabbinic Judaism* (London: Athlone, 1956) 224–46; Joachim Jeremias, "ΠΡΕΣΒΥΤΕΡΙΟΝ ausserchristlich bezeugt," *ZNW* 48 (1957) 129–30.

12 On ὑπακούειν τῇ πίστει, "obedient to the faith," see the commentaries on Rom 1:5.

6

The Attack on Stephen

8   And Stephen, full of grace and power, did great wonders and signs among the people. 9/ Then some of those who belonged to the synagogue of the Freedmen (as it was called), and of the Cyrenians, and of the Alexandrians, and of those from Cilicia and Asia, arose and disputed with Stephen. 10/ But they could not withstand the wisdom and the Spirit with which he spoke. 11/ Then they secretly instigated men, who said, "We have heard him speak blasphemous words against Moses and God." 12/ And they stirred up the people and the elders and the scribes, and they came upon him and seized him and brought him before the council, 13/ and set up false witnesses who said, "This man never ceases to speak words against this holy place and the law; 14/ for we have heard him say that this Jesus of Nazareth will destroy this place, and will change the customs which Moses delivered to us." 15/ And gazing at him, all who sat in the council saw that his face was like the face of an angel.

1   And the high priest said, "Is this so?"

Here we have the climax of the events which began with chapter 4.

■ **8** Compare vs 5. The portrayal of Stephen clashes with vss 3–4 (see above). Luke does not know of any concrete miracles performed by Stephen.

■ **9** συναγωγή, "synagogue," means the building as well as the congregation, but here the meaning is closer to the latter.[1] Luke is probably not thinking of several (Hellenistic) synagogues, but of *one,* which had a varied makeup. In regard to the synagogues of foreigners note the inscription from Jerusalem regarding the synagogue of Theodotos.[2] A synagogue of the Alexandrians is mentioned in *t. Meg.* 2.6 and *y. Meg.* 373d, 29; in the parallel (in *b. Meg.* 26a) the reference to the synagogue of the "Tarsusites" possibly indicates the same building. Most

understand the "Freedmen" as does Chrysostom *Hom. 15 on Acts:*[3] οἱ Ῥωμαίων ἀπελεύτεροι, "the freedmen of the Romans," that is, the liberated descendants of the Jews who had been taken to Rome by Pompey (Philo *Leg. Gai.* 155). Many interpreters have recourse to conjecture (following the example of the Armenian version), namely, "Libyans."[4]

■ **10** Compare 4:14 and Luke 21:15.

■ **11** On ὑποβάλλω, "instigate," compare *Mart. Pol.* 17.2. For the accusation, compare Josephus *Ant.* 20.200 (against James, the Lord's brother).

■ **12** The subject ("they") is not clear. This time the people are on the side of the opponents (in contrast to 5:26), and this goes back to the source. The report alternates between the description of a riot and of legal pro-

1   Wolfgang Schrage, "συναγωγή," *TDNT* 7 (1971) 837.
2   Adolf Deissmann, *Light from the Ancient East: The New Testament Illustrated by Recently Discovered Texts of the Graeco-Roman World* (rev. ed.; trans. L. R. M. Strachey; Garden City, NY: Doubleday, Doran, 1927) 439–41.
3   PG 60.120.
4   J. Rendel Harris, "The History of a Conjectural Emendation," *Expositor* VI, 6 (1902) 378–90; Theodor Nissen, "Philologisches zu Act. apost. 6,9," *Philologus* 95 (1942–43) 310–13.

ceedings (the same thing happens later: we find an alternation between a description of a lynching and an official execution). It is not possible, however, to distinguish two sources.[5] We have a source which Luke has worked over and the alternation corresponds to his intent: the authorities behave like a mob.

■ 13 The false witnesses are reminiscent of the trial of Jesus;[6] they are not found in Luke's account of the passion. We might ask in what sense they are "false" witnesses, since their charge appears to be confirmed by the speech which follows. But in Luke's view Stephen keeps the law (7:53)—thus they are lying. For τόπος, "place," used of the temple, compare 21:28; 2 Macc 5:17–20; the rabbis.

■ 14 What is presented here is the accusation against Jesus as found in Mark 14:58, again absent from Luke's passion account. "Thus in relating the trial of the first martyr, Luke had the trial of Jesus in mind and used material which might have been dangerous if applied to

the earlier occasion."[7] The *Gospel of Thomas* (Logion 71) transmits the saying of Jesus in the first person ("Jesus said, I will destroy this house . . .").

■ 15 The idea of an angel-like face here is found frequently in Judaism.[8] This motif is used in an artificial manner in *Paul and Thecla* 3, where Paul is described: "At times he looked like a man, and at times he had the face of an angel" (ποτὲ μὲν γὰρ ἐφαίνετο ὡς ἄνθρωπος, ποτὲ δὲ ἀγγέλου πρόσωπον εἶχεν). This verse, a Lukan insertion (it intrudes between vs 14 and 7:1),[9] shows us a picture of the Christian martyr in its nascent state (cf. *Mart. Pol.* 12.1). The natural continuation is the vision in 7:55–56. Luke has inserted the speech in the (expanded) martyrdom of Stephen which he had before him.[10]

---

5   In *Beginnings* 2.148–49, the two sources are identified as follows: (1) vss 9–11 and 7:54–58a, which describe the actions of a lynch mob; (2) vss 12–14 and 7:58b–60, which portray a trial and an execution.

6   See the commentaries on Mark 14:57–58.

7   Haenchen, p. 274. On the saying itself, see Marcel Simon, "Retour du Christ et reconstruction du Temple dans la pensée chrétienne primitive," *Aux sources de la tradition*, 247–57, and (especially on the negative formulation) Johann Bihler, "Der Stephanusbericht (Apg 6,8–15 und 7,54—8,2)," *BZ* n.s. 3

(1959) 257–59, who emphasizes that the wording of the accusation assumes the Lukan(!) conception of the temple.

8   Str-B 1.752; 2.665–66.

9   Hans Werner Surkau, *Martyrien in jüdischer und frühchristlicher Zeit* (FRLANT 54; Göttingen: Vandenhoeck & Ruprecht, 1938) 108–9.

10   Dibelius, *Studies,* 168–69.

7

**Stephen's Speech
before the Council**

2 And Stephen said:
"Brethren and fathers, hear me. The God of
glory appeared to our father Abraham,
when he was in Mesopotamia, before he
lived in Haran, 3/ and said to him, 'Depart
from your land and from your kindred and
go into the land which I will show you.'
4/ Then he departed from the land of the
Chaldeans, and lived in Haran. And after
his father died, God removed him from
there into this land in which you are now
living; 5/ yet he gave him no inheritance
in it, not even a foot's length, but promised to give it to him in possession and to
his posterity after him, though he had no
child. 6/ And God spoke to this effect,
that his posterity would be aliens in a
land belonging to others, who would
enslave them and ill-treat them four
hundred years. 7/ 'But I will judge the
nation which they serve,' said God, 'and
after that they shall come out and worship me in this place.' 8/ And he gave
him the covenant of circumcision. And so
Abraham became the father of Isaac, and
circumcised him on the eighth day; and
Isaac became the father of Jacob, and
Jacob of the twelve patriarchs.

9 "And the patriarchs, jealous of Joseph,
sold him into Egypt; but God was with
him, 10/ and rescued him out of all his
afflictions, and gave him favor and wisdom before Pharaoh, king of Egypt, who
made him governor over Egypt and over
all his household. 11/ Now there came a
famine throughout all Egypt and Canaan,
and great affliction, and our fathers could
find no food. 12/ But when Jacob heard
that there was grain in Egypt, he sent
forth our fathers the first time. 13/ And
at the second visit Joseph made himself
known to his brothers, and Joseph's
family became known to Pharaoh. 14/
And Joseph sent and called to him Jacob
his father and all his kindred, seventy-
five souls; 15/ and Jacob went down into
Egypt. And he died, himself and our
fathers, 16/ and they were carried back
to Shechem and laid in the tomb that
Abraham had bought for a sum of silver
from the sons of Hamor in Shechem.

17 "But as the time of the promise drew near,
which God had granted to Abraham, the
people grew and multiplied in Egypt 18/
till there arose over Egypt another king
who had not known Joseph. 19/ He dealt
craftily with our race and forced our
fathers to expose their infants, that they
might not be kept alive. 20/ At this time
Moses was born, and was beautiful
before God. And he was brought up for

three months in his father's house; 21/ and when he was exposed, Pharaoh's daughter adopted him and brought him up as her own son. 22/ And Moses was instructed in all the wisdom of the Egyptians, and he was mighty in his words and deeds.

23 "When he was forty years old, it came into his heart to visit his brethren, the sons of Israel. 24/ And seeing one of them being wronged, he defended the oppressed man and avenged him by striking the Egyptian. 25/ He supposed that his brethren understood that God was giving them deliverance by his hand, but they did not understand. 26/ And on the following day he appeared to them as they were quarreling and would have reconciled them, saying, 'Men, you are brethren, why do you wrong each other?' 27/ But the man who was wronging his neighbor thrust him aside, saying, 'Who made you a ruler and a judge over us? 28/ Do you want to kill me as you killed the Egyptian yesterday?' 29/ At this retort Moses fled, and became an exile in the land of Midian, where he became the father of two sons.

30 "Now when forty years had passed, an angel appeared to him in the wilderness of Mount Sinai, in a flame of fire in a bush. 31/ When Moses saw it he wondered at the sight; and as he drew near to look, the voice of the Lord came, 32/ 'I am the God of your fathers, the God of Abraham and of Isaac and of Jacob.' And Moses trembled and did not dare to look. 33/ And the Lord said to him, 'Take off the shoes from your feet, for the place where you are standing is holy ground. 34/ I have surely seen the ill-treatment of my people that are in Egypt and heard their groaning, and I have come down to deliver them. And now come, I will send you to Egypt.'

35 "This Moses whom they refused, saying, 'Who made you a ruler and a judge?' God sent as both ruler and deliverer by the hand of the angel that appeared to him in the bush. 36/ He led them out, having performed wonders and signs in Egypt and at the Red Sea, and in the wilderness for forty years. 37/ This is the Moses who said to the Israelites, 'God will raise up for you a prophet from your brethren as he raised me up.' 38/ This is he who was in the congregation in the wilderness with the angel who spoke to him at Mount Sinai, and with our fathers; and he received living oracles to give to us. 39/ Our fathers refused to obey him, but thrust him aside, and in their hearts they turned to Egypt, 40/ saying to Aaron, 'Make for us gods to go before us; as for this Moses who led us out from the land

of Egypt, we do not know what has become of him.' 41/ And they made a calf in those days, and offered a sacrifice to the idol and rejoiced in the works of their hands. 42/ But God turned [or: turned himself away] and gave them over to worship the host of heaven, as it is written in the book of the prophets:

'Did you offer to me slain beasts and sacrifices,
forty years in the wilderness, O house of Israel?
43/ And you took up the tent of Moloch,
and the star of the god Rephan,
the figures which you made to worship;
and I will remove you beyond Babylon.'

44 "Our fathers had the tent of witness in the wilderness, even as he who spoke to Moses directed him to make it, according to the pattern that he had seen. 45/ Our fathers in turn brought it in with Joshua when they dispossessed the nations which God thrust out before our fathers. So it was until the days of David, 46/ who found favor in the sight of God and asked leave to find a habitation for the God of Jacob. 47/ But it was Solomon who built a house for him. 48/ Yet the Most High does not dwell in houses made with hands; as the prophet says,

49/ 'Heaven is my throne,
and earth my footstool.
What house will you build for me, says the Lord,
or what is the place of my rest?
50/ Did not my hand make all these things?'

51 "You stiff-necked people, uncircumcised in heart and ears, you always resist the Holy Spirit. As your fathers did, so do you. 52/ Which of the prophets did not your fathers persecute? And they killed those who announced beforehand the coming of the Righteous One, whom you have now betrayed and murdered, 53/ you who received the law as delivered by angels and did not keep it."

The same introduction, "Brethren and fathers, hear . . . ," is found in 22:1.

■ 2–7 Abraham. In these *heilsgeschichtlich* (salvation-history) summaries the events selected from the stories of Abraham vary more widely than events selected from the time of Moses.[1]

■ 2 For "God of glory," see Ps 29 (28):3 LXX; for ὤφθη,

"appeared," compare Gen 12:7 LXX. 1QapGen 22.27 renders Gen 15:1 as follows: "After these things God appeared to Abram in a vision and spoke to him. . . ." Matthew Black concludes that in this passage Luke has taken material from an Aramaic Targum of his time.[2]

1   R. Storch, "Die Stephanusrede Ag 7:2–53" (Diss., Göttingen, 1967) 11ff; Nils A. Dahl, "The Story of Abraham in Luke-Acts," *Studies in Luke-Acts,* 139–58,

reprinted in his *Jesus in the Memory of the Early Church* (Minneapolis: Augsburg, 1976) 66–86.
2   Matthew Black, "Die Erforschung der Muttersprache

Actually it derives from Gen 12:7 LXX. ὄντι ἐν τῇ Μεσοποταμίᾳ, "when he was in Mesopotamia," is in contradiction to Gen 12:1. In recalling the travels of Abraham the stopover in Haran can be skipped over (cf. Gen 15:7; Neh 9:7; and to a certain degree Philo *Abr.* 62). Luke's strong emphasis on Haran, therefore, is striking.[3]

■ **3** This verse follows Gen 12:1, though omitting "and your father's house" because in Acts the departure, rather than from Haran, is from Ur, from which Abraham's father must also depart (cf. vs 4). It is not necessary to understand this as dependent upon the Palestinian Targum tradition.[4]

■ **4** "And after his father died" clashes with the numbers in Gen 11:26—12:4, but agrees with the Samaritan Pentateuch (Gen 11:32—145 years instead of 205) and with Philo *Migr. Abr.* 177.

■ **5** This verse combines a biblical expression (Deut 2:5) and a free quotation of Gen 17:8 (cf. 48:4; 12:7; 13:15).[5] The conception of promise is developed by reference to the paradox that Abraham as yet had no child (Rom 4:18–22).

■ **6–7** The reference to the time in bondage has this same sense of emphasizing the crisis through which God realized his promise. There are clear echoes of Gen 15:13–14, with a touch from Exod 2:22, and an expansion from Exod 3:12. ὄρος, "mountain," is replaced by τόπος, "place," thus Sinai is replaced by Jerusalem or the Temple (these two meaning essentially the same thing).[6] Compare 6:13–14. Luke applies Scripture to the situation of Stephen. This alteration does not prove that the passage was composed in Jerusalem (Holtz), but indicates the hand of Luke.

■ **8** Here is the introduction to the patriarchical history. For διαθήκη περιτομῆς, "covenant of circumcision," see Gen 17:10, 12—circumcision is the visible mark of historical continuity. There is no hint of criticism of any sort here. A comparison with the account in Ps.-Clem. *Recog.* 1.32–34 is interesting.[7] For καὶ οὕτως, "and so," compare 27:44; 28:14.

■ **9–16** Joseph. The bearers of the promise themselves bring about the crisis (Gen 37:11, 28; 39:21), thus placing the stress on divine guidance. The emphasis is not on an accusation against the patriarchs (4 *Macc* 7.19; 16.25; cf. Ps 105 [104]:17).

■ **10** Compare Gen 41:37–45 and Ps 105 (104):21. There are only hints at the θλίψεις, "afflictions," of Joseph.

■ **11** Here Gen 41:54–57 and 42:5 are followed, incorporating material from Ps 37 (36):19 LXX.

■ **12** Compare Gen 42:1–2. The narrator assumes that the reader is familiar with the material. The purpose is not to report the events, but to interpret them.

■ **14** Compare Deut 10:22. The number seventy-five follows Gen 46:27 LXX (cf. Exod 1:4; 4QExod[a];[8] Philo *Migr. Abr.* 198–207).

■ **15** Compare Gen 46:6; 49:33; Exod 1:6.

■ **16** Compare Gen 23:16–17. The author here mentions a fact earlier skipped over (vs 15), namely, Abraham's purchase of a grave. The designation of the place as "Shechem" results from a confusion with Jacob's purchase of land as reported in Gen 33:19 (cf. further the statement about Joseph in Josh 24:32). According to Gen 49:30 and 50:13, Jacob was buried in Hebron. According to Josephus *Ant.* 2.199, Joseph's brothers were buried there as well (cf. further *Jub.* 46.9). Jeremias suspects that a local Shechem tradition is responsible for the reference to Shechem.[9] For "from the sons of Hamor," compare Gen 33:19 and Josh 24:32 (not the LXX!).[10]

Jesu," *ThLZ* 82 (1957) 666.

3   Wilhelm Mundle, "Die Stephanusrede Apg. 7: Eine Märtyrerapologie," *ZNW* 20 (1921) 140.

4   Max Wilcox, *The Semitisms of Acts* (Oxford: Clarendon, 1965) 26–27.

5   For the negative οὐ, "not," with the participle, see BDF § 430.2.

6   Arguing for the Temple: Holtz, *Zitate*, 98; Storch, "Stephanusrede," 30–31.

7   Hans Joachim Schoeps, *Aus frühchristlicher Zeit: Religionsgeschichtlicher Untersuchungen* (Tübingen:

Mohr [Siebeck], 1950) 24ff; Strecker, *Judenchristentum,* 221–54.

8   Milik, *Ten Years,* 24.

9   Joachim Jeremias, *Heiligengräber in Jesu Umwelt (Mt. 23,29; Lk. 11,47): Eine Untersuchung zur Volksreligion der Zeit Jesu* (Göttingen: Vandenhoeck & Ruprecht, 1958) 37–38.

10   On the Joseph and Moses narratives in Philo, see E. R. Goodenough, *The Politics of Philo Judaeus: Practice and Theory* (New Haven: Yale University, 1938; reprinted Hildesheim: Olms, 1967) 32–39, 43–63.

Joseph is often understood as a type of the innocent. But it is precisely the sufferings of Joseph that are all but ignored. The emphasis does not fall on typological significance, but on the notion that God carries through his saving work contrary to human probability. This account is based on adherence to the biblical pattern: Canaan—Egypt—deliverance—return (the last anticipated in the burial of the patriarchs).

■ **17–43** Moses.

■ **17** The fulfillment of the promise, as in Exod 1:7.

■ **18** This verse quotes Exod 1:8 LXX almost verbatim.

■ **19** Compare Exod 1:10–11. For ἐκάκωσεν, "forced," compare Num 20:15 with 1 Kgs 17:20.[11] For ζωογονεῖσθαι, "be kept alive," compare Exod 1:17–18 and Luke 17:33.

■ **20** Moses is ἀστεῖος, "beautiful" (cf. Exod 2:2 LXX; Heb 11:23; Philo *Vita Mos.* 1.9,18; Josephus *Ant.* 2.224, 231–32).[12] Beauty is an attribute of the θεῖος ἀνήρ, "divine man" (Lucian *Alex.* 3).[13]

■ **21–22** Compare Exod 2:3–10. The biographical scheme ἐγεννήθη—(ἀν)ετράφη—ἐπαιδεύθη, "born—brought up—instructed," lies in the background;[14] Philo *Vita Mos.* 2.1: "The former treatise dealt with the birth and nurture of Moses; also with his education and career as a ruler" (Ἡ μὲν προτέρα σύνταξίς ἐστι περὶ γενέσεως τῆς Μωυσέως καὶ τροφῆς, ἔτι δὲ παιδείας καὶ ἀρχῆς).[15] The relationship of Moses to proverbial Egyptian wisdom (cf. 1 Kgs 5:10)[16] is also dealt with in Philo *Vita Mos.* 1.20–24, though with a different emphasis (1.32, 80).[17] δυνατός, "mighty": the Moses of the Old Testament was slow of speech (Exod 4:10); however, the handicap is

already glossed over as early as Sir 45:3 and is missing completely in Josephus *Ant.* 2.271–72. δύναμις τῶν λόγων, "mighty in words," is also a θεῖος ἀνήρ, "divine man," motif.[18]

■ **23** The number forty comes from Jewish tradition about Moses.[19] It is based on the forty years in the wilderness and Moses' age of one hundred and twenty years (Deut 34:7). In this way Moses' life is divided into three epochs of forty years each. For ἀναβαίνειν, compare the Hebrew, עָלָה עַל לֵב, "it came into (his) heart."

■ **24** Compare Exod 2:12. ἀμύνεσθαι can be understood as "defend" (Philo *Vita Mos.* 1.40) or as "help" (the middle used for the classical active form).[20] "The" Egyptian: the author presupposes that the reader is familiar with the material. The tendency to excuse Moses by assigning a noble motive to his actions is more marked in Philo *Vita Mos.* 1.43–44.

■ **25** This verse interrupts the course of the narrative with an interpretation.[21] It prepares for vss 33–38 by announcing the Moses typology.

■ **26** In Exod 2:13 Moses takes the side of one of the quarreling parties. In Acts, on the other hand, he wants to bring about "peace" (a work of the θεῖος ἀνήρ, "divine man"; Lucian *Demon.* 9; Philostratus *Vita Apoll.* 1.15; 6.38).[22]

■ **27** The modification of Exod 2:13 makes the reaction sharper. This is further emphasized through the ἀπώσατο αὐτόν, "thrust him aside" (cf. vss 35, 39).

■ **29** Here Moses' flight is caused by his brothers, not by the Pharaoh, as in Exod 3:15.

11 On the infinitive τοῦ ποιεῖν, "to make," see BDF § 400.8.

12 Str-B 1.678.

13 Bieler, *Theios Aner* 1.51–54; Betz, *Lukian,* 104–5; differently BAG (*s.v.* θεός 3 g B) argues that τῷ θεῷ should be taken as an ethical dative ("in the sight of God") and thus that it serves as a superlative (= "exceedingly"; cf. Jonah 3:3).

14 Plato *Crito* 50e and 51c; W. C. van Unnik, *Tarsus or Jerusalem: The City of Paul's Youth* (London: Epworth, 1962); see below on 22:3.

15 See also Philo *Flacc.* 158.

16 Cf. Herodotus 2; Plato *Tim.* 21e–22b; Lucian *Philops.* 34; Ps.-Callisth. 1.1.1; see Betz, *Lukian,* 104ff.

17 Georg Bertram, "Praeparatio Evangelica in der Septuaginta," *VT* 7 (1957) 229–30.

18 Lucian *Demon.* 13ff; Demosthenes *Encomium* 14–15; Betz, *Lukian,* 135 n. 3.

19 Str-B 2.679–80.

20 Isa 59:16; BDF § 316.1.

21 See the excursus "Stephen's Speech" below.

22 On the portrayal of Moses in Hellenistic Judaism, see Bieler, *Theios Aner* 2.5–8; Joachim Jeremias, "Μωϋσῆς," *TDNT* 4 (1967) 849–51.

■ **30** Compare Exod 3:1–2.[23]

■ **32** Compare Exod 3:6. The wording here does not follow the LXX exactly (cf. 3:13).

■ **33** Compare Exod 3:5.[24]

■ **34** Compare Exod 3:7, 10.[25]

■ **35** Here we have a change of style. Note the series of demonstratives: τοῦτον, "this," occurs twice in vs 35; οὗτος, "this one," introduces vss 36, 37, 38. Norden sees the style of the encomium here.[26] The Moses typology is responsible for certain stylized expressions here.[27] The words ἄρχοντα καὶ λυτρωτήν, "ruler and deliverer," sound the first theme of the Moses typology, connecting Moses and Jesus (cf. 5:31; Luke 1:68; 2:38; 24:21).

■ **36** Moses as miracle worker is also understood typologically. This motif grows out of Exod 7:3 where *God* is the one who does miracles (cf. Ps 105 [104]:27 and Josephus *Ant.* 2.276). Note also *T. Mos.* 3.11: "Moses, who suffered many things in Egypt and at the Red Sea and in the wilderness for forty years" (qui multa passus est in Aegypto et in mari rubro et in heremo annis quadraginta).

■ **37** Compare Deut 18:15.[28] Simon sees a connection with the Samaritan expectation of Taheb.[29] Taheb, however, was not originally identical with the Mosaic prophet.[30]

■ **38** A further theme of the typology appears here: Moses is "mediator" (Philo *Vita Mos.* 2.166; Gal 3:19–20).[31]

γίνεσθαι ἐν, "to be together with," is not a translation of וּבֵין . . . בֵּין "between."[32] For ἐκκλησία, "congregation," compare Deut 4:10; 9:10; 18:16. With regard to the giving of the Law through an angel[33] the passage from Josephus *Ant.* 15.136, which is usually cited as evidence for such a tradition, certainly does not refer to an angel[34] (compare the connection between Josephus *Ant.* 15.136 and *C. Apion.* 1.37). In his Sinai narrative Josephus makes no mention of angels. Deut 33:2 LXX provides some solid evidence. Paul uses this conception in order to prove the inferiority of the Law from a Jewish perspective. Here the motif has a positive sense (cf. vs 53). This is far removed from the perspective of Ezek 20:25. To the λόγια ζῶντα, "living oracles," compare rather Deut 32:47.

■ **39** Here the line of thought in vss 25 and 27 is continued. Num 14:3 is translated into psychological terms —an inward turning to the gods (cf. Ezek 20:8, 13).

■ **40** Compare Exod 32:1. Josephus skips the story of the golden calf.[35]

■ **41** For the formation of the word μοσχοποιεῖν, "to make a calf" (after Exod 32:4), compare the Greek εἰδωλοποιεῖν, "to make an image" (cf. also Justin *Dial.* 19.5). The plural ἔργα, "works," is part of the terminology of Jewish polemic against idols: ἔργα χειρῶν ἀνθρώπων, "works of men's hands," Ps 115:4 (= 113:12 LXX), Wis 13:10; Ep Jer 50. The accusation is not against Aaron,

23 On "forty years," see the commentary on vs 23.

24 See the commentaries on Exod 3:5; L. Dürr, "Zur religionsgeschichtlichen Begründung der Vorschrift des Schuhausziehens an heiliger Stätte," *OLZ* 41 (1938) cols. 410–12.

25 On δεῦρο, "come," with the aorist subjunctive (hortatory), see BDF § 364.1.

26 Norden, *Agnostos Theos,* 163ff. For the Greek form οὗτος, "this one," with honorific nouns and adjectives in apposition, cf. Aelius Aristides 2 (B. Keil [1898] p. 346); for the oriental form οὗτός [ἐστιν], "this [is]," followed by a substantive participle as predicate, cf. Philo *Leg. Gai.* 145–47, where the style appropriate to praise of God is applied to the emperor: οὗτός ἐστιν Καῖσαρ ὁ . . . χειμῶνας εὐδιάσας κτλ. ("This is the Caesar who calmed the torrential rains . . .").

27 On this topic, see Joseph Comblin, "La Paix dans la théologie de saint Luc," *EThL* 32 (1956) 447–48; Comblin, however, accords more importance to the typology than it deserves.

28 See the commentary on 3:22.

29 Simon, *St Stephen,* 61–62; also see Paul Kahle,

"Untersuchungen zur Geschichte des Pentateuchtextes," *ThStK* 88 (1915) 400–401.

30 Hans Gerhard Kippenberg, *Garizim und Synagoge: Traditionsgeschichtliche Untersuchungen zur samaritanischen Religion der aramäischen Periode* (RVV 30; Berlin/New York: de Gruyter, 1971) 276–305.

31 Albrecht Oepke, "μεσίτης," *TDNT* 4 (1967) 617–18.

32 Against *Beginnings* 4.78.

33 See the commentaries on Gal 3:19.

34 W. D. Davies, "A Note on Josephus, Antiquities 15.136," *HTR* 47 (1954) 135–40; Francis R. Walton, "The Messenger of God in Hecataeus of Abdera," *HTR* 48 (1955) 255–57 (with reference to Hecataeus in *FGH* 264 frg. 6).

35 On the nominative preceding the relative clause, see BDF § 466.1.

but against the people.

■ **42–43** It is not clear whether ἔστρεψεν here has an active meaning, "God turned the Israelites toward the heavenly bodies,"[36] or a reflexive meaning, "God turned away from them."[37] For παρέδωκεν, "gave them over," compare Rom 1:24–32, where moral perversion is the punishment for idolatry. Here idolatry itself is the punishment. The notion of "measure for measure" shines through.[38] For the expression "the host of heaven" compare Jer 7:18 and 19:13.

The quotation of Amos 5:25–27[39] is taken from the LXX almost verbatim;[40] however, "Damascus" is replaced by "Babylon"—a reference to the historical fulfillment of the threat. In its original context the passage said that during the time in the wilderness (as the ideal time) no sacrifices were offered. Now, as quoted in Acts, it says that apostasy existed even during the time in the wilderness (cf. Ezekiel 20!). The train of thought is best understood if we interpret: "They did not offer sacrifices to *me*, but to other gods."[41] This could be construed in two ways: (1) that they should have offered sacrifices to *God*, or (2) offering sacrifices was in itself idolatry (thus a fundamental opposition to the cult).[42] According to the latter interpretation, the progression of thought from vs 42 to vs 43 is not understandable. The quotation is transformed into a single reproach by vs 42a. If we assume further that μοι, "me," is not emphasized, then we should

translate: "Did you *offer* anything to me?" The sense of the reproach is then: "You have ceased offerings in order to turn to idols." There is, however, no substantial difference between the two interpretations. The Amos passage also appears in the Qumran writings with a quite different application in CD 7.14–16;[43] there it is connected with Amos 9:11.[44] What the author of Acts and the Qumran sectarians share is the interpretation of סכות as סכּות, "tent." The transmission of the name of the god Rephan is completely confused;[45] the LXX has Ραιφαν, "Raiphan."

■ **44** The logic is difficult to follow. Verses 44 and 43 do not fit together. The strange result is that two tents were brought along. Apparently the author has returned to his source, after having made an interpolation (note the change in style). In this source vs 44 probably followed vs 38 (or vs 34?). The connection of vs 43 and vs 44 occurs in the catchword σκηνή, "tent," which brought about the peculiar duplication, probably not noticed by the author.[46] σκηνὴ τοῦ μαρτυρίου, "tent of witness," is the LXX translation for אהל מועד, "tent of meeting," or אהל העדות, "tent of the testimony." Following Exod 25:40 (cf. Heb 8:5; Bar 4:5), the tent is traced back to a heavenly prototype and thus is evaluated positively. In

---

36   BAG *s.v.* στρέφω, 1 a *a*; this would be the normal usage and would correspond with παρέδωκεν, "gave them over."

37   BAG *s.v.* στρέφω, 1 b; cf. ἀναστρέφειν, "to return," Acts 15:16; 5:23.

38   Joachim Jeremias, "Zu Rm 1:22–23," *ZNW* 45 (1954) 119–21, now in his *Abba*, 290–92.

39   On the citation formula, see Bruce M. Metzger, "The Formulas Introducing Quotations of Scripture in the NT and the Mishnah," *JBL* 70 (1951) 297–307, reprinted in his *Historical and Literary Studies: Pagan, Jewish, and Christian* (NTTS 8; Leiden: Brill; Grand Rapids: Eerdmans, 1968) 52–63.

40   On the relation of the MT to the LXX, see Haenchen, p. 284 n. 1.

41   For offerings to demons instead of to God, cf. *Sib. Or.* frg. 1.20–22.

42   Thus Marcel Simon ("Saint Stephen and the Jerusalem Temple," *JEH* 2 (1951) 127–42; idem, *St Stephen*, 49, with an appeal to Jer 7:21–22; cf. Justin *Dial.* 22.2–6; see the commentary on vs 51. On the protest of the Ps.-Clem. against sacrifice, see

Strecker, *Judenchristentum*, 179–84; Hans Joachim Schoeps, *Theologie und Geschichte des Judenchristentums* (Tübingen: Mohr [Siebeck], 1949) 220–33, esp. 227: Amos 5:25 was disputed by the school of Hillel; Str-B 2.671; for a very different interpretation, see Munck, *Paul*, 222 n. 1.

43   See Chaim Rabin, *The Zadokite Documents* (2d ed.; Oxford: Clarendon, 1958) 29–30.

44   See the commentary on 15:16.

45   On the Hebrew text, see *BHK ad loc.*

46   Marcel Simon ("Saint Stephen and the Jerusalem Temple," *JEH* 2 [1951] 127–42) interprets the two tents as symbols of the line of proper worship and of apostasy, arguing that the images need not be viewed realistically.

this way the reprehensible nature of idol worship is accented all the more and—at least in this present context[47]—preparation is made for the contrast between the "tent" and the temple (which is χειροποίητον, "made with hands"). Philo too speaks of the tent as χειροποίητον (*Vita Mos.* 2.88), but without any deprecatory sense.

■ **45** For ἦν εἰσήγαγον, "which they brought in," see Josh 3:14. The fulfillment of vs 5 is announced by ἐν τῇ κατασχέσει, "in the dispossessing" (a *dispossession*, rather than simply possession). With διαδεξάμενοι, "in turn," supply "from generation to generation."

■ **46** On the basis of vs 48 we ought not too quickly read vs 46 as a reproach against David. Instead of οἴκῳ, "house," read θεῷ, "God," following Ps 132 (131):5 (A C 𝔑 etc.). With the reading θεῷ the connection with the next verse is clearer.[48]

■ **47** Verse 47 only becomes a reproach in light of vs 48 (for the positive evaluation of the statement, cf. 1 Kgs 6:2; 8:20).

■ **48** Here "tent" (which is not a dwelling place) and house (as God's dwelling place—that which cannot be) are contrasted. Until we get to vs 48 there is a line progressing from the tabernacle (tent), through David's wish, to the construction of the Temple. In the Old Testament the two traditions about tent and Temple parallel one another, and are even interwoven (the prayer dedicating the Temple in 1 Kgs 8:22–53 = 2 Chr 6:12–42). Criticism of the cult as in vs 48 can thus be derived from Old Testament traditions like those in 1 Kgs 8:27 = 2 Chr 6:18, passages, however, which certainly do not exclude the building of the Temple. In Acts, though, the quotation from Isaiah which follows is a clear rejection of the Temple. χειροποίητος, "made with hands," is used in Isa 16:12 LXX as a designation for a temple.[49]

Excursus: Criticism of the Temple

Criticism of the Temple has its beginnings in the spiritualizing of the cultic as found in late Judaism[50] (cf. Philo *Cher.* 99–105; Josephus *Ant.* 8.107–8. But even in this material one finds a concern to justify the existence of the Temple. In *Tg. Ps.-J.* Exod 39:43, Moses prays "that the shekinah of Yahweh might dwell in the works of your hands" (similarly *Tg. Neof.*, which is strengthened by a marginal note).[51] Nor is there a fundamental opposition to the Temple at Qumran (cf. 1QM 2.5). Luke goes beyond these Jewish beginnings to pick up Christian modifications of motifs from Jewish polemics against Gentiles, and then uses these motifs against Judaism. These motifs in turn employ arguments from Greek religious critiques.[52] The style of his criticism assumes the destruction of the Temple.[53]

■ **49** Was Isa 66:1(–2) a text often used in criticism of the Temple? *Barn.* 16.2 uses the same text, with only slight deviation from the LXX form (τίς, "what," instead of ποῖος, "what kind of"); compare Justin *Dial.* 22.11. For the idea of the world as the temple of God, see Seneca *Nat. quaest.* 7.30.

■ **51–53** The summary and application: the attack which the martyr makes against those persecuting him (2 Macc 7:14–19; *4 Macc.* 5–12).

■ **51** This is a reproach in biblical style. Compare Deut 10:16. For σκληροτράχηλος, "stiff-necked," compare Exod 33:3, 5, etc.; for ἀπερίτμητος, "uncircumcised," compare Lev 26:41, etc.; 1QS 5.5; 1QpHab 11.13, etc.; and for resistance against the Spirit, compare Isa 63:10.

■ **52** The notion that all the prophets were persecuted derives from Jewish tradition based on passages like 1 Kgs 19:10, 14; Neh 9:26; 2 Chr 36:16.[54] The emphasis

47   See the commentary on vs 48.
48   Schoeps (*Theologie*, 238) advocates the reading οἴκῳ. The verse alludes, he argues, not to Ps 132:5 but to 2 Sam 7:26.
49   For χειροποίητος, "made with hands," see the commentary on 17:24; for ὕψιστος, "Most High," see the commentaries on Mark 5:7.
50   Hans Wenschkewitz, *Die Spiritualisierung der Kultbegriffe: Temple, Priester und Opfer im Neuen Testament* (Angelos Beiheft 4; Leipzig: Pfeiffer, 1932).
51   Roger Le Déaut, "*Actes* 7,48 et *Matthieu* 17,4 (par.) à la lumière du targum palestinien," *RechSR* 52 (1964) 85–90.
52   Zeno (in *SVF* 1 frgs. 264–65); Clement Alex. *Strom.* 5.12.76; Plutarch *Mor.* 1034b: "Further, it is a doctrine of Zeno not to build sanctuaries of the gods" (ἔτι δόγμα Ζήνωνός ἐστιν ἱερὰ θεῶν μὴ οἰκοδομεῖν); cf. *Barn.* 16.
53   O'Neill, *Theology* [1st ed.], 89; see Klaus Baltzer, "The Meaning of the Temple in the Lukan Writings," *HTR* 58 (1965) 263–77.
54   Cf. esp. *Mart. Isa.*; Luke 13:34; 1 Thess 2:15; Heb 11:36–38; Justin *Dial.* 16.4.

here is not on the idea of martyrdom, nor is there a biographical interest in the destiny of the prophets. The focus is rather on a picture of Israel (based on the Deuteronomic history) which portrays Israel as the wrongdoer. The elements making up this picture include: the disobedient people, the patience of God, admonition by the prophets, stubbornness (resisting the Spirit: Neh 9:30; Zech 7:12), and judgment. This kind of thinking was also alive in Judaism (Josephus *Ant.* 9.265–66; 10.3–4; the rabbis). The interpretation of the suffering of the righteous and the formation of legends about the prophets arose out of such reflection.[55]

■ **53** See Gal 3:19.[56]

Excursus:
Stephen's Speech

Stephen's speech poses a whole series of difficult problems. How does it relate to the martyrdom of Stephen, and to the rest of the speeches in the book? What is its value as a historical source?

1. It seems strange that the content of the speech (with the exception of the closing remarks) has no connection with the charges against Stephen.[57] The attempts to understand the speech as a defense are artificial. Both style and theme indicate that this is not a martyr's speech.[58] It has been secondarily inserted into the martyrdom of Stephen;[59] note that it breaks the connection between 7:1 and 54. This means that it fits the situation as *Luke* understands it. The speech relates the martyrdom to Luke's whole view of history and furnishes the theoretical preparation for the transition to the mission to the Gentiles (cf. the reference to Stephen in 22:20). This becomes even clearer as one compares the supplement which Luke himself has composed, the speech in 13:16–41.

2. The speech certainly exhibits a number of highly individual features (in both style and content). This leads one to ask whether a source may have been used.

The fact is that literary seams are evident, precisely at those points where transitions are made from positive biblical matters to polemics. These polemic sections can be isolated (vss 35, 37, 39–42, 48–53, perhaps 25, 27). Then it becomes evident that beneath the present polemic surface lies a substratum of another kind. There we discover an edifying meditation on the history of salvation, which finds its meaning for the present in the retelling of history for instruction and warning. There is a long tradition behind this retelling.[60] The continuity in the history is not to be found in the programmatic proclamation of the events. It is rather the continuity of certain constant factors on the one hand (promise, circumcision), and of conduct (of the people) on the other.[61] The whole style of this retrospective view prohibits us from postulating either a unified tendency (say a typology), or a whole pattern which is worked out strictly, or a logical progression of thoughts. Motifs emerge and then disappear again. Typology can be hinted at (Joseph), clearly worked out (Moses), or also ignored (David). The wandering people of God (cf. the theme of Hebrews!) is not consistently worked out as a pattern for the whole either. That theme was not present, and it is Luke who interjects it into the speech. The consistent focus of Luke's source is the subject or theme, namely, the holy promise, which is dishonored time and again by the disobedience of the people.

3. A final question: How close to the historical Stephen does the source take us? To answer the question we must go beyond this example. Here we come to know how a Hellenistic Jewish-Christianity of a non-Pauline type views the Bible and history. There are still traces of this viewpoint elsewhere (in Luke himself, Hebrews, *Barnabas*, Justin, etc.).[62] It is surely not methodologically correct to seek to reconstruct the whole thought world of this group from a single text like this. Conclusions from silence (e.g., from the absence of a thematic christological section) ought not be drawn. Of course there are certain points of contact

---

55 Odil Hannes Steck, *Israel und das gewaltsame Geschick der Propheten: Untersuchungen zur Überlieferung des deuteronomistischen Geschichtsbildes im Alten Testament, Spätjüdentum und Urchristentum* (WMANT 23; Neukirchen-Vluyn: Neukirchener, 1967) 265ff. On ἔλευσις, "coming," see George D. Kilpatrick, "Acts vii. 52 ΕΛΕΥΣΙΣ," *JTS* 46 (1945) 136–45; for a contrary position, see Jacques Dupont, *Sun Christo: L'union avec le Christ suivant saint Paul* (Bruges: L'Abbaye de Saint-André, 1952) 55–59.

56 See the commentary on vs 38.

57 Dibelius, *Studies,* 167–70.

58 Surkau, *Martyrien,* 109.

59 Dibelius, *Studies,* 168.

60 Cf. Deuteronomy; Joshua 24; Ezekiel 20; Nehemiah 9; Psalm 105 (104); Josephus *Bell.* 5.377–400; Ps.-Clem. *Recog.* 1.22ff; see Strecker, *Judenchristentum,* 221–54.

61 See Georg Fohrer, *Ezechiel* (HAT 13; Tübingen: Mohr [Siebeck], 1955) 107–17, on Ezekiel 20.

62 Simon, *St Stephen,* 98–116; Ceslas Spicq, "L'Épître aux Hébreux, Apollos, Jean-Baptiste, les Hellénistes et Qumran," *RevQ* 1 (1958–59) 365–90.

with the Qumran texts; however, the specific ideas
and themes of the sect are lacking.[63]

63 Literature:
Johannes Bihler, *Die Stephanusgeschichte im
Zusammenhang der Apostelgeschichte* (MThS 1;
Historische Abteilung 16; Munich: Hueber, 1963)
33–86, who argues that the entire speech has been
fashioned by Luke. Against this view it may be
objected that the plan of the speech presupposes a
Jewish substratum (see Holtz, *Zitate,* 85–127).
A. F. J. Klijn, "Stephen's Speech—Acts VII.2–53,"
NTS 4 (1957–58) 25–31.
Munck, *Paul,* 220–28.
Wilhelm Mundle, "Die Stephanusrede Apg. 7: Eine
Märtyrerapologie," *ZNW* 20 (1921) 133–47.
Albrecht Oepke, *Das Neue Gottesvolk in Schrifttum,
Schauspiel, bildender Kunst und Weltgestaltung*
(Gütersloh: Bertelsmann, 1950) 190–94.
O'Neill, *Theology,* 77–99, an attempt to interpret the
passage from its placement in Acts as a whole.
Simon, *St Stephen.*
R. Storch, "Die Stephanusrede," who believes he can
reconstruct two Hellenistic-Jewish sources (one
the story of Abraham, the other the story of
Moses), which in various situations justify the
extension of the mission beyond Palestine, for
which reason Luke reworked them. The linguistic
and material evidences for such a difficult source
analysis are, however, inadequate.
Hartwig Thyen, *Der Stil der jüdisch-hellenistischen
Homilie* (FRLANT n.s. 47–65; Göttingen:
Vandenhoeck & Ruprecht, 1955) 19–20.

7 The Martyrdom of Stephen and the Outbreak of Persecution

54 Now when they heard these things they were enraged, and they ground their teeth against him. 55/ But he, full of the Holy Spirit, gazed into heaven and saw the glory of God, and Jesus standing at the right hand of God; 56/ and he said, "Behold, I see the heavens opened, and the Son of man standing at the right hand of God." 57/ But they cried out with a loud voice and stopped their ears and rushed together upon him. 58/ Then they cast him out of the city and stoned him; and the witnesses laid down their garments at the feet of a young man named Saul. 59/ And as they were stoning Stephen, he prayed, "Lord Jesus, receive my spirit." 60/ And he knelt down and cried with a loud voice, "Lord, do not hold this sin against them." And when he had said this, he fell asleep.

8 8:1/ And Saul was consenting to his death.

And on that day a great persecution arose against the church in Jerusalem; and they were all scattered throughout the region of Judea and Samaria, except the apostles. 2/ Devout men buried Stephen, and made great lamentation over him. 3/ But Saul was ravaging the church, and entering house after house, he dragged off men and women and committed them to prison.

4 Now those who were scattered went about preaching the word.

■ **54** The analysis of 7:54—8:4 is uncertain. It is best to understand vs 54 (which connects with the redactional vs 15 of chap. 6) as the redactional transition to vs 55. Hans Werner Surkau believes that vss 55–57 are also Lukan.[1] Johann Bihler believes that vs 55 is a Lukan interpretation of vs 56, because vs 55 presupposes the Lukan account of the passion;[2] but things are just the reverse. In the present context the vision is the heavenly confirmation of the truth of the speech. For ἀτενίσας κτλ., "gazed etc.," see *4 Macc.* 6.5–6. For the visions of the martyrs, compare *Asc. Is.* 5.7; *Mart. Carpi* 39, 42.

■ **56** Compare Luke 22:69 from which the concept of the Son of man may have been taken. This is the only place in the New Testament where "Son of man" occurs on the lips of someone other than Jesus. A single manuscript,

P[74], has the reading τὸν υἱὸν τοῦ θεοῦ, "the Son of God."[3] ἑστῶτα, "standing," is striking (especially when compared with Luke 22:69!). Had the Son of man stood up to receive the martyr? In any case it is assumed that Stephen entered directly into heaven at the moment of his death. H. P. Owen would interpret ἑστῶτα in a broader context as a stage in the completion of the events of salvation history: Luke 9:31 ἔξοδυς, "exodus"; 24:26 entrance; Acts 1:2, 11, 22 = 2:34 ascension; Luke 20:42, 22:69, Acts 2:34 sitting; and here, standing, that is, readiness to come.[4] In Oscar Cullmann's view he stands as a *witness* at

---

1   Surkau, *Martyrien,* 109.

2   Bihler, "Der Stephanusbericht."

3   George D. Kilpatrick, "Acts vii.56: Son of Man?" *ThZ* 21 (1965) 209.

4   H. P. Owen, "Stephen's Vision in Acts VII. 55–6," *NTS* 1 (1954–55) 224–26.

the judgment.[5] In C. K. Barrett's opinion he is ready to come to Stephen and every Christian may hope for the same.[6] On the basis of the total Lukan structure Rudolf Pesch interprets as follows: The text as a whole is not so much concerned with the fate of Stephen as with the significance of these events for the spread of the church. The Exalted One sanctions the departure from the Jews and the transition to the Gentiles. The Son of man rises up as Judge against his people (cf. Yahweh in *T. Mos.* 10.3).[7] But the judging function of the Son of man is not emphasized in Luke.[8]

■ **57** The listeners stop their ears to avoid hearing any blasphemy.[9] Verses 57 and 58a are not doublets to 58b from another source, but Lukan redactional anticipations characteristic of the author: the authorities provide their own characterization by their actions. Luke does not report any formal verdict, with the result that the account continues to alternate between the description of an act of a mob and a legal process.[10]

■ **58b** The last part of this verse also serves as a redactional link as Luke introduces Saul, who was not present in the original martyrdom of Stephen.[11] According to *Sanh.* 6.4, stoning is carried out by the witnesses. Stoning is the punishment for blaspheming God (Lev 24:10–23; *Sanh.* 7.4), but it is also the fate of the prophets (2 Chr 24:21; Josephus *Ant.* 20.200—James!). For ἔξω τῆς πόλεως, "out of the city," see Lev 24:14 and Deut 17:2–5.

Regulations for stoning (as they apply to witnesses and execution) are given in *Sanh.* 6.1–4, though these certainly include some later artificial elaborations.[12] Luke himself does not have a precise idea of Jewish law. Thus a comparison of the Lukan report with the Mishnah will not answer the question as to whether or not the legal regulations were observed here.[13]

■ **59** Stephen's death is reminiscent of the death of Jesus (Luke 23:46; there is a reminiscence of Ps 31:6).[14] Compare also, however, Seneca *Herc. oet.* 1703–4: "Admit this soul, I pray thee, to the stars" (spiritum admitte hunc precor in astra); and 1725–26: "But lo! now doth my father call me and he opens heavens; father, I come" (vocat ecce iam me genitor et pandit polos; venio, pater); also Lucian *Pergr. mort.* 36: "Spirits of my mother and my father, receive me with favor" (Δαίμονες μητρῷοι καὶ πατρῷοι δέξασθέ με εὐμενεῖς).

■ **60** Compare Luke 23:34. The story of the martyrs of Lyons preserved in Eusebius *Hist. eccl.* 5.2.5 takes up our text. Does ἱστάναι mean "mete out" here? Lake and Henry J. Cadbury refer to 1 Macc 13:38–39 and 15:5, where the word is used as the opposite of ἀφιέναι, "cancel."[15] κοιμᾶσθαι, "to sleep," is a widespread euphemism for death.

■ **8:1** The note about Saul is again a redactional link. The following summary also comes from Luke (who is composing from the conclusion of the source document) and

5   Oscar Cullmann, *The Christology of the New Testament* (rev. ed.; Philadelphia: Westminster, 1963) 157–58; similarly, John A. T. Robinson, *Jesus and His Coming: The Emergence of a Doctrine* (London: SCM, 1957; reprinted Philadelphia: Westminster, 1979) 55; see further H. E. Tödt, *The Son of Man in the Synoptic Tradition* (Philadelphia: Westminster, 1965) 303–5.

6   C. K. Barrett, "Stephen and the Son of Man," *Apophoreta*, 32–38.

7   Rudolf Pesch, *Die Vision des Stephanus: Apg 7:55–56 im Rahmen der Apostelgeschichte* (Stuttgarter Bibelstudien 12; Stuttgart: Katholisches Bibelwerk, 1966).

8   H. E. Tödt, *The Son of Man in the Synoptic Tradition* (Philadelphia: Westminster, 1965) 108–12; for a standing deity alongside one sitting on a throne, see Hans Haas, *Bilderatlas zur Religionsgeschichte,* fasc. 9–11: *Die Religionen in der Umwelt des Urchristentums* (Leipzig: Deichert, 1926) pls. 151, 175–77, 191.

9   Str-B 2.684.

10   See the commentary on 6:12.

11   Haenchen, p. 293; Burchard (*Der dreizehnte Zeuge,* 26–31) believes that Luke found Stephen and Saul

     connected in his source. A judgment on this matter depends upon the overall results of our examination of "Saul and Jerusalem" (see the commentary on 22:3).

12   Cf. George Foot Moore, *Judaism in the First Centuries of the Christian Era: The Age of the Tannaim* (3 vols.; Cambridge: Harvard University, 1927–30) 2.187; Paul Winter, *On the Trial of Jesus* (2d ed.; StJud 1; Berlin: de Gruyter, 1974) 97–99.

13   For literature on stoning, see Wilhelm Michaelis, "λιθάζω," *TDNT* 4 (1967) 267–68.

14   An evening prayer; Str-B 2.269.

15   *Beginnings* 4.86.

fits the martyrdom into the whole of his historical picture. In actuality the persecution could not have affected the whole Christian community except for the "apostles," because this community continues to exist later, both in fact and in Luke's own account (Luke is somewhat constrained by his sources). The Hellenistic group was driven out.

■ **2** Luke does not take account of the Jewish regulation concerning the burial of one who has been executed (i.e., there can be no public lamentation, *Sanh.* 6.6).

■ **3** In the immediately preceding account Saul was a young man. Now he is the organizer of the persecution. The tension does not arise from Luke's reworking of the source material. It is rather a result of Luke's literary purposes: at the death of Stephen it was necessary for Saul to play a relatively harmless role, but for the continuation of Luke's account Saul must be the main character.[16] Verses 58b, 8:1, and 8:3 all tie in with the deliberate intensification in this redactional section.[17] For λυμαίνεσθαι, "to ravage," in connection with the persecution of Jews in Alexandria, see Philo *Leg. Gai.* 134. According to an edict of Claudius, it was requested of the Alexandrians that they "offer no outrage to them [that is, "the Jews"] in the exercise of their traditional worship but permit them to observe their customs as in the time of Divus Augustus."[18]

■ **4** Bultmann finds the remnant of an (Antiochene) source here. He believes the sentence has been broken off (that is, διῆλθον, "went about," should have an indication of where they went) and is continued in 11:19.[19]

Excursus:
The Martyrdom of Stephen

The literary seams in the account (between 6:11 and 12; the unevenness of 7:54—8:4) indicate that Luke is using a source document. This source contained information about the person and activity of Stephen (6:8–10), about a riot (6:11a, 12), the stoning, a last word(?), and the burial. No conclusions about the right of the Jewish court to execute capital punishment can be drawn, because the source does not depict a real trial but only the action of a mob. Luke has reworked and supplemented his source material in the following ways: he has framed the martyrdom with a sketch of a trial before the Sanhedrin; the picture of the martyr has been stereotyped; Saul has been inserted; and the story has been made into the turning point in the relationship between the church and Judaism, as part of Luke's overarching view of history.[20] The source, a piece of Hellenistic tradition, took no note of the Twelve.[21]

---

16 Haenchen, p. 298.
17 Klein, *Die zwölf Apostel,* 115–20.
18 μηδὲν τῶν πρὸς θρησκείαν αὐτοῖς νενομισμένων τοῦ θεοῦ λοιμένωνται [read λυμαίνωνται] ἀλλὰ ἐῶσιν αὐτοὺς τοῖς ἔθεσιν χρῆσθαι ὓς [read οἷς] καὶ ἐπὶ τοῦ θεοῦ Σεβαστοῦ. The text and trans. are from H. Idris Bell, ed., *Jews and Christians in Egypt: The Jewish Troubles in Alexandria and the Athanasian Controversy* (Oxford: Oxford University, 1924; reprinted Milan: Cisalpino, 1977) text 25; trans. 28–29.
19 Bultmann, "Quellen," 78 = *Exegetica,* 422.
20 Johannes Bihler, *Die Stephanusgeschichte im Zusammen-* *hang der Apostelgeschichte* (MThS 1; Historische Abteilung 16; Munich: Hueber, 1963); idem, "Der Stephanusbericht."
21 In addition to Bihler (previous note), see Surkau, *Martyrien,* 105–19, and Martin Blumenthal, *Formen und Motive in den apokryphen Apostelgeschichten* (TU 48:1; Leipzig: Hinrichs, 1933) 60, for a comparison of Stephen's martyrdom with accounts of martyrs in later, apocryphal acts of the apostles.

8
Philip's Mission in Samaria and the Conversion of Simon Magus

5   Philip went down to a city of Samaria, and proclaimed to them the Christ. 6/ And the multitudes with one accord gave heed to what was said by Philip, when they heard him and saw the signs which he did. 7/ For unclean spirits came out of many who were possessed, crying with a loud voice; and many who were paralyzed or lame were healed. 8/ So there was much joy in that city.

9   But there was a man named Simon who had previously practiced magic in the city and amazed the nation of Samaria, saying that he himself was somebody great. 10/ They all gave heed to him, from the least to the greatest, saying, "This man is that power of God which is called Great." 11/ And they gave heed to him, because for a long time he had amazed them with his magic. 12/ But when they believed Philip as he preached good news about the kingdom of God and the name of Jesus Christ, they were baptized, both men and women. 13/ Even Simon himself believed, and after being baptized he continued with Philip. And seeing signs and great miracles performed, he was amazed.

■ **5–25** Hellenistic (written?) traditions (Philip in Acts 6:5) lie behind the report of the mission in Samaria (1:8). These traditions originally took no account of the Twelve. In contrast to John (4:39–42), Luke does not trace the founding of the Samaritan Christian community back to Jesus himself.[1]

■ **5** Luke believes that the region of Samaria has only one city—the city of the same name. Whether a source meant a different location here can no longer be determined. On the technical Christian language (κηρύσσειν τὸν χριστόν, "proclaimed the Christ"), compare 9:20. For a more detailed description of what this meant, compare vs 12 and 10:42.

■ **6–8** These verses offer a preliminary redactional summary of the activities in the city. On the style, compare Ps.-Clem. *Ep. ad Jas.* 19.2: "hearing the discourses preached by me in every city, and [seeing] my deeds" (ἐπακούων τῶν κατὰ πόλιν ὑπ᾿ ἐμοῦ κηρυχθέντων λόγων τε καὶ πράξεων).

■ **7b** The text here is corrupt or the expression is simply unintelligible "since the identification of the sick with their devils is in conflict with the distinction between them."[2] Two clauses are combined, πολλοὶ τῶν ἐχόντων . . . ἐθεραπεύθησαν, "many of those having unclean spirits were healed" (cf. Luke 6:18), and πολλὰ πνεύματα ἐξήρχετο, "many spirits went out." For the distinction between those possessed and those having other illnesses, compare 5:16 and Luke 4:40–41. The πολλοί, "many," here should not be understood as meaning "but not all." This account of results is positive, in line with the summaries in Luke's Gospel. Luke of course thinks of the Samaritans in a national-religious sense (Luke 9:52–53; 10:33; 17:16). Simon also appears as a Samaritan, though this was hardly the case. There is no trace here of the Hellenistic character of the capital city, Samaria/Sebaste.

■ **9** The verb προϋπῆρχεν is probably to be taken with both μαγεύων, "practicing magic," and ἐξιστάνων, "amazing";

---

1   Conzelmann, *Theology,* 65–73.
2   Haenchen, p. 302.

thus "Simon who had previously practiced magic . . . and amazed . . ." (cf. Luke 23:12).[3]

■ **10** οὗτός ἐστιν κτλ., "This man is, etc.," corresponds to an implied ἐγώ εἰμι, "I am," statement which was spoken by Simon; compare Origen *Cels.* 7.8–9: "I am God (or a son of God, or a divine Spirit)" (ἐγὼ ὁ θεός εἰμι ἢ θεοῦ παῖς ἢ πνεῦμα θεῖον). The "great power" was a self-designation of the historical Simon. ἡ καλουμένη, "which is called," is Luke's addition, which still recognizes that "great" is part of a title. Reporting on Simon's success, Justin defines the "great power" (*Apol.* 1.26.3): "Almost every Samaritan, and even a few from other religions, worship him and call him the first god" (καὶ σχεδὸν πάντες μὲν Σαμαρεῖς . . . , ὡς τὸν πρῶτον θεὸν ἐκεῖνον ὁμολογοῦντες, ἐκεῖνον καὶ προσκυνοῦσιν). Thus he would have been the manifestation of the highest God.[4] The Targum on the Samaritan Pentateuch translates Gen 17:1 אל, "God," with חילה, "Power."[5] Then θεοῦ, "of God," would have to be an addition (from Luke?); compare the Jewish circumlocution for the name of God in Mark 14:62. However, δύναμις, "power," could also indicate the second rank of divinity, the revealer. The variety of meanings of δύναμις is evident from the *Gos. Heb.* frg. 1.[6] In this latter case the genitive θεοῦ would be in the original text; compare the inscription: εἷς θεὸς ἐν οὐρανοῖς, μέγας. μὴν οὐράνιος, μεγάλη δύναμις τοῦ ἀθανάτου θεοῦ ("The one God in the heavens is great. Indeed heavenly, great is the power of the immortal God"),[7] also, ἐπικαλοῦμαί σε τὴν μεγίστην δύναμιν τὴν ἐν τῷ οὐρανῷ ὑπὸ κυρίου θεοῦ τεταγμένην ("I call upon you, the greatest power in heaven appointed by the lord god").[8]

Excursus: Simon (Magus)

Simon (Magus) appears in the ancient sources sometimes as a magician, at other times as the father of Gnosticism. Luke stresses only the first, though there is still a hint of the second in vss 9–10. The two are not mutually exclusive. Simon appears as a θεῖος ἀνήρ, "divine man," with miraculous powers and teachings about redemption.[9] Whether Luke knew about his companion Helena (the "Ennoia") or is intentionally silent cannot be determined; it is even disputed whether she was a historical figure at all.[10] Perhaps Simon was not yet expounding a developed Gnostic doctrine about the preexistence of the soul, but rather a conception of epiphany in *statu nascendi* in Gnosticism (contrary to Haenchen). In Justin, Simon does not yet appear as a Gnostic. In the later tradition he calls himself "he who stands" (Hippolytus *Ref.* 6.13, cf. 6.17.1–2; Ps.-Clem. *Hom.* 2.22, 24; 18.12, 14). G. Widengren assumes that there is a connection with Samaritan ideas as they are found in the Marqa-liturgies.[11] The matter of dating is only one of several reasons why this is improbable.[12]

3 BAG *s.v.* προϋπάρχω; for another view, BDF § 414.1.
4 Cf. Irenaeus *Adv. haer.* 1.23.1; Ps.-Clem. *Recog.* 2.12.5; also Hegesippus in Eusebius *Hist. eccl.* 2.2.13.
5 Hans Gerhard Kippenberg, *Garizim und Synagoge: Traditionsgeschichtliche Untersuchungen zur samaritanischen Religion der aramäischen Periode* (RVV 30; Berlin/New York: de Gruyter, 1971) 328–49.
6 *NTApoc.* 1.163.
7 Josef Keil and Anton v. Premerstein, "Bericht über eine zweite Reise in Lydien," *Denkschriften der kaiserlichen Akademie der Wissenschaften* (phil.-hist. Klasse 54; Vienna: Hölder, 1911) no. 211.
8 *PGM* 1.116 (IV 1275–76). On the use of the term δύναμις in Gnostic writings, see Lucien Cerfaux, "La Gnose Simonienne: Nos sources principales," *RechSR* 15 (1921) 489–511, reprinted in *Recueil Cerfaux* 1.191–23; idem, "Simon le Magicien à Samarie," *RechSR* 27 (1937) 615–17, reprinted in *Recueil Cerfaux* 1.259–62; Friedrich Preisigke, *Die Gotteskraft der frühchristlichen Zeit* (Papyrus-Institut Heidelberg 6; Berlin/Leipzig: de Gruyter, 1922).
9 Bieler, *Theios Aner* 1.48, 84.
10 L.-H. Vincent ("Le culte d'Hélène à Samarie," *RB* 45 [1936] 221–32 + 1 pl.) argues that Helena was a historical figure (though his reference to a Helena cult in Samaria supports the opposite view); against a historical figure are: Gilles Quispel, "Simon en Helena," *NedThT* 5 (1952) 339–75; Georg Kretschmar, "Zur religionsgeschichtlichen Einordnung der Gnosis," *EvTh* 13 (1953) 354–61; Ernst Haenchen, "Gab es eine vorchristliche Gnosis?" *ZThK* 49 (1952) 316–49, reprinted in his *Gott und Mensch*, 265–98.
11 Geo Widengren, *The Ascension of the Apostle and the Heavenly Book (King and Saviour III)* (UUÅ 7; Uppsala: Lundequistska, 1950) 48–58.
12 Sources (see *Beginnings* 5.151–63): Justin *Apol.* 1.26.56; *Dial.* 120.6; Irenaeus *Adv. haer.* 1.23; Ps.-Clem. passim; Hippolytus *Ref.* 6.2–15 (Μεγάλη ἀπόφασις); Epiphanius *Adv. haer.* 21.2ff; *Acts Pet.* 4ff.
   In addition to the literature cited above, see PW, 2d ser., 3.180–84; Robert McL. Wilson, "Gnostic Origins," *VC* 9 (1955) 193–211; idem, "Simon, Dositheus and the Dead Sea Scrolls," *ZRGG* 9 (1957) 21–30; Walter Schmithals, *The Office of Apostle in the*

■ **11** This verse is a Lukan explanation.

■ **12** The content of Philip's preaching is given in Luke's own style. What is implied by ἐβαπτίζοντο, "they were baptized," is clarified only subsequently in vss 15–16.

■ **13** The narrative is not historical. Simon is amazed after he has already been converted. This arises from Luke's desire, in making the transition to the following episode, to establish some connection with the events in vss 18–24, and from his concern to illustrate the superiority of Christian power over magic. A simple account about the success of Philip could lie behind this material;[13] even this would be a secondary (already pre-Lukan) stage in the tradition.[14] The impression that the narrative, as Haenchen says, "comes to a sudden and disappointing end"[15] arises only if one already knows more about Simon than is found in Luke. The other sources say nothing about Simon's conversion (and reversion). Philip is no longer important for what is occurring in Samaria. The circles of the Hellenists and the Twelve disciples touch but do not overlap—a hint as to the history of this particular bit of tradition: the two pieces were secondarily combined but certainly prior to Luke.

Early Church (Nashville/New York: Abingdon, 1969) 159–74.

13 Bauernfeind.

14 Dibelius, *Studies,* 17; Bauernfeind; Haenchen, pp. 307–8.

15 Haenchen, p. 303.

<table>
<tr><td rowspan="2">**8**</td><td>**The Annexation of the New Church</td></tr>
<tr><td>to the Earliest Congregation and
Peter's Clash with Simon Magus**</td></tr>
</table>

14	Now when the apostles at Jerusalem heard that Samaria had received the word of God, they sent to them Peter and John, 15/ who came down and prayed for them that they might receive the Holy Spirit; 16/ for it had not yet fallen on any of them, but they had only been baptized in the name of the Lord Jesus. 17/ Then they laid their hands on them and they received the Holy Spirit. 18/ Now when Simon saw that the Spirit was given through the laying on of the apostles' hands, he offered them money, 19/ saying, "Give me also this power, that anyone on whom I lay my hands may receive the Holy Spirit." 20/ But Peter said to him, "Your silver perish with you, because you thought you could obtain the gift of God with money! 21/ You have neither part nor lot in this matter, for your heart is not right before God. 22/ Repent therefore of this wickedness of yours, and pray to the Lord that, if possible, the intent of your heart may be forgiven you. 23/ For I see that you are in the gall of bitterness and in the bond of iniquity." 24/ And Simon answered, "Pray for me to the Lord, that nothing of what you have said may come upon me."
25	Now when they had testified and spoken the word of the Lord, they returned to Jerusalem, preaching the gospel to many villages of the Samaritans.

■ **14** In the Lukan portrayal of the Christian mission the establishment of a congregation (in the capital) represents the conversion of that province. The apostles function as a supervisory body. Yet, their authority in the concrete does not appear as jurisdiction, but as the authority to ordain. Luke knows nothing specific about the activity of the two. There must necessarily be two, but once again John's role is peripheral.[1]

■ **15** ὅστις, "whoever," takes the place of the simple relative ὅς, "who," as in 17:10.[2]

■ **16** The picture of a baptism without receiving the Spirit does not come from an ancient non- or pre-pneumatic understanding of baptism. This is an ad hoc construction (cf. 10:44–48; 19:1–7) which presupposes precisely the intimate connection between baptism and the Spirit. The point here is not the idea of baptism, but an understanding of the church: the Samaritan church is legitimate if it has been sanctioned by Jerusalem.

■ **17** The laying on of hands must have been customary at baptism, even if Tertullian is the first to state it explicitly (*Bapt.* 8).[3]

■ **18–24** These verses offer the first detailed example of

---

1   On this passage, see Eduard Schweizer, "πνεῦμα," *TDNT* 6 (1968) 414–15; Nikolaus Adler, *Taufe und Handauflegung: Eine exegetisch-theologische Untersuchung von Apg 8,14–17* (NTAbh 19:3; Münster: Aschendorff, 1951); Gerhard Delling, *Die Taufe im Neuen Testament* (Berlin: Evangelische Verlagsanstalt, 1963).

2   Albert Debrunner, *Grundfragen und Grundzüge des nachklassischen Griechisch,* vol. 2 of Otto Hoffmann, *Geschichte der griechischen Sprach* (Sammlung Göschen 114; Berlin: de Gruyter, 1954) 66–67.

3   See the excursus on 1 Tim 4:14 in Dibelius-Conzelmann, *Pastoral Epistles,* 70–71; Klein ("Synkretismus," 40–82, reprinted in his *Rekonstruktion,* 262–301) holds a different view. He argues that Luke struggles here not against magic, but against syncre-

the Lukan distinction between miracle and magic.[4]

■ **18** The narrator does not consider that theoretically Simon must also be a bearer of the Spirit. Wickedness can stifle even the Spirit!

■ **19** We would expect that he would want to buy the power to work miracles, not the power to impart the Spirit.[5] That must have been what the story originally said. Luke appears to have changed this, after careful reflection (note the involved expression here).

■ **20** An apostolic curse; compare $\pi\alpha\rho\alpha\delta\acute{\iota}\delta\omega\mu\acute{\iota}$ $\sigma\epsilon$ $\epsilon\grave{\iota}s$ $\tau\grave{o}$ $\mu\acute{\epsilon}\lambda\alpha\nu$ $\chi\acute{\alpha}os$ $\grave{\epsilon}\nu$ $\tau\alpha\hat{\iota}s$ $\grave{\alpha}\pi\omega\lambda\epsilon\acute{\iota}\alpha\iota s$ ("I deliver you into the black chaos in perdition"),[6] and $\epsilon\hat{\iota}\nu\alpha\iota$ $\epsilon\grave{\iota}s$ $\grave{\alpha}\pi\acute{\omega}\lambda\epsilon\iota\alpha\nu$, "perish" (Dan 2:5 [Th]; cf. 3:96 [Th]).

■ **21** For $\mu\epsilon\rho\acute{\iota}s/\kappa\lambda\hat{\eta}\rho os$, "part/lot," compare Deut 12:12, etc.; Col 1:12. On "your heart is not right before God," compare Ps 78(77):37.

■ **22** With this verse the curse appears to be conditional (without taking seriously the possibility of Simon's repentance). This is a word directed to the reader as general instruction about magic. $\epsilon\grave{\iota}$ $\check{\alpha}\rho\alpha$, "if possible," maintains God's freedom, in the style of Jewish penitential piety (cf., e.g., Dan 4:27).

■ **23** For $\epsilon\grave{\iota}s$ $\chi o\lambda\grave{\eta}\nu$ $\pi\iota\kappa\rho\acute{\iota}\alpha s$, "in the gall of bitterness," compare Deut 29:17 LXX.[7] A comparison with the paraphrase of the Deuteronomy passage in 1QS 2.11–12 is instructive.[8] For $\kappa\alpha\grave{\iota}$ $\sigma\acute{\upsilon}\nu\delta\epsilon\sigma\mu o\nu$ $\grave{\alpha}\delta\iota\kappa\acute{\iota}\alpha s$, "and (in the) bond of iniquity," see Isa 58:6.

■ **24** This verse documents the powerlessness of the magician before the one who bears the Spirit.

■ **25** The verse is a literary connective. The story breaks off: Luke does not report Simon's apostasy nor could he make the well-known rival into a Christian!

---

tism within the church. Yet Luke certainly avoids any hint of such difficulties within the church.

4   On this theme, cf. Tertullian *Apol.* 22.11–12; Ps.-Clem. *Hom.* 2.33–34; A. Fridrichsen, *The Problem of Miracle in Primitive Christianity* (Minneapolis: Augsburg, 1972) 89–95; Hermann Schlingensiepen, *Die Wunder des Neuen Testaments: Wege und Abwege ihrer Deutung in der alten Kirche bis zur Mitte des fünsten Jahrhunderts* (BFCTh: Sammlung Wissenschaftlicher Monographien 28; Gütersloh: Bertelsmann, 1933) 62–73; F. Pfister, "Epode," PWSup 4.325, 342–43.

5   Bauernfeind.

6   *PGM* 1.114 (IV 1247–48); see *The Greek Magical Papyri in Translation*, vol. 1, *Texts* (ed. Hans Dieter Betz; Chicago/London: University of Chicago, 1986) 62.

7   For the construction $\epsilon\hat{\iota}\nu\alpha\iota$ $\epsilon\grave{\iota}s$, "(you) are in" (different from vs 20), see BDF § 145.1

8   Otto Betz, *Offenbarung und Schriftforschung in der Qumransekte* (Tübingen: Mohr [Siebeck], 1960) 170–76 (on Deut 29:17–20 with 1QS 2.11–18).

8 The Conversion of an Ethiopian Official

26 But an angel of the Lord said to Philip, "Rise and go toward the south [or: at noon] to the road that goes down from Jerusalem to Gaza." This is a desert road. 27/ And he rose and went. And behold, an Ethiopian, a eunuch, a minister of the Candace, queen of the Ethiopians, in charge of all her treasure, had come to Jerusalem to worship 28/ and was returning; seated in his chariot, he was reading the prophet Isaiah. 29/ And the Spirit said to Philip, "Go up and join this chariot." 30/ So Philip ran to him, and heard him reading Isaiah the prophet, and asked, "Do you understand what you are reading?" 31/ And he said, "How can I, unless some one guides me?" And he invited Philip to come up and sit with him. 32/ Now the passage of the scripture which he was reading was this:

"As a sheep led to the slaughter
or a lamb before its shearer is dumb,
so he opens not his mouth.
33/ In his humiliation justice was denied him.
Who can describe his generation?
For his life is taken up from the earth."

34/ And the eunuch said to Philip, "About whom, pray, does the prophet say this, about himself or about some one else?" 35/ Then Philip opened his mouth, and beginning with this scripture he told him the good news of Jesus. 36/ And as they went along the road they came to some water, and the eunuch said, "See, here is water! What is to prevent my being baptized?" 38/ And he commanded the chariot to stop, and they both went down into the water, Philip and the eunuch, and he baptized him. 39/ And when they came up out of the water, the Spirit of the Lord caught up Philip; and the eunuch saw him no more, and went on his way rejoicing. 40/ But Philip was found at Azotus, and passing on he preached the gospel to all the towns till he came to Caesarea.

The story was apparently told in Hellenistic circles as the first conversion of a Gentile (cf. Ps 68[67]:32). The story thus rivals the account of Cornelius's conversion in chapters 10—11. Luke has placed the story here so that it now functions as a prelude to Cornelius's conversion. It is a self-contained episode and does not presuppose 8:4–25. We get the impression that Philip was originally not sent out from Samaria, but from Jerusalem. The style is markedly legendary.[1] The motif of miraculous divine guidance dominates, thereby making the significance of the first conversion all the more impressive.

■ **26** For ἄγγελος κυρίου, "angel of the Lord," compare 5:19–20. The order is given in biblical language. κατὰ μεσημβρίαν means either "toward the south" (Dan 8:4, 9 LXX)[2] or "at noon" (22:6). The objection to the latter interpretation, that no traveling took place in that region at midday because of the heat, does not hold; this depends on the time of year (cf. 10:9; 22:6). ἔρημος, "desert," refers to the road not to the city of Gaza, despite the note in Strabo 16.759 (which he took from a source): "but (Gaza) was razed to the ground by Alexander and remains uninhabited" (κατεσπασμένη δ᾽ ὑπὸ Ἀλεξάνδρου καὶ μένουσα ἔρημος). The intention here is not to describe a place, but simply to furnish some scenic detail.[3] There is no need to ask which of the possible roads from Jerusalem to Gaza Luke has in mind.[4] This statement is not part of the angel's speech—it is Luke's explanation.[5]

■ **27** Note that the carrying out of the order is reported by repeating the verbs; this is biblical style (Gen 43:13–15, etc.). "Ethiopia" was the kingdom of Napata-Meroe, which occupied both the fantasy and politics of that time; Luke certainly has no geographical or ethnological interest in the area. The territory was usually ruled by kings, but occasionally by queens.[6] Candace is a title. Note Pliny *Nat. hist.* 6.186: "They said that it is ruled by a woman, Candace, a name that has passed on through a succession of queens for many years" (regnare feminam Candacen, quod nomen multis iam annis ad reginas

transiit).[7] In Jer 34:19 = 41:19 LXX סרים, "eunuch," is translated by δυνάστης, "court official." Nevertheless εὐνοῦχος, "eunuch," as used here does not refer to a position (that would be δυνάστης), but to one who has been castrated. Eunuchs are mentioned as γαζοφύλακες, "treasurers," among the Persians (Plutarch *Demetr.* 25.900).[8] Luke purposely leaves the religious status of the eunuch vague. Apparently he did not venture to describe him as a proselyte because of what he found in his sources; he could not let him appear as a Gentile, because the Gentile mission really begins in chapter 10.

■ **28** The treasurer was reading aloud, following the ancient custom.[9]

■ **29** The intervention of the Spirit cannot be distinguished from that of the angel (vs 26; cf. chap. 10).

■ **30** For the paronomasia, compare 2 Cor 3:2. The interrogative particle ἆρά (γε) is found only in the writings of Paul and Luke in the New Testament.

■ **31** The potential optative with ἄν is unusual.[10] The risen Christ opens up the understanding of the Scriptures for the church (Luke 24:25–27, 44–49). The central content of the Scriptures is "that the Christ should suffer and rise from the dead" (παθεῖν τὸν χριστὸν καὶ ἀναστῆναι ἐκ νεκρῶν, Luke 24:46; cf. vs 26). On this basis the quotation from Isaiah has been selected; in doing so, it takes up neither the title "servant of the Lord" nor the idea of atonement from Isaiah 52—53.

■ **32–33** The quotation cites Isa 53:7–8 (verbatim). The conclusion of 53:8 ("stricken for the transgression of my people") is omitted because it is anticlimactic if αἴρειν, "taken up," is understood as referring to the exaltation.[11]

1   Dibelius, *Studies*, 15.
2   So Erwin Preuschen, *Die Apostelgeschichte* (HNT 4:1; Tübingen: Mohr [Siebeck], 1912); Haenchen, p. 310.
3   W. K. Clarke (*Beginnings* 2.101) cites Zeph 2:4—3:10 for comparison.
4   On this, see C. Kuhl, "Römische Straken und Strakenstationen in der Umgebung von Jerusalem," *PJ* 24 (1928) 113–40.
5   W. C. van Unnik ("Der Befehl an Philippus," *ZNW* 47 [1956] 181–91) has a different view. He reads the text to mean that the command is deliberately paradoxical: the missionary is sent from flourishing success into the "desert" as a test of his obedience.
6   Henry J. Cadbury, *The Book of Acts in History* (New York: Harper, 1955) 15–18.
7   See also Strabo 17.280; Ps.-Callisth. 3.18ff.
8   On the historical circumstances, see Stephan Lösch,

    "Der Kämmerer der Königin Kondake (Apg. 8,27)," *ThQ* 111 (1930) 477–519.
9   Cadbury, *Acts in History*, 18, 30 n. 29; Betz, *Lukian*, 2 n. 6.
10   See BDF § 385; for the future indicative after ἐάν, see § 373.2.
11   Erich Fascher, *Jesaja 53 in christlicher und jüdischer Sicht* (Aufsätze und Vorträge zur Theologie und Religionswissenschaft 4; Berlin: Evangelische Verlagsanstalt, 1958) 8.

The context of the quotation is not considered. To what extent did Luke take into account the meaning of this partially incomprehensible passage? We cannot say. He may have interpreted the "taking away of justice" as referring to the resurrection.

■ **34** The verse formulates a fundamental problem of early Christian hermeneutics (cf. Justin *Dial.* passim). The eunuch asks the questions which the ideal non-Christian Bible reader *should* ask, but which only the Christian reader *can* ask.[12]

■ **35** For ἀρξάμενος, "beginning," compare Luke 24:27; for the content of the sermon, compare 5:42 and 17:18.[13]

■ **36** Philip's well lies between Eleutheropolis and Ashkelon, according to the *Itinerarium Antoninianum* 32; another tradition locates it near Ain Dirweh, on the road between Jerusalem and Hebron.[14] Cullmann sees in τί κωλύει, "What is to prevent," a component of the baptismal ritual[15] (cf. 10:47; 11:17; Matt 3:14; Ps.-Clem. *Hom.* 13.5.1, 11.2).

■ **(37)** Western textual witnesses (E gig p sy[h]; cf. Irenaeus *Adv. haer.* 3.12.8) contain an additional verse, which approximates the baptismal rite (baptismal confession): "And Philip said, 'If you believe with all your heart, you may.' And he replied, 'I believe that Jesus Christ is the Son of God.'" Its secondary nature is confirmed by the variants to 11:17.

■ **39** This is the stylistically proper conclusion for the legend[16] (cf. 2 Kgs 2:16; Ezek 11:24; *Gos. Heb.* frg. 3).[17] The reading found in A p sy[h], etc., πνεῦμα ἅγιον ἐπέπεσεν ἐπὶ τὸν εὐνοῦχον· ἄγγελος δὲ κυρίου ἥρπασεν τὸν Φίλιππον, "the Holy Spirit fell on the Eunuch, and an angel of the Lord caught up Philip," is a secondary assimilation to vs 26; was its motivation anti-Gnostic?[18]

■ **40** This verse apparently results from Luke's editing of reports about Philip's stay in Caesarea (21:8). Again, Philip and Peter are in the same area, but their paths do not cross.

---

12 On the application of the passage to the prophet himself, see Joachim Jeremias, "παῖς θεοῦ," *TDNT* 5 (1967) 686.

13 For ἀνοίξας, "(Philip) opened his mouth,," see the commentaries on Matt 5:2.

14 C. Kuhl, "Römische Straken und Strakenstationen in der Umgebung von Jerusalem," *PJ* 24 (1928) 116 n. 4; Peter Thomsen, *Loca Sancta: Verzeichnis der im 1. bis 6. Jahrhundert n. Chr. erwahnten Ortschaften Palastinas mit besonderer Berücksichtigung der Lokalisierung der biblischen Statten* (Halle: Haupt, 1907; reprinted Hildesheim: Olms, 1966) 34, under Bethsura.

15 Oscar Cullmann, *Baptism in the New Testament* (SBT 1; London: SCM, 1950; reprinted Naperville, IL: Allenson, 1956) 71–80.

16 Martin Dibelius, "Zur Formgeschichte des Neuen Testaments (ausserhalb der Evangelien)," *ThR* n.s. 3 (1931) 235.

17 *NTApoc.* 1.164.

18 Eduard Schweizer ("πνεῦμα," *TDNT* 6 [1968] 409) offers a somewhat different interpretation. He provides parallels to the miraculous snatching away; cf. also Philostratus *Vita Apoll.* 8.10.

9

The Conversion of Paul:
The First Account

1   But Saul, still breathing threats and murder
     against the disciples of the Lord, went to
     the high priest 2/ and asked him for
     letters to the synagogues at Damascus,
     so that if he found any belonging to the
     Way, men or women, he might bring
     them bound to Jerusalem. 3/ Now as he
     journeyed he approached Damascus, and
     suddenly a light from heaven flashed
     about him. 4/ And he fell to the ground
     and heard a voice saying to him, "Saul,
     Saul, why do you persecute me?" 5/ And
     he said, "Who are you, Lord?" And he
     said, "I am Jesus, whom you are perse-
     cuting; 6/ but rise and enter the city, and
     you will be told what you are to do." 7/
     The men who were traveling with him
     stood speechless, hearing the voice but
     seeing no one. 8/ Saul arose from the
     ground; and when his eyes were opened,
     he could see nothing; so they led him by
     the hand and brought him into Damas-
     cus. 9/ And for three days he was with-
     out sight, and neither ate nor drank.

10   Now there was a disciple at Damascus
     named Ananias. The Lord said to him in a
     vision, "Ananias." And he said, "Here I
     am, Lord." 11/ And the Lord said to him,
     "Rise and go to the street called Straight,
     and inquire in the house of Judas for a
     man of Tarsus named Saul; for behold, he
     is praying, 12/ and he has seen in a vision
     a man named Ananias come in and lay
     his hands on him so that he might regain
     his sight." 13/ But Ananias answered,
     "Lord, I have heard from many about this
     man, how much evil he has done to thy
     saints at Jerusalem; 14/ and here he has
     authority from the chief priests to bind all
     who call upon thy name." 15/ But the
     Lord said to him, "Go, for he is a chosen
     instrument of mine to carry my name
     before the Gentiles and kings and the
     sons of Israel; 16/ for I will show him
     how much he must suffer for the sake of
     my name." 17/ So Ananias departed and
     entered the house. And laying his hands
     on him he said, "Brother Saul, the Lord
     Jesus who appeared to you on the road
     by which you came, has sent me that you
     might regain your sight and be filled with
     the Holy Spirit." 18/ And immediately
     something like scales fell from his eyes
     and he regained his sight. Then he rose
     and was baptized, 19a/ and took food
     and was strengthened.

The intent of the composition is clear: Before the first conversion of a Gentile the agent for the great mission to the Gentiles is prepared, whereby once again the meaning of both the preceding and the following episodes is clarified.

■ **1–19a** Saul's Call

■ **1** ὁ δέ, "but," connects with 8:3. For ἐμπνέω, "breathing," see Ps 18 (17):16; Euripides *Bacc.* 620, of the persecutor Pentheus: "breathing fury" (θυμὸν ἐκπνέων).

■ **2** The spread of Christianity to Damascus is simply assumed. We see how many gaps there are in the story as given in Acts. Connections between Christians in Damascus and the sectarians who produced the Damascus document cannot be demonstrated.[1] Contrary to Acts, Paul did not proceed from Jerusalem to Damascus. In regard to the Jews in Damascus, see Josephus *Bell.* 2.559–61 and 7.368. Luke gives no account of the (actual) legal situation. He mentions neither the Nabateans[2] nor that the city belongs to the Decapolis (Pliny *Nat. hist.* 5.74). In defense of the historicity of the portrait Luke sketches (the right of the Sanhedrin to make an arrest outside Palestine, or the right to demand extradition), reference is made to 1 Macc 15:16–21. However, the genuineness of the letter referred to in 1 Maccabees has been disputed.[3] Even if it is genuine, it lays down no permanent regulations, but is concerned only with fugitives. Its validity for Syria during the Roman period is completely out of the question. Moreover, Josephus *Bell.* 1.474 offers counterevidence. Compare also the legal situation which Paul himself assumes in 2 Cor 11:32.

Acts exhibits a unique use of the word ὁδός, "Way" (19:9, 23; 22:4; 24:14, 22), which denotes Christian teaching as well as Christians as a group. This sense cannot be derived from the Greek background of the word.[4] The Qumran texts offer something of an analogy (though not with this pregnant meaning); for example, 1QS 9.17b–20; 8.13–18, 21.[5]

■ **3** Appearances of light are part of the apparatus of epiphanies. Luke avoids saying that Paul saw the figure of the Lord (despite vs 5; contrast *Acts Thom.* 34; *Acts John* 97; *4 Macc.* 4.10).

■ **4** Compare *4 Macc.* 3.27. In vs 7 and also in 22:7 ἀκούειν, "to hear," is used with the genitive, while here it appears with the accusative; there is no difference in meaning.[6] Paul is addressed by the Hebrew form of his name (26:14); for the repetition of the name, compare 1 Sam 3:4, 6 LXX, etc. When the disciples are persecuted, the Lord himself is persecuted (Luke 10:16; cf. Euripides *Bacc.* esp. 784–91). Gerhard Lohfink compares the theophany dialogues of the Old Testament and of Judaism to the course of the conversion here (Gen 31:11–13; 46:2–3; Exod 3:4–10; *Jub.* 44.5; *Jos. Asen.* 14.6–8, etc.).[7]

■ **5** The question is formulated in view of the ἐγώ εἰμι, "I am," of the one who appears in the vision.

■ **6** In contrast to Gal 1:12–13 Paul does not learn of the gospel in the vision itself. He is directed to the church, which is the mediator of this teaching.

■ **7** Compare Maximus of Tyre 9 (15 Dübner) 7d–f: "In this place sailors often saw a young man with yellow hair leaping in golden armor. Some by no means saw him, but heard him singing the song of victory; others both saw and heard" (Εἶδον ἤδη ναῦται πολλάκις ἄνδρα ἠίθεον, ξανθὸν τὴν κόμην, πηδῶντα ἐν ὅπλοις. τὰ ὅπλα χρυσᾶ. οἱ δὲ εἶδον μὲν οὐδαμῶς, ἤκουσαν δὲ παιωνίζοντος. οἱ δὲ καὶ εἶδον καὶ ἤκουσαν).

The parallel accounts contain a number of differences in detail. The intention is on the one hand to establish Paul's companions as witnesses,[8] but on the other hand to reserve the appearance to Paul alone. For similarities

---

1   CD! Jean Daniélou, "L'Étoile de Jacob et la mission chrétienne à Damas," *VC* 11 (1957) 121–38.

2   See the excursus on 2 Cor 11:32 in Hans Lietzmann, *An die Korinther I / II* (HNT 9; Tübingen: Mohr [Siebeck], 1969) 152.

3   K. D. Schunck, *Die Quellen des 1. und 2. Makkabäerbuches* (Halle [Saale]: Niemeyer, 1954) 32ff.

4   On this, see Werner Jaeger, *The Theology of the Early Greek Philosophers* (Oxford: Clarendon, 1947; reprinted 1960) 98–100.

5   S. Vernon McCasland, "The Way," *JBL* 77 (1958) 222–30; Eero Repo, *Der "Weg" als Selbstbezeichnung*

des Urchristentums: Eine traditionsgeschichtliche und semasiologische Untersuchung (Annales Academiae Scientiarum Fennicae ser. B, vol. 132:2; Helsinki: Suomalainen Tiedeakatemia, 1964).

6   Horst R. Moehring, "The Verb AKOYEIN in Acts IX 7 and XXII 9," *NovT* 3 (1959) 80–99.

7   Gerhard Lohfink, "Eine alttestamentliche Darstellungsform für Gotteserscheinungen in den Damaskusberichten (Apg 9: 22, 26)," *BZ* n.s. 9 (1965) 246–57.

8   For ἐνεός, "speechless," see BAG *s.v.*

in wording, but not in meaning, compare Deut 4:12; Dan 10:7; Wis 18:1.

■ **8** The blinding is not a punishment, but indicates the helplessness of one formerly so powerful (22:11).

■ **9** Paul's abstention from food and drink can be understood as a consequence of the vision, or as an act of repentance and a preparation for baptism (*Did.* 7.4; Justin *Apol.* 1.61; Tertullian *Bapt.* 20).

■ **10** Ananias is thought of as a converted Jew (cf. 22:12). For the motif of corresponding visions, see chapter 10. It seems artificial that information about the others is given in the vision. This is the stylistic consequence of the double vision.[9] The double dream became a typical motif found in fictional literature.[10]

■ **11** Events attach themselves to well-known places. "Straight" street was the main street running from east to west (today the street lies further to the north).

■ **12** For the combination prayer and vision, compare Luke 1:10–11; 3:21; 9:28–36; Acts 10:3, 30; 22:17. ἐν ὀράματι, "in a vision," after ἄνδρα, "man," as in B and C, is to be preferred as the more difficult reading.

■ **13–14** The reply of Ananias is "incomprehensible"[11] only if one starts out from the psychological condition of the man. His hesitation actually serves to emphasize the incredible nature of this conversion (vss 15–16). Both verses are redactional. οἱ ἐπικαλούμενοι κτλ., "who call upon, etc.," had already become a technical designation of Christians by Paul's time (1 Cor 1:2).

■ **15** For the expression σκεῦος ἐκλογῆς, "chosen instrument," compare Jer 50:25 = 27:25 LXX; Ps.-Clem. *Recog.* 3.49: Simon has become "a choice vessel for the wicked one" (vas electionis maligno). The program as outlined here is carried out item by item. The reference to kings (Luke 21:12) is not unusual, even in the time of the empire.[12] Does the expression "to carry my name before," intend to describe Paul as a witness and to answer the question of where he will bear testimony? Or does it picture him as a missionary and seek to describe the destination of his calling? The former is closer to general usage. If it is preferred, the story here would be not about a calling, but about a conversion. In this case a pre-Lukan wording would be visible.[13]

■ **17** We are not to ask how Ananias now knows about Paul's vision. This time the conferring of the Spirit is reported only indirectly.

■ **18** The verse reflects a popular conception of being healed from blindness (cf. Tob 11:12).[14]

Excursus: Paul's Call

There are two more accounts of Paul's call, in 22:1–16 and 26:9–18. The three versions are generally in agreement, but there are differences and even contradictions in details. Does this mean that Luke used various sources?[15] No. The repetition is for stylistic reasons,[16] and the differences can be explained as literary variations (and, in part, as carelessness); they are linked with the adaptation of the material for the particular situation. The source is not an autobiographical account of an experience (for this reason a psychological explanation is wrongheaded), but a legend, with typical features.[17] The features include: the appearance of light, a falling down (Ezek 1:28), and the limitation of the appearance exclusively to the one

---

9   Alfred Wikenhauser, "Doppelträume," *Bib* 29 (1948) 100–111; *Herm. Vis.* 3.1.2; Dionysius Halic. 1.57.4; Josephus *Ant.* 11.327, 333–34; Valerius Maximus 1.7.3; Apuleius *Met.* 11.27; etc.

10   Karl Kerényi, *Die griechisch-orientalische Romanliteratur in religionsgeschichtlicher Beleuchtung* (Tübingen: Mohr [Siebeck], 1927; reprinted, with additions by the author, Darmstadt: Wissenschaftliche Buchgesellschaft, 1962) 166–67.

11   Preuschen.

12   See the comment of Nicholas of Damascus in *FGH* 90 frg. 137.2. On the relation of this perspective to Paul's own, see Olaf Linton, "The Third Aspect: A Neglected Point of View: A Study in Gal. i–ii and Acts ix and xv," *StTh* 3 (1949) 79–95.

13   See the excursus below.

14   See the commentary on 13:11. ἀναβλέπειν: for the

meaning "regain sight," see BAG *s.v.*

15   Emanuel Hirsh, "Die drei Berichte der Apostelgeschichte über die Bekehrung des Paulus," *ZNW* 28 (1929) 305–12.

16   Ernst von Dobschütz, "Die Berichte über die Bekehrung des Paulus," *ZNW* 29 (1930) 144–47.

17   Friedrich Smend, "Untersuchungen zu den Acta-Darstellungen von der Bekehrung des Paulus," *Angelos* 1 (1925) 34–45; Hans Windisch, "Die Christusepiphanie vor Damaskus (Act 9, 22 und 26) und ihre religionsgeschichtlichen Parallelen," *ZNW* 31 (1932) 1–23; Alfred Wikenhauser, "Doppelträume," *Bib* 29 (1948) 100–111; idem, "Die Wirkung der Christophanie vor Damaskus auf Paulus und seine Begleiter nach den Berichten der Apostelgeschichte," *Bib* 33 (1952) 313–23.

for whom the vision is intended (Maximus of Tyre [see above, vs 7]; Apollonius Rhod. *Arg.* 4.852; Philo *Exsecr.* 165). The appearance serves first of all not to convert a sinner, but to put down the persecutor. Compare especially the Heliodorus legend in 2 Macc 3:28–29 and the motifs of Euripides' *Bacc.,* though there is no question of any literary dependence upon the latter.[18] Nor is there a close relationship to the Heliodorus legend. There the persecutor is thrown down, but not converted. *Jos. Asen.* offers further comparative material for the conversion. Christoph Burchard sees two layers of meaning in this material: the first, a pre-Lukan, which tells the story as Paul's conversion to be a witness; the second, a Lukan over-lay, which sees the events as Paul's call to be a mission-ary. The latter interpretation is impressed upon the second (Acts 22) and especially the third version of Paul's conversion (Acts 26).[19]

It is important to note that Luke has not assimilated this event to the Easter appearance of Jesus. He distinguishes this vision fundamentally from those appearances—contrary to what Paul himself does. Through this experience Paul does not become an apostle. There is no anti-Pauline tendency operating here. Luke is simply yielding to the constraints of his salvation-historical scheme. Paul is *the* connecting link between the apostolic time and Luke's own time. As such, he is incorporated into the existing church (which is represented by Ananias). This same emphasis then governs vss 26–30.[20] The significance of this vision is stressed by its repetition.[21]

---

18   See the commentary on 26:9–18.
19   Burchard, *Der dreizehnte Zeuge,* 59–88.
20   Klein, *Die zwölf Apostel,* 144–59.
21   Literature:
     Beginnings 5.188–95.
     Klein, *Die zwölf Apostel,* 120–27, 144–59.
     Johannes Munck, "La vocation de l'Apôtre Paul," *StTh* 1 (1948) 131–45.
     William Prentice, "St. Paul's Journey to Damascus," *ZNW* 46 (1955) 250–55.
     Gillis P. Wetter, "Die Damaskusvision und das paulinische Evangelium," *Festgabe für Adolf Jülicher* (Tübingen: Mohr [Siebeck], 1927) 80–92.
     H. G. Wood, "The Conversion of St Paul: Its Nature, Antecedents and Consequences," *NTS* 1 (1954–55) 276–82.

On geographical matters:
Eric F. Bishop, "The Great North Road," *TToday* 4 (1947–48) 383–99.
On "conversion" in antiquity in general:
Burchard, *Der dreizehnte Zeuge.*
Gerhard Lohfink, *The Conversion of St. Paul: Narrative and History in Acts* (Herald Scriptural Library; Chicago: Franciscan Herald Press, 1976).
Arthur Darby Nock, *Conversion: The Old and the New in Religion from Alexander the Great to Augustine of Hippo* (Oxford: Clarendon, 1933).

9

Saul's Appearance in Damascus and His Escape

19b For several days he was with the disciples at Damascus. 20/ And in the synagogues immediately he proclaimed Jesus, saying, "He is the Son of God." 21/ And all who heard him were amazed, and said, "Is not this the man who made havoc in Jerusalem of those who called on this name? And he has come here for this purpose, to bring them bound before the chief priests." 22/ But Saul increased all the more in strength, and confounded the Jews who lived in Damascus by proving that Jesus was the Christ.

23 When many days had passed, the Jews plotted to kill him, 24/ but their plot became known to Saul. They were watching the gates day and night, to kill him; 25/ but his disciples took him by night and let him down over the wall, lowering him in a basket.

■ **19b** According to the plan of Acts Paul cannot yet turn to the Gentiles, because the Gentile mission has not yet been sanctioned. On the other hand, he ought not to remain inactive: the effects of his conversion must be demonstrated. In fact, at this point Paul went to Arabia (Gal 1:17), and his mission there may have been the reason for the Nabatean plot against him (2 Cor 11:32). Luke skips over these things (was it because he did not know about them?). Thus he needs a new motive for the hostile action against Paul.

■ **20** The summary of the sermon is in accord with a common confessional formula. On the Son of God title, compare Luke 22:67–71.[1]

■ **21** For πορθεῖν, "to make havoc of," see Gal 1:13, 23. Menoud would understand the word in a purely moral sense and exclude the actual shedding of blood: it does not mean persecution through actions, but through preaching.[2]

■ **22** χριστός, "Christ," is used throughout Acts as a title.[3]

■ **23** The fulfillment of vs 16 is announced by way of a concrete illustration. A comparison with Galatians shows that this is an abridged account.

■ **25** Compare 2 Cor 11:33; Josh 2:15 (Josephus *Ant.* 5.15); Poseidonius.[4] λαμβάνειν, "to take," is used pleonastically here.[5] The αὐτοῦ, "his," with μαθηταί, "disciples" (P[74] B ℵ A C) is difficult to understand here, and runs counter to Lukan usage. Is this a scribal error (for αὐτόν, which would then read, "the disciples took him")? Compare 14:20 D (E).

1   Conzelmann, *Theology,* 171–72; Wilckens, *Missions-reden,* 177.

2   Philippe H. Menoud, "The Meaning of the Verb πορθεῖν (Gal. 1:13, 23; Acts 9:21)," *Jesus Christ and the Faith,* 47–60.

3   Conzelmann, *Theology,* 170–84; Wilckens, *Missions-reden,* 156–63.

4   For the latter, see *FGH* 87 frg. 36.

5   BAG *s.v.* λαμβάνω.

9 Saul in Jerusalem (and Tarsus)

26 And when he had come to Jerusalem he attempted to join the disciples; and they were all afraid of him, for they did not believe that he was a disciple. 27/ But Barnabas took him, and brought him to the apostles, and declared to them how on the road he had seen the Lord, who spoke to him, and how at Damascus he had preached boldly in the name of Jesus. 28/ So he went in and out among them at Jerusalem, 29/ preaching boldly in the name of the Lord. And he spoke and disputed against the Hellenists; but they were seeking to kill him. 30/ And when the brethren knew it, they brought him down to Caesarea, and sent him off to Tarsus.

31 So the church throughout all Judea and Galilee and Samaria had peace and was built up; and walking in the fear of the Lord and in the comfort of the Holy Spirit it was multiplied.

■ **26** As in verse 19b, this verse also abridges the time span and in so doing creates a false impression (Gal 1:17–24). The historical Paul maintains his own independence, while the Lukan Paul is linked to and legitimized by Jerusalem (cf. further 22:17–21).[1]

■ **27** Luke apparently concluded from the later cooperation of Barnabas and Paul that Barnabas was the intermediary. The account here should not be assimilated to Gal 1:18–19.

■ **28-29** The conflict with Galatians is even greater here (cf. Gal 1:22). The entire description contains no concrete material. Paul appears as the one who steps into the gap left by the death of Stephen.

■ **30** The time spent in Tarsus serves as a pause. In fact, Paul carried on missionary activity there for more than a dozen years (Gal 2:1). But in Luke's view, the foundation for that activity must first be laid. Tarsus at this time was a famous cultural center (see Strabo 14.673 and the speeches of Dio Chrysostom to the people of Tarsus).[2]

■ **31** This is a Lukan summary; compare 2:47. ἐκκλησία, "church" (singular), here means the church as a whole (cf. 20:28). καὶ Γαλιλαίας, "and Galilee," is surprising, because no account of a mission there has been given. But this was also the case with Damascus, and besides, Galilee was the area where Jesus had worked (Acts 10:37). The geographical picture which Luke sketches is actually incorrect, though it corresponds to that of Pliny *Nat. hist.* 5.70: "Beyond Idumaea and Samaria stretches the wide expanse of Judaea. The part of Judaea adjoining Syria is called Galilee" (supra Idumaeam et Samariam Iudaea longe lateque funditur. pars eius Syriae iuncta Galilaea vocatur). According to this, Galilee would have been directly connected to Judea.[3]

1   J. Cambier, "Le voyage de S. Paul à Jerusalem en Act. IX. 26ss. et le schéma missionnaire théologique de S. Luc," *NTS* 8 (1961–62) 249–57.

2   Hans Böhlig, *Die Geisteskultur von Tarsus im augusteischen Zeitalter mit Berücksichtigung der paulinischen Schriften* (FRLANT n.s. 19; Göttingen: Vandenhoeck & Ruprecht, 1913); David Magie, *Roman Rule in Asia Minor to the End of the Third Century after Christ* (2 vols.; Princeton: Princeton University, 1950; reprinted New York: Arno, 1975) 2.1146–48.

3   Conzelmann, *Theology,* 68–69.

9
**Peter Heals Aeneas
and Raises Tabitha**

32   Now as Peter went here and there among them all he came down also to the saints that lived at Lydda. 33/ There he found a man named Aeneas, who had been bed-ridden for eight years and was paralyzed. 34/ And Peter said to him, "Aeneas, Jesus Christ heals you; rise and make your bed." And immediately he rose. 35/ And all the residents of Lydda and Sharon saw him, and they turned to the Lord.

36   Now there was at Joppa a disciple named Tabitha, which means Dorcas. She was full of good works and acts of charity. 37/ In those days she fell sick and died; and when they had washed her, they laid her in an upper room. 38/ Since Lydda was near Joppa, the disciples, hearing that Peter was there, sent two men to him entreating him, "Please come to us without delay." 39/ So Peter rose and went with them. And when he had come, they took him to the upper room. All the widows stood beside him weeping, and showing tunics and other garments which Dorcas made while she was with them. 40/ But Peter put them all outside and knelt down and prayed; then turning to the body he said, "Tabitha, rise." And she opened her eyes, and when she saw Peter she sat up. 41/ And he gave her his hand and lifted her up. Then calling the saints and widows he presented her alive. 42/ And it became known throughout all Joppa, and many believed in the Lord. 43/ And he stayed in Joppa for many days with one Simon, a tanner.

The "instrument" is ready. Now the mission to the Gentiles must get under way, proceeding, naturally, from Jerusalem. These two local legends serve as connecting links. In comparison with the Synoptic miracle stories they are stylistically polished; nevertheless, the typical elements (as in 3:1–10) can still be recognized.

■ **32** This is not a missionary journey, but an inspection tour (cf. 8:14–25). Nothing is said about Philip's presence here (8:40; 21:8). Once again, the original independence of these traditions is apparent. πάντων, "all," can refer either to people or places. Lydda (Diospolis) lies on the road from Jerusalem to Joppa, about three hours distant from Joppa.[1]

■ **33–34** In ancient miracle stories names are almost entirely lacking. The old elements of the miracle story still shine through: length of the illness and a healing word (on the relationship between the healing Christ and the human mediator, cf. 3:6, 12, 16). Moreover, στρῶσον σεαυτῷ, "make your bed," serves as the demonstration that healing has taken place (cf. Mark 2:11).[2]

■ **35** The effect upon the observers comes next, following the style of the miracle story.[3] For ἐπιστρέφειν κτλ., "to

---

1   Schürer, *History* 2.190–98; *DB* 4.444–47.

2   Rudolf Bultmann, *The History of the Synoptic Tradition* (New York/Evanston: Harper, 1963) 224–25; for another opinion, see *Beginnings* 4.109, where Lake and Cadbury take the expression to mean "set the table for yourself," i.e., "get yourself something to eat." But the passage where this translation should apply speaks against it, Ezek 23:41: "and sat on a

made bed, and before it a table had been set" (καὶ ἐκάθου ἐπὶ κλίνης ἐστρωμένης, καὶ τράπεζα κεκοσμημένη πρὸ προσώπου αὐτῆς).

3   Rudolf Bultmann, *The History of the Synoptic Tradition* (New York/Evanston: Harper, 1963) 225–26.

turn, etc.," see 11:21 (cf. 2 Cor 3:16). Sharon is the coastal plain near Joppa and Caesarea. On this form of description (the conversion of the whole region), compare 8:14.

■ **36** This account of the raising of a dead person originally circulated independently, as the beginning indicates. Secondary stylistic features can be detected: the name (see above) and the pious characterization of Tabitha. Old Testament prototypes are incorporated (cf. 1 Kgs 17:17–24; 2 Kgs 4:32–37). The portrayal of the apostle is assimilated to the picture of Jesus as miracle worker (according to sayings like Matt 10:8).[4] In regard to Joppa, see Strabo 16.759 (with a false conception of its distance to Jerusalem) and Josephus *Bell.* 3.419–20. Tabitha is טָבִיתָא or טְבִיתָא; compare צְבִיָא, "Zibia," in 1 Chr 8:9; צִבְיָה, "Zibiah," in 2 Kgs 12:2; 2 Chr 24:1. Both the Aramaic and the Greek word for "Gazelle" were used as names. The expression αὕτη ἦν κτλ., "She was, etc.," conflates two ideas: "she was full of good works" and "she did good works."[5]

■ **37** Washing of the corpse was a common ancient custom (cf. Lucian *De luctu* 11).[6] For ὑπερῷον, "upper room," see 1 Kgs 17:17–24.

■ **38** ἐγγύς, "near," that is, about three hours distant. Compare the use of δύο, "two," here with 10:7.

■ **39** The ritual of mourning for the dead here is psychologically motivated. The widows do not appear as a social class, but as poor people (cf. 6:1–6).

■ **40** Compare 2 Kgs 4:33 and Mark 5:40. The words which bring about the rising from the dead—טְבִיתָא קוּם, "Tabitha cum," "Tabitha, rise"—recall the words in Mark 5:41, טְלִיתָא קוּם, "Talitha cum," "Little girl . . . arise." In Luke 8:54, however, the author chose not to use the Aramaic. For Peter's action here, compare 2 Kgs 4:35; for the demonstration, compare Luke 7:15. ἀνιστάναι, "to rise," is a technical term for the resurrection from the dead (Lucian *Alex.* 24; *Philops.* 26).[7]

■ **41** The original meaning of the gesture (it brings about healing) has been lost.

■ **42** Compare vs 35.

■ **43** The fact that tanners were despised by the rabbis has no significance here.[8]

---

4   On the tendency to portray the thaumaturge as self-sufficient, deemphasizing the external source of his power, see Bihler, *Theios Aner* 2.28.

5   Haenchen, p. 339.

6   J. J. Wettstein, Η ΚΑΙΝΗ ΔΙΑΘΗΚΗ: *Novum Testamentum Graecum* (2 vols.; Amsterdam, 1751–52) 2.515; Betz, *Lukian*, 72.

7   Betz, *Lukian*, 161 n. 3; for comparative material

from Philostratus, see the commentary on 5:12–16.

8   Str-B 2.695.

10

The First Gentile Conversion
(through Peter)

1 At Caesarea there was a man named Cornelius, a centurion of what was known as the Italian Cohort, 2/ a devout man who feared God with all his household, gave alms liberally to the people, and prayed constantly to God. 3/ About the ninth hour of the day he saw clearly in a vision an angel of God coming in and saying to him, "Cornelius." 4/ And he stared at him in terror, and said, "What is it, Lord?" And he said to him, "Your prayers and your alms have ascended as a memorial before God. 5/ And now send men to Joppa, and bring one Simon who is called Peter; 6/ he is lodging with Simon, a tanner, whose house is by the seaside." 7/ When the angel who spoke to him had departed, he called two of his servants and a devout soldier from among those that waited on him, 8/ and having related everything to them, he sent them to Joppa.

9 The next day, as they were on their journey and coming near the city, Peter went up on the housetop to pray, about the sixth hour. 10/ And he became hungry and desired something to eat; but while they were preparing it, he fell into a trance 11/ and saw the heaven opened, and something descending, like a great sheet, let down by four corners upon the earth. 12/ In it were all kinds of animals and reptiles and birds of the air. 13/ And there came a voice to him, "Rise, Peter; kill and eat." 14/ But Peter said, "No, Lord; for I have never eaten anything that is common or unclean." 15/ And the voice came to him again a second time, "What God has declared clean, you must not call common." 16/ This happened three times, and the thing was taken up at once to heaven.

17 Now while Peter was inwardly perplexed as to what the vision which he had seen might mean, behold, the men that were sent by Cornelius, having made inquiry for Simon's house, stood before the gate 18/ and called out to ask, "Is Simon, also called Peter, staying here?" 19/ And while Peter was pondering the vision, the Spirit said to him, "Behold, three men are looking for you. 20/ Rise and go down, and accompany them without hesitation; for I have sent them." 21/ And Peter went down to the men and said, "I am the one you are looking for; what is the reason for your coming?" 22/ And they said, "Cornelius, a centurion, an upright and God-fearing man, who is well spoken of by the whole Jewish nation, was directed by a holy angel to send for you to

come to his house, and to hear what you have to say." 23/ So he called them in to be his guests.

The next day he rose and went off with them, and some of the brethren from Joppa accompanied him. 24/ And on the following day they entered Caesarea. Cornelius was expecting them and had called together his kinsmen and close friends. 25/ When Peter entered, Cornelius met him and fell down at his feet and worshiped him. 26/ But Peter lifted him up, saying, "Stand up; I too am a man." 27/ And as he talked with him, he went in and found many persons gathered; 28/ and he said to them, "You yourselves know how unlawful it is for a Jew to associate with or to visit any one of another nation; but God has shown me that I should not call any man common or unclean. 29/ So when I was sent for, I came without objection. I ask then why you sent for me?"

30   And Cornelius said, "Four days ago, about this hour, I was keeping the ninth hour of prayer in my house; and behold, a man stood before me in bright apparel, 31/ saying, 'Cornelius, your prayer has been heard and your alms have been remembered before God. 32/ Send therefore to Joppa and ask for Simon who is called Peter; he is lodging in the house of Simon, a tanner, by the seaside.' 33/ So I sent to you at once, and you have been kind enough to come. Now therefore we are all here present in the sight of God, to hear all that you have been commanded by the Lord."

34   And Peter opened his mouth and said: "Truly I perceive that God shows no partiality, 35/ but in every nation any one who fears him and does what is right is acceptable to him. 36/ You know the word which he sent to Israel, preaching good news of peace by Jesus Christ (he is Lord of all), 37/ the word which was proclaimed throughout all Judea, beginning from Galilee after the baptism which John preached: 38/ how God anointed Jesus of Nazareth with the Holy Spirit and with power; how he went about doing good and healing all that were oppressed by the devil, for God was with him. 39/ And we are witnesses to all that he did both in the country of the Jews and in Jerusalem. They put him to death by hanging him on a tree; 40/ but God raised him on the third day and made him manifest; 41/ not to all the people but to us who were chosen by God as witnesses, who ate and drank with him after [God] raised him from the dead. 42/ And he commanded us to preach to the people, and to testify that he is the one ordained by God to be judge of the living

and the dead. **43/ To him all the prophets bear witness that every one who believes in him receives forgiveness of sins through his name.**

44 **While Peter was still saying this, the Holy Spirit fell on all who heard the word. 45/ And the believers from among the circumcised who came with Peter were amazed, because the gift of the Holy Spirit had been poured out even on the Gentiles. 46/ For they heard them speaking in tongues and extolling God. Then Peter declared, 47/ "Can any one forbid water for baptizing these people who have received the Holy Spirit just as we have?" 48/ And he commanded them to be baptized in the name of Jesus Christ. Then they asked him to remain for some days.**

We begin with a general analysis of this material by looking at the account of the conversion of Cornelius:[1]

Excursus:
The Cornelius Story

The present form of the story about Cornelius according to which the Gentile mission was inaugurated in a single act (recognized as programmatic from the outset) does not fit the facts. It reflects the Lukan view of history and Luke's concept of the church. Nevertheless there are some indications by which to determine Luke's sources. Literary seams are noticeable. Verses 27–29 prove to be an insertion (vs 30 connects with vs 26). Peter's companions have been added as a secondary element.

Luke found the vision somewhere else (he did not construct it himself)[2] and inserted it here. The original account of the arrival of the messengers in Joppa has been covered over by the redactional connection.[3] Consideration of the content of the vision adds further support: the original intention of the vision does not conform with Luke's use of it. Its original point did not have to do with human relationships (Jews and Gentiles), but with foods—that is, with the issue of clean and unclean (cf. vs 15b). This was an issue present in Jewish Christianity, and goes back to the Jesus tradi-

tion. The vision is an artifice, but pre-Lukan. Luke could incorporate it because at his time the two themes (Jews and Gentiles, foods) were already mixed together.

In general, all passages in this chapter which elevate the singular story into one of principle may be assigned to Luke. These include the transition to the vision, the interpretation of the same in vs 28, Peter's speech, elements of the concluding scene, and above all the repetition in chapter 11, where Luke's intention is clearly expressed. Thus the motif of table fellowship emerges here, and it assumes fundamental significance for the story of Cornelius's conversion.[4] Chapter 11 applies the individual case to the whole of the church (represented by Jerusalem) and then sets forth a general principle; this in turn prepares for chapter 15 (cf. the references back to these events in 15:7, 14).

What is left as a source is a conversion legend in edifying style.[5] This corresponds to the first Gentile conversion through Philip. A historical kernel (Peter's mission in these cities, conversions, tradition about the names of the converted) is not denied but rather assumed. In the composition of Acts as a whole, this story serves as the preparation for chapter 15.[6]

■ **1** Caesarea was refounded by Herod the Great and provided with a manmade harbor (Josephus *Ant.*

1　Dibelius, *Studies,* 109–22; Munck, *Paul,* 228–31; see also the commentaries by Bauernfeind and Haenchen.

2　Contrary to Haenchen, p. 362; see below.

3　Dibelius, *Studies,* 120.

4　Ibid., 114–20.

5　With Dibelius, *Studies,* 13, cf. 109–22, esp. 120; against Haenchen, pp. 360–63.

6　See the commentary on 15:7. On the exegesis of Acts 10:1—11:18 in the ancient church, see François Bovon, *De Vocatione Gentium: Histoire de l'interprétation d'Act. 10, 1–11, 18 dans les six premiers siècles* (BGBE 8; Tübingen: Mohr [Siebeck], 1967; idem, "Tradition et rédaction en Actes 10, 1–11, 18," *ThZ* 26 (1970) 22–45.

15.331–41).[7] In 6 C.E. it became the seat of the Roman procurator and the major garrison of the province. The population was predominantly Gentile (Josephus *Bell.* 3.409).[8] There is evidence for a cohors II Italica civium Romanorum . . . exercitus Syriaci ("Second Italian cohort of Roman citizens belonging to the Syrian army"),[9] or cohors miliaria Italica voluntariorum quae est in Syria ("Italian cohort of one thousand volunteers, which is in Syria"),[10] in Syria(!) from the time before 69 C.E. on into the second century. Only auxiliary troops were quartered in Caesarea (a unit of cavalry, five cohorts of infantry).[11] During the years 41–44 (the administration of Agrippa I, see 12:1–23; Josephus *Ant.* 19.343–52), there were no Roman troops stationed in the city. This is no sure clue for dating this episode, however, because the situation from a different time may have been transferred to this setting. For Luke, Caesarea is the station midway between Jerusalem and Antioch. The name Cornelius is common after the time of Cornelius Sulla (who freed thousands of slaves).

■ **2** The "God-fearers" (cf. σεβόμενος [*RSV*, "devout"] 13:50; "worshiper" 16:14; etc.) were looked upon as Gentiles.[12] On prayer and almsgiving, see Tob 12:8; Matt 6:2–8; *Did.* 15.4. For διὰ παντός, "constantly," see Ps 34 (33):2. ὁ λαός, "the people," is used as a technical term for Israel.

■ **3** The mention of the time of day (cf. the hour of prayer,

3:1) shows the reader that a delusion is excluded.

■ **4** ἀνέβησαν εἰς μνημόσυνον, "ascended as a memorial," is a paraphrase for ἐμνήσθησαν, "were remembered" (vs 31). This is biblical language (cf. Exod 17:14; Sir 35:6; 50:16; Tob 12:12; Mark 14:8).[13]

■ **8** The distance from Caesarea to Joppa amounts to about fifty kilometers.

■ **9–16** Peter's Vision of the Clean and Unclean.

■ **9** Luke does not really make it clear that the messengers could not set out until afternoon. He is probably not thinking of a journey during the night, but of a journey over two days (as in vss 23–24). The sixth hour was the time for lunch.[14] For another example of a vision at midday, see 22:6.

■ **10** For ἔκστασις, "trance," compare 22:17; Gen 15:12; Philo *Rer. div. her.* 264.[15]

■ **12** For the classification of animals, compare Gen 1:24; 6:20; Rom 1:23.

■ **13** θύειν means "kill"—the meaning "sacrifice" does not fit here.[16] The command means eat, without worrying about clean and unclean!

■ **14** Compare Ezek 4:14. κοινός, "common," has the sense "cultically unclean"; this meaning would derive from Greek-speaking Jews.[17]

■ **15** Here the point of the vision is made. ἐκαθάρισεν, "has declared clean" (*RSV*, "has cleansed"), does not mean that the declaration occurs now in the vision. There is no

---

7   Thomas Corbishley ("The Chronology of the Reign of Herod the Great," *JTS* 36 [1935] 29–30) dates the refounding of the city not at 10 but 12 C.E.

8   Leo Haefeli, *Caesarea am Meer: Topographie und Geschichte der Stadt nach Josephus und Apostelgeschichte* (NTAbh 10:5; Münster: Aschendorff, 1923); also see the review of Haefeli by Peter Thomsen in *Philologische Wochenschrift* 45 (1925) cols. 19–20; A. H. M. Jones, *The Cities of the Eastern Roman Provinces* (Oxford: Clarendon, 1937) 273–81; regarding the military, see *Beginnings* 5.441–43.

9   *ILS* 3:2.9168.

10 *CIL* 11.6117.

11 Theodor Mommsen, "Die Conscriptionsordnung der römischen Kaiserzeit," *Hermes* 19 (1884) 217–18, reprinted in his *Gesammelte Schriften* (8 vols.; Berlin: Weidmann, 1905–13) 6.101–2.

12 Str-B 2.715–23; Karl Georg Kuhn, "προσήλυτος," *TDNT* 6 (1968) 740–44.

13 W. C. van Unnik, "De achtergrond en betekenis van Handelingen 10:4 en 35," *NedThT* 3 (1948–49) 260–83, 336–54; idem, "Kanttekeningen bij een nieuwe

verklaring van de anamnese-woorden," *NedThT* 4 (1949–50) 369–77; Joachim Jeremias, "Mc 14:9," *ZNW* 44 (1952–53) 105–7, rev. and reprinted in his *Abba*, 117–20, as "Markus 14,9"; idem, *The Eucharistic Words of Jesus* (trans. Norman Perrin from the German 3d ed. with author revisions; New York: Scribner's, 1966) 244–52.

14 PW 3.1895; for Jewish practices, see Str-B 2.204–6.

15 For vs 11, see the commentary on 7:56.

16 For another opinion, see Josef Sint, "Schlachten und Opfern: Zu Apg 10,13; 11,7," *ZKTh* 78 (1956) 194–205.

17 Friedrich Hauck, "κοινός," *TDNT* 3 (1965) 790–91.

reflection about the moment when this declaration was made (cf. the explanation in 15:9; 1 Tim 4:4).[18]

■ **17-33 The First Gentile Conversion (continued)**
■ **17** This verse is a literary seam which marks the transition from the vision to the narrative into which Luke has incorporated it (see the analysis above). Luke intends that the narrative action interpret the vision for the reader. For literary reasons, Peter does not discover the meaning of the vision until later (vs 28). For τί ἂν εἴη, "what (the vision which he had seen) might mean," compare 5:24. On πυλών, "gate," see the commentary on 12:13.
■ **18** εἰ Σίμων κτλ. should be understood as a direct question, "Is Simon, also called Peter, staying here?"
■ **19** For "three men," the various manuscripts have three or two, or omit the number (cf. vs 7 and 11:11). The intervention of the Spirit in this passage is artificial.
■ **20** With ἀλλά (before an imperative)[19] Luke is already leading up to the sense of μηδὲν διακρινόμενος, "without hesitation."
■ **22** τὸ ἔθνος τῶν Ἰουδαίων, "the Jewish nation," appears in documents as an official designation (see 1 Macc 10:25; 11:30, 33; Josephus *Ant.* 14.248; etc.).[20]
■ **23** Here we see the first results of the divine instructions. When it came to relationships with non-Jews,[21] Jewish practice certainly did not coincide with theory (cf. to a degree Josephus *Ant.* 20.34–53). In the Diaspora, relationships with non-Jews were apparently not avoided in principle. The accompanying brethren serve as witnesses (cf. 11:12); this is an official action of the church.[22]
■ **24** ἀναγκαῖος means "close" when used of relatives and friends.[23]
■ **25** The Western text has an expansion, which was initiated by a misunderstanding of εἰσελθεῖν, "to enter"

(taking it to mean entering the city, as in vs 24, rather than the house): προσεγγίζοντος δὲ τοῦ Πέτρου εἰς τὴν Καισάριαν προδραμὼν εἰς τῶν δούλων διεσάφησεν παραγεγονέναι αὐτόν. ὁ δὲ Κορνήλιος ἐκπηδήσας καὶ . . . , "And as Peter was drawing near to Caesarea, one of the servants ran ahead and announced that he had arrived. And Cornelius jumped up and . . ." Falling down before someone is a favorite motif of the apocryphal acts of the apostles[24] (cf. 28:6). Here the motif is taken up in order to be rejected.[25]
■ **26** Compare 14:15 and 3:12. This is not a matter of "exemplary humility,"[26] but is rather an established motif (for a counterpart, see 28:6). On ἄνθρωπος, "man," compare, for a contrast, 12:22–23. Philip of Macedon ordered that someone say to him each morning, "Philip, you are a man" (Φίλιππε, ἄνθρωπος εἶ; Aelian *Var. hist.* 8.15).
■ **27-29** These verses are a Lukan insertion, evident in that they presuppose the vision. Following after vs 25, the situation seems artificial (συνομιλῶν, "as he talked with"). Here Luke gives *his* interpretation of the ὅραμα, "vision."[27]
■ **30** The wording here is impossible because two statements have been combined in a confusing manner: a reference to the vision four days ago at the ninth hour has been combined with the statement that Cornelius has been continually at prayer for four days (vs 2). Luke more often uses the periphrastic subjunctive with προσεύχεσθαι, "to pray." D (ἀπὸ τῆς τρίτης ἡμέρας, "Three days ago") smoothed the text over, introduced the three-day fast before baptism, and perhaps adjusted the date in the light of vss 9 and 24.
■ **34-43 Peter's Speech**
The speech follows the usual structure, but the kerygma is expanded into an outline of the "gospel."[28]

---

18 For πάλιν ἐκ δευτέρου, "again a second time" (LXX; see the commentaries on Matt 26:42), and ἐπὶ τρίς, "three times" (vs 16), see the comments of Harald Riesenfeld, "Lagercrantz' Beiträge zum N.T.," *ConNT* 3 (1939) 24.
19 See BDF § 448.3; and BAG *s.v.*
20 On χρηματίζεσθαι, "to be directed," see the commentaries on Matt 2:12.
21 For the Jewish view of relationships with non-Jews, see Str-B 4.374–75; cf. John 18:28.
22 See further on vs 37.
23 BAG *s.v.*

24 Söder, *Die apokryphen Apostelgeschichten*, 95ff.
25 For ἐγένετο with the genitive of the articular infinitive, see BDF § 400.7.
26 Haenchen, p. 350.
27 See the commentary on vs 23.
28 Ulrich Wilckens, "Kerygma und Evangelium bei Lukas (Beobachtungen zu Acta 10:34–43)," *ZNW* 49 (1958) 223–37.

■ **34–35** These verses establish the connection with the context and introduce a scriptural passage. On the subject under discussion, compare Rom 2:10–11. Peter's words should not be understood as abstract reflection about the possibility of attaining salvation apart from Christian preaching (although analogous considerations may already be found in Judaism).[29] Rather, what we have here is reflection from within the Christian community about the fundamental possibility of a mission to the Gentiles (vs 36b should be kept in mind), as the context already indicates.

■ **36–41** The kerygma is given here in particularly detailed form. The grammar of this section is rough; it seems to be a collection of smaller units (with doublets?).

■ **36** Compare Ps 107 (106):20 and Acts 13:26. Grammatically speaking, this is not a properly constructed sentence (the *RSV* smooths it over). If need be, ὅν, "which," could be eliminated (as dittography with the preceding λόγ-ον) and this would yield a sentence; however, the tendency toward the use of relative clauses in the "kerygma" argues for the originality of the ὅν. If we understand τὸν λόγον, "the word," as the object of οἴδατε, "you know" (vs 37), the doublet with τὸ ῥῆμα, "the word," in vs 37 seems even more objectionable. διὰ Ἰησοῦ Χριστοῦ, "by Jesus Christ," should be connected with εὐαγγελιζόμενος, "preaching good news" (compare Luke 4:16–19). "Peter" makes a connection with the preaching of Jesus, which means that Luke connects it to his "gospel."

πάντων κύριος, "Lord of all," is an expression found in classical religions (Pindar *Isthm.* 5.35: "Zeus, the Lord of all" [Ζεὺς ὁ πάντων κύριος]),[30] as well as Hellenistic (at the birth of Osiris a voice sounds, "The Lord of all advances to the light" [ὡς ὁ πάντων κύριος εἰς φῶς πρόεισιν] Plutarch *Is. et Osir.* 355e). The expression has also passed over into Judaism[31] (Wis 6:7; 8:3, etc.); Hecataeus refers to the God of Moses as τῶν ὅλων κύριος, "Lord of all."[32] But the expression is also used politically, as in Epictetus 4.1.12: "Caesar, the lord of all" (ὁ πάντων κύριος Καῖσαρ). Our passage is not yet cosmologically oriented. It is dealing with the universality of salvation for all peoples (supplementing vs 35).

■ **37–38** Verse 37 parallels vs 36 (they are concurrent transitions to the christological topic).[33] ὑμεῖς οἴδατε, "you know" (*RSV* places this in vs 36), is surprising, because the audience is made up of non-Jews from outside Jerusalem. This is simply part of the stereotyped scheme.[34] The content of the ῥῆμα, "word," is specifically Lukan: the "beginning from Galilee" after John's baptism, the extension over "all Judea" (on both style and substance, cf. Luke 23:5; 24:47;[35] on the subject, cf. also 13:24), the "anointing" (Luke 4:16–19; Acts 4:27), and the description of Jesus' works, to which Luke's Gospel provides the commentary. Ἰησοῦν κτλ., "Jesus, etc.," must be construed as part of the ὡς-clause which follows; to see it as the object of οἴδατε, "you know" (vs 37; *RSV* vs 36), and thus as parallel to τὸ ῥῆμα, "the word," would be stretching the grammar to its limit.[36]

The θεῖος ἀνήρ, "divine man," style dominates here. Compare Epictetus 2.16.44, concerning Heracles: "Come, how many acquaintances and friends did he have with him as he went up and down through the whole world? Nay, he had no dearer friend than God. That is why he was believed to be a son of God [Zeus], and was. It was therefore in obedience to His will that he went about clearing away wickedness and lawlessness" (ἄγε, πόσους δὲ περιερχόμενος τὴν οἰκουμένην συνήθεις ἔσχεν, φίλους; ἀλλ᾽ οὐδὲν φίλτερον τοῦ θεοῦ· διὰ τοῦτο ἐπιστεύθη Διὸς υἱὸς εἶναι καὶ ἦν. ἐκείνῳ τοίνυν πειθόμενος περιῄει καθαίρων ἀδικίαν καὶ ἀνομίαν). Also compare fragments of the *Acts of Paul*: "Raising the dead, healing the sick, cleansing lepers, giving sight to the blind, healing the lame, raising up paralytics, purging those possessed by demons" ([νε]κροὺς ἐγείρων καὶ νόσους θεραπεύων κα[ὶ λε]προὺς καθαρίζων, τυφλοὺς θεραπεύω[ν] καὶ κυλλοὺς ἰώμενος, παρ[αλυτι]κοὺς ἐγ[είρων?], δαιμονιζομένους

29   *Beginnings* 5.209; Karl Georg Kuhn, "προσήλυτος," *TDNT* 6 (1968) 741–42.

30   Werner Foerster, "κύριος," *TDNT* 3 (1965) 1047.

31   Richard Wünsch, "Deisidaimoniaka," *ARW* 12 (1909) 39; *Beginnings* 5.361–62.

32   *FGH* 264 frg. 6.

33   See Dibelius, *Studies*, 111 n. 5.

34   Wilckens (*Missionsreden*, 67) offers a different interpretation: Luke allows the brethren (vs 23) to accompany Peter to make such a point of contact possible. Now he can permit those assembled to be addressed as a gathering of Christians called together by God (from Jews and Gentiles).

35   See the comment on Acts 1:22 in *Beginnings* 4.14.

36   διῆλθεν, "he went around": on the complexive (constative) aorist, see BDF § 332.1.

$\kappa\alpha\theta\alpha[\rho i\zeta\omega\nu])$.[37] But one also senses the influence of Ps 107 (106):20 (vs 36) in the $i\dot\omega\mu\epsilon\nu$os, "healing." For $\epsilon\dot\nu\epsilon\rho\gamma\epsilon\tau\hat\omega\nu$, "doing good," compare the predicate of Hellenistic rulers (Luke 22:25, RSV "benefactors") and, to a degree, the picture of the "benefactor" in Philostratus Vita Apoll. 8.7. In the passage from Plutarch Is. et Osir. which is mentioned above, a variant to the voice at the birth of Osiris reads "a mighty and beneficent king, Osiris, had been born" ($\mu\dot\epsilon\gamma\alpha$s $\beta\alpha\sigma\iota\lambda\epsilon\dot\upsilon$s $\epsilon\dot\upsilon\epsilon\rho\gamma\dot\epsilon\tau\eta$s $"O\sigma\iota\rho\iota$s $\gamma\dot\epsilon\gamma o\nu\epsilon$). The word $\epsilon\dot\upsilon\epsilon\rho\gamma\dot\epsilon\tau\eta$s never means to give alms, but rather to render assistance.[38] The conclusion to vs 38 evidences the Lukan subordinationist Christology.

■ **39** The concept of eyewitnesses comes from Luke ($\pi\dot\alpha\nu\tau\omega\nu$ $\kappa\tau\lambda$., "all, etc.," is explained by 1:21–22). For $\kappa\rho\epsilon\mu\dot\alpha\sigma\alpha\nu\tau\epsilon$s, "hanging," compare 5:30.

■ **40** With the word $\dot\epsilon\mu\phi\alpha\nu\dot\eta$s, "manifest," the stress is not on the element of visibility, but rather on the fact that he appeared. D ($\mu\epsilon\tau\dot\alpha$ $\tau\dot\eta\nu$ $\tau\rho i\tau\eta\nu$ $\dot\eta\mu\dot\epsilon\rho\alpha\nu$, "after the third day") conflates the expressions "on the third day" and "after three days" (D tends toward the latter, Matt 16:21; 17:23; Luke 9:22). The expression "on the third day" (or "after three days") belongs to the early kerygma (1 Cor 15:4). There have been a number of attempts to explain it: (1) The first appearance took place on the third day. (2) "Three" is a typical number; the soul lingers in the grave three days, etc.; these analogies, however, are vague. (3) On the third day the empty tomb was discovered.[39] (4) The date has been taken from Scripture; Hos 6:2 is the text in question (or Gen 22:4).[40]

■ **41** "Eating and drinking" (1:4?; Luke 24:30, 42–43) certified the reality of the resurrection (the $\sigma\dot\alpha\rho\xi$, "flesh," in Luke 24:39). $\dot\alpha\nu\alpha\sigma\tau\hat\eta\nu\alpha\iota$ is ambiguous: is it transitive ("after [God] raised him from the dead") or intransitive ("after he rose from the dead")? Luke has apparently taken the word (with intransitive meaning) from the

tradition, but has understood it as transitive, in the sense of a subordinationist Christology; compare the analogous $\dot\alpha\nu\alpha\sigma\tau\dot\eta\sigma\alpha$s $\alpha\dot\upsilon\tau\dot o\nu$ $\dot\epsilon\kappa$ $\nu\epsilon\kappa\rho\hat\omega\nu$, "by raising him from the dead," in 17:31 and $\tau o\hat\upsilon\tau o\nu$ $\dot o$ $\theta\epsilon\dot o$s $\dot\eta\gamma\epsilon\iota\rho\epsilon\nu$, "God raised him," in vs 40.[41]

■ **42** For the schema consisting of salvation—events—witnesses—proclamation, compare Luke 24:45–49. The initial limitation of preaching to Israel ($\tau\hat\omega$ $\lambda\alpha\hat\omega$, "to the people") corresponds to the "necessary" course of salvation history (13:46). For Luke's view of the judgment, compare 17:31. In both passages the emphasis is only on the reality of judgment, not on its imminence.[42]

■ **43** After the earlier speeches, scriptural proof can now simply be referred to. For "all," compare 3:24. The concluding condition for salvation is formulated in an emphatically universalistic manner, in accord with the situation (cf. vs 35 and 13:39). A call to repent is lacking, but it would be unnecessary with this audience.

■ **44–48** The First Gentile Conversion (concluded)

■ **44** An interruption occurs and with that the speech concludes. Despite the formal contradiction with 11:15, both passages are Lukan redactional constructions. The coming down of the Spirit before baptism (cf. its counterpart in 8:15–17) is an ad hoc construction: heaven itself points the way to the admission of the "Gentiles."

■ **45** $\dot\epsilon\pi\dot\iota$ $\tau\dot\alpha$ $\dot\epsilon\theta\nu\eta$, "on the Gentiles," is a deliberately general formulation.[43]

■ **47** For $\kappa\omega\lambda\dot\upsilon\epsilon\iota\nu$, "to forbid," compare 8:36 and 11:17.

■ **48** Here an interval is created during which the people in Jerusalem can learn about these events. Peter himself does not baptize. This corresponds to what has become the traditional view of the apostle in Luke's day: The apostle is above those office bearers who are responsible for baptizing (cf. the description in Acts 8:14–17).

37 Pap. Mich. 1317:8–12, ed. Henry A. Sanders, "A Fragment of the Acta Pauli in the Michigan Collection," HTR 31 (1938) 80.

38 See Hendrik Bolkestein, Wohltätigkeit und Armenpflege im vorchristlichen Altertum: Ein Beitrag zum Problem "Moral und Gesellschaft" (Utrecht: Oosthoek, 1939; reprinted New York: Arno, 1979) 98–102; for synonyms, compare Pollux 5.140.

39 Hans von Campenhausen, Tradition and Life in the Early Church: Essays and Lectures in Church History (Philadelphia: Fortress, 1968) 42–89.

40 Hans Grass, Ostergeschehen und Osterberichte (2d ed.;

Göttingen: Vandenhoeck & Ruprecht, 1962) 134–38; Karl Lehmann, Auferweckt am dritten Tag nach der Schrift: Früheste Christologie, Bekenntnisbildung und Schriftauslegung im Lichte von 1 Kor 15, 3–5 (Quaestiones Disputatae 38; Freiburg/Basil/Vienna: Herder, 1968).

41 See Wilckens, Missionsreden, 138–39.

42 Erich Grässer, Das Problem der Parusieverzögerung in den synoptischen Evangelien und in der Apostelgeschichte (2d ed.; BZNW 22; Berlin: Töpelmann, 1960) 210.

43 For "speaking in tongues and extolling God" (vs 46), see the commentary on 2:11; 19:6.

11 Peter's Report in Jerusalem

1 Now the apostles and the brethren who were in Judea heard that the Gentiles also had received the word of God. 2/ So when Peter went up to Jerusalem, the circumcision party criticized him, 3/ saying, "Why did you go to uncircumcised men and eat with them?" 4/ But Peter began and explained to them in order: 5/ "I was in the city of Joppa praying; and in a trance I saw a vision, something descending, like a great sheet, let down from heaven by four corners; and it came down to me. 6/ Looking at it closely I observed animals and beasts of prey and reptiles and birds of the air. 7/ And I heard a voice saying to me, 'Rise, Peter; kill and eat.' 8/ But I said, 'No, Lord; for nothing common or unclean has ever entered my mouth.' 9/ But the voice answered a second time from heaven, 'What God has cleansed you must not call common.' 10/ This happened three times, and all was drawn up again into heaven. 11/ At that very moment three men arrived at the house in which we were, sent to me from Caesarea. 12/ And the Spirit told me to go with them, making no distinction. These six brethren also accompanied me, and we entered the man's house. 13/ And he told us how he had seen the angel standing in his house and saying, 'Send to Joppa and bring Simon called Peter; 14/ he will declare to you a message by which you will be saved, you and all your household.' 15/ As I began to speak, the Holy Spirit fell on them just as on us at the beginning. 16/ And I remembered the word of the Lord, how he said, 'John baptized with water, but you shall be baptized with the Holy Spirit.' 17/ If then God gave the same gift to them as he gave to us when they [or: we] believed in the Lord Jesus Christ, who was I that I could withstand God?" 18/ When they heard this they were silenced. And they glorified God, saying, "Then to the Gentiles also God has granted repentance unto life."

This section is a redactional repetition. As Haenchen points out, "The speech . . . is comprehensible only to the readers of the book, not to Peter's audience in Jerusalem."[1] Note, for example, vs 13! Here the significance of the baptism of the Gentiles is spelled out as a matter of principle for the life of the church. The formulation of

1   Haenchen, p. 355.

the theme in vs 3 points ahead to chapter 15.

■ **1** For $\tau\grave{\alpha}$ $\check{\epsilon}\theta\nu\eta$, "the Gentiles," compare 10:45. The Western text connects vs 1 with the preceding and begins vs 2 with $\acute{o}$ $\mu\grave{\epsilon}\nu$ $o\check{\upsilon}\nu$, "Therefore [Peter]," and extends the journey.

■ **2** $\grave{\alpha}\nu\alpha\beta\alpha\acute{\iota}\nu\epsilon\iota\nu$, "to go up," is the term for travel to Jerusalem (cf. the corresponding $\kappa\alpha\tau\acute{\epsilon}\rho\chi\epsilon\sigma\theta\alpha\iota$, "to come down," of 9:32). For Luke $o\acute{\iota}$ $\grave{\epsilon}\kappa$ $\pi\epsilon\rho\iota\tau o\mu\hat{\eta}s$, "the circumcision party," is not a group, but the whole Jerusalem congregation; they are so designated here in order to point to the problem.

■ **3** $\check{o}\tau\iota$ introduces direct discourse (but not in P⁴⁵ B 33).[2]

■ **5** $\check{\alpha}\chi\rho\iota$ $\grave{\epsilon}\mu o\hat{\upsilon}$, "to me," is only an attempt to be more vivid than $\grave{\epsilon}\pi\grave{\iota}$ $\tau\hat{\eta}s$ $\gamma\hat{\eta}s$, "upon the earth" (10:11).

■ **6** For $\theta\eta\rho\acute{\iota}\alpha$, "beasts of prey," alongside $\tau\epsilon\tau\rho\acute{\alpha}\pi o\delta\alpha$, "animals," compare Gen 1:24–25.

■ **14** For "all your household," compare 16:15, 31–32; 18:8; 1 Cor 1:16.

■ **15** The contradiction with 10:44 does not result from using various sources, but rather from the way in which the account is put together. The intent in both cases is the same, namely, to indicate the divine initiative. For Luke speaking in tongues is identical with "prophecy." $\grave{\epsilon}\nu$ $\grave{\alpha}\rho\chi\hat{\eta}$, "at the beginning," is used in a technical sense.[3]

■ **16** This verse is a Lukan retrospective (as in Luke 22:61; 24:6), pointing back to 1:5, with an expression which apparently originally belonged to paraenetic tradition (*1 Clem.* 13.1; 46.7; Polycarp *Phil.* 2.3).

■ **17** The argument assumes the firm connection between baptism and the Spirit. Eduard Schweizer believes that the quotation in vs 16b makes sense only if no water baptism followed, or if it was at least not essential.[4] On the contrary! $\pi\iota\sigma\tau\epsilon\acute{\upsilon}\sigma\alpha\sigma\iota\nu$, "believed," can relate to $\alpha\grave{\upsilon}\tauo\hat{\iota}s$, "when they believed,"[5] or to $\grave{\eta}\mu\hat{\iota}\nu$, "when we believed,"[6] or to both.[7] In support of the first possibility, the text speaks not of the apostles' coming to faith some time ago, but of the present coming to faith of these Gentiles (cf. 10:43).[8]

■ **18** For $\delta o\hat{\upsilon}\nu\alpha\iota$ $\mu\epsilon\tau\acute{\alpha}\nuo\iota\alpha\nu$, "to grant repentance," compare 5:31.[9]

2 For this use ($\check{o}\tau\iota$ *recitativum*), see BDF § 470.1.

3 Hans Conzelmann, "'Was von Anfang war,'" *Neutestamentliche Studien für Rudolf Bultmann* (ed. Walther Eltester; BZNW 21; Berlin: Töpelmann, 1954) 196 nn. 10, 11.

4 Eduard Schweizer, "$\pi\nu\epsilon\hat{\upsilon}\mu\alpha$," *TDNT* 6 (1968) 413.

5 Preuschen.

6 Wendt.

7 Bauernfeind; Haenchen, p. 355.

8 For $\pi\iota\sigma\tau\epsilon\acute{\upsilon}\epsilon\iota\nu$ $\grave{\epsilon}\pi\acute{\iota}$, "to believe in," with the accusative, see Rudolf Bultmann, "$\pi\iota\sigma\tau\epsilon\acute{\upsilon}\omega$," *TDNT* 6 (1968) 210–11.

9 See the commentary on 5:31.

11   The Church Spreads to Antioch:
                                     The First Mixed Congregation

19   **Now those who were scattered because of the persecution that arose over Stephen traveled as far as Phoenicia and Cyprus and Antioch, speaking the word to none except Jews. 20/ But there were some of them, men of Cyprus and Cyrene, who on coming to Antioch spoke to the Greeks also, preaching the Lord Jesus. 21/ And the hand of the Lord was with them, and a great number that believed turned to the Lord. 22/ News of this came to the ears of the church in Jerusalem, and they sent Barnabas to Antioch. 23/ When he came and saw the grace of God, he was glad; and he exhorted them all to remain faithful to the Lord with steadfast purpose; 24/ for he was a good man, full of the Holy Spirit and of faith. And a large company was added to the Lord. 25/ So Barnabas went to Tarsus to look for Saul; 26/ and when he had found him, he brought him to Antioch. For a whole year they met with the church, and taught a large company of people; and in Antioch the disciples were for the first time called Christians.**

According to Harnack, an Antioch-Jerusalem source lay behind this material.[1] To it may be assigned 6:1—8:4; 11:19–30; 12:25(13:1)—15:35 (the authority behind this material was Silas). The view of Jeremias is similar (an Antiochene source to which he also assigns 9:1–30, but not 15:1–33).[2] According to Bultmann, vs 19 may be the continuation of the sentence in 8:4, which has been broken off: "Now those who were scattered traveled as far as . . ."[3] It is clear that Luke had access to written source material concerning Antioch (13:1–3). But if this consisted of a continuous Antiochene chronicle we would expect more concrete material, and that the mission history would encompass a larger area (including Syria and Cilicia) from the perspective of Antioch. Thus Dibelius envisioned a Lukan adaptation of various accounts while Bauernfeind spoke of the anecdotal character of the material.[4] It is clear that Luke has extensively reworked the material.

■ **19–20** Here we encounter Luke's mission terminology[5]

and his schema: first to the Jews, then to the Gentiles. Pre-Lukan material appears in vs 20, since the details do not fit in with Luke's conception of the historical sequence. Taken by itself, this verse says that the Hellenists take the first step toward a Gentile mission (the sense of the passage here demands the reading Ἕλληνας, "Greeks," at the end of vs 20, rather than Ἑλληνιστάς, "Hellenists"). It knows nothing about Peter and Cornelius, and nothing at all of the fundamental significance of that episode.

The mission on Cyprus does not fit with 13:4–12. The source for this information also manifests itself in 4:36 and 13:1. Luke has used the information here because it could now be seen in the light of 10:1—11:18. Characteristically, there is no evidence for an inner Hellenizing of Christianity, nor of the problem of the coexistence of Jewish and Gentile Christians in the same congregation

1   Harnack, *Acts*, 201.
2   Jeremias, "Quellenproblem," 213–20, reprinted in his *Abba*, 247–54.
3   Bultmann, "Quellen," 77–78 = *Exegetica*, 422.
4   Dibelius, *Studies*, 11; Bauernfeind.
5   Bauernfeind.

(Gal 2:11–21); by Luke's time such problems belonged to the past. The borders of Φοινίκη, "Phoenicia," are given in a variety of ways, a result of the frequent changes in administration; thus Pliny counts Joppa as part of this territory (*Nat. hist.* 5.69), and Strabo (16.749, 760) includes Philistia (corresponding to the division made by Pompey).[6] The significance of Antioch on the Orontes (Strabo 16.750; Josephus *Bell.* 3.29; Jews in Antioch: *Bell.* 7.41–62)[7] as a center for the early church is only hinted at in the sources.[8]

■ **21** For χείρ, "hand," compare 2 Sam 3:12 LXX.

■ **22** Compare 8:14. In Luke's view the apostles did not travel to foreign countries (but cf. Gal 2:11–12!); this was the task of the legates. Apparently Luke's account here grows out of his concept of the church and is assembled from reports about the activity of Barnabas in Jerusalem and in Antioch. On the phrase ἠκούσθη δὲ ὁ λόγος εἰς τὰ ὦτα τῆς ἐκκλησίας, "News of this came to the ears of the church," compare Isa 5:9 LXX.[9]

■ **23** Note the paronomasia χάρις—ἐχάρε, "grace—he was glad." For τῇ προθέσει τῆς καρδίας, "with steadfast purpose," compare Ps 10:17 Symm (= 9:38 LXX).

■ **24a** This is a typical Lukan substantiation (Luke 1:6; 2:25; 23:50; Acts 6:3), just as vs 24b is a typical note about the expansion of the church (cf. 2:47).

■ **25** We get the impression that the time since Paul's trip to Tarsus (9:30) is short (contrary to the actual facts, Gal 1:18; 2:1); this compressing of time fits ancient style. Luke may have inferred Barnabas's journey from his presence in Antioch and from his subsequent cooperation with Paul.[10]

■ **26** For the sentence construction, compare 22:6.[11]

Excursus:
The Word χριστιανός, **"Christian"**

The word χριστιανός, "Christian," is Latin and indicates in its formation that χριστός, "Christ," was thought of as a proper name, as is the case in the more ancient Roman witnesses: Suetonius *Claud.* 25(?); Tacitus *Ann.* 15.44; Pliny *Ep.* 10.96; Josephus *Ant.* 20.200 (for his Roman readers).[12] It is customarily assumed in the quotation from Tacitus *Ann.* 15.44: "a class of men, loathed for their vices, whom the crowd styled Christians" (quos per flagitia invisos vulgus Chrestianos appellabat).[13] Erik Peterson understands χρηματίζειν as a passive. The name may have been created by the Roman authorities in order to designate the Christians as a political entity, thereby making them liable to punishment under the law.[14] Elias Bickermann conceives of χρηματίζειν as a reflexive: This was a *self*-designation of the Christians, namely, as servants or officers in the kingdom of Christ.[15] However, the phraseology of our passage clearly indicates that this title was given to the "Christians" from outside the group. χρηματίζειν does occur with a passive meaning (Philo *Deus imm.* 121, etc.).[16] We certainly do not have an "official" term here (against Peterson and Bickermann); compare Rom 7:3 and above all Josephus *Ant.* 8.157, where χρηματίζειν is used for the "private" and καλεῖν for the official appellation of Caesar (in Philo *Deus imm.* 121 the two are used synonymously); the meaning is *appellare*, "to name" (Tacitus *Ann.* 15.44). Those who interpret the phrase as official language view our sentence as the report of a definite event, faithfully recorded in official minutes. But Luke would not have recorded an official action against Christians in this way, because it did not fit in

---

6 Gustav Hölscher, *Palästina in der persischen und hellenistischen Zeit: Eine historisch-geographische Untersuchung* (Quellen und Forschungen zur alten Geschichte und Geographie 5; Berlin: Weidmann, 1903) 52–54; on Cyprus, see the commentary on 13:4.

7 *RGG* 1.454; Glanville Downey, *A History of Antioch in Syria: From Seleucus to the Arab Conquest* (Princeton: Princeton University, 1961).

8 Bauer, *Orthodoxy and Heresy*, passim.

9 Nigel Turner, "The Relation of Luke I and II to Hebraic Sources and to the Rest of Luke-Acts," *NTS* 2 (1955–56) 103.

10 On Tarsus, see the commentary on 9:30.

11 See BDF § 409.4.

12 On the form χρηστ- (א*), see the literature cited in BAG *s.v.;* Tertullian *Apol.* 3.5; *Nat.* 1.3; Theophilus

Autol. 1.1; Justin *Apol.* 1.4.3.

13 Harald Fuchs, "Tacitus über die Christen," *VC* 4 (1950) 65–93.

14 Erik Peterson, "Christianus," *Miscellanea Giovanni Mercati. Volume I: Bibbia-Letteratura cristiana antica* (Studi e testi 121; Vatican: Biblioteca Apostolica Vaticana, 1946) 355–72; reprinted in his *Frühkirche, Judentum und Gnosis: Studien und Untersuchungen* (Rome/Freiburg/Vienna: Herder, 1959) 64–87.

15 Elias J. Bickermann, "The Name of Christians," *HTR* 42 (1949) 109–24; reprinted in his *Studies in Jewish and Christian History* (3 vols.; AGJU 9; Leiden: Brill, 1976–86) 3.139–51.

16 *RAC* 2.1131–38.

with his apologetic intention. Rather, he makes reference to the well-known popular name for Christians (cf. 26:28).[17]

---

17 See further J. Moreau, "Le nom des Chrétiens," *La Nouvelle Clio* 1–2 (1949–50) 190–92; C. Cecchelli, "Il nome e la 'setta' dei Cristiani," *Rivista di archeologia cristiana* 31 (1955) 55–73; C. Spicq, "Ce que signifie le titre de chrétien," *StTh* 15 (1961) 68–78.

11 The Prophecy of Agabus and
the Collection for Jerusalem

27 Now in these days prophets came down
from Jerusalem to Antioch. 28/ And one
of them named Agabus stood up and
foretold by the Spirit that there would be
a great famine over all the world; and this
took place in the days of Claudius. 29/
And the disciples determined, every one
according to his ability, to send relief to
the brethren who lived in Judea; 30/ and
they did so, sending it to the elders by the
hand of Barnabas and Saul.

Here again the problem of sources arises, and beyond that the question of the relationship of this section to chapter 15. The particulars given here are more concrete than in the preceding section. The discussion here is not about delegates from Jerusalem, but about free charismatics (cf. 13:1; on wandering prophets: *Did.* 11.7–12). The note about Agabus may be the oldest component of this section; as a whole, it has been shaped by Luke.[1]

■ **28** The Western text (not Irenaeus *Adv. haer.* 3.14.1) has a "we"-passage here: ἦν δὲ πολλὴ ἀγαλλίασις· συνεστραμμένων δὲ ἡμῶν ἔφη εἷς ἐξ αὐτῶν ὀνόματι Ἄγαβος σημαίνων . . . , "And there was much rejoicing; and when we were gathered together one of them named Agabus spoke. . . ." Bultmann defends it as original, because there is no motive for a secondary insertion.[2] But there is—namely, the later identification of Luke with Lucius in 13:1! (cf. Ephraem's commentary on this passage and also on 20:13).[3] On Agabus, compare 21:10–14.

σημαίνειν, "to foretell," means a clear announcement; the word has another sense in Heraclitus, frg. 93, where it is said of the lord of the Delphic oracle: "The lord whose oracle is that at Delphi neither speaks nor conceals, but

indicates"[4] (. . . οὔτε λέγει οὔτε κρύπτει, ἀλλὰ σημαίνει).

Excursus:
Famines

Famines are mentioned in various parts of the empire during the time of Claudius. Josephus tells of a famine in Palestine during the governorship of Tiberius Alexander (46/48 c.e.): "It was in the administration of Tiberius Alexander [reading ἐπὶ τούτου][5] that the great famine occurred in Judea, during which Queen Helena bought grain from Egypt for large sums and distributed it to the needy, as I have stated above" (ἐπὶ τούτοις [Niese: τούτον!] δὲ καὶ τὸν μέγαν λιμὸν κατὰ τὴν Ἰουδαίαν συνέβη γενέσθαι, καθ᾽ ὅν καὶ ἡ βασίλισσα Ἑλένη πολλῶν χρημάτων ὠνησαμένη σῖτον ἀπὸ τῆς Αἰγύπτου διένειμεν τοῖς ἀπορουμένοις, ὡς προεῖπον; Ant. 20.101; cf. 20.51 and also 3.320). The year 47/48 was a sabbatical year, which made the situation all the more acute.[6]

It is certain, however, that there was no worldwide famine. Luke did not note the inconsistency that Antioch would also have been involved in such a famine; he also dates it too early (before or during the reign of Agrippa I).[7]

1 Georg Strecker, "Die sogenannte zweite Jerusalemreise des Paulus (Act 11:27–30)," *ZNW* 53 (1962) 67–77.
2 Bultmann, "Quellen," 77 = *Exegetica*, 421–22.
3 See *Beginnings* 3.416, 442.
4 Trans. from Kathleen Freeman, *Ancilla to the Pre-Socratic Philosophers: A Complete Translation of the Fragments in Diels* (Fragmente der Vorsokratiker; Cambridge: Harvard University, 1966) 31.
5 If the variant reading, ἐπὶ τούτοις, is chosen, the translation would begin "Under these circumstances . . ." or "In their [Fadus's and Tiberius Alex-

ander's] time . . ."; see Haenchen, pp. 62–63.
6 Joachim Jeremias, "Sabbathjahr und neutestamentliche Chronologie," *ZNW* 27 (1928) 98–103; see further Tacitus *Ann.* 12.43 (51 c.e. in Rome); Eusebius *Chron.* 181, Helm p. 181 (in the ninth year of Claudius in Greece, in the tenth year of Claudius in Rome); Orosius 7.6 (50 c.e.); Suetonius *Claud.* 18; Dio Cassius 60.11.
7 Jacques Dupont, "Notes sur les Actes des Apôtres: IV. La famine sous Claude (Actes XI,28)," *RB* 62 (1955) 52–55; reprinted in his *Études,* 163–71.

■ **29** Whether the disciples made their decision (ὥρισαν, "determined") at the time of the prophecy, or when the prophecy was fulfilled, is not a real alternative for Luke. He is simply depicting a spontaneous action. According to Haenchen, the tradition about Paul's collection (Gal 2:10, etc.) had been fused with that of his trip with Barnabas (Acts 15; Gal 2:1).[8] Luke found the tradition in this form and tied it to the prophecy of Agabus.

■ **30** This verse could stem from a source, because the elders appear unexpectedly and the apostles are not named. If we take vs 30 together with 12:24–25, we get the impression that Paul and Barnabas were in Jerusalem during the persecution (12:1–2). But nothing is said about this in the main part of chapter 12. We have in this passage a typical literary seam.[9] This item is often taken as a doublet to 15:1–4. On that hypothesis the two journeys would in reality be identical, and the Apostolic Council, to be historically correct, would have to be dated prior to the first missionary journey. But even if vs

30 came from a source, this section as a whole has been fashioned by Luke out of originally separate accounts,[10] and thus cannot be historically localized.[11] It is not possible to harmonize the data of Galatians and this combination of traditions in Acts. Galatians excludes the possibility that Paul and Barnabas brought a collection with them to the Jerusalem council. The council took place *after* the "first missionary journey," that is, after the period to which Gal 2:1 refers. In Luke's understanding this section illustrates the relationship between the mother and daughter congregation, this time from the standpoint of the latter.[12]

8   Haenchen, pp. 378–79.
9   W. L. Knox, *The Acts of the Apostles* (Cambridge: Cambridge University, 1948) 35–36.
10 Kümmel, "Urchristentum III," 31–32.
11 Georg Strecker, "Die sogenannte zweite Jerusalemreise des Paulus (Act 11:27–30)," *ZNW* 53 (1962) 67–77.
12 The following scholars have attempted to locate this journey historically: Kenneth Sperber Gapp, "The Universal Famine under Claudius," *HTR* 28 (1935) 258–65; Dupont, "La famine"; Robert W. Funk, "The Enigma of the Famine Visit," *JBL* 75 (1956) 130–36; J. R. Porter ("The 'Apostolic Decree' and Paul's Second Visit to Jerusalem," *JTS* 47 [1946] 169–74), who wants to identify the prophecy of Agabus with the ἀποκάλυψις, "revelation," mentioned by Paul in Gal 2:2; Pierre Benoit, "La deuxième visite

de Saint Paul à Jérusalem," *Bib* 40 (1959) 778–92, reprinted in his *Exégèse et théologie* (Paris: Cerf, 1968) 3.285–99. On the constitution of the Jerusalem church (the oldest), see Hans von Campenhausen, *Ecclesiastical Authority and Spiritual Power in the Church of the First Three Centuries* (London: Black; Stanford, CA: Stanford University, 1969) 83–84; Günther Bornkamm, "πρέσβυς," *TDNT* 6 (1968) 662–63.

12
The Persecution in Jerusalem;
Peter's Imprisonment and Miraculous Escape

1 About that time Herod the king laid violent hands upon some who belonged to the church. 2/ He killed James the brother of John with the sword; 3/ and when he saw that it pleased the Jews, he proceeded to arrest Peter also. This was during the days of Unleavened Bread. 4/ And when he had seized him, he put him in prison, and delivered him to four squads of soldiers to guard him, intending after the Passover to bring him out to the people. 5/ So Peter was kept in prison; but earnest prayer for him was made to God by the church.

6 The very night when Herod was about to bring him out, Peter was sleeping between two soldiers, bound with two chains, and sentries before the door were guarding the prison; 7/ and behold, an angel of the Lord appeared, and a light shone in the cell; and he struck Peter on the side and woke him, saying, "Get up quickly." And the chains fell off his hands. 8/ And the angel said to him, "Dress yourself and put on your sandals." And he did so. And he said to him, "Wrap your mantle around you and follow me." 9/ And he went out and followed him; he did not know that what was done by the angel was real, but thought he was seeing a vision. 10/ When they had passed the first and the second guard, they came to the iron gate leading into the city. It opened to them of its own accord, and they went out and passed on through one street; and immediately the angel left him. 11/ And Peter came to himself, and said, "Now I am sure that the Lord has sent his angel and rescued me from the hand of Herod and from all that the Jewish people were expecting."

12 When he realized this, he went to the house of Mary, the mother of John whose other name was Mark, where many were gathered together and were praying. 13/ And when he knocked at the door of the gateway, a maid named Rhoda came to answer. 14/ Recognizing Peter's voice, in her joy she did not open the gate but ran in and told that Peter was standing at the gate. 15/ They said to her, "You are mad." But she insisted that it was so. They said, "It is his angel!" 16/ But Peter continued knocking; and when they opened, they saw him and were amazed. 17/ But motioning to them with his hand to be silent, he described to them how the Lord had brought him out of the prison. And he said, "Tell this to James and to the brethren." Then he departed and went to another place.

18 Now when day came, there was no small
stir among the soldiers over what had
become of Peter. 19/ And when Herod
had sought for him and could not find
him, he examined the sentries and
ordered that they should be put to death.
Then he went down from Judea to Caesarea, and remained there.

■ **1** For ἐπιβάλλειν τὰς χεῖρας, "to lay violent hands upon,"
see 1 Esdr 9:20 LXX.

**Excursus:
"Herods"**

Luke distinguishes between "Herod," namely Julius
Agrippa I,[1] and "Agrippa" (II). Agrippa I was a grandson of Herod the Great. In 37 C.E. he received from
Caligula the tetrarchy of Philip (and of Lysanias?—the
sources do not agree on this). In 40 C.E. his territory
was expanded by the addition of the tetrarchy of his
uncle Antipas; from 41 to 44 he possessed all of Judea
as king (βασιλεὺς μέγας Ἀγρίππας φιλόκαισαρ, "Great
King Agrippa, friend of Caesar").[2] As king of Judea, he
displayed a Judaism of a Pharisaic type (Josephus *Ant.*
19.292–316). Thus the motivation for his action
reported in vs 3 is credible. He died in 44 C.E. (Josephus
Bell. 2.219; *Ant.* 19.343–52).[3]

■ **2** This comment serves as the backdrop for the story of
the miraculous protection of Peter, upon which the
accent falls. Luke knows nothing about an execution of
James's brother at the same time.[4]

■ **3–10** This section is a detailed personal legend (5:18–23
offers a less colorful doublet). It is complete in itself and
has been preserved essentially intact (Luke is responsible
for the transitions). We have here the purest example of
the "realistic" legend style in the New Testament;[5] there
is an interest in details which themselves serve a purpose
in the narrative, because they are intended to be edifying.

■ **3** The designation of time reminds the reader of the

time of Jesus' passion (Luke 22:1). There is, however, no
thoroughgoing Passover symbolism here.[6] For προστί-
θεσθαι, "to proceed," with the infinitive, compare the
LXX.

■ **4** In popular usage "Passover" (on the fourteenth of
Nisan) and the "Feast of Unleavened Bread" (the following week) blend together (cf. Josephus *Ant.* 14.21).[7] This
verse is probably one of Luke's typical redactional anticipations.[8] Thus the author twice mentions the prison and
the intent to bring Peter before the people. For the
military procedures here (groups of four, which are
relieved after three hours), compare Philo *Flacc.* 111;
Vegetius *Epit. rei mil.* 3.8: "And because it used to seem
impossible for sentries [at their posts] to maintain successful watches, the watches therefore were divided into
four parts by the waterclock, so that it not be necessary
to stand watch for more than three nighttime hours" (et
quia impossibile videbatur in speculis vigilantes singulos
permanere, ideo in quattuor partes ad clepsydram sunt
divisae vigiliae, ut non amplius quam tribus horis noc-
turnis necesse sit vigilare).

■ **5** For ἐκτενῶς, "earnest," compare *1 Clem.* 34.7.[9]

■ **6** Compare Seneca *Ep.* 5.7: "the same chain fastens the
prisoner and the soldier who guards him" (eadem catena
et custodiam et militem copulat); compare Josephus *Ant.*
18.196.

■ **7** For a shining light, compare Luke 2:9. For πατάξας,
"he struck," compare Curtius Rufus 4.13.20 (49), "then
at last [Parmenion] entered the tent, and after often
calling the king often by name, when he could not waken
him with his voice, he did so by touching him" (tunc

1   On the name, see PWSup 2.167; Agrippa is called
    "Herod" only by Luke.
2   Schürer, *History* 1.451 n. 40.
3   See below on 12:20–23, and the excursus there; see
    also PW 10.143–50; on chronology, see *Beginnings*
    5.446–52; Haenchen, pp. 61–62.
4   See the commentaries on Mark 10:39; Walter Bauer,
    Das Johannesevangelium (3d ed.; HNT 2:2; Tübingen:
    Mohr [Siebeck], 1933) 242–43.
5   Dibelius, *Studies*, 21–23.
6   Contrary to August Strobel, "Passa-Symbolik und
    Passa-Wunder in Act. XII. 3ff.," *NTS* 4 (1957–58)

210–15.
7   See the commentaries on Mark 14:1.
8   Dibelius, *Studies*, 22.
9   See the excursus on *1 Clem.* 34.7 in *Die Apostolischen
    Väter*, vol. 1, Rudolf Knopf, *Die Lehre der Zwölf
    Apostel; Die Zwei Clemensbriefe* (HNT Ergänzungs-
    band; Tübingen: Mohr [Siebeck], 1920) 102–3.

demum intrat tabernaculum saepiusque nomine compellatum, cum voce non posset, tactu excitavit); Homer *Il.* 10.157–59, "To his side came the horseman, Nestor of Gerenia, and woke him, stirring him with a touch of his heel" (τὸν παρστὰς ἀνέγειρε Γερήνιος ἱππότα Νέστωρ, λὰξ ποδὶ κινήσας . . .). The miraculous falling off of chains and opening of doors are often connected; thus Euripides *Bacc.* 447–48, "The fetters from their feet self-sundered fell; Doors, without mortal hand, unbarred themselves" (αὐτόματα δ᾽ αὐταῖς δεσμὰ διελύθη πεδῶν, κλῇδές τ᾽ ἀνῆκαν θύρετρ᾽ ἄνευ θνητῆς χερός). There is, however, no literary dependence of Luke upon Euripides here, but rather the appropriation of a widespread motif;[10] compare, for example, Ovid *Metam.* 3.699–700, "Of their own accord the doors flew open wide; of their own accord, with no one loosing them, the chains fell from the prisoner's arms" (sponte sua patuisse fores lapsaeque lacertis sponte sua fama est nullo solvente catenas). In Philostratus *Vita Apoll.* 7.34, 38 and 8.30, the θεῖος ἀνήρ, "divine man," can loose his chains, while in Luke all is ascribed to the intervention of God.

■ **9** ἐδόκει κτλ., "he . . . thought, etc.," serves to heighten the παράδοξον, "wonder" (cf. vs 11).

■ **10** Apparently the guards are assumed to be sleeping.

Excursus: The Miracle of the Opening of the Gate[11]

There is an abundance of comparative material for the miraculous opening of the gate as indicated above.[12] αὐτόματος, "of its own accord," is a thematic word: (1) in connection with the opening of the doors of heaven,

Homer *Il.* 5.749 = 8.393; the voice is numinous, Callimachus *Hymni* 2 (to Apollo). The motif is transferred to the doors of the temple as in Josephus *Bell.* 6.293 (Tacitus *Hist.* 5.13). (2) It is found in the mystery cults;[13] (3) in magical openings;[14] and finally (4) in legends, thus of Moses in Artapanus (Eusebius *Praep. ev.* 9.27.23) frg. 14:[15] "But when night came the doors of the prison opened of their own accord and some of the guards died, while some were beset with sleep and their weapons were broken" (νυκτὸς δὲ ἐπιγινομένης τάς τε θύρας πάσας αὐτομάτως ἀνοιχθῆναι τοῦ δεσμωτηρίου καὶ τῶν φυλάκων οὓς μὲν τελευτῆσαι, τινὰς δὲ ὑπὸ τοῦ ὕπνου παρεθῆναι τά τε ὅπλα κατεαγῆναι).

The place of imprisonment cannot be located, not even with the help of the undeservedly famous seven steps which are mentioned in D (which says that Peter and the angel "walked down the seven steps" [κατέβησαν τοὺς ζ βαθμούς]), d, and p (for local knowledge, compare the "Western" recension of 3:1–3).

■ **12** Local tradition lies in the background here—it is assumed that the house is well known. Haenchen understands the verse differently, with this note serving Luke's dramatic purposes and preparing for vs 25 and 13:5.[16] It may be said against this interpretation that Luke does indeed make this connection, but he had factual support for it in his material. Since the sixth century the house has been identified as the site of the Last Supper and of the outpouring of the Spirit.[17] For the identification of Mary by means of her son, compare Mark 15:(21), 40; for Mark, compare Col 4:10; Phlm 24; 2 Tim 4:11.

■ **13** ὑπακούειν, "to answer," is used technically for the task

---

10   Vögeli, "Lukas und Euripides," 415–38.
11   Literature:
      Karl Deichgräber, *Parmenides' Auffahrt zur Göttin des Rechts: Untersuchungen zum Prooimion seines Lehrgedichts* (Mainz: Akademie der Wissenschaften und der Literatur, 1958) 35.
      Paul Fiebig, "Zu den Wundern der Apostelgeschichte," *Angelos* 2 (1926) 157–58.
      Joachim Jeremias, "θύρα," *TDNT* 3 (1965) 176–77.
      Richard Reitzenstein, *Hellenistische Wundererzählungen* (Leipzig: Teubner, 1906; reprinted 1963) 120–22.
      Above all:
      Otto Weinreich, "Türöffnung im Wunder-, Prodigien- und Zauberglauben der Antike, des Judentums und Christentums," *Genethliakon W. Schmid zum 70. Geburtstag* (Tübinger Beiträge zur Altertumswissenschaft 5; Stuttgart: Kohlhammer, 1929) 200–264, esp. 222ff.
12   See especially the comments on vs 7.
13   Otto Weinreich, *Gebet und Wunder: Zwei Abhandlungen zur Religions- und Literatur-Geschichte* (Stuttgart: Kohlhammer, 1929) 222–28.
14   Ibid., 412ff.
15   *FGH* 3 frg. 222.
16   Haenchen, pp. 384–85.
17   Clemens Kopp, *Die Heiligen Stätten der Evangelien* (Regensburg: Pustet, 1959) 381–82.

of the doorkeeper (Plato *Phaedr.* 593, etc.). πυλών, "gateway," was the gateway which separated the courtyard from the street (cf. 10:17).

■ **14** For another example of the indirect heightening of the miraculous, compare Luke 24:11.

■ **15** The guardian angel is imagined as a celestial double (see *Herm. Vis.* 5.7).[18]

■ **17** James, the Lord's brother, is introduced abruptly, as a well-known person. This note belongs to the Lukan redaction, rather than to the source[19] as Luke could assume that James was well known to his readers. The conclusion of the verse, however, is actually the conclusion of the old Peter legend.[20] The εἰς ἕτερον τόπον, "to another place" (cf. Plutarch *Mor.* 108 d), should not be understood as a reference to a specific place, here intentionally kept secret. The meaning is that he left safely.[21]

■ **18–19** Compare 5:21–24. The connection between the Peter legend and the Herod legend is secondary; the latter has its own motivation for the terrible end of the ruler: his hubris. The litotes (οὐκ ὀλίγος, "no small") is frequent in Luke.[22] For ἀπαχθῆναι, literally "to be led away," that is, to execution (as the D reading expressly states by using instead ἀποκτανθῆναι, "to be killed"), compare Luke 23:26; *Pap. Oxy.* 1.33, col. 2.14ff; Charito 3.4.18. The guards were liable for the prisoners (cf. *Code of Justinian* 9.4.4). The statement here gives the impression that Agrippa went immediately to Caesarea, but—as a redactional statement—it should not be used for dating.

---

18   Wilhelm Bousset, *Die Religion des Judentums im spät-hellenistischen Zeitalter* (3d ed.; ed. Hugo Gressmann; HNT 21; Tübingen: Mohr [Siebeck], 1926) 324.

19   With Haenchen, p. 391, against Dibelius, *Studies,* 96–97.

20   Dibelius, *Studies,* 96 n. 8.

21   Helge Almqvist, *Plutarch und das Neue Testament: Ein Beitrag zum Corpus Hellenisticum Novi Testamenti*

(ASNU 15; Uppsala: Appelberg; Copenhagen: Munksgaard, 1946) 78–79.

22   On the (apparent) asyndetic string of participles, see Gunnar Rudberg, "Zu den Partizipien im Neuen Testament," *ConNT* 12 (1948) 1–38; cf. vs 21; 14:21–23; 16:9, 22–23.

12

The Terrible Death of the Persecutor

20 Now Herod was angry with the people of Tyre and Sidon; and they came to him in a body, and having persuaded Blastus, the king's chamberlain, they asked for peace, because their country depended on the king's country for food. 21/ On an appointed day Herod put on his royal robes, took his seat upon the throne, and made an oration to them. 22/ And the people shouted, "The voice of a god, and not of man!" 23/ Immediately an angel of the Lord smote him, because he did not give God the glory; and he was eaten by worms and died.

24 But the word of God grew and multiplied.

25 And Barnabas and Saul returned from Jerusalem when they had fulfilled their mission, bringing with them John whose other name was Mark.

■ **20–23** By its incorporation into this context the originally independent legend receives an additional nuance. Agrippa's death is due not only to his hubris, but to his role as persecutor. The year of his death was 44 C.E.

Excursus:
The Death of "Herod" (Agrippa I)

A variant to the death of "Herod" (Agrippa I) is found in Josephus *Ant.* 19.343–52. Here also the king dies (of stomach pains), after being acclaimed as a god. The occasion for his visit to Caesarea was the games, which were celebrated there every five years as a salute to Caesar (nothing is said about a conflict with the Phoenicians). In Josephus as well as in Luke the Jewish origin of the legend is clear. The Lukan version is more naive and appears to be an abridged rendering of a more detailed (written) version. In the abridgment, details such as the position of Blastus, the course of the legal process, the significance of the robes (Josephus *Ant.* 19.344!), and the motivation for the acclamation have become obscured. For an evaluation of the style here, Josephus *Bell.* 7.451–53 is informative (Hellenistic psychologizing of the motif), and also Philo *Flacc.* 188–91 (elevated style).

■ **20** Phoenicia's dependence upon Palestine for food is also expressed elsewhere (cf. 1 Kgs 5:23; Ezek 27:17).

■ **21** In regard to the ruler's robes on an official occasion, compare Suetonius *Nero* 25; Josephus *Ant.* 19.344, "clad in a garment woven completely of silver" (στολὴν ἐνδὺς ἐξ ἀργύρου πεποιημένην πᾶσαν). καθίζειν ἐπὶ (τοῦ) βήματος, "to sit upon (the) judgment seat" or "tribunal" (*RSV*, "throne"), is a fixed expression (cf. John 19:13).[1]

■ **22** ἐπεφώνει, "shouted," is in accord with courtly style.[2] Stephen Lösch compares the veneration of the divine voice of Nero to the glorification of the voice here;[3] for example, Dio Cassius 62.20.5, where the crowd pays homage to Nero as he returns from Greece: "Hail to Nero, our Hercules! Hail to Nero, our Apollo! . . . Augustus! Augustus! O, Divine Voice!" (Νέρωνι τῷ Ἡρακλεῖ, Νέρωνι τῷ Ἀπόλλωνι . . . Αὔγουστε, Αὔγουστε, ἱερὰ φωνή); compare Tacitus *Ann.* 14.15; 16.22; etc.). However, the analogy is only apparent because in our case we do not have the veneration of the voice, but of the person (who is recognized as "divine" by his voice).[4]

■ **23** To be eaten by worms (or by lice) is the typical death

---

1 On βῆμα, "judgment seat," see *RAC* 2.129–30.

2 Erik Peterson, "Die Einholung des Kyrios," *ZSTh* 7 (1929–30) 697.

3 Stephen Lösch, *Dietas Jesu und Antike Apotheose: Ein Beitrag zur Exegese und Religionsgeschichte* (Rottenberg a.N. [Württ.]: Bader, 1933) 17–26.

4 Franz Joseph Dölger, "ΘΕΟΥ ΦΩΝΗ: Die 'Gottes-Stimme' bei Ignatius von Antiochien, Kelsos und Origenes," *Antike und Christentum: Kultur- und Religionsgeschichtliche Studien* (5 vols.; Münster: Aschendorff, 1929–36) 5.218–23. On the imperial cult in general: L. Cerfaux and J. Tondriau, *Le culte des souverains dans la civilisation gréco-romaine* (Bibliothèque de Théologie ser. 3, vol. 5; Paris: Desclée, 1957); Fritz Taeger, *Charisma: Studien zur Geschichte des antiken Herrscherkultes* (2 vols.; Stuttgart: Kohl-

for one who despises God.[5] Criticism of the cult of the ruler was often disguised as criticism of the "tyrant" and was a prominent motif in the portrayals of Alexander the Great (his hubris, that is, his self-deification).

■ **25** Bultmann assigns this verse to the Antiochene source.[6] The manuscripts vary between εἰς, "to," and ἐκ (or ἀπό), "from," Ἰερουσαλήμ, "Jerusalem." εἰς is possible only if it is connected with the following participial clause. ἐκ should probably be read since this fits with the details (συμπαραλαβόντες, "bringing with them," etc.).[7]

hammer, 1957–60) [vol. 1 covers Hellenistic ruler cult; vol. 2 Roman ruler cult].

5 See Herodotus 4.205; Pausanius 9.7.2–3; Pliny *Nat. hist.* 7.172; Lucian *Alex.* 59; 2 Macc 9:9 (Antiochus Epiphanes); Josephus *Ant.* 17.169; *Bell.* 1.656 (Herod the Great). See further: Wikenhauser, *Apostelgeschichte,* 398–401; Wilhelm Nestle, "Legenden vom Tod der Gottesverächter," *ARW* 33 (1936) 246–69; Betz, *Lukian,* 3 n. 5; 178 nn. 2–3. On common ancient criticism of the cult of the ruler, see Fritz Taeger, "Zum Kampf gegen den antiken Herrscherkult," *ARW* 32 (1935) 282–92; Martin P.

Nilsson, *Geschichte der griechischen Religion,* vol. 2, *Die hellenistische und römische Zeit* (HKAW 5:2.2; Munich: Beck, 1950) 374–75.

6 Bultmann, "Quellen," 77, 80 n. 13, reprinted in his *Exegetica,* 421–22.

7 Finally, on the problem, see Jacques Dupont, "La mission de Paul 'à Jérusalem' (Act XII 25)," *NovT* 1 (1956) 275–303, reprinted in his *Études,* 217–41; Pierson Parker, "Three Variant Readings in Luke-Acts," *JBL* 83 (1964) 168–70.

The First Missionary Journey [13—14]

13

Saul (Paul) and Barnabas in Cyprus

1 Now in the church at Antioch there were prophets and teachers, Barnabas, Simeon who was called Niger, Lucius of Cyrene, Manaen a foster brother of Herod the tetrarch, and Saul. 2/ While they were worshiping the Lord and fasting, the Holy Spirit said, "Set apart for me Barnabas and Saul for the work to which I have called them." 3/ Then after fasting and praying they laid their hands on them and sent them off.

4 So, being sent out by the Holy Spirit, they went down to Seleucia; and from there they sailed to Cyprus. 5/ When they arrived at Salamis, they proclaimed the word of God in the synagogues of the Jews. And they had John to assist them. 6/ When they had gone through the whole island as far as Paphos, they came upon a certain magician, a Jewish false prophet, named Bar-Jesus. 7/ He was with the proconsul, Sergius Paulus, a man of intelligence, who summoned Barnabas and Saul and sought to hear the word of God. 8/ But Elymas the magician (for that is the meaning of his name) withstood them, seeking to turn away the proconsul from the faith. 9/ But Saul, who is also called Paul, filled with the Holy Spirit, looked intently at him 10/ and said, "You son of the devil, you enemy of all righteousness, full of all deceit and villainy, will you not stop making crooked the straight paths of the Lord? 11/ And now, behold, the hand of the Lord is upon you, and you shall be blind and unable to see the sun for a time." Immediately mist and darkness fell upon him and he went about seeking people to lead him by the hand. 12/ Then the proconsul believed, when he saw what had occurred, for he was astonished at the teaching of the Lord.

Luke understands this as a "model journey," furnishing the pattern for subsequent missionary activity.[1] It sets forth the problem, which is then solved in chapter 15. In actual fact it replaces the thirteen years of missionary work mentioned in Gal 1:21 and 2:1. Luke has created the conception of "journey." The course of the first journey as a whole is determined by the reference to Antioch as the starting point and the goal. This city appears as the *historical* center for the expansion of Christianity into Gentile territory. It is subordinate to the *dogmatic* center (Jerusalem), and in this way the unity of the church, made up of Jews and Gentiles, is portrayed. In this section a gradual shift in emphasis begins. Up to this point Barnabas, as the mediator between Jerusalem and Paul,

---

1 Menoud, "The Plan of the Acts of the Apostles," *Jesus Christ and the Faith*, 121–32.

ranked ahead of Paul. But now Paul gradually takes precedence over him, not in relationship to Jerusalem, but in relationship to the mission congregations.[2] Dibelius assumes that underlying the material from this point on is an "itinerary," which Luke has filled out with concrete reports about individual stations along the way.[3] Bultmann's view is similar.[4] From chapter 13 he believes the following should be assigned to the itinerary: vss 3–4, 13–14, 43–44, 48–49, (52?). With this hypothesis, however, the unevenness of the itinerary remains unexplained.

■ **1-3 The Sending of Barnabas and Saul**

These verses form the prelude. The list of prophets and teachers probably comes from an (Antiochene) source. The picture deviates from that of 11:19–21, 27–30, in that the "prophets and teachers" appear as settled in Antioch in chapter 13.

■ **1** For the participial construction, τὴν οὖσαν, compare 5:17 and 28:17.[5] As in Paul's writings, prophets and teachers are connected with specific congregations.[6] Except for Barnabas and Saul, the persons mentioned here are not otherwise known. Later, Lucius was occasionally identified with Luke.[7] Herod the "tetrarch" is Antipas (in distinction from "the king," 12:1).[8]

■ **2-3** Fasting is preparation for the reception of a revelation (10:30; *Herm. Vis.* 2.2.1; 3.1.2; 3.10.6; prayer and fasting, cf. 14:23). On this setting apart of individuals by prophets through the Spirit, compare 20:28 and 1 Tim 4:14. The laying on of hands here is blessing, not ordination;[9] it is not the transfer of the power of an office. There is no difference in rank between those blessed and

the others;[10] the concept of office is not developed in Luke as it is in the Pastoral Epistles. Bultmann assigns vs 3 to the itinerary. According to Dibelius the itinerary begins in vs 4.

■ **4-12 The Mission on Cyprus (Sergius Paulus, Bar-Jesus)**

■ **4-5** Luke could have constructed these data himself. Both style (μὲν οὖν, "so," with the participle) and content (initiative by the Spirit, the terminology used for preaching, and the first example of the schema of the connection with the synagogue, cf. vs 46) are Lukan. Cyprus had been a senatorial province since 22 C.E.[11] Salamis was the main harbor on the island, the nearest port to Syria. With regard to Jews on Cyprus, see Philo *Leg. Gai.* 282 and Josephus *Ant.* 13.284–87. Mark's position as ὑπηρέτης, "assistant," cannot be defined with precision.[12] He is mentioned only *after* the references to the Holy Spirit, and he soon withdraws from the work.[13]

■ **6** This travel note is redactional, created as the introduction to the following episode. This proves to be an independent tradition—it takes into account neither a previous mission on Cyprus (11:19) nor the presence of Barnabas. Paphos lies in the southwest part of the island.[14] Perhaps Luke had the story before him in two variant forms, one about a Jew named Bar-Jesus, and another about a magician named Elymas.[15] The connection with the proconsul (vs 7) would seem to be an addition. For ψευδοπροφήτης, "false prophet," compare Josephus *Ant.* 8.236–37.

■ **7** The governor of Cyprus was a *propraetor* with the title proconsul (ἀνθύπατος). Testimony from inscriptions (especially *IGR* 3 no. 930) concerning Sergius Paulus is

2   Klein, *Die zwölf Apostel*, 168–73.

3   Dibelius, *Studies*, 4–11.

4   Bultmann, "Quellen," 78, reprinted in his *Exegetica*, 423.

5   Edwin Mayser, *Grammatik der griechischen Papyri aus Ptolemäerzeit* (2 vols. [vol. 2 in 3 parts]; Berlin/Leipzig: de Gruyter, 1906–34; reprinted 1970) 2:1 pp. 347–48.

6   Heinrich Greeven, "Propheten, Lehrer, Vorsteher bei Paulus: Zur Frage der 'Amter' im Urchristentum," *ZNW* 44 (1952–53) 1–43.

7   See the commentary on 11:28. On the (incorrectly used) article "ὁ" Κυρηναῖος, "'the' Cyrene," see BDF § 268.1. On Manaen, see the commentary on 4:36.

8   On σύντροφος, "foster brother" (*RSV*, "member of the court"), see *OGIS* 247.

9   See the excursus on 1 Tim 4:14 in Dibelius-Conzel-

mann, *Pastoral Epistles*, 70–71; David Daube, *The New Testament and Rabbinic Judaism* (London: University of London, Athlone, 1956) 229–30, 239–41.

10 G. Sevenster, "De Wijding van Paulus en Barnabas," *Studia Paulina in honorem Johannis de Zwaan septuagenarii* (Haarlem: Bohn, 1953) 188–201.

11 *RAC* 3.481–99. On roads, see PW 12.97–98.

12 B. T. Holmes, "Luke's Description of John Mark," *JBL* 54 (1935) 63–72.

13 Haenchen, pp. 396–97.

14 *DB* 4.2077–78.

15 Dibelius, *Studies*, 16.

uncertain.[16]

■ **8** The magician's new name is surprising. The word Elymas is obscure. Luke apparently understands it (in Diodorus Sic. 20.17.1; 20.18.3, a Libyan name) as an appellative, "magician";[17] or does he equate Bar-Jesus and Elymas?[18] Some have proposed Semitic derivations: from the Aramaic אלימא = "strong," or the Arabic *alim*, which is close to $\mu\acute{a}\gamma o\varsigma$, "magician" (*'ālim*, "learned"; *'alīm*, "omniscient," used only of Allah), or from the Aramaic חלמא, "expert in the interpretation of dreams."[19] In an inscription Ηλειμ is found as a name (in Tyre).[20] Codex D has the form ΕΤ[Ο]ΙΜΟΣ, "Hetoimos," by which many are reminded of the Jew ΑΤΟΜΟΣ, "Atomos," who posed as a magician (Josephus *Ant.* 20.142). Jews enjoyed a certain fame as magicians (cf. 19:13).[21] At an early point $\mu\acute{a}\gamma o\varsigma$, "magician," had a derogatory connotation in Greek;[22] Philostratus (*Vita Apoll.* 1.2) rejects this designation for Apollonius of Tyana. Again, we recognize the Lukan criticism of magic. Its style is not that of the philosophical criticism of miracles.[23] Luke does not say that magic is a fraud (in the manner of Lucian, in his *Philops.*), but that it is destroyed by the power of Jesus (cf. Ignatius *Eph.* 19.3).

■ **9** Here we have the well-known permanent transition from Saul to Paul. This does not originate in a source (the itinerary, as Dibelius suggested).[24] Rather, Luke uses the opportunity provided by the name of "Paul's"

first convert (Sergius *Paulus*) to introduce Paul into the mission under his generally known name. The connection with Sergius Paulus is therefore purely literary, not historical. Luke also knows that Paul did not just assume this name, but it was his from the beginning (this is evident from the expression $\acute{o}$ $\kappa a\acute{\iota}$ = "alias"). We do not know whether "Paulus" was a praenomen or cognomen. In the eastern part of the Roman Empire the giving of names follows no recognizable rules (other than the widespread practice of giving an additional name, called a *signum*, which in this case was "Saul").[25]

■ **10** This declaration is biblical language (cf. Sir 1:30; Gen 32:11; Prov 10:9; Hos 14:10).

■ **11** For $\acute{a}\chi\rho\iota$ $\kappa a\iota\rho o\hat{\upsilon}$, "for a time," compare Luke 4:13. Note the stylistic features of the miraculous punishment here: the effective curse word,[26] the effect, the demonstration, and the reaction of the spectators; of course not all of these elements are present in full. The time limitation for the punishment is a stylistically secondary feature. $\acute{a}\chi\lambda\acute{\upsilon}\varsigma$, "mist," does not have a technical medical sense; compare rather Homer *Il.* 20.321 and Josephus *Ant.* 9.56–57.

---

16 PW 6.1780ff; *Beginnings* 5.455–59.

17 Wendt; Haenchen, p. 398.

18 BAG *s.v.*

19 L. Yaure, "Elymas—Nehelamite—Pethor," *JBL* 79 (1960) 297–314.

20 *OGIS* 594.

21 Marcel Simon, *Verus Israel: A Study of the Relations between Christians and Jews in the Roman Empire* (A.D. *135–425*) (trans. H. McKeating; Littman Library of Jewish Civilization; Oxford/London/New York: Oxford University, 1986) 339–68.

22 *Beginnings* 5.164–88; Gerhard Delling, "$\mu\acute{a}\gamma o\varsigma$," *TDNT* 4 (1967) 356–59; Bieler, *Theios Aner* 1.86–87.

23 Karl Prümm, *Religionsgeschichtliches Handbuch für den Raum der altchristlichen Umwelt* (Freiburg: Herder, 1943) 429–30, on the opinion of philosophers regarding manticism; on magic: 366–403.

24 Dibelius, *Studies*, 6 n. 13.

25 Cadbury, *Acts in History*, 69–71. The view of G. A. Harrer ("Saul Who Also Is Called Paul," *HTR* 33 [1940] 19–33) is ingenious—and in view of the anomalous character of name-giving, overly so.

26 On curses, see *SIG* 3 nos. 1174–81; Richard Wünsch, *Antike Fluchtafeln* (2d ed.; KlT 20; Bonn: Marcus & Weber, 1912); PWSup 7.202–4.

The First Missionary Journey [13—14]

13

Antioch in Pisidia (including
Paul's Speech, vss 16–41)

13　Now Paul and his company set sail from
Paphos, and came to Perga in Pamphylia.
And John left them and returned to Jerusalem; 14/ but they passed on from
Perga and came to Antioch of Pisidia.
And on the sabbath day they went into
the synagogue and sat down. 15/ After
the reading of the law and the prophets,
the rulers of the synagogue sent to them,
saying, "Brethren, if you have any word
of exhortation for the people, say it." 16/
So Paul stood up, and motioning with his
hand said:
"Men of Israel, and you that fear God,
listen. 17/ The God of this people Israel
chose our fathers and made the people
great during their stay in the land of
Egypt, and with uplifted arm he led them
out of it. 18/ And for about forty years he
bore with them in the wilderness. 19/
And when he had destroyed seven
nations in the land of Canaan, he gave
them their land as an inheritance, for
about four hundred and fifty years. 20/
And after that he gave them judges until
Samuel the prophet. 21/ Then they asked
for a king; and God gave them Saul the
son of Kish, a man of the tribe of Benjamin, for forty years. 22/ And when he
had removed him, he raised up David to
be their king; of whom he testified and
said, 'I have found in David the son of
Jesse a man after my heart, who will do
all my will.' 23/ Of this man's posterity
God has brought to Israel a Savior, Jesus,
as he promised. 24/ Before his coming
John had preached a baptism of repentance to all the people of Israel. 25/ And
as John was finishing his course, he said,
'What do you suppose that I am? I am not
he. No, but after me one is coming, the
sandals of whose feet I am not worthy to
untie.'

26　"Brethren, sons of the family of Abraham,
and those among you that fear God, to us
has been sent the message of this salvation. 27/ For those who live in Jerusalem
and their rulers, because they did not
recognize him nor understand the utterances of the prophets which are read
every sabbath, fulfilled these by con-
demning him. 28/ Though [or: because]
they could charge him with nothing
deserving death, yet they asked Pilate to
have him killed. 29/ And when they had
fulfilled all that was written of him, they
took him down from the tree, and laid
him in a tomb. 30/ But God raised him
from the dead; 31/ and for many days he
appeared to those who came up with him
from Galilee to Jerusalem, who are now

his witnesses to the people. 32/ And we bring you the good news that what God promised to the fathers, 33/ this he has fulfilled to us their children by raising Jesus; as also it is written in the second psalm,

'Thou art my Son,
today I have begotten thee.'

34/ And as for the fact that he raised him from the dead, no more to return to corruption, he spoke in this way,

'I will give you the holy and sure blessings of David.'

35/ Therefore he says also in another psalm,

'Thou wilt not let thy Holy One see corruption.'

36/ For David, after he had served the counsel of God in his own generation, fell asleep, and was laid with his fathers, and saw corruption; 37/ but he whom God raised up saw no corruption. 38/ Let it be known to you therefore, brethren, that through this man forgiveness of sins is proclaimed to you, 39/ and by him every one that believes is freed from everything from which you could not be freed by the law of Moses. 40/ Beware, therefore, lest there come upon you what is said in the prophets:

41/ 'Behold, you scoffers, and wonder, and perish;
for I do a deed in your days,
a deed you will never believe, if one declares it to you.'"

42   As they went out, the people begged that these things might be told them the next sabbath. 43/ And when the meeting of the synagogue broke up, many Jews and devout converts to Judaism followed Paul and Barnabas, who spoke to them and urged them to continue in the grace of God.

44   The next sabbath almost the whole city gathered together to hear the word of God. 45/ But when the Jews saw the multitudes, they were filled with jealousy, and contradicted what was spoken by Paul, and reviled him. 46/ And Paul and Barnabas spoke out boldly, saying, "It was necessary that the word of God should be spoken first to you. Since you thrust it from you, and judge yourselves unworthy of eternal life, behold, we turn to the Gentiles. 47/ For so the Lord has commanded us, saying,

'I have set you to be a light for the Gentiles
that you may bring salvation to the uttermost parts of the earth.'"

48   And when the Gentiles heard this, they were glad and glorified the word of God; and as many as were ordained to eternal life believed. 49/ And the word of the Lord spread throughout all the region.

50/ But the Jews incited the devout women of high standing and the leading men of the city, and stirred up persecution against Paul and Barnabas, and drove them out of their district. 51/ But they shook off the dust from their feet against them, and went to Iconium. 52/ And the disciples were filled with joy and with the Holy Spirit.

■ **13** These details, which Dibelius and Bultmann ascribe to an itinerary,[1] could have been inferred (e.g., with the help of a map). Travel experiences are absent in Acts until the last journey (and what an opportunity for recounting experiences this first stretch must have offered!).

According to *Stadiasmus* 219,[2] Perga could be reached by ship on the Cestrus River; in reality, however, it was situated eight kilometers away from the river.[3] The expression οἱ περὶ (Παῦλον), "(Paul) and his company," can be used even if only *one*, or even if no companion is present (Xenophon Eph. 2.2.1–2).[4] Here the expression indicates that by this time Paul is the leader. The note about John Mark is illumined by 15:38.

■ **14** Information about roads and travel in this region is given in Strabo 12.570–71; the area was not yet open to Roman civilization. The distance from Perga to Antioch is about 160 kilometers (by air).

Excursus: Antioch

Antioch is called ἡ πρὸς (τῇ) Πισιδίᾳ, "on the Pisidian border," by Strabo (12.569, 577).[5] It lies in "Pisidian" Phrygia; the adjectival use of Πισιδία, "Pisidia," is unusual. The city was officially called Colonia Caesarea (Pliny *Nat. hist.* 5.94),[6] and was one of the Roman colonies which offered protection against the highlanders. It was also the administrative center for the southern part of the province of Galatia.[7] The Roman character of the city is not recognizable in Acts (in contrast to 16:12). Evidence for the presence of the Jewish community is provided by an inscription in Apollonia.[8]

Contact with the synagogue is indicated in schematic fashion.[9] The ἀρχισυνάγωγος, "leader of the synagogue," was in charge of the service. Luke thinks in terms of a council (cf. Mark 5:22). The title also occurs as an honorary title.

■ **16** It was the custom for the Jewish preacher to sit (cf. Luke 4:20);[10] however, compare Philo *Spec. leg.* 2.62: "while one of special experience rises and sets forth what is the best and sure to be profitable" (ἀναστὰς δέ τις τῶν ἐμπειροτάτων ὑφηγεῖται τὰ ἄριστα καὶ συνοίσοντα). According to Luke, Paul opens his speech with the appropriate rhetorical gesture. The content of the speech is a fundamental encounter between church and synagogue, based upon salvation history. It is of mixed type, falling somewhere between the speeches of Peter and that of Stephen. The survey of salvation history replaces the usual introductory scriptural quotation. It establishes the continuity between Israel and the church. The story is traced as far as David, the ancestor of Jesus. The time of the patriarchs and of Moses is passed over

1   Dibelius, *Studies*, 4–11; Bultmann, "Quellen," 78, reprinted in his *Exegetica*, 423.
2   *Stadiasmus Maris Magni*, in *Geographi Graeci minores* (ed. C. Müller; 3 vols.; Paris: Firmin-Didot, 1855–82) 1.489.
3   PW 19.694–704; Magie, *Roman Rule* 2.1134–35; for Pamphylia, see PW 18:3.354–407; for a map, see *Anatolian Studies* 7 (1957) supplement, "A Classical Map of Asia Minor."
4   BAG *s.v.*
5   Victor Schultze, *Altchristliche Städte und Landschaften* (3 vols.; Gütersloh: Bertelsmann, 1913–30) 2:2.350–

52, 357–64. For inscriptions, see William M. Ramsay, *The Social Basis of Roman Power in Asia Minor* (Aberdeen: University Press, 1941) passim.
6   For numismatic evidence, see Magie, *Roman Rule* 2.1319–20.
7   A. H. M. Jones, *The Cities of the Eastern Roman Provinces* (Oxford: Clarendon, 1937) 128–40.
8   See *BCH* 17 (1893) 257.
9   For the course of the synagogue service (with the Shema, prayer, reading from the Law, from the prophets, interpretation), see Str-B 4.153–88.
10   Ibid., 185.

(because Stephen's speech dealt with these in such detail?[11] However, beginning with the exodus from Egypt does have a precedent in the OT).[12] Then follows a detailed presentation of the kerygma, proof from Scripture, and the announcement of forgiveness, concluded by a warning.[13] For "you that fear God," compare 10:2.[14]

■ **17** The style here is biblical (Isa 1:2; Exod 6:6; Deut 5:15).

■ **18** Compare Exod 16:35 and Num 14:34. In Deut 1:31 LXX (B*), τροποφορεῖν, "to bear with," is found, along with the probably original τροφοφορεῖν, "care for," as the translation for נשׂא, "bear" (cf. 2 Macc 7:27).

■ **19** Compare Deut 7:1 and Josh 14:1–2.

■ **20** The calculation of the time involved is not clear, and the text is uncertain. P74, B, ℵ, A, C, sa, bo, and syh all count 450 years as the time between the settlement and the period of the Judges, which is impossible. The problem cannot be solved by appeal to the 400-year stay in Egypt mentioned in Acts 7:6. The difficulty may rather be with a clumsy expression. What is probably meant is, "He gave them the land for 450 years, and after the conquest, he gave them judges." The Western and Koine text types have (secondarily) made corrections. The date agrees with the data given in the Hebrew text of Judges (along with 1 Sam 4:18). The reference in Acts, however, likely did not go back directly to the Hebrew text. The number was probably kept alive in the tradition. Josephus also gives dates which deviate from the Bible (1 Kgs 6:1, where the MT and the LXX differ), and which are not consistent within his own writings (cf. *Ant.* 8.61 and 10.147–48, with 11.112–13 and 20.230.

■ **21** The time given for the reign of Saul is the same as in Josephus *Ant.* 6.378 (10.143 differs, giving twenty years. Is the text corrupt?). The quotation combines several passages (cf. Ps 89[88]:21; 1 Sam 13:14; Isa 44:28). The similarity with *1 Clem.* 18.1 leads one to ask whether now and again the author uses a collection of testimonies.

■ **22** On the subject of ἤγειρεν, "he raised up," see 1 Sam 16:12–13. With David, the goal of the proof from Scripture has been reached.

■ **23** For the emphatic οὗτος, "of this man's," compare 7:35–38. On the subject of God's promise to David, see 2:30.

■ **24** This verse is Lukan in language and content—he avoids mentioning the baptism of Jesus, as in 1:21–22. For the portrayal of John here, compare Luke 3:15–20. For πρὸ προσώπου, "before," compare Mal 3:1; for βάπτισμα μετανοίας, "baptism of repentance," compare Acts 19:4.

■ **25** On ἐπλήρου τὸν δρόμον, "(John) was finishing his course," compare 20:24.[15] Is τί, "what," or τίνα, "whom," here a relative pronoun[16] or an interrogative (cf. John 1:19–22)? Luke concluded that John said this at the end of his career, because he found the Baptist's messianic prophecy at the conclusion of the account about him. As the composition of Luke's Gospel makes clear,[17] in the careers of John and Jesus two epochs of salvation history adjoin.[18]

■ **26** The word of salvation here refers to the kerygma described elsewhere in Acts. ἡμῖν, "to us," provides an interesting contrast to ὑμῖν, "to you," in 2:39 and ὑμεῖς, "to you," in 3:25–26.

■ **27** Here, as in other "kerygmatic" passages, there is some inconsistency reflected in the structure. The idea that the Jerusalemites and their rulers did not recognize Jesus and thus fulfilled the Scriptures (vs 29) is not expressed clearly, because in the middle of the sentence their guilt must be stressed. The Western text paraphrases and understands the ἄγνοια, "ignorance" (*RSV*,

11   Thus Haenchen, p. 415.
12   Martin Noth, *Überlieferungsgeschichte des Pentateuch* (Stuttgart: Kohlhammer, 1948) 48–67.
13   Wilckens, *Missionsreden*, 50–55; Otto Glombitza, "Akta XIII.15–41: Analyse einer lukanischen Predigt vor Juden," *NTS* 5 (1958–59) 306–17.
14   Louis H. Feldman, "Jewish 'Sympathizers' in Classical Literature and Inscriptions," *TAPA* 81 (1950) 200–208; Lars Hartman ("David's son: Apropa Acta 13, 16–41," *SEÅ* 28–29 [1963–64] 117–34) argues that the speech is a homily based on 2 Samuel 7. On the use of Scripture, see Rese, *Alttestamentliche Motive*,

80–93; Holtz (*Zitate*, 131–45) assumes the existence of a source, comprising an outline of salvation history, in which the conception of the covenant is displaced by the idea of election.
15   See Dibelius-Conzelmann, *Pastoral Epistles*, 121, on 2 Tim 4:7.
16   BDF § 298.4.
17   Conzelmann, *Theology*, 22–27.
18   Wilckens, *Missionsreden*, 102–6.

"they did not recognize him"), as an excuse.[19] γάρ, "for," is not emphasizing the opposition between Jews from Jerusalem and other Jews, but is only a transitional particle, indicating the reason why salvation can now be proclaimed. Consideration is of course given to the fact that those present were neither eyewitnesses nor participants. ἄγνοια, "ignorance" (*RSV*, "they did not recognize him"), is understood as guilt (other than in 3:17). This corresponds to the thrust of the following sentences.

■ **28** Compare 3:13–14. The most natural rendering of the participle εὑρόντες would be "*though* they found no guilt" (*RSV*, "though they could charge him with nothing"), but we might ask whether Luke did not intend something more pointed: "*because* (or *when*) they found no guilt."[20]

■ **29** The wording has led to the assumption of a special tradition, according to which the *Jews* buried Jesus.[21] But the form here is kerygmatic, not narrative. This is simply a concise summary of the events. The burial is also mentioned in a formula in 1 Cor 15:3–8. The reference to burial is intended not as an allusion to traditions about the empty tomb, but to establish the reality of Jesus' death (cf. 2:29).

■ **30–31** As in 10:40–43, the section dealing with Easter is expanded; note the use of relative clauses ("who appeared to those . . ."). ὤφθη, "he appeared," is a thematic word (cf. 1 Cor 15:5). ἐπὶ ἡμέρας πλείους, "for many days," is a reference back to 1:3, varying the expression. Because in Luke's view Paul was not an eyewitness to the resurrection, the circle of witnesses must be limited τοῖς συναναβᾶσιν κτλ., "to those who came up, etc. . . ." This

corresponds to the plan of Luke's Gospel, with the journey to Jerusalem as the middle section (cf. also 1:11 and 2:7). These witnesses included more than just the Twelve.[22]

■ **32** This verse establishes the connection between the witnesses and those who bring the good news.

■ **33** The text is corrupt: τοῖς τέκνοις ἡμῶν, "to our children" (p⁷⁴ B ℵ A C D) is impossible; ἡμῖν, "to us," has virtually no textual support (MS 142); αὐτῶν ἡμῖν, "to us, their (children)" (the Koine tradition, E [sy]), and αὐτῶν, "their (children)" (MS 1175 gig sa), are conjectures (cf. 2:39; 3:25–26). ἀναστήσας could be understood to mean "God *sent* Jesus" (as God "raised up" prophets for Israel, cf. 3:22, 26)[23] or "God raised him up," meaning his resurrection.[24] The context demands the latter.[25] The reference to Ps 2:7 does not mean, in Luke's understanding, that Jesus became Son only with the resurrection (cf. Luke 3:22).[26] D, gig, and Origen have πρώτῳ, "first," based on a differing enumeration of the Psalms.[27]

■ **34–35** Isa 55:3 is cited in such a fragmentary manner that the quotation is unintelligible by itself. Had Luke found it already combined with the quotation from Ps 16:10 which follows? On this latter passage, compare Acts 2:27 where the promise to David is seen as fulfilled in the resurrection of Christ.[28] There is a correspondence in the two quotations: δώσω—δώσεις, "I will give—thou wilt . . . let," τὰ ὅσια—τὸν ὅσιον, "the blessings—thy Holy One." τὰ πιστά, "sure," is understood as "imperishable"—thus the word cannot refer to David, as the next verse indicates (cf. 2:29–34).

19 Epp (*Theological Tendency*, 46–48) interprets the Alexandrian text in this way as well.

20 Conzelmann, *Theology*, 90.

21 Maurice Goguel, *The Birth of Christianity* (London: Allen & Unwin, 1953) 30–33; on possible apocryphal traces of such a tradition, see J. N. Bakhuizen van den Brink, "Eine Paradosis zu der Leidensgeschichte," *ZNW* 26 (1927) 213–19.

22 Against Haenchen, p. 411.

23 This interpretation is favored by Zahn, *Beginnings* 4.154–55 (with some reservation), and Wendt.

24 Arguments for this interpretation are offered by Haenchen, p. 411, Wilckens, *Missionsreden*, 51 n. 3, and Jacques Dupont, "'Filius meus es Tu': l'Interprétation de Ps. II,7 dans le Nouveau Testament," *RechSR* 35 (1948) 522–43.

25 Evald Lövestam (*Son and Savior: A Study of Acts 13,*

32–37 [*ConNT* 18; Lund: Gleerup; Copenhagen: Munksgaard, 1961]) analyzes the connection between the quotations and the structure of the promise.

26 See the commentary on 2:36.

27 Cf. Justin *Apol.* 1.40; Tertullian *Adv. Marc.* 4.22; Str-B 2.725.

28 Jacques Dupont ("ΤΑ ῾ΟΣΙΑ ΔΑΥΙΔ ΤΑ ΠΙΣΤΑ [Ac XIII 34 = Is LV 3]," *RB* 68 (1961) 91–114, reprinted in his *Études*, 337–59) offers a different interpretation. The τὰ ὅσια means "the holiness"—in its concrete manifestations, such as forgiveness of sins and justification. For contrary interpretations, see Evald Lövestam, *Son and Savior: A Study of Acts 13, 32–37* (*ConNT* 18; Lund: Gleerup; Copenhagen: Munksgaard, 1961) 71–81, and Mussner, "Die Idee der Apokatastasis," 298–99.

■ 36 J. W. Doeve suggests dependence upon the Hebrew text here.[29] There are reminiscences of 1 Kgs 2:10 and Judg 2:10.[30] The analysis of the sentence is unclear: (1) He fell asleep according to God's will, after he had served his generation; (2) He fell asleep, after he had served his generation according to God's will; or (3) He fell asleep in his generation . . . (that is, as a prophet).[31] In any case, the meaning of the quotation is made clear: David was mortal. This leads to the inference drawn about Jesus in vss 37 and 38–39.

■ 38–39 Here the concomitants of salvation are detailed with some effort to express them in a Pauline manner. The controlling concept ἄφεσις ἁμαρτιῶν, "forgiveness of sins," is, however, non-Pauline (cf. rather the speeches of Peter). By means of the "forgiveness of sins," the understanding of "justification" is modified. What Luke understands as the insufficiency of the Law (Rom 8:3) is indicated in chapter 15, namely, that it was just too great a burden. It had no active role as it did for Paul (Rom 7:7–25). πίστις, "faith," is used as it was generally understood in the church. It is not legitimate to infer from the expression ἀπὸ πάντων κτλ., "from everything, etc.," that one could gain partial, but not complete, justification through the Law.

■ 40–41 In the familiar style the promise is followed by the concluding admonition, citing Hab 1:5 LXX. 1QpHab 2:1–10, like the LXX, presupposes the reading בוגדים, "traitors, scoffers," instead of בגוים, "among the nations,"[32] and interprets: "[This statement refers to the] traitors who are with the man of lies; for [they have] not [obeyed the words] of the teacher of righteousness from the mouth of God—and to the trai[tors who have betrayed the] new [covenant]."

■ 42–43 These verses appear to be doublets. But this impression stems from the fact that Luke first sets forth a more general statement, then follows it with a specific one. The Koine text introduces the transition to the Gentile mission here, but this does not make sense, and later results in a contradiction. μεταξύ is commonly used with the meaning of ἑξῆς, "next" (D; cf. 23:24 v.l.). Is προσηλύτων, "converts to Judaism," a gloss, or is this a careless expression?

■ 44–45 For the exchange of ἐρχόμενος, "next" (B ℵ C* D), and the grammatically correct, but here secondary, ἐχόμενος (A E*), compare Luke 13:33; Acts 20:15; 21:26.[33] How this crowd could find room is beside the point. The conduct of the Jews is poorly motivated, or has been recorded at the wrong place in the narrative. D has made improvements, including the alteration of ". . . almost the whole city gathered together to hear the word of God. But when the Jews saw the multitudes . . ." to ". . . gathered together to hear Paul. And when he had delivered a long discourse about the Lord and the Jews saw the multitudes . . ." (Παύλου πολύν τε λόγον ποιησαμένου περὶ τοῦ κυρίου). On βλασφημεῖν, "to revile," compare 26:11.

■ 46 Here a basic principle within salvation history is formulated and from this perspective subsequent scenes are formed (14:1; 16:13; 17:1, 10, 17; 18:4, 19; 19:8); compare the repetition in 18:6 and 28:28. Thus to the end of the book the decision remains one which belongs to Israel.[34]

■ 47 In Luke 2:32, Isa 49:6 is applied to Jesus, but here (with a slight abridgment of the LXX) it is applied to the missionaries. For the light symbolism, compare 2 Cor 4:3–6. The use of "enlightenment" for conversion is attested in the terminology of Jewish mission literature.[35]

■ 48–49 In spite of the expression ὅσοι ἦσαν τεταγμένοι, "as many as were ordained," the notion of election in Luke is not worked out in the sense of a predestination of the individual. "Ordained to eternal life" is a Jewish expression (cf. CD 3.20).[36]

■ 50 The picture here is meant to be typical. On the place of women in Judaism, see Josephus Bell. 2.560. The use of οἱ Ἰουδαῖοι, "the Jews," is pregnant: after they have rejected the gospel, they are "Jews" in a qualified sense (cf. 14:1–2). For οἱ πρῶτοι, "leading men," compare 25:2

29 J. W. Doeve, *Jewish Hermeneutics in the Synoptic Gospels and Acts* (Assen: Van Gorcum, 1954) 172–75.
30 But cf. Wilckens, *Missionsreden*, 141 n. 2.
31 *Beginnings* 4.156.
32 Karl Elliger, *Studien zum Habakuk-Kommentar vom Toten Meer* (BHTh 15; Tübingen: Mohr [Siebeck], 1953) 167–68.
33 Also see Thucydides 6.3.2; 1 Macc 4:28; Josephus

Ant. 6.174, 235.
34 On πρῶτον, "first" (Rom 1:16; 2:9–10; 3:1–2), see the commentary on 3:26.
35 See the commentary on 26:18.
36 Cf. Str-B 2.726–27.

and 28:17.[37]

■ **51** Compare Luke 9:4 and 10:11. In Luke's Gospel the shaking off of dust is a final sentence, while in Acts the gesture is weakened to a symbolic act.[38] Iconium, the modern Konya, about 140 kilometers from Antioch, was reckoned partly with Phrygia (Pliny *Nat. hist.* 5.245), and partly with Lycaonia (Strabo 12.568; Pliny *Nat. hist.*

5.95), but politically it belonged to the province of Galatia. The city was important as a crossroads for traffic.[39] It was also a Roman colony (Claudiconium)—but since what time? Since Claudius?[40] Neo-Phrygian inscriptions have been found.[41] The *Via Sebaste* went either from Antioch to Lystra[42] or from Antioch to Iconium.[43]

37 BAG *s.v.*

38 On this, see *Beginnings* 5.269–77; Str-B 1.571.

39 William M. Ramsay, *The Cities of St. Paul: Their Influence on His Life and Thought* (London: Hodder & Stoughton, 1907) 317–82; Schultze, *Altchristliche Städte*, 2:2.328–33.

40 This is the view in PW 9.991; according to Magie (*Roman Rule* 1.622 and 2.1405–6 and 1484) it was a Roman colony first under Hadrian.

41 Magie, *Roman Rule*, 2.1312.

42 This is the view of William M. Ramsay, *The Cities of St. Paul: Their Influence on His Life and Thought*

(London: Hodder & Stoughton, 1907) 410–11, and PW 13.2259.

43 This is the position espoused by Magie, *Roman Rule* 2.1325; thus also Konrad Miller, ed., *Die Peutingersche Tafel* (Ravensburg: Otto Maier, 1888; reprinted Stuttgart: Brockhaus, 1962) section 10.2; Ramsay, *Social Basis*, 180–81.

First Missionary Journey [13—14]

14

Iconium

1   Now at Iconium they entered together [or: also] into the Jewish synagogue, and so spoke that a great company believed, both of Jews and of Greeks. 2/ But the unbelieving Jews stirred up the Gentiles and poisoned their minds against the brethren. 3/ So they remained for a long time, speaking boldly for the Lord, who bore witness to the word of his grace, granting signs and wonders to be done by their hands. 4/ But the people of the city were divided; some sided with the Jews, and some with the apostles. 5/ When an attempt was made by both Gentiles and Jews, with their rulers, to molest them and to stone them, 6/ they learned of it and fled to Lystra and Derbe, cities of Lycaonia, and to the surrounding country; 7/ and there they preached the gospel.

■ 1 The schema recurs in a colorless account. Luke had no concrete information, only general reports about the founding of the congregations and persecutions. κατὰ τὸ αὐτό means "together" [RSV] or "likewise, also" (cf. κατὰ τὸ εἰωθός, "as was his custom," 17:2).

■ 2 This verse is a Lukan synopsis whose purpose is to move at once to the pattern he wishes to present. This gives rise to an awkwardness in the narrative. Hence the Western recension revised the whole passage, though the result does not make sense. For ἀπειθεῖν, "to be disobedient," that is, to the faith, compare 6:7.

■ 3 The ἐπί, "to," after μαρτυρεῖν, "to bear witness," has very poor textual support and is not Lukan. For διδόντι κτλ., "granting, etc.," compare 5:12–16. The activity of the two missionaries, Paul and Barnabas, is described in language used of the apostles. In fact, in the next verse and in vs 14 (only in these two places) Paul and Barnabas are actually called apostles!

■ 4 The usage of the term apostle here has apparently been taken over from a source. Since vs 4 is Lukan (ἐσχίσθη, "divided," is used to form a typical scene; concrete material is absent), the author has probably been influenced here by vs 14,[1] which comes from a source. Others assume that ἀπόστολος, "apostle," is used here in a general, nontitular sense.[2] But this would be unique in Luke.[3]

■ 5 The word ὁρμή (RSV, "attempt") does not refer to an attack, but to a plot. λιθοβολεῖν, "to stone," anticipates vs 19.

■ 6 Iconium is no longer considered as part of Lycaonia.[4] This region belonged politically to the province of Galatia.[5] Dibelius assigned this verse (with vs 7) to the itinerary. He found a discrepancy, however, as Derbe is mentioned here with a story from Lystra following, but the apostles arrive in Derbe only in vs 20. Thus vss 8–20a could have been inserted secondarily.[6] But again, we have here a redactional anticipation.[7]

Whether Lystra (about forty kilometers south of Iconium), modern Hatunsaray, lay on the *Via Sebaste* continues to be debated. Under Augustus the city became a colony (Colonia Julia Felix Gemina Lustra);[8] again, Luke does not take note of this.[9]

1   Haenchen, p. 420 n. 10.
2   Eduard Lohse, "Ursprung und Prägung des christlichen Apostolates," *ThZ* 9 (1953) 273 n. 46.
3   For a very different opinion, see Trocmé, *Livre des Actes*, 60; above all, see Klein, *Die zwölf Apostel*, 210–13.
4   See the commentary on 13:51.
5   PW 13.2257; *DB* 4.437–40; Magie, *Roman Rule* 1.455–59.
6   Dibelius, *Studies*, 6.
7   *Beginnings* 4.167; Haenchen, p. 421 n. 6.
8   *CIL* 3.6786.
9   Ramsay, *Social Basis*, 180–83; Magie, *Roman Rule* 2.1324; *DB* 4.460–64. On the declension (Λύστραν, "Lystran," a feminine accusative singular form, vs 6; but Λύστροις, "Lystrois," a neuter dative plural, vs 8), see BDF § 57.

The First Missionary Journey [13—14]

14   Lystra

8   Now at Lystra there was a man sitting, who could not use his feet; he was a cripple from birth, who had never walked. 9/ He listened to Paul speaking; and Paul, looking intently at him and seeing that he had faith to be made well, 10/ said in a loud voice, "Stand upright on your feet." And he sprang up and walked. 11/ And when the crowds saw what Paul had done, they lifted up their voices, saying in Lycaonian, "The gods have come down to us in the likeness of men!" 12/ Barnabas they called Zeus, and Paul, because he was the chief speaker, they called Hermes. 13/ And the priest of Zeus, whose temple was in front of the city, brought oxen and garlands to the gates and wanted to offer sacrifice with the people. 14/ But when the apostles Barnabas and Paul heard of it, they tore their garments and rushed out among the multitude, crying, 15/ "Men, why are you doing this? We also are men, of like nature with you, and bring you good news, that you should turn from these vain things to a living God who made the heaven and the earth and the sea and all that is in them. 16/ In past generations he allowed all the nations to walk in their own ways; 17/ yet he did not leave himself without witness, for he did good and gave you from heaven rains and fruitful seasons, satisfying your hearts with food and gladness." 18/ With these words they scarcely restrained the people from offering sacrifice to them.

19   But Jews came there from Antioch and Iconium; and having persuaded the people, they stoned Paul and dragged him out of the city, supposing that he was dead. 20a/ But when the disciples gathered about him, he rose up and entered the city;

■ **8-18** Episode in Lystra

Dibelius classified this as an isolated story.[1] There is no trace of the Lukan schema in which contact is first made with the Jews.[2] For the healing of a lame man, compare 3:1–10. The similarity of these two incidents results from the typical style of miracle stories. Luke transforms the story into literature by inserting a speech and in general fashioning the material into an episode with its own denouement. In this way the miracle acquires a didactic sense and is drawn into the whole course of the mission, without losing its individuality.[3]

■ **8** In accord with the style of the miracle story the exposition offers details about the duration and severity of the illness (cf. 3:2). The repetition of the details seems

1   Dibelius, *Studies*, 20–21.
2   Lösch (*Dietas Jesu*, 38–46) provides comparative material.
3   Plümacher, *Apostelgeschichte*, 92–95.

affected. Is the unusual word order for reasons of euphony (ἀδύνατος, "could not use," before ἐν Λύστροις, "in Lystra")?

■ **9** In view of vs 11 one might ask how the man could understand Paul. The problem probably never entered the narrator's mind. He assumes that in the cities people understand Greek (he does not deal with the knowledge of Latin in this Roman colony). Note the Hellenistic coloring which is given by the names of the gods. Faith is a presupposition for the healing, as in 3:6 (cf. Mark 5:34; Luke 8:48).

■ **10** The effective word ("stand upright on your feet") is another standard feature, modeled on Ezek 2:1. Manuscripts C, D, and E insert a calling upon the name of Jesus, and thereby ruin the progress of the story (because of the following misunderstanding). The result of the healing and demonstration is only hinted at.

■ **11** The effect on the observers is extensively developed. This is no longer the recitation of a naive legend, but the development of a literary motif.[4] The remark about the use of the native language is necessary. Paul and Barnabas are not to grasp what is going on at first (but later they must be able to make themselves understood—in Greek). The use of the native language by Galatians is still attested by Jerome.[5]

■ **12** The superior ranking of Barnabas is only apparent. As Zeus, Barnabas has no actual role to play but is merely an extra. It need not be asked whether Paul and Barnabas were seen as Zeus and Hermes, the Greek gods, or whether we have here a Greek interpretation of the native gods in this place. For the author (from his "classical" perspective) they are recognized simply as Zeus and Hermes. In fact, the two gods appear together on an inscription from this region.[6] Compare ὁ ἡγούμενος κτλ., "the chief speaker," with Iamblichus *Myst.* 1.1, where Hermes is called θεὸς ὁ τῶν λόγων ἡγεμών, "the god who is the leader in speaking" (cf. Aelius Aristides 46.398 [Dindorf ed.]). It is true that usually Hermes is so called only as messenger, not as one who speaks in the presence of Zeus. There is a story about Philemon and Baucis which took place in Phrygia, in which these two gods appear in human form (Ovid *Metam.* 8.611–725).[7]

■ **13** πρὸ πόλεως, "in front of the city," is used almost adjectivally.[8] The temple of Zeus in Lystra has not been found.[9] It is not clear whether the πυλῶνες, "gates," are those of the city or those of the temple. S. Eitrem refers to the rite of ἄφιξις, "departure," which took place outside the city.[10] The legend does not need to concern itself with such matters as the amount of time necessary for the scene to be played out.

■ **14–15** Refusing veneration as gods (cf. 10:26) is also a motif in profane literature; for example, Ps.-Callisth. 2.22.12 (Alexander), "I decline the honors equal to God, for I was born a mortal man" (παραιτοῦμαι τὰς ἰσοθέους

4 Arthur Darby Nock, "The Emperor's Divine *Comes*," *JRomS* 37 (1947) 106n.

5 The source is Lactantius; see Friedrich Müller, "Der zwanzigste Brief des Gregor von Nyssa," *Hermes* 74 (1939) 68ff. For further details, see Karl Holl, "Das Fortleben der Volkssprachen in Kleinasien in nachchristlicher Zeit," *Gesammelte Aufsätze zur Kirchengeschichte*, vol. 2, *Der Osten* (Tübingen: Mohr [Siebeck], 1928) 238–48. On the topic of veneration as gods, see the commentary on 28:6.

6 W. M. Calder, "A Cult of the Homonades," *ClR* 24 (1910) 76–81; idem, "The 'Priest' of Zeus at Lystra," *Expositor* 7:10 (1910) 148–55; *DACL* 10.411–14; Heinrich Swoboda, Josef Keil, and Fritz Knoll, eds., *Denkmäler aus Lykaonien, Pamphylien und Isaurien* (Brno/Leipzig/Vienna: Rohrer, 1935) no. 146.

7 On this, see Ludolf Malten, "Motivgeschichtliche Untersuchungen zur Sagenforschung," *Hermes* 74 (1939) 176–206; idem, "Motivgeschichtliche Untersuchungen zur Sagengeschichte," *Hermes* 75 (1940) 168–76. On the milieu, see S. Eitrem, "De Paulo et Barnaba Deorum numero habitis (Act. 14:12),"

ConNT 3 (1938) 9–12; Arthur Darby Nock, "The Emperor's Divine *Comes*," *JRomS* 37 (1947) 106n.; Cadbury, *Acts in History,* 22–23.

8 Cf. *CIG* 2.2963c; *IG* 12.420, 522; the latter two inscriptions are from the island of Thera— 522: . . . ἱερέα διὰ γένους τοῦ πρὸ πόλεως Διονύσου.

9 On "Zeus" for the temple of Zeus, see BAG *s.v.*

10 S. Eitrem, "De Paulo et Barnaba Deorum numero habitis (Act. 14:12)," *ConNT* 3 (1938) 9–12; yet see Hans Oppermann, *Zeus Panamaros* (RVV 19:3; Giessen: Töpelmann, 1924) 5ff. On bulls (*RSV,* "oxen"), see Ludolf Malten, "Der Stier in Kult und mythischem Bild," *Jahrbuch des deutschen archäologischen Instituts* 43 (1928) 90–139; Jack Randolf Conrad, *The Horn and the Sword: The History of the Bull as Symbol of Power and Fertility* (New York: Dutton, 1957; London: MacGibbon & Kee, 1959). On garlands, see Karl Baus, *Der Kranz in Antike und Christentum: Eine religionsgeschichtliche Untersuchung mit besonderer Berücksichtigung Tertullians* (Theophaneia: Beiträge zur Religions- und Kirchengeschichte des Altertums 2; Bonn: Hanstein, 1940; reprinted

τιμὰς· ἐγὼ γὰρ ἄνθρωπος φθαρτὸς γεγένημαι).[11] For the scene which is described here, compare Dio Cass. 48 and 37.7; Dio Chrys. *Or.* 35.9: If someone is reputed to be a philosopher, and he is not yet ready for that vocation, "he should tear off his garments and leap forth naked upon the public highways, proving to all the world that he is no better than any other man" (δεῖ περιρρηξάμενον ἐκπηδᾶν γυμνὸν εἰς τὰς ὁδούς, ἐπιδεικνύντα πᾶσιν ὅτι μηδενός ἐστι βελτίων).[12] The speech is a preparation for the Areopagus speech and a concise summary of preaching directed to Gentiles as presented by Luke. For ὁμοιοπαθής, "of like nature," compare Wis 7:3 and Jas 4:17.[13] The title "apostle" (see vs 4) probably comes from the source. Lucien Cerfaux and Günter Klein favor the "Western" reading, in which the title "the apostles" is absent.[14] We find here a good number of key words from Jewish mission literature, which Christians have appropriated: τὰ μάταια, "vain things";[15] ἐπιστρέφειν, "to turn"; θεὸς ζῶν, "living God."[16] The existence of *one* God is not demonstrated by means of philosophical argumentation, but is proclaimed in biblical phraseology. This is the presupposition for the reference to God's self-attestation in nature (vs 17).

■ **16** On God's forbearance (since Gentiles are excused at least in part because of their ἄγνοια, "ignorance"), see 17:30. Paul says something quite different in Rom 1:20–32.

■ **17** Compare 17:24–31 (also Justin *Apol.* 2.5.2; cf. 1.13.2).[17] On "gladness," compare Xenophon *Mem.* 4.3.5–6: "Now, seeing that we need food, think how they make the earth to yield it, and provide to that end appropriate seasons which furnish in abundance the diverse things that minister not only to our wants but to our enjoyment" (τὸ δ᾽, ἐπεὶ τροφῆς δεόμεθα, ταύτην ἡμῖν ἐκ τῆς γῆς ἀναδιδόναι καὶ ὥρας ἁρμοττούσας πρὸς τοῦτο παρέχειν, αἳ ἡμῖν οὐ μόνον ὧν δεόμεθα πολλὰ καὶ παντοῖα παρασκευάζουσιν, ἀλλὰ καὶ οἷς εὐφραινόμεθα). Dio Chrys. *Or.* 30.28–44 serves as a commentary.

■ **19–20a** This appears to be an insertion as the transition is abrupt. Did the author supplement the narrative with an account from another source? 2 Tim 3:10–11 indicates that reports about experiences of Paul circulated in this region (cf. the reference to stoning in 2 Cor 11:25). For Luke this segment says something about the conduct of the Jews and is the fulfillment of 9:16. C and Western witnesses offer various forms of infelicitous paraphrases.

1965) 7–12 (for the one offering the sacrifice); 12–17 (the sacrifice; Lucian *Sacr.* 12).

11 Cf. Plutarch *Mor.* 341b; Arrian *Anab.* 4.9.6; Tacitus *Ann.* 4.38; Ps.-Clem. *Recog.* 10.70, etc. See the commentary on 3:12; Fritz Taeger, "Zum Kampf gegen den antiken Herrscherkult," *ARW* 32 (1935) 282–92; Lösch, *Dietas Jesu*, 42–46.

12 Cf. Appian *Bell. civ.* 1.66; Bertil Gärtner, "Paulus und Barnabas in Lystra: Zu Apg. 14, 8–15," *SEÅ* 27 (1962) 85–88.

13 See also Pap. Berol 8877 line 26; the text is found in Musurillo, *Acts of the Pagan Martyrs*, 23–24, and idem, *Acta Alexandrinorum*, 17.

14 Lucien Cerfaux, "Pour l'histoire du titre *Apostolos* dans le Nouveau Testament," *RechSR* 48 (1960) 88 n. 35; Klein, *Die zwölf Apostel*, 212–13.

15 See the commentaries on Rom 1:21.

16 On this style, compare Epistle of Jeremiah; Bel and the Dragon; 1 Thess 1:9–10; *Herm. Vis.* 1.1.6; Rudolf Bultmann, *Theology of the New Testament* (trans. Kendrick Grobel; 2 vols.; New York: Scribner's, 1951–55) 1.65–92.

17 On the repeated hendiadys, "fruitful seasons" and "gladness over food," see O. Lagercrantz, "Act 14:17," *ZNW* 31 (1932) 86–87; cf. 23:6 (ἐλπὶς καὶ ἀνάστασις, "hope and resurrection").

The First Missionary Journey [13—14]

14   Derbe and Return

20b   and on the next day he went on with Barnabas to Derbe. 21/ When they had preached the gospel to that city and had made many disciples, they returned to Lystra and to Iconium and to Antioch, 22/ strengthening the souls of the disciples, exhorting them to continue in the faith, and saying that through many tribulations we must enter the kingdom of God. 23/ And when they had appointed elders for them in every church, with prayer and fasting they committed them to the Lord in whom they believed.

24   Then they passed through Pisidia, and came to Pamphylia. 25/ And when they had spoken the word in Perga, they went down to Attalia; 26/ and from there they sailed to Antioch, where they had been commended to the grace of God for the work which they had fulfilled. 27/ And when they arrived, they gathered the church together and declared all that God had done with them, and how he had opened a door of faith to the Gentiles. 28/ And they remained no little time with the disciples.

■ **20b–21** Details about the journey and the reference to Derbe are again given only in bare outline. The location of Derbe, disputed for a long time, may now be identified in light of an inscription as Kerti Hüyük, twenty-two kilometers north-northeast of Karaman-Laranda.[1] εὐαγγελιζόμενοι, "when they had preached the gospel," refers back to vs 7. The recent persecutions in Iconium and Antioch do not appear to be taken into consideration, which seems most peculiar in view of vs 19. The simplest explanation would undoubtedly be that Luke was using a list of stopping places. In fact, however, vs 21 is already aimed toward vss 22 and 23, which are certainly redactional, and which Luke has shaped precisely in view of the earlier persecutions.

■ **22** ἡ πίστις, "the faith," means Christianity. Out of these events is extracted a general rule of life. Its formulation fits with Lukan metaphysics in that the focus is not on the "coming" of the kingdom of God, but on the earthly path to it and the entry into it at death. The Greek motif of

παιδεία, "education" (through suffering—"per aspera ad astra," "through adversity to the stars"—cf. Sophocles *Phil.* 1418–22 regarding Heracles), is absent.

■ **23** This verse gives one of the few hints which Acts provides about congregational organization. The un-Pauline[2] form of polity, in which elders are the principal officeholders, is assumed to be the general form of organization (as in the Pastorals, see Tit 1:5; cf. further 20:17–38).[3] χειροτονεῖν, "to appoint," here means installation (not election by a congregational laying on of hands).[4]

■ **24–25** Attalia is the port city near Perga. Here also the hypothesis of an itinerary is superfluous. The details about route and place seem to be as redactional as the remark about the sermon in Perga.

■ **26–27** These verses form a redactional conclusion, connecting up with 13:1–3. Thereby the connection is made to the report that Paul traveled from Antioch to the council. For ποιεῖν with "μετά," "all that God had done

1   M. Ballance, "The Site of Derbe: A New Inscription," *Anatolian Studies* 7 (1957) 147–51; George Ogg, "Derbe," *NTS* 9 (1962–63) 367–70.

2   von Campenhausen, *Ecclesiastical Authority,* 65–66.
3   Ibid., 80–82.
4   See BAG *s.v.*

with them," where a dative might be expected, compare the LXX and the papyri. Preparation for the generalization "to the Gentiles" has been made by 10:45 and 11:1.[5]

■ **28** This verse creates one of the Lukan pauses.

5   On "the door of faith," see Hans Conzelmann, *A Commentary on the First Epistle to the Corinthians* (ed. George MacRae; Hermeneia; Philadelphia: Fortress, 1975) 297, on 16:9.

15 The Apostolic Council

1 But some men came down from Judea and were teaching the brethren, "Unless you are circumcised according to the custom of Moses, you cannot be saved." 2/ And when Paul and Barnabas had no small dissension and debate with them, Paul and Barnabas and some of the others were appointed to go up to Jerusalem to the apostles and the elders about this question. 3/ So, being sent on their way by the church, they passed through both Phoenicia and Samaria, reporting the conversion of the Gentiles, and they gave great joy to all the brethren. 4/ When they came to Jerusalem, they were welcomed by the church and the apostles and the elders, and they declared all that God had done with them. 5/ But some believers who belonged to the party of the Pharisees rose up, and said, "It is necessary to circumcise them, and to charge them to keep the law of Moses."

6 The apostles and the elders were gathered together to consider the matter. 7/ And after there had been much debate, Peter rose and said to them, "Brethren, you know that in the early days God made choice among you, that by my mouth the Gentiles should hear the word of the gospel and believe. 8/ And God who knows the heart bore witness to them, giving them the Holy Spirit just as he did to us; 9/ and he made no distinction between us and them, but cleansed their hearts by faith. 10/ Now therefore why do you make trial of God by putting a yoke upon the neck of the disciples which neither our fathers nor we have been able to bear? 11/ But we believe that we shall be saved through the grace of the Lord Jesus, just as they will."

12 And all the assembly kept silence; and they listened to Barnabas and Paul as they related what signs and wonders God had done through them among the Gentiles. 13/ After they finished speaking, James replied, "Brethren, listen to me. 14/ Simeon has related how God first visited the Gentiles, to take out of them a people for his name. 15/ And with this the words of the prophets agree, as it is written,

16/ 'After this I will return,
and I will rebuild the dwelling of David,
which has fallen;
I will rebuild its ruins,
and I will set it up,
17/ that the rest of men may seek the Lord,
and all the Gentiles who are called by my name,

18/ says the Lord, who has made these things
known from of old.'
19/ Therefore my judgment is that we should not trouble those of the Gentiles who turn to God, 20/ but should write to them to abstain from the pollutions of idols and from unchastity and from what is strangled and from blood. 21/ For from early generations Moses has had in every city those who preach him, for he is read every sabbath in the synagogues."

22 Then it seemed good to the apostles and the elders, with the whole church, to choose men from among them and send them to Antioch with Paul and Barnabas. They sent Judas called Barsabbas, and Silas, leading men among the brethren, 23/ with the following letter: "The brethren, both the apostles and the elders, to the brethren who are of the Gentiles in Antioch and Syria and Cilicia, greeting. 24/ Since we have heard that some persons from us have troubled you with words, unsettling your minds, although we gave them no instructions, 25/ it has seemed good to us, having come to one accord, to choose men and send them to you with our beloved Barnabas and Paul, 26/ men who have risked their lives for the sake of our Lord Jesus Christ. 27/ We have therefore sent Judas and Silas, who themselves will tell you the same things by word of mouth. 28/ For it has seemed good to the Holy Spirit and to us to lay upon you no greater burden than these necessary things: 29/ that you abstain from what has been sacrificed to idols and from blood and from what is strangled and from unchastity. If you keep yourselves from these, you will do well [or: it will be well with you]. Farewell."

It is not by chance that the Apostolic Council occupies the middle of the book. It is the great turning point, the transition from the primitive church to the "contemporary" church. From this point on the apostles disappear, even in Jerusalem itself (cf. 21:15–26, etc.). In Jerusalem continuity is represented by James, in the Gentile Christian church by Paul.

■ 1–5 Here the problem is set forth. It does not have to do with the admission of the Gentiles as such, but with the conditions for their entrance. According to the Lukan concept of the church, the criteria must be established only by the earliest congregation.

■ 1 This verse is reminiscent of Gal 2:12; however, the conflict described there takes place *after* the conference

(we find an echo of that conflict in Acts 15:39). Luke avoids saying that these Jewish Christians come from "Jerusalem." Instead he uses the general term "Judea" to indicate that they were not agitating under orders from the Jerusalem church (cf. vs 24). Their demand is described more exactly in vs 5, but already here in vs 1 D, sy^{hmg}, and sa add "*and walk* ($\kappa\alpha\grave{\iota}$ . . . $\pi\epsilon\rho\iota\pi\alpha\tau\hat{\eta}\tau\epsilon$) in the way of Moses."

■ 2 The $\sigma\tau\acute{\alpha}\sigma\iota\varsigma$, "dissension," was not a split within the congregation at Antioch, but is rather a result of the visit of the Judeans. Paul and Barnabas are the spokesmen for the congregation and they go to Jerusalem as delegates (contrast Gal 2:1!). In accord with Luke's ecclesiology they do not take an active part in the discussion or in issuing the decree, they merely represent one of the groups whose position is under consideration. Luke certainly does not intend to degrade them. They find themselves in a role similar to that of Peter in 11:1–18. Titus (Gal 2:1, 3) is not mentioned, as is the case throughout Acts. John's name (Gal 2:9) also does not appear. For the elders in Jerusalem, compare 11:30. The Western text makes the subject of ἔταξαν, "appointed," the Judeans, not the Antiochenes. It replaces the arrangements made by the Antiochene church with a request from the Judeans to go to Jerusalem. The Western text fails to observe the need in this case to alter vs 3 in accord with this change. These readings are not motivated by an anti-Pauline tendency. The intention is rather a positive one, that is, to emphasize the unity and authority of the church.[1] Pierre Benoit explains vss 1–2 as redactional.[2] The author of these verses, Benoit argues, says "Paul and Barnabas," which is the order that appears in the Pauline tradition (13:43–50; 15:35), while additional traditional material the author uses reversed the order of the two names (cf. 12:25). Acts 15:3–33 would then connect with 11:30. The account in chapters 13 and 14 should thus be understood as an independent piece of tradition in Benoit's view. The episode reported in 11:27–30 would then originally have introduced the journey described in 15:3–33. Thus, for Benoit, the differences between Galatians and Acts would disappear.[3]

■ 3 This verse sets the mood for the scene that follows—a scene set among Jewish Christians (cf. τῶν ἐθνῶν, "of the Gentiles," and 11:19).

■ 4-5 These verses harken back to 14:27 and are thus clearly from Luke. It is somewhat strange that the problem about Gentiles is not mentioned as part of the report of the delegation, but that the dispute now arises anew within the Jerusalem church. This does not provide evidence that vss 3–33 and vss 1–2 are based on different sources. A literary explanation is sufficient since only in this way can the solution be depicted in a scene that will

have a lasting impact.[4] Haenchen correctly points out that for Luke the Gentile mission, with freedom from the Law, is no longer an open question, and consequently it can no longer be an open question for Paul, Barnabas, Peter, and James. Because it was necessary, however, to make the fundamental principle clear, he allows the "circumcision party" to appear. They can still express themselves because there has not yet been any official decision. The proponents of a more Jewish view regarding observance of the Law (Gal 2:4–5, 12) appear from the outset as a special group (Pharisees; cf. 26:5; αἵρεσις, "party," is still used with a neutral sense here).[5] Verses 4–5 provide a summary of the discussion which follows. They make clear that the author is not describing two assemblies here, one in vss 4–5 and another in vss 6–21, but one plenary assembly (vs 12).

■ 6-29 In comparison with Galatians, the passivity of Paul and Barnabas is striking (see above, vs 2).

■ 7 Here the formative hand of Luke is apparent as he has Peter refer back to the events of chapters 10—11, where Luke has described a scene that can serve as a model. Here Peter offers Luke's own interpretation.[6] The "speech" contains (1) factual evidence, vss 7–9, and (2) appropriate inferences. The expression ἀφ᾽ ἡμερῶν ἀρχαίων, "in the early days," transforms the story of Cornelius into the "classic" prototype. According to Luke, Peter's audience had heard the story about Cornelius from Peter himself on a previous occasion. Acts does not give the impression that this occurred long ago, yet when the need arises, Luke can either condense periods of time or, as is done here, extend them (cf. the use of ἐν ἀρχῇ, "at the beginning," referring to Pentecost, in 11:15). The harsh ἐκλέγεσθαι ἐν, "to make choice among," has a prototype (to be sure, only a formal one) in the LXX (there used for בָּחַר בְּ, "he chose"). The Gentiles have believed (καὶ πιστεῦσαι, "and believe") without accepting the burden of the Law (cf. vss 9, 28).

■ 8 For καρδιογνώστης, "who knows the heart," compare 1:24. For καθὼς καὶ ἡμῖν, "just as . . . to us," compare

1   Epp, *Theological Tendency*, 96–98, cf. 101–3.
2   Pierre Benoit, "La deuxième visite de saint Paul à Jérusalem," *Bib* 40 (1959) 778–92, reprinted in his *Exégèse et théologie III* (Paris: Cerf, 1968) 285–99.
3   Trocmé also attempts a source analysis (*Livre des Actes*, 156–63).
4   Haenchen, pp. 457–58; idem, "Quellenanalyse und Kompositionsanalyse in Act 15," *Judentum, Urchris-* *tentum, Kirche: Festschrift für Joachim Jeremias* (ed. Walter Eltester; BZNW 26; Berlin: Töpelmann, 1960) 153–64.
5   See the commentary on 5:17.
6   The Western text differs: Peter rose "in the Holy Spirit" (ἐν πνεύματι [ἁγίῳ]); see Joseph Crehan, "Peter according to the D-Text of Acts," *TS* 18 (1957) 596–603.

10:47 and 11:15–17.

■ **9** οὐθὲν διέκρινεν, "he made no distinction," is an interpretation of the vision of 10:9–16 (cf. 10:20; 11:2–17).

■ **10** For πειράζειν, "make trial of," compare Exod 17:2 (with the infinitive, Ps 78 [77]:18), that is, after God has made his will known. The concept of the Law as an unbearable burden is neither the common Jewish view (the Jewish expression, "the yoke," does not imply something unbearable and impossible to fulfill)[7] nor is it Pauline. It expresses the view of a Christian at a time when the separation from Judaism already lies in the past. On this basis we can also understand why Luke does not draw the conclusion which logic demands, that this yoke should also be removed from Jewish Christians. For Luke Jewish Christianity no longer has any present significance, but it is of fundamental significance in terms of salvation history.

■ **11** Here Peter speaks as Paul does in 13:38–39. Luke knows nothing of various types of theology and terminology. The Pauline view of grace as the antithesis to works is absent (Gal 2:15–16).

■ **12** Peter's vote has silenced the ζήτησις, "debate" (ἐσίγησεν, "and the assembly kept silence"). Bultmann,[8] following Wilhelm Bousset,[9] again asks whether the passages which mention Paul and Barnabas might not be secondary additions, namely vss 2, 3, 5, 12, and σὺν τῷ Παύλῳ καὶ Βαρναβᾷ, "with Paul and Barnabas," in vss 22, 25–26. The speeches of Peter and James would then belong to a source concerning a gathering at which the apostolic decree would have been decided upon (as distinguished from the Apostolic Council). But the speeches are Lukan compositions, as is evident from the reference to chapters 10 and 11. The reference to the "signs and wonders God had done through them among the Gentiles" in this verse may seem like a doublet after vs 4,

but can be explained by Luke's custom of giving a preliminary survey of what is to follow (vs 4).

■ **13** When James (who was introduced in 12:17) now casts his vote, the testimony of two "witnesses" agrees. Of course Luke possessed reports about the significance of this man at the discussion in Jerusalem (Gal 2:9). The scriptural proof is now added to the evidence.

■ **14** The form Simeon (an Aramaicism) is archaic.[10] There are connections between the speeches of Peter and James, as shown by πρῶτον/ἀφ᾽ ἡμερῶν ἀρχαίων, "first/in the early days"; ἐπεσκέψατο/ἐξελέξατο, "visited/made choice" (cf. Luke 1:68, 78; 7:16). ἐξ ἐθνῶν λαόν, "a people out of the Gentiles," is a consciously paradoxical formulation. Jacques Dupont compares Deut 14:2 LXX, as well as other passages.[11] Contrast Deut 26:18–19 (the distinction between עַם, "people," and גּוֹיִם, "nations"). However, this is not an allusion to a specific passage, but Luke's biblical style. The same is true also for τῷ ὀνόματι αὐτοῦ, "for his name."[12]

■ **16–18** The proof from Scripture first of all follows the LXX of Amos 9:11, with some influence from Jer 12:15. This is followed by Amos 9:12 LXX, quoted almost verbatim, and the passage concludes with three words from Isa 45:21. The author may have found this combination of verses in a collection of testimonies.[13] The Hebrew text would not have been suitable for the proof; however, compare the citation of the Amos passage in CD 7.16 and in 4QFlor 1.12–13. The three words quoted from Isa 45:21 ("known from of old") provide Luke with a salvation-historical background for his ἀφ᾽ ἡμερῶν ἀρχαίων, "in the early days" (vs 7), a motif in his history of the church.

■ **19** κρίνειν, "to judge," does not refer to the "decision" (the whole assembly makes that, vs 22), but rather to the proposal. μὴ παρενοχλεῖν, "not to trouble," corresponds

---

7 Str-B 1.608–10.

8 Bultmann, "Quellen," 73 n. 6, reprinted in his *Exegetica*, 417 n. 6.

9 Wilhelm Bousset, "Der Gebrauch des Kyriostitels als Kriterium für die Quellenscheidung in der ersten Hälfte der Apostelgeschichte," *ZNW* 15 (1914) 141–62.

10 Cf. my comment on Σαούλ, "Saul," in 26:14.

11 Jacques Dupont, "ΛΑΟΣ ΕΞ ΕΘΝΩΝ (Act. XV.14)," *NTS* 3 (1956–57) 47–50, now in his *Études*, 361–65; Paul Winter, "Miszellen zur Apostelgeschichte," *EvTh* 17 (1957) 399–406.

12 This is contrary to the view of Nils A. Dahl ("A People for His Name [Acts XV.14]," *NTS* 4 [1957–58] 319–27) who cites passages from the Targums for comparison; however, these show a different use of language from לשם.

13 On the text, see Cerfaux, "Citations," 48–49, reprinted in his *Recueil Cerfaux* 2.100–101, who defends the priority of D. Against this view, see Haenchen, "Schriftzitate," 164, reprinted in his *Gott und Mensch* 1.168.

to vss 10–11. What is added here is the positive proposal of the "apostolic decree."

■ **20** The intention of the decree is not to retain the Law as valid, not even symbolically or "in principle." The fundamental prescription of circumcision is not imposed. The decree is conceived rather as a concession to the Gentile Christians, which would enable Jewish Christians to live with them, and particularly to have table fellowship.[14] The Western text inserts the "golden rule" here.[15]

Excursus:
The Apostolic Decree

1. The text. The text of the decree is repeated in vs 29 and in 21:25. It has been transmitted in two versions. The one (B, etc.) gives cultic stipulations, the other (D, etc.) ethical stipulations. Further variants have sprung from these two basic forms.[16] In P[45] πορνείας, "unchastity," is absent (in the two parallels—vs 29 and 21:25—the text has not been preserved), as is the case in a part of the Ethiopic version and in Origen *Cels.* 8.29.[17] In texts where this prohibition is absent, however, we probably do not have a genuine variant, but a mistake.[18] In all three passages D omits καὶ πνικτοῦ, "and from what is strangled" (likewise Irenaeus in 15:20, 29;

gig in 15:20 and 21:25; Ephraim in 15:20) and inserts the "golden rule" in its place (καὶ ὅσα μὴ θέλουσιν ἑαυτοῖς γείνεσθαι ἑτέροις μὴ ποιεῖτε, ". . . and not to do to others whatever they do not wish to be done to themselves"), both here and in vs 29 (likewise sa, Irenaeus, etc.; only in vs 29: 614, sy[h], and Old Latin).

The cultic version (with four regulations) is the original, because the development from it to the ethical is understandable, but not the reverse.[19] G. Strothotte demonstrates that in rabbinic literature there was a triad of "things which are unclean," namely, idolatry, unchastity, and the shedding of blood (e.g., *Šeb.* 7b, in a Baraita which refers to Lev 16:16).[20] His conclusion, that the Western text is closest to the original and that the account in Acts 15 is (together with the apostolic decree) historically accurate, is wrong. At most, the rabbinic material provides a hint as to how the D version later arose, namely, through the influence of Jewish paraenesis upon Christian paraenesis, which can also be demonstrated elsewhere. T. Bowman also defends the originality of the Western text,[21] basing his argument on a hypothetical Aramaic version.

2. The stipulations. These are the prohibitions of Leviticus 17—18 (in vs 29 they are even in the same order),[22] which were also valid for non-Jews living in Israel.[23] ἀλισγήματα τῶν εἰδώλων, "the pollutions of idols," is explained by εἰδωλόθυτα, "what has been

14 Dibelius, *Studies*, 97.

15 See the excursus which follows, and Albrecht Dihle, *Die Goldene Regel: Eine Einführung in die Geschichte der antiken und frühchristlichen Vulgärethik* (Studienheft zur Altertumswissenschaft 7; Göttingen: Vandenhoeck & Ruprecht, 1962).

16 With Werner Georg Kümmel ("Die älteste Form des Aposteldekrets," *Spiritus et Veritas* [Festschrift für Karl Kundsin] [Eutin, Germany: Ozolins, 1953] 83–98, reprinted in his *Heilsgeschehen und Geschichte: Gesammelte Aufsätze 1933–64* [Marburger theologische Studien 3; Marburg: Elwert, 1965] 278–88) and against Philippe H. Menoud ("The Western Text and the Theology of Acts," *Bulletin of the Studiorum Novi Testamenti Societas* 2 [1951] 19–32, reprinted in his *Jesus Christ and the Faith*, 61–83) who assumes that there were four versions. Menoud views as original those regulations which are common to all four versions, that is, only the prohibition of pollutions of idols and of blood.

17 See Preuschen on vs 29.

18 Werner Georg Kümmel, "Die älteste Form des Aposteldekrets," *Spiritus et Veritas* [Festschrift für Karl Kundsin] (Eutin, Germany: Ozolins, 1953) 87, reprinted in his *Heilsgeschehen und Geschichte: Gesammelte Aufsätze 1933–64* (Marburger theologische Studien 3; Marburg: Elwert, 1965) 280–81.

19 See below; of another opinion is Harnack, *Acts*, 248–63; idem, *Neue Untersuchungen zur Apostelgeschichte und zur Abfassungszeit der synoptischen Evangelien* (Beiträge zur Einleitung in das Neue Testament 4; Leipzig: Hinrichs, 1911) 22–24.

20 G. Strothotte, "Das Apostelkonzil im Lichte der jüdischen Rechtsgeschichte" (Diss., Erlangen, 1955).

21 Thorleif Bowman, "Das textkritische Problem des sogenannten Aposteldekrets," *NovT* 7 (1964–65) 26–36.

22 Hans Waitz, "Das Problem des sog. Aposteldekrets und die damit zusammenhängenden literarischen und geschichtlichen Probleme des apostolischen Zeitalters," *ZKG* 55 (1936) 227–63.

23 Schoeps (*Theologie*, 259–60) believes otherwise: this is a matter of the Noachic minimum. On the Noachic regulations, cf. Str-B 3.37–38; Luke himself certainly designates these as Mosaic, vs 21.

sacrificed to idols," in vs 29 (cf. Lev 17:8; 1 Cor 8:1–13; 10:19–30; Justin *Dial.* 34.8). The prohibition of πορνεία, "unchastity" (according to Lev 18:6–30) is an established component of early Christian paraenesis (1 Thess 4:3; Gal 5:19, etc.; with εἰδωλολάτραι, "idolaters," 1 Cor 6:9). πνικτόν, "what is strangled," is meat from animals which have not been slaughtered ritually (Gen 9:4; cf. the expansion of the instructions regarding "what is torn" in Lev 17:15; also Origen *Cels.* 8.30; Philo *Spec. leg.* 4.122–23).[24] The prohibition of αἷμα, "blood," is in accordance with Lev 17:10–14. It is significant that "blood" is mentioned after πνικτόν, "what is strangled," that is, first the partaking of meat is forbidden, then of the blood. Both stipulations are explained by Lev 17:10–14 (cf. further Josephus *Ant.* 3.260).

As a whole, these stipulations had to do with those ritual prohibitions which enabled the Jew to live together with the Gentile Christian. The Western text has transformed this regulation of the church for a specific time into a timeless precept by striking out the prohibition of πνικτόν, "what is strangled," and adding the "golden rule" (see above). By this means the remaining stipulations were changed to moral stipulations (αἷμα, "shedding of blood" = murder). The pattern of the three mortal sins stands out. In this way there was not only a failure to recognize the original historical setting and meaning, but also to recognize the importance Luke attaches to the decree. For Luke, of course, the issue of table fellowship in mixed congregations was no longer a live issue. Yet he saw these stipulations as of fundamental significance. That

significance, however, was not ethical, but salvation-historical, since the decree provided continuity between Israel and the church, which was free from the Law.

3. The historical setting. Gal 2:6 excludes the possibility that the decree was decided upon at the Apostolic Council. Furthermore, it does not deal at all with the main point of contention, circumcision. Gal 2:11–14 indicates that the problem of table fellowship between Jewish and Gentile Christians had not yet been brought before the council. Moreover, Paul does not mention the decree when he deals with εἰδωλόθυτα, "what has been sacrificed to idols" (along with πορνεία, "unchastity"), in 1 Corinthians.[25] The stipulations would fit well with the conflict in Antioch (Gal 2:11–14). They would fill in the gaps left open by the council and thus make table fellowship possible. It is at least correct that the decree certainly arose in mixed congregations. O. Linton believes that Luke possessed reports, traces of which may still be detected in Paul—but that Paul rejected them as false.[26] For example, Gal 2:6 can be understood as a polemic against rumors that at the council further conditions had been imposed, that is, the decree. There are many indications that the decree was circulated in the church: Rev 2:14, 20; Justin *Dial.* 34.8; Minucius Felix 30.6; the martyrs of Lyons in Eusebius *Hist. eccl.* 5.1.26; Tertullian *Apol.* 9.13; Ps.-Clem. *Hom.* 7.4.2; 7.8.1; 8.19 (here in connection with demonology; cf. the connection between εἰδωλόθυτον, [εἰδωλολατρία], "what has been sacrificed to idols" ["idolatry"], and demon worship in 1 Cor 10:19–22).[27]

---

24 Strothotte ("Das Apostelkonzil im Lichte der jüdischen Rechtsgeschichte" [Diss., Erlangen, 1955] 129) offers a somewhat different interpretation.

25 C. K. Barrett ("Things Sacrificed to Idols," *NTS* 11 [1964–65] 138–53) judges the situation in Corinth differently. Cf. also the repetition of the decree in 21:25, and the commentary on that passage.

26 Linton, "Third Aspect."

27 Schoeps, *Theologie*, 303; idem, *Aus frühchristlicher Zeit: Religionsgeschichtlicher Untersuchungen* (Tübingen: Mohr [Siebeck], 1950) 78; A. F. J. Klijn, "The Pseudo-Clementines and the Apostolic Decree," *NovT* 10 (1968) 305–12.

In addition to the literature cited in the above notes, see the article of Kümmel (n. 16, above) which concludes with a survey of literature, and the following:

Jacques Dupont, *Les problèmes du livre des Actes d'après les traveaux récents* (Analecta Lovaniensia Biblica et Orientalia 2:17; Louvain: Publications Universitaires de Louvain, 1950) 67ff, now in his *Études*, 72–75.

Haenchen, pp. 468–72.

Klijn, *Survey*, 19–20.

Hans Lietzmann, "Der Sinn des Aposteldekretes und seine Textwandlung," *Amicitiae Corolla: A Volume of Essays Presented to James Rendel Harris* (ed. H. G. Wood; London: University of London, 1933) 203–11, reprinted in his *Kleine Schriften*, vol. 2, *Studien zum Neuen Testament* (ed. Kurt Aland; TU 68; Berlin: Akademie-Verlag, 1958) 292–98.

Bo Reicke, "Der geschichtliche Hintergrund des Apostelkonzils und der Antiochia-Episode, Gal. 2, 1–14," *Studia Paulina in honorem Johannis de Zwaan* (Haarlem: Bohn, 1953) 172–87.

On the Pseudo-Clementines, see Einar Molland, "La circoncision, le baptême et l'autorité du décret apostolique (Actes XV,28sq.) dans les milieux judéo-chrétiens des Pseudo-Clémentines," *StTh* 9 (1955) 1–39.

■ **21** The logic here is unclear: What is to be substantiated? Does the "preaching of Moses in every city" relate to James's interpretation of Amos 9, with the implication that this interpretation can be assumed as commonly known? But then why is Moses mentioned, and why is no application made to those present? Perhaps the verse intends to substantiate the *decree*. This is necessary because of the obligation of the Jews (Jewish Christians) to the universally known Law of "Moses" (vs 28). The explanation which is given in 21:20–25 fits with this. Étienne Trocmé understands vs 21 as an explanation of vs 19 (both came from one source).[28] Verse 20 would be an addition from Luke, to prepare for the letter in vss 23–29. James would then be explaining that no Jewish messengers need be sent to the Gentile Christian congregations—the existing synagogues are sufficient for making the Law of Moses known (Philo *Spec. leg.* 2.61–64).

■ **22** Here is the official decision. Silas = שׁאִילָא, the Aramaic equivalent of Saul.[29]

■ **23–29** Did Luke have the letter before him? The notable address argues for this. It fits with Gal 1:21, but not with the account in Acts up to this point; Cilicia has not been mentioned as a sphere of mission activity to this point. The address may seem to limit the territory in which the decree is valid. This impression is altered, however, when Cilicia is actually mentioned in vs 41 as a new sphere of Paul's missionary activity. And Haenchen points out that the address—measured by the mission as described to this point—is not a limitation, but an expansion, and that furthermore this communication with its purposive structure is not a real letter, but a literary creation.[30] It is not an answer to a question which has been submitted, but the frame for a "decree." The language is literary (e.g., there is evidence of the influence of the LXX, and also ecclesiastical language). The form of the prescript with one member is typical of Greek letters, as in 23:26 and Jas 1:1 (in distinction from the oriental form with two members).[31] ἀδελφοί,

"brethren," seems strange in apposition to apostles and elders. If we bracket ἀπόστολοι καὶ οἱ πρεσβύτεροι, "apostles and the elders," understanding these as a secondary (Lukan) addition,[32] then we must also postulate that Luke has removed a reference to a place ("in Jerusalem"). Haenchen suggests that Luke may have created the unusual expression after the example of ἄνδρες ἀδελφοί, "brethren" (literally, "men, brothers").

■ **24–26** Outside of Luke 1:1–4, this is the only "period" in Luke-Acts, that is, the "organization of a considerable number of clauses and phrases into a well-rounded unity."[33] There are indeed some obscurities. Does λόγοις, "with words," belong with ταράσσειν, "to trouble," or with ἀνασκευάζειν, "to unsettle"? The reading ἐκλεξαμένοις, "to choose" (dative; P45 B A) is better Greek than ἐκλεξαμένους, "to choose" (accusative with infinitive).[34] The text—οἷς οὐ διεστειλάμεθα, "although we gave them no instructions"—does not imply "although we gave them no instructions to trouble you" (as if someone suspected that those in Jerusalem had intended to create confusion); it simply means the troublers went to Antioch on their own authority, without any commission.

■ **26** On this honorific expression ("men who have risked their lives"), compare Rom 16:4.

■ **27** This fits better in a fictitious letter than in a real one.

■ **28** This verse contains the Lukan concept of church and Spirit. ἔδοξεν κτλ., "it has seemed, etc.," follows the style of an official letter; compare Josephus *Ant.* 16.163, "it has been decided by me and my council" (ἔδοξέ μοι καὶ τῷ ἐμῷ συμβουλίῳ). μηδὲν πλέον, "no greater," does not mean that in place of a heavy burden a light one will now be imposed, but that there will be no burden at all. "These necessary things" are explained by the Lukan understanding of Law and church.[35]

■ **29** By the addition φερόμενοι ἐν τῷ ἁγίῳ πνεύματι, "being carried along by the Holy Spirit" (D, Irenaeus, Tertullian), εὖ πράξετε, "you will do well" (*RSV*), is understood as good conduct. This is in line with the ethical tendency of the Western text. Perhaps well-being is also in view.

---

28   Trocmé, *Livre des Actes,* 160–61.
29   See the commentaries on 1 Pet 5:12. On the construction of the sentence: ἔδοξε τοῖς ἀποστόλοις . . . ἐκλεξαμένους, "it seemed/good/to the apostles . . . to choose" (accusative with the infinitive as in vs 25; *v.l.* is -οις, the dative plural), see BDF § 410; on . . . γράψαντες, "having written" (relating the participle to the logical subject), see BDF § 468.3. The *RSV*

30   Haenchen, "Quellenanalyse," 153–64.
31   See the commentaries on Rom 1:1.
32   Schwartz, "Chronologie," 271 n. 1; also see Preuschen.
33   BDF § 464.
34   See the comments on vs 22; BDF § 410.

simplifies the sentence construction by translating the participle "having written" as "with the letter."

Excursus:
The Apostolic Council

The problems involve: (1) the relationship between Paul's trips to Jerusalem as described in Acts and in Galatians; (2) the time of the meeting (before or after the "first missionary journey"?), thus the relationship between 11:27–30 and chapter 15; and (3) the content and results of the discussions (already touched on above in connection with the apostolic decree).[35]

1. A solution to this first question presupposes a satisfactory literary-critical analysis of the chapter. Both Dibelius[36] and Haenchen[37] have shown that Luke has shaped the account as a whole. Both conclude that Luke had no sources for chapter 15. The investigation of Luke's composition of the material must precede any attempt at a reconstruction of the events. The relative unity of the presentation, however, does not *eo ipso* exclude the use of sources.[38] Luke could indeed have reworked them and fashioned them to serve his purpose. In any case, he found the names of Peter and James in his material, but not John (Gal 2:9). Whether he knew nothing about Titus or intentionally passed over him is difficult to say. Since he is altogether silent about him, the latter is more probable. Bultmann asks whether a report about the origin of the apostolic decree could not be the basic source, into which the author first inserted Paul and Barnabas.[39] Then Acts 11:30 would correspond to the journey of Gal 2:1 and Acts 15 would deal with events after the conflict described in Gal 2:11–14. This hypothesis is improbable, however, because speeches and discussions do not come from a pre-Lukan source. And one ought not maintain that the decree harmoniously grew out of the discussion.[40] The account is easier to explain if one assumes that Luke has fashioned scenes from reports about the council, and has inserted the decree into such reports for his own reasons.

2. The time is established to some extent by Galatians: the council took place after the fourteen-year mission in Syria and Cilicia (cf. Gal 1:23). To this extent chapter 15 is in the historically correct place, if we assume that the years in Acts are contracted into a brief missionary journey. The chronological evidence (Galatians 1—2 and the date for the stay in Corinth)[41] points to about the year 48. A harmonization of the data about the journeys to Jerusalem in Galatians and in Acts is not possible. In any case, Acts has one journey too many between the conversion and the council. We could assume that the journeys of 11:30 and 15:1–4 are doublets. But even then it would not be certain that the council took place at that earlier time. Only Galatians remains as the source for the reconstruction of the events. Only from it can the actual decisions be set forth: the council agreed that Gentile Christians would be free from the Law, and that Paul would take up a collection for the Jerusalem church in his missionary travels. Paul's role was that of an independent participant in the discussions, not that of one who received orders. Behind Paul's passive role in Acts there is certainly no intention to degrade him. This is simply a necessary consequence of Luke's understanding of the church: freedom from the Law can be declared only from Jerusalem.

3. The questions about communal life in mixed congregations remain open. It appears that there were no difficulties in this respect in the Pauline congregations. In Luke's mind, the way to the great mission—after the prelude of chapters 13—14—is now open. Thus chapter 15 is not only the literary center, but also the real center of the whole book.[42] Peter and the apostles disappear from the field of view. From now on the whole history of the church is compressed into the story of Paul's work. He represents the connection between the early days of the church and the present.[43]

35   See the excursus above on "The Apostolic Decree."
36   Dibelius, *Studies,* 93–101.
37   Haenchen, "Quellenanalyse," 160.
38   Bultmann, "Quellen," 71–74, reprinted in his *Exegetica,* 412–23.
39   Ibid.; see the commentary on vs 12.
40   Haenchen, "Quellenanalyse," 160.
41   See the commentary on 18:12.
42   Menoud, *Jesus Christ and the Faith,* 121–32.
43   For an account of the scholarly discussion of the Apostolic Council, see Kümmel, "Das Urchristentum," 28–33; idem, "Urchristentum III," 26–29;

Jacques Dupont, *Les Problèmes du livre des Actes d'après les travaux récents* (Analecta Lovaniensia Biblica et Orientalia 2:17; Louvain: Publications Universitaires de Louvain, 1950) 51ff, now in his *Études,* 56–75.

For a review of English and American hypotheses, see G. B. Caird, *The Apostolic Age* (London: Duckworth, 1955) 202–8; *Beginnings* 5.195–212; Dibelius, *Studies,* 93–101; Trocmé, *Livre des Actes,* 156–63; Pierre Benoit, "La deuxième visite de saint Paul à Jérusalem," *Bib* 40 (1959) 778–92 (see the comment on vs 2 above); Lucien Cerfaux, "Le chapitre XVᵉ du livre des Actes à la lumière de la littérature ancienne," *Miscellanea Giovanni Mercati,* vol. 1, *Bibbia-Letteratura Christiana antica* (Studi e testi 121; Vatican City: Biblioteca Apostolica Vaticana, 1946) 107–26, reprinted in *Recueil Cerfaux* 2.105–24; Bo Reicke, "Der geschichtliche Hintergrund des Apostelkonzils und der Antiochia-Episode, Gal. 2, 1–14," *Studia Paulina in honorem Johannis de Zwaan* (Haarlem: Bohn, 1953) 172–87; G. Strothotte, "Das Apostelkonzil im Lichte der jüdischen Rechtsgeschichte" (Diss., Erlangen, 1955); Günter Klein, "Galater 2,6–9 und die Geschichte der Jerusalemer Urgemeinde," *ZThK* 57 (1960) 275–95, reprinted in his *Rekonstruk-tion,* 99–118; Walter Schmithals, *Paul and James* (SBT 46; London: SCM, 1965) 28–62. For a totally different interpretation, see Munck, *Paul,* 231–38; Franz Mussner, "Die Bedeutung des Apostelkonzils für die Kirche," *Ekklesia: Festschrift für Bischof Dr. Matthias Wher* (TThSt 15; Trier: Paulinus-Verlag, 1962) 35–46.

The Great Missionary Journey [15:36—21:26]	**15**	The Return of Paul and Barnabas to Antioch; Their Clash and Separation

30 So when they were sent off, they went down to Antioch; and having gathered the congregation together, they delivered the letter. 31/ And when they read it, they rejoiced at the exhortation. 32/ And Judas and Silas, who were themselves prophets, exhorted the brethren with many words and strengthened them. 33/ And after they had spent some time, they were sent off in peace by the brethren to those who had sent them. 35/ But Paul and Barnabas remained in Antioch, teaching and preaching the word of the Lord, with many others also.

36 And after some days Paul said to Barnabas, "Come, let us return and visit the brethren in every city where we proclaimed the word of the Lord, and see how they are." 37/ And Barnabas wanted to take with them John called Mark. 38/ But Paul thought best not to take with them one who had withdrawn from them in Pamphylia, and had not gone with them to the work. 39/ And there arose a sharp contention, so that they separated from each other; Barnabas took Mark with him and sailed away to Cyprus, 40/ but Paul chose Silas and departed, being commended by the brethren to the grace of the Lord. 41/ And he went through Syria and Cilicia, strengthening the churches.

■ **32** For prophecy and παράκλησις, "encouragement," compare 1 Cor 14:3.

■ **(34)** This verse, "But it seemed good to Silas to remain there," is a widely attested addition (C D etc.) which attempts to eliminate the contradiction between vs 33 and vs 40: Paul cannot take Silas with him unless Silas is still in Antioch. The verse succeeds only in creating a more serious tension with vs 33 since "they" in vs 33 can refer only to Judas and Silas (vs 32).[1]

■ **35** Compare 13:1. The καὶ, "and," after μετά, "with," here is pleonastic, as in Phil 4:3 (cf. also *1 Clem.* 65.1).[2]

■ **36** Here the great missionary journey begins,[3] now with Paul on his own. All other mission territories and missionary efforts are almost completely ignored (Apollos is an exception, 18:24–28). Paul takes the initiative himself, in contrast to 13:1–3. On the other hand, 15:36—16:5 deliberately establishes a connection with everything done thus far, and with the decision made in Jerusalem.

■ **37** How and when Mark[4] again came to Antioch from Jerusalem (13:13) "is a detail with which Luke does not concern himself."[5]

■ **38–39** The incident reported in Gal 2:11–14 is apparently behind this account; here in Acts it has been transposed from the functional into the personal.[6] The story may have come to Luke in a somewhat similar form. We cannot speak of a "suppressing" of the clash with Peter, because Luke does not appear to know Galatians and the events in Antioch were far removed from him personally. Of course he must have known that Mark later

---

1 Dibelius, *Studies*, 87.
2 BDF § 442.13.
3 See the commentary on 13:4.

4 See the commentary on 13:4–5.
5 Haenchen, p. 474.
6 On the imperfect ἠξίου, "thought best" (of unfulfilled

came back to Paul (Phlm 24; Col 4:10; cf. 2 Tim 4:11; there is no reason to doubt the identity of that Mark with John Mark). For Cyprus, compare 4:36 and 13:4.

■ **40–41** According to vs 33 Silas had gone back to Jerusalem. Has another source been inserted here, or is this due to the author's carelessness (as with his treatment of Mark, see above, vs 37)?[7] For παραδοθείς, "being commended," compare 14:26. In actuality, Paul could probably not have succeeded in his dispute with Peter and Barnabas, and left for that reason. If 18:22 is trustworthy, he later sought to restore the relationship. The note about "Syria and Cilicia" could be redactional. Luke of course knew that there were congregations in these regions, but he apparently had no further information. Thus he mentions them in passing (cf. the mention of Galilee in 9:31, and Damascus in 9:1–25).[8]

---

desire), see BDF § 328.
7   Haenchen, p. 477.
8   See further the comments on vs 23.

The Great Missionary Journey [15:36—21:26]	**16**	The Visit to the Congregations of the First Journey; Circumcision of Timothy

1 And he came also to Derbe and to Lystra. A disciple was there, named Timothy, the son of a Jewish woman who was a believer; but his father was a Greek. 2/ He was well spoken of by the brethren at Lystra and Iconium. 3/ Paul wanted Timothy to accompany him; and he took him and circumcised him because of the Jews that were in those places, for they all knew that his father was a Greek. 4/ As they went on their way through the cities, they delivered to them for observance the decisions which had been reached by the apostles and elders who were at Jerusalem. 5/ So the churches were strengthened in the faith, and they increased in numbers daily.

■ **1–2** Compare 14:6. ἐκεῖ, "there," that is, in Lystra.[1] The picture of Timothy in Acts does not do justice to his real significance. In Acts, Timothy, like all of Paul's fellow workers, stands completely in Paul's shadow. In reality, he carried out important assignments independently. This anecdote takes no account of the presence of Silas, nor that Timothy was converted by Paul (1 Cor 4:17).

Mixed marriages were illegal according to Jewish law.[2] Nevertheless, the children of a Jewish mother were counted as Jews.

■ **3** Circumcision can be performed by any Israelite.[3] The question whether Paul would perform circumcision as a matter of principle is beside the point. Timothy was already a Christian, therefore circumcision would not even be considered in his case(!) (Gal 5:11). Were rumors perhaps circulating that in Jerusalem Paul had agreed to the circumcision of Titus (Gal 2:3)?[4] The motivation Luke offers for circumcision (cf. 15:21) presupposes a view of the Law as having lost its power—thus largely in agreement with the historical Paul (1 Cor 9:20 cannot be cited in support of a contrary opinion). This would also fit the view of a non-Jew. For Luke, Timothy's circumcision is required because of the schematic portrayal of Paul's mission in Acts which requires that Paul always go first to the synagogue. For that reason he must be accompanied by Jewish associates (therefore, for example, not Titus). In regard to ᾔδεισαν γὰρ κτλ., "for they . . . knew, etc.," a reference to the mother—instead of the father—would have been better (see above, vss 1–2)! Apparently Luke does not have a precise understanding of Jewish law.

■ **4** This statement serves as an indication of the continuity within the church.

■ **5** Here is a short summary (cf. 6:7; 9:31); for the phraseology, compare Col 2:5 and 1 Pet 5:9. Trocmé emphasizes the definite break after vs 5.[5]

1   See Dibelius-Conzelmann, *Pastoral Epistles*, 98, on 2 Tim 1:3–5.
2   Str-B 2.741.
3   Ibid., 4.28–29.
4   Linton, "Third Aspect," 86–95.
5   Trocmé, *Livre des Actes*, 163 n. 4.

The Great Missionary Journey [15:36—21:26]

16

**The Journey to Troas
and Paul's Vision
(Call to Macedonia)**

6   And they went through the region of
Phrygia and Galatia, having been forbidden by the Holy Spirit to speak the
word in Asia. 7/ And when they had
come opposite Mysia, they attempted to
go into Bithynia, but the Spirit of Jesus
did not allow them; 8/ so, passing by
Mysia, they went down to Troas. 9/ And
a vision appeared to Paul in the night: a
man of Macedonia was standing be-
seeching him and saying, "Come over to
Macedonia and help us." 10/ And when
he had seen the vision, immediately we
sought to go on into Macedonia, concluding that God had called us to preach
the gospel to them.

■ **6–10** The description of this journey is most remarkable: it is an intentional nonmissionary journey! In reality, Paul had worked in this region for a long time. Evidence of this work can still be detected in Acts, since
there is reference to congregations in Galatia and Phrygia (18:23). One senses the gaps in Luke's knowledge
about central Asia Minor (with the exception of the
region from Pisidian Antioch to Derbe). Since Luke's
account is devoid of all specifics regarding stopping
places, the itinerary hypothesis can be held only by
assuming that Luke must have abridged his source to
convey the distinct impression of movement toward the
new goal, Europe.[1] In fact, the account creates the impression of being a summary (similar to 18:21b–23);
compare the parts of 2 Maccabees in which the abridgment of a source is obvious (e.g., 2 Macc 13:18–26). On
the other hand, there are no gaps or breaks which could
give conclusive proof that a summarizing process had
taken place. Nor can any motive be advanced for such
epitomizing. Luke could well have created the same
impression in another way—for example, by providing a
simple list of stopping places (cf. the journeys in 20:13–
17 and 21:1–16) in which there is also a clear destina-

tion. In fact, Luke fashioned the route from a minimum
of hard data. Nothing about Paul's real plans or work
during this period can be concluded from these notes.
■ **6** A comparison with 18:23 indicates that this verse is
redactional. Φρυγία, "Phrygia," is not an adjective, despite the similar adjective Πισιδία, "Pisidian," in 13:14 (cf.
18:23; in the Greek of this time, the adjective Φρύγιος
has two endings). The territory of Phrygia in Luke's day
was divided up between the provinces of Asia and Galatia. Γαλατικὴ χώρα, "Galatian region" (for the absence of
the article, cf. Luke 3:1), probably means the *region* of
Galatia, thus the northern part of the province of the
same name. χώρα, "region," is not an official term (*regio*
meaning an administrative district) as William M. Ramsay supposed.[2] Luke certainly distinguishes "Galatia"
from the territory covered on the first journey, which
did extend into the province of Galatia. The names here
are those of regions, and not the names of provinces, as is
clear from the juxtaposition of Phrygia, Galatia, Asia,
and Mysia.[3] Similarly, "Asia" should be understood in
the narrower sense as referring to the territory around
Ephesus (cf. 19:10, 22). Mysia, which Luke distinguishes
from Asia, actually belongs to the province of Asia.

1   Dibelius, *Studies*, 4–6, 148–49, 199–201, 209–10;
     Haenchen, pp. 484–85.

2   William M. Ramsay, *St. Paul the Traveler and the
     Roman Citizen* (7th ed.; London: Hodder &
     Stoughton, 1895; reprinted Grand Rapids: Baker,
     1949) 102–3, cf. 194.

3   On Ramsay's views, see *Beginnings* 5.228–36; T. R. S.
     Broughton, "Three Notes on Saint Paul's Journeys in

Asia Minor," *Quantulacumque: Studies Presented to
Kirsopp Lake* (ed. Robert P. Casey, Silvia Lake, and
Agnes Lake; London: Christophers, 1937) 133–34.

The meaning of the participial sentence is not clear. Ramsay explains, "They traveled through Phrygia and Galatia and were *then* prevented," but this breaks down for grammatical reasons.[4] Therefore one must interpret that they wanted to travel on the great main highway to Asia (Ephesus), but were then prevented from doing so and turned toward the north.[5] It must be taken into account that Luke apparently did not know the interior of Asia Minor. He views Asia Minor, as he views Palestine, from the perspective of someone who lives on the coast. It is at least clear what Luke intends here: the comments make obvious God's guidance on the way to Europe.

■ **7–8** Mysia is the northern portion of the province of Asia (Strabo 12.564–65, 571). Bithynia, which connects with it to the northeast, belonged to the province of Bithynia and Pontus. Because they were prevented from going to the left (Asia) and right (Bithynia), the only way remaining was to the west, and the coast. For κατά, "opposite," compare 27:7 and Luke 10:32. παρελθόντες (the Western text has διελθόντες, "go through") does not mean "pass by" but "pass through" (1 Macc 5:48).[6] The significance of the imminent crossing is indicated by the intervention of the Spirit. Alexandria Troas (2 Cor 2:12–13) at that time was a Roman colony (Pliny *Nat. hist.* 5.124). The congregation there is mentioned in 20:6–12.

■ **9** Revelations that occur in dreams are well known in the Old Testament and in the whole of the ancient world; for example, Herodotus 7.12: "It seemed to Xerxes that a tall and goodly man stood over him and said . . ." (ἐδόκεε ὁ Ξέρξης ἄνδρα οἱ ἐπιστάντα μέγαν τε καὶ εὐειδέα εἰπεῖν . . .); compare Philostratus *Vita Apoll.* 4.34.[7]

■ **10** The transition to the first person follows, completely without preparation.[8] However, with βοήθησον ἡμῖν, "help us," the author appears to intend a transition, and to indicate the meaning of the "we" or the perspective from which it is spoken. Quite apart from the question of a "we-source"[9] this creates the impression of an eyewitness account. This impression continues for the coastal region of the northern Aegean and for the last two journeys (Philippi-Jerusalem and Caesarea-Rome). Apparently there are reflected here connections among congregations of this area during Luke's time.[10] Or the author is pointing to the region from which he himself has collected material, thus being conscious of possessing authentic traditions. Haenchen believes that for the ancient reader the "we" would have pointed to Silas and Timothy.[11] But these two were with Paul for a long time without the narrative shifting into the first person. "We" rather gives the impression that at this point the narrator has become Paul.

---

4   The aorist participle is not to be compared with that of 25:13; see the comment on 25:13.

5   Haenchen, p. 486.

6   Regarding the route, see T. R. S. Broughton, "Three Notes on Saint Paul's Journeys in Asia Minor," *Quantulacumque: Studies Presented to Kirsopp Lake* (ed. Robert P. Casey, Silvia Lake, and Agnes Lake; London: Christophers, 1937) 135.

7   Wilhelm Michaelis, "ὁράω," *TDNT* 5 (1967) 329, 350–51; Alfred Wikenhauser, "Die Traumgesichte des Neuen Testaments in religionsgeschichtlicher Sicht," *Pisciculi: Studien zur Religion und Kultur des Altertums [Festschrift] Franz Joseph Dölger* (ed. Theodor Klauser and Adolf Rücker; Antike und Christentum Sup 1; Münster: Aschendorff, 1939) 320–33. On the apocryphal acts, see Söder, *Die apokryphen Apostelgeschichten*, 171–80. On the significance of this

move toward Europe within the context of Luke's view of history, see Otto Glombitza, "Der Schritt nach Europa: Erwägungen zu Act 16:9–15," *ZNW* 53 (1962) 77–82.

8   Cadbury, "'We' and 'I' Passages," 128–32.

9   See the Introduction, pp. xxxviii–xl.

10   Cf. also the singular prominence of Philippi; Ramsay, *St. Paul*, 206–8; Wilfred L. Knox, *St Paul and the Church of Jerusalem* (Cambridge: Cambridge University, 1925) xxiv.

11   Haenchen, p. 490.

The Great Missionary Journey [15:36—21:26]

16

Philippi

11 Setting sail therefore from Troas, we made a direct voyage to Samothrace, and the following day to Neapolis, 12/ and from there to Philippi, which is the leading city of the district of Macedonia, and a Roman colony. We remained in this city some days; 13/ and on the sabbath day we went outside the gate to the riverside, where we supposed there was a place of prayer; and we sat down and spoke to the women who had come together. 14/ One who heard us was a woman named Lydia, from the city of Thyatira, a seller of purple goods, who was a worshiper of God. The Lord opened her heart to give heed to what was said by Paul. 15/ And when she was baptized, with her household, she besought us, saying, "If you have judged me to be faithful to the Lord, come to my house and stay." And she prevailed upon us.

16 As we were going to the place of prayer, we were met by a slave girl who had a spirit of divination and brought her owners much gain by soothsaying. 17/ She followed Paul and us, crying, "These men are servants of the Most High God, who proclaim to you the way of salvation." 18/ And this she did for many days. But Paul was annoyed, and turned and said to the spirit, "I charge you in the name of Jesus Christ to come out of her." And it came out that very hour.

19 But when her owners saw that their hope of gain was gone, they seized Paul and Silas and dragged them into the market place before the rulers; 20/ and when they had brought them to the magistrates they said, "These men are Jews and they are disturbing our city. 21/ They advocate customs which it is not lawful for us Romans to accept or practice." 22/ The crowd joined in attacking them; and the magistrates tore the garments off them and gave orders to beat them with rods. 23/ And when they had inflicted many blows upon them, they threw them into prison, charging the jailer to keep them safely. 24/ Having received this charge, he put them into the inner prison and fastened their feet in the stocks.

25 But about midnight Paul and Silas were praying and singing hymns to God, and the prisoners were listening to them, 26/ and suddenly there was a great earthquake, so that the foundations of the prison were shaken; and immediately all the doors were opened and every one's fetters were unfastened. 27/ When the jailer woke and saw that the prison doors were open, he drew his sword and was

about to kill himself, supposing that the prisoners had escaped. 28/ But Paul cried with a loud voice, "Do not harm yourself, for we are all here." 29/ And he called for lights and rushed in, and trembling with fear he fell down before Paul and Silas, 30/ and brought them out and said, "Men, what must I do to be saved?" 31/ And they said, "Believe in the Lord Jesus, and you will be saved, you and your household." 32/ And they spoke the word of the Lord to him and to all that were in his house. 33/ And he took them the same hour of the night, and washed their wounds, and he was baptized at once, with all his family. 34/ Then he brought them up into his house, and set food before them and he rejoiced with all his household that he had believed in God.

35   But when it was day, the magistrates sent the police, saying, "Let those men go." 36/ And the jailer reported the words to Paul, saying, "The magistrates have sent to let you go; now therefore come out and go in peace." 37/ But Paul said to them, "They have beaten us publicly, uncondemned, men who are Roman citizens, and have thrown us into prison; and do they now cast us out secretly? No! let them come themselves and take us out." 38/ The police reported these words to the magistrates, and they were afraid when they heard that they were Roman citizens; 39/ so they came and apologized to them. And they took them out and asked them to leave the city. 40/ So they went out of the prison, and visited Lydia; and when they had seen the brethren, they exhorted them and departed.

■ 11 The fact that the trip goes so well is a confirmation of the ὅραμα, "vision." The distance from Troas to Neapolis (= Kavalla) is two hundred kilometers by air. Favorable winds made it possible to cover the distance in the time indicated.[1] Samothrace is midway between Troas and Neapolis—compare the trip in the opposite direction (20:6).

■ 12 Philippi lay about fourteen kilometers inland, separated from the coast by a mountain range.

Excursus:
Philippi

Philippi = *Colonia Julia August Philippensis.*[2] It possessed *ius Italicum*, "Italian law," rights that citizens of an Italian city had.[3] In the following verses the accuracy of detail and intensity of local coloring are striking. In this instance it is important for the course

1   On the speed of ancient ships, see the literature cited in the excursus after 27:44.

2   Paul Collart, "Le Sanctuaire des Dieux Égyptiens,"

3   *BCH* 53 (1929) 84–85; idem, "Inscriptions de Philippes," *BCH* 56 (1932) 129; *CIL* 3 Sup 14206.4. PW 10.1238–53; cf. 4.511–88.

of events that the city is a Roman colony.[4] (This was not so in Antioch of Pisidia, etc.; does Luke have any information at all of its status as a colony?) With regard to the language, Latin dominates the inscriptions in the first two centuries, but Greek apparently continued to be a spoken language (cf. the correspondence of both Paul and Polycarp with the congregation).[5]

πρώτη τῆς μερίδος κτλ., "leading city . . . of the district, etc.," can scarcely be translated in its present form. Macedonia was not a μερίς, "district," rather the *province* of Macedonia was divided into four "districts" (Livy 45.29).[6] πρώτη, "first" (*RSV*, "leading"), designates a city as the capital,[7] but can also be a title of honor.[8] The Western text gives an interpretation by replacing πρώτη with κεφαλή, "head" (cf. Isa 7:6–9 LXX). But Philippi, as a colony, was neither a provincial capital nor a district capital. Should one conjecture the reading πρώτης μερίδος, "first district," thus yielding "a city in the first district"—which would fit?

■ **13** The river is the Gangites (or Angites), two kilometers west of the city. Near it was a gate which marked the border of the pomerium. προσευχή, "place of prayer," can mean a synagogue.[9] If such is the case here, it is strange that the author then says οὗ ἐνομίζομεν, "where we *supposed* there was a place of prayer." It is even stranger that only women were there. Is the author thinking of a place for prayer out in the open? The textual tradition is confused. The following readings occur: B and A read ἐνομίζομεν προσευχή [*sic*] εἶναι, "we supposed there was a place of prayer" (προσευχήν, an accusative instead of the nominative, is grammatically

correct; the reading includes a mistake); א and C employ the correct accusative form, προσευχήν, but א has ἐνόμιζεν, "he supposed"; P[74] has ἐνόμιζεν προσευχή; C has ἐνομίζαμεν; D offers ἐδόκει προσευχὴ εἶναι, "there appeared to be a place of prayer"; and the Koine tradition has ἐνομίζετο, "it was supposed." The variants can be explained in the simplest way if the original had an incorrect nominative (προσευχή) instead of the accusative (προσευχήν).

■ **14** Lydia was a well-known name, especially because of Horace (*Odes* 1.8, etc.). In this case the woman actually comes from the land of Lydia. πόλεως θυατίρων, "the city of Thyatira," is the genitive form of πόλις θυάτειρα, "city Thyatira" (cf. 11:5, ἐν πόλει Ἰόππῃ, "in the city Joppa"); the genitive does not designate the inhabitants (for that, cf. 2 Cor 11:32).[10] Thyatira (Rev 2:18) was famous as a center for the purple dyeing industry.[11] On a damaged inscription from Philippi, the word *PV]RPVRARI[*, "purple," can still be made out.[12] This first convert is not mentioned in Philippians. For διήνοιξεν, "opened," compare Luke 24:45 and 2 Macc 1:4. For προσέχειν, "to give heed," compare 8:6.

■ **15** Here is a case of the baptism of a household (cf. 1 Cor 1:16). This expression provides no information about the baptism of children or infants.[13] For house fellowship as religious fellowship, compare the inscription of Pompeia Agrippinilla.[14] πιστήν, "faithful," is used here instead of σεβομένη, "worshiper" (cf. vs 14), to reflect the change which has occurred in the life of this woman. On hospitality, compare Matt 10:40; Rom 12:13; 1 Tim 5:10; *1 Clem.* 1.2; 10–12.

4 For information about the city, see Paul Collart, *Philippes: Ville de Macédoine, depuis ses origines jusqu'à la fin de l'époque romaine* (2 vols.; École Française d'Athènes: Travaux et Mémoires 5; Paris: Boccard, 1937); *DACL* 14.712–41, esp. 720 and 731.

5 PW 19.2206–44; Ernst Kirsten and Wilhelm Kraiker, *Griechenlandkunde: Ein Führer zu klassischen Stätten* (5th ed.; Heidelberg: Winter, 1967) 655–69, esp. 657–58.

6 PW 14.767.

7 BAG *s.v.* μερίς.

8 Schultze, *Altchristliche Städte* 2.1, 13; *Beginnings* 4.188.

9 In addition to the literature cited in BAG *s.v.*, see PW 4 A 1284–1316. On the place of the synagogue in Paul's mission as an element in Luke's schema, see the commentary on 13:5.

10 BDF § 167.

11 BAG *s.v.*

12 *CIL* 3.664.

13 Joachim Jeremias believes otherwise, see *Infant Baptism in the First Four Centuries* (Library of History and Doctrine; London: SCM, 1960); idem, *The Origins of Infant Baptism: A Further Study in Reply to Kurt Aland* (SHT 1; London: SCM, 1963); for a contrary interpretation, see Kurt Aland, *Did the Early Church Baptize Infants?* (2d ed.; trans. G. R. Beasley-Murray; Library of History and Doctrine; London: SCM, 1963); idem, *Die Stellung der Kinder in den frühen christlichen Gemeinden—und ihre Taufe* (ThExH 138; Munich: Kaiser, 1967).

On οἶκος, "household," see Peter Weigandt, "Zur sogenannten 'Oikosformel'," *NovT* 6 (1963) 49–74; Gerhard Delling, "Zur Taufe von 'Häusern' in Urchristentum," *NovT* 7 (1964–65) 285–311;

■ **16–40** The account which follows provides a good example of the way Luke works. From the information he has gathered he fashions a plot, connecting it to the story of Lydia, a plot with a double denouement (the first in vs 19, the second brought about by the miracle). The building blocks are the local stories, the exorcism, information about Paul's suffering in Philippi (apparently including local coloring), and the legend about the release from jail.[15]

■ **16–18** This little scene serves once again to delimit mantic phenomena.[16] The exploitation of such diviners for commercial gain regularly drew criticism (Lucian). The word πύθωνα which the *RSV* translates "divination" is the name of the dragon Apollo killed at Delphi.[17] Later (attested at the time of the empire) the word was used of a ventriloquist as a soothsayer; Plutarch *Defect. orac.* 414e: "Certainly it is foolish and childish in the extreme to imagine that the god himself after the manner of ventriloquists (who used to be called 'Eurycleis,' but now 'Pythones') enters into the bodies of his prophets and prompts their utterances, employing their mouths and voices as instruments" (εὔηθες γάρ ἐστι καὶ παιδικὸν κομιδῇ τὸ οἴεσθαι τὸν θεὸν αὐτὸν ὥσπερ τοὺς ἐγγαστριμύθους, Εὐρυκλέας πάλαι νυνὶ δὲ Πύθωνας προσαγορευομένους, ἐνδυόμενον εἰς τὰ σώματα τῶν προφητῶν ὑποφθέγγεσθαι, τοῖς ἐκείνων στόμασι καὶ φωναῖς χρώμενον ὀργάνοις).[18] Luke transfers the label from the ventriloquist to a spirit which speaks through the ventriloquist (in fact, Luke is probably not thinking of ventriloquism at all; the use of the verb κράζω, "to cry out," in vs 17 is appropriate for spirit possession). In this way the account is more closely patterned after the Synoptic exorcisms.

■ **17** καὶ ἡμῖν, "and us," seems to be a secondary assimilation to the "we" of the framework (the first-person plural is not found again until 20:5). In the Gospels demons also speak objective truths (Mark 1:24; Luke 4:41, etc.), but they are not *allowed* to continue speaking. The name for God, ὕψιστος, "Most High," is also found in Mark 5:7 and Luke 8:28 in connection with demons. For ὁδὸς σωτηρίας, "way of salvation," compare 2:28.

■ **18a** The reference to "many days" does not fit with vs 16 (ἐγένετο ὑπαντῆσαι, "we were met"). The original version probably told of only a single encounter between Paul and the young woman and an immediate exorcism. This extension of time seems artificial and tendentious: it wants to suggest that, in view of the consequences of this encounter, Paul must have been carrying on missionary activity for some time. For the effect, compare Ps.-Clem. *Hom.* 9.16.3: "For pythons prophesy, yet they are cast out by us as demons, and put to flight" (ὅτι καὶ πύθωνες μαντεύονται, ἀλλ᾽ ὑφ᾽ ἡμῶν ὡς δαίμονες ὁρκιζόμενοι φυγαδεύονται). αὐτῇ τῇ ὥρᾳ, "that very hour," is not a "Lukan Aramaism";[19] the expression is found in the papyri (cf. also Dan 3:15; 4:33; 5:5 [Th]).[20]

■ **19** Paul refers to his suffering in Philippi in 1 Thess 2:2. ἄρχοντες, "rulers," and στρατηγοί, "magistrates" (vs 20), do not indicate different stages in a legal process.[21]

■ **20–21** στρατηγοί, "magistrates," is a popular name for the *duumviri* (Cicero *De leg.* 2.34, 93); ἀγορά, "market place" = the forum; ῥαβδοῦχοι, "police" (vs 35) = lictors. The formulation of the accusation is instructive for understanding the Lukan apologetic—the charge is delivered in such a way that it can be denied. It is clear that Luke is not trying to recommend Christianity to the Romans as true Judaism; rather he distinctly sets Christianity apart from Judaism. Moreover, he does not enter into the Roman legal principles (e.g., Cicero *De leg.* 2.8.19: "No one shall have gods to himself, either new gods or alien gods, unless recognized by the State. Privately they shall worship those gods whose worship they

August Strobel, "Der Begriff des 'Hauses' im griechischen und römischen Privatrecht," *ZNW* 56 (1965) 91–100.

14   The inscription is found in Nilsson, *Geschichte* 2.359–63.

15   Plümacher, *Apostelgeschichte,* 95–97; on the analysis also see Gottfried Schille, *Anfänge der Kirche: Erwägungen zur apostolischen Frühgeschichte* (BEvTh 43; Munich: Kaiser, 1966) 43–53.

16   On this, see Nilsson, *Geschichte* 2.97–107, 447–65; Prümm, *Handbuch,* 413–34.

17   Werner Foerster, "ὄφις," *TDNT* 5 (1967) 569 n. 47.

18   Werner Foerster, "πύθων," *TDNT* 6 (1968) 917–20.

19   Matthew Black, *An Aramaic Approach to the Gospels and Acts* (3d ed.; Oxford: Clarendon, 1967; reprinted 1971) 111.

20   Joachim Jeremias, "Ἐν ἐκείνῃ τῇ ὥρᾳ (ἐν) αὐτῇ τῇ ὥρᾳ," *ZNW* 42 (1949) 214–17.

21   On the officials in Philippi (Roman system!), see *DACL* 14.719; W. C. van Unnik, "Die Anklage gegen die Apostel in Philippi (Apostelgeschichte 16,20f)," *Mullus: Für Theodor Klauser* (ed. Alfred Stuiber and Alfred Hermann; JAC Sup 1; Münster: Aschendorff, 1964) 366–73, reprinted in *Sparsa collecta: The*

have duly received from their ancestors" [Separatim nemo habessit deos neve novos neve advenas nisi publice adscitos privatim colunto quos rite a patribus cultos acceperint]). From Cicero we can conclude that it was a punishable act for a Roman citizen to convert to Judaism. In actual fact, the application of criminal law was inconsistent. When necessary, the state could intervene in an individual case (as in the case of Flavius Clemens and of Domitilla concerning "atheism"; Dio Cass. 67.14).[22]

■ **22** For tearing off the garments (before being beaten), compare Livy 8.32, 11; Tacitus *Hist.* 4.27; Diodorus Sic. 17.35.7: "others, ripping off their clothing, drove them with blows of their hands . . . against their naked bodies" (οἱ δὲ τὰς ἐσθῆτας περιρρηγνύντες καὶ γυμνοῖς τοῖς σώμασιν ἐπιβάλλοντες τὰς χεῖρας). On Paul's beatings (by the Romans), compare 2 Cor 11:25.[23]

■ **23–24** ἀσφαλῶς and ἀσφαλίζεσθαι, "safely" (vs 23) and "fastened" (vs 24), sets up the miraculous nature of the release; the inner prison and the stocks are mentioned for the same reason. This area in the prison ("Martyrs of Lyons" in Eusebius *Hist. eccl.* 5.1.27; *Pass. Perp.* 3.5–6; *Mart. Pionii* 11) was dark, and the prisoners were chained. The miraculous release was an independent legend, in agreement with Dibelius[24] and against Haenchen,[25] who explains it as a creation of Luke. Luke, however, does not freely invent such stories. Of course the legend is not stylistically pure, since the conversion motif is mixed in with the release motif.

■ **25** The midnight hour is part of the "numinous" mood. Singing hymns of praise is a common motif of the δεσμόλυτα, "prison release";[26] the imprisoned Bacchae praise

Dionysus, Epictetus 2.6.26: "And then we shall be emulating Socrates, when we are able to write paeans in prison" (καὶ τότ᾽ ἐσόμεθα ζηλωταὶ Σωκράτους, ὅταν ἐν φυλακῇ δυνώμεθα παιᾶνας γράφειν); *T. Jos.* 8.5: "When I was in fetters, the Egyptian woman was overtaken with grief. She came and heard the report how I gave thanks to the Lord and sang praise in the house of darkness" (καὶ ὡς ἦμεν ἐν τοῖς δεσμοῖς, ἡ Αἰγυπτία συνείχετο ἀπὸ τῆς λύπης, καὶ ἐπηκροατό μου πῶς ὕμνουν κύριον ἐν οἴκῳ σκότους). The miracle is the heavenly response to the joyous confession of faith.

■ **26** The combination of door opening and unfastening of chains is also widespread.[27] The miracle is spiritualized in the apocryphal acts of the apostles.[28] One is not to ask whether the city also felt the earthquake. In the original form of the story there was probably also no thought given to the rest of the prisoners.[29]

■ **27** The warden was responsible for the prisoners. The higher authorities would certainly have exonerated him (*Dig.* 12.48.3). His behavior is portrayed in a legendary rather than realistic manner.

■ **28–29** The style of the legend dominates all the more here. How did Paul, in the inner prison, know that the jailer was about to kill himself? How did he know that all the prisoners were still there? How did his cry reach the jailer? How did the jailer know for which prisoners the miracle had taken place (because all were released from their chains)? These are all questions about which the legend does not concern itself; as in the theater, some details must be left to the imagination of the audience.

■ **29** This time there is no gesture refusing the man's

Collected Essays of W. C. van Unnik (2 vols.; NovTSup 29–30; Leiden: Brill, 1973–80) 374–85.

22 Jean Juster, *Les Juifs dans l'Empire romain: Leur condition juridique, économique et sociale* (2 vols.; Paris: Geuthner, 1914) 1.254–63.
    For literature on anti-Semitism in antiquity, see Bo Reicke, *Diakonie, Festfreude und Zelos, in Verbindung mit der altchristlichen Agapenfeier* (UUÅ 1951:5; Uppsala: Lundequist; Wiesbaden: Harrassowitz, 1951) 312 n. 29.

23 On the procedures, see Theodor Mommsen, "Die Rechtsverhältnisse des Apostels Paulus," *ZNW* 2 (1901) 89–90; yet it should be noted that the earliest form of the narrative knew nothing of Paul's rights as a Roman citizen.

24 Dibelius, *Studies*, 23–24.

25 Haenchen, pp. 501–4.

26 Otto Weinreich, "Gebet und Wunder," *Genethliakon: Festschrift für W. Schmid* (Stuttgart: Kohlhammer, 1929) 321–22.

27 See the commentary on 12:6–11; Euripides *Bacc.* 447–48; Ovid *Metam.* 15.669–74; Origen *Cels.* 2.34. On shaking, see the commentary on 4:31; Lucian *Philops.* 22.

28 Erik Peterson, *Frühkirche, Judentum und Gnosis: Studien und Untersuchungen* (Freiburg/Rome/Vienna: Herder, 1959) 183–208.

29 For the form ἀνέθη (without augment), "were unfastened," see BDF § 67.2.

action. In 10:26 Peter declines the gesture of respect offered by Cornelius—there is no such comment in this verse (cf. also 14:15).

■ **30** D and sy^h—contrary to the style of the legend—concern themselves with the rest of the prisoners (τοὺς λοιποὺς ἀσφαλισάμενος, "having secured the rest"). Luke's failure to mention Paul's preaching to the rest of the prisoners is evidence that this is a rather clumsy, secondary expansion. For the question formulated in catechetical style, compare 2:37 and Luke 3:10. The jailer's question (as formulated) assumes that the miracle would no longer be understood.

■ **31** The answer is given by the shortest version of the confession of faith (cf. Rom 10:9; John 20:28). For "and your household," compare vs 15 and 11:14.

■ **32-33** The instruction for baptism is resumed. The content of this instruction is anticipated by vs 31. Are vss 32-33 a redactional expansion of the source, which has confused the details about the setting for the sermon and the baptism?[30] Compare vs 30 with vs 33.

■ **34** παρατιθέναι τράπεζαν, "set food before them," is not a circumlocution for the Eucharist,[31] but is an act of kindness, like the washing of the wounds. With this verse the legend is concluded.

■ **35** This verse leads back without transition to the action which frames the miracle story. The narrative continues without any indication that a miracle has occurred. Thus the miracle was inserted secondarily into the narrative. The attempt of D and sy^{hmg} to connect the two (by referring to the magistrates: ἀναμνησθέντες τὸν σεισμὸν τὸν γεγονότα ἐφοβήθησαν, "recollecting the earthquake that had taken place, they were afraid") is done crudely.

■ **36** For the greeting, compare Luke 8:48.

■ **37** This prepares for an apologetic point: Roman law did not hinder the mission. Roman courts could occasionally make mistakes, but the Romans themselves would have to say, from the viewpoint of their own law, that Paul's arrest and beating were improper. Thus Luke has Paul not only insist upon his own innocence in general (for

this, cf. Lucian *Tox.* 33), but also make a special appeal to Roman law. In view of the events it may seem artificial that Luke reports Paul's appeal here for the first time. But in view of Luke's apologetic purpose it makes sense, since the point receives special emphasis when made at the conclusion.[32] The Roman citizen enjoyed legal protection against being put in chains and against flogging; Livy 10.9.4: "Yet the Porcian law alone seems to have been passed to protect the persons of the citizens, imposing, as it does, a heavy penalty if anyone should scourge or put to death a Roman citizen" (Porcia tamen lex sola pro tergo civium lata videtur, quod gravi poena, siquis verberasset necassetve civem Romanum, sanxit); compare Cicero *Rab. post.* 4.12–13; Paulus *Sent.* 5.26.1: "By the Julian law on public violence he is condemned who, endowed with some power, will have killed, or ordered to be killed, should torture, scourge, condemn by law or order to be incarcerated in the state prison a Roman citizen appealing previously to the people and now to the emperor" (Lege Julia de vi publica damnatur, qui aliqua potestate praeditus civem Romanum antea ad populum, nunc imperatorem appellantem necaverit necarive iusserit, torserit, verbaverit, condemnaverit iure publica vincula duci iusserit). But offenses against these laws are also recorded (cf. Cicero *Verr.*;[33] *Fam.* 10.32; "Martyrs of Lyons" in Eusebius *Hist. eccl.* 5.1.44, 50; Josephus *Bell.* 2.308).

■ **39** The evangelists leave with complete freedom (1 Thessalonians does not tell of this rehabilitation). In retrospect it would appear that the concrete material which Luke had concerning Philippi consisted of an anecdote, a legend, and the conversion of Lydia. The nature of this material indicates that it had already passed through many hands before Luke received it, perhaps with the exception of the report about Lydia.

---

30   Dibelius, *Studies*, 23.

31   Contrary to the opinion of Philippe H. Menoud, "The Acts of the Apostles and the Eucharist," *Jesus Christ and the Faith*, 89–90.

32   A. N. Sherwin-White, *The Roman Citizenship* (Oxford: Clarendon, 1939); idem, "The Early Persecutions and Roman Law Again," *JTS* n.s. 3 (1952) 199–213; Cadbury, *Acts in History*, 73–82. On Jews as Roman

citizens, see Josephus *Ant.* 14.228–67; Mommsen, "Rechtsverhältnisse," 82–83; Juster, *Les Juifs* 2.25–27.

33   See the commentary on 22:25.

The Great Missionary Journey [15:36—21:26]

17

Thessalonica

1 Now when they had passed through Amphipolis and Apollonia, they came to
Thessalonica, where there was a synagogue of the Jews. 2/ And Paul went in,
as was his custom, and on three sabbath
days he argued with them from the scriptures, 3/ explaining and proving that it
was necessary for the Christ to suffer
and to rise from the dead, and saying,
"This Jesus, whom I proclaim to you, is
the Christ." 4/ And some of them were
persuaded, and joined Paul and Silas; as
did a great many of the devout Greeks
and not a few of the leading women. 5/
But the Jews were jealous, and taking
some wicked fellows of the rabble, they
gathered a crowd, set the city in an
uproar, and attacked the house of Jason,
seeking to bring them out to the people.
6/ And when they could not find them,
they dragged Jason and some of the
brethren before the city authorities,
crying, "These men who have turned the
world upside down have come here also,
7/ and Jason has received them; and
they are all acting against the decrees of
Caesar, saying that there is another king,
Jesus." 8/ And the people and the city
authorities were disturbed when they
heard this. 9/ And when they had taken
security from Jason and the rest, they let
them go.

■ **1** Luke required no access to an itinerary for this data
since the only route from Philippi to Thessalonica was
the Egnatian Way.[1] A personal knowledge of the road,
inquiry or examination of a description of the road, or a
map would suffice (cf. the *Peutinger Table!*). According to
this work, the distances amount to the following: Philippi
to Amphipolis (capital of the first district of Macedonia)
ca. 33 miles; Amphipolis to Apollonia, ca. 30 miles;
Apollonia to Thessalonica, ca. 38 miles.[2] Thessalonica
(Salonika) was a free city, the most important city of
Macedonia.[3] It was the residence of the Roman governor.[4] Following the familiar schema, Paul goes first to
the synagogue.

■ **2–3** Here is the proof from Scripture, a typical element
in the Lukan schema (cf. 3:18; 26:23; Luke 24:26, 46).[5]
To the conception of the Messiah derived from the Old
Testament he adds the notion that this Messiah must
suffer. From this perspective conclusions can be made
about Jesus: (1) He did suffer, thus the prophecy applied
to him; and (2) by means of the Scriptures, his suffering
is shown to be "necessary" (2:23: τῇ ὡρισμένῃ βουλῇ κτλ.,
"according to the definite plan, etc."). πάσχειν, "to

1 PW 5.1988–93.
2 Konrad Miller, *Die Peutingersche Tafel* (Ravensburg:
Otto Meier, 1887–88; reprinted Stuttgart: Brockhaus, 1962); cf. further *Itinerarium Antoninianum*
320, 331; and *Itinerarium Hieros* 605.
3 PW 6.A.143–63; *DACL* 15.624–713.
4 Regarding the local administration (politarchy), see
Beginnings 4.202.

5 Conzelmann, *Theology*, 153–54.

suffer," has a pregnant significance, as in the parallel passages, and it means "to die."[6] ἀπὸ τῶν γραφῶν, "from the scriptures," should be connected with the participles which follow. ἐπὶ, "on, for" (cf. 16:18), σάββατα τρία, "three sabbaths" means "on three sabbath days," and not "for three weeks" (as in *RSV*). The brevity of Paul's stay does not fit with 1 Thessalonians and Phil 4:9.

■ **4** A, D, gig, and Vg insert καί, "and," after σεβόμενοι, "devout," and thereby distinguish between two groups: the devout or God-fearers, *and* the Greeks. γυναικῶν κτλ., "women, etc.," is explained by vs 12. "But it is strange that neither here nor in Beroea could these influential women avert the persecution of Christians."[7]

■ **5** Note the usage of οἱ Ἰουδαῖοι, "the Jews," which has hardened into an expression with the meaning "the 'disobedient' Jews." Jason is introduced as someone who is well known. This is not sufficient, however, to conclude that a written source was being used, but rather this fits Luke's narrative style (cf. 19:33). προαγαγεῖν εἰς τὸν δῆμον, "to bring . . . out to the people," taken by itself is a juristic expression (presentation before a public assembly; cf. 25:26). Nevertheless here a tumult is being described (δῆμος, "people" = ὄχλος, "mob"), compare the *RSV* and 14:19. Compare with the scene here Plutarch *Aem. Paulus* 38: "Appius saw Scipio rushing into the forum attended by men who were of low birth and had lately been slaves, but who were frequenters of the forum and able to gather a mob and force all issues by means of solicitations and shouting" (ὡς οὖν ἐμβάλλοντος εἰς ἀγορὰν τοῦ Σκηπίωνος κατεῖδε παρὰ πλευρὰν ὁ Ἄππιος ἀνθρώπους ἀγεννεῖς καὶ δεδουλευκότας, ἀγοραίους δὲ καὶ δυναμένους ὄχλον συνάγαγειν καὶ σπουδαρχίᾳ καὶ κραυγῇ πάντα πράγματα βιάσασθαι). Through these intrigues the accusers of vs 6 are unmasked in advance for the reader: it is they who complain about causing a riot![8]

■ **6** πολιτάρχης, "politarch" (*RSV*, "city authority"), as a title for a city magistrate is attested in Macedonia, even in Thessalonica itself.[9] On τὴν οἰκουμένην, "the world," compare Pap. London 1912, lines 96–100,[10] where Claudius commands the Alexandrian Jews "not to introduce or invite Jews who sail down to Alexandria from Syria or Egypt, thus compelling me to conceive the greater suspicion; otherwise I will by all means take vengeance on them as fomenting a general plague for the whole world" (μηδὲ ἐπάγεσθαι ἢ προσείεσθαι ἀπὸ Συρίας ἢ Αἰγύπ(τ)ου καταπλέοντας Ἰουδαίους ἐξ οὗ μείζονας ὑπονοίας ἀναγκασθήσομε λαμβάνειν· εἰ δὲ μή, πάντα τρόπον αὐτοὺς ἐπεξελεύσομαι καθάπερ κοινήν τεινα τῆς οἰκουμένης νόσον ἐξεγείροντας); also recension C of the *Acts of Isidore*, Pap. Berol. 8877, lines 22–24: "I accuse them [the Jews] of wishing to stir up the entire world" (ἐγκ[αλῶ αὐτοῖς] [ὅτι κ]αὶ ὅλην τὴν οἰκουμένην [θέλουσι] [ταράς]σειν).[11]

■ **7** In recension A of the same *Acts of Isidore*,[12] Caesar is called βασιλεύς, "king."[13] It is questionable, however, whether Luke really means the emperor, since elsewhere he always calls the emperor Καῖσαρ, "Caesar" (Luke 23:2; Acts 25:8). Once again, Luke has formulated the charge in line with his apologetic purpose.

■ **9** λαμβάνειν τὸ ἱκανόν, "to take security," is equivalent to the legal term *satis accipere*, "to take/receive bail."[14]

---

6   Wilhelm Michaelis, "πάσχω," *TDNT* 5 (1967) 913–16.

7   Haenchen, p. 507.

8   Conzelmann, *Theology*, 140–44.

9   Ernest DeWitt Burton, "The Politarchs," *AJT* 2 (1898) 598–632.

10   The text and trans. are from Bell, *Jews and Christians*, 25, 29.

11   The text and trans. are available in Musurillo, *Acts of the Pagan Martyrs*, 23, 25; idem, *Acta Alexandrinorum*, 17 (text).

12   Musurillo, *Acts of the Pagan Martyrs*, 18–19; idem, *Acta Alexandrinorum*, 12–13.

13   For examples of this title used for Caesar, see BAG *s.v.*

14   See *OGIS* 484.50–51; 629.100–101.

The Great Missionary Journey [15:36—21:26]

17

Beroea

10 The brethren immediately sent Paul and Silas away by night to Beroea; and when they arrived they went into the Jewish synagogue. 11/ Now these Jews were more noble than those in Thessalonica, for they received the word with all eagerness, examining the scriptures daily to see if these things were so. 12/ Many of them therefore believed, with not a few Greek women of high standing as well as men. 13/ But when the Jews of Thessalonica learned that the word of God was proclaimed by Paul at Beroea also, they came there too, stirring up and inciting the crowds. 14/ Then the brethren immediately sent Paul off on his way to the sea, but Silas and Timothy remained there. 15/ Those who conducted Paul brought him as far as Athens; and receiving a command for Silas and Timothy to come to him as soon as possible, they departed.

■ 10 Beroea, modern Verria, lies to the south of the Egnatian Way (about 80 kilometers from Thessalonica) on the highway toward central and southern Greece.[1] At the time of Nero the city was the assembling place for the Macedonian κοινόν, "council," with the title μητρόπολις, "capital city";[2] Lucian (*Lucius* 34) calls it large and populous.

■ 11 εὐγενέστεροι, "more noble"—Chrysostom: τουτέστιν ἐπιεικέστεροι, "that is, more gentle."[3] Expressions such as μετὰ πάσης προθυμίας, "with all eagerness," are common in inscriptions.[4]

■ 13 On this action, compare 14:19.[5]

■ 14 ἕως (*v.l.* ὡς) ἐπί, "to," is equivalent to ἕως πρός, "as far as," in Luke 24:50;[6] compare *Peripl. Erythr.* 4: ὡς εἰς πέλαγος, "as far as the sea."[7] It is not said that they only took Paul "as if" to the sea, that is, to deceive his pursuers, but that he really traveled by land.[8] D certainly assumes a journey by land (in Codex D the sea is first reached in Athens). It follows from 1 Thess 3:1–2 that Timothy traveled with Paul to Athens, and from there he was again sent back to Thessalonica. Not until then did he follow Paul to Corinth, where Paul had gone in the meantime (cf. 18:4); thus the Lukan picture is simplified.

1   PW 3.304–5.
2   PWSup 4.930–31.
3   J. A. Cramer, *Catenae Graecorum Patrum in Novum Testamentum* (8 vols.; Oxford: Oxford University, 1838–44) 3.282.
4   See the commentary on 4:29; 19:29; BAG *s.v.*
5   On ἀπό, "of," to indicate belonging to a place, see BDF § 209.2.
6   BDF § 453.4.
7   For the text of this document, see Frisk, *Le Périple.*
8   So Preuschen; Bauernfeind.

The Great Missionary Journey [15:36—21:26]

17

Athens
(including the Areopagus Speech)

16 Now while Paul was waiting for them at Athens, his spirit was provoked within him as he saw that the city was full of idols. 17/ So he argued in the synagogue with the Jews and the devout persons, and in the market place every day with those who chanced to be there. 18/ Some also of the Epicurean and Stoic philosophers met him. And some said, "What would this babbler say?" Others said, "He seems to be a preacher of foreign divinities"—because he preached Jesus and the resurrection [or: Anastasis (the goddess)]. 19/ And they took hold of him and brought him to the Areopagus, saying, "May we know what this new teaching is which you present? 20/ For you bring some strange things to our ears; we wish to know therefore what these things mean." 21/ Now all the Athenians and the foreigners who lived there spent their time in nothing except telling or hearing something new.

22 So Paul, standing in the middle of the Areopagus, said: "Men of Athens, I perceive that in every way you are very religious. 23/ For as I passed along, and observed the objects of your worship, I found also an altar with this inscription, 'To an [or: the] unknown god.' What therefore you worship as unknown, this I proclaim to you. 24/ The God who made the world and everything in it, being Lord of heaven and earth, does not live in shrines made by man, 25/ nor is he served by human hands, as though he needed anything, since he himself gives to all men life and breath and everything. 26/ And he made from one every nation of men to live on all the face of the earth, having determined allotted periods and the boundaries of their habitation, 27/ that they should seek God, in the hope that they might feel after him and find him. Yet he is not far from each one of us, 28/ for

'In him we live and move and have our being';

as even some of your poets have said,

'For we are indeed his offspring.'

29/ Being then God's offspring, we ought not to think that the Deity is like gold, or silver, or stone, a representation by the art and imagination of man. 30/ The times of ignorance God overlooked, but now he commands all men everywhere to repent, 31/ because he has fixed a day on which he will judge the world in righteousness by a man whom he has appointed, and of this he has given assurance to all men by raising him from the dead."

32 Now when they heard of the resurrection of the dead, some mocked; but others said, "We will hear you again about this." 33/ So Paul went out from among them. 34/ But some men joined him and believed, among them Dionysius the Areopagite and a woman named Damaris and others with them.

Athens has deliberately been chosen as the stage for a paradigmatic encounter. The scenery is redactional, sketched to fit the speech. It fluctuates somewhat, because on the one hand Luke wants to bring the representatives of the universal Greek culture into play, but on the other hand he uses vivid local color to characterize the audience as typical Athenians. Dibelius understands the matter differently, assigning vss 17 and 34 and "perhaps" also vss 19 and 20 or 32 to the "itinerary";[1] H. Hommel assigns vss 16–18 and 34 to the itinerary.[2] But style and content (a lack of concrete material) indicate rather that the author has used the well-known tour-guide motif, with freedom.

Excursus:
Athens

The might of Athens had been broken long ago, but the city still enjoyed great respect; Cicero *Pro Flacco* 26.62: "Here present are men from Athens, where men think humanity, learning, religion, grain, rights, and laws were born, and whence they were spread through all the earth. . . . It has, moreover, such renown that the now shattered and weakened name of Greece is supported by the reputation of this city" (Adsunt Athenienses, unde humanitas, doctrina, religio, fruges, iura, leges ortae atque in omnes terras distributa putantur . . . auctoritate autem tanta est, ut iam fractum prope ac debilitatum Graeciae nomen

huius urbis laude nitatur). It should not be called a "quiet little city." It was a tourist center, site of great festivals, and still the classical university city (*doctae Athenae*, "learned Athens," Ovid *Ep.* 2.83; cf. Philostratus *Vita Apoll.* 4.17); Cicero *Fin.* 5.2.5: "Though in fact there is no end to it in this city; wherever we go we tread on historic ground" (Quamquam id quidem infinitum est in hac urbe: quacumque enim ingredimur, in aliqua historia vestigium ponimus).[3]

■ **16** The word κατείδωλος, "full of idols," is not attested in pre-Christian writings, but is grammatically correct. On this subject, compare Livy 45.27: "Athens . . . has . . . statues of gods and men—statues notable for every sort of material and artistry" (Athenas . . . habentes . . . simulacra deorum hominumque omni genere et materiae et artium insignia); compare also Strabo 9.396; Pausanius 1.17.1. παρωξύνετο, "was provoked," sets the mood for Paul's speech to the Athenians in vss 22–31. The aesthetic point of view which characterized classical culture is absent. The Jewish-Christian rejection of "idols" dominates.

■ **17** This verse does not come from a source, but simply carries out the Lukan schema. This time the transition to the Gentiles follows smoothly, which means that Luke has no source material and has composed this verse independently. He has chosen the agora as the setting because it was one of the best-known localities; it lay to

1 Dibelius, *Studies*, 73–75.
2 Hommel, "Areopagrede," 174.
3 Literature:
   Ernst Curtius, *Die Stadtgeschichte von Athen* (Berlin: Weidmann, 1891).
   Paul Graindor, *Athènes de Tibère à Trajan* (Cairo: Société anonyme égyptienne, 1931) esp. 166–71.
   Idem, *Athènes sous Auguste* (Cairo: Société anonyme égyptienne, 1927).
   Idem, *Athènes sous Hadrien* (Cairo: Boulac, 1934).
   Ida Thallon Hill, *The Ancient City of Athens: Its Topography and Monuments* (Cambridge: Harvard University, 1953).
   Walther Judeich, *Topographie von Athen* (2d ed.; Munich: Beck, 1931).
   Kirsten and Kraiker, *Griechenlandkunde*, 49–75.

the north of the Areopagus.[4] διελέγετο, "he argued" (in the agora), awakens memories of Socrates (Plato *Apol.* 19d); but with Luke the word has already taken on the sense "preach" (17:2; 18:4, 19; 19:8–9; 20:7, 9).[5]

■ **18** The scene is supplied with local color; for that reason it should be seen as a literary creation. Stoics and Epicureans are mentioned as representatives of the two schools best known to the general public. Luke does not side with the Stoics, though later he actually works with Stoic ideas. The speech which follows does not begin with philosophical teachings (such as the monotheistic tendencies of the time), but with popular religion. The juxtaposition of the two schools merely serves to create a milieu. The author is striving for a cultured style: τί ἂν θέλοι, "What would" (the optative!).[6] σπερμολόγος, "babbler," is an Athenian term of derision, but it was also in use elsewhere (Philo *Leg. Gai.* 203). ξένων κτλ., "of foreign, etc.," is again reminiscent of Socrates; Xenophon *Mem.* 1.1.1: "Socrates is guilty of rejecting the gods acknowledged by the state and of bringing in strange deities" (ἀδικεῖ Σωκράτης οὓς μὲν ἡ πόλις νομίζει θεοὺς οὐ νομίζων, ἕτερα δὲ καινὰ δαιμόνια εἰσφέρων); compare Plato *Apol.* 24b. In this scene Luke seeks not to provide detailed information about legal proceedings, but to create a mood. Is Luke playing on a misunderstanding, attributing to the audience an interpretation of the word "anastasis" as a name for a goddess rather than a word meaning resurrection (*RSV*)? (Chrysostom understood the text this way.) The plural δαιμόνια, "divinities," certainly does not prove this. In any case, the Christian reader understands that here has been summarized the central theme of Christian preaching—according to Lukan theology—and he or she will take the speech which follows as the development of that theme.

■ **19** At first glance, vss 18 and 19 might seem to be dou-

blets. But this is Lukan style for the exposition of a scene. Exegetes have interpreted this in various ways, some seeing here a hostile "arrest" and an arraignment before the "Council of the Areopagus," others a friendly invitation to seek a quiet place for the discussion. ἐπιλαμβάνεσθαι, "to take hold," can support either interpretation ("arrest": 16:19; 18:17; 21:30, 33; "take": 9:27; 23:19). Ἄρειος πάγος, "Areopagus," refers, first of all, to the Hill of Ares. But the word is also used as an abbreviation for the council which derives its name from the hill; Cicero *Fam.* 13.1.5; Pollux 8.117: "courts of law at Athens; the Hill of Ares" (δικαστήρια Ἀθήνησιν· Ἄρειος πάγος);[7] Charito 1.11.6–7: "So they all [the pirates!] thought it best to sail down to Athens. But Theron did not care for the peculiar officiousness of that town. 'Is it possible,' he said, 'that you have not heard of the meddlesome curiosity of the Athenians? They are a talkative people and fond of lawsuits. . . . The Areopagus is near at hand"[8] (ἐδόκει δὴ πᾶσιν καταπλεῖν εἰς Ἀθήνας· οὐκ ἤρεσκε δὲ Θήρωνι τῆς πόλεως ἡ περιεργία· μόνοι γὰρ ὑμεῖς οὐκ ἀκούετε τὴν πολυπραγμοσύνην τῶν Ἀθηναίων; δῆμός ἐστι λάλος καὶ φιλόδικος . . . Ἄρειος πάγος εὐθὺς ἐκεῖ). The fact that the council (or a committee drawn from it) also dealt with educational questions (Plutarch *Vita Cic.* 24) does not prove that *here* a trial is being described; it would rather prove the opposite.[9] In general, the whole scene—as a redactional creation—should not be interpreted as a supposedly historical event, but should rather be read according to the Lukan intention. Luke makes it very clear when he is describing a trial. Nor is the speech an apology Paul offers in his

---

4   For the plan of the city, see *Westermanns Atlas zur Weltgeschichte. Teil I: Vorzeit und Altertum* (ed. Hans-Erich Stier and Ernst Kirsten; Braunschweig: Georg Westermann Verlag, 1963) 12. Information about the American excavations and reconstructions is provided in the periodical *Hesperia* (1–, 1932–); a summary is offered in *The Athenian Agora: Results of Excavations Conducted by the American School of Classical Studies at Athens* (22 vols. to date; Princeton: American School of Classical Studies at Athens, 1953–82).

5   Dibelius, *Studies*, 74.

6   See BDF § 385.1.

7   Hellanicos in *FGH* 323a, frg. 1; Androtion in *FGH* 324, frg. 3 (with commentary); an inscription in Benjamin D. Meritt, "Greek Inscriptions," *Hesperia* 21 (1952) 356, pls. 89–90—on this, see Cadbury, *Acts in History,* 57 n. 43.

8   English translation from Warren E. Blake, *Chariton's Chaereas and Callirhoe* (Ann Arbor: University of Michigan; London: Oxford University, 1939) 13.

9   On the powers of the council, see B. Keil, *Beiträge zur Geschichte des Areopag* (Leipzig: Teubner, 1920); Paul Graindor, *Athènes de Tibère à Trajan* (Cairo: Société anonyme égyptienne, 1931) 62–69, 116.

own defense.[10] The scene and speech are woven together to form a whole. At issue here is not a legal problem, but an epistemological one (cf. the role of the stem γινώσκειν—γνῶσις, "to know, knowledge"). The progression here is: καινὴ διδαχή—(ξενίζοντά τινα)—τὶ καινότερον—καταγγελεύς, "new teaching—(strange things)—something new—preacher."

■ **20** The key word ξένος, "strange," is combined with the Athenian curiosity (used in a nonpejorative sense).[11] In this way we are prepared for the explanation that the God whom Paul now proclaims is no stranger. For the meaning of such a hearing one cannot rely upon the bookish learning of Josephus (C. Apion. 2.267, of Athens): "and the penalty decreed for any who introduced a foreign god was death" (τιμωρία κατὰ τῶν ξένον εἰσαγόντων θεὸν ὥριστο θάνατος); compare Strabo 10.471: "for they welcomed so many of the foreign rites" (πολλὰ γὰρ τῶν ξενικῶν ἱερῶν παρεδέξαντο); Lucian Scytha 1, the Athenians give an ironic description of the Scythian Toxarias: "And the Athenians sacrifice to him as 'The Foreign Physician'" (καὶ ἐντέμνουσιν αὐτῷ Ξένῳ Ἰατρῷ οἱ Ἀθηναῖοι). The location on the Areopagus is chosen simply because it is a famous place, in dependence on information Luke has received about Dionysius the Areopagite. Thus the discussion about whether the narrow place on the Hill of Ares was adequate for a speech is pointless. Βουλόμεθα γνῶναι, "we wish to know," is a rhetorical statement. Note the rhetorical technique here: "May we know" occurs in vs 19, the wish is given a reason and explained in vs 20a, and then is repeated, with a variation in vocabulary, in vs 20b.[12] Compare Euripides Bacc. 650: "Strange and ever strange thine answers are" (τοὺς λόγους γὰρ εἰσφέρεις καινοὺς ἀεί); also see Sophocles Ajax 148–49.

■ **21** The absence of the article before Ἀθηναῖοι, "Athe-nians," is classical.[13] For the description of the "Athenians and foreigners" here,[14] note Demosthenes Orat. 4.10: "Are you content to run round and ask one another, 'Is there any news today?' Could there be any news more startling . . ." (ἢ βούλεσθε . . . περιιόντες αὐτῶν πυνθάνεσθαι· "λέγεταί τι καινόν"; γένοιτο γὰρ ἄν τι καινότερον). On the curiosity of the Athenians, compare Charito (above vs 19); Thucydides 3.38.4–7; Aristophanes Eq. 1260–63.

■ **22** ἐν μέσῳ, "in the middle," that is, of the place (see above). The proem follows (vss 22b and 23)[15]—in substance essentially a captatio-benevolentiae (a "currying of favor"). Therefore δεισιδαιμονία should be understood in a positive sense as "religious"[16]—though the reader knows what was said in vs 16. ὡς, "very," with the comparative is equal to a superlative. The piety of the Athenians was as well known as their curiosity; Sophocles Oed. col. 260: "Athens is held of States the most devout" (τάς γ' Ἀθήνας φασὶ θεοσεβεστάτας εἶναι); Josephus C. Apion. 2.130: "by common consent . . . the most pious of the Greeks" (τοὺς δὲ εὐσεβεστάτους τῶν Ἑλλήνων ἅπαντες λέγουσιν).

■ **23** σεβάσματα, "objects of . . . worship," is neutral, without pejorative intent, but compare Wis 14:20 and 15:17. Paul's use of the altar inscription as his point of contact with the Athenians is a purely literary motif,[17] since there was no inscription in this form. Rather, Luke has taken up a type of inscription well known in Athens, and has altered it to suit his purposes; compare Pausanius 1.1.4 (in Athens): ". . . and altars of the gods named Unknown and of heroes, and of the children of Theseus and Phalerus" (βωμοὶ δὲ θεῶν τε ὀνομαζομένων ἀγνώστων καὶ ἡρώων καὶ παίδων τῶν Θησέως καὶ Φαλήρου); Philostratus Vita Apoll. 6.3: "especially at Athens, where altars are set up in honor even of unknown gods" (καὶ ταῦτα

10 Dibelius, Studies, 68.
11 Hommel, "Areopagrede," 150–51.
12 Ibid., 175. Norden comments on the change from ξένος, "strange," to καινός, "new" (Agnostos Theos, 53 n. 3). On εἰσφέρειν, "to bring," see the commentary on vs 18.
13 BDF § 262.3.
14 Norden, Agnostos Theos, 333, overestimates the Attic character of the style; it is also found in the papyri.
15 Hommel, "Areopagrede," 158.
16 See BAG s.v.; P. J. Koets, Δεισιδαιμονία: A Contribution to the Knowledge of the Religious Terminology in Greek (Purmerend: Muusses, [1929]); Hendrik Bolkestein, Theophrastos' Charakter der Deisidaimonia als religionsgeschichtliche Urkunde (RVV 21:2; Giessen: Töpelmann, 1929).
17 Norden, Agnostos Theos, 31–56.

Ἀθήνησιν, οὗ καὶ ἀγνώστων δαιμόνων βωμοὶ ἵδρυνται); see also Tertullian *Nat.* 2.9. The restoration of an inscription from Pergamum is uncertain: θεοῖς ἀγ[νώστοις?] Καπίτ[ων] δαδοῦχο[s] ("Capit[o], Torch-bear[er] to the un[known?] gods").[18] Jerome's observation, *Comm. in Tit.* 1.12, is correct: "In actuality, the altar inscription read 'to the unknown, foreign gods of Asia, Europe and Africa,' not 'to the unknown god' as Paul would have it" (Inscriptio autem arae non ita erat, ut Paulus asseruit "ignoto deo," sed "diis Asiae et Europae et Africae, diis ignotis et peregrinis"). Even if such an inscription in the singular had existed (which cannot be proved from Diogenes L. 1.110),[19] the sense would have implied a thoroughgoing polytheism. Even in antiquity various explanations were given for altars such as those mentioned (cf. Pausanius 1.1.4).[20] ἄγνωστος, "unknown," does not mean the unknown god of Gnosticism,[21] but reflects the common Jewish and Christian conviction that the Gentiles do not know the "true" God.[22] Nor is Luke taking over the terminology of philosophical monotheism. The emphasis is on ἀγνοοῦντες—καταγγέλλω, "unknown—I proclaim." Luke is interested neither in theories about the origins of this ignorance nor about the development of idol worship (in contrast to Wisdom of Solomon and Philo).

The section which follows may be divided into two parts: (1) vss 24–26: creator and creation, (2) vss 27–29: the destiny of humanity; or into three:[23] (1) vss 24–25: the creator, (2) vss 26–27: God and humanity, and (3) vss 28–29: humanity and God.

■ **24** First of all, the theme which had already been touched upon in 14:15 (God the creator) is expanded further. The introductory phraseology is dependent on the Bible, but at the same time shows Greek influence (κόσμος, "world"); this has been mediated through Hellenistic Judaism. For ποιεῖν, "to make," compare on the one hand: Gen 1:1; 3:14; Isa 42:5; 2 Macc 7:28; Philo; Aristobulus frg. 5;[24] on the other hand: Plato *Tim.* 28c; 76c (ὁ ποιῶν, "the one who makes"); Epictetus 4.7.6: "God has made all things in the universe" (ὁ θεὸς πάντα πεποίηκεν τὰ ἐν τῷ κόσμῳ); *Corp. Herm.* 4.1. For κόσμος, compare 2 Macc 7:23; Wis 9:9; Aristobulus frg. 5.[25] For the division into heaven and earth: Gen 1:1; Philo *Op. mundi* 2: "for the cosmos is a whole compounded of heaven, earth, and all that is contained within them" (κόσμος μὲν οὖν ἐστι σύστημα ἐξ οὐρανοῦ καὶ γῆς καὶ τῶν ἐν τούτοις περιεχομένων φύσεων). For καὶ πάντα, compare 1QH 1.13–14: earth—seas—deeps, וכול אשר בם, "and all within them"; Aristobulus frg. 5. πάντα, "everything," prepares for vs 25: creation means lordship (κύριος, "Lord"; Hecataeus:[26] τῶν ὅλων κύριος, "lord of all") and care. Based on the essence of God, a conclusion is drawn as to how he should be worshiped; the same process is found in the Stoa—Plutarch *Mor.* 1034b: "Moreover, it is a doctrine of Zeno's 'not to build temples of the gods'" (ἔτι δόγμα Ζήνωνός ἐστιν "ἱερὰ θεῶν μὴ οἰκοδομεῖν . . .").[27] This saying has been transmitted in a variety of ways;[28] Seneca in Lactantius *Inst.* 6.25: "Temples are not to be built to him with stones piled up on high; he is to be consecrated by each man in his own breast" (Non templa illi congestis in altitudinem saxis exstruenda sunt: in suo cuique consecrandus est pectore); Ps.-Heraclitus 4th Letter: "But where is god? . . . Uneducated men, you do not know that god is not wrought by hand, . . . but the whole world is a temple to him" (ποῦ δ᾽ ἐστὶν ὁ θεός; . . . ἀπαίδευτοι, οὐκ ἴστε ὅτι οὐκ ἔστι θεὸς χειρόκμητος, . . . ἀλλ᾽ ὅλος ὁ κόσμος αὐτῷ ναός ἐστι . . .). Lucian (*Sacr.* 11) pokes fun at the idea that the gods live in their temples.[29] Judaism makes use of the same kind of polemic, but of

---

18 PWSup 1.28–30; cf. Adolf Deissmann, *Paul: A Study in Social and Religious History* (2d ed.; Hodder & Stoughton, 1927) 288–91.

19 Against T. Birt, "Ἄγνωστοι θεοί und die Areopagrede des Apostels," *RhM* 69 (1914) 342–92.

20 Regarding remnants of these explanations in the church fathers, particularly for Isho'dad of Merv, see Wickenhauser, *Apostelgeschichte*, 373–77.

21 Against Norden, *Agnostos Theos*, 56–83.

22 Rudolf Bultmann, "ἄγνωστος," *TDNT* 1 (1964) 119–21.

23 With Dibelius, *Studies*, 27, and Hommel, "Areopagrede," 158.

24 See Appendix 7; see BAG *s.v.*

25 See Appendix 7.

26 *FGH* 264, frg. 6.

27 On οὐκ ἐν χειροποιήτοις, "not made by man," see the commentary on 7:48.

28 *SVF* 1, nos. 264–67; É. des Places, "Des temples faits de main d'homme (Actes des Apôtres 17,24)," *Bib* 42 (1961) 217–23.

29 Betz, *Lukian*, 40.

course turns it only against pagan temples; instructive here is Josephus *Ant.* 8.227–29 and *Sib. Or.* 4.8–11.

■ **25** For θεραπεύειν, "to serve," compare Epistle of Jeremiah 25, 38 and Philo *Det.* 55. The play on words ζωή-πνοή, "life-breath," no doubt has prototypes in Gen 2:7, Isa 42:5, and 2 Macc 7:23. The statement is again formulated as a contrast: God takes nothing, he gives everything. This is a favorite contrast; *Corp. Herm.* 5.10: "For all things are in Thee, all things from Thee, having given all things and receiving nothing" (πάντα δὲ ἐν σοί, πάντα ἀπὸ σοῦ, πάντα δίδως καὶ οὐδὲν λαμβάνεις); compare *Corp. Herm.* 2.16. The notion that God needs nothing is a commonplace of Greek philosophy; Euripides *Herc. fur.* 1345–46: "For God hath need, if God indeed he be, of naught" (δεῖται γὰρ ὁ θεός, εἴπερ ἔστ᾿ ὀρθῶς θεός, οὐδενός); Seneca *Ep.* 95.47:[30] "for God seeks no servants. Of course not; he himself does service to mankind, everywhere and to all he is at hand to help" (non quaerit ministros deus. quidni? ipse humano generi ministrat, ubique et omnibus praesto est); also compare *Corp. Herm.* 6.1 and *Asclepius* 41. Lucian (*Charon* 12.24) notes sarcastically that the gods must be poor if they require things which must be given through ἀναθήματα, "votive offerings"; if they receive no sacrifices, they suffer need (*Jup. trag.* 18).[31] The motif—that God requires nothing—has also penetrated into Judaism: 2 Macc 14:35 (in reference to the building of the temple!); Josephus *Ant.* 8.111; *T. Naph.* (Jerachmeel) 1.6: "It is not that he hath need of any creature. . . ."

■ **26** ἐποίησεν, "he made," can be understood as a helping verb with the infinitive κατοικεῖν: "he made them live," meaning "he let them live";[32] or it can be understood as an independent statement: "he made them," in which case the infinitive κατοικεῖν should be taken as parallel with the infinitive ζητεῖν, "to seek," in vs 27, both describ-

ing the purpose of God's creating.[33] Both interpretations regard ζητεῖν in vs 27 as a statement of purpose; the only question is the function of κατοικεῖν. Those who view ἐποίησεν as a helping verb argue that God created men not for inhabiting but for seeking; those who argue for the latter interpretation must admit the resulting grammatical difficulty (two parallel infinitives indicating purpose). Nevertheless the latter interpretation is to be preferred. A difficult construction of this sort is quite possible given the style of the passage.[34] The context favors this interpretation as well, particularly the reminiscence of the biblical creation story; in the light of vs 24 (ποιεῖν—"God who made the world"), ἐξ ἑνός ("from one") here means Adam. Given the first interpretation, this ἐξ ἑνός hardly makes sense; with the second, it prepares for the summary statement about humanity and the earth, and thereby the universality of revelation. αἵματος, "blood," after ἑνός, "one" (the Koine tradition, D), is a secondary gloss. πᾶν ἔθνος ἀνθρώπων, "every nation of men," means "every nation" (14:16)[35] or "the whole human race."[36] Actually, there is little difference between the two alternatives. It is clear that Luke is not advancing a proof for the existence of God *e consensu gentium,* "by common consent";[37] nor is he following up the development from a primeval unity of the human race to a current diversity of the human race, as Poseidonius does.[38] The formulation is aimed at summing up and prepares for what is said about the destiny of all humankind in vs 27. For ἐπὶ παντὸς προσώπου, "on all the face," compare Gen 11:9 and Luke 21:35.

Max Pohlenz and Bertil Gärtner understand καιροὶ καὶ ὁροθεσίαι, "periods and boundaries," as referring to the epochs in the histories of the nations and to their national boundaries;[39] compare Deut 32:8 and the apocalyptic vision of world history as found in Daniel.[40]

30 Is this from Poseidonius? See Willy Theiler, *Die Vorbereitung des Neuplatonismus* (Problemata 1; Berlin: Weidmann, 1930) 106–9.

31 See further Dibelius, *Studies,* 43 n. 48.

32 Max Pohlenz, "Paulus und die Stoa," *ZNW* 42 (1949) 84–85; Walther Eltester, "Gott und die Natur in der Areopagrede," *Neutestamentliche Studien für Rudolf Bultmann,* 211 n. 13.

33 Dibelius, *Studies,* 35; Haenchen, p. 523 and n. 1; Hommel, "Areopagrede," 161.

34 Hommel, "Areopagrede," 161.

35 A. D. Nock ("Book of Acts," 505, reprinted in his

Essays 2.830) refers to 2:5 and 10:35.

36 Dibelius, *Studies,* 35; Haenchen, p. 523; Hommel, "Areopagrede," 161 and n. 27.

37 Against Pohlenz, "Paulus."

38 Against Stig Hanson, *The Unity of the Church in the New Testament: Colossians and Ephesians* (ASNU 14; Uppsala: Almqvist & Wiksells, 1946; reprinted Lexington, KY: American Theological Library Association, 1963) 101–5.

39 Gärtner, *Areopagus Speech,* 147–51; Pohlenz, "Paulus," 86–87.

40 Cf. also Luke 21:24; *T. Mos.* 12.4(?); *T. Naph.* (Jerach-

Though in its own distinctive style, ancient historiography was also concerned with the theme of historical epochs (cf. Dionysius Halic. 1.2; Appian *proem;* Diodorus). Dibelius, on the other hand, would understand the passage in terms of a philosophy of nature, seeing the "order" of the seasons and the natural boundaries of the zones which are habitable for humankind (as opposed to the uninhabitable zones) as a proof for the existence of God.[41] Walther Eltester shows that καιροί, "periods" (instead of the classical ὧραι, "times"), can have the meaning "seasons" in Hellenistic Greek;[42] the reader has already encountered this meaning in 14:17.[43] τάσσειν, "to determine, fix," and derivatives (here προστεταγμένους, "allotted") are in this context thematic words (cf. *Pss. Sol.* 18.10; *1 Enoch* 2.1; Aristobulus frg. 5).[44] *1 Clem.* 20.2–12 (and 40) is especially instructive. This passage points in the direction of an interpretation from natural philosophy. However, the stylistic differences in comparison with our passage should not be overlooked. The concept of ὁροθεσίαι, "boundaries," causes difficulties with this "philosophical" interpretation; D argues for the historical interpretation with its reading κατὰ ὁροθεσίαν, "according to the boundary" for "and the boundaries."[45] Dibelius would understand here a reference to the "boundaries" of the two inhabitable (temperate) zones as against the three uninhabitable zones.[46] Pohlenz objects that we are then faced with the strange notion that God has shown his care for humankind by making the greater part of the earth uninhabitable![47] But this objection is not valid. In the literature both views may be found: (1) the skeptical view, declaring that the space for humankind is very small; (2) the grateful view, seeing that the gods have made two zones inhabitable for humankind.[48] Nevertheless, Dibelius's interpretation does not fit the tenor of the context, which is determined by πᾶν, πάντα, "every, all": the whole earth is a dwelling place. The participial clause does indeed define κατοικεῖν, "to live."[49] Compare rather Philo *Prov.* 2.84[50] (cf. *Prov.* 2.74):[51] "For you have thought it over while paying very little attention to this, namely, that a portion of land has been properly set aside for human habitation as well as for space for use relating to the sentient gods. For the sectors granted to us through distribution are more than adequate for habitation" (nam minimum id considerans ruminasti, quod recte disposita sit sectio terrae pro habitatione hominum proque spatio ad usum deorum respectu sensibilium. nobis enim per distributionem concessae partes plus quam satis sunt pro habitatione). Eltester sees the difficulty. He would escape it by understanding the ὁροθεσίαι, "boundaries," as the boundaries of all the land as against the sea. That the sea has been enclosed in "boundaries" is in fact a commonplace.[52] It may be identified as one of the elements of chaos which has been tamed (Jer 38:36 LXX [= 31:35 MT]; Ps 74(73):13–14; Luke 21:25!). The base of the menorah on the arch of Titus in Rome appears to offer evidence from a monument.[53] But elsewhere in Luke there is no hint that the sea is viewed as an element of chaos (Luke 21:25 is concerned with an apocalyptic event); it is simply a part of creation (4:24; 14:15). This has an analogy in the Qumran texts, at least to the extent that God is pictured as having created the deeps (1QH 1.10–15;

---

41 Dibelius, *Studies,* 29–34.

42 Eltester, "Gott und die Natur," 206–9.

43 The development: Gen 1:14 LXX; Psalm 74(73); Wis 7:18; *Diogn.* 4.5; Philo *Op. mundi* 59; *Spec. leg.* 2.56–57; Plutarch *Mor.* 378–79 (alongside 379a!); the inscription on a coin, εὐτυχεῖς καιροί, "favorable seasons," appearing beside the figure of four boys, which stands for the seasons (see Nock, "Book of Acts," 505, reprinted in his *Essays* 2.830).

44 See Appendix 7.

45 Dibelius, *Studies,* 56 n. 91.

46 Ibid., 31.

47 Pohlenz, "Paulus," 85–87.

48 Cf. Cicero *Tusc. disp.* 1.28, 68–69; Virgil *Georg.* 1.237–38; Ovid *Metam.* 1.45–88; Dibelius, *Studies,* 31–32.

meel) 10.1–2.

49 Nock, "Book of Acts," 505, reprinted in his *Essays* 2.830.

50 *SVF* 2.1149–50.

51 *SVF* 1.548.

52 Cf. Eltester's evidence ("Gott und die Natur," 209–12); above all: *Const. Ap.* 7.34; 8.12; *Ep. Apost.* 3 (14); *Corp. Herm.* 5.4: "Who is he having cast bounds about the sea?" (τίς τῇ θαλάσσῃ τοὺς ὅρους περιβαλών;).

53 See also *1 Clem.* 20; *Diogn.* 7; *Const. Ap.* 7.33–34.

1QM 10.12–13). The whole controversy, however, about whether the text is to be understood historically or philosophically perhaps expects too much from Acts. It assumes a degree of abstraction which corresponds neither to popular Greek tradition nor to the Jewish tradition, which is recognizable in the background. For the latter, compare the Qumran texts which have already been mentioned in which both historical and philosophical features are interwoven; 1QH 1.16–17: "Thou hast allotted their service unto them in all their generations according to their times (בקציהם). And [Thou hast ordained their] ju[dg]ment in conformity with the seasons [במועדיה]." 1QM 10.12–16: "(It is Thou) who hast created the earth and the laws of its divisions (מפלגיה חוקי) into desert and pleasant land . . . the globe of the seas . . . and the dispersion of the peoples (מפרד עמים), the abode of the clans and the division of territories . . . the sacred moments and the circuits of the years and the everlasting . . . ages."

■ **27-29** The Destiny of Humanity

■ **27-28** ζητεῖν, "to seek," is parallel to κατοικεῖν, "to live" (see above). The seeking which is mentioned here is not a matter of will, as in the Old Testament (Deut 4:29; Amos 5:6; Isa 55:6, etc.), but of the intellect.[54] Systematic reflection, that is, the distinction which we see between the formulation of the question εἰ ἔστι τὸ θεῖον, "whether the deity exists," and τί ἐστι κατ᾽ οὐσίαν, "what the deity is in essence" (Philo *Spec. leg.* 1.32; similarly, Cicero *Nat. deor.* 2.4, 12), is absent. Luke does not ask about the method of this seeking. εἰ ἄρα γε, "in the hope that," with the infrequently used optative, leaves the finding in suspension; Philo *Spec. leg.* 1.36: "For nothing is better than to search for the true God, even if the discovery of him eludes human capacity" (ἄμεινον γὰρ οὐδὲν τοῦ ζητεῖν τὸν ἀληθῆ θεόν, κἂν ἡ εὕρεσις αὐτοῦ διαφεύγῃ δύναμιν ἀνθρωπίνην). For ψηλαφᾶν, "to feel after," compare Philo *Mut. nom.* 126. On the subject, compare Dio Chrysostom 12.60: "[all men have a strong yearning] to honor and worship the deity from close at hand, approaching and

laying hold of him . . ." (ἐγγύθεν τιμᾶν καὶ θεραπεύειν τὸ θεῖον προσιόντας καὶ ἁπτομένους . . .); also compare *Corp. Herm.* 5.2. Do we detect here a trace of Poseidonius?[55] The question arises later as well. The reason given here ("he is not far from each one of us") is reminiscent of Dio Chrysostom 12.28: "For inasmuch as these earlier men were not living dispersed far away from the divine being or beyond his borders apart by themselves, but had grown up in the very center of things, or rather had grown up in his company . . . they could not for any length of time continue to be unintelligent beings" (ἅτε γὰρ οὐ μακρὰν οὐδ᾽ ἔξω τοῦ θείου διῳκισμένοι καθ᾽ αὑτούς, ἀλλ᾽ ἐν αὐτῷ μέσῳ πεφυκότες μᾶλλον δὲ συμπεφυκότες ἐκείνῳ . . . οὐκ ἐδύναντο μέχρι πλείονος ἀσύνετοι μένειν). Hommel concludes that there was a literary connection between Luke and Poseidonius through a Hellenistic-Jewish mediator.[56] But the litotes οὐ μακράν, "not far," is widespread; note Mark 12:34; Josephus *Ant.* 8.108: ὅτι πάρει καὶ μακρὰν οὐκ ἀφέστηκας ("that Thou art present and not far removed"); also compare Deut 30:11 LXX. On the subject, compare, on the one hand, Ps 139(138):7–12, and, on the other hand, Seneca *Ep.* 41.1: "God is near you, he is with you, he is within you" (prope est a te deus, tecum est, intus est).

■ **28** This verse combines οὐ μακράν, "not far," with a pantheistic triad and a pantheistic (Stoic) quotation. The triad is not evidenced elsewhere. But Luke probably took this from some tradition available to him, since he has no interest of his own in the distinction among stages of being.[57] Hommel refers again to Poseidonius as mediator between Luke and Plato from whom the thought of this triad ultimately derives.[58] *Tim.* 37c is the ultimate source for this tradition: "And when the Father that engendered it perceived it in motion and alive, a thing of joy to the eternal gods, He too rejoiced" (ὡς δὲ κινηθὲν αὐτὸ καὶ ζῶν ἐνόησεν τῶν ἀϊδίων θεῶν γεγονὸς ἄγαλμα ὁ γεννήσας πατήρ, ἠγάσθη). For the connection between ζῆν, "to live," and κινεῖσθαι, "to move," see further Plutarch *Mor.* 477cd (with a rejection of the worship of

54 Dibelius, *Studies*, 32–33.

55 Willy Theiler, *Die Vorbereitung des Neuplatonismus* (Problemata 1; Berlin: Weidmann, 1930) 101–4; Hommel, "Areopagrede," 163–70.

56 Hommel, "Areopagrede," 170.

57 On the appropriation of Stoic pantheistic triads into Christianity (mediated by Hellenistic Judaism, where they are altered to fit in with the OT idea of God),

see below; see the commentaries on Rom 11:36.

58 Hommel, "Areopagrede," 169; also see Pohlenz, "Paulus," 90; Gärtner, *Areopagus Speech*, 183.

images),[59] 591b, 957d, 979d; Quintilian *Inst. orat.* 10.1.16. For εἶναι, "to be," see Plato *Rep.* 2.369d and, above all, *Soph.* 248e: κίνησιν καὶ ζωὴν καὶ ψυχὴν καὶ φρόνησιν ("motion and life and soul and mind"), where the two latter concepts circumscribe "being"[60] (cf. *Symp.* 206b–c). This evidence indicates that "ζῶμεν ['we live'] involves the physical life, ἐσμέν ['we have our being'] the spiritual-intellectual in contrast to it, while the third, κινούμεθα ['we move'], transposes both into the cosmic sphere."[61] Of course Luke no longer knows how to interpret the formula exactly.[62] The quotation which serves both as proof and explanation comes from Aratus's *Phaenomena* 5. The plural, "poets" (καθ᾽ ὑμᾶς, "your," replaces the possessive pronoun), does not prove that Luke was thinking of several poets,[63] referring, say, to Cleanthes' *Hymn to Zeus* in which there is a similar expression,[64] nor that he was designating the preceding triad as a quotation.[65] The plural is simply a literary convention.[66] On the relation between creatures and the gods, compare Dio Chrysostom 30.26: "They [the gods] are good and love us as being kin to them. For it is from the gods, he declared, that the race of men is sprung and not from Titans or from Giants" (ὡς ἀγαθοί τέ εἰσι καὶ φιλοῖεν ἡμᾶς, ἅτε δὴ ξυγγενεῖς ὄντας αὐτῶν. ἀπὸ γὰρ τῶν θεῶν ἔφη τὸ τῶν ἀνθρώπων εἶναι γένος, οὐκ ἀπὸ Τιτάνων οὐδ᾽ ἀπὸ Γιγάντων).

Both the understanding of God and of humanity in this passage are unique in the New Testament. Nevertheless, it should be observed that such statements had enjoyed currency for some time in Hellenistic Judaism as attempts to describe the Jewish idea of God; for example Philo *Leg. all.* 3.4: "For God fills and penetrates all things, and has left no spot void or empty of his presence" (πάντα γὰρ πεπλήρωκεν ὁ θεὸς καὶ διὰ πάντων διελή-λυθεν καὶ κενὸν οὐδὲν οὐδὲ ἔρημον ἀπολέλοιπεν ἑαυτοῦ); see

also 1.44. Aristobulus frg. 4[67] cites Aratus *Phaenomena* 1–9 to interpret the biblical creation story(!) and understands the verses as referring to the Creator's omnipresence and governance of the world. The intention of the statement as Luke uses it is not ontological—as if to say something about the essence of humanity as superior to nature. Rather it is intended as a criticism, aimed at the restoration of the proper kind of worship of God.

■ **29** It is in this sense that the author makes use of the quotation in vs 29. At first the logic is not clear. If humanity is related to God, one might infer that the "divine" could be represented in human form. But we understand the line of Luke's thinking if we see that two motifs intersect here: (1) the Greek, that the living can be represented only by something that is living[68] (cf. Dio Chrys. 12.83); (2) the Jewish, that the Creator is not to be represented by the created (Wis 13:5; 15:3–17). But the obvious synthesis, that humanity is in the image of the living God, is not spelled out. The neuter τὸ θεῖον, "the Deity," again is unique; but it too has already penetrated into Hellenistic Judaism (Philo, Aristobulus, Josephus).[69] Luke does not concern himself with the distinction between cultic images and dedicated statues, nor with that between the images and the gods themselves (on this latter distinction, e.g., Heraclitus frg. 5;[70] Plutarch *Mor.* 379cd; Lucian [*Jup. trag.* 7] ironically equates gods and statues). For Greek criticism of images, see Maximus of Tyre 2 on "Whether one must set up statues to the gods" (εἰ θεοῖς ἀγάλματα ἱδρυτέον). This criticism was certainly not successful.[71] Of course it played an important role in Hellenistic Judaism: Bel and the Dragon, Epistle of Jeremiah, and Wisdom 13—15. The non-Jewish world paid some attention to it: Strabo 16.2.35 = Poseidonius,[72] Hecataios of Abdera,[73] and Tacitus *Hist.* 5.4.

---

59 Hommel, "Areopagrede," 165–66.
60 Hildebrecht Hommel, "Platonisches bei Lukas: Zu Act 17:28a (Leben—Bewegung—Sein)," *ZNW* 48 (1957) 195–96.
61 Ibid., 198–99: "In ζῶμεν das physische, in ἐσμέν dagegen das seelisch-geistige Leben steckt, während das dritte, κινούμεθα, beides ins Kosmische überhöht."
62 Ibid.
63 Thus *Beginnings* 4.218.
64 In vss 3–4; see *SVF* 1.537.
65 Pohlenz ("Paulus," 101–4) has demonstrated that the material cannot be traced back to Epimenides.

66 Dibelius, *Studies*, 50 n. 76.
67 See Appendix 6.
68 Richard Reitzenstein, "Die Areopagrede des Paulus," *NJKlA* 31 (1913) 393–422.
69 See BAG *s.v.*
70 Diels 22 B 5.
71 B. von Borries, "Quid veteres philosophi de idolatria senserint" (Diss., Göttingen, 1918); PWSup 5.472–511.
72 *FGH* 87 frg. 70; otherwise Wolfgang Aly, *Strabons Geographie,* vol. 4, *Strabon von Amaseia: Untersuchungen über Text, Aufbau und Quellen der Geographika*

■ **30–31** The final, specifically Christian section follows without any obvious conceptual shift. Here again the style is not that of argumentation, but of proclamation. Hommel classifies this as an epilogue,[74] which would mean that these verses would be somehow distinguished from the author's major concern. But the setting of the scene had already pointed to the resurrection, the content of this final section, as central (vs 18). Thus the first, biblically colored portion of the speech and this final christological section form a bracket around the anthropological section in the middle. The whole of world history is viewed from the perspective of the *one*, decisive turning point that occurred in the resurrection of Christ. Thus there are two epochs: the one, of ἄγνοια, "ignorance,"[75] and the other, of proclamation, providing the opportunity for μετάνοια, "repentance"[76] (cf. Ps.-Clem. *Hom.* 1.7.6: "the time of repentance," ὁ τῆς μετανοίας καιρός).[77] The universalism of the speech (the key word πᾶς, "every, all," and derivatives) is actualized at this point. With the key word ἄγνοια, "ignorance," Luke refers back to the introduction of the speech (ἀγνώστῳ, "unknown," vs 23) and to the term γινώσκειν already found in the setting of the scene (the stem γινώσκειν— γνῶσις, "to know, knowledge").[78]

■ **31** Compare Pss 9:9; 96(95):13; 98(97):9. This is good Lukan eschatology, not focused on the imminence of the judgment but on the fact of judgment as such. The precondition is the general resurrection of the just and the unjust (24:15). As for ἐν ἀνδρὶ κτλ., "by a man, etc.," the name has already been mentioned in vs 18.[79] The meaning of πίστιν παρέχειν, "to give assurance," is to furnish proof, not to grant "faith" (Josephus *Ant.* 2.218; Vettius Valens 277.29–30). This idea is also Lukan.[80]

■ **32** The reference in vs 32 to the "strangeness" (cf. vs 20) of the message for Greek ears, which frames the speech, shows that with the concluding statement in vs 31, the author has achieved his purpose. For the Greek expectation, compare Aeschylus *Eum.* 647–48: "But when the dust hath drained the blood of man, once he is slain, there is no return to life" (ἀνδρὸς δ᾽ ἐπειδὰν αἷμ᾽ ἀνασπάσῃ κόνις ἅπαξ θανόντος, οὔτις ἔστ᾽ ἀνάστασις).[81] The scene here has its counterpart in 2:12–13 (cf. *Corp. Herm.* 1.29; *Sib. Or.* 1.171–72; Ps.-Clem. *Hom.* 1.101). Apparently we have here a style widespread in writing about missionary activity. The mocking is the foil for the superiority of the θεῖος ἀνήρ, "divine man."[82]

Excursus:
The Areopagus Speech

1. *The speech as literary creation.* This is not the abbreviated version of an actual speech given by Paul so that the original form could be recovered by a hypothetical filling out of hints given in the text.[83] It is not a resume but a specifically literary creation. The first to recognize this were Norden and Dibelius. Norden assigned it to a widespread type of literary missionary "speech." He compared the speech with *Corp. Herm.* 1.27–28; 7:1–2; *Odes Sol.* 33; *Kerygma of Peter*; Ps.-Clem. *Hom.* 1.7 (= *Recog.* 1.7); compare further *Sib. Or.* 1.150–98, frg. 1.3. Norden identified the following as elements of the genre: "A summons to a recognition of God as a spiritual being who is dissimilar to humankind, and to the requisite change of mind; attributes which are predicated of this God and the proper manner of

(Bonn: Hobelt, 1957) 191–210.

73 *FGH* 264 frg. 6.

74 Hommel, "Areopagrede," 158.

75 See the commentary on 13:27.

76 Conzelmann, *Theology*, 101.

77 Jacques Dupont, "Repentir et conversion d'après les Actes des Apôtres," *Sciences Ecclésiastiques* 12 (1960) 166–69, reprinted in his *Études*, 450–53. On πάντας πανταχοῦ, see Jacques Dupont, "The Salvation of the Gentiles and the Theological Significance of Acts," *The Salvation of the Gentiles: Studies in the Acts of the Apostles* (New York/Ramsey/Toronto: Paulist, 1979) 31–32.

78 See the commentary on vs 19.

79 For ἐν, "by," with κρίνειν, "to judge," cf. κριθέντω ἐν ἄνδροις τρίοις, "Let them be judged by three men"

(*SIG* 2 no. 850.8); for the forensic use of ἐν, see BAG *s.v.* ἐν I.3.

80 Conzelmann, *Theology*, 110–11, 205.

81 See also Celsus in Origen *Cels.* 5.14; Tertullian *Res.* 39; Robert M Grant, *Miracle and Natural Law in Greco-Roman and Early Christian Thought* (Amsterdam: North-Holland, 1952) 221–34.

82 Cf. Betz, *Lukian*, 111 n. 3.

83 Wilhelm Schmid, "Die Rede des Apostels Paulus vor den Philosophen und Areopagiten in Athen," *Philologus* 95 (1942–43) 79–120.

worshiping him (not bloody sacrifices, but in the spirit); and eternal life and blessedness as the reward for such a recognition."[84] To be sure, this does not sufficiently explain the details of the speech's structure (see below). In fact, Norden's thesis that the whole speech is an interpolation modeled after a speech given in Athens by Apollonius of Tyana is certainly wrong. Rather it has been composed by the author writing to Theophilus, in imitation of existing examples. In any case it has been recognized since Norden that for the interpretation of the speech it is not sufficient to identify individual motifs. The whole complex of motifs must be examined and the *composition* must be analyzed. To move beyond Norden one must ask further about the way in which the motifs came to the author, and about his own role in shaping the structure of the speech.[85]

A first step in this direction is to note the linking of the scene and the speech by means of the term γινώσκειν, "to know," the reference to the strange and unknown God, and to Jesus and the resurrection. In this way Luke gave the speech an individual-historical character, despite his dependence upon a literary type. The speech intends not simply to provide an example of typical Christian missionary preaching, but to show how that unique individual named Paul fared in this incomparable encounter with representatives of Greek civilization. In Luke's view Paul fared well in this encounter; the conclusion of the scene is not meant to portray any failure on Paul's part, but rather a failure on the part of the Greeks.[86] This "historical" sense of the speech is also evident in the *language*. Luke strives for an elevated style (e.g., the optative) and Attic coloring, and also employs rhetorical devices (parechesis, paronomasia, alliteration). To be sure there are limitations: he does not construct well-rounded periods; his grammatical construction can be very harsh (vss 26–27); word usage deviates from the usual on occasion (ὁροθεσία, χάραγμα); elements of Septuagintal Greek are evident.

2. *Luke and Paul.* The "genuineness" of the speech cannot be demonstrated by going through the Pauline letters and finding reminiscences. Some relationship is to be expected, since both stand in the ecclesiastical tradition and proceed from the same credo. Such reminiscences are found throughout early Christian writings. In Paul there are formulations which are taken directly from common church tradition (1 Thess 1:9–10). The question rather is whether, on the one hand, the theme of the Areopagus speech as a whole has a parallel in Paul, and on the other hand, whether specifically Pauline *theologumena* are to be found in it. Missing from the speech are Paul's doctrine of justification, the theme of the wrath of God, faith and law, works, the *theologia crucis,* the dialectical understanding of the present and the future, and the expectation of the imminent return of the Lord. And if elements of Stoic natural theology are found here, as in Romans 1, the extent and the way in which these are used theologically are completely different.[87] In place of the Pauline διὸ παρέδωκεν αὐτοὺς ὁ θεός, "therefore God gave them up," is the relative excusing of the Gentiles because of their ἄγνοια, "ignorance"; God permitted them to do as they chose. The stereotyped arrangement of motifs is not found in Paul (1 Thess 1:9–10 offers no counterargument, because in that passage Paul is following a given schema).[88] That God can be known is not a separate theme for Paul, he presupposes it (Rom 1:18–23; 1 Cor 1:18–25). Even the structure of Romans indicates that for him the judgment motif stands at the beginning. The structure of Paul's eschatology and soteriology is different from what we find here, thus affecting the whole direction of the development of thought.[89]

3. *The material and its prehistory.* The most recent investigations have confirmed the essentials of Norden's analysis: the speech includes an underlying Jewish-Christian motif as well as an accompanying Stoic motif. The piece that forms the heart of the speech is indeed Stoic (with Platonic components; Poseidonius!).[90] But the material has obviously come to Luke through the mediation of Hellenized Judaism, as the parallels—above all in Aristobulus and in *Const. Ap.*—indicate;[91] the parallels in *1 Clement* (19–20; 33; 40) point to the same trajectory. Even though the Stoic

---

84   Norden, *Agnostos Theos,* 129–30: "Afforderung zur Erkenntnis Gottes als eines menschenunähnlichen, geistigen Wesens und zu der dadurch bedingten Sinnesänderung, Prädikation dieses Gottes und die rechte Art seiner Verehrung (nicht blutige Opfer, sondern im Geiste), ewiges Leben und Seligkeit als Lohn solcher Erkenntnis. . . ."

85   Wolfgang Nauck, "Die Tradition und Komposition der Areopagrede," *ZThK* 53 (1956) 11–52.

86   Haenchen, p. 526.

87   As Pohlenz ("Paulus") especially has shown.

88   See the commentaries on 1 Thess 1:9–10.

89   Cf. also Günther Bornkamm, "Faith and Reason in Paul," *Early Christian Experience* (New York: Harper, 1969) 29–46.

90   Cf. Hommel, "Areopagrede," 169.

91   Nauck, "Areopagrede," 11–36; see Appendices 8–9.

central section of the speech seems so compact, one should not fail to note the absence of precisely the specific elements of Stoic philosophy: the speech establishes no connection between the understanding of the cosmos, the nature of human beings, and epistemology (knowledge of the world, of God, of oneself), nor between knowledge and the ethical life in the sense of philosophical existence. There is no development of a consistent picture of the world, God, or humankind (with the terminology of macro- and microcosm, φύσις, "nature," νόμος, "law," λόγος, "reason," νοῦς, "mind"). No natural epistemology is developed. Compared with Poseidonius, for example, there is lacking the concept of the development of ideas, the genetic explanation of the world, humankind, religion, and the motif of cosmos and sympathy. Finally, in comparison with Jewish and early Christian parallels, there is also absent any description of nature. Thus it is not sufficient simply to assemble motifs and to seek clarification by use of comparative material. We must also take note of the reduction which has occurred in the literary setting where these motifs now appear. The Stoic motifs, in other words, cannot be interpreted without some attention to the singular framework into which they have been inserted, which leads on to the next consideration.

4. *The composition.* In the composition of this speech the schema of a credal statement with two members stands out: God, the Creator—Jesus Christ, the coming Judge (1 Thess 1:9–10). The origin of this schema (God—Christ) may be seen, for example, in 1 Cor 8:6, and even here a connection is established between "objective" statements about God and Christ and human existence. In the present passage the first and second articles of the creed have become a literary frame; within this frame, the destiny of humanity has become an explicit theme. There are prototypes for individual features of the thematic arrangement of the speech. For example, one can find precedent for beginning with a reference to God the Creator (and Preserver) in *1 Clem.* 19.2; 33.2; *Const. Ap.* 7.34; 8.12; *Ep. Apost.* 3 (14); *Sib. Or.* 4.8–23. Concluding with a reference to judgment is a schematic feature which determines the structure of Q as well as Mark's presentation of Jesus' teachings, and determines the structure of speeches in Matthew.[92] The call to repentance consistently follows the speeches of "Peter" in Acts and occurs in the passages cited by Norden (*Corp. Herm.* 1.28; *Odes Sol.* 33.6; Ps.-Clem. *Hom.* 1.7.3, 6; *Sib. Or.* 1.16.8). Wolfgang Nauck argues, particularly in the case of Jewish missionary speeches, for a

schema with three elements: *creatio—conservatio—salvatio,* "creation, preservation, salvation."[93] In fact there is some linking of these motifs in the *Prayer of Manasseh,* which corresponds to Nauck's threefold structure. But there is no threefold structure attested anywhere that corresponds with the Areopagus speech in Acts 17. In this respect, Luke is original. This represents a new step in the reflection about human existence in light of the creed. Thus Luke's achievement goes beyond the literary to the theological. Here his new concept of eschatology is logically extended to anthropology.

5. *Theological motivation.* If we wish to evaluate the speech for the purpose of establishing a systematic natural theology, a doctrine of "connection" between the message and the world, both an appropriation and a reduction of theological motifs must be considered, as well as the historicality of every theological proposal. It is clear that Luke enlists the service of philosophy in establishing a point of contact between the missionary message and the non-Christian world; it is also apparent that he goes considerably further than Paul in establishing the connection. But that cannot simply be restated in the form of a thesis like "Luke advocates a natural theology," because it will not do to evaluate these statements in an unhistorical manner, whether to accept them or reject them. They intend to be understood in their historical setting and in their own context as an attempt to interpret the creed at a particular time. The modern abstract question about the uniqueness or the plurality of "sources of revelation" would have been unfamiliar to Luke because revelation had not yet been defined as an abstract concept. Since for Luke no split exists between creation and redemption, nor between *fides quae creditur* (the faith which is believed) and *fides qua creditur* (the faith by which [it] is believed), concern for the relationship between a "theological" and a "philosophical" monotheism would be anachronistic. Even what is said about God does not yet have the sense of an abstract concept of God. There is no reflection about the "natural" possibilities of reason (and nothing at all about a clouding of reason in a primeval fall). The meaning is quite simple: If the Gentiles understand that there is *one* God, the Creator, and if they repent, then they do indeed *believe.* And then they know that they should always have understood this. Here Luke provides an insight into the structure of faith: he knows that independent of our comprehension, God has always been near at hand; thus unbelief cannot be blamed on God's alleged distance.[94]

---

92   Günther Bornkamm, Gerhard Barth, and Heinz
      Joachim Held, *Tradition and Interpretation in Matthew*
      (Philadelphia: Westminster, 1963) 20–21, 46–47,

      59–60.
93   Nauck, "Areopagrede," 25.

■ **34** From the specifics here we catch some glimpse of the concrete accounts which Luke had from Athens—they were scanty. We can still perceive that no congregation was organized. The well-known collection of writings (of the mystic Ps.-Dionysius the Areopagite) was later attached to the name of Dionysius.[95]

---

94 Literature:

Basic studies include:

Martin Dibelius, "Paul on the Areopagus," *Studies,* 26–77.

Norden, *Agnostos Theos.*

For a comprehensive discussion (and an almost complete bibliography), see:

Gärtner, *Areopagus Speech,* which was brought up to date by Jacques Dupont, "La salut des Gentils et la signification théologique du Livre des Actes," *NTS* 6 (1959–60) 152–53 n. 4. (The footnotes were not included in the English translation in *The Salvation of the Gentiles.*)

Further studies:

T. Birt, "Ἄγνωστοι θεοί und die Areopagrede des Apostels," *RhM* 69 (1914) 342–92.

Hans Conzelmann, "The Address of Paul on the Areopagus," *Studies in Luke-Acts,* 217–30.

Walther Eltester, "Gott und die Natur in der Areopagrede," *Neutestamentliche Studien für Rudolf Bultmann,* 202–27.

Idem, "Schöpfungsoffenbarung und natürliche Theologie im frühen Christentum," *NTS* 3 (1956–57) 93–114.

Hommel, "Areopagrede."

Idem, "Platonisches bei Lukas."

Jürgen-Christian Lebram, "Der Aufbau der Areopagrede," *ZNW* 55 (1964) 221–42.

H.-U. Minke, "Die Schöpfung in der frühchristlichen Verkündigung nach dem Ersten Clemensbrief und der Areopagrede" (Diss., Hamburg, 1966).

Franz Mussner, "Anknüpfung und Kerygma in der Areopagrede," *TThZ* 67 (1958) 344–54, now in his *Praesentia salutis,* 235–43.

Idem, "Einige Parallelen aus den Qumrântexten zur Areopagrede (Apg 17,22–31)," *BZ* n.s. 1 (1957) 125–30.

Nauck, "Areopagrede."

H. P. Owen, "The Scope of Natural Revelation in Romans I and Acts XVII," *NTS* 5 (1958–59) 133–43.

Pohlenz, "Paulus," 69–104.

Richard Reitzenstein, "Die Areopagrede des Paulus," *NJKlA* 31 (1913) 393–422.

Wilhelm Schmid, "Die Rede des Apostels Paulus vor den Philosophen und Areopagiten in Athen," *Philologus* 95 (1942–43) 79–120.

Gottlob Schrenk, "Urchristliche Missionspredigt im 1. Jahrhundert," *Studien zu Paulus* (AThANT 26; Zurich: Zwingli, 1954) 131–48.

Eduard Schweizer, "Concerning the Speeches in Acts," *Studies in Luke-Acts,* 208–16.

F. Skutsch, "Ein neuer Zeuge der altchristlichen Liturgie," *ARW* 13 (1910) 291–305.

Ned B. Stonehouse, *Paul before the Areopagus and Other New Testament Studies* (Grand Rapids: Eerdmanns, 1957).

Philipp Vielhauer, "On the 'Paulinism' of Acts," *Studies in Luke-Acts,* 33–50.

95 On the name Δαμαρίς, see *SEG* 11 no. 903 (cf. *IG* 5:1, no. 972) and no. 669a and b; cf. further *IG* 5:1, no. 1302; the alteration to Δάμαλις is superfluous.

The Great Missionary Journey [15:36—21:26]

18

Corinth
(including the Trial before Gallio)

1 After this he left Athens and went to Corinth. 2/ And he found a Jew named Aquila, a native of Pontus, lately come from Italy with his wife Priscilla, because Claudius had commanded all the Jews to leave Rome. And he went to see them; 3/ and because he was of the same trade he stayed with them, and they worked, for by trade they were tentmakers. 4/ And he argued in the synagogue every sabbath, and persuaded Jews and Greeks.

5 When Silas and Timothy arrived from Macedonia, Paul was occupied with preaching, testifying to the Jews that the Christ was Jesus. 6/ And when they opposed and reviled him, he shook out his garments and said to them, "Your blood be upon your heads! I am innocent. From now on I will go to the Gentiles." 7/ And he left there and went to the house of a man named Titius Justus, a worshiper of God; his house was next door to the synagogue. 8/ Crispus, the ruler of the synagogue, believed in the Lord, together with all his household; and many of the Corinthians hearing Paul believed and were baptized. 9/ And the Lord said to Paul one night in a vision, "Do not be afraid, but speak and do not be silent; 10/ for I am with you, and no man shall attack you to harm you; for I have many people in this city." 11/ And he stayed a year and six months, teaching the word of God among them.

12 But when Gallio was proconsul of Achaia, the Jews made a united attack upon Paul and brought him before the tribunal, 13/ saying, "This man is persuading men to worship God contrary to the law." 14/ But when Paul was about to open his mouth, Gallio said to the Jews, "If it were a matter of wrongdoing or vicious crime, I should reasonably [or: of course] attend to your complaint, O Jews; 15/ but since it is a matter of questions about words and names [or: persons] and your own law, see to it yourselves; I refuse to be a judge of these things." 16/ And he drove them from the tribunal. 17/ And they all seized Sosthenes, the ruler of the synagogue, and beat him in front of the tribunal. But Gallio paid no attention to this.

**Excursus:
Corinth**

Corinth was destroyed by the Romans in 146 B.C.E. and then refounded by Caesar as a Roman colony (called *Laus Julia Corinthiensis*).[1] Thanks to its location on the isthmus, over which a great part of the east-west traffic passed (ships feared the journey around the Peloponnese), it soon became once again a flourishing commercial and industrial city. It became the capital of the province of Achaia in 27 B.C.E. (which became a senatorial province in 44 C.E.). The widespread notion that oriental influence on religious life must have been especially strong here has no basis in the literary or archaeological sources. The flourishing cult of Isis (Apuleius *Met.* 11) had long since been Hellenized. The immorality of the city was proverbial: "Not every man's is the voyage to Corinth" (οὐ παντὸς ἀνδρὸς ἐς κόρινθόν ἐσθ᾽ ὁ πλοῦς, Strabo 8.378); thus κορινθιάζεσθαι means to "practice fornication."[2]

Luke possessed some good individual pieces of information on Paul's activity in Corinth. There are factual details not previously encountered in such abundance in Acts—details about working conditions, lengths of time, names, places, and dates. But the total picture has been highly stylized here also, as is evident from a comparison with the Corinthian letters. There is no information about relationships with other congregations during this time (1 Thessalonians!), nothing about the variety of religious tendencies within the Corinthian congregation. There is no hint of their enthusiastic character, of the rapidly developing gnosis, and of the schismatic tendencies. This is not to deny the reliability of the individual accounts. Details such as those given in vs 2 are not invented. But the nature of Luke's sources can no longer be determined (his source, in any case, was not an old dairy).[3] Haenchen describes the way in which Luke put the material together into a continuous account.[4] The relationship between the source material and Luke's own shaping of it is especially evident in the description of Paul's relationship to the synagogue. Concrete details are

shaped according to the typical pattern found in Acts; compare the programmatic statement in vs 6 with 13:46 and 28:28.

■ **2** Aquila and Priscilla are called Jews, but this does not mean that they were not already Christians. This detail is mentioned only to indicate why they had to leave Rome. 1 Corinthians does not mention the conversion of this couple either. In fact, this letter rules out the possibility that they had been converted to Christianity through Paul's efforts (1:14–16; 16:15). Thus we find here an early indication of Christianity's presence in Rome—and in Corinth! Luke, of course, eliminates any such trace of an earlier Christian presence in Corinth because Paul must appear as the founder of the congregation. In fact, Paul *was* the founder of the congregation; that is certainly the way he understands his role (1 Cor 3:6). Whatever indications there may be of a pre-Pauline Christian presence in Corinth, there is no evidence of a congregation there before Paul. Priscilla is equivalent to Prisca (1 Cor 16:19; Rom 16:3; 2 Tim 4:19). Suetonius mentions the edict of Claudius in *Claud.* 25: "Since the Jews constantly made disturbances at the instigation of Chrestus/Christos?/, he [Claudius] expelled them from Rome" (Iudaeos impulsore Chresto assidue tumultuantis Roma expulit). Orosius (*Historiae adversum paganos* 7.6.15–16) dates it: "In his ninth year [= 49 C.E.] the Jews were expelled from the city by Claudius, Josephus reports" (anno eiusdem nono expulsos per Claudium urbe Judaeos Josephus refert).[5]

■ **3** At last we discover something about Paul's occupation (cf. 1 Thess 2:9; 1 Cor 4:12; 9). σκηνοποιός, "tentmaker," according to syᵖ and Rufinius, perhaps means "harness maker."

■ **4** This is a redactional, schematic note. On the Jews in

---

1   See *Corinth: Results of Excavations Conducted by the American School of Classical Studies at Athens* (vol. 1–; Princeton, NJ: American School of Classical Studies at Athens, 1929–) vol. 8, part 3, no. 130.

2   J. Weiss, "Griechenland in der apostolischen Zeit," *RE* 7.165–68; PWSup 4.991–1036 and 6.182–99; Kirsten and Kraiker, *Griechenlandkunde,* 312–29. On the American excavations, see *Corinth.*

3   See the comments on vs 8.

4   Haenchen, pp. 537–41.

5   CSEL 5.451. On the origin of this information, see Adolf Harnack, "Chronologische Berechnung des

'Tags von Damaskus'," SPAW, phil.-hist. Klasse (1912) 674–82. On Rome's political handling of Jews, see Simon, *Verus Israel*; on Claudius, see Bell, *Jews and Christians* (this includes the text of the London Papyrus 1912!).

Corinth, see Philo *Leg. Gai.* 36. An inscription has been found which reads: [συνα]γωγὴ ʽΕβρ[αίων], "synagogue of Hebrews."[6]

■ **5** Compare 17:14–15 and 1 Thess 3:1–2, 6. συνείχετω κτλ., "was occupied, etc.," can mean that from this point on Paul ceased doing manual labor and could preach every day (not just on the Sabbath) because he had received money from Macedonia (2 Cor 11:9).[7] The harsh transition from vs 4 to vs 5 is explained by Luke's intention in any case to carry through his schema (in vs 4!). The formulation of vs 5b is also Lukan. The content of the message is explained more fully in 17:3.

■ **6** For the meaning of Paul's shaking out of his garments, see the commentary on 13:51; cf. 2 Esdr 15:13 LXX. For the explanation of the underlying principle, "to the Jew first," see the commentary on 13:46. Paul's statement does not exclude the possibility that he will visit a synagogue again at the next location—it rather presumes that he will (vs 19).

■ **7** According to the explanation of vs 5 proposed by Haenchen, there may be a suggestion here that Paul ceased living and working with Aquila and Priscilla (so already D 614 h, which, rather than saying that "Paul moved [*RSV:* left] from there," have "Paul moved from Aquila" [ἀπὸ τοῦ ʼΑκύλα]). Yet the content suggests that Luke is describing a change in the location of Paul's teaching; for this reason Luke also emphasizes that the new room was next to the synagogue.

■ **8** For Crispus, see 1 Cor 1:14. Paul's first convert in Achaia, Stephanus (1 Cor 1:16; 16:15), is not mentioned here at all. If our passage were from an "itinerary," such an itinerary would have to be judged unreliable and highly abbreviated.[8] Once again the success is noted in a Lukan schematic formulation.[9]

■ **9–11** The vision explains not only the duration of Paul's stay in Corinth, but especially the significance of the Corinthian congregation at the time of Luke (for this cf. *1 Clement* which comes from the same time!); it also sheds light in advance on Paul's appearance before Gallio.[10] "Do not be afraid" is an ancient formula accompanying epiphanies.[11] It is also found among Greek writers: Herodotus 1.9; Arjstophanes *Ranae* 1092; Lucian *Dial. deor.* 20.7.

■ **12** This verse contains the single most important piece of information for sketching the chronology of Paul's career, and of early Christianity, because we can date the administration of Gallio with the help of the famous Gallio inscription from Delphi (four fragments in the museum at Delphi).

Excursus:
Lucius Junius Gallio Annaeus

Lucius Junius Gallio Annaeus[12] was the older brother of the philosopher Seneca (he was born M. Annaeus Novatus, then adopted by Junius Gallio). The inscription runs as follows (with attempted reconstruction):[13]

Τιβέρ[ιος Κλαύδιος Κ]αῖσ[αρ Σεβαστ]ὸς Γ[ερμανικός, ἀρχιερεὺς μέγιστος, δημαρχικῆς ἐξου]/σίας [τὸ ιβʹ, αὐτοκράτωρ τ]ὸ κςʹ, π[ατὴρ πα]τρί[δος, ὕπατος τὸ εʹ, τιμητής, Δελφῶν τῇ πόλει χαίρειν]./ Πάλ[αι μὲν] τῇ π[όλει τ]ῶν Δελφ[ῶν πρόθ]υμο[ς ἐγενόμην--καὶ εὔνους ἐς ἀρ]/χῆς, ἀεὶ[δʹ] ἐτήρη[σα τὴ]ν θρησκεί[αν τ]οῦ ʼΑπό[λ-λωνος τοῦ Πυθίου---ὅσα δὲ]/νῦν λέγεται καὶ [πολ]ειτῶν ἔρι[δες ἐ]κεῖναι ω---[καθὼς Λούκιος ʼΙού]/νιος Γαλλίων ὁ φ[ίλος] μου κα[ὶ ἀνθύ]πατος [τῆς ʼΑχαίας ἔγραψεν,---διὰ τοῦτο συγχωρῶ ὑμᾶς]/ἔτι ἔξειν τὸν πρ[ότερ]ο[ν---

Tiber[ius Claudius C]aes[ar August]us G[ermanicus, Pontifex Maximus, Holder of the Tribunician Po]wer [for the twelfth time, Imperator f]or the twenty-sixth time, F[ather of the c]ount[ry, Counsel

---

6   Deissmann, *Light from the Ancient East,* 13–14.
7   Haenchen, p. 534; E. Henschel, "Zur Apostel-geschichte 18:5," *ThViat* 2 (1950) 213–15.
8   Gottfried Schille, "Die Fragwürdigkeit eines Itinerars der Paulusreisen," *ThLZ* 84 (1959) 168.
9   On "house," see the commentary on 16:15.
10   On both, see Maurice Goguel, "La vision de Paul à Corinthe et sa comparution devant Gallion: Une conjecture sur la place originale d'*Actes* 18,9–11," *RHPhR* 12 (1932) 321–33.
11   Hugo Gressmann, "Die literarische Analyse Deutero-jesajas," *ZAW* 34 (1914) 254–97; L. Köhler, *Schweiz-erische Theologische Zeitschrift* 36 (1919) 33ff; Joachim Begrich, "Das priesterliche Heilsorakel," *ZAW* 52 (1934) 81–92.
12   *IG* 7.1676.
13   Deissmann, *Paul,* frontispiece, and *DBSup* 2.358–59, figs. 115–16 (see the literature in the following notes). Reconstruction in Deissmann, *Paul,* 272–73; *SIG* 2 no. 801 D; Edmund Groag, *Die römischen Reichsbeamten von Achaia bis auf Diokletian* (Akademie der Wissenschaften in Wien: Schriften der Balkan-kommission, Antiquarische Abteilung 9; Vienna: Hölder-Pichler-Tempsky, 1939) 32–35.

for the fifth time, and Censor, to the city of the Delphians, greetings.]
For some ti[me past I have been de]vot[ed] to the c[ity of t]he Delph[ians . . . and good will from the be]ginning; and I have ever obser[ved th]e worship[ping of Pythian] Apo[llo . . . But as for the many] current reports and those disco[rds] among the [citi]zens . . . [just as Lucius Ju]nius Gallio, my f[riend] an[d proc]onsul [of Achaia, wrote . . . Therefore I am granting that you] continue to enjoy your for[me]r. . . .

The year of Gallio's governorship may be determined from the twenty-sixth acclamation of the emperor (the only acclamation which is preserved). According to an inscription,[14] the twenty-fourth acclamation took place in the eleventh year of the tribunate, which is equivalent to the year of the reign of Claudius from 25 January 51 through 24 January 52. The twenty-seventh acclamation took place, according to another inscription,[15] in the twelfth year, in fact before the first of August 52 (according to Frontinus *Aq.* 13). An inscription from Carian has as a date the twelfth tribunate and the twenty-sixth acclamation.[16] By means of these inscriptions the Gallio stone may be dated in the period between 25 January 52 and 1 August 52. The proconsulate generally lasted for one year. In regard to the beginning of the term of office, newly appointed officials had to leave Rome before the middle of April, according to a decree of Claudius mentioned by Dio Chrysostom 60.17.3. All things considered, the year of Gallio's proconsulate was 51/52 (the more probable)[17] or 52/53. Unfortunately we do not know how Paul's one and one-half years in Corinth relate to Gallio's term of office.[18]

The βῆμα or judicial bench (*RSV,* "tribunal") has been located by the American excavations. It lies at the south side of the agora.[19]

■ **13** The scene has been shaped into an apologetic paradigm. This has determined the meaning of νόμος, "law." Since this account is not an official record of the trial, one should not ask which law the accusing Jews had in mind, the Jewish (which enjoyed the protection of the Roman government;[20] the singular form τὸν θεόν, "God," is cited in favor of this view—but the account has been written by Luke, and he certainly knows Jews would have spoken about God only in the singular) or the Roman.[21] Rather, one should ask what Luke intended here. He has the Jews formulate their charge in a deliberately ambiguous way (cf. 17:7); they seek, however clumsily, to deceive Gallio. But a capable Roman official is not so easily taken in. In this way Luke has laid the foundation for Gallio's explanation: he will have nothing to do with the whole dispute, since it is an inter-Jewish matter.[22]

■ **14–15** Here the legal situation from the standpoint of the Roman state is defined in a way that Luke would like to suggest as the ideal for Roman practice: the state should not become involved in controversies within the Jewish community involving Christians—the disputes lie outside the jurisdiction of Roman law. Gallio's statement is in the form of a contrary-to-fact condition! Luke does not actually reclaim for Christianity the recognized privileges of Judaism (as a *religio licita,* "legal religion"). This concept which is used without hesitation in modern literature was unknown to him, because there was no such conception. It does not fit with the historical and

14 *CIL* 3.1977.
15 *CIL* 6.1256.
16 *BCH* 11 (1887) 306–7.
17 Deissmann, *Paul,* 281–82; Haenchen, pp. 66–67; Groag, *Die römischen Reichsbeamten,* 33–34.
18 Literature:
   Beginnings 5.460–64.
   DBSup 2.355–73.
   Deissmann, *Paul,* 261–86.
   Maurice Goguel, "La vision de Paul à Corinthe et sa comparution devant Gallion: Une conjecture sur la place originale d'*Actes* 18,9–11," *RHPhR* 12 (1932) 321–33.
   Groag, *Die römischen Reichsbeamten,* 32–35.
   SEG 3.389.
19 *Corinth,* 1:3.91–111 and 124–32; Kirsten and Kraiker, *Griechenlandkunde,* 322; E. Dinkler, "Das

Bema zu Korinth: Archäologische, lexikographische, rechtsgeschichtliche und ikonographische Bemerkungen zu Apostelgeschichte 18,12–17," *Marburger Jahrbuch für Kunstwissenschaft* 13 (1941) 12–22 and 9 pls., reprinted in his *Signum Crucis: Aufsätze zum Neuen Testament und zur Christlichen Archäologie* (Tübingen: Mohr [Siebeck], 1967) 118–29, with an appendix, 129–33.
20 So Ramsay, *St. Paul,* 257–60, and Maurice Goguel, "La vision de Paul à Corinthe et sa comparution devant Gallion: Une conjecture sur la place originale d'*Actes* 18,9–11," *RHPhR* 12 (1932) 321–33.
21 So Theodor Zahn (*Die Apostelgeschichte des Lucas* [2 vols.; 3d and 4th eds.; KNT 5; Leipzig/Erlangen: Deichert, 1922–27]), Preuschen, and Haenchen, p. 536.
22 Conzelmann, *Theology,* 142–44.

legal evidence, nor with the intention of Luke. κατὰ λόγον (*RSV*, "have reason [to bear with"]) can mean "reasonably, rightly," or "as one wishes,"[23] or "of course."[24] ὀνόματα (*RSV*, "names") here means "persons" or "concepts." ἀνέχομαι, "bear with," is a technical term which means "to receive/attend to a complaint."[25]

■ **16** This verse demonstrates the disinterest of the author-

ities in Christianity, an attitude which, in Luke's opinion, is appropriate for them.

■ **17** The scene concludes with one of the burlesque episodes encountered in these chapters—the blow comes back upon the one who struck it. πάντες, "all," here means the people (surely not the Jews).

23   BAG *s.v.*
24   *Beginnings* 4.227.
25   Tabachovitz, "In Palladii," 102–3.

The Great Missionary Journey [15:36—21:26]

18

**The Journey to Palestine
via Ephesus and Return**

18 After this Paul stayed many days longer, and then took leave of the brethren and sailed for Syria, and with him Priscilla and Aquila. At Cenchreae he cut his hair, for he had a vow. 19/ And they came to Ephesus, and he left them there; but he himself went into the synagogue and argued with the Jews. 20/ When they asked him to stay for a longer period, he declined; 21/ but on taking leave of them he said, "I will return to you if God wills," and he set sail from Ephesus.

22 When he had landed at Caesarea, he went up and greeted the church, and then went down to Antioch. 23/ After spending some time there he departed and went from place to place through the region of Galatia and Phrygia, strengthening all the disciples.

■ **18** προσμείνας, "stayed," indicates that Paul was not driven out of the city by force (cf. 16:40). The transition from the "second" to the "third" missionary journey is not stressed and no longer indicates any real distinction between the two.[1] The details raise difficulties: Syria is given as the destination, but Paul arrives at Caesarea, "goes up," and only then arrives in Antioch. This is usually explained, on the historical level, as pragmatic: initially the goal of the trip was Antioch, but the wind drove the ship to Caesarea. If Luke had meant that he would have so indicated.[2] Does Syria include Palestine (as in 20:3)?

The mention of Priscilla and Aquila seems to be an insertion, because κειράμενος, "he cut [his hair]," refers to Paul; this indicates his faithful fulfilling of the Jewish prescription (cf. 21:23–24). One cannot argue against this grammatical observation, namely that the participle refers to Paul, by insisting that Paul would never have done such a thing—one is not dealing with the historical Paul here at all. Nor does the unusual word order allow us to conclude that Priscilla and Aquila were not mentioned at all in the source which Luke is using here. The analysis of vs 19 indicates that already the source reported a journey of Paul with fellow travelers. The exact wording of the source, however, can no longer be reconstructed. It may have mentioned the two in a second sentence, which Luke has combined with the first. From 1 Cor 16:19 one may conclude that the couple actually did move from Corinth to Ephesus. A (Nazarite) vow counted as a meritorious work; one could be released from it only at the Temple. Cutting the hair was not done at the beginning of the vow, but at the time of release from it (Num 6:1–21).[3] Certainly nothing would have prevented having one's hair cut before the vow as well. Luke, however, thinks of the cutting of the hair as an element of the vow itself.

■ **19–21** Other than the note about Priscilla's and Aquila's remaining behind there is no concrete data in these verses, but only the familiar schema of Paul's initial visit to the synagogue, without details, coupled with a brief statement by Paul, which Luke has composed. If αὐτός . . . τοῦ θεοῦ θέλοντος, "but he . . . if God wills"[4] (19b–21b), is bracketed, then the matter becomes clear. This insertion makes the course of events seem curious, but it also permits a glimpse of Luke's intention. He knows that there were already Christians in Ephesus when Paul arrived there (as the following episodes indicate), but he wants to have Paul appear as the first Christian preacher in the city. In objecting to this analysis one could argue that Priscilla's and Aquila's remaining behind in Ephesus and Paul's resolution to return belong together. That would imply that this passage should not be removed from its context. But this connection was first made by Luke; 19:1 proves that it was not present in the source

---

1 See the comments on vs 22.
2 See further on vs 22.
3 Str-B 2.747–51.

4 On τοῦ θεοῦ θέλοντος, "if God wills," see the commentaries on Jas 4:15.

material—when Paul returns, Priscilla and Aquila are not mentioned.

■ **22** Landing at Caesarea makes sense only if Paul intended to visit Jerusalem. ἀναβάς, "he went up," points toward such a visit (one "goes up" to Jerusalem). The vow points in the same direction. Unfortunately it can no longer be determined what the material from which Luke constructed these notes looked like. One might ask whether this trip between the Apostolic Council and the bringing of the collection is historically probable. The piece of source material which may be detected in 21:18–25 is unaware of such a trip, and the evidence from the letters of Paul (1 and 2 Corinthians, Galatians, Romans) plainly rules it out. On the other hand, this passage cannot be explained as a doublet to chapter 15,[5] basing this hypothesis on the parallelism between vs 23 and 16:6.[6] Haenchen assumes that Paul had initially intended to travel to Antioch, in order once again to improve relations after the unfortunate dispute with Peter and Barnabas (Gal 2:11–14; cf. on vs 18 above).

■ **23** The return journey seems to be a doublet to 16:6. In favor of the historicity of *two* visits to Galatia reference is made to Gal 4:13–14 (τὸ πρότερον, "at first"); the wording, however, cannot provide conclusive proof.[7] Verses 21b–23 give an even stronger impression of being an epitome than 16:6–10.[8] The details are understandable only to the author of the epitome, no longer to his readers. This impression is reinforced if one takes 19:1 into consideration as well. Of course there is also the possibility here that Luke himself took scattered reports and from them fashioned a journey. There is a remarkable parallel with the preceding journey, though in this latter case there is no "tendency" governing Luke's presentation. And 19:1 could belong wholly to the Lukan redaction.

---

5   On this hypothesis, see Haenchen, p. 544 n. 6.
6   For an overview of the various attempts at eliminating disagreements between the accounts of Paul's journeys (almost all of which historicize the problem, to the neglect of the literary character of the account), see Jacques Dupont, *Les problèmes du livre des Actes d'après les traveaux récents* (Analecta Lovaniensia Biblica et Orientalia 2:17; Louvain: Publica-

tions Universitaires de Louvain, 1950) 51ff, reprinted in his *Études*, 93, and G. B. Caird, *The Apostolic Age* (London: Duckworth, 1955) 202–9.
7   See BAG *s.v.* πρότερος.
8   See the commentary on 16:6–10.

The Great Missionary Journey [15:36—21:26]

18

Apollos

24 Now a Jew named Apollos, a native of Alexandria, came to Ephesus. He was an eloquent man, well versed in the scriptures. 25/ He had been instructed in the way of the Lord; and being fervent in spirit, he spoke and taught accurately the things concerning Jesus, though he knew only the baptism of John. 26/ He began to speak boldly in the synagogue; but when Priscilla and Aquila heard him, they took him and expounded to him the way of God more accurately. 27/ And when he wished to cross to Achaia, the brethren encouraged him, and wrote to the disciples to receive him. When he arrived, through grace he greatly helped those who had believed, 28/ for he powerfully confuted the Jews in public, showing by the scriptures that the Christ was Jesus.

■ **24-28** The fundamental component here is an independent episode. This is based on the observation that the episode does not fit with Luke's intention, since it deals with pre-Pauline Christianity in Ephesus.[1]

Excursus: Ephesus

Ephesus was the most important city in Asia (Strabo 14.641), the residence of the governor,[2] and the site of the temple of the Ephesian Artemis (whose cult had spread far beyond that city) as well as Ἐφέσια γράμματα, "Ephesian letters," mystic words engraved on the statue of the Ephesian Artemis, believed—when recited—to be a magic charm.[3]

The characterization of Apollos (an abbreviation for Apollonios; cf. D!),[4] is reminiscent of that of Stephen—it is typical, not individual. Whether λόγιος is understood as "eloquent" (*RSV*) or "learned" hardly makes any difference in view of the cultural ideal of that time (cf. 6:10!). Being well versed in the Scriptures is a presupposition for successful discussion (17:2–3). The impression which Apollos made (and his independence from Paul) is reflected in 1 Corinthians. It seems natural to connect his scriptural learning with Alexandria, his home.

■ **25** The reading in D and gig describes Apollos as already a Christian in Alexandria, for—following "He had been instructed"—they say ᾿εν τῇ πατρίδι, "in his

1   See the comments on vs 19. For an analysis of vss 24–28 (and 19:1–7), see Ernst Käsemann, "The Disciples of John the Baptist in Ephesus," *Essays on New Testament Themes* (SBT 41; London: SCM, 1964) 136–48; Eduard Schweizer, "Die Bekehrung des Apollos, Ag. 18,24–26," *EvTh* 15 (1955) 247–54.

2   PW 23.1024.

3   Literature:
     Inscriptions:
        C. T. Newton, ed., *The Collection of Ancient Greek Inscriptions in the British Museum*. Part 3, *Priene, Iasos and Ephesos* (ed. E. L. Hicks; Oxford: Clarendon, 1886) 67–291.
        Forschungen in Ephesos (vols. 1–; Vienna: Österreichischen Akademie der Wissenschaften, 1906–); the literary evidence is found in 1.237–74.

        PW 5.2773–2823.
        Schultze, *Altchristliche Städte* 2:2.86–120.
        CAH 11.916 (bibliography).
        Josef Keil, *Ephesos: Ein Führer durch die Ruinenstätte und ihre Geschichte* (Vienna: Alfred Hölder, 1915; 5th ed., 1964).
        Franz Miltner, *Ephesos: Stadt der Artemis und des Johannes* (Vienna: Deuticke, 1958).
        Magie, *Roman Rule* 1.74–77; 2.885–89.
     On Asia:
        RAC 1.740–49.
        F. Sokolowski, "A New Testimony on the Cult of Artemis of Ephesus," *HTR* 58 (1965) 427–31.

4   See Hans Conzelmann, *A Commentary on the First Epistle to the Corinthians* (ed. George W. MacRae; Hermeneia; Philadelphia: Fortress, 1975) 33, on 1:12.

own country."[5] ζέων τῷ πνεύματι, "fervent in spirit," appears to be a phrase from the language of Christian paraenesis (cf. Rom 12:11). There is a certain tension between vss 25b and 25c (in view of 19:1–7; 1:5; 11:16; Luke 3:16). The peculiarity of this "Christianity" becomes even more striking if, with Ernst Käsemann, vs 25c is taken as a Lukan addition (which is intended to demote Apollos in comparison with Paul);[6] then Luke would have intentionally allowed a sharp contradiction with his view of Christian baptism. In favor of Käsemann's interpretation it may be noted that vss 25c and 26 are disruptive in this context. If they are bracketed out, the contradiction that this eminent student of Scripture still needed some elementary instruction disappears. Perhaps Luke understood the matter in this fashion: Apollos knew the material of the "gospel" (as far as Luke 24), but not the events from Acts 2 and on. He could have taken the motif of the baptism of John from the other episode (19:1–7), because with its help (though not without difficulty) he could make clear in what way Apollos was subordinate to Paul.[7] There is still the difference that Apollos, in contrast to the disciples that Paul finds in Ephesus in the next episode, was not baptized again—an indication that originally the two episodes had nothing to do with one another. Schweizer assumes that in vss 24 and 25a Apollos is still being characterized as a Jew (ζέων τῷ πνεύματι, "fervent in spirit," could correspondingly mean simply his fiery eloquence).[8] Originally the story of his conversion would have been recounted here. But the Lukan style of characterization argues against Schweizer's view, as does the manner of expression, behind which we can detect no pre-Lukan stage.[9]

■ **27** This verse indicates the existence of a pre-Pauline Christian congregation. προτρεψάμενοι οἱ ἀδελφοί, "the brethren encouraged him": they encourage either Apollos to go to Corinth[10] or the recipients of the letter.[11] διὰ τῆς χάριτος, "through grace," is best applied to the activity of Apollos, and is therefore linked to συνεβάλετο, "he . . . helped." Luke avoids a meeting between Apollos and Paul (but contrast 1 Cor 16:12).

5   Bauer, *Orthodoxy and Heresy,* 46. For a discussion of ὁδός, "way," see Wilhelm Michaelis, "ὁδός," *TDNT* 5 (1967) 89–91.
6   Käsemann, "Disciples of John," 144.
7   This is Käsemann's view ("Disciples of John," 147–48), who speaks of a *communicatio idiomatum* (interchange of properties), which has taken place between the two episodes.

8   Eduard Schweizer, "Die Bekehrung des Apollos, Ag. 18,24–26," *EvTh* 15 (1955) 251–53; cf., from an earlier time, Wendt.
9   Käsemann, "Disciples of John," 143–44, 47.
10   Wendt; Bauernfeind.
11   Preuschen; cf. Haenchen, p. 551. In regard to letters of recommendation, see the commentaries on 2 Cor 3:1.

The Great Missionary Journey [15:36—21:26]

19

The "Johannine" Christians
in Ephesus

1 While Apollos was at Corinth, Paul passed
through the upper country and came to
Ephesus. There he found some disciples.
2/ And he said to them, "Did you receive
the Holy Spirit when you believed?" And
they said, "No, we have never even heard
that there is a Holy Spirit." 3/ And he
said, "Into what then were you baptized?" They said, "Into John's baptism."
4/ And Paul said, "John baptized with the
baptism of repentance, telling the people
to believe in the one who was to come
after him, that is, Jesus." 5/ On hearing
this, they were baptized in the name of
the Lord Jesus. 6/ And when Paul had
laid his hands upon them, the Holy Spirit
came on them; and they spoke with
tongues and prophesied. 7/ There were
about twelve of them in all.

It is easy to see how this and the preceding story came to be associated with one another. One might ask if Luke was the first to locate the story about these disciples in Ephesus. This episode could have occurred anywhere (the closer to Palestine the better), whereas the connection of Apollos with Ephesus in the preceding story is firmly established.[1] Priscilla and Aquila do not appear. One might also consider the possibility that Luke located the scene here in line with his tendency to portray Paul as the initiator. Haenchen describes the intention correctly: "Paul wins over the sects."[2] With the juxtaposition of these stories a definite structure appears: Apollos; an analogous event, through which Paul takes up the initiative; preaching in the synagogue; separation of the Christian congregation from the synagogue and the free development of Paul's activity (cf. Corinth, Acts 18:5–6). Originally, the annexation of the disciples of John the Baptist would have been related here; it is doubtful that the Spirit-less "Christianity" as described here existed anywhere.[3] For Luke, after the death of John the Baptist and after Jesus had superseded him in the history of salvation (Luke 16:16), there can no longer be a Baptist group. He has worked the matter out in his own way by making the disciples of the Baptist into a special Christian group.[4]

■ **1** The connection is redactional. This conclusion depends upon the judgment about the travel narrative in 18:21b–23.[5] τὰ ἀνωτερικὰ μέρη, "the upper country," denotes especially Galatia and Phrygia according to 18:23. In this expression, ἀνωτερικός, "upper," is not attested in other sources, though ἄνω, "upper," is (LXX; Charito 1.11.7).

■ **2–3** Paul's question is formulated ad hoc. The dialogue presupposes that baptism and the Spirit belong together.[6] ἀκούειν εἰ means "to hear that."[7] The peculiar expression "baptized into John's baptism" results from Luke's concern to avoid speaking about a baptism in John's *name*.

■ **4** Compare Luke 3:3, 15–18, and Acts 13:24.

■ **5–6** Here it becomes clear that this episode has nothing to do with the preceding episode, and that it tells of an annexation to the church (not of the correction of a type of Christianity). In its present form Paul exercises the same function here as the two Jerusalem apostles in 8:14–25.[8] Speaking in tongues and prophecy are iden-

---

1   Cf. Haenchen, p. 556.
2   Ibid., 557.
3   Käsemann, "Disciples of John," 144.
4   Klein, *Die zwölf Apostel*, 176–78; Walter Wink, *John
    the Baptist in the Gospel Tradition* (SNTSMS 7; Cam-
    bridge: Cambridge University, 1968) 84–86.
5   See the commentary on 18:23.
6   See the comments on 8:16.

7   Chr. Burchard, "Εἰ nach einem Ausdruck des Wissens
    oder Nichtwissens Joh 9:25, Act 19:2, 1 Cor 1:16,
    7:16," *ZNW* 52 (1961) 73–82.
8   Käsemann, "Disciples of John," 144–46.

tified; Luke no longer has any exact knowledge of the former.[9]

■ **7** The number twelve has no symbolic significance. ὡσεί, "about," before numbers is typical of Luke (cf. 2:41; 4:4; etc.).

---

9   Of a somewhat different opinion is Günther Born-kamm, "Faith and Reason in Paul," *Early Christian Experience* (New York: Harper, 1969) 38–39. On the topic here, see the excursus at 2:13.

The Great Missionary Journey [15:36—21:26]

19 Ephesus: The Sons of Sceva (13-17);
The Riot Caused by Demetrius (23-41).

8 And he entered the synagogue and for three months spoke boldly, arguing and pleading about the kingdom of God; 9/ but when some were stubborn and disbelieved, speaking evil of the Way before the congregation, he withdrew from them, taking the disciples with him, and argued daily in the hall of Tyrannus. 10/ This continued for two years, so that all the residents of Asia heard the word of the Lord, both Jews and Greeks.

11 And God did extraordinary miracles by the hands of Paul, 12/ so that handkerchiefs or aprons were carried away from his body to the sick, and diseases left them and the evil spirits came out of them. 13/ Then some of the itinerant Jewish exorcists undertook to pronounce the name of the Lord Jesus over those who had evil spirits, saying, "I adjure you by the Jesus whom Paul preaches." 14/ Seven sons of a Jewish high priest named Sceva were doing this. 15/ But the evil spirit answered them, "Jesus I know, and Paul I know; but who are you?" 16/ And the man in whom the evil spirit was leaped on them, mastered all [or: both] of them, and overpowered them, so that they fled out of that house naked and wounded. 17/ And this became known to all residents of Ephesus, both Jews and Greeks; and fear fell upon them all; and the name of the Lord Jesus was extolled. 18/ Many also of those who were now believers came, confessing and divulging their practices. 19/ And a number of those who practiced magic arts brought their books together and burned them in the sight of all; and they counted the value of them and found it came to fifty thousand pieces of silver. 20/ So the word of the Lord grew and prevailed mightily.

21 Now after these events Paul resolved in the Spirit to pass through Macedonia and Achaia and go to Jerusalem, saying, "After I have been there, I must also see Rome." 22/ And having sent into Macedonia two of his helpers, Timothy and Erastus, he himself stayed in Asia for a while.

23 About that time there arose no little stir concerning the Way. 24/ For a man named Demetrius, a silversmith, who made silver shrines of Artemis, brought no little business to the craftsmen. 25/ These he gathered together, with the workmen of like occupation, and said, "Men, you know that from this business we have our wealth. 26/ And you see and hear that not only at Ephesus but almost through all Asia this Paul has persuaded

and turned away a considerable company of people, saying that gods made with hands are not gods. 27/ And there is danger not only that this trade of ours may come into disrepute but also that the temple of the great goddess Artemis may count for nothing, and that she may even be deposed from her magnificence, she whom all Asia and the world worship."

28 When they heard this they were enraged, and cried out, "Great is Artemis of the Ephesians!" 29/ So the city was filled with the confusion; and they rushed together into the theater, dragging with them Gaius and Aristarchus, Macedonians who were Paul's companions in travel. 30/ Paul wished to go in among the crowd, but the disciples would not let him; 31/ some of the Asiarchs also, who were friends of his, sent to him and begged him not to venture into the theater. 32/ Now some cried one thing, some another; for the assembly was in confusion, and most of them did not know why they had come together. 33/ Some of the crowd prompted [or: informed] Alexander, whom the Jews had put forward. And Alexander motioned with his hand, wishing to make a defense to the people. 34/ But when they recognized that he was a Jew, for about two hours they all with one voice cried out, "Great is Artemis of the Ephesians!" 35/ And when the town clerk had quieted the crowd, he said, "Men of Ephesus, what man is there who does not know that the city of the Ephesians is temple keeper of the great Artemis, and of the sacred stone that fell from the sky? 36/ Seeing then that these things cannot be contradicted, you ought to be quiet and do nothing rash. 37/ For you have brought these men here who are neither sacrilegious nor blasphemers of our goddess. 38/ If therefore Demetrius and the craftsmen with him have a complaint against any one, the courts are open, and there are proconsuls; let them bring charges against one another. 39/ But if you seek anything further, it shall be settled in the regular assembly. 40/ For we are in danger of being charged with rioting today, there being no cause that we can give to justify this commotion." 41/ And when he had said this, he dismissed the assembly.

These verses tell of the completion of Paul's missionary work. Once again Luke possessed no "diary" as a source, but rather isolated data about times (cf. 18:11) and places, and individual episodes as well. Once more these episodes can be seen from two perspectives. On the one hand, they are woven together to form a plot. Paul's success causes the reaction, after he has already made his departure. This is different from the usual sequence of events. On the other hand, the scenes are understandable when taken by themselves. The riot caused by Demetrius, especially, is narrated in a dramatic rather than an epic manner: action is followed by speech, then comes the crisis and the denouement.[1] Here also the account seeks to develop one line of action. Events occurring in Corinth during this same time (1 and 2 Corinthians) remain outside the field of vision.

■ **8** The style, Paul's initial contact with the synagogue, and details of his preaching are Lukan.

■ **9** The designation of the "stubborn" as τινές, "some," is also Lukan. Nothing can be concluded about their number from this expression, because the term belongs to a widespread style of polemic language.[2] In this way the believing Jews are indirectly characterized as the true Jews. The breaking away of the congregation to become an independent group has its counterpart in 18:6. The detail about the lecture hall derives from local tradition. Paul is pictured here as a wandering philosopher.[3] It is not related whether Tyrannus was a lecturer or the owner of the hall. The Western text indicates the time of the lectures: from 11:00 A.M. until 4:00 P.M., thus during the time of the normal midday rest. Ambrosiaster says in regard to 2 Cor 11:23: "For here, from morning until the fifth hour, he used to seek his livelihood by means of his hands" (hic enim a mane usque ad quintam horam victum manibus quaerebat).

■ **10** The two years begin after the end of the three months referred to in vs 8 (cf. 20:31 where the whole period of time is referred to as τριετία, "three years"). Once again the Christianizing of a whole province is reported. In actual fact, Ephesus was the center of an organized mission carried out by fellow workers of Paul, as Colossians indicates (even if it was not written by Paul). But Luke makes no mention of this, emphasizing rather the personal importance of Paul.

■ **11–12** These verses contain no concrete material, but provide (on the basis of hearsay about handkerchiefs and aprons) a succinct picture of Paul the miracle worker, a picture from a later time (cf. 5:12–16). This note serves as the preparation for an episode: The miracle worker is contrasted to those who have no real power. οὐ τὰς τυχούσας (RSV, "extraordinary") is a Hellenistic expression (frequent in Vettius Valens) which means "unusual" (not "singular" in the sense of "exceptions which never recur"). For σιμικίνθιον, "apron," and σουδάριον, "handkerchief," compare Ammonius: "I think that both are made of linen, except that the handkerchiefs are worn upon the head, but those not able to wear handkerchiefs hold the aprons in their hands" (ἀμφότερα νομίζω λινοειδῆ εἶναι· πλὴν τὰ μὲν σουδάρια ἐπὶ τῆς κεφαλῆς ἐπιβάλλεται, τὰ δὲ σιμικίνθια ἐν ταῖς χερσὶν κατέχουσιν, οἱ μὴ δυνάμενοι ὀράρια [oraria] φορέσαι).[4]

■ **13–14** The Sons of Sceva

Verses 13–16 contain a legend with burlesque antecedents. Has a profane anecdote been appropriated, or is this a creation of popular Christianity? Luke employs the story to establish some distinction between miracle and magic: naming the name of Jesus does not have an automatic effect (contrast Mark 9:38–41; Luke 9:49–50). Klein reads the tendency differently; he believes that the story is a defense against Christian syncretism.[5] Luke's reworking of the language of the story is no proof that it is his creation (against Klein). In regard to Jews and exorcism, see Josephus *Ant.* 8.45–49; Justin *Dial.* 80.9–10; Lucian *Philops.* 16.[6] For ὁρκίζω, "I adjure," with the double accusative, compare Vettius Valens 172.31, etc. ὑμᾶς, "you," is plural in agreement with the plural πνεύματα, "spirits"; this is redactional—the original version knew of only *one* demon. Note the following from the Greek magical papyri: "I adjure you by Jesus, the God of the Hebrews" (ὁρκίζω σε κατὰ τοῦ θεοῦ τῶν Ἑβραίων Ἰησοῦ).[7] For the success of exorcists who employ the name of Jesus, see Origen *Cels.* 1.6 and 6.40.[8]

1   Plümacher, *Apostelgeschichte*, 98–100.
2   See my comments on 1 Tim 1:6 in Dibelius-Conzelmann, *Pastoral Epistles*, 21.
3   See the excursus on 1 Thess 2:12 in Martin Dibelius, *An die Thessalonicher I II, An die Philipper* (HNT 11; Tübingen: Mohr [Siebeck], 1937).
4   J. A. Cramer, *Catenae Graecorum Patrum in Novum Testamentum* (8 vols.; Oxford: Oxford University, 1838–44) 3.316–17.
5   Günter Klein, "Synkretismus," 40–82, now in his *Rekonstruktion*, 262–301.
6   Str-B 4.527–35; Heinrich Lewy, "Zum Dämonenglauben," *ARW* 28 (1930) 241–52; Wilfred Lawrence Knox, "Jewish Liturgical Exorcism," *HTR* 31 (1938) 191–203; Simon, *Verus Israel*, 339–68.
7   *PGM* 4.3019–20.
8   Samson Eitrem, "Some Notes on the Demonology in the New Testament," *SOSup* 12 (1950) 3–4; 2d ed., *SOSup* 20 (1966) 6–7.

■ **14** "Seven" serves to heighten the effect: Seven against one—and yet the seven are overpowered! The high priest Sceva is a purely legendary figure.

■ **15** The incorporation of the individual story into the context has resulted in some confusion. At this point more descriptive material should have been given (and originally was included) in which the encounter with the demon and the speaking of the formula of exorcism were described. But Luke has already anticipated that and immediately moves beyond it; he goes abruptly into the midst of the action. No setting is introduced until vs 16. The demon is not driven out, but begins to debate; with that it has already won the contest.

■ **16** Either the source spoke of two exorcists, in which case ἀμφοτέρων has the sense "both," or Luke uses the word with its loose Hellenistic sense, "all" (RSV).

■ **17** This statement is a redactional conclusion; compare the conclusions to the Synoptic miracle stories (cf. also Acts 1:19; 4:16).

■ **18** The application. Local coloring is apparent: the Ἐφέσια γράμματα ("Ephesian letters"—cf. on Ephesus at Acts 18:24–28, above) enjoyed a worldwide reputation.[9] πράσσειν, "to practice," and πρᾶξις, "practice," are widely used magical terms, as is περίεργος, "magic arts" (vs 19). ἐξομολογεῖσθαι, "to confess," is used of making confession of sins in worship (*Did.* 4.14; *2 Clem.* 8.3; *Barn.* 19.12). Luke seems unaware that according to his wording these Christians still continued their "practices" even after their conversion. He wants simply to highlight the striking success of the conversion.

■ **19** The magnitude of the success is realistically demon-strated. "Silver" probably refers to silver drachmas. The collection of Greek magical papyri offers an abundance of comparative material regarding ancient books of magic.[10]

■ **20** Rome is the stereotyped goal of missionaries and wonderworkers.[11] The verse might be translated "the word grew and prevailed in accordance with the power of the Lord," taking the genitive τοῦ κυρίου, "of the Lord," with κράτος, "power," except that κατὰ κράτος is a widespread adverbial expression meaning "mightily."

■ **21** The formulation of this verse comes from Luke (δεῖ, "must": 23:11; 27:24).[12] He says nothing about the real reason for the journey, which was the collection. The actual events were much more complicated (cf. 1 Cor 16:5–9; 2 Cor 1:15; etc.). The placement of this verse prior to the story of Demetrius means that the story which follows must be read in light of Paul's earlier decision to move on. According to Luke, in other words, Paul's plans have not been frustrated by the riot caused by Demetrius.

■ **22** Compare 1 Cor 4:17 and 16:10. Luke makes no mention of Timothy's return, Paul's stay in Corinth, or the two missions of Titus (2 Cor 2:12–13; 7:6; 8:16–24). The actual journey is narrated beginning with chapter 20. Erastus is again mentioned in Rom 16:23 and 2 Tim 4:20.[13]

■ **23-40** The riot caused by Demetrius. The local coloring in this narrative is vivid.[14] A glance at 1 Cor 15:32 and 2 Cor 1:8–11 reveals that the real events have been toned down to fit the style of the narrative. Haenchen supposes that the author created the whole account based on only

---

9 PW 5.2771–73.

10 In addition to the collection of Preisendanz (*PGM*), see: Prümm, *Handbuch*, 357–464; Ps.-Clem. *Recog.* 4.27; Joseph Bidez and Franz Cumont, *Les mages hellénisés: Zoroastre, Ostanès et Hystaspe d'après la tradition grecque* (2 vols.; Paris: Société d'édition "Les Belles-Lettres," 1938; reprinted, 2 vols. in 1, New York: Arno, 1975) 1.149; 2.243; Martin P. Nilsson, *Die Religion der griechischen Zauberpapyri* (Lund: Gleerup, 1948).

   For information about ancient and early Christian critiques of magic, in addition to the collection of Preisendanz (*PGM*), see: Herbert Braun, "Plutarchs Kritik am Aberglauben im Lichte des NT," *Gesammelte Studien*, 120–35; Hermann Schlingensiepen, *Die Wunder des Neuen Testaments: Wege und Abwege ihrer Deutung in der alten Kirche bis zur Mitte des fünsten*

Jahrhunderts (BFCTh: Sammlung Wissenschaftlicher Monographien 28; Gütersloh: Bertelsmann, 1933) 62–76.

   Regarding the burning of books, see Livy 40.29 and 39.16.8; Suetonius *Aug.* 31; C. A. Forbes, "Books for the Burning," *TAPA* 67 (1936) 114–25; Arthur Stanley Pease, "Notes on Book-Burning," *Munera Studiosa: Studies Presented to W. H. P. Hatch* (ed. Massey Hamilton Shepherd and Sherman Elbridge Johnson; Cambridge, MA: Episcopal Theological School, 1946) 145–60.

11 Betz, *Lukian*, 110.

12 Erich Fascher, "Theologische Beobachtungen zu δεῖ," *Neutestamentliche Studien für Rudolf Bultmann*, 247–48.

13 Henry J. Cadbury, "Erastus of Corinth," *JBL* 50 (1931) 42–58.

a minimum of information (including a vague recollection of one Demetrius).[15] Nevertheless, while Luke does compose scenes, he does not invent stories such as this. The intermezzo with Alexander remains unexplained (reference to the Alexander of 1 Tim 1:20 and 2 Tim 4:14 is not an explanation).

■ **24** ποιῶν ναούς, "who made . . . shrines": A νεωποιός ("temple official") named Demetrius is mentioned in an inscription from the first century.[16] A νεωποιός, however, is not one who manufactures small souvenir temples, but one who belongs to the administrative staff of the temple of Artemis.[17] In regard to the Ephesian Artemis and her world-famous temple, see Strabo 14.1.20–23; Pausanius 2.2.5 and 4.31; Achilles Tatius 7–8; Xenophon Eph. 1.[18] ναοί, "shrines," were probably copies of the temple.[19] Though such copies have not been found in Ephesus, they have been discovered elsewhere;[20] they served as souvenirs or amulets.[21]

■ **26** The genitives, Ἐφέσου, "at Ephesus," and πάσης τῆς Ἀσίας, "throughout all Asia," are probably dependent on ὄχλος, "company."[22] For the Christian reader, the charge against Paul is a testimony to the victorious advance of the mission. Demetrius naively identifies the temple replicas with the gods (is Luke intentionally portraying him as stupid?); the reader remembers 17:24–25.

■ **27** The three infinitives ἐλθεῖν, "come," λογισθῆναι, "count," and μέλλειν, "may . . . be," are dependent upon κινδυνεύειν, "to be in danger." μέλλειν replaces the future indicative. The expression εἰς ἀπελεγμὸν ἐλθεῖν, "come into disrepute," is not attested elsewhere; it corresponds to the Latin *redargutionem venire* (d Vg).[23] The damage which Christianity caused to various trades[24] is illustrated by the famous letter of Pliny the Younger to Trajan:

'Tis certain at least that the temples, which had been almost deserted, begin now to be frequented [that is, after the suppression of Christianity]. And the sacred festivals, after a long intermission, are again revived; while there is a general demand for sacrificial animals, which for some time past have met with but few purchases (Certe satis constat prope iam desolata templa coepisse celebrari et sacra sollemnia diu intermissa repeti pastumque venire victimarum, cuius adhuc rarissimus emptor inveniebatur).[25]

■ **28** For μεγάλη, "great," as an attribute of the Ephesian Artemis, compare Xenophon Eph. 1.11.5: "our ancestral goddess [cf. vs 37!], the great Artemis of the Ephesians" (τὴν πάτριον ἡμῖν θεόν, τὴν μεγάλην Ἐφεσίων Ἄρτεμιν). An inscription reads: "the greatest goddess Artemis" (τὴν μεγίστην Θεὸν Ἄρτεμιν).[26] In D the definite article before Artemis is absent. Ramsay regards this reading as original, since the article was lacking in the ancient acclamation.[27] Forms of the acclamation are known, however, that include the article as well; Aelius Aristides 24: "Great is Asclepius" (μέγας ὁ Ἀσκλήπιος).[28] Peterson points out that in the ancient novel such acclamations could be woven into the narrative for animation.[29] The worship of the Ephesian goddess had spread to other cities also (Pausanius 4.31.6).[30]

14 Cadbury, *Acts in History,* see the index under Ephesus and Artemis.
15 Haenchen, p. 577.
16 Newton, *Inscriptions,* no. 578.
17 PW 16.2433.
18 *Beginnings* 5.251–56; *RAC* 1.714–18; Hermann Thiersch, *Artemis Ephesia: Eine archäologische Untersuchung* (AGG 3:12; Göttingen: Vandenhoeck & Ruprecht, 1935).
19 Artemidorus 2.33 (p. 130.3 Hercher).
20 Cadbury, *Acts in History,* 5.
21 Nilsson, *Zauberpapyri* 1.520; *RAC* 3.866.
22 See BDF § 186.1.
23 George D. Kilpatrick, "Acts XIX.27 ἀπελεγμόν," *JTS* n.s. 10 (1959) 327.
24 BAG *s.v.* μέρος.
25 Pliny *Ep.* 2.405.
26 *Ancient Greek Inscriptions of the British Museum* 3, no. 481, cols. 12–13, pp. 117 and 127; cf. col. 6.278, pp. 122 and 132.
27 William Ramsay, *The Church in the Roman Empire Before A.D. 170* (5th ed.; London: Hodder & Stoughton, 1897) 139–42.
28 Dindorf, p. 471; Keil 2.399. See also B. Müller, ΜΕΓΑΣ ΘΕΟΣ (Dissertationes philologicae Halenses 21 [1913]) 331–33.
29 Erik Peterson, Εἷς θεός: *Epigraphische, formgeschichtliche und religionsgeschichtliche Untersuchungen* (FRLANT n.s. 24; Göttingen: Vandenhoeck & Ruprecht, 1926) 196–208.
30 PW 2.1372–73 and 5.2753–71.

■ **29** Compare the inscription from Cnidus: "The people [cf. vvs 30, 33], falling into immoderate confusion, . . . having come together with all eagerness into the theater" ([ὁ μὲν] δᾶμος ἐν οὐ μετρίᾳ συγχύ[σει γε]νόμενος . . . [μετὰ] πάσης προθυμίας συνελ[θὼν ε]ὶς τὸ θέατρον). For (Gaius and) Aristarchus, see 20:4. The theater at Ephesus had a seating capacity of twenty-four thousand.

■ **31** The precise position of the Asiarchs is debated.[31] Their office was apparently more representative than administrative. At that time such a position included cultic responsibilities (the official Roman cult—in Ephesus there was a temple of Augustus and of the goddess Roma).

■ **32** Compare Charito 1.5.3: "The whole populous, too, rapidly assembled in the market place, with various shouts and exclamations" (ἀλλὰ καὶ ὁ δῆμος ἅπας εἰς τὴν ἀγορὰν συνέτρεχεν ἄλλων ἄλλα κεκραγόντων).[32]

■ **33** The sense of συμβιβάζειν, "prompted," is not clear (as the variants indicate). Does it mean "inform" here? What was Alexander supposed to do? As a trusted representative of the Jews, was he to explain that they had nothing to do with this matter? Did Luke no longer understand his source here?

■ **34** The verse provides some feel for ancient "anti-Semitism."[33]

■ **35** The γραμματεύς (τοῦ δήμου),[34] "town clerk," was one of the ranking functionaries of the city.[35] νεωκόρος, "temple keeper," is a title used of cities. Most often it is used to designate a city as the location of the imperial cult.[36] It also occurs, though infrequently, in connection with other cults; it is used, for example, for the cult of Artemis:[37] "doubly temple keeper of the emperors . . . and temple keeper of Artemis" (δὶς νεωκόρος τῶν Σεβαστῶν . . . καὶ νεωκόρος τῆς Ἀρτέμιδος).[38] διοπετής, "fell from the sky": this claim is not made for the Ephesian image other than in this passage. Euripides, however, uses the word in connection with the image of the Taurian Artemis (*Iph. Taur.* 78–79, 1384–85). Copies of the Ephesian image (Strabo 4.179; Minucius Felix 22.5) have been preserved.[39] Recently both a life-size statue and a statue larger than life-size have been found in Ephesus itself.[40]

■ **37** For the charge of sacrilege (against Jews), compare Rom 2:22 and Josephus *Ant.* 4.207: Jews were prohibited from blaspheming strange foreign gods and robbing shrines.[41]

■ **38** With ἀγοραῖοι, "courts" (supply ἡμέραι, "days," σύνοδοι, "sessions"), and ἄγονται, "are open," compare the Latin *conventus agere,* "to hold the assizes [court sessions]." Reference is to the regular court sessions, which the proconsul held at various locations in the province.

■ **39** Alongside this institution of the Roman government the organ of self-government is named, the "regular" assembly (cf. the inscription: "in the lawful assemblies" [ἐν ταῖ ἐννόμωι ἐκκλησίαι]).[42] The expression may also connote "legal" gatherings, in contrast to this mob.

■ **40** With regard to μηδενὸς αἰτίου (from τὸ αἴτιον, "the cause") ὑπάρχοντος κτλ., "there being no cause, etc.," apparently two expressions are mixed together: "We have no cause" and "we can provide no information (about a cause)." The expression would be simpler if the οὐ, "not," were left out, as do D, gig, etc. (it could have entered the text through dittography).

31   PW 2.1564–78; another opinion is expressed in PW 7.1753; PWSup 4.936; *Beginnings* 5.256–62; Magie, *Roman Rule* 1.449–50 and 2.1298–1301.

32   English trans. from Warren E. Blake, *Chariton's Chaereas and Callirhoe* (Ann Arbor: University of Michigan; London: Oxford University, 1939) 8.

33   See the commentary on 16:21. On the construction, see BDF § 466.4.

34   *OGIS* 493. He can also be an Asiarch, Newton, *Inscriptions,* no. 500; *SEG* 19 no. 984, lines 34–35. One can also find γραμματεὺς τῆς βουλῆς ("clerk of the council"), and sometimes both.

35   PW 7.1747–52; Magie, *Roman Rule* 2.848–49,

36   *OGIS* 493; Nilsson, *Zauberpapyri* 2.367–68.

37   *CIG* 2.2972; *Ephesos* 3, nos. 5, 8.

38   *Ephesos* 2, p. 163, no. 40; see also PW 16.2422–28.

39   On coins: for example, Barclay Vincent Head, "The Coins [of Ephesus]," in David G. Hogarth, *Excavations at Ephesus: The Archaic Artemisia* (London, 1908) 74–93, see table 5, 2–6.

40   Franz Miltner, *Ephesos: Stadt der Artemis und des Johannes* (Vienna: Deuticke, 1958) pls. 31, 87–89.

41   On ἡ θεός, see the commentary on vss 27–28; *Ephesos* 3, index.

42   *SIG* 2 no. 672.37.

1510–11.

The Great Missionary Journey [15:36—21:26]

20

The Journey through Macedonia to Corinth and Return to Troas

1 After the uproar ceased, Paul sent for the disciples and having exhorted them took leave of them and departed for Macedonia. 2/ When he had gone through these parts and had given them much encouragement, he came to Greece. 3/ There he spent three months, and when a plot was made against him by the Jews as he was about to set sail for Syria, he determined to return through Macedonia. 4/ Sopater of Beroea, the son of Pyrrhus, accompanied him; and of the Thessalonians, Aristarchus and Secundus; and Gaius of Derbe, and Timothy; and the Asians, Tychicus and Trophimus. 5/ These went on ahead and were waiting for us at Troas, 6/ but we sailed away from Philippi after the days of Unleavened Bread, and within five days we came to them at Troas, where we stayed for seven days.

■ **1** Luke avoids saying that Paul was expelled or banished from Ephesus, although it follows from vss 17–18 that he could no longer risk entering the city (cf. 2 Cor 1:8–11). Here we have travel notes (vss 1–6, 13–16) interspersed with episodes. The list indicates that Luke was in possession of some very early material. Once again, however, the events are simplified (cf. 1 Cor 16:5; 2 Cor 2:12–13; 7:6–7, 13–16). Nothing is said about Paul's stay in Troas after his journey there, although later the existence of a congregation in the city is assumed (vs 6). Since no specific locations are mentioned, it is difficult to assume that Luke was using an itinerary here. Dibelius must assume that the precise journey had not been recorded, or that Luke has abbreviated it.[1]

■ **2** Luke's use of the word Ἑλλάς, "Greece," here indicates that he is not bound to using official names of provinces (this would be "Achaia"). "Greece" is distinguished from τὰ μέρη ἐκεῖνα, "these parts" = Macedonia, and thus does not refer to the whole of Greece.

■ **3** During this stay in Corinth Paul wrote the Letter to the Romans. In it he expressed his apprehensions about the Jews, especially those in Judea. Originally, Paul intended to travel directly from Corinth to Palestine.

This is evident because he already had the collection from the Macedonian congregations with him, a fact Luke does not mention.[2]

■ **4** Those named here are actually the delegates who were to deliver the collection. But since Luke only speaks of the collection later, mentioning it only in passing (24:17), one gets the impression that this is simply a representative escort. There is mention of a "Gaius" in 19:29, identified as a Macedonian. Because of this, D* and gig have changed Δερβαῖος, "of Derbe" (the correct form would be Δερβήτης) to Δουβ[ε]ριος, "from Doberus," or "Doverius" (referring to the Macedonian city of Doberus, southwest of Philippi). It may be concluded, however, that Δερβαῖος, "of Derbe," is the original reading, because Paul's companions are listed here according to the districts from which they came.[3] For Tychicus, compare Col 4:7;[4] for Trophimus, compare 21:29 and 2 Tim 4:20; for Aristarchus, compare 19:29 and 27:2.

■ **5** The reading προσελθόντες, "went on," has better support, but the context here demands προ-, "went on

---

1 Dibelius, *Studies*, 5; cf. 170, 210–11; see the commentary on 16:6–10 and 18:23.

2 On ἐγένετο γνώμης, "he determined," see BDF

§ 162.7.

3 Haenchen, pp. 52–53.

4 See the commentaries on Col 4:7.

ahead."[5] Once again "we" appears (in Philippi! cf. 16:16) without any preparation. Either the whole company went on ahead to Troas, or only the Asians (so most exegetes). Paul's companion to which the "we" refers joined him in Philippi, or at least the narrator assumes this is the case. "We" is once again reserved for use in connection with a voyage, and it is found only in the framework of the itinerary, thus in sections composed by the author.

■ **6** For dating according to the Jewish calendar, compare 27:9 and 1 Cor 16:8.[6] Verse 16 shows why the date is mentioned. "Within" is an unusual use of the preposition $\check{\alpha}\chi\rho\iota$ ($\check{\alpha}\chi\rho\iota$ $\dot{\eta}\mu\epsilon\rho\hat{\omega}\nu$ $\pi\acute{\epsilon}\nu\tau\epsilon$, "within five days"). The difference in duration of the crossing reported in 16:11 and that reported here is not of particular note; it can be explained simply as due to wind conditions.

5   Hans Conzelmann, "Miszelle zu Act 20:4f.," *ZNW* 45 (1954) 266.
6   On $\alpha\dot{\iota}$ $\dot{\eta}\mu\acute{\epsilon}\rho\alpha\iota$ $\tau\hat{\omega}\nu$ $\dot{\alpha}\zeta\acute{\nu}\mu\omega\nu$, "the days of Unleavened Bread," see the commentaries on Mark 14:1.

The Great Missionary Journey [15:36—21:26]

20

**The Sermon in Troas and
the Raising of Eutychus**

7   **On the first day of the week, when we
were gathered together to break bread,
Paul talked with them, intending to
depart on the morrow; and he prolonged
his speech until midnight. 8/ There were
many lights in the upper chamber where
we were gathered. 9/ And a young man
named Eutychus was sitting in the
window. He sank into a deep sleep as
Paul talked still longer; and being over-
come by sleep, he fell down from the
third story and was taken up dead. 10/
But Paul went down and bent over him,
and embracing him said, "Do not be
alarmed, for his life is in him." 11/ And
when Paul had gone up and had broken
bread and eaten, he conversed with them
a long while, until daybreak, and so
departed. 12/ And they took the lad away
alive, and were not a little comforted.**

This episode is complete in itself. It is concerned only
with Paul; the "we" of vs 8 is obviously secondary.[1] Verse
7, which does not fit with vss 8 and 9, where the details
are repeated, is the usual redactional preview. Verse 11
is intrusive in its position between vss 10 and 12. If vss 7
and 11 are removed, then the unity of the piece is clear:
what remains is a secular story with a popular comic
touch. In the original form the liturgical embellishment
was absent. No conclusions about the course and the
components of the liturgy can be drawn from the redactional additions, since they do not intend to provide
ritual exactitude.[2] The unusual position for the Eucharist in the sequence of events cannot be explained on the
basis of the actual course of the celebration (neither at
the time of Paul nor of Luke). The note has simply been
inserted in an awkward manner.

■ **7** For Sunday as the day for gathering for worship, compare 1 Cor 16:2 and *Did.* 14.[3] It is not clear whether the
reference is to Saturday night and early Sunday morning, or Sunday night and early Monday morning. Lake
and Cadbury argue for the latter since Luke divides the
day in the manner of the Greeks, as is shown by comparison of Mark 15:42—16:2 with Luke 23:54—24:1. The

findings, however, are not unequivocal.[4]

■ **8** Here is the original exposition. Mention of the lights is
aimed at the main motif:[5] despite the bright lights, the
lad fell asleep. He is just a νεανίας, "youth" = παῖς, "lad"
(vs 12), and the sermon was excessively long. Others
interpret the mention of the lights as a reference to a
festive mood[6] or as an apologetic comment: when Christians got together, nothing occurred which needed to be
hidden from the light (cf. the well-known charges against
the Christians in Minucius Felix *Octavius* 9 and Tertullian
Apol. 8–9—but may we assume that these existed as early
as the time of Luke?).

■ **9** A similar accident is reported in *Pap. Oxy.* 3.475.[7]
νεκρός, "dead," should not be weakened to "as if" dead.

■ **10** In the same way this verse does not say that his life is
"still" in him. A real raising of the dead is meant, as in
9:36–41. For the manner of the raising, compare 1 Kgs
17:21–22 (2 Kgs 4:34–37), and for the command not to
be alarmed, compare Mark 5:39.

■ **12** Because of the redactional insertion in vs 11 (see
above), vs 12 is unclear. From where did they bring the
young man who had been brought back to life, and
where did they take him? Without vs 11 the answer is

---

1   For an analysis, see Dibelius, *Studies,* 17–19.
2   This is contrary to the view of Philippe H. Menoud,
    "The Acts of the Apostles and the Eucharist," *Jesus
    Christ and the Faith,* 84–106.
3   For τῇ μιᾷ τῶν σαββάτων, "On the first day of the
    week," see the commentaries on Mark 16:2 and 1
    Cor 16:2.
4   *Beginnings* 4.255; cf. in addition H. Riesenfeld,

    "Sabbat et Jour du Seigneur," *New Testament Essays:
    Studies in Memory of Thomas Walter Manson* (Man-
    chester: Manchester University, 1959) 210–17.
5   So Dibelius, *Studies,* 18.
6   Menoud, "The Acts of the Apostles and the
    Eucharist," *Jesus Christ and the Faith,* 93.
7   Cadbury, *Acts in History,* 9.

obvious: they took him from where he had fallen back up to the place of the meeting. The detail in vs 12 is the "demonstration" of the miracle which is stylistically appropriate to the miracle story.

The Great Missionary Journey [15:36—21:26]

20

The Journey to Miletus

13 But going ahead to the ship, we set sail for Assos, intending to take Paul aboard there; for so he had arranged, intending himself to go by land. 14/ And when he met us at Assos, we took him on board and came to Mitylene. 15/ And sailing from there we came the following day opposite Chios; the next day we touched at Samos; and the day after that we came to Miletus. 16/ For Paul had decided to sail past Ephesus, so that he might not have to spend time in Asia; for he was hastening to be at Jerusalem, if possible, on the day of Pentecost.

■ **13** Why does Paul travel by land? Use of an "itinerary" does not make this any more intelligible. All explanations for Paul's decision to travel by land are purely speculative. Luke himself no longer knew the reason. The distance from Troas to Assos is about thirty kilometers.

■ **14–15** Here we have a straightforward list of stations. Once again this does not prove that Luke was using a source. This is the construction of the author, for only in this way can we understand that Paul's route from Assos first takes him through Miletus (cf. the surprisingly similar style of description in Xenophon Eph. 1:11–12!). For this part of the journey, see Strabo 14.639. Μιτυλήνη, "Mitylene," is a later form of Μυτιλήνη, "Mytilene." The Koine and Western texts have inserted Trogyllium (a city and promontory opposite Samos) as another station.

■ **16** Given good weather conditions, it was possible to reach Jerusalem in the stated time (allowing for stops in Miletus, Tyre, and Caesarea). But Luke does not make further mention of this intention, and says nothing about the actual time of arrival in Jerusalem. In any case the reason Luke gives for the meeting between Paul and the Ephesian elders in Miletus—Paul's haste to reach Jerusalem—is strange. It would have taken at least five days for the Ephesians to reach Miletus (the distance from Miletus to Ephesus is about fifty kilometers by air; the distance by land was considerably greater). Samos would have been a more convenient meeting place. It is clear that Paul could no longer enter Ephesus, but Luke cannot say this. The accusative of time ("[on] the day") is used as the designation of a point in time.[1]

---

1   BDF § 161.3.

The Great Missionary Journey [15:36—21:26]

20

The Farewell to the Elders of
the Ephesian Congregation

17 And from Miletus he sent to Ephesus and called to him the elders of the church. 18/ And when they came to him, he said to them:

"You yourselves know how I lived among you all the time from the first day that I set foot in Asia, 19/ serving the Lord with all humility and with tears and with trials which befell me through the plots of the Jews; 20/ how I did not shrink from declaring to you anything that was profitable, and teaching you in public and from house to house, 21/ testifying both to Jews and to Greeks of repentance to God and of faith in our Lord Jesus Christ. 22/ And now, behold, I am going to Jerusalem, bound in the Spirit, not knowing what shall befall me there; 23/ except that the Holy Spirit testifies to me in every city that imprisonment and afflictions await me. 24/ But I do not account my life of any value nor as precious to myself, if only I may accomplish my course and the ministry which I received from the Lord Jesus, to testify to the gospel of the grace of God. 25/ And now, behold, I know that all you among whom I have gone preaching the kingdom will see my face no more. 26/ Therefore I testify to you this day that I am innocent of the blood of all of you, 27/ for I did not shrink from declaring to you the whole counsel of God. 28/ Take heed to yourselves and to all the flock, in which the Holy Spirit has made you overseers, to care for the church of God which he obtained with the blood of his own Son [or: with his (own) blood]. 29/ I know that after my departure fierce wolves will come in among you, not sparing the flock; 30/ and from among your own selves will arise men speaking perverse things, to draw away the disciples after them. 31/ Therefore be alert, remembering that for three years I did not cease night or day to admonish every one with tears. 32/ And now I commend you to God and to the word of his grace, which is able to build you up and to give you the inheritance among all those who are sanctified. 33/ I coveted no one's silver or gold or apparel. 34/ You yourselves know that these hands ministered to my necessities, and to those who were with me. 35/ In all things I have shown you that by so toiling one must help the weak, remembering the words of the Lord Jesus, how he said, 'It is more blessed to give than to receive.'"

36 And when he had spoken thus, he knelt down and prayed with them all. **37/** And they all wept and embraced Paul and kissed him, **38/** sorrowing most of all because of the word he had spoken, that they should see his face no more. And they brought him to the ship.

Since the journey is interrupted, the "we" also ceases. Apparently the only source material which Luke had was the report about the meeting in Miletus as such. He has composed the details as well as the speech itself. When compared with the previous speeches in Acts, this one represents a new type.[1] It is the only one of Paul's speeches which is delivered to Christians. It contains elements of the edifying speech,[2] but above all it serves a "historical" purpose in the framework of the whole: it marks the conclusion of Paul's mission. Stylistic elements of the farewell speech are used for this purpose.[3] The speech is more easily structured on the basis of content than in terms of formal elements.[4] The threefold καὶ νῦν ἰδού, "and now, behold," or καὶ τὰ νῦν, "and now," yields only an apparent structure; in actuality, these do not mark off the major sections of the speech.[5]

On the basis of content the speech may be divided as follows: (1) Retrospect 18–21; (2) Prospect 22–27; (3) Testament 28–31; and (4) Blessing 32–35. Each section includes a reference to Paul (Paul's self-defense and Paul as paradigm). As in 2 Timothy, the idealized picture of a later time is set forth as the enduring contribution (alongside the transmission of his teaching).[6]

■ **17** Contrary to the historical facts, the institution of elders is assumed for the Pauline congregations.[7]

■ **18** In such reminiscences one is directed to the first day, the time of beginnings (cf. 1 Sam 12:2; Phil 1:5; Col 1:6),

and then to a survey of the whole of the individual's activity.

■ **19** This verse sketches the picture of Paul as he should always be remembered. Flowery phrases from ecclesiastical language are woven into the speech: δουλεύειν κτλ., "serving, etc.," compare 1 Thess 1:9–10; Col 3:24; Eph 6:7; μετὰ δακρύων, "with tears," compare vs 31 and 2 Cor 2:4 (these are in part from popular rhetoric: μετὰ πάσης, "with all," cf. 4:29; 17:11; Eph 4:2).

■ **20** The assertion of innocence also fits the style of this type of speech (cf. 1 Sam 12:2–5; *T. 12 Patr.*;[8] 1 Thess 2:1–12; 2 Cor 7:2).[9] The assertion that he did not withhold anything is so strongly emphasized with the repetition in vs 27 and also by vs 30 that it cannot be explained simply by referring to the style of the speech.[10] This pointed remark is undoubtedly aimed at an actual target—apparently it is directed against advocates of a secret gnostic teaching, which was traced back to Paul.[11]

■ **21** Here is a good example of a Lukan summary of doctrine, in dependence on a formal schema (cf. 1 Thess

---

1   Dibelius, *Studies,* 155–58.
2   Bo Reicke, "A Synopsis of Early Christian Preaching," *The Root of the Vine: Essays in Biblical Theology* (Anton Fridrichsen et al.; New York: Philosophical Library; London: Dacre, 1953) 154–55.
3   Johannes Munck, "Discours d'adieu dans le Nouveau Testament et dans la littérature biblique," *Aux sources de la tradition,* 155–70. For the farewell speech, cf. *T. 12 Patr.*; John 13—17; 2 Timothy; and 2 Peter; see my comments on 1 Tim 4:1 and 2 Tim 3:1–5 in Dibelius-Conzelmann, *Pastoral Epistles,* 64–72.
4   In agreement with Dibelius (*Studies,* 157) and against Haenchen, pp. 595–96.
5   On the speech as a whole, see J. Dupont, *Paulus an die Seelsorger* (Düsseldorf: Patmos, 1966); Heinz Schürmann, "Das Testament des Paul für die Kirche," *Traditionsgeschichtliche Untersuchungen zu den*

synoptischen Evangelien (Düsseldorf: Patmos, 1968) 310–40.
6   On the significance of the speech within the framework of Luke's overall sketch (that is, Luke's image of Paul), see Klein, *Die zwölf Apostel,* 178–84.
7   See the commentary on 14:23.
8   See the comments on vs 26.
9   See Hans Windisch, *Der zweite Korintherbrief* (9th ed.; KEK 6; Göttingen: Vandenhoeck & Ruprecht, 1924; reprinted 1970) on this passage; also see H. Aschermann, "Die paränetischen Formen der 'Testamente der zwölf Patriarchen' und ihr Hachwirken in der frühchristlichen Mahnung" (Diss., Berlin, 1955).
10   So also Haenchen, p. 596.
11   On the development of Gnosticism in the areas of Paul's missionary work, see Bauer, *Orthodoxy and Heresy,* esp. 232–36.

1:9–10; Acts 14:15; 16:31; 26:18).[12] The unique expression μετάνοια "εἰς θεόν," "repentance to God," may be explained by the relationship of μετάνοια, "to repent," to the more usual ἐπιστρέφειν, "turn." μετάνοια, "repentance," and πίστις, "faith," indicate the appropriate response to the first and second articles of the creed respectively. "Jews and Greeks" is a consistent element in Luke's depiction of Christian mission.

■ 22 καὶ νῦν ἰδού, "and now, behold," is a LXX expression (cf. 13:11). In accord with the style of the speech, the retrospect is followed by the prospect. Haenchen is of a different opinion, namely, that the speech at this point is not yet dealing with the future, but first with the uncertain present.[13] The present is uncertain, however, precisely because of the future. From Paul's standpoint the threat is still anticipated. δεδεμένος κτλ., "bound, etc.," does not mean Paul considers himself shackled by the Spirit; rather he travels to Jerusalem under the constraint of the Spirit (in contrast to 19:21). δέω, "bind," is being used in reference to a supernatural "binding."[14] μὴ εἰδώς, "not knowing," leads immediately to an ominous announcement in vs 23: "except that the Holy Spirit testifies."[15]

■ 23 Thus Paul knows essentially what awaits him because of the testimony of the Spirit, that is, the testimony mediated by prophets;[16] compare 21:4, 10–11, where there are traces of the reports upon which Luke based this generalization. With this vacillation between not knowing and knowing, Luke can indicate both the divine guidance of Paul's life and also Paul's willingness to endure suffering. He avoids speaking directly of Paul's death.

■ 24–25 In these verses, however, he clearly hints at death (τελειοῦν τὸν δρόμον, "accomplish the course," cf. 13:25).[17] οὐδενὸς λόγου ποιοῦμαι τὴν ψυχὴν τιμίαν

ἐμαυτῷ[18] means either "I do not consider my life worth mention" (thus τίμιος = ἄξιος, "worth")[19] or we have here a mixture of two expressions: οὐδενὸς λόγον ποιοῦμαι, "I have regard for nothing" (cf. variants), and "I do not consider my life precious." For τῆς χάριτος, "of the grace," compare vs 32. Joy at the opportunity for self-sacrifice is a favorite motif in ceremonial inscriptions and in rhetorical historiography;[20] note Dionysius Halic. 3.16.2; 5.65.4: "They would freely expose their persons and lives, which were all they had left, to any dangers" (τὰ δὲ σώματα καὶ τὰς ψυχὰς . . . ἀφειδῶς εἰς τοὺς . . . κινδύνους ἐπιδιδόντες).

■ 25 This verse presupposes that Luke is looking back at Paul's death. The wording excludes the possibility that he was set free from Roman imprisonment (and succeeded in making another visit to the East). This also agrees with the Pastorals, which know only *one* imprisonment of Paul.[21]

■ 26 This assertion means: if anyone now forfeits eternal life, Paul is innocent—he has carried out his missionary charge faithfully. The following verse provides the basis for this statement, repeating vs 20.

■ 27 Initiation into the "whole counsel" of God takes place through public preaching. The opposite of this is the esoteric teaching of the Gnostics, where only the initiates experience the whole (cf. also the esoteric teachings and practices of the Qumran sect, 1QpHab 7.1–14; 1QS 3.13–14; 11.5–9). On this polemical formulation, compare Irenaeus *Adv. haer.* 1.1 and Tertullian *Praescr. haer.* 22–23.[22] What is actually being affirmed here is the sufficiency of the historical revelation and the transmission of that revelation through the preached word.

■ 28 This verse offers paraenesis for the postapostolic age. It is the only passage in Acts which refers explicitly to false doctrine within the church. This is also a typical

---

12 See the commentaries on 1 Thess 1:9–10.

13 Haenchen, p. 591.

14 Deissmann, *Light from the Ancient East*, 304–7.

15 On the expression πλὴν ὅτι, see BDF § 449.1.

16 Eduard Schweizer, "πνεῦμα," *TDNT* 6 (1968) 408 n. 491.

17 See my comments on 2 Tim 4:7 in Dibelius-Conzelmann, *Pastoral Epistles*, 121.

18 B ℵ* C; A D E and the Koine have smoothed out the text.

19 BAG *s.v.* λόγος.

20 Cf. *SIG* 2 no. 613. 25ff.

21 See my excurses to 1 Tim 1:3 and 2 Tim 4:21 in Dibelius-Conzelmann, *Pastoral Epistles*, 15–16, 126–28.

22 Walter Bauer, "Matthiasüberlieferungen," *Neutestamentliche Apokryphen* (ed. Edgar Hennecke; 2d ed.; Tübingen: Mohr [Siebeck], 1924) 139. On the concept of βουλή, see Conzelmann, *Theology*, 151–54.

feature of farewell speeches (originally connected with an eschatological outlook; cf. Mark 13:22 and the speeches in Matthew); compare 1 Tim 4:1–7; 2 Tim 3:1—4:4; 2 Pet 2:1—3:18. There is correspondence "in the last, evil days" between external threats, through persecution, and internal threats, through heresy. With Luke can be observed the transposition of what was originally eschatological style into a style appropriate to ecclesiastical history and its connection with the concept of tradition. Luke expresses this conception of authority by attributing to Paul the bequest of a normative teaching authority to the elders at Miletus.

The other established factor in the battle against heresy is the conception of office. Indeed, Paul's speech is delivered to officeholders. "Overseers" (*RSV*, "guardians") or "bishops" here denotes the *task* of the elders. From the standpoint of institutional history, this passage reflects the blending together of Pauline congregational polity (with bishops and deacons) and the institution of elders.[23] The conception of office (as "overseeing") is described by the picture of the shepherd. Compare Philostratus *Vita Apoll.* 8.22, where Apollonius protects his ποίμνη, "flock," from the wolves, the representatives of worldly affairs.[24] The institution and the Spirit are tied together (for ordination, cf. 14:23).[25] This synthesis, however, is not yet understood in a catholic manner, because it is not yet secured by a notion of succession, and the office still does not confer to its bearer any indelible "character."

The blood of Christ plays no independent role in Luke's theology (ἣν περιεποιήσατο κτλ., "which he obtained, etc.").[26] Here Luke reproduces early Christian tradition; the key word ἴδιος, "his own" (Rom 8:32; Heb 9:12), also belongs to this material. Especially because of the uncertainty of the text, it is not clear (1) whether the subject is God or Christ; or (2) whether ἴδιος is used as an adjective or a substantive: "with his (own) blood" or "with the blood of his Own." If, with B and ℵ, τοῦ θεοῦ, "of God," is read after "the church," then the construction of the sentence points toward God as the subject of the relative clause. In this case ἴδιος must be understood as a substantive ("with the blood of his Own"). The patripassianistic statement that God shed his own blood is not suited to this period in time. It would be completely impossible for Luke, who advocates a clear subordinationism; thus the translation "which He (God) obtained with the blood of his Own." ἴδιος would then be used in a way similar to ὁ ἀγαπητός, "the beloved," and μονογενής, "only begotten" (cf. also Rom 8:32–33 with Gen 22:16).[27] On the other hand, the expression could simply have been appropriated as a whole, as its non-Lukan character argues. Then, of course, it would have referred to Christ from the beginning, and the unusual impression (that God is the subject) would have resulted only because of the connection with the expression, "the church of God," which is itself a common expression (cf. 1 Tim 3:5, 15). Thus, in this case, it would be translated "which he (Christ) obtained with his blood." ἴδιος does not need to bear the meaning "own"; it can take the place of the possessive pronoun.[28]

■ **29** Is ἄφιξις, "departure," here a euphemism for death? The designation of false teachers as wolves is a common one: Matt 7:15; *Did.* 16.3; Ignatius *Phld.* 2.2; *2 Clem.* 5.2–4; Justin *Apol.* 1.16.13 and *Dial.* 35.3. Its use is especially graphic in connection with the picture of the shepherd and the flock. Klein interprets the prophecy in the light of Luke's whole view of history: the original epoch of peace in the church comes to an end with Paul.[29]

■ **31** γρηγορεῖν, "to be alert," is a key word in eschato-

---

23   von Campenhausen, *Ecclesiastical Authority*, 80–82.
24   Wilhelm Jost, ΠΟΙΜΗΝ: *Das Bild von Hirten in der biblischen Überlieferung und seine christologische Bedeutung* (Giessen: Munich University, 1939); R. Schnackenburg, "Episkopos und Hirtenamt," *Episcopus: Studien über des Bischofsamt seiner Eminenz Michael Kardinal von Faulhaber, Erzbischof von München-Freising, zum 80. Geburtstag* (Regensburg: Gregorius, 1949) 66–88; Wolfgang Nauck, "Probleme des frühchristlichen Amtsverständnisses (I Ptr 5: 2f.)," *ZNW* 48 (1957) 200–220.
25   See my excursus to 1 Tim 4:14 in Dibelius-Conzel-

mann, *Pastoral Epistles*, 70–71.
26   Conzelmann, *Theology*, 201, 220 n. 1.
27   See *Beginnings* 4.261–62.
28   BAG *s.v.*
29   Klein, *Die zwölf Apostel*, 180–81. On what occurred in Asia after Paul's death, see Bauer, *Orthodoxy and Heresy*, 82–89.

logical paraenesis, which Luke here transposes into his ecclesiastical style, in accord with his construction of history. For μετὰ δακρύων, "with tears," compare vs 19; for τριετία, "three years," see 19:8–10.

■ **32** This statement comprises the actual testament.

■ **33** Once again, compare 1 Sam 12:3.

■ **34–35** Passages such as 1 Thess 2:9 and 4:11 are now formed into a timeless prototype. "πάντα" ὑπέδειξα probably does not mean "I have shown you 'all things'" (this would be the third statement of this kind, after vss 20 and 27; such a repetition in itself would be quite legitimate stylistically), but rather, "in every respect" (*RSV,* "In all things"). The alleged word of the Lord is actually a Greek aphorism with a slight Christian touch, namely, the selection of μακάριον, "blessed," instead of ἥδιον, "more gladly."[30] According to Thucydides 2.97.4, it was originally a Persian axiom. μᾶλλον, "more," should not be understood in a Semitic, exclusive sense (giving is blessed, receiving is not), but as a genuine comparative.[31]

Compare here *1 Clem.* 2.1: "giving more gladly than receiving" (ἥδιον διδόντες ἢ λαμβάνοντες); Plutarch *Mor.* 173d: "(Artaxerxes) used to say that it is more kingly to give to one who has than to take away" (ἔλεγεν ὅτι τὸ προσθεῖναι τοῦ ἀφελεῖν βασιλικώτερόν ἐστιν); compare also Plutarch *Mor.* 181–82 and 778c; *Vita Caes.* 16. Note the comparative in 5:29! The logical connection with the context should not be overemphasized; the saying only serves to strengthen the appeal. On this appeal, compare Sir 29:9, and on the expression, compare 2 Chr 28:15.

■ **36–38** The farewell scene is intended to underscore the character of the speech as a testament. It, too, clearly points back to the death of Paul.

■ **37** On this verse, compare Gen 33:4; 45:14; Tob 7:6; Luke 15:20.

30   Rengstorf argues for a different interpretation in "Geben ist seliger denn Nehmen," *Die Leibhaftigkeit des Wortes* [Festschrift Adolf Köberle] (ed. Otto Michel and Ulrich Mann; Hamburg: Furche, 1958) 23–33.

31   The English translations of the aphorism are thus appropriate. See Haenchen, p. 594 n. 5, and Joachim Jeremias, *Unknown Sayings of Jesus* (trans. Reginald H. Fuller; 2d ed.; London: SPCK, 1964) 34.

The Great Missionary Journey [15:36—21:26]

21

From Miletus to Caesarea

1   And when we had parted from them and set sail, we came by a straight course to Cos, and the next day to Rhodes, and from there to Patara. 2/ And having found a ship crossing to Phoenicia, we went aboard, and set sail. 3/ When we had come in sight of Cyprus, leaving it on the left we sailed to Syria, and landed at Tyre; for there the ship was to unload its cargo. 4/ And having sought out the disciples, we stayed there for seven days. Through the Spirit they told Paul not to go on to Jerusalem. 5/ And when our days there were ended, we departed and went on our journey; and they all, with wives and children, brought us on our way till we were outside the city; and kneeling down on the beach we prayed and bade one another farewell. 6/ Then we went on board the ship, and they returned home.

7   When we had finished the voyage from Tyre, we arrived at Ptolemais; and we greeted the brethren and stayed with them for one day. 8/ On the morrow we departed and came to Caesarea; and we entered the house of Philip the evangelist, who was one of the seven, and stayed with him. 9/ And he had four unmarried daughters, who prophesied. 10/ While we were staying for some days, a prophet named Agabus came down from Judea. 11/ And coming to us he took Paul's girdle and bound his own feet and hands, and said, "Thus says the Holy Spirit, 'So shall the Jews at Jerusalem bind the man who owns this girdle and deliver him into the hands of the Gentiles.'" 12/ When we heard this, we and the people there begged him not to go up to Jerusalem. 13/ Then Paul answered, "What are you doing, weeping and breaking my heart? For I am ready not only to be imprisoned but even to die at Jerusalem for the name of the Lord Jesus." 14/ And when he would not be persuaded, we ceased and said, "The will of the Lord be done."

■ 1 This is simply a list of stopping points in "we-style." The presence of such a list of stations on the journey, given for its own sake, without any information about occurrences in any of the cities, is not a sign that Luke is copying a source in rather mechanical fashion. Rather, Luke is tracing the footsteps of Paul, or perhaps relying on information from one of Paul's companions.[1] Compare once again the description of the journey in Xenophon Eph. 1.11–12; Ps.-Clem. *Hom.* 13.1.2–3; (*Recog.* 7.25.3). P⁴¹, D, gig, and sa add an extra stop, at Myra (cf. 27:5).

■ **3** The route runs in a southerly direction from Cyprus; this is the direct way. The stretch from Rhodes to Tyre (ca. 420 kilometers) is covered in four [*sic*] days in Xenophon Eph. 1.11–12; 1.14.6.[2] ἀναφαίνειν, "come in sight" (with Doric aorist), is probably a nautical term meaning "to cause the land to appear," that is, "to sight."

■ **4–5** The haste mentioned in 20:16 is forgotten. Acts only hints in passing at the founding of congregations in Phoenicia (11:19); in Luke's Gospel, the seacoast belongs to the area within which Jesus preaches (Luke 6:17). Verses 4–5 link up with vss 10–11 and 20:23. The warning about continuing the journey should be interpreted in light of these passages (the present infinitive!). "Through the Spirit" does not imply that Paul is now commanded not to go to Jerusalem. The warning arises from the concern of those to whom the Spirit unveils the future. Luke also does not thereby seek to characterize the disciples as somewhat weak in faith. He simply wants to demonstrate Paul's willingness to suffer for the faith.[3] Is ἐπιβαίνειν, "to go" (vs 4), a technical term ("to secure a place on board ship"), or does it simply mean "to set foot on" (20:18; 25:1)?

■ **7** διανύειν usually means "to complete." Thus one could conclude that Paul traveled from Ptolemais to Caesarea by land (about 50 kilometers). But in Xenophon Eph. 1.11.2, 5; 1.14.6, the word is used of the "continuation" of a journey.

■ **8** The title "evangelist" is rare in the New Testament. It seems to be closely tied, however, to the person of Philip (6:5; 8:4, 40).

■ **9** There appears to be no reason for the mention of the four prophetic daughters, because in this instance they do not prophesy; but the comment does contribute to the mood for the following episode. Does this comment come from the source, or does Luke mention the daughters because they were well known throughout the church?[4]

■ **10–14** The prophecy of Agabus is an independent episode, complete in itself. Agabus (11:28) is introduced as someone who is unknown; the "we" comes from Luke. The prophecy originally took no account of the earlier (redactional) predictions with the same message (nor of the presence of the prophetesses!). In this context it builds to a final climax.

■ **11** As in the Old Testament, the prophecy is taken as God's own word (here he is represented by the Spirit). It is accompanied by a symbolic act (Isa 20:2; Jer 13:1–11).[5] That the Jews will bind Paul should not be understood as a contradiction to vs 33. In Luke's view they are the guilty ones; for the terminology, compare Mark 15:1.

■ **12–13** Furthermore, Luke sees no contradiction that Paul is warned by the Spirit and nevertheless goes to Jerusalem.[6] This is in accord with the common notion of prophecies and prodigies: they are fulfilled, but not to the exclusion of human decision. Paul "must" go, but he freely affirms his destiny. For suffering "for the name," compare 5:41.[7]

■ **14** This verse is not an expression of resignation, but a positive affirmation of the will of God (cf. Luke 22:42; *Mart. Pol.* 7.1).

---

1   Thus Haenchen, pp. 86–87.
2   Lionel Casson, "Speed Under Sail of Ancient Ships," *TAPA* 82 (1951) 141.
3   See the comments on vs 12.
4   Cf. Papias in Eusebius *Hist. eccl.* 3.39.9; he speaks of the "apostle" Philip.
5   Georg Fohrer, *Die symbolischen Handlungen der Propheten* (2d ed.; AThANT 54; Zurich: Zwingli, 1968).
6   See the comments on vs 4.
7   Conzelmann, *Theology,* 177–78.

The Great Missionary Journey [15:36—21:26]

21   The Arrival in Jerusalem

15   After these days we made ready and went
up to Jerusalem. 16/ And some of the
disciples from Caesarea went with us,
bringing us to the house of Mnason of
Cyprus, an early disciple, with whom we
should lodge.

17   When we had come to Jerusalem, the
brethren received us gladly. 18/ On the
following day Paul went in with us to
James; and all the elders were present.
19/ After greeting them, he related one
by one the things that God had done
among the Gentiles through his ministry.
20/ And when they heard it, they glorified God. And they said to him, "You see,
brother, how many thousands there are
among the Jews of those who have
believed; they are all zealous for the law,
21/ and they have been told about you
that you teach all the Jews who are
among the Gentiles to forsake Moses,
telling them not to circumcise their
children or observe the customs. 22/
What then is to be done? They will
certainly hear that you have come. 23/
Do therefore what we tell you. We have
four men who are under a vow; 24/ take
these men and purify yourself along with
them and pay their expenses, so that
they may shave their heads. Thus all will
know that there is nothing in what they
have been told about you but that you
yourself live in observance of the law.
25/ But as for the Gentiles who have
believed, we have sent a letter with our
judgment that they should abstain from
what has been sacrificed to idols and
from blood and from what is strangled
and from unchastity." 26/ Then Paul took
the men, and the next day he purified
himself with them and went into the
temple, to give notice when the days of
purification would be fulfilled and the
offering presented for every one of them.

This is the last "we-section" before the journey to Rome;
again, the "we" fades away when Paul journeys on land.
■ **15** ἐπισκευάζεσθαι here means "make ready." The itinerary hypothesis cannot explain why the stopovers in
between Caesarea and Jerusalem are not mentioned here
(Luke knows that one day is not enough for this journey
of ca. 100 kilometers, cf. 23:32).

■ **16** The geography has been improved in D and sy[hmg],
allowing for a stop on the way to Jerusalem "at a certain
village" where "we stayed with" Mnason of Cyprus. This
is not to dispute the possibility that some source lies
behind Luke's account. It is true, however, that we can
no longer recognize precisely what the source com-
prised.[1]

---

1   See the comments on vs 25. For the genitive τῶν
μαθητῶν, "some of the disciples," see BDF § 164.2 A;
for the relative clause with final meaning, § 378; for
the incorporation of the noun into the relative
clause, § 294.5.

■ 17 Verse 17 is somewhat awkward between vss 16 and 18.[2] Because of vs 22, "the brethren" cannot be identical with the whole congregation. Is Luke thinking of a circle of Hellenistic Christians around Mnason, or is "the brethren received us gladly" a Lukan anticipation? If it were, however, the continuation in vs 18 (τῇ δὲ ἐπιούσῃ, "but[!] on the following day") would be harsh.

■ 18–19 These verses are reminiscent of 15:4, 12, and thus can be ascribed to the Lukan redaction. What lies behind these verses is anybody's guess. It is striking that *James* emerges only for a moment. The absence of the "Twelve" in the narrative is surely in accord with the actual facts: leadership of the congregation has already passed over to James.[3] The absence of the Twelve is also in accord with the thrust of the Lukan portrayal of history: the Apostolic Council was the turning point from the apostolic to the postapostolic epoch, represented by James in Jerusalem and by Paul in the world.

■ 20 This verse sheds light on 15:21; the issue here, however, concerns Jewish *Christians*.

■ 21 The reader of Acts knows that these accusations are false. Paul has always been observant of the Law; he had circumcised Timothy. The accusations (which are denied) shed light on Paul's trial: we know in advance that the charges (24:5–6) are without foundation (24:13–21; 25:8). Paul's fate is settled precisely as he fulfills obligations of Jewish Law. The real facts were certainly otherwise. A Jew would have understood Rom 10:4 precisely in the sense of these charges (if he did not also take note of the complex train of thought in Romans 3 and 7). Paul certainly anticipated trouble from Jews who disagreed with him (cf. Rom 15:31).

■ 22 This verse is to be understood on the basis of vs 21. τί οὖν ἐστιν, "What then is to be done?" does not mean that the church leadership entertains any doubt about Paul's innocence (we ought not seek in this expression such a meaning in pre-Lukan tradition). They ask only what is to be done in this situation. "They will certainly hear" seems to make more sense in reference to Jews than to

Jewish *Christians*. Thus it has been suggested that vs 20 originally referred to Jews.[4] The focus of this passage, however, is not yet on the attack against Paul, but rather on settling the situation within the church.

■ 23 The elders' proposal corresponds to the Lukan understanding of the church—the proposal testifies to the continuity which runs from Israel through Jewish Christianity and Gentile Christianity (through the apostolic decree). The account which follows certainly raises difficulties if we look closely at Jewish prescriptions about vows, but these result from Luke's inexact knowledge of these prescriptions. Considered in itself, his account contains no contradiction. εὐχή, "vow," can mean a Nazirite vow (Num 6:1–21; Philo *Ebr.* 2);[5] shaving the head is a part of the Nazirite vow.[6] After "four men who have taken a vow" (*RSV*, "are under a vow"), the reading ἐφ᾽ ἑαυτῶν, "upon themselves" (P⁷⁴ A C D), as opposed to ἀφ᾽ ἑαυτῶν, "on their own initiative" (B ℵ), is to be preferred (cf. Num 6:7; 30:7).[7] The vow was considered as a good work. Its duration was at least thirty days. The release from the vow (shaving the head and bringing the hair as an offering, plus other offerings, Num 6:13–21) entailed a considerable expense. Making this contribution on behalf of a Nazirite also counted as a good work (Josephus *Ant.* 19.294).

■ 24 What is here described is certainly no longer in accord with the requirements. ἁγνίσθητι κτλ., "purify, etc.," can only be understood as "enter into the vow with them!" But that could not be done for a period of only seven days (vs 27). Luke has misunderstood a report here. The period of purification for Levitical uncleanliness lasted seven days (Num 19:12 LXX; note the same verb, ἁγνίζεσθαι!). Did Luke erroneously combine this passage with Num 6:4? Haenchen supposes that the source did in fact tell of such a purification of Paul: he had come from abroad; thus it was necessary for him to be purified in order for him to participate in the absolution ceremony for the Nazirites.[8]

■ 25 This verse seems to be an insertion, and is therefore

---

2 For the grammatically improper genitive absolute, see BDF § 423.2.

3 Hans von Campenhausen, "Die Nachfolge des Jakobus: Zur Frage eines urchristlichen 'Kalifats,'" *ZKG* 63 (1950–51) 133–44.

4 Schwartz, "Chronologie," 290; Preuschen.

5 Str-B 2.80–88, 747–51, 755–61.

6 See the comments on 18:18.

7 Heinrich Greeven, "εὔχομαι," *TDNT* 2 (1964) 777.

8 Haenchen, pp. 611–12.

not to be assigned to the source material but rather to the Lukan redaction.[9] Others believe that here Paul is informed about the decree as something new. If so, this material would derive from a source which had not tied the decree to the Apostolic Council. But even the formulation should be understood as redactional. The wording is not for Paul's benefit, but for the readers'.

■ **26** For τὴν ἐκπλήρωσιν κτλ., "fulfillment (of the days of purification)," compare Num 6:3–8, 13; 1 Macc 3:49.

---

9   This reference to the decree is quite significant, see the comments on vs 23.

21 Paul's Arrest

27 When the seven days were almost completed, the Jews from Asia, who had seen him in the temple, stirred up all the crowd, and laid hands on him, 28/ crying out, "Men of Israel, help! This is the man who is teaching men everywhere against the people and the law and this place; moreover he also brought Greeks into the temple, and he has defiled this holy place." 29/ For they had previously seen Trophimus the Ephesian with him in the city, and they supposed that Paul had brought him into the temple. 30/ Then all the city was aroused, and the people ran together; they seized Paul and dragged him out of the temple, and at once the gates were shut. 31/ And as they were trying to kill him, word came to the tribune of the cohort that all Jerusalem was in confusion. 32/ He at once took soldiers and centurions, and ran down to them; and when they saw the tribune and the soldiers, they stopped beating Paul. 33/ Then the tribune came up and arrested him and ordered him to be bound with two chains. He inquired who he was and what he had done. 34/ Some in the crowd shouted one thing, some another; and as he could not learn the facts because of the uproar, he ordered him to be brought into the barracks. 35/ And when he came to the steps, he was actually carried by the soldiers because of the violence of the crowd; 36/ for the mob of the people followed, crying, "Away with him!"

37 As Paul was about to be brought into the barracks, he said to the tribune, "May I say something to you?" And he said, "Do you know Greek? 38/ Are you not the Egyptian, then, who recently stirred up a revolt and led the four thousand men of the Assassins out into the wilderness?" 39/ Paul replied, "I am a Jew, from Tarsus in Cilicia, a citizen of no mean city; I beg you, let me speak to the people." 40/ And when he had given him leave, Paul standing on the steps, motioned with his hand to the people; and when there was a great hush, he spoke to them in the Hebrew language, saying:

■ 27 The seven days are mentioned here as something which is already known. This is either an indication that the source mentioned the seven days, or that the author has Numbers 6 in mind. What is striking about the whole account is that the real purpose of the journey, the delivering of the collection, is resolutely concealed, although Luke knows about it (24:17). Haenchen conjectures that in view of the increasingly critical situation in Jerusalem (Rom 15:31) the collection could no longer be accepted without hesitation; but for the sake of church unity, it could not be refused either. As a way out of this dilemma, according to Haenchen, it was decided to use a part of the collection for the release of some poor Christian Nazirites. In this way it would have been possible for the collection to be accepted. Luke no longer understood that they hesitated to accept the collection, and thus did not mention it at all.[1] Haenchen's conjecture, however, reads too much into the account here. Even Luke's source apparently did not offer a historically accurate picture of Paul, but rather a tendentious one, along the lines of 16:3.[2]

By Asia here, Ephesus is meant (compare vs 29 with 20:4).

■ **28** Compare 6:13. The theme of Paul's trial is carefully introduced here into the formulation of this verse. From the preceding section the reader already knows what part of the accusation is valid.

■ **29** This verse explains how the misunderstanding came about. Two copies of the inscriptions which denied non-Jews access to the inner courts of the Temple have been discovered. The inner courts were marked off by the סורג, δρύφακτος, "balustrade" (see *Mid.* 2.3; Josephus *Bell.* 5.193–94; 6.124–25; *Ant.* 15.417; Philo *Leg. Gai.* 212). The text runs as follows: "Let no foreigner enter within the screen and enclosure surrounding the sanctuary. Whosoever is taken so doing will be the cause that death overtaketh him" (Μηθένα ἀλλογενῆ εἰσπο/ρεύεσθαι ἐντὸς τοῦ πε/ρὶ τὸ ἱερὸν τρυφάκτου καὶ/περιβόλου. ὃς δ᾽ ἂν λη//φθῇ ἑαυτῷ αἴτιος ἔς/ται διὰ τὸ ἐξακολου/θεῖν θάνατον).[3] Of course, Luke has a simplified picture of the Temple and the area around it.[4] He does not distinguish between the various courts, but rather sees the ἱερόν, "temple," as a unified precinct, to which only Jews had access. The Roman military were not in an outer court, but rather intervened at the boundary of the Temple area, ἔξω τοῦ ἱεροῦ, "out of the Temple."

■ **31** φάσις here means "notification." On the desecration of the holy place through murder, compare 2 Chr 24:20–22 and Matt 23:35. According to Luke, the Roman garrison consisted of one cohort. The Roman military included:

a. *cohors peditata,* "infantry"
1. *quingenaria,* "a cohort of 500 foot soldiers"
2. *miliaria,* "a cohort of 1,000 foot soldiers"
b. *cohors equitata,* "cavalry and infantry"
1. *quingenaria,* "a cohort of 500 troops: 380 infantry and 120 cavalry"
2. *miliaria,* "a cohort of 1,000 troops: 760 infantry and 240 cavalry"

Luke assumes the presence of the larger unit (23:23). The actual size of the force is unknown. The barracks were in the fort, called the Antonia, at the northwest corner of the Temple area; the fort was connected to the Temple complex by two staircases (Josephus *Bell.* 5.238–47).

■ **33–34** Compare 19:32.[5] For "two chains," see 12:6; for γνῶναι τὸ ἀσφαλές, "learn the facts," compare 22:30 and 25:26.

■ **35** Do we detect hints here of an account which said that Paul was no longer able to walk because of the beating he had just received?[6] But this would be something Luke could not report, since Paul must immediately deliver his speech.[7]

■ **36** For αἶρε αὐτόν, "away with him," compare Luke 23:18; Acts 22:32; John 19:15; *Mart. Pol.* 3.2 and 9.2.

■ **37–38** This scene is purely redactional; it contains no concrete data. It is intended to establish the first contact with the Roman commander. The author intentionally withholds information about Paul's Roman citizenship[3] in order to heighten the effect of this announcement later. For the present it is enough that Paul is a *Jew,* and therefore is permitted to enter the Temple, and that he is from Tarsus, thus not "the Egyptian," as is evident from his knowledge of Greek. On this latter point, compare Lucian *Navig.* 2 (of an Egyptian boy): "He spoke in a slovenly manner, one long, continuous prattle; he spoke Greek, but his accent and intonation pointed to his native land" (καὶ ἐφθέγγετο ἐπισεσυρμένον τι καὶ συνεχὲς καὶ ἐπίτροχον, Ἑλληνιστὶ μέν, ἐς τὸ πάτριον δὲ τῷ ψόφῳ καὶ τῷ τῆς φωνῆς τόνῳ). In regard to the "Egyptian," see

1   Haenchen, pp. 612–14.
2   G. Klein, review of Ernst Haenchen, *Die Apostel-geschichte,* in *ZKG* 68 (1957) 366.
3   The text is found in *OGIS* 598; Deissmann, *Light from the Ancient East,* 80–81; *SEG* 8 no. 169; *CII* 2.1400; Elias J. Bickermann, "The Warning Inscriptions of Herod's Temple," *JQR* 37 (1947) 387–405, reprinted in his *Studies in Jewish and Christian History*

(3 vols.; AGJU 9; Leiden: Brill, 1976–86) 2.210–24.
4   See the commentary on 3:1–10.
5   See the commentary on 22:24–29.
6   Haenchen, p. 618.
7   For the location, see the comments on vs 31.

Josephus *Bell.* 2.261–63 and *Ant.* 20.169–72. He led his followers (according to *Bell.* from the wilderness, and according to *Ant.* from Jerusalem) to the Mount of Olives. Felix intervened and some were killed, others captured; according to *Ant.* there were four hundred dead and two hundred captured, while *Bell.* speaks of a group of thirty thousand followers. Can this discrepancy be explained by a confusion between $\Delta = 4$ and $\Lambda = 30$?[8] The leader escaped. His movement must be distinguished from that of the Sicarii (from *sica*, "dagger," Josephus *Bell.* 2.254–57; *Ant.* 20.186).[9] Luke is simply putting together all that he knew about Jewish political movements in order to set Christianity apart from all of them. Josephus also tells about the Egyptian, the Sicarii, and movements out into the wilderness, all in the same passage (*Bell.* 2.259–60).[10]

■ **39** οὐκ ἄσημος, "no mean," is a favorite litotes; used of cities, it occurs in Dionysius Halic. 2.35.7; Achilles Tatius 8.3.1: "though I am a free man and a citizen of no mean city" (ἐλεύθερός τε ὢν καὶ πόλεως οὐκ ἀσήμου). Tarsus: "Tarsus, the first and greatest and most beautiful metropolis" (Τάρσος, ἡ πρώτη κ[αὶ] μεγίστη/καὶ καλλίστη μ/ητρόπολις);[11] Strabo 14.673. According to Luke, Paul had a dual citizenship (Tarsus and Rome); this had been possible since the time of the empire.[12] The edicts of Augustus found at Cyrene are instructive for this development.[13] Paul's request to speak to the people and the granting of that request are inconceivable.

■ **40** "Hebrew" here means Aramaic;[14] compare John 5:2; Josephus *Ant.* 18.228. For the oratorical gesture, compare 12:17; 13:16; 26:1.

---

8 As proposed in *Beginnings* 4.277.

9 Hengel, *Die Zeloten*, 47–54.

10 See Appendix 5.

11 *OGIS* 578.7–8.

12 A. N. Sherwin-White, *The Roman Citizenship* (Oxford: Clarendon, 1939) 245–50; Simeon L. Guterman, *Religious Toleration and Persecution in Ancient Rome* (London: Aiglon, 1951) 19–25; Mason Hammond, "Germana Patria," *HSCP* 60 (1951) 147–74; *CAH* 11.458–59.

13 On this, see Anton von Premerstein, "Die fünf neugefundenen Edikte des Augustus aus Kyrene," *Zeitschrift der Savigny-Stiftung,* Rom Abt 48 (1928) 448ff; Cadbury, *Acts in History,* 81–82.

14 For a different opinion, see H. Ott, "Um die Muttersprache Jesu; Forschungen seit Gustaf Dalman," *NovT* 9 (1967) 22.

22

The Speech before the People

1 "Brethren and fathers, hear the defense which I now make before you."

2 And when they heard that he addressed them in the Hebrew language, they were the more quiet. And he said:

3 "I am a Jew, born at Tarsus in Cilicia, but brought up in this city, educated at the feet of Gamaliel according to the strict manner of the law of our fathers, being zealous for God as you all are this day. 4/ I persecuted this Way to the death, binding and delivering to prison both men and women, 5/ as the high priest and whole council of elders bear me witness. From them I received letters to the brethren, and I journeyed to Damascus to take those also who were there and bring them in bonds to Jerusalem to be punished.

6 "As I made my journey and drew near to Damascus, about noon a great light from heaven suddenly shown about me. 7/ And I fell to the ground and heard a voice saying to me, 'Saul, Saul, why do you persecute me?' 8/ And I answered, 'Who are you, Lord?' And he said to me, 'I am Jesus of Nazareth whom you are persecuting.' 9/ Now those who were with me saw the light but did not hear the voice of the one who was speaking to me. 10/ And I said, 'What shall I do, Lord?' And the Lord said to me, 'Rise, and go into Damascus, and there you will be told all that is appointed for you to do.' 11/ And when I could not see because of the brightness of that light, I was led by the hand by those who were with me, and came into Damascus.

12 "And one Ananias, a devout man according to the law, well spoken of by all the Jews who lived there, 13/ came to me, and standing by me said to me, 'Brother Saul, receive your sight.' And in that very hour I received my sight and saw him. 14/ And he said, 'The God of our fathers appointed you to know his will, to see the Just One and to hear a voice from his mouth; 15/ for you will be a witness for him to all men of what you have seen and heard. 16/ And now why do you wait? Rise and be baptized, and wash away your sins, calling on his name.'

17 "When I had returned to Jerusalem and was praying in the temple, I fell into a trance 18/ and saw him saying to me, 'Make haste and get quickly out of Jerusalem, because they will not accept your testimony about me.' 19/ And I said, 'Lord, they themselves know that in every synagogue I imprisoned and beat those who believed in thee. 20/ And

> when the blood of Stephen thy witness
> was shed, I also was standing by and
> approving, and keeping the garments of
> those who killed him.' 21/ And he said to
> me, 'Depart; for I will send you far away
> to the Gentiles.'"

Like the preceding speeches, the entire defense speech given before the people is Luke's creation. The issue which was most important at the moment, the charge of defiling the temple, is not dealt with; this is a proven literary technique. At the conclusion, once again the device of interruption is employed, after Luke has allowed Paul to say everything that he wants him to in this passage.[1] Here Luke is setting forth the fundamental debate between Christianity and Judaism.

■ **1** For the address here, compare 7:2 (but in that passage members of the Sanhedrin are being addressed!).[2] Vocabulary associated with ἀπολογεῖσθαι, "to defend oneself," emerges in these chapters; compare Philostratus *Vita Apoll.* 7.29, 32–35, 40–41, and 8.1 with the major speech in 8.7.

■ **2** Compare 21:40. The variants in the reports of Paul's conversion have been discussed in connection with 9:1–19a.

■ **3** The autobiographical retrospect has been formulated to fit the situation. Paul must present himself as a Jew and must at the same time explain his associations (known to the crowd, 21:28–29) with non-Jews. Luke does not allow Paul to explain that these associations did not affect his faithfulness to the Law, for reasons connected with the composition of the speech. For the biographical schema: γεγεννημένος—ἀνατεθραμμένος—πεπαιδευμένος, "born—brought up—educated,"[3] compare Arrian *Bithynica* frg. 1.2, concerning himself:[4] "For he declares his race to be Nikomedian in this history, and that he was born and raised and educated there" (Νικομήδειον γάρ [τι] τὸ γένος αὑτοῦ ἐν ταύτῃ τῇ συγγραφῇ

διορίζει, ἐν αὐτῇ τε γεννηθῆναι καὶ τραφῆναι καὶ παιδευθῆναι); Ovid *Tr.* 4.10.3–16: "Sulmo is my native place . . . there I first saw the light . . . while still of tender age we began our training, and through our father's care we came to attend upon men of the city distinguished in the liberal arts" (Sulmo mihi patria est . . . editus hinc ego sum . . . protinus excolimur teneri curaque parentis imus ad insignes urbis ab arte viros).[5] Luke assumes that Paul's family moved to Jerusalem (26:4; but for a contrary view, cf. Gal 1:22).

Gamaliel[6] was a Hillelite. Paul's exegetical method utilized elements of the school of Hillel, which had appropriated the principles of Hellenistic hermeneutics.[7] παρὰ τοὺς πόδας, "at the feet" (Luke 8:35; 10:39) should (on the basis of the schema) be connected with παιδεύειν, "educated." For πατρῷος νόμος, ζηλωτής, "law of our fathers, being zealous," compare Gal 1:14. This does not fit with the Lukan(!) picture of Gamaliel (but cf. 26:5), where the key word ἀκριβής, "strict," is found. For ἀκρίβεια, "strictness," in connection with νόμος, "law," see Isocrates 7.40; compare Josephus *Bell.* 2.162; *Vita* 191. For ζηλωτὴς θεοῦ, "zealous for God," see C. Musonius Rufus 37.3 and Epictetus 2.14.13; compare Num 25:13 and Rom 10:2. ζηλωτής, "zealot," is also a key word in biography (used of the pupil), as may be seen in Nicholas of Damascus[8] and Marcellinus *Vita Thuc.* 35. Unlike the historical Paul (Phil 3:4–11), the Lukan Paul does not reject his earlier zeal for the Law, he only condemns the false conclusions that he once drew from it.

■ **4** For ἡ ὁδός, "the Way," compare 9:2. For ἄρχι θανάτου, "to the death," compare 9:1 (φόνος, "murder," 26:10).

1 Dibelius, *Studies,* 160.
2 On the plea for a hearing, see the commentary on 2:14 (the style of a defense speech!). For the forward position of the possessive pronoun, see BDF § 473.1.
3 See the commentary on 7:21–22.
4 Vol. 2.197 in the Roos edition; cf. vol. 2.xliii.
5 Compare also Nicholas of Damascus in *FGH* 90 frg. 126; Procopius *Arc.* 10.1. See W. C. van Unnik, *Tarsus or Jerusalem: The City of Paul's Youth* (London: Epworth, 1962). On Jewish upbringing, see Werner Jentsch, *Urchristliches Erziehungsdenken: Die Paideia Kyriu im Rahmen der hellenistisch-jüdischen Umwelt*

(BFCTh 45:3; Gütersloh: Bertelsmann, 1951) 85–139.
6 See the comments on 5:34.
7 Joachim Jeremias, "Paulus als Hillelit," *Neotestamentica et Semitica: Studies in Honour of Matthew Black* (ed. E. E. Ellis and M. Wilcox; Edinburgh: T. & T. Clark, 1969) 88–94.
8 *FGH* 90 frg. 132.

■ **5** Luke compresses the time. The impression is given that the same high priest is still in power (although in 23:5, Paul does not know the high priest!). The character of an autobiographical account is maintained. In the report found in 9:1–19a, it said πρὸς τὰς συναγωγάς, "to the synagogues." *Here* Paul the Jew speaks of his "brethren." πρεσβυτέριον, "council of elders," equals the Sanhedrin (Luke 22:66).[9]

■ **6** The note about the time of day is absent in the first version (9:3).[10]

■ **9** Hearing and seeing exchange places in comparison with 9:7. This is connected with the intensification of the light imagery. There is no longer any difference between the use of the accusative (here and 26:14) and the genitive (9:7) with ἀκούειν, "to hear."[11]

■ **11** ἐμβλέπειν, "to look at," is used in an unusual way here. Should we read ΟΥΔΕΝΕΒΛΕΠΟΝ, "I saw nothing" (B)?

■ **13** ἀναβλέπειν means "to open the eyes" or "to see again." Here we have the latter meaning, though εἰς αὐτόν, "to him," does not fit with it. Haenchen thinks that εἰς αυτόν is an interpolation, which corresponds to the similarly inappropriate ἐμβλέπειν in vs 11.[12]

■ **14–15** The coloring is—again, to suit the situation—more biblical than 9:17: Ananias speaks as a Jewish Christian. The "will" of God encompasses the whole of his plan of salvation (cf. 20:27).[13] For ὁ δίκαιος, "the Just One,"[14] compare 3:14. In Luke, μάρτυς, "witness," is first of all the eyewitness to the ministry and the resurrection of Jesus.[15] Here the concept is expanded so that Paul is also included, and so that he can become the connecting

link between the apostolic and the postapostolic times.[16] Paul's speech also belongs to this "witness" he is to bear (cf. 2 Macc 3:34–36!).[17]

■ **16** τί μέλλεις, "why do you wait?" is not to be pressed psychologically, as if Paul still had some final doubts. It is an expression, already found in classical Greek, like "Get up!" Perhaps it was a cultic formula used with initiation rites; compare *Corp. Herm.* 1.26; Apuleius *Met.* 11.22; also *Acts Thom.* 73 and 78.[18] Luke ties the Greek expression together with the Jewish καὶ νῦν, "and now."[19]

■ **17–21** Paul's preaching in Damascus and Jerusalem is replaced by the vision in the temple, which is absent in both parallel accounts. It belongs to that traditionary complex which connects Paul biographically to Jerusalem (vs 3; 23:16) and which determines the Lukan picture of Paul. It can no longer be determined where Luke received these reports. In any case, they reflect a split in the tradition about Paul which already existed in the early period.[20] The account here cannot be harmonized with Gal 1:17—2:2. Nor does the episode fit with 9:29–30. Taken by itself, it assumes no previous call. Indeed, it does not fit in with such a call, and it forms a concurrent variant to the account of the call on the way to Damascus.[21] Of course Luke has had a hand in shaping the material. From Luke stems the reference back to Stephen, corresponding to Luke's earlier introduction of Paul into the story of Stephen. He takes up this story because with it he can set forth the continuity between the original congregation in Jerusalem and the present church, and also because in this special situation he can clarify the relationship of Paul (and Christ)[22] to the

9   On the word πρεσβυτέριον, see Joachim Jeremias, "ΠΡΕΣΒΥΤΕΡΙΟΝ ausserchristlich bezeugt," *ZNW* 48 (1957) 127–32.

10   See the commentary on 26:13.

11   Horst R. Moehring, "The Verb AKOYEIN in Acts IX 7 and XXII 9," *NovT* 3 (1959) 80–99.

12   Haenchen, p. 626.

13   For προχειρίζω, "appoint," see the commentary on 3:20.

14   On the placement of "seeing" before "hearing," see Conzelmann, *Theology,* 192 n. 2.

15   See the commentary on 1:21–22.

16   Wilckens, *Missionsreden,* 146; Klein, *Die zwölf Apostel,* 117.

17   Brox, *Zeuge und Märtyrer,* 55–61.

18   Gustav Anrich, *Das antike Mysterienwesen in seinem Einfluss auf das Christentum* (Göttingen: Vandenhoeck

& Ruprecht, 1894) 82 n. 5. See the commentary on the stylistically related τί κωλύει, "what is to prevent?" in 8:37.

19   See the commentary on 3:17.

20   On this problem, see Linton, "Third Aspect," 79–95.

21   Burchard (*Der dreizehnte Zeuge,* 164–65) is of another opinion: the narrative assumes a converted Paul; consequently, it does not entirely conflict with the Damascus vision, especially since the latter originally narrated not the call, but the conversion.

22   Conzelmann, *Theology,* 75–78, 164–65.

Temple. By linking the authority of Paul with this place so significant in the history of salvation, Luke creates some additional reality that mediates between the commissioning Christ and the commissioned Paul in addition to Ananias, who represents the church. This is in accord with Luke's portrait of Paul.[23]

■ **17** On the impossible construction here, compare Luke 3:21.[24]

■ **18** The notion that the mission to the Gentiles is caused by the obduracy of Israel has already been worked into the parable of the banquet (Luke 14:16–24). In comparison with Paul (Romans 9—11), we note that the hope for the conversion of Israel before the end of the world is absent. Israel's turning away from salvation is final, as is clear in Paul's concluding statement in 28:8.

■ **19** An objection to God's commission is a motif widespread in the Old Testament. The testimony of a "convert" counts as especially convincing—even to this day.

■ **20** See above on vss 14–15. The word $\mu\acute{\alpha}\rho\tau\upsilon\varsigma$, "witness," develops in the direction of "martyr," even if the technical sense has not yet been reached.[25] Norbert Brox disputes this "martyriological" sense but must concede that the meaning of the word in this passage is singular.[26]

23   Klein, *Die zwölf Apostel*, 152–55.
24   BDF § 378, § 423.4.
25   With Haenchen, p. 627 n. 7.

26   Brox, *Zeuge und Märtyrer*, 61–69.

22   Paul Identifies Himself as a Roman Citizen

22   Up to this word they listened to him; then they lifted up their voices and said, "Away with such a fellow from the earth! For he ought not to live." 23/ And as they cried out and waved their garments and threw dust into the air, 24/ the tribune commanded him to be brought into the barracks, and ordered him to be examined by scourging, to find out why they shouted thus against him. 25/ But when they had spread out his hands for [or: with] the thongs, Paul said to the centurion who was standing by, "Is it lawful for you to scourge a man who is a Roman citizen, and uncondemned?" 26/ When the centurion heard that, he went to the tribune and said to him, "What are you about to do? For this man is a Roman citizen." 27/ So the tribune came and said to him, "Tell me, are you a Roman citizen?" And he said, "Yes." 28/ The tribune answered, "I bought this citizenship for a large sum." Paul said, "But I was born a citizen." 29/ So those who were about to examine him withdrew from him instantly; and the tribune also was afraid, for he realized that Paul was a Roman citizen and that he had bound him.

■ **22** The interruption by the "Jews" at the mention of salvation for the Gentiles is deliberate.[1] In actuality the speech is complete.[2]

■ **23** ῥιπτεῖν [*sic*], "to throw off," can mean actually casting off clothing (Lucian *Syr. dea.* 51) or waving it;[3] compare iactare togas, "toss [one's] toga," as in Ovid *Am.* 3.2.74: "and toss your togas in signal from every side" (et date iactatis undique signa togis). For this scene, compare Philo *Flacc.* 144 and Lucian *Salt.* 83. Compare further Pap. London 2785.36–37:[4] "the speaker cast off his garment with his right hand" (ῥήτωρ τῇ δεξι[ᾷ]/τὸ ἱμάτιον ἔρρι[ψεν]). The reconstruction is uncertain, however; Herbert A. Musurillo now reconstructs as follows after Heliodorus *Aeth.* 6.8: καὶ τότε ὁ]/ ῥήτωρ, τῇ δεξι[ᾷ περρηξάμενος . . .] / τὸ ἱμάτιον, ἔρρι [ψεν ἑαυτὸν χαμαὶ] /

καὶ εἶπεν κτλ. ("then the speaker, tearing off his garment, threw himself on the ground, and said . . .").[5]

■ **24** The use of torture was prescribed for noncitizens and slaves.[6]

■ **25** προτείνειν, "to stretch out [the hands]," can mean "with thongs," for the scourging, or better "for the thongs." εἰ (untranslatable particle) used with a direct question is Hellenistic (cf. 21:37).[7] Either "without a hearing" (16:37) or "without sentence" may be added to κατακρίνειν, "condemn"; Cicero *Verr.* 2.5.66: "To bind a Roman citizen is a crime, to flog him is an abomination, to slay him is almost an act of murder" (Facinus est vincire civem Romanum, scelus verberare, prope parricidium necare).[8] The reason for Paul's delay in appealing to his rights as a citizen should be sought in Luke's tech-

1   Dibelius, *Studies,* 160. For the interruption as a literary device, see above.

2   For the imperfect καθῆκεν, "he ought (not)," see BDF § 358.2.

3   *Beginnings* 5.275–76.

4   The text is in Musurillo, *Acts of the Pagan Martyrs,* 22 (*Acta Isidori* recension B; see Musurillo's comment on p. 137).

5   Musurillo, *Acts Alexandrinorum,* 15 (apparatus).

6   Mommsen, "Rechtsverhältnisse," 90 n. 7; idem, *Römisches Strafrecht* (Leipzig: Duncker & Humblot, 1899) 938–39.

7   BDF § 440.3.

8   For the legal problem here, see the comments on 16:20–21. Cf. further Leopold Wenger, *Die Quellen des römischen Rechts* (Vienna: Holzhausen, 1953) 292.

nique as a writer. A short dialogue furnishes the basis for the further course of the legal process.

■ **28** κεφάλαιον means "capital, sum of money." Concerning the purchase of citizenship rights under Claudius, see Dio Cass. 60.17.5ff.[9] On the higher esteem accorded citizens by birth, compare Ovid *Tr.* 4.10.7–8: "I was heir to rank (if rank is aught) that came from forefathers of older time—Knight fresh made by fortune's gift" (Si quid id est, usque a proavis vetus ordinis heres, non modo fortunae munere factus eques).[10]

---

9   A. N. Sherwin-White, *The Roman Citizenship* (Oxford: Clarendon, 1939) esp. 237–50.

10 For Jews as Roman citizens, see the commentary on 21:39; Juster, *Les Juifs* 2.15–17. For vs 29, see the comments on 16:21.

22

The Presentation before the Council

30 But on the morrow, desiring to know the real reason why the Jews accused him, he unbound him, and commanded the chief priests and all the council to meet,

23

and he brought Paul down and set him before them. 23:1/ And Paul, looking intently at the council, said, "Brethren, I have lived before God in all good conscience up to this day." 2/ And the high priest Ananias commanded those who stood by him to strike him on the mouth. 3/ Then Paul said to him, "God shall strike you, you whitewashed wall! Are you sitting to judge me according to the law, and yet contrary to the law you order me to be struck?" 4/ Those who stood by said, "Would you revile God's high priest?" 5/ And Paul said, "I did not know, brethren, that he was the high priest; for it is written, 'You shall not speak evil of a ruler of your people.'"

6 But when Paul perceived that one part were Sadducees and the other Pharisees, he cried out in council, "Brethren, I am a Pharisee, a son of Pharisees; with respect to the hope and the resurrection of the dead I am on trial." 7/ And when he had said this, a dissension arose between the Pharisees and the Sadducees; and the assembly was divided. 8/ For the Sadducees say that there is no resurrection, nor angel, nor spirit; but the Pharisees acknowledge them all. 9/ Then a great clamor arose; and some of the scribes of the Pharisees' party stood up and contended, "We find nothing wrong in this man. What if a spirit or an angel spoke to him? 10/ And when the dissension became violent, the tribune, afraid that Paul would be torn in pieces by them, commanded the soldiers to go down and take him by force from among them and bring him into the barracks.

11 The following night the Lord stood by him and said, "Take courage, for as you have testified about me at Jerusalem, so you must bear witness also at Rome."

■ **30** This incident is historically impossible: the tribune is afraid because he has seized a Roman citizen, but he leaves him overnight in chains; he does not interrogate Paul himself, but rather allows the Roman citizen to be presented before Jewish authorities. The statements about the meeting room of the Sanhedrin differ in Josephus and the Mishnah.[1]

■ **23:1**Compare 24:16.[2] As Haenchen says, "How this squares with the (alleged) participation in the killing of Stephen and other Christians, one may of course not ask."[3]

■ **2** Ananias had been high priest since about 48 (Josephus *Ant.* 20.103); it follows from *Ant.* 20.179 that he was deposed during the time when Felix was in office. He was murdered by a mob in the year 66 (*Bell.* 2.441–42).

■ **3** It is not necessary to explain this verse as a *vaticinium ex eventu* ("a prophecy [created] out of the event"). τύπτειν κτλ., "strike, etc.," is a Jewish curse. Was "whitewashed wall" also a current term of abuse (with an allusion to Ezek 13:10–16; cf. CD 8.12)? Of course one ought not psychologize about the character of Ananias (Josephus *Ant.* 20.205–7). Luke is characterizing Judaism through its representatives—its relation to the Law is broken and hypocritical (cf. 7:50–53). The entire scene is inconceivable: How could Paul not have known the one who was presiding? Behind this scene lie some vague details, not a historically accurate account.

■ **4–5** The reaction is impossibly feeble and Paul's statement unthinkable. An "explanation" for Paul's failure to recognize Ananias because of alleged nearsightedness can only be viewed as comic. Paul's reply, however, is appropriate to Luke's intent. Once again Paul shows himself as obedient to the Law[4] and in accord with the developing story Luke has composed, conflict cannot yet arise.[5] The quotation comes from Exod 22:27.

■ **6** The anecdotal style shines through in this scene in which Paul's action is naively portrayed as an adroit chess move (cf., in contrast, Phil 3:3–5). The aorist participle ("when Paul perceived that") would seem more appropriate in a single anecdote than in the context of a historical account in which Paul is considered as a former

trusted member of this body (see 22:5 with the present tense of μαρτυρεῖ, "as the high priest and the whole council of elders bear me witness"!). One would expect a present participle here. What Paul says about his faith is tailored to fit Luke's design—the belief in a general resurrection is the link between (genuine) Judaism and Christianity. Hence the Jews should realize that their faith comes to fulfillment in Christianity. ἐλπίς, "hope," and ἀνάστασις, "resurrection," form a hendiadys;[6] in this way Luke avoids a double genitive. Thus one ought not distinguish this ἐλπίς from belief in resurrection (taking it, perhaps, as referring to messianic hope; the Messiah is not mentioned intentionally).[7] The question which, according to 22:30, was the reason for bringing Paul before this group does not arise at all. The scene rather serves to set forth the fundamental relationship between Judaism and Christianity. Looking ahead to the subsequent course of events, it has already been demonstrated here that this ζήτησις, "dispute," has nothing to do with Roman law.[8]

■ **7** This verse points to the hopelessness of a Judaism that denies belief in the resurrection; it is divided within itself.

■ **8** Luke knows that the Sadducees reject belief in the resurrection (Luke 20:27–33; cf. Josephus *Bell.* 2.165), but he does not know why—namely their limiting Scripture to the Torah and their rejection of tradition. Thus he alters the picture of them by depicting them as skeptics. In his opinion they are not true Jews. τὰ ἀμφότερα, "all" (literally "both"), is loose Hellenistic usage (cf. 19:16).

■ **9** The desired result occurs immediately, and the reader sees that the Jews are not clear about their own religion.

■ **11** For δεῖ, "must," compare 19:21; Josephus *Vita* 208–9.

1   Str-B 1.997–1001.
2   For the concept of the "good conscience," see my excurus on 1 Tim 1:5 in Dibelius-Conzelmann, *Pastoral Epistles,* 18–20; Johannes Stelzenberger, *Syneidesis im Neuen Testament* (Abhandlungen zur Moraltheologie 1; Paderborn: Schöningh, 1961) 49–50.
3   Haenchen, p. 637.
4   W. M. L. de Wette, *Kurze Erklärung der Apostelgeschichte* (4th ed.; rev. and enlarged by Franz Overbeck; Kurzgefasstes exegetisches Handbuch zum Neuen Testament 1:4; Leipzig: Hirzel, 1870)

402.
5   Haenchen, p. 638.
6   O. Lagercrantz, "Act 14:17," *ZNW* 31 (1932) 86–87; Gudmund Björk, "Quelques Cas de ἐν διὰ δύοιν dans le Nouveau Testament et Ailleurs," *ConNT* 4 (1940) 2–3.
7   See the commentary on 25:19.
8   See the commentary on 18:15.

23   The Plot on Paul's Life;
Transfer to Caesarea

12   When it was day, the Jews made a plot and bound themselves by an oath neither to eat nor drink till they had killed Paul. 13/ There were more than forty who made this conspiracy. 14/ And they went to the chief priests and elders, and said, "We have strictly bound ourselves by an oath to taste no food till we have killed Paul. 15/ You therefore, along with the council, give notice now to the tribune to bring him down to you, as though you were going to determine his case more exactly. And we are ready to kill him before he comes near."

16   Now the son of Paul's sister heard of their ambush; so he went and entered the barracks and told Paul. 17/ And Paul called one of the centurions and said, "Take this young man to the tribune; for he has something to tell him." 18/ So he took him and brought him to the tribune and said, "Paul the prisoner called me and asked me to bring this young man to you, as he has something to say to you." 19/ The tribune took him by the hand, and going aside asked him privately, "What is it that you have to tell me?" 20/ And he said, "The Jews have agreed to ask you to bring Paul down to the council tomorrow, as though they were going to inquire somewhat more closely about him. 21/ But do not yield to them; for more than forty of their men lie in ambush for him, having bound themselves by an oath neither to eat nor drink till they have killed him; and now they are ready, waiting for the promise from you." 22/ So the tribune dismissed the young man, charging him, "Tell no one that you have informed me of this."

23   Then he called two of the centurions and said, "At the third hour of the night get ready two hundred soldiers with seventy horsemen and two hundred spearmen to go as far as Caesarea. 24/ Also provide mounts for Paul to ride, and bring him safely to Felix the governor." 25/ And he wrote a letter to this effect:

26   "Claudius Lysias to his Excellency the governor Felix, greeting. 27/ This man was seized by the Jews, and was about to be killed by them, when I came upon them with the soldiers and rescued him, having learned that he was a Roman citizen. 28/ And desiring to know the charge on which they accused him, I brought him down to their council. 29/ I found that he was accused about questions of their law, but charged with nothing deserving death or imprisonment. 30/ And when it was disclosed to

me that there would be a plot against the man, I sent him to you at once, ordering his accusers also to state before you what they have against him."

31   So the soldiers, according to their instructions, took Paul and brought him by night to Antipatris. 32/ And on the morrow they returned to the barracks, leaving the horsemen to go on with him. 33/ When they came to Caesarea and delivered the letter to the governor, they presented Paul also before him. 34/ On reading the letter, he asked to what province he belonged. When he learned that he was from Cilicia 35/ he said, "I will hear you when your accusers arrive." And he commanded him to be guarded in Herod's praetorium.

This extended account appears once again to derive from an independent anecdote, which knows nothing about a trial before the Sanhedrin[1] and even conflicts with such an event. Luke repeats the motif of the attempt on Paul's life in chapter 25.

■ **12** συστροφή means "plot" here (cf. vs 13). For ἀναθεμα-τίζεσθαι, "to bind with an oath," compare *1 Enoch* 6.4–5.[2]

■ **13–15** The Western text has smoothed out this section.

■ **15** This proposal makes sense only in an individual anecdote, not in the present context. σὺν τῷ συνεδρίῳ, "with the council," should come after ὑμεῖς, "you." διαγινώσκειν, "decide, determine" (a legal term), here means simply γινώσκειν, "find out about" (it does not refer to the judicial decision!). For ἀκριβέστερον, "more exactly," compare vs 20.

■ **16** Did the notion that Paul's parents had lived in Jerusalem (22:3) arise from information about relatives of Paul who lived in Jerusalem? Visits to people in prison were possible (Matt 11:2; 25:36; *Pass. Perp.*; etc.). The style is peaceful and idyllic; details are expanded for their own sake.

■ **20** The reading μέλλων, "you (singular) were going to," is well attested; but vs 15 demands μέλλον, "they were going to": the Sanhedrin wants to be informed. μέλλων could be an accommodation to 22:30.[3]

■ **21–22** These verses awaken some anticipation of the burlesque: What will happen to the conspirators who have so bound themselves by their oath?[4]

■ **22** This sentence provides one of the examples of alternation between indirect and direct discourse (then cf. vs 24, where direct speech changes to indirect).

■ **23** The display of troops here is sheer fantasy (half the garrison in the capital city).[5] The display intends to illustrate the importance of the prisoner, the enormity of the danger, and the quality of the measures taken by Roman military officials. Luke is unaware that secrecy and such a display do not fit. For τινὰς δύο, "two," compare 19:14 and Luke 7:18. The type of troops called δεξιολάβοι, *RSV*, "spearmen," appear elsewhere only in late (Byzantine) documents.

■ **24** ἡγεμών, "governor," is also used as a designation for the procurator in Josephus (cf. Luke 3:1).[6]

Excursus: Antonius Felix

Claudius (?, as in the mss. of Josephus *Ant.* 20.137) Antonius Felix was a freedman, the brother of Pallas who was a powerful figure under Claudius. Because of this connection, despite his origins, he became procurator. According to Suetonius (*Claud.* 28), he married three princesses in succession. The anger at his being named to a position which had formerly been reserved for nobility is reflected in Tacitus *Hist.* 5.9: "The princes now being dead or reduced to insignificance, Claudius made Judea a province and entrusted it to Roman knights or to freedmen; one of the latter, Antonius Felix, practiced every kind of cruelty and lust, wielding the power of king with all the instincts of a slave" (Claudius, defunctis regibus aut ad modicum redactis, Iudaeam provinciam equitibus Romanis aut libertis permisit, e quibus Antonius Felix per omnem saevitiam ac libidinem ius regium servili ingenio exercuit; *Ann.* 12.54: "(Felix) considered that with such influences behind him all malefactions would be

1   Preuschen.
2   Str-B 2.767; 4.293–333.
3   Preuschen.
4   See the commentary on vs 12.
5   See the commentary on 21:31.
6   On the rank of procurator, see PW 23.1240–79.

venial" (cuncta malefacta sibi inpune ratus tanta potentia subnixo). He receives poor marks from Josephus as well. During his term of office the situation in Palestine worsened considerably with the appearance of the Sicarii and zealots, against whom he fiercely struggled. The dates for his time of office are debated. According to Tacitus (*Ann.* 12.54), in the year 52 he "for a while past had held the governorship of Judea" (iam pridem Iudaeae impositus). According to Josephus *Bell.* 2.247 and *Ant.* 20.137–38, he arrived in the year 52/53. The latter is more probable; in Tacitus the relationships in Palestine are described with some confusion. Scholars do not agree about the end of his term either. In *Ant.* 20.182, Josephus writes that after he was deposed a delegation of Jews from Caesarea complained to Nero about him, but Felix was protected by Pallas. This would have to have occurred before the downfall of Pallas (the end of 55). This would place Felix's term at about 53–55. Acts 24:27 (διετία, "two years") cannot be invoked in support of this proposed dating.[7] According to Eusebius *Chron.*,[8] Festus had already taken office in the year 54; according to Jerome *Chron.*[9] in the year 56, which fits with the dates proposed for Felix.[10] Perhaps one ought not in fact build too much on Josephus's note about the help of Pallas; it is gossip.[11] The early dating nevertheless remains possible and probable.

■ **25** For ἔχουσαν κτλ., "to this effect," compare (περι)ἔχουσαι τὸν τρόπον τοῦτον, "its contents were as follows," in 1 Macc 11:29; 15:2; Josephus *Ant.* 11.215; etc. For τύπος, "content" (*RSV,* "effect"), compare *3 Macc.* 3.30; Aristeas 34. The letter is redactional; it serves to illumine the situation from the Roman standpoint (as Luke understands it). Legal innocence is acknowledged by the first Roman functionary who dealt with the matter. The view is the same as in the Gallio scene: the Roman does not state that Christianity is identical with Judaism, but rather that the whole matter is of no concern to Rome.

■ **26** The form of greeting in the letter is the normal one as in 15:23. Compare κράτιστος: egregius, "excellency," with the following inscription from the time of Nero: "to Julius Vestinus, his excellency the governor" (ἐπὶ ᾽Ιουλίου Οὐηστίνου τοῦ κρατίστου ἡγεμόνος).[12]

■ **27–35** There is a good deal of juristic terminology here: συλλαμβάνειν, "to seize"; ἐγκαλεῖν/ἔγκλημα, "accused/accusation"; κατήγορος, "accuser"; ἄξιος θανάτου, "deserving death"; μηνύειν, "to disclose"; παραγγέλλειν, "to order"; compare vs 33, παριστάνειν, "to present"; vs 35, διακούειν, "to give someone a hearing";[13] ἄξιον . . . ἔγκλημα, "deserving . . . charge," that is, "a charge deserving death or imprisonment."[14]

■ **30** The conclusion in this verse prepares for 24:1–23.[15] With παραγγείλας κτλ., "ordering, etc.," the redactional character is especially clear. "This instruction the tribune could only transmit to the accusers when Paul was safely out of Jerusalem."[16]

■ **31** Antipatris is situated between Lydda and Caesarea, about sixty kilometers from Jerusalem and forty kilometers from Caesarea. On the distance between Jerusalem and Caesarea, compare the anecdote in Josephus *Bell.* 1.79.

■ **34** The question about the home province is in accord with the order of the legal process.[17] ποίας equals τίνος, "what."

---

7   See the comments on 24:27.

8   The text is found in Josef Karst, *Eusebius: Werke V: Die Chronik* (GCS 20; Berlin: Akademie-Verlag, 1911) 215.

9   The text is found in Rudolf Helm, *Eusebius: Werke VII: Die Chronik des Hieronymus* (GCS 47; Berlin: Akademie-Verlag, 1956) 182.

10 In favor of this dating the change of office in the year 55/56, see *Beginnings* 5.464–67; Haenchen, pp. 68–71; Schwartz, "Chronologie," 284–99; PW 22.224. Against this view see, for example, Schürer, *History* 1.459–66: two years would be too short a period for all the events of his term to have taken place.

11 PW 22.224.

12 *OGIS* 667.3–4.

13 See Otto Eger, *Rechtsgeschichtliches zum Neuen Testament* (Basel: Reinhardt, 1919) 10–11.

14 BAG *s.v.* ἔγκλημα.

15 On the construction here (partial transformation of a nominative with infinitive, ἐμηνύθη ἐπιβουλὴ ἔσεσθαι, "a plot was disclosed to be," into a genitive absolute), see BDF § 424.

16 Haenchen, p. 648.

17 Cf. *Mart. Carpi.* 24–27; *Mart. Justin* 4.7–8. See Mommsen, "Rechtsverhältnisse," 92; A. N. Sherwin-White, *Roman Society and Roman Law in the New Testament* (Oxford: Clarendon, 1963) 55–57.

■ **35** The site of the praetorium is no longer known.[18]
The conduct of Felix is correct; we cannot read into the
text here that he is seeking a delay.

18   See the excursus on Phil 1:13 in Martin Dibelius, *An
      die Thessalonicher I II, An die Philipper* (HNT 11;
      Tübingen: Mohr [Siebeck], 1937) 64–65.

24

The Trial before Felix

1 And after five days the high priest Ananias came down with some elders and a spokesman, one Tertullus. They laid before the governor their case against Paul; 2/ and when he was called, Tertullus began to accuse him, saying:

"Since through you we enjoy much peace, and since by your provision, most excellent Felix, reforms are introduced on behalf of this nation, 3/ in every way and everywhere we accept this with all gratitude. 4/ But, to detain you no further, I beg you in your kindness to hear us briefly. 5/ For we have found this man a pestilent fellow, an agitator among all the Jews throughout the world, and a ringleader of the sect of the Nazarenes. 6/ He even tried to profane the temple, but we seized him. 8/ By examining him yourself you will be able to learn from him about everything of which we accuse him.

9 The Jews also joined in the charge, affirming that all this was so.

10 And when the governor had motioned to him to speak, Paul replied:

"Realizing that for many years you have been judge over this nation, I cheerfully make my defense. 11/ As you may ascertain, it is not more than twelve days since I went up to worship at Jerusalem; 12/ and they did not find me disputing with any one or stirring up a crowd, either in the temple or in the synagogues, or in the city. 13/ Neither can they prove to you what they now bring up against me. 14/ But this I admit to you, that according to the Way, which they call a sect, I worship the God of our fathers, believing everything laid down by the law or written in the prophets, 15/ having a hope in God which these themselves accept, that there will be a resurrection of both the just and the unjust. 16/ So I always take pains to have a clear conscience toward God and toward men. 17/ Now after some years I came to bring to my nation alms and offerings. 18/ As I was doing this, they found me purified in the temple, without any crowd or tumult. But some Jews from Asia— 19/ they ought to be here before you and to make an accusation, if they have anything against me. 20/ Or else let these men themselves say what wrongdoing they found when I stood before the council, 21/ except this one thing which I cried out while standing among them, 'With respect to the resurrection of the dead I am on trial before you this day.'"

22 But Felix, having a rather accurate knowl-

edge of the Way, put them off, saying, "When Lysias the tribune comes down, I will decide your case." 23/ Then he gave orders to the centurion that he should be kept in custody but should have some liberty, and that none of his friends should be prevented from attending to his needs.

■ **1** A spokesman can represent the accusers as well as the accused; compare Achilles Tatius 7 and 8; also note the examples in the papyri! ἐμφανίζειν, "laid . . . case," is a technical term meaning "to bring formal charges against someone."[1] What follows here is the only *debate* in the book, with extensive use of rhetorical devices.[2] Of course it does not follow from the juristic-rhetorical terminology that the speech (or an original on which it is based) is authentic; rather, it means that Luke has composed it in accord with rhetorical style. Compare the parody in Lucian *Bis acc.* 16ff, which, also, is not an extended speech. The point of the accusation is mentioned, but not developed rhetorically.

■ **2** The genitive absolute κληθέντος, "when (he) was called," is part of official legal style.[3] Taken by itself, the word is used for the summons to a trial, not for the bringing forward (ἄγεσθαι, "to bring") of one who is already in custody. The speech begins with the *captatio benevolentiae*, "currying of favor," which is part of the rhetorical style (cf. Lucian *Bis acc.* 17). For examples of πολύς, "much," at the beginning of a speech,[4] compare Thucydides 1.80.1; 2.35.1; 3.37.1; etc.[5] For the style in general, compare Dionysius Halic. 5.1.4: "It appeared that the kings had been the authors of a great many advantages to the commonwealth" (πολλῶν καὶ μεγάλων ἀγαθῶν αἴτιοι γεγονέναι τοῖς κοινοῖς πράγμασιν ἔδοξαν οἱ βασιλεῖς).[6]

Since this praise is a part of rhetorical style, it is unnecessary to explain the praise of Felix by appeal to contemporary events (by a reference, say, to Felix's struggle against guerrilla organizations; see Josephus *Bell.* 2.253–63; *Ant.* 20.160–61). Other key words are also typical of rhetorical style: διόρθωμα, "reform" (and κατόρθωμα, "good order," Koine text), πρόνοια, "provision." εἰρήνη, "peace," and πρόνοια appear on coins.[7] "Tertullus" is not trying to distance himself from the Jews by using the expression τὸ ἔθνος τοῦτο, "this nation"; compare the use of "we" in the speech. Paul uses the same expression in vs 10. It is not necessary to understand ἔθνος here in a technical administrative sense as *provincia*, "province" or "provincial administration."[8]

■ **3** πάντη—πανταχοῦ, "in every way and everywhere," occurs in petitions.[9]

■ **4** With yet another rhetorical expression this sentence leads into the actual subject at hand. ἐγκόπτειν perhaps means "to weary" (as in the LXX—Job 19:2; Isa 43:23); note Lucian *Bis acc.* 26: "But not to prolong my introduction when the water has been running for some time [a water clock!], I will begin my complaint" (ἀλλὰ γάρ, ἵνα μὴ μακρὰ προοιμιάζωμαι, τοῦ ὕδατος πάλαι εἰκῆ ῥέοντος ἄρξομαι τῆς κατηγορίας).[10] ἐπὶ πλεῖον, "further," and συντόμως, "briefly," are expressions characteristic of administrative style.[11] For the request for a hearing, compare Lucian *Bis. acc.* 16: "Listen first, gentlemen of

1   BAG *s.v.* Examples are cited in Stephan Lösch, "Die Dankesrede des Tertullus: Apg 24,1–4," *ThQ* 112 (1931) 295–319.
2   Lösch, "Die Dankesrede des Tertullus."
3   Ibid., 301.
4   Ibid., 306.
5   See the commentaries on Luke 1:1.
6   Eiliv Skard, "Epigraphische Formeln bei Dionys von Halikarnass," SO 11 (1932) 55–60.
7   Joseph Vogt, *Die alexandrinischen Münzen: Grundlegung einer alexandrinischen Kaisergeschichte* (2 vols.; Stuttgart: Kohlhammer, 1924) 1.28–39 and passim; cf. the Münzverzeichnis (= vol. 2). An inscription in Dittenberger (*OGIS* 669) provides a beautiful illustration of laudatory style and of official expressions of well-being.
8   Thus Eger, *Rechtsgeschichtliches*, 13; cf. Moulton-

Milligan, *s.v.*
9   Friedrich Preisigke, *Wörterbuch der griechischen Papyrusurkunden mit Einschluss der griechischen Inschriften, Aufschriften, Ostraka, Mumienschilder, usw. aus Ägypten* (ed. E. Kiessling; 3 vols.; Berlin and Marburg, 1925–31) 2.228–29.
10 Lucian *Hist. conscr.* 27; see Betz, *Lukian*, 188 n. 1.
11 Preisigke, *Wörterbuch* 2.315, 554.

the jury" (ἀκούετε, ὦ ἄνδρες δικασταί); *Acta Isidori*: "My Lord Caesar, I beseech you to hear my account of my native city's suffering" (κύριέ μου Καῖσαρ, τῶν γονά[των σου δέομαι] ἀκοῦσαί μου τὰ πονοῦν[τα τῇ πατρίδι]).[12]

■ **5–6** The accusation concerns *seditio*, "sedition," and profaning the temple[13] (the mere attempt was enough; cf. 25:8). The apologetic intent appears in the inclusion of the whole "sect of the Nazarenes."[14] In this way we are prepared for Paul's arguments in vss 14–16. Here he appears as the representative of the ecumenical church.

■ **(7)** The Western text inserts an invective against Lysias: "And we would have judged him according to our law. But the chief captain Lysias came and with great violence took him out of our hands, commanding his accusers to come before you." It refers παρ' οὗ, "from him," in vs 8 to Lysias.

■ **8** The invitation here extended to Felix to determine Paul's wrongdoing is in vs 20 directed back at Paul's accusers: "or else let these men themselves say what wrongdoing they found. . . ."

■ **10** Paul's own *captatio benevolentiae* (see on vs 2, above) is limited to an appeal to the professional expertise of Felix (cf. vs 22). Thereby Paul can discuss the religious issues with the hope of convincing Felix that there is no legal case at issue here (not just that Christianity and Judaism are to be equated). ἐκ πολλῶν ἐτῶν, "for many years," taken by itself could be understood in light of Tacitus *Ann.* 12.54: "for a while past had held the governorship of Judaea" (iam pridem Iudaeae inpositus).[15] But here again we have an example of flowery language. In his letter to the Alexandrians, written during the first year of his reign, Claudius refers to the benevolence that he has demonstrated to them ἐκ πολλῶν χρόνων, "for a long time."[16]

■ **11** "As you may ascertain" refers back to vs 8 and prepares for the rebuttal (vss 13, 20). The reference to the brevity of his stay is probably not intended to indicate that the time was too short for a στάσις, "insurrection," but rather that his stay is easily reviewed. The twelve

days arise simply by adding the seven days of 21:27 and the five of 24:1. προσκυνήσων, "to worship," is more precisely defined in vs 17.

■ **13** Paul calls upon the fundamental legal principle that one is innocent until proven guilty.

■ **14–15** The contemptuous designation αἵρεσις, "sect" (cf. vs 5), is corrected by the term ὁδός, "Way." The explanation about the essence of Christianity is fundamental: It is the true fulfillment of Judaism. Belief in the resurrection, in its general Lukan form, appears alongside the conception of God and the theme of promise and fulfillment (cf. Luke 24:44–45) as central doctrines.[17] No mention of the special resurrection of Jesus is made until 25:19 (because this was a controversial matter).

■ **16** ἐν τούτῳ, "so" or "for this reason," is not to be taken with ἀσκεῖν, "take pains." "Toward God and toward men" is a widespread expression; compare Prov 3:4; Philo *Abr.* 208: "holiness to God and justice to men" (ὁσιότης μὲν πρὸς θεόν, δικαιοσύνη δὲ πρὸς ἀνθρώπους).[18]

■ **17** Finally the collection is mentioned, but only in passing and ad hoc, in order to refute the charge of στάσις, "insurrection," and to demonstrate the solidarity of Paul with his people. The reader of Acts can scarcely understand the allusion here; it is clear that Luke knows more than he says. For προσφοραί, "offerings," compare 21:26.

■ **18–19** The sentence is not completed. There is no verb for τινὲς δέ, "but some" (perhaps: "stirred up a riot"). If need be, one could explain as follows: τινὲς δέ is, on the one hand, the subject of εὗρον, "they found"; on the other hand, the δέ, "but," hints at a contrasting thought, which is not expressed. Thus: "It was not I who stirred up the tumult, but rather some Jews from Asia." ἡγνισμένον, "purified," makes a special point: They have charged him with profaning the Temple—while he was there making an offering. For εἴ τι ἔχοιεν, "if they have anything" (optative), the correct form would be εἴ τι ἔχουσιν or ἐάν τι ἔχωσιν.[19] The optative is used with the intent of lessening the degree of probability.

12   BGU 511.30ff; the text is according to Musurillo, *Acta Alexandrinorum*, 12.

13   See the comments on 21:29.

14   C. Cecchelli, "Il nome e la 'setta' dei Cristiani," *Rivista di archeologia cristiana* 31 (1955) 55–73.

15   See the excursus on (Claudius) Antonius Felix following 23:24 above.

16   Pap. London 1912; Bell, *Jews and Christians*.

17   Conzelmann, *Theology*, 226–27, 230–31.

18   *SIG* 2 no. 900.9–10, etc.; cf. Luke 18:2, 4.

19   BDF § 385.2.

■ **20** The statement in vs 8 proves to be hollow. Paul's accusers have no witnesses.

■ **21** ἤ, "except" (before περί, "concerning," not translated in *RSV*), refers back to an ἄλλο, "other," which should be supplied before ἀδίκημα, "wrongdoing" (for this word, cf. 18:14).

■ **22** ἀναβάλλειν is a legal term meaning "to adjourn." Felix's expertise is explained by vs 24—his wife is a Jewess.

■ **23** For ἄνεσις, "liberty," compare Josephus *Ant.* 18.235 (describing Agrippa's custody); one ought not miscon-strue, however, Paul's custody as idyllic in light of this passage, and *Ant.* 18.204.[20] Note also Constantine *Cod. Theod.* 11.7.3: "in free and open military custody, as is established by ordinary usage" (aperta et libera et in usum hominum constituta custodia militaris).[21]

---

20 On arrest, see Mommsen, "Rechtsverhältnisse," 93. On such directions in official records, see Eger, *Rechtsgeschichtliches*, 12 n. 23.

21 Trans. from Clyde Pharr, *The Theodosian Code and Novels and the Sirmondian Constitutions* (Princeton: Princeton University, 1952) 299.

24

Paul and Felix

24   **After some days Felix came with his wife Drusilla, who was a Jewess; and he sent for Paul and heard him speak upon faith in Christ Jesus. 25/ And as he argued about justice and self-control and future judgment, Felix was alarmed and said, "Go away for the present; when I have an opportunity I will summon you." 26/ At the same time he hoped that money would be given him by Paul. So he sent for him often and conversed with him. 27/ But when two years had elapsed, Felix was succeeded by Porcius Festus; and desiring to do the Jews a favor, Felix left Paul in prison.**

Once again, no concrete material was necessary for the construction of this scene. The interest in Christianity shown by those in high places is a Lukan theme. Women of high rank play a prominent role in the apocryphal acts of apostles. Is this scene reminiscent of the story involving Herod, Herodias, and John the Baptist, a story which Luke omitted in his Gospel?[1]

■ **24** Drusilla was the youngest daughter of Agrippa I. The scandalous story of how Felix won her is told in Josephus *Ant.* 20.141–44.

■ **25** Here is a summary of Christianity formulated to fit the situation, but nevertheless typically Lukan: Paul's discussion focuses on ethics and future judgment. In the apocryphal acts, "self-control" develops into a recurring motif which can determine the whole plot (*Paul and Thecla; Acts of Peter* 33–34; Aristeas 278: "and commands them to respect self-control and justice more highly. God directs all these matters" (ἐγκράτειαν δὲ κελεύει καὶ δικαιοσύνην προτιμᾶν· ὁ δὲ θεὸς πάντων ἡγεῖται τούτων).

■ **26** This is reminiscent of the picture of Felix as given by Tacitus and Josephus. Luke assumes that the insinuations concerning Felix in vss 25 and 26 are enough for the reader. At the same time he shows why Paul, despite his proven innocence, was not released. With respect to the delay,[2] there were no legal means available for forcing the disposition of Paul's case.

■ **27** Here we are given a further reason—of the same kind. In this context διετία, "two years," refers to the length of Paul's imprisonment. Others understand it as referring to the time Felix was in office, at least in the source which Luke used.[3] But no source for this detail can be detected.

---

1   Haenchen, p. 661.
2   Mommsen, "Rechtsverhältnisse."
3   Haenchen, p. 661.

25

**Paul before Festus;
Appeal to Caesar**

1 Now when Festus had come into his province, after three days he went up to Jerusalem from Caesarea. 2/ And the chief priests and the principal men of the Jews informed him against Paul; and they urged him, 3/ asking as a favor to have the man sent to Jerusalem, planning an ambush to kill him on the way. 4/ Festus replied that Paul was being kept at Caesarea, and that he himself intended to go there shortly. 5/ "So," said he, "let the men of authority among you go down with me, and if there is anything wrong about the man, let them accuse him."

6 When he had stayed among them not more than eight or ten days, he went down to Caesarea; and the next day he took his seat on the tribunal and ordered Paul to be brought. 7/ And when he had come, the Jews who had gone down from Jerusalem stood about him, bringing against him many serious charges which they could not prove. 8/ Paul said in his defense, "Neither against the law of the Jews, nor against the temple, nor against Caesar have I offended at all." 9/ But Festus, wishing to do the Jews a favor, said to Paul, "Do you wish to go up to Jerusalem, and there be tried on these charges before me?" 10/ But Paul said, "I am standing before Caesar's tribunal, where I ought to be tried; to the Jews I have done no wrong, as you know very well. 11/ If then I am a wrongdoer, and have committed anything for which I deserve to die, I do not seek to escape death; but if there is nothing in their charges against me, no one can give me up to them. I appeal to Caesar." 12/ Then Festus, when he had conferred with his council, answered, "You have appealed to Caesar; to Caesar you shall go."

■ 1 We know practically nothing about Porcius Festus; we know him only through Acts and Josephus (*Bell.* 2.271–72; *Ant.* 20.182–88). He took office around 55/56 C.E.[1] and died about 62. In the interim, before the arrival of his successor Albinus, the high priest Ananus had James, the brother of Jesus, put to death (Josephus *Ant.* 20.200). τῇ ἐπαρχίᾳ, "into his province" (cf. 23:34), is better attested (by B, etc.) than (the infrequent) τῇ ἐπαρχείῳ (supply χώρᾳ; ℵ* A P⁷⁴ [ΕΠΑΡΧΙΩ]).

■ 2 According to Josephus *Ant.* 20.179 (cf. 20.194), Ishmael, son of Phabi, was still high priest at the time of Felix. Luke says nothing about a change.

■ 3 It appears that the motif of a plot against Paul's life has simply been taken over from 23:12–30.

1　See the excursus to 23:24.

■ 4 The infinitive with an accusative subject identical with that of the governing verb (ἑαυτὸν δὲ μέλλειν, "and . . . he himself intended") is frequent in the New Testament. In this case the construction is classical, because it is formed in contrast to the correct accusative with infinitive τηρεῖσθαι κτλ., "was being kept, etc."[2]

■ 6 ἀχθῆναι, "to be brought forward," is more exact than καλεῖσθαι, "to summon," in 24:2.[3]

■ 7 The scene is only sketched. Paul's opponents have nothing new to express. The reader is familiar with the old accusations, even if Festus is not.

■ 8 The fundamental problem is formulated more sharply than before:[4] (1) From the standpoint of the Jews, no charge can be made against the Christians. Here also no claim is made that Christianity should be recognized as a legitimate group within Judaism. Rather, the Jewish charges are denied—there has been no infringement of Roman law. This is also important in view of the favor Festus intends to do for the Jews (vs 9)—he has no reason to send Paul to Jerusalem. (2) The second point certainly does have to do with Roman law, because this law guaranteed the protection of the Temple.[5] But the issue here concerns the specific charge against Paul, and not the general legal status of Christianity. (3) The government, represented by Caesar, is finally addressed: There has been no offense.

■ 9 At this point Luke certainly has to explain why once again Paul was not set free. The reason is the human failure of the official; he breaks down. This change in his attitude is constructed to suit Luke's apologetic purposes.

■ 10 Paul's rejoinder seems illogical. In Jerusalem he would be before Caesar's tribunal no less than in Caesarea. But in the first place, the reader knows about the Jewish plot, and second, Luke presents Paul as grasping the real intent of Festus, which is to please the Jews. We have here the most severe judgment on a Roman official in the entire book. Festus alone(!) is to blame for the continuation of Paul's trial. Paul is compelled to appeal to Caesar, and the δεῖ, "must," which was prophesied

(19:21; 23:11) is fulfilled.

With "before Caesar's tribunal" (βῆμα), compare Ulpian *Dig.* 1.19.1: "Things that have been conducted and accomplished by a procurator of Caesar are approved by him just as if they were administered by Caesar himself" (quae acta gestaque sunt a procuratore Caesaris, sic ab eo comprobantur, atque si a Caesare ipso gesta sint).

■ 11 This fundamental acknowledgment of law and rights is a common theme. It is already the basic theme in Plato's *Apology* and *Crito;* note Josephus *Vita* 141: "If I deserve to die, I ask no mercy" (θανεῖν μὲν εἰ δίκαιόν ἐστιν, οὐ παραιτοῦμαι).

■ 12 For συμβούλιον, "council" = *concilium,* compare Philo *Leg. Gai.* 234–60; 350.[6]

Excursus:
The Appeal

Details of the law of appeals are still as unclear as ever. Whatever clarity has come about has resulted from the study of Acts. Acts is not, however, a legal protocol. Unfortunately, the Alexandrian *Acts of the Pagan Martyrs* and the *Edict of Claudius from Cyrene* give no exact picture with regard to the matter of appeal either. Originally, at the time of the republic, there was (1) the *provocatio,* the right of the citizen to demand the verdict of the people (instead of that of the official); (2) the *appellatio,* the appeal to the colleagues of an official or to a superior magistrate or to the people's tribune, that is, the request for intercession. Neither of these resulted in the intervention in a trial which was in process nor in overturning a sentence which had already been made. This argues against the assumption[7] that the right of appeal during the time of the empire grew out of a combining of the *provocatio* and *appellatio* because Caesar had combined the various official duties into his own office. If we do follow this hypothesis, the following points remain uncertain:[8] (1) Could only Roman citizens appeal? Paul's failure to mention his rights as a citizen in this passage certainly is of no significance in this connection.[9] The reader already knows about his citizenship. For Luke, in any

---

2   BDF § 406.1.
3   See the comments there.
4   Conzelmann, *Theology,* 142–44.
5   See the comments on 21:28.
6   Moulton-Milligan, *s.v.*
7   Held by Mommsen, "Rechtsverhältnisse"; L. Wenger, "Appellation," *RAC* 1.564–71.

8   Cadbury provides a summary in *Beginnings* 5.316–17.
9   It is on this matter that Mommsen sees difficulty; see J. Bleiken, "Senatsgericht und Kaisergericht," AGG phil-hist Kl. 3. F Nr 53 (1962) 178ff.

case, the rights of the citizen and the right of appeal are connected. (2) Was the governor obligated to allow an appeal? Was it possible only in trials involving capital crimes? (3) Was the appeal possible only before the governor had passed sentence, or could it also be made afterward? Could the governor no longer set the accused free after such an appeal, even in the case of proven innocence?

Some of these questions are based on too formalistic a conception of the right of appeal, and they can be answered.[10] The foundation for the legal system of the early empire was apparently neither the strictly defined republican laws regarding *provocatio* and *appellatio,* nor the strict definition of the particular official roles of the emperor. It was rather a new development which grew out of his actual political power. Only in this way can we explain the reforming impact of the appeal at this time. It began with the emperor's willingness to grant extraordinary legal assistance upon request. This was gradually institutionalized. The development in the imperial provinces was of special significance. Here, where the legate represented the emperor, there was the possibility that all proceedings and sentences could in principle be laid before the emperor as the adjudicator, and this was of course possible at any stage in the trial, including after the sentence. After an appeal, it would have been difficult for the governor to deny the transfer to Rome.[11] Of course an appeal was not the only possible cause for a transfer to Rome—this could also be ordered by the official or the court (cf. the Second Edict of Augustus).[12] An appeal by the citizens involved is surely not excluded.[13] On the *remissio,* "sending back," of Roman citizens, see Pliny *Ep.* 10.96. For the transferring of Jews, note Josephus *Bell.* 2.243 = *Ant.* 20.131; *Bell.* 2.253 = *Ant.* 20.161; compare the case of Ignatius of Antioch.

---

10   See ibid.

11   In addition to the literature already cited, see *RAC* 1.564–71 and the bibliography there; A. N. Sherwin-White, *Roman Society and Roman Law in the New Testament* (Oxford: Clarendon Press, 1963) 63–69.

12   See Appendix 10.

13   von Premerstein, "Edikte des Augustus," 461.

25

Festus and Agrippa

13 Now when some days had passed, Agrippa the king and Bernice arrived at Caesarea to welcome Festus. 14/ And as they stayed there many days, Festus laid Paul's case before the king, saying, "There is a man left prisoner by Felix; 15/ and when I was at Jerusalem, the chief priests and the elders of the Jews gave information about him, asking for sentence against him. 16/ I answered them that it was not the custom of the Romans to give up any one before the accused met the accusers face to face, and had opportunity to make his defense concerning the charge laid against him. 17/ When therefore they came together here, I made no delay, but on the next day took my seat on the tribunal and ordered the man to be brought in. 18/ When the accusers stood up, they brought no charge in his case of such evils as I supposed; 19/ but they had certain points of dispute with him about their own superstition and about one Jesus, who was dead, but whom Paul asserted to be alive. 20/ Being at a loss how to investigate these questions, I asked whether he wished to go to Jerusalem and be tried there regarding them. 21/ But when Paul had appealed to be kept in custody for the decision of the emperor, I commanded him to be held until I could send him to Caesar." 22/ And Agrippa said to Festus, "I should like to hear the man myself." "Tomorrow," said he, "you shall hear him."

23 So on the morrow Agrippa and Bernice came with great pomp, and they entered the audience hall with the military tribunes and the prominent men of the city. Then by command of Festus Paul was brought in. 24/ And Festus said, "King Agrippa and all who are present with us, you see this man about whom the whole Jewish people petitioned me, both at Jerusalem and here, shouting that he ought not to live any longer. 25/ But I found that he had done nothing deserving death; and as he himself appealed to the emperor, I decided to send him. 26/ But I have nothing definite to write to my lord about him. Therefore I have brought him before you, and, especially before you, King Agrippa, that, after we have examined him, I may have something to write. 27/ For it seems to me unreasonable, in sending a prisoner, not to indicate the charges against him."

■ **13–22** This scene is also a free literary composition. It appears to be superfluous, but it serves to illumine the legal situation from the Roman viewpoint more sharply, and to cause it to be more flexible from the Jewish viewpoint (by means of a Jewish authority who did not belong to the Jewish establishment in Jerusalem). At the same time it presents the fulfillment of 9:15.

■ **13** The aorist participle ἀσπασάμενοι, "to welcome," is usually explained with the sense of simultaneity or even of purpose.[1] But Albert Wifstrand objects, arguing that there are no examples for this use.[2] However, in Byzantine Greek the aorist participle is used for subsequent action, if this unambiguously follows upon the preceding action; compare Apollodorus (first century C.E.) 3.5.9 of Oedipus: "And having come with Antigone to Colonus in Attica . . . he sat down there as a suppliant, was kindly received by Theseus . . ." (παραγενόμενος δὲ σὺν Ἀντιγόνῃ τῆς Ἀττικῆς εἰς Κολωνόν . . . καθίζει ἱκέτης, προσδεχθεὶς ὑπὸ Θησέως). What is most important for the narrator is reported with the finite verb.

**Excursus:
Agrippa II**

Agrippa II was the son of Agrippa I (the "Herod" of chapter 12) and thus the brother of Drusilla. He had been brought up in Rome and reigned ca. 50–100 C.E. over a territory that was enlarged several times. His sister Bernice[3] was widowed at the time and lived at her brother's court. There was gossip about the relationship between the brother and sister (Josephus *Ant.* 20.145; Juvenal *Sat.* 6.156–60). Later she became world famous because of her relationship with Titus (Suetonius *Titus* 7; Dio Cass. 66.15).[4]

■ **14** Festus's reason for bringing the case before Agrippa is finally mentioned in vs 26.

■ **15** Here is an intensification of what was said in vs 2. In this way Paul's appeal becomes somewhat more justified.

■ **16** Disavowing personal responsibility, Festus acknowl-

edges his disapproval.[5] But he himself has not held to the Roman principle which he has extolled. πρὶν ἔχοι . . . λάβοι, "before [he] had . . . to make," is the oblique optative "used in indirect discourse for the subjunctive (with ἄν) of the direct."[6] For τόπος = "opportunity" (= *locus*, "place"), compare Josephus *Ant.* 16.258. On the Roman principle note the following: Ulpian *Dig.* 48.17.1: "And we employ this right lest those who are absent be condemned, for the concept of equity does not allow anyone to be condemned with case unheard" (et hoc iure utimur, ne absentes damnentur, neque enim inaudita causa quemquam damnari aequitatis ratio patitur); Appian *Bell. civ.* 3.54.222: "Our law, Senators, requires that the accused shall himself hear the charge preferred against him and shall be judged after he has made his own defense" (ὁ μὲν νόμος, ὦ βουλή, δικαιοῖ τὸν εὐθυνόμενον αὐτὸν ἀκοῦσαί τε τῆς κατηγορίας καὶ ἀπολογησάμενον ὑπὲρ αὐτοῦ κρίνεσθαι). Luke appeals to the most basic principles of Roman government, as the apologists do later; Justin *Apol.* 1.3; Athenagoras *Supplication* 3; Tertullian *Apol.* 1.3; 2.2: "There is freedom to answer, to cross-question, since in fact it is against the law for men to be condemned, undefended and unheard" (Respondendi, altercandi facultas patet, quando nec liceat indefensos et inauditos omnino damnari). It is a sign of inner corruption if this principle is disregarded (Tacitus *Hist.* 1.6).[7]

■ **17** On "I made no delay," note the contrast to 24:22.

■ **18–19** Compare 18:15. Here the apologetic aim becomes quite clear: the goal is not to achieve the recognition of Christianity by the state, but to urge Rome's withdrawal from the legal proceedings.[8] δεισιδαιμονία, "religion," has no derogatory connotation; Festus is speaking with a high-ranking guest who is himself a Jew (cf. 17:22; Josephus *Bell.* 2.174; *Ant.* 10.42). In 17:32 Luke described the Greeks' inability to understand the resurrection faith. Now the same is said about the Romans, and in this way preparation is made for 26:24. Here, however, Jesus is finally mentioned. Luke assumes

---

1   BDF § 339.1.
2   Albert Wifstrand, "Apostelgeschichte 25,13," *Eranos* 54 (1956) 123–37.
3   Bernice = Φερενίκη, "Veronica"; the B in place of Φ is Macedonian; the dropping of the ε in the form Βερνίκη, "Bernice," is a vulgarization.
4   Emile Mireaux, *La reine Bérénice* (Paris: Michel, 1951).
5   On the connection by means of the relative pronoun,

6   see Haenchen, p. 139 n. 7; Albert Debrunner, *Gnomon* 28 (1956) 188.
   BDF § 386.4.
7   Jacques Dupont, "*Aequitas Romana:* Notes sur Actes 25,16," *RechSR* 49 (1961) 354–85, reprinted in his *Études*, 527–52.
8   G. Strothotte, "Das Apostelkonzil im Lichte der jüdischen Rechtsgeschichte" (Diss., Erlangen, 1955)

that one could not think of the resurrection without also thinking of Jesus. But in situations such as 23:6, Paul could not explicitly name him.

■ **20** The motivation here is purposely different from that given in vs 9. The reader is shown the incompetence of the authorities to deal with questions of religion.

■ **21** ὁ Σεβαστός, "the emperor" = Augustus. διάγνωσις, "decision," is a technical term.[9] ἐπὶ . . . διαγνώσεων τοῦ Σεβαστοῦ, "upon . . . decision of the emperor," was used of an official title (= a cognitionibus Augusti, which referred to a secretary to the emperor for judicial matters). Luke likes to use ἐπί, "upon," in forensic contexts.[10]

■ **23–27** The display of ostentation is Luke's creation and is without a historical core. One ought not ask whether a legal procedure is present here. Does Luke mean it to be such? Yes! Compare vs 26. But the meaning is to be inferred exclusively from the literary purpose: Paul, and with him Christianity, steps into the great public arena (cf. 9:15 with 26:26).

■ **23** For φαντασία, "pomp," compare Vettius Valens 38.25–26: "But wealthy and rich and supporting themselves with very great pomp" (εὐπόρους δὲ καὶ πλουσίους καὶ μετὰ πλείστης φαντασίας διεξάγοντας). ἀκροατήριον is equivalent to "auditorium."

■ **24** For καὶ ἐνθάδε, "and here," see 25:7. For βοῶντες, "shouting," see 22:22.

■ **25** Compare 23:29 and 25:18. One thinks of Pilate's

threefold declaration of Jesus' innocence in the Lukan passion narrative (Luke 23:22).

■ **26** This verse provides the reason for this spectacle in an artificial manner. What Festus says is self-contradictory. He had enough material! The contradiction results from Luke's literary aim.

κύριος, "lord," as an imperial title was used since the time of Claudius/Nero.[11] This passage seems to be the earliest known evidence for the absolute use of ὁ κύριος (during the time of Domitian!). In any case, the title is already used as if it needed no explanation. The language (ἀσφαλής, "definite"; πρόαγω, "bring before"; ἐφ᾽ ὑμῶν, "before you"; ἀνάκρισις, "examination") is again technical juristic vocabulary.

■ **27** Festus's rather elegant statement appears somewhat hollow; in reality he *must* submit a report; Ulpian *Dig.* 49.6.1: "After an appeal has been entered, records must be furnished by the one who made the appeal to the person who is going to conduct the examination concerning the appeal" (Post appellationem interpositam litterae dandae sunt ab eo, a quo appellatum est, ad eum, qui de appellatione cogniturus est).

9   IG 14.1072.
10   G. Schulze, "Das Paulusbild des Lukas" (Diss., Kiel, 101, refers to Josephus *Ant.* 14.195.
1961) 263–64.
11   Werner Foerster, "κύριος," *TDNT* 3 (1965) 1054–55.

26

Paul Speaks before Agrippa II and Festus

1 Agrippa said to Paul, "You have permission to speak for yourself." Then Paul stretched out his hand and made his defense:

2 "I think myself fortunate that it is before you, King Agrippa, I am to make my defense today against all the accusations of the Jews, 3/ because you are especially familiar with all customs and controversies of the Jews; therefore I beg you to listen to me patiently.

4 "My manner of life from my youth, spent from the beginning among my own nation and at Jerusalem, is known by all the Jews. 5/ They have known for a long time, if they are willing to testify, that according to the strictest party of our religion I have lived as a Pharisee. 6/ And now I stand here on trial for hope in the promise made by God to our fathers, 7/ to which our twelve tribes hope to attain, as they earnestly worship night and day. And for this hope I am accused by Jews, O king! 8/ Why is it thought incredible by any of you that God raises the dead?

9 "I myself was convinced that I ought to do many things in opposing the name of Jesus of Nazareth. 10/ And I did so in Jerusalem; I not only shut up many of the saints in prison, by authority from the chief priests, but when they were put to death I cast my vote against them. 11/ And I punished them often in all the synagogues and forced them to blaspheme; and in raging fury against them, I persecuted them even to foreign cities.

12 "As [or: thus] I journeyed to Damascus with the authority and commission of the chief priests. 13/ At midday, O king, I saw on the way a light from heaven, brighter than the sun, shining round me and those who journeyed with me. 14/ And when we had all fallen to the ground, I heard a voice saying to me in the Hebrew language, 'Saul, Saul, why do you persecute me? It hurts you to kick against the goads.' 15/ And I said, 'Who are you, Lord?' And the Lord said, 'I am Jesus whom you are persecuting. 16/ But rise and stand upon your feet; for I have appeared to you for this purpose, to appoint you to serve and bear witness to the things in which you have seen me and to those in which I will appear to you, 17/ delivering you from the people and from the Gentiles—to whom I send you 18/ to open their eyes, that they may turn from darkness to light and from the power of Satan to God, that they may receive forgiveness of sins and a place among those who are sanctified by faith

19   in me.'

    "Wherefore, O King Agrippa, I was not
    disobedient to the heavenly vision, 20/
    but declared first to those at Damascus,
    then at Jerusalem and throughout all the
    country of Judea, and also to the Gen-
    tiles, that they should repent and turn to
    God and perform deeds worthy of their
    repentance. 21/ For this reason the Jews
    seized me in the temple and tried to kill
    me. 22/ To this day I have had the help
    that comes from God, and so I stand here
    testifying both to small and great, saying
    nothing but what the prophets and
    Moses said would come to pass: 23/ that
    the Christ must suffer, and that, by being
    the first to rise from the dead, he would
    proclaim light both to the people and to
    the Gentiles."

24   And as he thus made his defense, Festus
    said with a loud voice, "Paul, you are
    mad; your great learning is turning you
    mad." 25/ But Paul said, "I am not mad,
    most excellent Festus, but I am speaking
    the sober truth. 26/ For the king knows
    about these things, and to him I speak
    freely; for I am persuaded that none of
    these things has escaped his notice, for
    this was not done in a corner. 27/ King
    Agrippa, do you believe the prophets? I
    know that you believe." 28/ And Agrippa
    said to Paul, "In a short time you think to
    make me a Christian!" 29/ And Paul said,
    "Whether short or long, I would to God
    that not only you but also all who hear me
    this day might become such as I am—
    except for these chains."

30   Then the king rose, and the governor and
    Bernice and those who were sitting with
    them; 31/ and when they had with-
    drawn, they said to one another, "This
    man is doing nothing to deserve death or
    imprisonment." 32/ And Agrippa said to
    Festus, "This man could have been set
    free if he had not appealed to Caesar."

The thrust of the speech leads from the apology, addressing the situation, to a missionary appeal. Now that Luke has dealt with the juristic problem, there is opportunity to introduce religious issues. In introducing the scene Luke overlooks the comment in vs 29 that Paul is chained. ἐκτείνας κτλ., "stretched out, etc.," refers to the familiar orator's gesture; compare the "Arringatore" in the archaeological museum in Florence and the statue of Augustus in the Vatican; compare Apuleius *Met.* 2.21.
■ **2–3** *Captatio benevolentiae,* "currying of favor" (cf. 24:2, 10). Note the alliteration (περὶ πάντων, "against all");

compare the beginning of 24:3.
■ **3** On the reference to expertise in these matters, compare vs 26 and 24:10.[1] μάλιστα, "especially," can be taken with γνώστην, "familiar," or it could mean "especially because you are familiar." The accusative γνώστην σε ὄντα, "you are familiar," is a solecism.[2] κατά ("*of the* Jews") takes the accusative here in order to avoid two genitives in a row.[3] Paul's praise of Agrippa is not meant as a sarcastic jab at Festus; it is simply appropriate style.
■ **4–5** The details given at 22:3 are not repeated because they are already known to the reader.[4] In keeping with

---

1   On the request for a hearing, see the comments on 24:4.
2   BDF § 136.2 and § 137.3.
3   BDF § 224.1.
4   For the style of the autobiographical survey, see the comments on 22:3.

the situation the essential point is stressed: Paul is known in Jerusalem, and those living there must attest to Paul's faithfulness to the Jewish religion. Paul's designation of himself as a Pharisee fits in with his description to this point and prepares for the announcement of the resurrection. Luke has Paul speak in an "educated" manner; classical forms appear which otherwise have fallen out of use: the superlative ἀκριβέστατος, "strictest";[5] the Attic ἴσασιν, "know" (the future infinitive in B is surely secondary; it is found elsewhere in the New Testament only in Acts and Hebrews). Friedrich Blass believes that Paul wants to show that he knows how to handle Attic Greek.[6] On the other hand, however, we have the solecism in vs 3, the nonclassical βίωσις, "manner of life," in vs 4, and the style of vss 4–5 and 6–7, which is unimpressive. The piling up of the expressions ἐκ νεότητος, ἀπ' ἀρχῆς, ἄνωθεν, "from (my) youth, from the beginning, for a long time," results from the use of fixed elements of biographical style with an apologetic intent; Lucian *Pergr. mort.* 8: ἀκούσατέ μου ἐξ ἀρχῆς παραφυλάξαντος τὴν γνώμην αὐτοῦ καὶ τὸν βίον ἐπιτηρήσαντος ("give me your ears, for I have observed his character and kept an eye on his career from the beginning"). ἄνωθεν, "for a long time," (Marcellinus *Vita Thuc.* 1.2, 1 p 1 [Hude ed.]) is practically synonymous with ἀπ' ἀρχῆς, "from the beginning"; compare Luke 1:2–3.[7] Of course ἔθνος, "nation," does not refer to Paul's home province, Cilicia.[8]

■ **6–7** Compare 24:14–15. The conception of promise and fulfillment is expressed more clearly than before: The true Jew must become a Christian, in order to remain a Jew. For λατρεύειν κτλ., "worship etc.," compare Luke 2:37. For ἐν ἐκτενείᾳ, "earnestly," see Jdt 4:9. In place of the aorist καταντῆσαι, "to attain," the future infinitive would be grammatically preferable,[9] but it has practically disappeared from use.

■ **8** The change in person from "they" to "you" indicates the actual difference between Christians and Jews at the time; the style is that of the missionary appeal. εἰ (cf. vs 23) comes close to the sense of "that." The formulation here (εἰ ὁ θεός κτλ., "that God, etc.") hovers between reference to the doctrine of a general resurrection and to the raising of Christ, which has already occurred (present tense!). The Jews believe in the former (17:31); they could not deny the possibility of the latter. Thus the progress of thought runs logically from vs 8 to vs 9; compare what has already been expressed in 25:19, and then in 26:23.

■ **9** The senselessness of the conduct of the Jews is demonstrated by the former conduct of Paul the Pharisee.

■ **10–11** Paul's activity as a persecutor is intensified here over against 22:3–4.[10] κατήνεγκα ψῆφον, "I cast my vote," is not to be weakened to συνευδοκεῖν, "agree with." According to Luke, Paul actively participated in the voting. It is assumed that the Jewish authorities had the *ius gladii*, the right to execute capital criminals. εἰς τὰς ἔξω πόλεις, "to foreign cities," is a generalization of Damascus. ἠνάγκαζον is not a conative imperfect, "I tried to make them,"[11] but rather a descriptive imperfect, "I forced them (to blaspheme)," like ἐδίωκον, "I persecuted." Nothing is said about the results of this effort. On the connotation of βλασφημεῖν, "blaspheme," note Pliny *Ep.* 10.96.5: He who maintains that he is not a Christian must offer sacrifices and *maledicere Christo . . . quorum nihil posse cogi dicuntur qui sunt re vera Christiani*, "curse Christ—none of which acts, it is said, those who are really Christians can be forced to perform."

■ **12** ἐν οἷς refers to time, "then (I journeyed)," or to the situation, "under these circumstances" (cf. *RSV*, "thus").

■ **13** The time is given as in 22:6; note the intensification in comparison with that passage.

■ **14** Here again we find an intensification (cf. 9:4).[12] "In the Hebrew language" (that is, Aramaic, as in 21:40): this explains the form of the name Σαούλ, "Saul," which is found in all three variations of Paul's call. But then the voice quotes a Greek proverb. This is found in Euripides *Bacc.* 794–95, in connection with the pursuit of the new god. But we need not assume any literary dependence of Luke on Euripides, because the saying was widespread;

---

5   BDF § 60.1.
6   Friedrich Blass, *Philology of the Gospels* (London: Macmillan, 1898) 9–10.
7   This is contrary to the view of Cadbury, "'We' and 'I' Passages," 130.
8   As is held in *Beginnings* 4.315.
9   BDF § 350.
10 On καί after a relative, see Haenchen, p. 140 n. 8.

For ἕως, "in combination with prepositions, see the comments on 17:14.
11 So *RSV* and BDF § 326.
12 For the accusative φωνήν, "voice," see the comments on 22:9.

cf. further Aeschylus *Agam.* 1624; Euripides *Iph. Taur.* 1396; Julian *Or.* 8.246b: "or as the proverb says (not to) kick against the goads" (μηδέ, ὅ φησιν ἡ παροιμία᾿ πρὸς κέντρα λακτίζειν). The sense is: "It is useless, being human, to strive against fate" (οὐ συμφέρει τῇ τύχῃ ἄνθρωπον ὄντα διαμάχεσθαι).[13] Of course the proverb has nothing at all to say about Paul's inner experience.

■ **16–18** A further development of the incident in biblical style (motifs from the call of the Servant of God)[14] replaces the episode with Ananias (the loss of sight is accordingly omitted). In chapter 22, in a speech delivered to Jews, Paul mentions the cooperation of the devout Jew, Ananias. Here, before the ruler, the speech turns to the irresistibility of God's power.

■ **16** For στῆθι κτλ., "stand, etc.," compare Ezek 2:1, 3; for προχειρίζειν, "to appoint," see 22:14; for ὑπερέτης, "servant," see Luke 1:2. For μάρτυς, "witness," see the comments on 22:15. ὧν τε εἶδες κτλ., "to the things in which you have seen, etc.": Is the text corrupt? Did it originally say ὧν τε εἶδες ὧν τε ὀφθήσεταί σοι, "which you have seen and which will be shown to you"?[15]

■ **17** ἐξαιρεῖσθαι probably does not mean "choose" here, but rather, "deliver," as in Jer 1:7–8; 1 Chr 16:35; Acts 7:10, 34; 12:11; 23:27. εἰς οὕς, "to whom," refers to Jews and Gentiles (cf. 9:15; 22:15, and vs 20 of this chapter). One ought not infer from this passage a favorable outcome of the trial which Luke allegedly knew; it means simply that until now everything has gone well (vs 22). And in any case, a "favorable" course of events would be one which allows Paul to fulfill his destiny, namely, to bear witness.

■ **18** This is pious Christian language with a biblical touch (cf., Isa 42:7, 16). "From darkness to light" is an expression from the language of conversion: Eph 5:8; Col 1:12–13; 1 Pet 2:9; *Jos. Asen.* 8.9: "God . . . who gave life to all (things) and called (them) from the darkness to the light, and from the error to the truth, and from the death to the life" (here the conversion to Judaism is being described; cf. further *Jos. Asen.* 15:12).[16]

■ **19** "The address 'King Agrippa' shows that the words of Christ are ended."[17] The overall result of Paul's defense is twofold: (1) The mission of Paul was a matter of obedience to God. For this motif, compare Plato *Apol.* 33c; Epictetus 2.16.44, where it is said of Heracles: "It was therefore in obedience to His [Zeus's] will that he went about clearing away wickedness and lawlessness" (Ἐκείνῳ τοίνυν πειθόμενος περιῄει καθαίρων ἀδικίαν καὶ ἀνομίαν).

■ **20** The second result is: (2) The mission had to begin with the Jews and then extend to the Gentiles (22:17–21). For Paul's preaching in Jerusalem, see 9:28–29. "And throughout all the country of Judea" does not fit the construction; is it a gloss?[18] On the range of Paul's missionary activity, compare Rom 15:19. μετανοεῖν καὶ ἐπιστρέφειν, "repent and turn," are important terms for Luke.[19] For ἄξια τῆς μετανοίας ἔργα, "deeds worthy of repentance," compare Luke 3:8. This is a variation of the final motif in the speeches of Peter.

■ **22–23** The speech is brought to an end with a concluding summary of the essence of faith. This agrees essentially with the preceding verses, but is expressed more clearly. For the prophets and Moses, compare Luke 24:44–47 and Acts 3:22–23.[20] As in vs 8, εἰ means "that." For παθητός, "must suffer," compare Ignatius *Eph.* 7.2; *Pol.* 3.2; Justin *Dial.* 34.2; 36.1, among others; πάσχειν, "suffer," may have the sense "die."[21] πρῶτος, "first," explains ἀρχηγός, "Author," in 3:15 (cf. 1 Cor 15:20).

One detects formalized expressions here (cf. Rom 1:3–4; Col 1:18). In connection with φῶς καταγγέλλειν, "proclaim light," compare Aeschylus *Pers.* 300–301: "The

---

13 *Scholia Vetera in Pindari Carmina* II 60. On the relationship of Luke to Euripides, see Haenchen, p. 685 n. 3; Dibelius, *Studies,* 188–91; Vögeli, "Lukas und Euripides." Also see the comments on vs 24 below.

14 Jeremias; Hans Windisch, *Paulus und Christus: Ein biblisch-religionsgeschichtlicher Vergleich* (UNT 24; Leipzig: Hinrichs, 1934) 137–38.

15 Dibelius, *Studies,* 92.

16 Trans. from *The Old Testament Pseudepigrapha* (ed. James H. Charlesworth; 2 vols.; Garden City, NY: Doubleday, 1983–85) 2.213; for ἐπὶ τὸν θεόν, "to

God," see the commentaries on 1 Thess 1:9–10.

17 Haenchen, p. 686.

18 Haenchen (p. 687) suggests the whole is "an old and false gloss."

19 Conzelmann, *Theology,* 99–101. For ἐπὶ τὸν θεόν, "to God," see the comments on vs 18 and 20:21.

20 On the form of the proof from Scripture, see the commentary on 17:2–3. On the use of the title χριστός, see Conzelmann, *Theology,* 171.

21 Wilhelm Michaelis, "πάσχω," *TDNT* 5 (1967) 912–23.

words thou utterest bring a great light of joy into my house, and bright day after night wrapped in gloom" (ἐμοῖς μὲν εἶπας δώμασιν φάος μέγα καὶ λευκὸν ἦμαρ νυκτὸς ἐκ μελαγχίμου). On this topic, compare 13:47 and Luke 2:32.

■ **24** Again we have the interruption as an artistic device, this time actually a demonstration of the Roman's incomprehension (25:19); in this way Paul's learning is acknowledged (and the incompetence of the authorities is certified). εἰς μανίαν περιτρέπει, "is turning you mad," appears to be a common expression (Lucian *Abdic.* 30). On the charge, compare *Sib. Or.* 1.171–72; Pliny *Ep.* 10.96.4.

■ **25** Compare Pap. Oxy. 33.4.9–15 (*Acta Appiani*): "The emperor: 'Appian, I am accustomed to chasten those who rave and have lost all sense of shame. You speak only so long as I permit you.' Appian: 'By your *genius,* I am neither mad nor have I lost my sense of shame'" (Αὐτοκράτωρ· Ἀππιανέ, ἰῶθα//μεν καὶ ἡμεῖς μαινομένους καὶ/ἀπονενοημένους σωφρονίζειν./ Λαλεῖς ἐφ᾽ ὅσον ἐγώ σε θέλω λα/λεῖν. Ἀππιανός· Νὴ τὴν σὴν τύ/χην οὔτε μαίνομαι οὔτε ἀπονενό/ημαι . . .).[22]

■ **26** ἐν γωνίᾳ, "in a corner," is a Greek expression (Plato *Gorg.* 485d; Epictetus 2.12.17; Plutarch *Mor.* 516b and 777b). For Luke the expression οὐκ ἐν γωνίᾳ, "not in a corner," is programmatic: "These words light up Luke's presentation in Acts from beginning to end."[23]

■ **28** Note the play on the expression ἐν ὀλίγῳ, "in a short time," in the next verse. Χριστιανὸν ποιῆσαι, "to make a Christian," probably means "to play the Christian" (cf. 1 Kgs 20:7 LXX B);[24] ποιεῖν is used with this sense in

Johannes Climacus[25] and Johannes Malalas 338. Anton Fridrichsen explains the phrase in light of Xenophon *Mem.* 1.2.49: "'But,' said his accuser, 'Socrates taught sons to treat their fathers with contempt: he persuaded them that he made his companions wiser than their fathers'" (ἀλλὰ Σωκράτης γ᾽, ἔφη ὁ κατήγορος, τοὺς πατέρας προπηλακίζειν ἐδίδασκε, πείθων μὲν τοὺς συνόντας αυτῷ σοφωτέρους ποιεῖν τῶν πατέρων). According to Fridrichsen the complete sentence should be: . . . πείθων τοὺς συνόντας αὐτῷ (ἑαυτὸν) σοφωτέρους ποιεῖν (αὐτοὺς) τῶν πατέρων. Thus Acts 26:28 is completely analogous: ἐν ὀλίγῳ με πείθεις (σεαυτὸν) χριστιανὸν ποιῆσαί (με). Fridrichsen translates as follows: "You will make me believe that you, in small time, have made me a Christian."[26] Walter Bauer conjectures that there is present here a combination of two expressions: "in a short time you are persuading me to become a Christian," and "in a short time you will make me a Christian."[27]

■ **29** This is the only passage in the New Testament where a potential optative (with ἄν) is found in the main clause (also in the direct questions in 8:31; 17:18).[28] In regard to a Roman citizen being in chains during the investigation, compare again Augustus's Second Edict from Cyrene;[29] Roman citizens were brought to Rome in chains.[30]

■ **31** This is the last word from the Roman and from the Jewish political standpoint, the final impression with which Luke sends the reader on the journey. Paul's appeal to Rome and the continuation of his trial are due solely to the Romans' mishandling of the case.

■ **32** Compare 25:25.

---

22 Hans Lietzmann, *Griechische Papyri* (2d ed.; KlT 14; Bonn: Marcus & Weber, 1910) 24. Musurillo, *Acta Alexandrinorum,* 55, under Commodus?; idem, *Acts of Pagan Martyrs,* 67 (text), 70 (trans.).

23 Haenchen, p. 691.

24 Ibid., 689 n. 2.

25 *PG* 88.693d.

26 Anton Fridrichsen, "Acts 26,28," *ConNT* 3 (1939) 13–16.

27 BAG *s.v.* πείθω.

28 BDF § 359.2 and § 385.1.

29 Appendix 10.

30 von Premerstein, "Edikte des Augustus," 463–64.

27 The Voyage to Rome

1 And when it was decided that we should sail for Italy, they delivered Paul and some other prisoners to a centurion of the Augustan Cohort, named Julius. 2/ And embarking in a ship of Adramyttium, which was about to sail to the ports along the coast of Asia, we put to sea, accompanied by Aristarchus, a Macedonian from Thessalonica. 3/ The next day we put in at Sidon; and Julius treated Paul kindly, and gave him leave to go to his friends and be cared for. 4/ And putting to sea from there we sailed under the lee of Cyprus, because the winds were against us. 5/ And when we had sailed across the sea which is off Cilicia and Pamphylia, we came to Myra in Lycia. 6/ There the centurion found a ship of Alexandria sailing for Italy, and put us on board. 7/ We sailed slowly for a number of days, and arrived with difficulty off Cnidus, and as the wind did not allow us to go on, we sailed under the lee of Crete off Salmone. 8/ Coasting along it with difficulty, we came to a place called Fair Havens, near which was the city of Lasea.

9 As much time had been lost, and the voyage was already dangerous because the fast had already gone by, Paul advised them, 10/ saying, "Sirs, I perceive that the voyage will be with injury and much loss, not only of the cargo and the ship, but also of our lives." 11/ But the centurion paid more attention to the captain and to the owner of the ship than to what Paul said. 12/ And because the harbor was not suitable to winter in, the majority advised to put to sea from there, on the chance that somehow they could reach Phoenix, a harbor of Crete, looking northeast and southeast, and winter there.

13 And when the south wind blew gently, supposing that they had obtained their purpose, they weighed anchor and sailed along Crete, close inshore. 14/ But soon a tempestuous wind, called the northeaster, struck down from the land; 15/ and when the ship was caught and could not face the wind, we gave way to it and were driven. 16/ And running under the lee of a small island called Cauda, we managed with difficulty to secure the boat; 17/ after hoisting it up, they took measures to undergird the ship; then, fearing that they should run on the Syrtis, they lowered the gear, and so were driven. 18/ As we were violently storm-tossed, they began next day to throw the cargo overboard; 19/ and the third day

213

they cast out with their own hands the tackle of the ship. 20/ And when neither sun nor stars appeared for many a day, and no small tempest lay on us, all hope of our being saved was at last abandoned.

21   As they had been long without food, Paul then came forward among them and said, "Men, you should have listened to me, and should not have set sail from Crete and incurred this injury and loss. 22/ I now bid you take heart; for there will be no loss of life among you, but only of the ship. 23/ For this very night there stood by me an angel of the God to whom I belong and whom I worship, 24/ and he said, 'Do not be afraid, Paul; you must stand before Caesar; and lo, God has granted you all those who sail with you.' 25/ So take heart, men, for I have faith in God that it will be exactly as I have been told. 26/ But we shall have to run on some island."

27   When the fourteenth night had come, as we were drifting across the sea of Adria, about midnight the sailors suspected that they were nearing land. 28/ So they sounded and found twenty fathoms; a little further on they sounded again and found fifteen fathoms. 29/ And fearing that we might run on the rocks, they let out four anchors from the stern, and prayed for day to come. 30/ And as the sailors were seeking to escape from the ship, and had lowered the boat into the sea, under pretense of laying out anchors from the bow, 31/ Paul said to the centurion and the soldiers, "Unless these men stay in the ship, you cannot be saved." 32/ Then the soldiers cut away the ropes of the boat, and let it go.

33   As day was about to dawn, Paul urged them all to take some food, saying, "Today is the fourteenth day that you have continued in suspense and without food, having taken nothing. 34/ Therefore I urge you to take some food; it will give you strength, since not a hair is to perish from the head of any of you." 35/ And when he had said this, he took bread, and giving thanks to God in the presence of all he broke it and began to eat. 36/ Then they all were encouraged and ate some food themselves. 37/ (We were in all two hundred and seventy-six persons in the ship.) 38/ And when they had eaten enough, they lightened the ship, throwing out the wheat into the sea.

39   Now when it was day, they did not recognize the land, but they noticed a bay with a beach, on which they planned if possible to bring the ship ashore. 40/ So they cast off the anchors and left them in the sea, at the same time loosening the ropes

that tied the rudders; then hoisting the foresail to the wind they made for the beach. 41/ But striking a shoal they ran the vessel aground; the bow stuck and remained immovable, and the stern was broken up by the surf. 42/ The soldiers' plan was to kill the prisoners, lest any should swim away and escape; 43/ but the centurion, wishing to save Paul, kept them from carrying out their purpose. He ordered those who could swim to throw themselves overboard first and make for land, 44/ and the rest on planks or on pieces of the ship [or: on the shoulders of some]. And so it was that all escaped to land.

■ **1** In this account of a voyage which is the only real description of a journey in the book, the "we" clearly seems to be a literary device. One could ask whether it did not originate here (see below) and then was extended to the other voyages. The Western text, by adding "and Secundus" (καὶ Σεκοῦνδος) at the end of vs 2 (cf. 20:4), has seen the difficulty that "we" is used, even though Paul is the only Christian prisoner (but cf. Phlm 24 and Col 4:10: Aristarchus the συναιχμάλωτος, "fellow prisoner"). σπεῖρα Σεβαστή, "Augustan Cohort," was an honorary title which could be used for auxiliary troops: Ἐπὶ βασιλέω[s μεγάλου Μάρκου Ἰου]/λίου Ἀγρίππα, [ἔτους.., ------]/ Χάρητος, ἔπα[ρχος-----------]/ σπείρης Αὐ[γούστης καὶ στρατηγ]//ὸς Νομάδων-----------/- ης καὶ Χαλ[κιδηνῆς-----------] ("During the reign of king Marcus Julius the Great, Agrippa . . . Charitos, prefect . . . of the Augustan Cohort and commander of the Nomads . . . and of Chalkis. . . .")[1] An Augustan Cohort I (this same one?) was stationed in Syria during the time of Quirinius.[2] The imperfect παρεδίδουν, "they delivered," is used as the tense of narrative.[3]

■ **2** τόπος is used with the sense of "port."[4] κατά with the accusative indicating places is normal and means simply

"in" Asia (= Asia Minor). The mention of Aristarchus (19:29; 20:4) is striking and ought to be viewed as an indication of how the material came to Luke.

■ **3** From Caesarea to Sidon is about seventy nautical miles. φιλανθρώπως χρῆσθαι, "to treat kindly," and ἐπιμελείας τυγχάνειν, "to be cared for," were both common expressions; such expressions also appear later (vss 13, 20, 29, 33).

■ **4** ὑποπλεῖν means "to sail under the lee of," that is, taking advantage of the island's protection from the wind (it lay to the left). At this time of the year the prevailing winds were from the northwest.[5] Similarly, ships carrying grain from Alexandria sailed to the western tip of Cyprus, and from there to Myra. The voyage of the "Isis" provides an interesting parallel.[6]

■ **5** At this time of year along the southern coast of Asia Minor the winds frequently blow at right angles to the coast (onshore during the day, offshore during the night); there was, in addition, a westerly current. Thus the voyage to the west was possible.[7]

■ **6** Myra was an important stopping point for Egyptian grain ships.[8] The size of the "Isis" was 2,900 gross registered tons according to August Köster; 1,200 according

1 The text is in *OGIS* 421 (from El Hît, Batanäa).
2 *ILS* 1.2683; *Beginnings* 5.443.
3 Radermacher, *Grammatik,* 153.
4 Frisk, *Le Périple,* 8, 10, 17, etc.
5 See *Sailing Directions for the Mediterranean* (US Navy Hydrographic Office Nr 154 A, 1942) 32–33.
6 See Appendix 1; Lionel Casson, "The Isis and Her Voyage," *TAPA* 81 (1950) 43–56.
7 A. Breusing, *Die Nautik der Alten* (Bremen: Schünemann, 1886) 155–56; Hans Balmer, *Die Romfahrt des Apostels Paulus und die Seefahrtskunde im römischen Kaiserzeitaltern* (Bern: Sutermeister, 1905) 294; see

the literature listed under the excursus on "The Report about the Voyage" which follows the end of this chapter.
8 See the comments on vs 4. On the system of transportation, see Suetonius *Claud.* 18; compare also Seneca *Ep.* 77.1–2 (Puteoli); PW 7.126–87.

to Lionel Casson.[9]

■ **7** Luke apparently assumes that the normal route was the one which ran to the north of Crete. But for the route which went around the southern coast of Crete, in the lee of the island, compare Lucian *Navig.* 9.[10] κατὰ τὴν Κνίδον means "off Cnidus."[11] Salmone is on the northeast tip of Crete (Strabo 10.472, 475; Pliny *Nat. hist.* 4.58.71; *Stad.* 318, 355).

■ **8** Καλοὶ Λιμένες, "Fair Havens," is not mentioned elsewhere. Lasea (the spelling varies) perhaps lay to the east of Cape Matala/Lithinae.[12] A bay was there (open to the east) which is known today as Καλοὶ Λιμένες. παραλέγεσθαι means "to coast along."[13]

■ **9–11** This is an inserted episode about Paul, which disrupts the context; vs 12 connects with vs 8[14] or with vs 9a.[15] It is a free composition. Such a role for a prisoner is inconceivable.

■ **9** For dating according to the Jewish calendar, compare 20:6. νηστεία, "fast," was the Day of Atonement on the tenth of Tishri (September/October), five days before the feast of booths.[16] The rabbis counted the beginning of the time when sailing was dangerous from the time of the feast of booths. Is the fast mentioned here in order to suggest that Paul observed it? If so, the datum is part of the insertion (see above). This dating gives rise to a difficulty later on. The stay on Malta was supposed to have lasted for three months (28:11; cf. Josephus *Bell.* 2.203). This would result in a date probably too early for the continuation of the voyage to Rome. But Luke has obviously not squared the dates with one another, particularly since the reference to three months is a schematic detail. The difficulties are diminished if we see this as based on the Syrian-Jewish calendar, which Josephus used (the year begins on the nineteenth of October and the tenth of Tishri would then be the twenty-eighth of

October);[17] compare Vegetius *Epit. rei mil.* 4.39: "After this time [i.e., supply the eighteenth of the Kalends of October = September fourteenth] up until November eleventh, navigation is uncertain and more disposed to danger" (post hoc tempus usque in tertium idus Novembres incerta navigatio est et discrimini propior). From the eleventh of November until the tenth of March sailing ceased. For an illustration, compare the extraordinary measures of Claudius (Suetonius *Claud.* 18). Pliny (*Nat. hist.* 2.122) dates the resumption of sailing earlier.[18] *Mare clausum*, "closed sea," certainly does not mean that no ships traveled at all (cf., perhaps, Josephus *Bell.* 1.279, cf. 281).[19]

■ **10** The mixed construction ὅτι . . . μέλλειν ἔσεσθαι, "that . . . will be" (ὅτι with the accusative and infinitive), is possible because of the weakening of ὅτι.[20] ὕβρις means "injury."[21]

■ **11** Only in this passage are ranks distinguished; elsewhere only the general term ναῦται, "sailors," is used. It seems odd that later on the ναύκληρος = "owner of the ship" and the κυβερνήτης = "captain" do not appear at the time of the shipwreck—this is a further indication that this passage is an insertion. For the relationship between ranks, compare Plutarch *Mor.* 807b: "a pilot selects sailors and a ship-captain selects a pilot" (ναύτας μὲν ἐκλέγεται κυβερνήτης καὶ κυβερνήτην ναύκληρος). Oddly enough, it appears from our passage as if the centurion could make decisions about the voyage. But Luke does not really mean that. He only wants to show that all of the important people on the ship disagreed with Paul. Later on, we see that Paul was absolutely right. Ramsay concludes that this was a ship of the imperial merchant marine;[22] therefore the command would fall to the centurion (a lower-ranking officer!) if he were to come on board. Disregarding the actual impossibility of this, there

9 August Köster, *Das antike Seewesen* (Berlin: Schoetz & Parrhysius, 1923) 165; Casson, "The Isis," 55.

10 See Appendix 1; James Smith, *The Voyage and Shipwreck of St. Paul* (4th ed.; London: Longmans & Green, 1880) 75–76; Casson, "The Isis," 47–48.

11 For κατά as "off," see Frisk, *Le Périple*, 25: ὁ κατ' αὐτὴν διάπλους, "the voyage off it."

12 Cf. *Peutinger Table* 9.1 (see the note at 13:51, above) (Lisia?).

13 Frisk, *Le Périple*, 60.

14 Dibelius, *Studies*, 205.

15 Paul Wendland, *Die urchristlichen Literaturformen* (HNT 1:3; Tübingen: Mohr [Siebeck], 1912) 334; Haenchen, p. 700.

16 Str-B 2.771–72; Johannes Behm, "νῆστις," *TDNT* 4 (1967) 925.

17 E. Schwartz, *Christliche und jüdische Ostertafeln* (AGG 8:6; Berlin: Weidmann, 1905) 149.

18 See the comments on 28:11.

19 *SIG* 2 no. 810.

20 BDF § 397.6; Radermacher, *Grammatik*, 195–96.

21 BAG *s.v.*

22 Ramsay, *St. Paul*, 324–25.

is no evidence for an imperial merchant marine. There were corporations made up of shipowners, which provided supplies for the city of Rome (again, see Suetonius *Claud.* 18–19).[23]

■ **12** This connects with vs 8 or with vs 9a (see on vss 9–11 above). Now the basic plot continues. The various ranks no longer play a role. Originally οἱ πλείονες, "the majority," meant the majority of the sailors. With vs 11, the meaning is changed, that is, from vs 12 we see how this insertion came about:

Luke has pondered these words carefully. He gathers from them that there was a deliberation. Naturally only the important men took part. For Luke these were Paul, the centurion, the owner and the captain. The majority was for the fateful continuation of the voyage—thus Paul was against it, because he foresaw the outcome; not as a meteorologist or thanks to his great experience as a traveller . . . but from prophetic alliance with God.[24]

On the stretch from Lasea to Phoenix, see *Stad.* 323ff.[25] Φοῖνιξ, "Phoenix," is usually thought to be located in the bay east or west of the peninsula called Muros.[26] James Smith favors the eastern location (Lutro), arguing that it would be the best harbor on the southern coast of Crete, west of Cape Matala.[27] But this bay "looks" toward the east. We could certainly ask whether κατὰ λίβα, "toward the southwest," is reliable. A. Breusing argues for the eastern bay by taking the expression βλέπων κτλ., "looking, etc.," in a technical sense: looking in the direction in which these winds blow (and thus protected from them), contrary to the colloquial use of the term.[28] If this detail is correct, then the western bay is meant. For evaluating a harbor according to the wind conditions, compare

Arrian *Periplus maris Euxini* 4 (where λίψ means approximately west-southwest). The evaluation of the western harbor in terms of present unfavorable conditions for anchorage cannot simply be assumed for Luke's time. One must reckon with some changes since ancient times.[29] It is also possible that Luke confused the two bays. Ptolemy 3.17.3 distinguishes between Φοινικοῦς λιμήν (the western bay) and Φοίνιξ πόλις (the city Phineka) which lies to the east of it.[30] λίψ in classical Greek means the southwest, in the LXX it is most often the translation for נֶגֶב, "south," as well as דָּרוֹם, "south," and מַעֲרָב תֵּימָן, "the west"; in Egyptian papyri it means "the west."[31] χῶρος, "northwest," is equivalent to the Latin *caurus* or *corus*, according to Pliny *Nat. hist.* 2.119, "west-northwest."[32]

■ **13** Under normal conditions the distance could be covered in a day. αἴρω, "weigh anchor," is a technical term.[33]

■ **14** For the personification with ἔβαλεν, "struck down" (intransitive), compare Luke 8:23.[34] κατ᾽ αὐτῆς, "from the land," means from Crete, that is, from Mount Ida (after they had sailed around Cape Matala). εὐρακύλων, "northeaster," is a hybrid expression formed from εὖρος (east-southeast wind) and *Aquilo* (north-northeast wind) and is therefore self-contradictory; here it must mean "approximately northeast."[35]

■ **15** Since it was no longer possible to bring the bow of the ship into the wind, they allowed it to be driven by the wind.[36] τῷ ἀνέμῳ, "to the wind," may be taken (1) with

---

23 PW 16 "Navicularii," 1899–1932, esp. 1907 "Römische Zeit"; "Ναύκληρος," 1937–38; Jean Dauvillier, "A propos de la venue de saint Paul à Rome: Notes sur son procès et son voyage maritime," *BLE* 61 (1960) 17–21.

24 Haenchen, p. 709.

25 For κατανᾶν εἰς, "reach," see Frisk, *Le Périple*, 60.

26 Strabo 10.475; *Stad.* 328: "[Phoenix] the city has a harbor and an island" ([Φοῖνιξ] πόλις ἔχει λιμένα καὶ νῆσον); Smith, *Voyage*, 86ff; Balmer, *Romfahrt*, 319–26.

27 See Mittelmeerhandbuch IV (1935) 198.

28 Breusing, *Nautik*, 163.

29 R. M. Ogilvie, "Phoenix," *JTS* n.s. 9 (1958) 308–14.

30 PW 20.431–35.

31 Ibid.; see Appendix 1.

32 On the names for the winds, see *Beginnings* 5.338–44.

33 For ἆσσον, "close," with a positive (rather than comparative) sense, cf. BDF § 244.2.

34 Radermacher, *Grammatik*, 23.

35 *Beginnings* 5.344.

36 Breüsing, *Nautik*, 167–68; Chr. Voigt, "Die Romfahrt des Apostels Paulus," *Hansa* 53 (1916) 728; see

ἐπιδιδόναι, "gave way" (Lucian *Hermot.* 28: ἐπιδιδόναι τῇ πνεούσῃ αὐτόν, "surrenders himself to the wind"; compare the expansion in the Western text, which takes τῷ ἀνέμῳ with ἀντοφθαλμεῖν, "to face"!)[37] or (2) with ἀντοφθαλμεῖν, "to face."[38]

■ **16** ὑποδραμόντες means "screened from the wind by." Clauda (like most names from this region, this name has been passed on in various forms), modern Gozzo, lies about forty kilometers south of Phoenix (Pliny *Nat. hist.* 4.61; *Stad.* 328; Ptolemy 3.17.11). The lifeboat was to be hauled in so that it would not be destroyed by the waves.[39]

■ **17** The transition to the third person in this verse is striking. Is this intentional, or is it carelessness? The meaning of βοήθειαι, "measures," is not clear; is it a technical term? Compare Philo *Jos.* 33: ὥσπερ γὰρ κυβερνήτης ταῖς τῶν πνευμάτων μεταβολαῖς συμμεταβάλλει τὰς πρὸς εὔπλοιαν βοηθείας ("The pilot is helped to a successful voyage by means which change with the changes of the wind"). Does it mean that they used a block and tackle to take the lifeboat in, or that they provided the ship with "helps" (with the sense of a technical term) in that they "undergirded" it (this is evidenced for ancient warships)? How that would have been handled technically is debated: (1) With lines running the length of the ship, that is, over the deck. This corresponds to Egyptian pictures, but is out of the question for huge grain-hauling vessels. (2) With lines running lengthwise around the ship.[40] (3) With lines running transversely, inside the hold. Or (4) with lines running transversely around the ship.[41]

There are four possible meanings for χαλάσαντες κτλ., "lowered, etc.": (1) reefing the sail;[42] (2) the opposite—setting the sail (χαλᾶν as the opposite of συστέλλειν, "shorten"; cf. vs 15 as found in syp and others, συστέλλειν

τὰ ἱστία, "shorten the sails"; ἱστία is found instead of σκεῦος, "gear");[43] (3) lowering the main yard, which they had still been using, but with a storm sail;[44] or (4) letting down a sea anchor, in order to reduce the speed; see Plutarch *Mor.* 507a: "So when a ship has been caught by a wind, they try to check it, deadening its speed with cables and anchors" (νεὼς μὲν γὰρ ἁρπαγείσης ὑπὸ πνεύματος ἐπιλαμβάνονται σπείραις καὶ ἀγκύραις τὸ τάχος ἀμβλύνοντες). In Lucian *Tox.* 19[45] cables were thrown out as drags, not because of speed, but rather in order to cut down the impact of the waves.[46] The waters of Syrtis were feared because they were so shallow; Josephus *Bell.* 2.381: "Syrtes, whose very name strikes terror" (αἱ φοβεραὶ καὶ τοῖς ἀκούουσιν Σύρτεις); Strabo 17.835; Dio Chrys. 5.8–11.

■ **18** ἐκβολή, "throw the cargo overboard," is a technical term; compare vs 38; Jonah 1:5 LXX; Lucian *Merc. cond.* 1; Achilles Tatius 3.2.9: "The helmsman gave orders to jettison the cargo" (καὶ ὁ κυβερνήτης ἐκέλευε ῥίπτειν τὸν φόρτον); Josephus *Bell.* 1.279–80.

■ **20** Compare Thucydides 1.65. For the imperfect as the tense of narrative, compare vs 1. Compare Achilles Tatius 3.2.4: ῥίψαντες τὰς ἐλπίδας, "giving up all hope." At that time the only means of orientation was observation of the stars.

■ **21–26** A second inserted episode; vs 27 connects with vs 20. Verses 21–22 pick up the theme of vss 10–11. Now Paul can return to center stage after he has been proven right. But this scene is completely unreal:[47] a speech delivered on board ship at a time of extreme distress in the midst of a hurricane is highly unlikely. σταθείς, "came forward": like an orator before the tribune.

■ **21** ἀσιτία, "without food," does not refer to a lack of available food, but rather loss of appetite (seasickness! vss 33–36).

Köster, *Das antike Seewesen*, 140–41, regarding the reduced maneuverability of ancient ships.

37 Preuschen; *Beginnings* 4.331.
38 BAG *s.v.*
39 See further the comments on vs 30; Breusing, *Nautik*, 168–69.
40 Ibid., 170–84.
41 Smith, *Voyage*, 210–15; Balmer, *Romfahrt*, 160ff; see further *Beginnings* 5.345–54; PWSup 5.944–45 and Sup 4.776–82 (where it is argued that ὑποζωννύναι, "undergird," means the same as ζευγνύναι, "connect,

join," and would thus refer merely to repairing the damage).

42 Ramsay, *St. Paul*, 329.
43 *Beginnings* 4.333.
44 Balmer, *Romfahrt*, 355ff.
45 See Appendix 2.
46 Breusing, *Nautik*, 177–82.
47 Haenchen, pp. 709–10.

■ **22** This is an example of brachylogy.

■ **23-24** παρίσταμαι, "stand by," is a technical term in epiphanies;[48] ἐκολάσθην ὑπὸ τοῦ θεοῦ πολλὰ [κ]αὶ ὀνείροις μοι παρεστάθη καὶ ἐπενπόδων . . . ("I was chastened by God often, and he stood by me both in dreams and before my eyes").[49] The word order θεοῦ ἄγγελος, "an angel of the God," is Lukan.[50] The motif of a rescue from distress at sea by the intervention of a god (Isis, Serapis, Dioscuri) is widespread (Lucian *Navig.* 9).[51] Moreover, special divine protection in danger is a θεῖος ἀνήρ, "divine man," motif.[52]

■ **27** This verse originally connected with vs 20. In its present context, the prophecy of Paul is now fulfilled. διαφέρεσθαι means "to drift across." "Adria" was the name used for the sea at that time; compare Josephus *Vita* 15 which reports a shipwreck κατὰ μέσον τὸν Ἀδρίαν, "in the midst of the Sea of Adria," that is, on the journey to Rome; Ptolemy 3.17.1 "(Crete) is bounded on the West by the Adriatic sea" (περιορίζεται ἀπὸ μὲν δυσμῶν ὑπὸ τοῦ Ἀδριατικοῦ πελάγους); 3.4.1 "Silicia is encompassed on the East by the Adrian sea" (ἡ Σικελία περιέχεται . . . ἀπὸ δὲ ἀνατολῶν ὑπὸ τοῦ Ἀδρίου πελάγους; compare also 3.15.1). The distance from Clauda to Malta is about 470 nautical miles by air.[53] When the sailors "suspected" (ὑπενόουν) that they were nearing land, it was either because of the raging of the breakers[54] or because the sea anchor was dragging.[55] The objection against the latter interpretation, that the depth was too great—at first, still more than thirty meters—is invalid. Indeed, the mention of the number is for effect—Luke hardly stood by and counted as they were taking soundings! For the expression "land was drawing near to them," compare the paraphrase for "sight" in 21:3.

■ **28** ὀργυιά, "fathom" = 6 feet = 1.80 meters.

■ **29** Compare the following situations: Dio Chrys. 7.2: "when such a storm arose that we had great difficulty in reaching the Hollows of Euboea in safety; the crew ran their boat up a rough beach under the cliffs, where it was wrecked" (χειμῶνος δὲ γενομένου χαλεπῶς καὶ μόλις διεσώθημεν πρὸς τὰ κοῖλα τῆς Εὐβοίας· τὸ μὲν δὴ ἀκάτιον [lightweight vessel] εἰς τραχύν τινα αἰγιαλὸν ὑπὸ τοῖς κρημνοῖς ἐκβαλόντες διέφθειραν . . .); Lucian *Ver. hist.* 1.6: after a storm of seven days "at no great distance we saw a high, wooded island ringed about with sounding surf, which, however, was not rough" (καθορῶμεν οὐ πόρρω νῆσον ὑψηλὴν καὶ δασεῖαν, οὐ τραχεῖ περιηχον μένην τῷ κύματι).[56] The anchors had to be thrown out from the stern because in the storm it was no longer possible to turn the ship.[57]

■ **30** The conduct of the sailors is defended by those skilled in nautical affairs; they were certainly not planning to abandon ship. An escape by night, into the midst of the storm and the breakers, going toward an unknown shore, would have been suicidal. What we have here was a necessary maneuver—they wanted to cast out anchors from the bow as well. In the face of a prevailing wind, these had to be taken from the ship in the lifeboat,[58] then pulling on the anchor ropes would secure the ship.[59] According to this view the soldiers and Paul made a disastrous mistake. They were responsible for the shipwreck. It should be noted, however, that the escape of the crew is a motif in fiction (Achilles Tatius 3.3;

---

48 F. Pfister, "Epiphanie," PWSup 4.280; A. Cameron, "Inscriptions Relating to Sacral Manumission and Confession," *HTR* 32 (1939) 158, 161–62.

49 *Monumenta Asiae Minoris Antiqua* 4.279, lines 10ff.

50 Haenchen, p. 704.

51 See Appendix 1; Söder, *Die apokryphen Apostelgeschichten*, 162–71; PWSup 4.277–323.

52 Bieler, *Theios Aner* 1.119–20.

53 Breusing, *Nautik*, 189.

54 Smith, *Voyage*, 121; cf. B: προσαχεῖν which is a corruption for προσηχεῖν, "to resound"; gig s: *resonare*, "to resound."

55 Breusing, *Nautik*, 193.

56 See Appendix 3; cf. also Ps.-Clem. *Ep. ad Jas.* 14.4, included in the comments on vs 41 below.

57 Wolfgang Stammler, *Apostelgeschichte 27 in nautischer Beleuchtung und die ostdeutsche Bibelübersetzung des*

Mittelalters (Greifswalder Studien zur Lutherforschung und neuzeitlichen Geistesgeschichte 4; Berlin/Leipzig: de Gruyter, 1931), is of a different opinion.

58 σκάφη/scapha, "lifeboat," see E. Zinn, "ΑΠΟΡΟΣ ΣΩΤΗΡΙΑ, Horaz Carm III 29,62," ERANION: Festschrift für Hildebrecht Hommel (ed. Jürgen Kroymann; Tübingen: Niemeyer, 1961) 185ff.

59 Breusing, *Nautik*, 193–94.

Petronius 102, cf. 114). One might ask how the whole crew would have found places in the lifeboat, which would have to be assumed for such a planned escape?

■ **31** In any case, with his own new addition (vs 31), Luke allows no room for any interpretation other than his own.

■ **32** This verse again belongs to the source.

■ **33** This verse marks the beginning of another insertion devoted to Paul. Here, however, it is difficult to determine precisely where it begins, because Luke interferes in the composition of his source. Verse 39 could be connected with vs 32, but the reference to 276 persons in vs 37 is unmotivated, and must already have belonged to the source.[60] This source must have reported that they threw out the cargo until daybreak; note the doublet ἄχρι δὲ οὗ ἡμέρα ἤμελλεν γίνεσθαι, "as day was about to dawn" (vs 33), and ὅτε δὲ ἡμέρα ἐγένετο, "Now when it was day" (vs 39). κορεσθέντες δὲ τροφῆς, "And when they had eaten enough," could also derive from the source, and Luke himself could have developed his motif from it (as with vs 12). Thus the interpolation probably included vss 33–36.

■ **34** πρός with the genitive occurs only here in the New Testament; compare Thucydides 3.59.1 οὐ πρὸς τῆς ὑμετέρας δόξης τάδε ("These things are not consistent with your honor"); Josephus *Ant.* 16.313. For the imagery here, compare 1 Sam 14:45; 2 Sam 14:11; Luke 12:7; 21:18.

■ **35** This is not a reference to a celebration of the Eucharist (though the Western text hints at such by adding, after "eat," "having given also to us [ἐπιδοὺς καὶ ἡμῖν]"). The scene describes the way Christians customarily eat.[61]

■ **37** The number 276 is quite possible (Josephus *Vita* 15!);[62] here a piece of material from the source is present. The number has been explained as a "triangular number" (the sum of the numbers 1–24).[63] There is nothing in the passage, however, to suggest that the numbers are symbolic.

■ **38** Compare vs 18. This measure was necessary because they no longer had a lifeboat; therefore the entire ship had to be brought as close to land as possible.

■ **39** The present-day St. Paul's Bay on the northeast coast of Malta does not have a good beach. ἐξωθεῖν is a technical term meaning "to let run aground." For the whole impression here (storm—past the Syrtis—an unfamiliar beach—shipwreck—natives),[64] compare *1 Enoch* 101:4–5: "Do you not see the sailors of the ships, how their ships are tossed up and down by the billows and are shaken by the winds, and they become anxious? On this account (it is evident that) they are seized by fear, for they will discharge all their valuable property—the goods that are with them—into the sea" ([ὁρᾶ]τε τοὺς ναυκλήρους τοὺς πλωι[ζο]μένους τὴν θάλασσαν, ὑπὸ τοῦ κ[λύδω]νος καὶ χειμῶνος σεσα[λευ]μέ[να τὰ] πλοῖα αὐτῶν, καὶ χειμαζόμενοι πά[ν]τες φοβοῦνται, ἔξω δὲ τὰ [ἀγαθὰ πάντα] καὶ τὰ ὑπάρχοντα αὐτῶν ἐκβάλλο[υσιν] εἰς τὴν θάλασσαν).

■ **40** The ship is set free by throwing the anchor ropes into the sea. The rudders had been tied during the storm.[65] ἀρτέμων = *artemo*, the "foresail"; only with this sail set is the ship maneuverable.[66]

■ **41** The τόπος διθάλασσος, "shoal," could be a shoal or sandbank. There is such a shoal in St. Paul's Bay (today twelve meters below the water), but we must take into account changes since the time of Paul. Other interpretations for τόπος διθάλασσος include "spit of land" (cf. Ps.-Clem. *Ep. ad Jas.* 14.4: "the promontories and the rugged rocks of those places . . . and the meetings of the two seas, and the wild places" [τὰ ἀκρωτήρια καὶ τὰ τραχέα (vs 29!) τῶν τόπων . . . διθάλασσοι δὲ καὶ θηριώδεις τόποι], which Rufinus paraphrases: "headlands—rocky places—

---

60 Dibelius, *Studies*, 205.

61 Bo Reicke ("Die Mahlzeit mit Paulus auf den Wellen des Mittelmeers Act. 27,33–38," *ThZ* 4 [1948] 401–10) disagrees, though he must qualify his view: since non-Christian passengers also take part in the meal, this must be a "prefiguration" of the Eucharist. This is a curious ad hoc invention for the purpose of underlining the historicity of the scene.

62 B and sa read 76; this probably came about by taking ΠΛΟΙΩ‾COF‾ as ΠΛΟΙΩΩCOF, "about 76 in the boat," remembering that Luke usually used ὡς before numbers.

63 F. H. Colson, "Triangular Numbers in the New Testament," *JTS* 16 (1914–15) 72.

64 Cadbury, *Acts in History*, 24–25.

65 Breusing, *Nautik*, 102–3.

66 Ibid., 79–80; Köster, *Das antike Seewesen*, 121, 172–76.

but in fact promontories, that is, spits of land, which are beaten on both sides by the seething of a treacherous sea" [promontoria—loca confragosa—bithalassa vero loca, quae duplicibus undae fallacis aestibus verberantur]) or, finally, "channel," in this case between Malta and the island of Salmonetta.[67] ἐπικέλλειν τὴν ναῦν, "to run the vessel aground," is found in Homer *Od.* 9.148–49, 546. ἐρείδω, "stick," is also found in Homer; compare Virgil *Aen.* 5.206: "the bow hung where it crashed" (inlisaque prora pependit); on ἐλύετο, "was broken up," compare Achilles Tatius 3.5.1.

■ **42–43** Luke apparently inserted the reference to Paul into the source.

■ **44** Should ἐπί τινων, "on pieces," be understood as masculine ("on the shoulders of some," cf. 12:1; 15:5)? In this way one could at least understand the change of case with ἐπὶ. But the context favors taking it as a neuter. Xenophon Eph. 2.11.10: "But as they were held back by a contrary wind, and after the ship was torn apart almost into planks, some people arrived after being saved on a certain beach" (ἐναντίῳ δὲ πνεύματι κατεχόμενοι καὶ τῆς νεὼς διαρραγείσης μόλις ἐν σανίσι τινὲς σωθέντες ἐπ᾽ αἰγιαλοῦ τινος ἦλθον).

Excursus:
The Report about the Voyage

The report about the voyage is the only real account of travel experiences in Acts. Thus it cannot be explained with the help of the itinerary hypothesis. The style of Acts 27 differs totally and precisely from the earlier reports of voyages in which "we" appears. Of course Dibelius, the most resolute advocate of the itinerary, saw this. He extended the hypothesis (suggested by Wellhausen, Wendland), saying that here an existing literary description of a journey "served as a pattern, basis or source." It had been fitted into the book by the insertion of several episodes in which Paul "appears."[68] The theme of the insertions is Paul the deliverer. The fact of the matter is that the episodes in which Paul appears can be excised without leaving any gaps; indeed, at some points only in this way does the course of the narrative become understandable (vs 12!). That which remains is of a higher literary quality than any other part of the book.[69]

Haenchen points out that in Hellenistic novels travel adventures are closely tied to the characters in the plot. Thus one could not just appropriate a ready-made description from somewhere or other. But one need not conceive of the process in such a mechanical way. One need only recognize that there was an established stylistic model and that, as such, it could be detached from the characters in the plot, as we see quite clearly in Achilles Tatius. The first-person plural is a typical device in these descriptions. Haenchen argues that since soldiers are already mentioned in the source, this must already have been an account of real adventures. But he passes too quickly over the observation that Paul fails to appear and that for this reason we cannot really speak of an actual recounting of an experience. We also ought to note that there is a discrepancy between the description of events up to Malta, and the account from Malta to Rome: after Malta, Paul no longer appears as a prisoner. Thus, the sense of "we" shifts correspondingly. One could take this as an indication that in chapter 27 Luke was using a source document from a companion of Paul.[70] The other possibility is that Luke was working according to a model which he had in his mind.[71]

67 Smith, *Voyage*, 143; Balmer, *Romfahrt*, 413ff.

68 Dibelius, *Studies*, 204–6; cf. Julius Wellhausen, "Noten zur Apostelgeschichte," NGG (1907) 17; idem, "Kritische Analyse der Apostelgeschichte," AGG Neue Folge Band 15, Nro. 2 (1914) and (Berlin: Weidmann, 1914) 2; Paul Wendland, *Die urchristlichen Literaturformen* (HNT 1:2–3; 2d ed.; Tübingen: Mohr [Siebeck], 1912) 324 n. 4.

69 Cf. the material in Norden, *Agnostos Theos*, 313, and the examples from Lucian and Achilles Tatius included in the appendices.

70 Haenchen, pp. 708–11.

71 In addition to the literature cited in the notes for this chapter, see the following: August Köster, *Die Nautik im Altertum* (Berlin: Mittler, 1914); E. de St. Denis, "La vitesse des navires anciens," *Revue Archéologique*, 6th ser. 28 (1941) 121ff; for a different view, Casson, "Speed Under Sail," and idem, "The Isis"; B. H. D. Hermesdorf, "Sint Paulus temidden van zeerechtlijke vraagstukken," *Stud. Cath.* 9 (1954) 237–48; PWSup 4.776–82 and Sup 5.906–62; E. Haenchen, "Acta 27," *Zeit und Geschichte: Dankesgabe an Rudolf Bultmann zum 80. Geburtstag* (ed. Erich Dinkler; Tübingen: Mohr [Siebeck], 1964) 235–54.

28

The Stay in Malta; Continuation of the Journey and Arrival in Rome

1 After we had escaped, we then learned that the island was called Malta. 2/ And the natives showed us unusual kindness, for they kindled a fire and welcomed us all, because it had begun to rain and was cold. 3/ Paul had gathered a bundle of sticks and put them on the fire, when a viper came out because of the heat and fastened on his hand. 4/ When the natives saw the creature hanging from his hand, they said to one another, "No doubt this man is a murderer. Though he has escaped from the sea, justice [or: Dike] has not allowed him to live." 5/ He, however, shook off the creature into the fire and suffered no harm. 6/ They waited, expecting him to swell up or suddenly fall down dead; but when they had waited a long time and saw no misfortune come to him, they changed their minds and said that he was a god.

7 Now in the neighborhood of that place were lands belonging to the chief man of the island, named Publius, who received us and entertained us hospitably for three days. 8/ It happened that the father of Publius lay sick with fever and dysentery; and Paul visited him and prayed, and putting his hands on him healed him. 9/ And when this had taken place, the rest of the people on the island who had diseases also came and were cured. 10/ They presented many gifts to us; and when we sailed, they put on board whatever we needed.

11 After three months we set sail in a ship which had wintered in the island, a ship of Alexandria, with the Twin Brothers as figurehead. 12/ Putting in at Syracuse, we stayed there for three days. 13/ And from there we made a circuit and arrived at Rhegium; and after one day a south wind sprang up, and on the second day we came to Puteoli. 14/ There we found brethren, and were invited to stay with them for seven days. And so we came to Rome. 15/ And the brethren there, when they heard of us, came as far as the Forum of Appius and Three Taverns to meet us. On seeing them Paul thanked God and took courage. 16/ And when we came into Rome, Paul was allowed to stay by himself, with the soldier that guarded him.

■ **1** For Malta, see Strabo 17.832–34.[1]

■ **2** βάρβαροι, "natives": they spoke a Punic dialect.[2] As soon as a concrete scene is described the "we" becomes a distinct group. Luke has certainly given no indication that the "we" has shifted its meaning. That Paul is a prisoner is now forgotten. The military retinue disappears completely.

■ **3–4** This anecdote of secular character[3] is recounted in a polished episodic style. It appears to be based on a literary motif; compare the epitaph from the *Palatine Anthology* 7.290:[4] "The shipwrecked mariner had escaped the whirlwind and the fury of the deadly sea, and as he was lying on the Libyan sand not far from the beach, deep in his last sleep, naked and exhausted by the unhappy wreck, a baneful viper slew him. Why did he struggle with the waves in vain, escaping then the fate that was his lot on the land?" (Λαίλαπα καὶ μανίην ὀλοῆς προφυγόντα θαλάσσης ναυηγόν, Λιβυκαῖς κείμενον ἐν ψαμάθοις, οὐχ ἑκὰς ἠιόνων, πυμάτῳ βεβαρημένον ὕπνῳ, γυμνόν, ἀπὸ στυγερῆς ὡς κάμε ναυφθορίης, ἔκτανε λυγρὸς ἔχις. τί μάτην πρὸς κύματ᾽ ἐμόχθει, τὴν ἐπὶ γῆς φεύγων μοῖραν ὀφειλομένην). Concerning ἔχιδνα, "viper," one ought not ask whether there are or were poisonous snakes on Malta; moreover, poisonous snakes do not bite and then hang on. The intention here is to tell of a genuine miracle. Nor should one ask whether there was a Punic equivalent to the deity Δίκη, "Justice." The author puts these words into the mouths of the natives.

■ **6** The present participle ("expecting") is used for something which happened previously (it represents the imperfect).[5] The construction in vs 6b (genitive absolute with the following participle μεταβαλόμενοι, "they changed their minds") is grammatically very harsh. The incident is the most extreme example of the θεῖος ἀνήρ, "divine man," motif in Acts. Unlike the incident reported in 14:11–18, no critical reservations are expressed,[6] nevertheless, one should recall that the motif has analogies in Jewish apocalyptic literature.[7] In the apocryphal acts the motif is widespread; *Acts Thom.* 106: "But the crowd worshiped him as a god" (τὸ δὲ πλῆθος ὥσπερ θεὸν προσεκύνουν αὐτόν); compare *Acts of Peter* 5.29.[8] For the motif of the θεῖος ἀνήρ and the harmless beasts, compare Plutarch *Cleom.* 39; Lucian *Philops.* 11.[9]

■ **7** For ὁ πρῶτος τῆς νήσου, "the chief man of the island," compare the following inscriptions: [munic]ipi Mel(itensium) primus omni[um],[10] "the foremost citizen of all those of the town of the Maltese"; πρῶτος Μελιταίων καὶ πάτρων (patronus) . . . ,[11] "chief man of the Militians and patron. . . ."[12]

■ **8** The plural πυρετοί, "fever," was usual medical terminology. But specialized medical knowledge (on the part of Luke the physician) is as little evident here as in vs 6.

■ **9–10** It is quite absurd to read out of ἡμᾶς, "us," and ἐθεραπεύοντο, "were cured" (Harnack: they were "treated"), that Luke the physician gave assistance.[13] The cures did not come about because of medical treatment, but because of miraculous power. The intention is to give a final impression of Paul before his entrance into Rome. This passage is instructive for our evaluation of the we-narrative: it was not an eyewitness account.

■ **11** On "three months," compare Josephus *Bell.* 2.203: sailing resumed in February/March; according to Vegetius on the tenth of March;[14] according to Pliny *Nat. hist.* 2.122, with the Favonian wind in February. The *navigium Isidis*, "voyage of Isis," is the fifth of March (the proclamation of the πλοιαφέσια, launching of the ship of Isis at the Isis festival, Apuleius *Met.* 11.5, 17).[15] Is παράσημον, "figurehead," used as an adjective? A better explanation is that this is a mechanically attached dative (cf. ὀνόματι, "by name").[16] παράσημον was the ship's

---

1   A. Mayr, *Die Insel Malta im Altertum* (Munich: Beck, 1909); *DACL* 10.1318–42.

2   Bilingual inscriptions are found in *CIG* 3.5753, and *CIS* 1.124.

3   Dibelius, *Studies*, 8, 204–6.

4   The translation is from LCL, *Greek Anthology* 2.159.

5   BDF § 339.3.

6   According to Dibelius (*Studies*, 214) this represents "not a Christian but a pagan point of view."

7   O'Neill, *Theology*, 142–46.

8   Söder, *Die apokryphen Apostelgeschichten*, 95–99.

9   Bieler, *Theios Aner* 1.108.

10   *CIL* 10.7495 (= Dessau 5415).

11   *IG* 14.601.

12   A. Mayr, *Die Insel Malta im Altertum* (Munich: Beck, 1909) 106–7; Wikenhauser, *Apostelgeschichte*, 345–46.

13   Cf. Adolf Harnack, *Luke the Physician: The Author of the Third Gospel and the Acts of the Apostles* (Crown Theological Library 19; London: Williams & Norgate; New York: Putnam, 1907) 15–16, 61–62.

14   See the comments on 27:9.

15   Nilsson, *Geschichte* 2.624–26.

16   BDF § 198.7: "a ship, insignia the Dioscuri."

figurehead (Plutarch *Mor.* 247–48: "[He sailed] in a vessel which had a lion as its figurehead at the prow, and a serpent at the stern" [πλοίῳ λέοντα μὲν ἔχοντι πρῴραθεν ἐπίσημον, ἐκ δὲ πρύμνης δράκοντα]), or a picture painted on both sides of the bow beneath which was the name of that which was portrayed. Thus the word παράσημον also came to be used for the ship's name; compare the "Isis," Lucian *Navig.* 5: At the rear of the ship, as a figurehead, was a goose, "and correspondingly at the opposite end, the prow juts right out in front, with figures of the goddess, Isis, after whom the ship was named, on either side" (καταντικρὺ δ᾽ ἀνάλογον ἡ πρῷρα ὑπερβέβηκεν ἐς τὸ πρόσω ἀπομηκυνομένη, τὴν ἐπώνυμον τῆς νεὼς θεὸν ἔχουσα τὴν Ἶσιν ἑκατέρωθεν); Plutarch *Mor.* 162a: "he had ascertained the name of the captain and of the pilot, and the ship's emblem" (πυθόμενον τοῦ τε ναυκλήρου τοὔνομα καὶ τοῦ κυβερνήτου καὶ τῆς νεὼς τὸ παράσημον).

The Dioscuri (Castor and Pollux, twin sons of Zeus) were deliverers in times of distress at sea (cf. Lucian *Navig.* 9; Epictetus 2.18.29).[17] No further mention is made of a military escort.

■ **13** περιελθόντες, "we sailed along the coast," is used of the voyage along the coast;[18] περιελόντες B, ℵ*, "they took away," does not make sense.[19] The explanation of this as "weigh anchor" is only speculation. From Rhegium to Puteoli is about 350 kilometers. This would mean an average speed of five knots, which would be fitting for that time.[20] At that time of year Puteoli (modern Pozzuoli) was still the most important port in Italy for overseas traffic. Later it was surpassed by Ostia, which was built up by Claudius (Seneca *Ep.* 77).[21] The usual route leaving Puteoli was the Via Campana to Capua, and from there the Via Appia.

■ **14** Paul's time was at his own disposal. Verse 14b (cf. vs 16) is apparently a Lukan anticipation, preparing for the meeting with the brethren from Rome.[22]

■ **15** Here is the only mention of the Roman congregation. The Forum of Appius was forty-three miles from Rome;[23] Horace *Sat.* 1.5.3: "Next came Appii Forum, crammed with boatmen and stingy tavern-keepers" (inde Forum Appi differtum nautis cauponibus atque malignis). "Three Taverns" was thirty-three miles from the city.

■ **16** Luke has redactionally anticipated Paul's arrival in Rome in vs 14b. After vs 16, the "we" disappears, once again after the arrival at a destination (cf. Europe/Philippi, Palestine/Jerusalem before his arrest). The description is in purely Lukan style. Luke knows that there already is a congregation in Rome; nevertheless, he wishes to depict Paul as the pioneer of Christianity. For that reason the congregation appears—only to be greeted by Paul—and then just as quickly disappears from Luke's account. The Koine and Western texts have inserted a surrendering of the prisoners to the στρατοπεδάρχης (or -os), "captain of the guard." This probably means the prefect of the Praetorian guard; compare Pliny *Ep.* 10.57.2: Trajan orders, "He must be sent in chains to the officers in command of my imperial guards" (vinctus mitti ad praefectos praetorii mei). The Western text also mentions the παρεμβολή, the Praetorian barracks at the Porta Viminalis (Tacitus *Hist.* 1.31, etc.). The Old Latin MS gig freely translates στρατοπεδάρχης as *princeps peregrinorum* = commander of the courier corps (the *frumentarii*), but apparently this was first organized by Trajan.[24] The translator has anachronistically inserted the conditions of a later time into the time of Paul. As a rule, a prisoner was given over to two soldiers.[25] It was possible to inquire about his affairs (Ulpian *Dig.* 4.6.10). In regard to the rented house, see Ulpian *Dig.* 48.2.3. For the conditions during an investigation,

17 For the passage from Lucian, see Appendix 1; F. G. Dölger, "Dioskuroi," *Antike und Christentum* 6 (1950) 276–85; PW 5.1087–1123; *RAC* 3.1122–38; Betz, *Lukian*, 173.

18 Preuschen.

19 See BAG *s.v.* περιαιρέω.

20 Casson, "Speed Under Sail," 140.

21 On the decline of Puteoli, see *OGIS* 595; *DACL* 14.1673–87; Michael Rostovtzeff, *Gesellschaft und Wirtschaft im römischen Kaiserreich* (2 vols.; Leipzig: Quelle & Meyer, 1929) 1.134–40. For a description of the arrival of a new god in the city from Phoenicia

22 Haenchen (p. 719) understands this differently: 14a was inserted by Luke.

23 The forty-third milestone has been discovered, cf. *CIL* 10.6825; see *Peutinger Table* 6.2; *Itinerarium Antoninianum*, p. 107 Wessely.

24 PW 7.122–25.

25 The type of arrest envisioned here, *militi tradere*, is described by Theodor Mommsen, *Römisches Strafrecht* (Leipzig: Duncker & Humblot, 1899) 317 n. 5; PW 4.1896–99.

(in the year 79 C.E.), see the comments on 13:8; also see *OGIS* 594.

compare also the Second Edict of Augustus from Cyrene.[26]

---

26   See Appendix 10.

28

In Rome

17 After three days he called together the local leaders of the Jews; and when they had gathered, he said to them, "Brethren, though I had done nothing against the people or the customs of our fathers, yet I was delivered prisoner from Jerusalem into the hands of the Romans. 18/ When they had examined me, they wished to set me at liberty, because there was no reason for the death penalty in my case. 19/ But when the Jews objected, I was compelled to appeal to Caesar—though I had no charge to bring against my nation. 20/ For this reason therefore I have asked to see you and speak with you, since it is because of the hope of Israel that I am bound with this chain." 21/ And they said to him, "We have received no letters from Judea about you, and none of the brethren coming here has reported or spoken any evil about you. 22/ But we desire to hear from you what your views are; for with regard to this sect we know that everywhere it is spoken against."

23 When they had appointed a day for him, they came to him at his lodging in great numbers. And he expounded the matter to them from morning till evening, testifying to the kingdom of God and trying to convince them about Jesus both from the law of Moses and from the prophets. 24/ And some were convinced by what he said, while others disbelieved. 25/ So, as they disagreed among themselves, they departed, after Paul had made one statement: "The Holy Spirit was right in saying to your fathers through Isaiah the prophet:

26/ 'Go to this people, and say,
You shall indeed hear but never understand,
and you shall indeed see but never perceive.
27/ For this people's heart has grown dull,
and their ears are heavy of hearing,
and their eyes they have closed;
lest they should perceive with their eyes,
and hear with their ears,
and understand with their heart,
and turn for me to heal them.'

28/ Let it be known to you then that this salvation of God has been sent to the Gentiles; they will listen."

30 And he lived there two whole years at his own expense, and welcomed all who came to him, 31/ preaching the kingdom of God and teaching about the Lord Jesus Christ quite openly and unhindered.

■ **17** This is the final example of Paul's schematized preaching first to Jews at the synagogue. For this purpose Luke cannot make use of any already existing Christian congregation—Paul must preach first to the Jews. The fundamental significance of the schema becomes crystal clear. At the same time, the goal of the book is evident: the (spatial) goal of the world mission has been reached, and the transition from the primitive church to the church of Luke's day is portrayed. The Lukan picture of Paul and his understanding of the Law, the Old Testament, and Israel within the context of salvation history are once more unveiled. The reader recognizes that the Jews had a part in Paul's imprisonment by the indication, "from Jerusalem . . . into the hands of the Romans." The formulation is reminiscent of the passion-kerygma (Luke 9:22; 24:7). Jews in Rome had not formed themselves into an organized whole.[1] For πρῶτοι, "leaders," compare Luke 19:47; Acts 13:50; 25:2; Josephus *Ant.* 11.141.

■ **18–19** The account here is not consistent with what has been said earlier. What had previously been suppressed comes out here: the role of "the Jews" [*sic*]. Compare 23:29; 25:8, 25; 26:31. To make a point, Luke permits the contradiction to his own account to stand (25:9–25!).

■ **20** Compare 26:6–7. The construction is unclear and grammatically difficult, whether translated "I have asked to be permitted to see you," or "I have asked you here, to see you."

■ **21–22** The Jews speak as if there were still no Christians in Rome.[2]

■ **23** This is a typical Lukan summary of the Christian message, as in 8:12 and 19:8.[3] περὶ τοῦ Ἰησοῦ, "about Jesus," includes the whole ministry (including death and resurrection), therefore the content of the Gospel or of the kerygmatic summaries such as we find in 2:22–23. On the proof from the Scriptures relating to Jesus, com-

pare Luke 24:26–27.[4] For τάσσεσθαι ἡμέραν, "to appoint a day," compare 2 Macc 3:14 and 14:21. ξενία, "lodging" (cf. vs 30, μίσθωνα, "hired dwelling"; *RSV* margin) occurs with the concrete meaning "inn."[5]

■ **24–25** The picture of Judaism divided within itself is presented here for the last time. Luke no longer counts on the success of the Christian mission with "the Jews." In οἱ μὲν ἐπείθοντο, "some were convinced," the emphasis is not that, nevertheless, some were converted (cf. 23:9).[6] The scene has been constructed with the express purpose of conveying the impression that the situation with the Jews was hopeless. In contrast to Paul (Romans 9—11), Luke does not look beyond the present hardening to a future conversion of Israel. Rather, the time of the Gentile church has now broken in—this church has taken possession of the inheritance of Israel. The schema is completed. This third declaration about turning away from the Jews and turning toward the Gentiles (cf. in Asia Minor 13:46; in Greece 18:6) is final. It is not "by chance" and it cannot be explained psychologically, but rather is shown from the Scriptures to be God's plan. For καλῶς, "right," compare Mark 7:6 and Papyrus Egerton II: καλῶς Ἡ[σαίας περὶ ὑ]μῶν ἐπ[ρο]φ(ήτευσεν) εἰπών . . . ("rightly did Isaiah prophesy about you, saying . . .").[7]

■ **26–27** The quotation (Isa 6:9–10) follows the LXX almost exactly. This passage also plays a role elsewhere (cf. Mark 4:12 and pars.; John 12:39–40; Justin *Dial.* ‡2.2; 33.1; 69.4). The agreement with Matt 13:14–15 is striking. There we also find the wording of the LXX— contrary to the usual situation in Matthew, and contrary to Mark.[8]

■ **28** A summary, in Lukan language.

■ **30–31** The final point is made clearly: ἀκωλύτως, "unhindered"—an appeal to Rome. The reference to the διετία, "two years," certainly assumes that this situation of Paul

1   Schürer, *History* 3:1.95–102. Jean-Baptiste Frey, "Les communautés juives à Rome aux premiers temps de l'Église," *RechSR* 20 (1930) 269–97, 21 (1931) 129–68; idem, *CII* 1.53–55; H. J. Leon, *The Jews of Ancient Rome* (Philadelphia: Jewish Publication Society of America, 1960). Of a different opinion is George La Piana, "Foreign Groups in Rome during the First Centuries of the Empire," *HTR* 20 (1927) 183–403.

2   See the comments on vs 17.

3   Conzelmann, *Theology*, 218; on βασιλεία τοῦ θεοῦ, "Kingdom of God," see ibid., 113–19.

4   See the comments on 3:21–26 and 17:3.

5   BAG *s.v.*; Gustav Stählin, "ξένος," *TDNT* 5 (1967) 19 n. 137.

6   Haenchen, pp. 723–24.

7   Joachim Gnilka, *Die Verstockung Israels: Isaias 6,9–10 in der Theologie der Synoptiker* (SANT 3; Munich: Kösel, 1961).

8   Is this an interpolation in Matthew? That is the view of Krister Stendahl, *The School of St. Matthew and Its Use of the Old Testament* (Uppsala, 1954; reprinted Philadelphia: Fortress, 1968) 131.

was terminated. The farewell speech in Miletus leaves no doubt as to how this came about: Paul was executed. But Luke did not wish to tell about that. The purpose of the book has been fully achieved; therefore we ought to reject all hypotheses which understand the book as incomplete or which declare the ending to be accidental.

Excursus:
Four Hypotheses Regarding the Conclusion of the Book

There are four hypotheses regarding the ending of the book. (1) Luke had planned to write a third volume.[9] He hinted at this already in the proem, when he called the Gospel of Luke the πρῶτος, "first," rather than the πρότερος λόγος, "former book." But this "philology" is misleading,[10] and this view fails to recognize the well-planned design of the work as a whole: here is expressed a comprehensive theological conception, an understanding of the epochs of salvation history and of the history of the church, of the continuity between the primitive church and the present, which is both established and represented by Paul. (2) Acts was composed before Paul's trial had been completed.[11] But the farewell address in 20:18–35 argues against

this. Furthermore, Luke's Gospel was not written until after 70 (Luke 21:20–24) and its existence is presupposed in Acts. (3) According to Roman law, the case would have been dismissed after two years if the plaintiff had failed to appear by that time (in this case the plaintiff was the representative of the Sanhedrin).[12] But was a plaintiff necessary in the case of a *remissio* (Pliny *Ep.* 10.96!)? The Second Edict of Cyrene allows us to answer the question in the negative.[13] In any case, Luke does not hint at anything like this. The decisive text is the edict cited in Appendix 11.[14] Neither this text nor the others which have been cited lend support to this hypothesis (Pliny *Ep.* 10.56; Philo *Flacc.* 128–29: The case of Lampou was drawn out for more than two years; nothing is said, however, about this being the longest duration allowed); Josephus *Vita* 13–14 speaks against it.[15] (4) Paul's martyrdom was originally narrated, but was then removed (in order to connect up with the *Actus Vercellenses;* this begins with the departure for Spain).[16] The ending of the book does not appear to be fragmentary, however, and nothing can be proved by the enigmatic passage in the *Muratorian Canon.*[17]

---

9   Ramsay, *St. Paul,* 27–28; Theodor Zahn, "Das dritte Buch des Lukas," *NKZ* 28 (1917) 373–95.

10 See the comments on 1:1.

11 Adolf Harnack, *Neue Untersuchungen zur Apostelgeschichte und zur Abfassungszeit der synoptischen Evangelien* (Beiträge zur Einleitung in das Neue Testament 4; Leipzig: Hinrich, 1911) 68–69; cf. the English trans., *The Date of the Acts and of the Synoptic Gospels* (New Testament Studies 4; Crown Theological Library 33; London: Williams & Norgate; New York: Putnam, 1911) 93–99.

12 Thus Eger, *Rechtsgeschichtliches.*

13 See Appendix 10. ̈

14 The reconstruction of BGU 628 in Appendix 11 is by Ludwig Mitteis in L. Mitteis and U. Wilcken, *Grundzüge und Chrestomathie der Papyruskunde* (2 vols.; Leipzig/Berlin: Teubner, 1912) 2:2.417–48.

15 For the rest, see Haenchen, p. 724 n. 3.

16 Fridrich Pfister, "Die zweimalige römische Gefangenschaft und die spanische Reise des Apostels Paulus und der Schluss der Apostelgeschichte," *ZNW* 14 (1913) 216–21; cf. *Beginnings* 5.336–37, 495.

17 See the Introduction, p. xxxii. On this whole question, see Trocmé, *Livre des Actes,* 34–37, and O'Neill, *Theology,* passim.

**Appendices
Bibliography
Indices**

Appendix 1
Lucian *Navigium* 7–9

(Karl Jacobitz, ed., *Luciani Samosatensis Opera* [Bibliotheca scriptorum graecorum et romanorum Teubneriana; Leipzig: Teubner, 1909–12] 3.216–17)

7 .... ΛΥΚ. Οὔχ, ὦ Τιμόλαε, ἀλλὰ νῦν ἡδέως ἂν ἀκούσαιμεν. ΤΙΜ. Ὁ ναύκληρος αὐτὸς διηγεῖτό μοι, χρηστὸς ἀνὴρ καὶ προσομιλῆσαι δεξιός. ἔφη δὲ ἀπὸ τῆς Φάρου ἀπάραντας οὐ πάνυ βιαίῳ πνεύματι ἑβδομαίους ἰδεῖν τὸν Ἀκάμαντα, εἶτα ζεφύρου ἀντιπνεύσαντος ἀπενεχθῆναι πλαγίους ἄχρι Σιδῶνος, ἐκεῖθεν δὲ χειμῶνι μεγάλῳ περιπεσόντας δεκάτῃ ἐπὶ Χελιδονέας διὰ τοῦ Αὐλῶνος ἐλθεῖν, ἔνθα δὴ παρὰ μικρὸν ὑποβρυχίους δῦναι ἅπαντας. 8. οἶδα δέ ποτε καὶ αὐτὸς παραπλεύσας Χελιδονέας ἡλίκον ἐν τῷ τόπῳ ἀνίσταται τὸ κῦμα, καὶ μάλιστα περὶ τὸν λίβα, ὁπόταν ἐπιλάβῃ καὶ τοῦ νότου· κατ' ἐκεῖνο γὰρ δὴ συμβαίνει μερίζεσθαι τὸ Παμφύλιον ἀπὸ τῆς Λυκιακῆς θαλάττης, καὶ ὁ κλύδων ἅτε ἀπὸ πολλῶν ῥευμάτων περὶ τῷ ἀκρωτηρίῳ σχιζόμενος— ἀπόξυροι δέ εἰσι πέτραι καὶ ὀξεῖαι παραθηγόμεναι τῷ κλύσματι—καὶ φοβερωτάτην ποιεῖ τὴν κυματωγὴν καὶ τὸν ἦχον μέγαν, καὶ τὸ κῦμα πολλάκις αὐτῷ ἰσομέγεθες τῷ σκοπέλῳ. 9. τοιαῦτα καὶ σφᾶς καταλαβεῖν ἔφασκεν ὁ ναύκληρος ἔτι καὶ νυκτὸς οὔσης καὶ ζόφου ἀκριβοῦς· ἀλλὰ πρὸς τὴν οἰμωγὴν αὐτῶν ἐπικλασθέντας τοὺς θεοὺς πῦρ τε ἀναδεῖξαι ἀπὸ τῆς Λυκίας, ὡς γνωρίσαι τὸν τόπον ἐκεῖνον, καί τινα λαμπρὸν ἀστέρα Διοσκούρων τὸν ἕτερον ἐπικαθίσαι τῷ καρχησίῳ καὶ κατευθῦναι τὴν ναῦν ἐπὶ τὰ λαιὰ ἐς τὸ πέλαγος ἤδη τῷ κρημνῷ προσφερομένην· τοὐντεῦθεν δὲ ἅπαξ τῆς ὀρθῆς ἐκπεσόντας διὰ τοῦ Αἰγαίου πλεύσαντας ἑβδομηκοστῇ ἀπ' Αἰγύπτου ἡμέρα πρὸς ἀντίους τοὺς ἐτησίας πλαγιάζοντας ἐς Πειραιᾶ χθὲς καθορμίσασθαι τοσοῦτον ἀποσυρέντας ἐς τὸ κάτω, οὓς ἔδει τὴν Κρήτην δεξιὰν λαβόντας ὑπὲρ τὴν Μαλέαν πλεύσαντας ἤδη εἶναι ἐν Ἰταλίᾳ. ΛΥΚ. Νὴ Δία, θαυμάσιόν τινα φὴς κυβερνήτην τὸν Ἥρωνα ἢ τοῦ Νηρέως ἡλικιώτην, ὃς τοσοῦτον ἀπεσφάλη τῆς ὁδοῦ.

[7] . . . *Lycinus*

No, Timolaus, but I'd very much like to.

Timolaus

The captain himself told me—a good man, and good company. When they left Pharos, he said, the wind was not very strong, and they sighted Acamas in seven days. Then it blew against them from the west, and they were driven abeam to Sidon. After Sidon a severe storm broke and carried them through Aulon to reach the Chelidonenses on the tenth day. There they were all nearly drowned. [8] I myself have sailed by the Chelidonenses, and I know the size of the waves there, especially in a sou'westerly gale with a touch of south; this, you see, happens to be where the Pamphylian and Lycian seas divide. The swell is driven by numerous currents and is split on the headland—the rocks are knife-edged, razor-sharp at the sea's edge. So the breakers are terrifying and make a great din, and the wave is often as high as the cliff itself. [9] This is what the captain said they found when it was still night and pitch dark. But the gods were moved by their lamentations, and showed fire from Lycia, so that they knew the place. One of the Dioscuri put a bright star on the masthead, and guided the ship in a turn to port into the open sea, just as it was driving on to the cliff. Then, having now lost their course, they sailed across the Aegean beating up with the trade winds against them, and yesterday, seventy days after leaving Egypt, they anchored in Piraeus, after being driven so far downwind. They should have kept Crete to starboard, and sailed beyond Malea so as to be in Italy by now.

Lycinus

Upon my word, that's an amazing pilot you speak of, this Heron, as old as Nereus, who went so far astray.

Appendix 2
Lucian *Toxaris* 19–20

(Karl Jacobitz, ed., *Luciani Samosatensis Opera* [Bibliotheca scriptorum graecorum et romanorum Teubneriana; Leipzig: Teubner, 1909–12] 2.276–78)

19. ΜΝΗΣ . . . διηγεῖτο δέ μοι περὶ αὐτοῦ Σίμυλος ὁ ναύκληρος ὁ Μεγαρικὸς ἐπομοσάμενος ἦ μὴν αὐτὸς ἑωρακέναι τὸ ἔργον· πλεῖν μὲν γὰρ ἔφη ἐξ Ἰταλίας Ἀθήναζε περὶ δύσιν Πλειάδος συλλογιμαίους τινὰς ἀνθρώπους κομίζων, ἐν δὲ τούτοις εἶναι καὶ τὸν Εὐθύδικον καὶ μετ' αὐτοῦ Δάμωνα, Χαλκιδέα καὶ τοῦτον, ἑταῖρον

[19] *Mnesippus*

. . . It was repeated to me by Simylus, the sea-captain of Megara, who took his solemn oath that he himself had seen the deed. He said that he was making a voyage from Italy to Athens at about the season of the setting of the Pleiades [26 October], carrying a

αὐτοῦ· ἡλικιώτας δὲ εἶναι, τὸν μὲν Εὐθύδικον ἐρρωμένον καὶ καρτερόν, τὸν δὲ Δάμωνα ὕπωχρον καὶ ἀσθενικόν, ἄρτι ἐκ νόσου μακρᾶς, ὡς ἐδόκει, ἀνιστάμενον. ἄχρι μὲν οὖν Σικελίας εὐτυχῶς διαπλεῦσαι ἔφη ὁ Σίμυλος σφᾶς· ἐπεὶ δὲ τὸν πορθμὸν διαπεράσαντες ἐν αὐτῷ ἤδη τῷ Ἰονίῳ ἔπλεον, χειμῶνα μέγιστον ἐπιπεσεῖν αὐτοῖς. καὶ τὰ μὲν πολλὰ τί ἄν τις λέγοι, τρικυμίας τινὰς καὶ στρο-βίλους καὶ χαλάζας καὶ ἄλλα ὅσα χειμῶνος κακά· ἐπεὶ δὲ ἤδη σφᾶς κατὰ τὴν Ζάκυνθον εἶναι ἀπὸ ψιλῆς τῆς κεραίας πλέοντας, ἔτι καὶ σπείρας τινὰς ἐπισυρομένους, ὡς τὸ ῥόθιον ἐπιδέχεσθαι τῆς ὁρμῆς, περὶ μέσας νύκτας οἷον ἐν τοσούτῳ σάλῳ ναυτιάσαντα τὸν Δάμωνα ἐμεῖν ἐγκεκυφότα εἰς τὴν θάλατταν· εἶτα, οἶμαι, τῆς νεὼς βιαιότερον ἐς ὃ ἐκεκύφει μέρος ἐπικλιθείσης καὶ τοῦ κύματος συναπώσαντος, ἐκπεσεῖν αὐτὸν ἐπὶ κεφαλὴν ἐς τὸ πέλαγος, οὐδὲ γυμνὸν τὸν ἄθλιον, ὡς ἂν καὶ ῥᾷον δύνασθαι νεῖν· εὐθὺς οὖν βοᾶν πνιγόμενον καὶ μόγις ἑαυτὸν ὑπερέχοντα τοῦ κλύδωνος. 20. τὸν δὲ Εὐθύδικον, ὡς ἤκουσε—τυχεῖν δὲ γυμνὸν ἐν τῇ εὐνῇ ὄντα—ῥῖψαι ἑαυτὸν εἰς τὴν θάλατταν καὶ καταλαβόντα τὸν Δάμωνα ἤδη ἀπαγορεύοντα—φαίνεσθαι γὰρ ἐπὶ πολὺ ταῦτα τῆς σελήνης καταλαμπούσης—συμπαρανήχεσθαι καὶ συγκουφίζειν· σφᾶς δὲ ἐπιθυμεῖν μὲν αὐτοῖς βοηθεῖν καὶ ἐλεεῖν τὴν συμφορὰν τῶν ἀνδρῶν, μὴ δύνασθαι δὲ μεγάλῳ τῷ πνεύματι ἐλαυνομένους· πλὴν ἐκεῖνά γε ποιῆσαι, φελλούς τε γὰρ πολλοὺς ἀφεῖναι αὐτοῖς καὶ τῶν κοντῶν τινας, ὡς ἐπὶ τούτων ἀπονήξαιντο, εἴ τινι αὐτῶν περιτύχοιεν, καὶ τέλος καὶ τὴν ἀποβάθραν αὐτὴν οὐ μικρὰν οὖσαν. ἐννόησον τοίνυν πρὸς θεῶν, ἥντινα ἄν τις ἄλλην ἐπίδειξιν ἐπιδείξαιτο εὐνοίας βεβαιοτέραν πρὸς ἄνδρα φίλον ἐν νυκτὶ ἐκπεσόντα ἐς πέλαγος οὕτως ἠγριωμένον ἢ κοινωνήσας τοῦ θανάτου; καί μοι ἐπ᾽ ὀφθαλμῶν λαβὲ τὴν ἐπανάστασιν τῶν κυμάτων, τὸν ἦχον τοῦ ὕδατος ἐπικλωμένου, τὸν ἀφρὸν περιζέοντα, τὴν νύκτα, τὴν ἀπόγνωσιν, εἶτα ἀποπνιγόμενον ἐκεῖνον καὶ μόγις ἀνακύπτοντα καὶ τὰς χεῖρας ὀρέγοντα τῷ ἑταίρῳ, τὸν δὲ ἐπιπηδῶντα εὐθὺς καὶ συννέοντα καὶ δεδιότα μὴ προαπόληται αὐτοῦ ὁ Δάμων· οὕτω γὰρ ἂν μάθοις ὡς οὐκ ἀγεννῆ σοι καὶ τοῦτον φίλον τὸν Εὐθύ-δικον διηγησάμην.

miscellaneous collection of passengers, among whom was Euthydicus, and with him Damon, also of Chalcis, his comrade. They were of the same age, but Euthydicus was vigorous and strong, while Damon was pale and sickly, just convalescing, it seemed, from a prolonged illness.

As far as Sicily they had made a fortunate passage, said Simylus; but when they had run through the straits [of Messina] and in due time were sailing in the Adriatic itself, a great tempest fell upon them. Why repeat the many details of his story—huge seas, cyclones, hail, and all the other evils of a storm? But when they were at last abreast of Zacynthos, sailing with the yard bare, and also dragging hawsers in their wake to check the fury of their driving, towards midnight Damon became seasick, as was natural in weather so rough, and began to vomit, leaning outboard. Then, I suppose because the ship was hove down with greater force towards the side over which he was leaning and the high sea contributed a send, he fell overboard head-first; and the poor fellow was not even without his clothes, so as to have been able to swim more easily. So he began at once to call for help, choking and barely able to keep himself above the water.

[20] When Euthydicus, who happened to be undressed and in his bunk, heard him, he flung himself into the sea, got to Damon, who was already giving out (all this was visible at a long distance because the moon was shining) and helped him by swimming beside him and bearing him up. The rest of them, he said, wanted to aid the men and deplored their misfortune, but could not do it because the wind that drove them was too strong; however, they did at least something, for they threw them a number of pieces of cork and some spars, on which they might swim if they chanced upon any of them, and finally even the gang plank, which was not small.

Think now, in the name of the gods! what firmer proof of affection could a man display towards a friend who had fallen overboard at night into a sea so wild, than that of sharing his death? I beg you, envisage the tumult of the seas, the roar of the breaking water, the boiling spume, the night, the despair; then one man strangling, barely keeping up his head, holding his arms out to his friend, and the other leaping after him at once, swimming with him, fearing that Damon would perish first. In that way you can appreciate that in the case of Euthydicus too it is no common friend whom I have described.

Appendix 3
Lucian *Verae historiae* 1.6

(Karl Jacobitz, ed., *Lucian Samosatensis Opera* [Biblio-theca scriptorum graecorum et romanorum Teub-neriana; Leipzig: Teubner, 1909–12] 2.32)

Ἡμέραν μὲν οὖν καὶ νύκτα οὐρίῳ πλέοντες ἔτι τῆς γῆς ὑποφαινομένης οὐ σφόδρα βιαίως ἀνηγόμεθα, τῇ ἐπιούσ

Well, for a day and a night we sailed before the wind without making very much offing, as land was still

δὲ ἅμα ἡλίῳ ἀνατέλλοντι ὅ τε ἄνεμος ἐπεδίδου καὶ τὸ κῦμα ηὐξάνετο καὶ ζόφος ἐπεγίγνετο καὶ οὐκέτ᾽ οὐδὲ στεῖλαι τὴν ὀθόνην δυνατὸν ἦν. ἐπιτρέψαντες οὖν τῷ πνεύματι καὶ παραδόντες ἑαυτοὺς ἐχειμαζόμεθα ἡμέρας ἐννέα καὶ ἑβδομήκοντα, τῇ ὀγδοηκοστῇ δὲ ἄφνω ἐκλάμψαντος ἡλίου καθορῶμεν οὐ πόρρω νῆσον ὑψηλὴν καὶ δασεῖαν, οὐ τραχεῖ περιηχουμένην τῷ κύματι· καὶ γὰρ ἤδη τὸ πολὺ τῆς ζάλης κατεπέπαυτο. προσσχόντες οὖν καὶ ἀποβάντες ὡς ἂν ἐκ μακρᾶς ταλαιπωρίας πολὺν μὲν ἐπὶ τῆς γῆς χρόνον ἐκείμεθα, διαναστάντες δὲ ὅμως ἀπεκρίναμεν ἡμῶν αὐτῶν τριάκοντα μὲν φύλακας τῆς νεὼς παραμένειν, εἴκοσι δὲ σὺν ἐμοὶ ἀνελθεῖν ἐπὶ κατασκοπὴ τῶν τῇ νήσῳ.

dimly in sight; but at sunrise on the second day the wind freshened, the sea rose, darkness came on, and before we knew it we could no longer even get our canvas in [cf. Acts 27:15]. Committing ourselves to the gale and giving up, we drove for seventy-nine days. On the eightieth day, however, the sun came out suddenly and at no great distance we saw a high, wooded island ringed about with sounding surf, which, however, was not rough, as already the worst of the storm was abating.

Putting in and going ashore, we lay on the ground for some time in consequence of our long misery, but finally we arose and told off thirty of our number to stay and guard the ship and twenty to go inland with me and look over the island.

Appendix 4
Achilles Tatius 3.1–5

(Rudolf Hercher, ed., *Erotici scriptores graeci* [2 vols.; Leipzig: Teubner, 1858–59] 1.88–93) [Reprinted by permission of the publishers and The Loeb Classical Library from *Achilles Tatius,* translated by S. Gaselee, Cambridge, Massachusetts: Harvard University Press, 1969]

Τρίτην δὲ ἡμέραν πλεόντων ἡμῶν, ἐξ αἰθρίας πολλῆς αἰφνίδιον ἀχλὺς περιχεῖται καὶ τῆς ἡμέρας ἀπωλώλει τὸ φῶς· ἐγείρεται δὲ κάτωθεν ἄνεμος ἐκ τῆς θαλάσσης κατὰ πρόσωπον τῆς νεώς, καὶ ὁ κυβερνήτης περιάγειν ἐκέλευσε τὴν κεραίαν. Καὶ σπουδῇ περιῆγον οἱ ναῦται, πῆ μὲν τὴν ὀθόνην ἐπὶ θάτερα συνάγοντες ἄνω τοῦ κέρως βίᾳ (τὸ γὰρ πνεῦμα σφοδρότερον ἐμπεσὸν ἀνθέλκειν οὐκ ἐπέτρεπε), πῆ δὲ πρὸς θάτερον μέρος, φυλάττοντες τοῦ πρόσθεν μέτρου καθ᾽ ὃ συνέβαινεν οὔριον εἶναι τῇ περιαγωγῇ τὸ πνεῦμα. Κλίνεται δὲ κοῖλον τοιχίσαν τὸ σκάφος καὶ ἐπὶ θάτερα μετεωρίζεται καὶ πάντη πρηνὲς ἦν, καὶ ἐδόκει τοῖς πολλοῖς ἡμῶν περιτραπήσεσθαι καθάπαξ ἐμπίπτοντος τοῦ πνεύματος. Μετεσκευαζόμεθα οὖν ἅπαντες εἰς τὰ μετέωρα τῆς νεώς, ὅπως τὸ μὲν βαπτιζόμενον τῆς νεὼς ἀνακουφίσαιμεν, τὸ δὲ τῇ προσθήκῃ βιασάμενοι κατὰ μικρὸν καθέλοιμεν εἰς τὸ ἀντίρροπον. Πλέον δὲ ἠνύομεν οὐδέν· ἀνέφερε γὰρ ἡμᾶς μᾶλλον κορυφούμενον τὸ ἔδαφος τῆς νεώς, ἢ πρὸς ἡμῶν κατεβιβάζετο. Καὶ χρόνον μέν τινα διαταλαντουμένην οὕτω τὴν ναῦν τοῖς κύμασιν ἐπαλαίομεν εἰς τὸ ἀντίρροπον καθελεῖν· αἰφνίδιον δὲ μεταβάλλεται τὸ πνεῦμα ἐπὶ θάτερα τῆς νεὼς καὶ μικροῦ βαπτίζεται τὸ σκάφος, τοῦ μὲν τέως εἰς κῦμα κλιθέντος ἀναθορόντος ὀξείᾳ ῥοπῇ, θατέρου δέ, ὃ ἠώρητο, καταρραγέντος εἰς τὴν θάλατταν. Κωκυτὸς οὖν αἴρεται μέγας ἐκ τῆς νεώς, καὶ μετοικία πάλιν καὶ δρόμος μετὰ βοῆς ἐπὶ τὰς ἀρχαίας ἕδρας. Καὶ τρίτον καὶ τέταρτον καὶ πολλάκις τὸ αὐτὸ πάσχοντες κοινὴν ταύτην εἴχομεν [ἐν] τῷ σκάφει τὴν πλάνην. Πρὶν μὲν γὰρ μετασκευάσασθαι τὸ πρῶτον, δίαυλος ἡμᾶς διαλαμβάνει δεύτερος. 2. Σκευοφοροῦντες οὖν κατὰ τὴν ναῦν διὰ πάσης ἡμέρας δόλιχόν τινα τοῦτον δρόμον μυρίον ἐπονοῦμεν, ἀεὶ τὸν θάνατον προσδοκῶντες. Καὶ ἦν, ὡς εἰκός, οὐ μακράν. Περὶ γὰρ μεσημβρίαν δείλην ὁ μὲν ἥλιος τέλεον ἁρπάζεται, ἑωρῶμεν δὲ ἑαυτοὺς ὡς ἐν

1. On the third day of our voyage, the perfect calm we had hitherto experienced was suddenly overcast by dark clouds and the daylight disappeared, a wind blew upwards from the sea full in the ship's face, and the helmsman bade the sailyard be slewed round. The sailors hastened to effect this, bunching up half the sail upon the yard by main force, for the increasing violence of the gusts obstructed their efforts; for the rest, they kept enough of the full spread to make the wind help them to tack. As a result of this, the ship lay on her side, one bulwark raised upward into the air and the deck a steep slope, so that most of us thought that she must heel over when the gale next struck us. We transferred ourselves therefore to that part of the boat which was highest out of water, in order to lighten that part which was down in the sea, and so if possible, by our own added weight depressing the former, to bring the whole again to a level; but all was of no avail: the high part of the deck, far from being weighed down by our presence, merely lifted us higher still away from the water. For some time we thus ineffectually struggled to bring to an equilibrium the vessel thus balanced on the waves: but the wind suddenly shifted to the other side so that the ship was almost sent under water, and instantly that part of the boat which had been down in the waves was now violently thrown up, and the part formerly raised on high was crushed down into the waters. Then arose a great wailing from the ship, and all changed their station, running, with shouts and cries, to the position in which they had been before they moved; and the same thing happening a third and a fourth, nay, many times, we thus imitated the motion of the ship; and even before we had

σελήνη. Πῦρ μὲν ἀπ᾽ αὐτῆς ἵπταται, μυκᾶται δὲ βροντῶν [ὁ] οὐρανός, καὶ τὸν ἀέρα γεμίζει βόμβος, ἀντεβόμβει δὲ κάτωθεν τῶν κυμάτων ἡ στάσις, μεταξὺ δὲ οὐρανοῦ καὶ θαλάσσης ἀνέμων ποικίλων ἐσύριζε ψόφος. Καὶ ὁ μὲν ἀὴρ εἶχε σάλπιγγος ἦχον, οἱ δὲ κάλοι περὶ τὴν ὀθόνην πίπτουσιν, ἀντιπαταγοῦντες δὲ ἐτετρίγεσαν· ἐφόβει δὲ καὶ τὰ ξύλα τῆς νεὼς ῥηγνύμενα μὴ κατὰ μικρὸν ἀνοιχθείη τὸ σκάφος τῶν γόμφων ἀποσπωμένων· γέρρα δὲ περὶ πᾶσαν τὴν ναῦν ἐκεκάλυπτο. Καὶ γὰρ ὄμβρος ἐπέκλυζε πολύς, ἡμεῖς δὲ τὰ γέρρα ὑποδύντες ὥσπερ εἰς ἄντρον ἐμένομεν, παραδόντες ἑαυτοὺς τῇ τύχῃ, ῥίψαντες τὰς ἐλπίδας. Τρικυμίαι δὲ πολλαὶ καὶ πάντοθεν, αἱ μὲν κατὰ πρόσωπον, αἱ δὲ κατ᾽ οὐρὰν τῆς νεὼς ἀλλήλαις ἀντέπιπτον. Ἡ δὲ ναῦς ἀεὶ πρὸς μὲν τὸ κυρτούμενον τῆς θαλάσσης ἠγείρετο, πρὸς δὲ τὸ παραδραμὸν ἤδη καὶ χθαμαλὸν τοῦ κύματος κατεδύετο. Ἐῴκει δὲ τῶν κυμάτων τὰ μὲν ὄρεσι, τὰ δὲ χάσμασιν. Ἦν δὲ καὶ τὰ ἐγκάρσια τῶν κυμάτων ἑκατέρωθεν φοβερώτερα. Ἀναβαίνουσα μὲν γὰρ ἐπὶ τὴν ναῦν ἡ θάλασσα διὰ τῶν γέρρων ἐκυλίετο καὶ ἐκάλυπτε πᾶν τὸ σκάφος. Τὸ γὰρ κῦμα αἰρόμενον ὑψοῦ, ψαῦον αὐτῶν τῶν νεφῶν, πόρρωθεν μὲν πρὸς ἀντιπρόσωπον ἐφαίνετο τῷ σκάφει μέγετος οἷον ** προσιὸν δὲ βλέπων καταποθήσεσθαι τὴν ναῦν προσεδόκησας. Ἦν οὖν ἀνέμων μάχη καὶ κυμάτων· ἡμεῖς δὲ οὐκ ἠδυνάμεθα κατὰ χώραν μένειν ὑπὸ τοῦ τῆς νεὼς σεισμοῦ. Συμμιγὴς δὲ πάντων ἐγίνετο βοή· ἐρρόχθει τὸ κῦμα, ἐπάφλαζε τὸ πνεῦμα, ὀλολυγμὸς γυναικῶν, ἀλαλαγμὸς ἀνδρῶν, κελευσμὸς ναυτῶν, πάντα θρήνων καὶ κωκυτῶν ἀνάμεστα. Καὶ ὁ κυβερνήτης ἐκέλευε ῥίπτειν τὸν φόρτον· διάκρισις δ᾽ οὐκ ἦν ἀργύρου καὶ χρυσοῦ πρὸς ἄλλο τι τῶν εὐτελῶν, ἀλλὰ πάνθ᾽ ὁμοίως ἠκοντίζομεν ἔξω τῆς νεώς· πολλοὶ δὲ καὶ τῶν ἐμπόρων αὐτοὶ τῶν οἰκείων λαμβάνοντες, ἐν οἷς εἶχον τὰς ἐλπίδας, ἐώθουν ἐπειγόμενοι. Καὶ ἦν ἤδη ἡ ναῦς τῶν ἐπίπλων γυμνή· ὁ δὲ χειμὼν οὐκ ἐσπένδετο. 3. Τέλος ὁ κυβερνήτης ἀπειπὼν ῥίπτει μὲν τὰ πηδάλια ἐκ τῶν χειρῶν, ἀφίησι δὲ τὸ σκάφος τῇ θαλάσσῃ καὶ εὐτρεπίζει ἤδη τὴν ἐφολκίδα, καὶ τοῖς ναύταις ἐμβαίνειν κελεύσας τῆς ἀποβάθρας ἦρχεν· οἱ δὲ εὐθὺς κατὰ πόδας ἐξήλλοντο. Ἔνθα δὴ καὶ τὰ δεινὰ ἦν καὶ ἦν μάχη χειροποίητος. Οἱ μὲν γὰρ ἐπιβάντες ἤδη τὸν κάλων ἔκοπτον, ὃς συνέδει τὴν ἐφολκίδα τῷ σκάφει· τῶν δὲ πλωτήρων ἕκαστος ἔσπευδον μεταπηδᾶν ἔνθα καὶ τὸν κυβερνήτην ἑωράκεσαν, ἐφειλκοντό [τε] τὸν κάλων· οἱ δ᾽ ἐκ τῆς ἐφολκίδος μεταβαίνειν οὐκ ἐπέτρεπον· εἶχον δὲ καὶ πελέκεις καὶ μαχαίρας, καὶ πατάξειν ἠπείλουν, εἴ τις ἐπιβήσεται· οἱ δὲ ἐκ τῆς νεὼς ὁπλισάμενοι τὸ δυνατόν, ὁ μὲν κώπης παλαιᾶς τρύφος ἀράμενος, ὁ δὲ τῶν τῆς νεὼς σελμάτων, ἠμύνοντο. Θάλασσα γὰρ εἶχε νόμον τὴν βίαν καὶ ἦν ναυμαχίας καινὸς τρόπος. Οἱ μὲν γὰρ ἐκ τῆς ἐφολκίδος δέει τοῦ καταδῦναι τῷ τῶν ἐπεμβαινόντων ὄχλῳ πελέκεσι καὶ μαχαίρας τοὺς ἐξαλλομένους ἔπαιον· οἱ δὲ σκυτάλαις καὶ κώπαις ἅμα τῷ πηδήματι τὰς πληγὰς κατέφερον· οἱ δὲ καὶ ἄκρου ψαύοντες τοῦ σκάφους ἐξωλίσθανον· ἔνιοι δὲ καὶ ἐπιβαίνοντες τοῖς ἐπὶ τῆς ἐφολκίδος ἤδη διεπάλαιον· φιλίας γὰρ ἢ αἰδοῦς οὐκέτι θεσμὸς ἦν, ἀλλὰ τὸ οἰκεῖον ἕκαστος σκοπῶν ἀσφαλές, τὸ πρὸς τοὺς ἑτέρους εὔγνωμον οὐκ ἐλογίζετο. Οὕτως οἱ μεγάλοι κίνδυνοι καὶ τοὺς τῆς φιλίας λύουσι νόμους. 4.

finished one transmigration, the necessity for a second and contrary one was upon us.

2. The whole day long then we carried our baggage up and down the ship, running, as it were, a long-distance race a thousand times, with the expectation of death ever before our eyes. Nor did it seem far off, for about mid-day or a little after the sun totally disappeared, and we could see one another no better than by moonlight. Lightning flashed from the sky, the heaven bellowed with thunder so that the whole air rang with the din; this was answered from below by the turmoil of the waves, and between sky and sea whistled the noise of contending winds. In this manner the air seemed to be turned into one vast trumpet; the ropes beat against the sail, creaking as they crossed one another, and there was every reason to fear for the broken planks of the ship that the rivets would no longer keep together and that the whole would fall asunder. The wicker bulwarks were actually under water the whole ship round. For much rain fell too, washing over the decks, so we crept under the wattlings as if into a cave, and there we waited, trusting to luck but giving up all hope. Great waves came from every quarter; some from the bows, some dashed against one another at the ship's stern. The vessel rose first as the wave heaved beneath it, and then sank deep as it retired and sank low down; the billows were now like mountains, now like valleys. More terrifying still were those which struck us athwart from either side. For the water rose up, rolled over the bulwarks, and deluged the whole vessel; even from a distance the wave could be seen lifting its head on high so as almost to touch the clouds, and threatening the ship, as large as [a mountain]; and when one saw it as it approached nearer, one would think that it would swallow it up altogether. It was a fight between wind and water: we could never keep still in one spot owing to the shocks imparted to the vessel. A confused noise of all kinds arose—roaring of waves, whistling of wind, shrieking of women, shouting of men, the calling of the sailors' orders; all was full of wailing and lamentation. Then the helmsman ordered the jettison of the cargo. No difference was made between gold and silver and the cheapest stuff, but we hurled all alike from the ship's sides; many of the merchants themselves seized their goods, on which all their hopes were centred, and hastened to pitch them overboard. Now the ship was stripped of all its contents; but the storm was still unabated.

3. At length the helmsman threw up his task. He dropped the steering oars from his hands and left the ship to the mercy of the sea; he then had the jollyboat got ready, and bidding the sailors follow him, was the first to descend the ladder and enter her. They jumped in close after him, and then was confusion worse confounded and a hand-to-hand fight ensued. They who were already in the boat began to cut the rope which held her to the ship, while all the

Ἔνθα δή τις ἀπὸ τῆς νεὼς νεανίσκος εὔρωστος λαμβάνεται τοῦ κάλω καὶ ἐφέλκεται τὴν ἐφολκίδα, καὶ ἦν ἐγγὺς ἤδη τοῦ σκάφους, ηὐτρεπίζετο δὲ ἕκαστος ὡς εἰ πελάσειε πηδήσων ἐς αὐτήν. Καὶ δύο μὲν ἢ τρεῖς ηὐτύχησαν οὐκ ἀναιμωτί, πολλοὶ δὲ ἀποπηδᾶν πειρώμενοι ἐξεκυλίσθησαν τῆς νεὼς κατὰ τῆς θαλάσσης. Ταχὺ γὰρ τὴν ἐφολκίδα ἀπολύσαντες οἱ ναῦται, πελέκει κόψαντες τὸν κάλων τὸν πλοῦν εἶχον ἔνθα αὐτοὺς ἦγε τὸ πνεῦμα· οἱ δὲ ἐπὶ τῆς νεὼς ἐπηρῶντο καταδῦναι τὴν ἐφολκίδα. Τὸ δὲ σκάφος ἐκυβίστα περὶ τοῖς κύμασιν ὀρχούμενον, λανθάνει δὲ προσενεχθὲν ὑφάλῳ πέτρᾳ καὶ ῥήγνυται πᾶν· ἀπωσθείσης δὲ τῆς νεὼς ὁ ἱστὸς ἐπὶ θάτερα πεσὼν τὸ μέν τι κατέκλασε, τὸ δέ τι κατέδυσεν αὐτῆς. Ὁπόσοι μὲν οὖν παραχρῆμα τῆς ἄλμης πιόντες κατεσχέθησαν, οὗτοι μετριωτέραν ὡς ἐν κακοῖς ἔσχον τὴν συμφοράν, οὐκ ἐνδιατρίψαντες τῷ τοῦ θανάτου φόβῳ. Ὁ γὰρ ἐν θαλάττῃ θάνατος βραδὺς προαναιρεῖ πρὸ τοῦ παθεῖν· ὁ γὰρ ὀφθαλμὸς πελάγους γεμισθεὶς ἀόριστον ἐκτείνει τὸν φόβον, ὡς καὶ διὰ τούτων θάνατον δυστυχεῖν πλείονα· ὅσον γὰρ τῆς θαλάσσης τὸ μέγεθος, τοσοῦτος καὶ ὁ τοῦ θανάτου φόβος. Ἔνιοι δὲ κολυμβᾶν πειρώμενοι, προσραγέντες ὑπὸ τοῦ κύματος τῇ πέτρᾳ διεφθείροντο· πολλοὶ δὲ καὶ ξύλοις ἀπερρωγόσι συμπεσόντες δίκην ἰχθύων· οἱ δὲ καὶ ἡμιθνῆτες ἐνήχοντο. 5. Ἐπεὶ οὖν τὸ πλοῖον διελύθη, δαίμων τις ἀγαθὸς περιέσωσεν ἡμῖν τῆς πρώρας μέρος, ἔνθα περικαθίσαντες ἐγώ τε καὶ ἡ Λευκίππη κατὰ ῥοῦν ἐφερόμεθα τῆς θαλάσσης· ὁ δὲ Μενέλαος καὶ ὁ Σάτυρος σὺν ἄλλοις τῶν πλωτήρων ἐπιτυχόντες τοῦ ἱστοῦ καὶ ἐπιπεσόντες ἐνήχοντο. Πλησίον δὲ καὶ τὸν Κλεινίαν ἑωρῶμεν περινηχόμενον τῇ κεραίᾳ καὶ ταύτην ἠκούσαμεν αὐτοῦ τὴν βοὴν "ἔχου τοῦ ξύλου, Κλειτοφῶν"· ἅμα δὲ λέγοντα κῦμα ἐπεκάλυπτε κατόπιν· καὶ ἡμεῖς ἐκωκύσαμεν. Κατὰ ταὐτὸ καὶ ἡμῖν ἐπεφέρετο [τὸ] κῦμα· ἀλλὰ τύχῃ τινὶ πλησίον γενόμενον ἡμῶν κάτωθεν παρατρέχει, ὥστε ὑψούμενον μετέωρον τὸ ξύλον κατὰ τὸν αὐχένα τοῦ κύματος καὶ τὸν Κλεινίαν ἰδεῖν αὖθις. Ἀνοιμώξας οὖν "ἐλέησον" ἔφην "δέσποτα Πόσειδον, καὶ σπεῖσαι πρὸς τὰ τῆς ναυαγίας σου λείψαντα. Πολλοὺς ἤδη τῷ φόβῳ θανάτους ὑπεμείναμεν· εἰ δὲ ἡμᾶς ἀποκτεῖναι θέλεις, μὴ διαστήσῃς ἡμῶν τὴν τελευτήν· ἓν ἡμᾶς κῦμα καλυψάτω· εἰ δὲ καὶ θηρίων ἡμᾶς βορὰν πέπρωται γενέσθαι, εἷς ἡμᾶς ἰχθὺς ἀναλωσάτω, μία γαστὴρ χωρησάτω, ἵνα καὶ ἐν ἰχθύσι κοινῇ ταφῶμεν." Μετὰ μικρὸν δὲ τῆς εὐχῆς τὸ πολὺ τοῦ πνεύματος περιεπέπαυτο, τὸ δὲ ἄγριον ἐστόρεστο τοῦ κύματος. Μεστὴ δὲ ἦν ἡ θάλαττα νεκρῶν σωμάτων. Τοὺς μὲν οὖν ἀμφὶ τὸν Μενέλαον θᾶττον προσάγει τῇ γῇ τὸ κῦμα· καὶ ἦν ταῦτα τῆς Αἰγύπτου τὰ παράλια· κατεῖχον δὲ τότε λῃσταὶ πᾶσαν τὴν ἐκεῖ χώραν· ἡμεῖς δὲ περὶ δείλην ἑσπέραν τύχῃ τινὶ τῷ Πηλουσίῳ προσίσχομεν καὶ ἄσμενοι γῆς λαβόμενοι τοὺς θεοὺς ἀνευφημοῦμεν· εἶτα ὠλοφυρόμεθα τὸν Κλεινίαν καὶ τὸν Σάτυρον, νομίζοντες αὐτοὺς ἀπολωλέναι.

passengers made preparations to jump where they saw the helmsman holding on to the rope; the boat's crew objected to this, and, being armed with axes and swords, threatened to attack any who leaped in; many, on the other hand, of those still on the ship armed themselves as best they might, one picking up a piece of an old oar, another taking a fragment of one of the ship's benches, and so began to defend themselves. At sea might is right, and there now followed a novel kind of sea-fight; those already in the jolly-boat, fearing she would be swamped by the number of those desiring to enter her, struck at them as they jumped with their axes and swords, while the passengers returned the blows as they jumped with planks and oars. Some of them merely touched the edge of the boat and slipped into the sea; some effected their entry and were now struggling with the crew already there. Every law of friendship and pity disappeared, and each man, regarding only his own safety, utterly disregarded all feeling of kindliness towards his neighbours. Great dangers do away with all bonds, even the most dear.

4. At that point one of the passengers, a sturdy young man, seized the cable and drew up the jolly-boat until it was quite close to the ship's side, and everybody made ready to jump into it directly it should be close enough. Two or three were successful, though they effected their object not unscathed, and many made the attempt to leap only to fall from the ship into the sea; for the crew cut the rope with an axe, cast the boat off, and set sail wherever the wind was driving them, while the passengers did their best to sink it. Our vessel, after much plunging and tossing upon the waves, drove unexpectedly on to a rock hidden under water, and was utterly broken in pieces; as she slipped off the rock the mast fell on one side, breaking up part of her and carrying the rest beneath the water. Those who instantly perished, their lungs full of salt water, experienced the most tolerable fate in our general evil plight, because they were not kept in suspense by the fear of death. For a slow death at sea lets a man suffer all its pangs before the actual moment of dissolution. The eye, satiated with the waste expanse of the waters, prolongs the agony of fear, so that perishing in these circumstances is far more wretched than in any other: the terror of such a death is great in proportion to the size of the ocean. Some tried to swim, and were killed by being dashed by the waves on to the rock: many others fell upon broken pieces of wood and were spitted upon them like fishes; others were swimming about already half dead.

5. The ship thus broken up, some favouring deity kept whole for us that part of the prow on which Leucippe and I were seated astride, and we floated as the sea carried us. Menelaus and Satyrus, together with some others of the passengers, happened upon the mast, and swam, using it as a support. Close by we saw Clinias swimming with his hands on the yardarm,

and we heard him cry; "Keep hold of your piece of wood, Clitophon." As he spoke, a wave overwhelmed him from behind. We cried out at the sight, and at the same time the wave bore down upon us too; but by good fortune when it came near it only heaved us up and passed by beneath us, and we once again saw the spar lifted up on high on the crest of the billow, with Clinias upon it. "Have pity," I wailed and cried, "Lord Poseidon, and make a truce with us, the remnants of your shipwreck. We have already undergone many deaths through fear; if you mean to kill us, do not put off longer our end; let one wave overwhelm us. If our fate is to become food for sea-beasts, let one fish destroy us and one maw swallow us, that even in the fish we may have a common tomb." It was but a short time after I had uttered this prayer that the wind dropped and the savagery of the waves subsided; the sea was full of the corpses of the dead; and the tide rapidly brought Menelaus and his servants to land. (This land was the coast of Egypt, then wholly infested by robbers.) We, towards evening, chanced to come ashore at Pelusium; in joy at our safe arrival we first gave thanks to the gods and then bewailed Clinias and Satyrus, thinking that they had both perished.

Appendix 5
Josephus *The Jewish War* 2.254–63
(Benedict Niese, ed., *Flavii Josephi Opera*, vol. 6: *De Bello Judaico Libros VII* [Berlin: Weidmann, 1894] 202–4)

254 Καθαρθείσης δὲ τῆς χώρας ἕτερον εἶδος λῃστῶν ἐν Ἱεροσολύμοις ἐπεφύετο, οἱ καλούμενοι σικάριοι, μεθ' ἡμέραν καὶ ἐν μέσῃ τῇ πόλει φονεύοντες ἀνθρώπους, 255 μάλιστα [δὲ] ἐν ταῖς ἑορταῖς μισγόμενοι τῷ πλήθει καὶ ταῖς ἐσθῆσιν ὑποκρύπτοντες μικρὰ ξιφίδια, τούτοις ἔνυττον τοὺς διαφόρους, ἔπειτα πεσόντων μέρος ἐγίνοντο τῶν ἐπαγανακτούντων οἱ πεφονευκότες, διὸ καὶ παντάπασιν ὑπὸ ἀξιοπιστίας ἦσαν ἀνεύρετοι. 256 πρῶτος μὲν οὖν ὑπ' αὐτῶν Ἰωνάθης ὁ ἀρχιερεὺς ἀποσφάττεται, μετὰ δ' αὐτὸν καθ' ἡμέραν ἀνῃροῦντο πολλοί· καὶ τῶν συμφορῶν ὁ φόβος ἦν χαλεπώτερος, ἑκάστου καθάπερ ἐν πολέμῳ καθ' ὥραν τὸν θάνατον προσδεχομένου. 257 προεσκοποῦντο δὲ πόρρωθεν τοὺς διαφόρους, καὶ οὐδὲ τοῖς φίλοις προσιοῦσιν πίστις ἦν, ἐν μέσαις δὲ ταῖς ὑπονοίαις καὶ ταῖς φυλακαῖς ἀνῃροῦντο· τοσοῦτον τῶν ἐπιβουλευόντων τὸ τάχος ἦν καὶ τοῦ λαθεῖν ἡ τέχνη. 258 Συνέστη δὲ πρὸς τούτοις στῖφος ἕτερον πονηρῶν χειρὶ μὲν καθαρώτερον, ταῖς γνώμαις δὲ ἀσεβέστερον, ὅπερ οὐδὲν ἧττον τῶν σφαγέων τὴν εὐδαιμονίαν τῆς πόλεως ἐλυμήνατο. 259 πλάνοι γὰρ ἄνθρωποι καὶ ἀπατεῶνες προσχήματι θειασμοῦ νεωτερισμοὺς καὶ μεταβολὰς πραγματευόμενοι δαιμονᾶν τὸ πλῆθος ἔπειθον καὶ προῆγον εἰς τὴν ἐρημίαν ὡς ἐκεῖ τοῦ θεοῦ δείξοντος αὐτοῖς σημεῖα ἐλευθερίας. 260 ἐπὶ τούτοις Φῆλιξ, ἐδόκει γὰρ ἀποστάσεως εἶναι καταβολή, πέμψας ἱππεῖς καὶ πεζοὺς ὁπλίτας πολὺ πλῆθος διέφθειρεν. 261 Μείζονι δὲ τούτου πληγῇ Ἰουδαίους

[254] But while the country was thus cleared of these pests, a new species of banditti was springing up in Jerusalem, the so-called *sicarii*, who committed murders in broad daylight in the heart of the city. [255] The festivals were their special seasons, when they would mingle with the crowd, carrying short daggers concealed under their clothing, with which they stabbed their enemies. Then, when they fell, the murderers joined in the cries of indignation and, through this plausible behaviour, were never discovered. [256] The first to be assassinated by them was Jonathan the high-priest; after his death there were numerous daily murders. The panic created was more alarming than the calamity itself; every one, as on the battlefield, hourly expecting death. [257] Men kept watch at a distance on their enemies and would not trust even their friends when they approached. Yet, even while their suspicions were aroused and they were on their guard, they fell; so swift were the conspirators and so crafty in eluding detection. [258] Besides these there arose another body of villains, with purer hands but more impious intentions, who no less than the assassins ruined the peace of the city. [259] Deceivers and impostors, under the pretence of divine inspiration fostering revolutionary changes, they persuaded the multitude to act like

ἐκάκωσεν ὁ Αἰγύπτιος ψευδοπροφήτης· παραγενόμενος γὰρ εἰς τὴν χώραν ἄνθρωπος γόης καὶ προφήτου πίστιν ἐπιθεὶς ἑαυτῷ περὶ τρισμυρίους μὲν ἀθροίζει τῶν ἠπατημένων, 262 περιαγαγὼν δὲ αὐτοὺς ἐκ τῆς ἐρημίας εἰς τὸ ἐλαιῶν καλούμενον ὄρος ἐκεῖθεν οἷός τε ἦν εἰς ʽΙεροσόλυμα παρελθεῖν βιάζεσθαι καὶ κρατήσας τῆς τε ʽΡωμαϊκῆς φρουρᾶς καὶ τοῦ δήμου τυραννεῖν χρώμενος τοῖς συνεισπεσοῦσιν δορυφόροις. 263 φθάνει δ᾽ αὐτοῦ τὴν ὁρμὴν Φῆλιξ ὑπαντήσας μετὰ τῶν Ρωμαϊκῶν ὁπλιτῶν, καὶ πᾶς ὁ δῆμος συνεφήψατο τῆς ἀμύνης, ὥστε συμβολῆς γενομένης τὸν μὲν Αἰγύπτιον φυγεῖν μετ᾽ ὀλίγων, διαφθαρῆναι δὲ καὶ ζωγρηθῆναι πλείστους τῶν σὺν αὐτῷ, τὸ δὲ λοιπὸν πλῆθος σκεδασθὲν ἐπὶ τὴν ἑαυτῶν ἕκαστον διαλαθεῖν.

madmen, and led them out into the desert under the belief that God would there give them tokens of deliverance. [260] Against them Felix, regarding this as but the preliminary to insurrection, sent a body of cavalry and heavy-armed infantry, and put a large number to the sword.

[261] A still worse blow was dealt at the Jews by the Egyptian false prophet. A charlatan, who had gained for himself the reputation of a prophet, this man appeared in the country, collected a following of about thirty thousand dupes, [262] and led them by a circuitous route from the desert to the mount called the mount of Olives. From there he proposed to force an entrance into Jerusalem and, after overpowering the Roman garrison, to set himself up as tyrant of the people, employing those who poured in with him as his bodyguard. [263] His attack was anticipated by Felix, who went to meet him with the Roman heavy infantry, the whole population joining him in the defence. The outcome of the ensuing engagement was that the Egyptian escaped with a few of his followers; most of his force were killed or taken prisoners; the remainder dispersed and stealthily escaped to their several homes.

Appendix 6
Aristobulus Fragment 4

(Eusebius *Preparation for the Gospel* 13.12.4–8 [trans. E. H. Gifford; Oxford: Clarendon, 1903] 719–20)

λέγει δ᾽ οὕτως . . . καὶ ʺΑρατος δὲ περὶ τῶν αὐτῶν φησιν οὕτως. . . . σαφῶς οἴομαι δεδεῖχθαι διότι διὰ πάντων ἐστὶν ἡ δύναμις τοῦ θεοῦ. καθὼς δὲ δεῖ, σεσημάγκαμεν περιαιροῦντες τὸν διὰ τῶν ποιημάτων Δία καὶ Ζῆνα· τὸ γὰρ τῆς διανοίας αὐτῶν ἐπὶ θεὸν ἀναπέμπεται, διόπερ οὕτως ἡμῖν εἴρηται. οὐκ ἀπεοικότως οὖν τοῖς ἐπεζητημένοις προενηνέγμεθα ταῦτα. πᾶσι γὰρ τοῖς φιλοσόφοις ὁμολογεῖται διότι δεῖ περὶ θεοῦ διαλήψεις ὁσίας ἔχειν, ὃ μάλιστα παρακελεύεται καλῶς ἡ καθ᾽ ἡμᾶς αἵρεσις. ἡ δὲ τοῦ νόμου κατασκευὴ πᾶσα τοῦ καθ᾽ ἡμᾶς περὶ εὐσεβείας τέτακται καὶ δικαιοσύνης καὶ ἐγκρατείας καὶ τῶν λοιπῶν ἀγαθῶν τῶν κατὰ ἀλήθειαν.

And this is what he says . . . [quotation] Aratus also speaks of the same subject thus [quotation of Aratus *Phaenomena* 1–9!]:

"It is clearly shown, I think, that all things are pervaded by the power of God: and this I have properly represented by taking away the name of Zeus which runs through the poems; for it is to God that their thought is sent up, and for that reason I have so expressed it. These quotations, therefore, which I have brought forward are not inappropriate to the questions before us.

"For all the philosophers agree, that we ought to hold pious opinions concerning God, and to this especially our system gives excellent exhortation; and the whole constitution of our law is arranged with reference to piety, and justice, and temperance, and all things else that are truly good."

Appendix 7
Aristobulus Fragment 5

(Eusebius *Preparation for the Gospel* 13.12.9–12 [trans. E. H. Gifford; Oxford: Clarendon, 1903] 720–21)

ʽΕχομένως δ᾽ ἐστὶν ὡς ὁ θεός, ὃς τὸν ὅλον κόσμον κατεσκεύακε, καὶ δέδωκεν ἀνάπαυσιν ἡμῖν, διὰ τὸ κακόπαθον εἶναι πᾶσι τὴν βιοτήν, ἑβδόμην ἡμέραν, ἣ δὴ καὶ πρώτη φυσικῶς ἂν λέγοιτο φωτὸς γένεσις, ἐν ᾧ τὰ πάντα συνθεωρεῖται. μεταφέροιτο δ᾽ ἂν τὸ αὐτὸ καὶ ἐπὶ τῆς σοφίας· τὸ γὰρ πᾶν φῶς ἐστιν ἐξ αὐτῆς. καί τινες εἰρήκασι τῶν ἐκ τῆς αἱρέσεως ὄντες ̦ τῆς ̦ ἐκ τοῦ Περι-

With this it is closely connected, that God the Creator of the whole world, has also given us the seventh day as a rest, because for all men life is full of troubles: which day indeed might naturally be called the first birth of light, whereby all things are beheld. The same thought might also be metaphorically applied in the case of wisdom, for from it all light

πάτου λαμπτῆρος αὐτὴν ἔχειν τάξιν· ἀκολουθοῦντες γὰρ
αὐτῇ συνεχῶς ἀτάροχοι καταστήσονται δι᾽ ὅλου τοῦ
βίου. σαφέστερον δὲ καὶ κάλλιον τῶν ἡμετέρων προ-
γόνων τις εἶπε Σολομῶν αὐτὴν πρὸ οὐρανοῦ καὶ γῆς
ὑπάρχειν· τὸ δὴ σύμφωνόν ἐστι τῷ προειρημένῳ. τὸ δὲ
διασαφούμενον διὰ τῆς νομοθεσίας ἀποπεπαυκέναι τὸν
θεὸν ἐν αὐτῇ, τοῦτο οὐχ, ὥς τινες ὑπολαμβάνουσι,
μηκέτι ποιεῖν τι τὸν θεὸν καθέστηκεν, ἀλλ᾽ ἐπὶ τῷ κατα-
πεπαυκέναι τὴν τάξιν αὐτῶν οὕτως εἰς πάντα τὸν χρόνον
τεταχέναι. σημαίνει γὰρ ὡς ἐν ἓξ ἡμέραις ἐποίησε τόν τε
οὐρανὸν καὶ τὴν γῆν καὶ πάντα τὰ ἐν αὐτοῖς, ἵνα τοὺς
χρόνους δηλώσῃ καὶ τὴν τάξιν προείπῃ τί τίνος προτερεῖ.
τάξας γάρ, οὕτως αὐτὰ συνέχει καὶ μεταποιεῖ. διασε-
σάφηκε δ᾽ ἡμῖν αὐτὴν ἔννομον ἕνεκεν σημείου τοῦ περὶ
ἡμᾶς ἑβδόμου λόγου καθεστῶτος, ἐν ᾧ γνῶσιν ἔχομεν
ἀνθρωπίνων καὶ θείων πραγμάτων.

proceeds. And it has been said by some who were of the Peripatetic School that wisdom is in place of a beacon-light, for by following it constantly men will be rendered free from trouble through their whole life.

But more clearly and more beautifully one of our forefathers, Solomon, said that it has existed before heaven and earth; which indeed agrees with what has been said above. But what is clearly stated by the Law, that God rested on the seventh day, means not, as some suppose, that God henceforth ceases to do anything, but it refers to the fact that, after He has brought the arrangement of His works to completion, He has arranged them thus for all time.

For it points out that in six days He made the heaven and the earth and all things that are therein, to distinguish the times, and predict the order in which one thing comes before another: for after arranging their order, He keeps them so, and makes no change. He has also plainly declared that the seventh day is ordained for us by the Law, to be a sign of that which is our seventh faculty, namely reason, whereby we have knowledge of things human and divine.

Appendix 8
Apostolic Constitutions 7.34.1–2, 6–8
(Franz Xaver Funk, ed., *Didascalia et Constitutiones Apostolorum* [2 vols. in 1; Paderborn: Schoeningh, 1905] 1.426, 428) [trans. from *The Ante-Nicene Fathers,* vols. 7 (Grand Rapids: Wm. B. Eerdmans); reprinted by permission]

Εὐλογητὸς εἶ, κύριε, "βασιλεῦ τῶν αἰώνων," ὁ διὰ
Χριστοῦ ποιήσας τὰ ὅλα καὶ δι᾽ αὐτοῦ ἐν ἀρχῇ
κοσμήσας τὰ ἀκατασκεύαστα, ὁ διαχωρίσας ὕδατα
ὑδάτων στερεώματι καὶ πνεῦμα ζωτικὸν τούτοις
ἐμβαλών, ὁ γῆν ἑδράσας καὶ οὐρανὸν ἐκτείνας καὶ τὴν
ἑκάστου τῶν κτισμάτων ἀκριβῆ διάταξιν κοσμήσας. 2.
σῇ γὰρ ἐνθυμήσει, δέσποτα, κόσμος πεφαίδρυται,
"οὐρανὸς δὲ ὡς καμάρα" πεπηγμένος ἠγλάϊσται ἄστροις
ἕνεκεν παραμυθίας τοῦ σκότους, φῶς δὲ καὶ ἥλιος εἰς
ἡμέρας καὶ καρπῶν γονὴν γεγένηνται, σελήνη δὲ εἰς
καιρῶν τροπὴν αὔξουσα καὶ μειουμένη, καὶ νὺξ
ὠνομάζετο καὶ ἡμέρα προσηγορεύετο, στερέωμα δὲ διὰ
μέσων τῶν ἀβύσσων ἐδείκνυτο . . .

6. καὶ τέλος τῆς δημιουργίας τὸ λογικὸν ζῷον, τὸν
κοσμοπολίτην, τῇ σῇ σοφίᾳ διαταξάμενος κατεσκεύασας
εἰπών· "ποιήσωμεν ἄνθρωπον κατ᾽ εἰκόνα καὶ καθ᾽
ὁμοίωσιν ἡμετέραν," κόσμου κόσμον αὐτὸν ἀναδείξας, ἐκ
μὲν τῶν τεσσάρων σωμάτων διαπλάσας αὐτῷ τὸ σῶμα,
κατασκευάσας δ᾽ αὐτῷ τὴν ψυχὴν ἐκ τοῦ μὴ ὄντος,
αἴσθησιν δὲ πένταθλον αὐτῷ χαρισάμενος καὶ νοῦν τὸν
τῆς ψυχῆς ἡνίοχον ταῖς αἰσθήσεσιν ἐπιστήσας. 7. καὶ
ἐπὶ πᾶσι τούτοις, δέσποτα κύριε, τίς ἐπαξίως διηγήσεται
νεφῶν ὀμβροτόκων φοράν, ἀστραπῆς ἔκλαμψιν, βροντῶν πάταγον, εἰς τροφῆς χορηγίαν καταλλήλου καὶ
κρᾶσιν ἀέρων παναρμόνιον; 8. παρακούσαντα δὲ τὸν
ἄνθρωπον ἐμμίσθου ζωῆς ἐστέρησας, οὐκ εἰς τὸ παντελὲς

Thou art blessed, O Lord, the King of ages, who by Christ hast made the whole world, and by Him in the beginning didst reduce into order the disordered parts; who dividedst the waters from the waters by a firmament, and didst put into them a spirit of life; who didst fix the earth, and stretch out the heaven, and didst dispose every creature by an accurate constitution. [2] For by Thy power, O Lord, the world is beautified, the heaven is fixed as an arch over us, and is rendered illustrious with stars for our comfort in the darkness. The light also and the sun were begotten for days and the production of fruit, and the moon for the change of seasons, by its increase and diminutions; and one was called Night, and the other Day. And the firmament was exhibited in the midst of the abyss.

[6] And at the conclusion of the creation Thou gavest direction to Thy Wisdom, and formedst a reasonable creature as the citizen of the world, saying, "Let us make man after our image, and after our likeness;" and hast exhibited him as the ornament of the world, and formed him a body out of the four elements, those primary bodies, but hadst prepared a soul out of nothing, and bestowedst upon him his five senses, and didst set over his sensations a mind as the conductor of the soul. [7] And besides all

ἀφανίσας, ἀλλὰ χρόνῳ πρὸις ὀλίγον κοιμίσας, ὅρκῳ εἰς παλιγγενεσίαν ἐκάλεσας, ὅρον θανάτου ἔλυσας, ὁ ζωοποιὸς τῶν νεκρῶν διὰ "Ἰησοῦ Χριστοῦ τῆς ἐλπίδος ἡμῶν."

these things, O Lord God, who can worthily declare the motion of the rainy clouds, the shining of the lightning, the noise of the thunder, in order to the supply of proper food, and the most agreeable temperature of the air? [8] But when man was disobedient, Thou didst deprive him of the life which should have been his reward. Yet didst Thou not destroy him for ever, but laidst him to sleep for a time; and Thou didst by oath call him to a resurrection, and loosedst the bond of death, O Thou reviver of the dead, through Jesus Christ, who is our hope.

Appendix 9
Apostolic Constitutions **8.12.12–16, 20**

(Franz Xaver Funk, ed., *Didascalia et Constitutiones Apostolorum* [2 vols. in 1; Paderborn: Schoeningh, 1905] 1.498–500, 502) [trans. from *The Ante-Nicene Fathers*, vol. 7 (Grand Rapids: Wm. B. Eerdmans); reprinted by permission]

12. ὁ τὴν μεγάλην θάλασσαν χωρίσας τῆς γῆς καὶ τὴν μὲν ἀναδείξας πλωτήν, τὴν δὲ ποσὶ βάσιμον ποιήσας, καὶ τὴν μὲν "ζῴοις μικροῖς καὶ μεγάλοις" πληθύνας, τὴν δὲ ἡμέροις καὶ ἀτιθάσσοις πληρώσας, φυτοῖς τε διαφόροις στέψας καὶ βοτάναις στεφανώσας καὶ ἄνθεσι καλλύνας καὶ σπέρμασι πλουτίσας· 13. ὁ συστησάμενος ἄβυσσον καὶ μέγα κύτος αὐτῇ περιθείς, ἁλμυρῶν ὑδάτων σεσωρευμένα πελάγη, "περιφράξας δὲ αὐτὴν πύλαις" ἄμμου λεπτοτάτης· ὁ πνεύμασί ποτε μὲν αὐτὴν κορυφῶν εἰς ὀρέων μέγεθος, ποτὲ δὲ στρωννύων αὐτὴν εἰς πεδίον, καί ποτε μὲν ἐκμαίνων χειμῶνι, ποτὲ δὲ πραΰνων γαλήνῃ ὡς ναυσιπόροις πνωτῆρσιν εὔκολον εἶναι πρὸς πορείαν· 14. ὁ ποταμοῖς διαζώσας τὸν ὑπὸ σοῦ διὰ Χριστοῦ γενόμενον κόσμον καὶ χειμάρροις ἐπικλύσας καὶ πηγαῖς ἀενάοις μεθύσας, ὄρεσιν δὲ περισφίγξας εἰς ἕδραν ἀτρεμῆ γῆς ἀσφαλεστάτην. 15. ἐπλήρωσας γάρ σου τὸν κόσμον καὶ διεκόσμησας αὐτὸν βοτάναις εὐόσμοις καὶ ἰασίμοις, ζῴοις πολλοῖς καὶ διαφόροις, ἀλκίμοις καὶ ἀσθενεστέροις, ἐδωδίμοις καὶ ἐνεργοῖς, ἡμέροις καὶ ἀτιθάσσοις, ἑρπετῶν συριγμοῖς, πτηνῶν ποικίλων κλαγγαῖς, ἐνιαυτῶν κύκλοις, μηνῶν καὶ ἡμερῶν ἀριθμοῖς, τροπῶν τάξεσιν, νεφῶν ὀμβροτόκων διαδρομαῖς εἰς καρπῶν γονὰς καὶ ζῴων σύστασιν, "σταθμὸν ἀνέμων" διαπνεόντων ὅτε προσταχθῶσιν παρὰ σοῦ, τῶν φυτῶν καὶ τῶν βοτανῶν τὸ πλῆθος. 16. καὶ οὐ μόνον τὸν κόσμον ἐδημιούργησας, ἀλλὰ καὶ τὸν κοσμοπολίτην ἄνθρωπον ἐν αὐτῷ ἐποίησας, κόσμου κόσμον αὐτὸν ἀναδείξας· εἶπας γὰρ τῇ σῇ σοφίᾳ "Ποιήσωμεν ἄνθρωπον κατ᾽ εἰκόνα ἡμετέραν καὶ καθ᾽ ὁμοίωσιν, καὶ ἀρχέτωσαν τῶν ἰχθύων τῆς θαλάσσης καὶ τῶν πετεινῶν τοῦ οὐρανοῦ."

20. ἀμελήσαντα δὲ τῆς ἐντολῆς καὶ γευσάμενον ἀπηγορευμένου καρποῦ ἀπάτῃ ὄφεως καὶ συμβουλίᾳ γυναικὸς τοῦ μὲν παραδείσου δικαίως ἐξῶσας αὐτόν, ἀγαθότητι δὲ εἰς τὸ παντελὲς ἀπολλύμενον οὐχ ὑπερεῖδες, σὸν γὰρ ἦν δημιούργημα, ἀλλὰ καθυποτάξας αὐτῷ τὴν κτίσιν δέδωκας αὐτῷ οἰκείοις ἱδρῶσιν καὶ πόνοις πορίζειν ἑαυτῷ τὴν τροφήν, σοῦ πάντα φύοντος καὶ αὔξοντος καὶ πεπαίνοντος· χρόνῳ δὲ πρὸς ὀλίγον αὐτὸν κοιμίσας ὅρκῳ εἰς παλιγγενεσίαν ἐκάλεσας, ὅρον

[12] Who didst separate the great sea from the land, and didst render the former navigable and the latter fit for walking, and didst replenish the former with small and great living creatures, and filledst the latter with the same, both tame and wild; didst furnish it with various plants, and crown it with herbs, and beautify it with flowers, and enrich it with seeds; [13] who didst ordain the great deep, and on every side madest a mighty cavity for it, which contains seas of salt waters heaped together, yet didst Thou every way bound them with barriers of the smallest sand; who sometimes dost raise it to the height of mountains by the winds, and sometimes dost smooth it into a plain; sometimes dost enrage it with a tempest, and sometimes dost still it with a calm, that it may be easy to seafaring men in their voyages; [14] who didst encompass this world, which was made by Thee though Christ, with rivers, and water it with currents, and moisten it with springs that never fail, and didst bind it round with mountains for the immovable and secure consistence of the earth: [15] for Thou hast replenished Thy world, and adorned it with sweet-smelling and with healing herbs, with many and various living creatures, strong and weak, for food and for labour, tame and wild; with the noises of creeping things, the sounds of various sorts of flying creatures; with the circuits of the years, the numbers of months and days, the order of the seasons, the courses of the rainy clouds, for the production of the fruits and the support of living creatures. Thou hast also appointed the station of the winds, which blow when commanded by Thee, and the multitude of the plants and herbs.

[16] And Thou hast not only created the world itself, but hast also made man for a citizen of the world, exhibiting him as the ornament of the world; for Thou didst say to Thy Wisdom: "Let us make man according to our image, and according to our likeness; and let them have dominion over the fish of

θανάτου λύσας ζωὴν ἐξ ἀναστάσεως ἐπηγγείλω.

the sea, and over the fowls of the heaven."

[20] But when he neglected that command, and tasted of the forbidden fruit, by the seduction of the serpent and the counsel of his wife, Thou didst justly cast him out of paradise. Yet of Thy goodness Thou didst not overlook him, nor suffer him to perish utterly, for he was Thy creature; but Thou didst subject the whole creation to him, and didst grant him liberty to procure himself food by his own sweat and labours, while Thou didst cause all the fruits of the earth to spring up, to grow, and to ripen. But when Thou hadst laid him asleep for a while, Thou didst with an oath call him to a restoration again, didst loose the bond of death, and promise him life after the resurrection.

Appendix 10
Second Edict of Augustus from Cyrene

(*SEG* 9, no. 8 ii [trans. from *Roman Civilization*, vol. 2: *The Empire*, ed. Naphtali Lewis and Meyer Reinhold (New York: Columbia University, 1955) 38])

Αὐτοκράτωρ Καῖσαρ Σεβαστὸς ἀρχιε|ρεὺς δημαρχικῆς ἐξουσίας τὸ ἑπτακαιδέκατον λέγει· φθόνος ψόγος | τε εἶναι Ποπλίωι Σεξστίωι Σκεύαι οὐκ ὀφείλει, ὅτι Αὖλον Στλάκκιον Λευ|κίου υἱὸν Μάξιμον καὶ Λεύκιον Στλάκκιον Λευκίου υἱὸν Μακεδόνα καὶ Πόπλι|ον Λακουτάνιον Ποπλίου ἀπελεύθερον Φιλέρωτα, ἐπειδὴ ἑατοὺς οὗτοι, || ὃ πρὸς τὴν ἐμὴν σωτηρίαν τά τε δημόσια πράγματ ⟨ α ⟩ ἀνῆκεν, ἐπίστασθαι καὶ | βούλεσθαι εἰπεῖν ἔφησαν, δεσμίους πρός με ἐκ τῆς Κυρηναϊκῆς ἐπαρχήας {α} | ἀναπεμφθῆναι ἐφρόντισεν· τοῦτο γὰρ ἐποίησεν Σέξστιος καθηκόντως καὶ ἐ|πιμελῶς. Λοιπὸν ἐπειδὴ τῶν πρὸς ἐμὲ καὶ τὰ δημόσια πράγματα ἀνηκόν|των οὐδὲν γεινώσ-κουσ(ι,τ)οῦτο δὲ ἐν τῆι ἐπαρχήαι εἶπαν ἑατοὺς πε|πλάσ-θαι καὶ ἐψεῦσθαι φανερὸν ἐποίησάν μοι, ἐλευθερωθέντας | αὐτοὺς ἐκ τῆς παραφυλακῆς ἀφείημι. Αὖλον δὲ Στλάκ-κιον | Μάξιμον, ὃν Κυρηναίων οἱ πρέσβεις αἰτιῶνται ἀνδριάντας ἐκ τῶν | δημοσίων τόπων ἠρκέναι, ἐν οἷς καὶ τὸν ὧι ἡ πόλεις τὸ ἐμὸν ὄνομα ὑπέγραψεν, ἕως |{s} ἂν περὶ τούτου τοῦ πράγματος διαγνῶ, ἀπελθεῖν ἄνευ τῆς ἐμῆς ἐπιταγῆς κω|λύω.

The Emperor Caesar Augustus, *pontifex maximus*, holding the tribunician power for the seventeenth year, declares:

Publius Sextius Scaeva does not merit reproach or censure for ordering Aulus Stlaccius Maximus son of Lucius, Lucius Stlaccius Macedo son of Lucius, and Publius Lacutanius Phileros, freedman of Publius, to be sent on to me from the province of Cyrene under guard because they had said that they had knowledge concerning my security and the commonwealth and wished to declare it. In so doing Sextius performed his duty conscientiously. However, since they have no information that concerns me or the commonwealth but have declared and convinced me that they had misrepresented and lied about this in the province, I have set them free and am releasing them from custody. But as for Aulus Stlaccius Maximus, whom the envoys of the Cyrenaeans accuse of having removed statues from public places, among them even the one on the base of which the city inscribed my name, I forbid him to depart without my order until I have investigated this matter.

Appendix 11
Imperial Edict concerning Appeals in Criminal Cases

(BGU 628; L. Mitteis and U. Wilcken, Grundzüge und Chrestomathie der Papyruskunde [2 vols. each in 2 parts; Leipzig and Berlin: Teubner, 1912] 2:2, no. 371) [trans. Kelly Del Tredici]

Col I

In multis bene factis consultisque divi parentiṣ mei id quoque|iure nobis praedicandum pu[t]o [q]uod causas qu(a)e a[d] principalem | notionem [vel] provocatae vel [rem]issae fuissen[t i]mposita qua|dạm nec[ess]itate de[c]idenda[s es]se pers[p]exit ne [aut] prob[i] h[o]mines| [c]onflitar[e]ntur diu[t]ina mor[a

Col. 1:

Among the many good legal decisions made by my divine parent, I think that with some right we also should proclaim this: that he perceived that cases which either had been appealed or remanded to the emperor's authority should, by the force of a certain necessity, be decided, lest either honest/upright men

a]ut call[id]iores fructum [ca]perel [ali]quem p[rot]ra-
hend[a] lite au[c]uparen[tu]r, quod [c]um animad-
ver|[ti]sset iam p[er] multo[s] annos ev[en]ire ed[i]xit
salub[ri]ter praefini|t[is] temp⟨o⟩r[ibus] intra qu⟨a⟩e
cum [ex p]rovinciis [a]d a[gend]um veni|[sse]nt
utrae[qu]ẹ [p]arte[s] nec disçe[de]rent priusqu[am]
ad disceptan|[du]m i[ntrodu]çṭị f[uis]ṣẹ[nt aut]
scirent fore u[t al]tera parte audi|ṭạ ser[v]aret[u]r
seṇteṇtia aut [sec]ụṇdum praese[nte]m
pronuntial[retur; sin vero] neut[er] ḷitiga[nti]em
adfuiṣṣet ex[cid]ere tum eas[]. | [lites ex or]dine
cognitionu[m] offici nostri. E[t . . .]rcules ịam |
[dudum] id obtinedum fuit [cu]m a presipto eius
edi[c]ti satis super|q[ue tempo]ris quasi
conive[n]tibus nobis tra[ns]cocurrerint | e[t . . . .
iu[d]ex in pr[. . . . . .] . . di . . . . [. . .inte]ṛposito
teṃ|[pore . . . .] io̧ [. . . . .] ation
[. . . . .] conti[. .]. | (Some lines lacking)
[. . . . .]ṣ Italia q[. . . . . . .] edi [. . .]. . . |
. . . . [. . . . .]t sex menses t[ran]salpinis
| [autem . . . .] ṃ annum qui nis[i] adfuerint vel |
defensi fuerint cum [cont]roversiae eorum noscantur
Col II
sciant fore et stetur sentent[i]ae eṭ acc[us]atores | ad
petendam poenam in re[c]ogantur. Sed quoniam |
capitale[s] causae aliquid ạ[u]xilium conctationis
ad|mittun[t e]t accusatoribus et rei[s] in It[a]lia
qu[i]dem | novem [me]ṇses dabuntur t[ra]nsalpinis
audem et trans|marins annus et sex menses iṇṭra quoṣ
misi ⟪a⟫ | adfuer[in]t fore iam nu[n]c sciant ut cu[m]
prosecu|toribus [v]eneant quod n[e]que grave
n[e]que darum | viderị pote⟨st⟩ si ⟨i⟩is tam pro|[i]xum
tempus i[nd]ulserim | et opinor qui aliqua di[gn]itate
censer[i] possunt | tanto [. . .]. .i deḅe[nt] so[lli]citi
[esse u]t iis quae praecepta | sunt ma[t]urato
obsequantur cu[m] praesentem repul|tent iṇteresse
hones[t]atis suae ut qụam primum | molestiạ careant.
Apella[ti]oneṣ ṿẹro quae ad magi|stratus et sacerdotia
et alios honores pertinebunt | habe[ant] formam
tem[po]ris sui. Set ea [qu]aequae sunt | eṛ[. . . . . . .]
rump [. . . . .] ụmqu [. . a]d notion[em]. | (Some lines
lacking) ço̧pṛ[. . . . .] . .f [. . . . . .] [. . . .] | bo [] [] []

be oppressed by a long delay or lest shrewd men
strive to win some advantage by protracting the case.
And when he had noticed that this was occurring for
many years he proclaimed an edict which defined
useful time periods within which, when both parties
had come from the provinces for a case, they should
not depart before they had been brought in to enter
their plea or before they knew, if one party had been
heard, that a decision would be reserved or else
pronounced in favor of the party which was present.
But if neither of the litigants had been present, then
he proclaimed that these cases be resolved in due
accord with the investigations of our office. And . . .
since by order of his edict enough and more than
enough time has transpired while we, as it were, let it
go unnoticed . . .

Col. 2:
They shall know that judgment will remain fixed and
accusers are constrained to seek a penalty in a case.
But because capital cases allow for some assistance
through delay, nine months will be granted to
accusers and defendants who come to Italy from
transalpine locales, but a year and a half to those who
come from across the sea, within which time they
must be present. Let them now know that they
should come accompanied by their official escorts,
which directive can appear neither weighty nor harsh
since I will have granted to them such an extended
period of time. I also think that persons to whom can
be attributed a certain standing should be concerned
all the more to follow these directives/commands . . .
Appeals, however, which pertain to magistrates,
priestly and other offices should have their own
period of time . . .

This list of studies on the Acts of the Apostles is highly selective and includes (1) items referred to frequently by Conzelmann, (2) older works that have made a significant scholarly contribution to the study of Acts and are still of value at the present time, and (3) works appearing after 1972.

1. Bibliographies

Bousset, Wilhelm
"Neueste Forschungen zur Apostelgeschichte," *ThR* 11 (185–205).

Clemen, Carl
"Apostelgeschichte und apostolisches Zeitalter," *ThR* 1 (1897–98) 371–77; 3 (1900) 50–56; 4 (1901) 66–79; 6 (1903) 79–90; 7 (1904) 278–86.

Dupont, Jacques
Les problèmes du Livre des Actes d'après les travaux récents (Analecta lovaniensia biblica et orientalia 2:17; Louvain: Louvain University, 1959). Reprinted in his *Etudes,* 11–124.

Grässer, Erich
"Acta-Forschung seit 1960," *ThR* 41 (1976) 141–94, 259–90; 42 (1977) 1–68.

Idem
"Die Apostelgeschichte in der Forschung der Gegenwart," *ThR* 26 (1960) 93–167.

Kümmel, Georg Werner
"Das Urchristentum," *ThR* n.s. 14 (1942) 81–95; 17 (1948–49) 3–50, 103–42; 18 (1950) 1–53; 22 (1954) 138–70, 191–211.

Mattill, A. J., Jr., and Mary Bedford Mattill
A Classified Bibliography of Literature on the Acts of the Apostles (NTTS 7; Leiden: Brill, 1966). List of works through 1961.

Mills, Watson E.
A Bibliography of the Periodical Literature on the Acts of the Apostles 1962–1984 (NovTSup 58; Leiden: Brill, 1986).

Plümacher, Eckhard
"Acta-Forschung 1974–1982," *ThR* 48 (1983) 1–56; 49 (1984) 105–69.

Stuehrenberg, Paul F.
"The Study of Acts before the Reformation: A Bibliographic Introduction," *NovT* 29 (1987) 100–136.

Wagner, Günter, ed.
An Exegetical Bibliography of the New Testament: Luke and Acts (Macon, GA: Mercer University, 1985).

Windisch, Hans
"Urchristentum," *ThR* n.s. 5 (1933) 186–200, 239–58, 289–301, 319–34.

See also Schneider, 1.11–52; Bieder; Bovon; Gasque (below).

2. Commentaries

Older Works

Cramer, John A.
Catenae graecorum patrum in Novum Testamentum (vol. 3; Oxford: Oxford University, 1844; reprinted Hildesheim: Olms, 1967).

Ephraem of Syria (306–73)
[In Armenian] = *Saint Ephrem: Commentary on the Acts of the Apostles* (ed. Fr. Nerses Akinean; Critical Editions of the Literature and Translations of the Ancient Armenians, II:1; Vienna: Mechitarist Brethren Press, 1921).

Idem
"The Commentary of Ephrem on Acts," by Frederick C. Conybeare in *Beginnings,* 3.373–453.

Chrysostom, John (c. 344/54–407)
PG 51.65–112.

Bede, The Venerable (c. 673–735)
Bedae Venerabilis expositio actuum apostolorum et retractatio, by M. L. W. Laistner (Cambridge: Harvard University, 1939).

Isho'dad of Merv (ninth century)
The Commentaries of Isho'dad of Merv, Bishop of Ḥaḍatha (c 850 A.D.) in Syriac and English: Vol. IV: Acts of the Apostles and Three Catholic Epistles in Syriac and English (ed. and trans. Margaret Dunlop Gibson; Horae Semiticae 10; Cambridge: Cambridge University, 1913).

Wettstein, John Jacob
Η ΚΑΙΝΗ ΔΙΑΘΗΚΗ, *Novum Testamentum graecum* (2 vols.; Amsterdam: ex Officina Dommeriana, 1751–52) 2.447–657.

Modern Works

Bauernfeind, Otto
Die Apostelgeschichte (ThHKNT 5; Leipzig: Deichert, 1939). Reprinted in his *Kommentar und Studien zur Apostelgeschichte* (ed. V. Metelmann; WUNT 22; Tübingen: Mohr [Siebeck], 1980) 1–282.

Beyer, Hermann Wolfgang
Die Apostelgeschichte (NTD 2:5; Göttingen: Vandenhoeck & Ruprecht, 1933; 4th ed. 1947). See Stählin.

Bruce, Frederick Fyvie
The Acts of the Apostles: The Greek Text with Introduction and Commentary (London: Tyndale, 1951; 2d ed. 1952).

Idem

Commentary on the Book of Acts: The English Text with Introduction, Exposition and Notes (New International Commentary on the New Testament; Grand Rapids: Eerdmans, 1954).

DeWette, Wilhelm Martin Leberecht

Kurze Erklärung der Apostelgeschichte (Kurzgefasstes exegetisches Handbuch zum Neuen Testament 1:4; Leipzig: Weidmann, 1938; 2d ed. 1841; 3d ed. 1848). 4th ed. rev. and expanded by Franz Overbeck (Leipzig: Hirzel, 1870).

Dillon, Richard Joseph, and Joseph A. Fitzmyer

"Acts of the Apostles," in *The Jerome Biblical Commentary* (ed. R. E. Brown, J. A. Fitzmyer, and R. E. Murphy; Englewood Cliffs, NJ: Prentice-Hall, 1968) 2.165–214.

Foakes-Jackson, Frederick John

The Acts of the Apostles (Moffatt New Testament Commentary; New York: Harper; London: Hodder & Stoughton, 1931).

Grosheide, Frederik Willem

De Handelingen der Apostelen (2 vols.; Kommentaar op het Nieuwe Testament 5; Amsterdam: Bottenburg, 1942–48).

Haenchen, Ernst

Die Apostelgeschichte (KEK 3; Göttingen: Vandenhoeck & Ruprecht, 1st ed. [= 10th ed.] 1956; 2d ed. [= 11th ed.] 1957; 3d ed. [= 12th ed.] 1959; 5th ed. [= 14th ed.] 1965; 7th ed. [= 16th ed.] 1977.

Idem

The Acts of the Apostles: A Commentary (Philadelphia: Westminster, 1971).

Hanson, Richard P. C.

The Acts in the Revised Standard Version, with Introduction and Commentary (New Clarendon Bible [New Testament]; Oxford: Clarendon, 1967).

Holtzmann, Heinrich Julius

Die Apostelgeschichte (Handkommentar zum Neuen Testament 1:2; Freiburg: Mohr [Siebeck], 1889; 2d ed. 1892; 3d ed. Tübingen/Leipzig, 1901).

Jacquier, Eugène

Les Actes des Apôtres (Études bibliques; Paris, Gabalda, 1926).

Knopf, Rudolf

Die Apostelgeschichte (Die Schriften des Neuen Testaments 3; Göttingen: Vandenhoeck & Ruprecht, 1906; 2d ed. 1907; 3d ed. 1917).

Knowling, Richard John

The Acts of the Apostles (Expositor's Greek Testament; London: Hodder & Stoughton, 1897; reprinted Grand Rapids: Eerdmans, 1951).

Krodel, Gerhard A.

Acts (Augsburg Commentary on the New Testament; Minneapolis: Augsburg, 1986).

Lake, Kirsopp, and Henry Joel Cadbury

The Acts of the Apostles: English Translation and Commentary and *Additional Notes to the Commentary*, in *Beginnings*, vols. 4–5 (London: Macmillan, 1933).

Loisy, Alfred

Les Actes des Apôtres (Paris: Emile Nourry, 1920; Paris: F. Rieder, 1925).

Macgregor, G. H. C.

"The Acts of the Apostles," in *Interpreter's Bible* (12 vols.; ed. G. A. Buttrick; New York/Nashville: Abingdon, 1951–57) 9.3–352.

Marshall, I. Howard

The Acts of the Apostles: An Introduction and Commentary (Tyndale New Testament Commentaries; Grand Rapids: Eerdmans, 1980).

Meyer, Heinrich August Wilhelm

Kritisch-exegetisches Handbuch über die Apostelgeschichte (KEK 3; Göttingen: Vandenhoeck & Ruprecht, 1835; 2d ed. 1854; 3d ed. 1861; 4th ed. 1869). [See Wendt and Haenchen.] Trans.: *Critical and Exegetical Handbook to the Acts of the Apostles* (2 vols.; trans. from 4th German ed. by P. J. Gloag; Edinburgh: T. & T. Clark, 1877). American ed., with supplementary notes by William Ormiston (New York: Funk & Wagnalls, 1883; 2d ed. 1884).

Munck, Johannes

The Acts of the Apostles (Anchor Bible 31; Garden City, NY: Doubleday, 1967).

Page, Thomas Ethelbert

The Acts of the Apostles, Being the Greek Text as Revised by Westcott and Hort, with Explanatory Notes (London: Macmillan, 1886; Introduction added in 1895). Often reprinted.

Preuschen, Erwin

Die Apostelgeschichte (HNT 4:1; Tübingen: Mohr [Siebeck], 1912).

Rackham, Richard Belward

The Acts of the Apostles: An Exposition (Westminster Commentaries; London: Methuen, 1901). Often reprinted.

Schneider, Gerhard

Die Apostelgeschichte (2 vols.; Herders theologischer Kommentar zum Neuen Testament; Freiburg/Basel/Vienna: Herder, 1980, 1982).

Stählin, Gustav

Die Apostelgeschichte (NTD 5; Göttingen: Vandenhoeck & Ruprecht, 1962; 16th ed. 1980). [See Beyer.]

Wendt, Hans Hinrich

Die Apostelgeschichte (KEK 3; Göttingen: Vandenhoeck & Ruprecht, 1st ed. [= 5th ed.] 1880; 2d ed. [= 6th & 7th eds.] 1888; 3d ed. [= 8th ed.] 1899; 4th ed. [= 9th ed.] 1913). [See Meyer and Haenchen.]

Wikenhauser, Alfred

Die Apostelgeschichte (Regensburger Neues Testament 5; Regensburg: Pustet, 1938; 2d ed. 1951; 3d ed. 1956).

Williams, Charles Stephen Conway

The Acts of the Apostles (Harper's New Testament Commentaries; New York: Harper; London: A. & C. Black, 1957; 2d ed. 1969).

Zahn, Theodor

Die Apostelgeschichte des Lucas (Kommentar zum Neuen Testament 5:1–2; Leipzig: Deichert, 1st & 2d eds. 1919–21; 3d & 4th eds. 1922–27).

3. Studies

Barrett, Charles Kingsley

"Is There a Theological Tendency in Codex Bezae?" in *Text and Interpretation: Studies in the New Testament Presented to Matthew Black* (ed. E. Best and R. McL. Wilson; Cambridge/New York: Cambridge University, 1979) 15–27.

Idem

Luke the Historian in Recent Study (A. S. Peake Memorial Lecture 6; London: Epworth, 1961; reprinted Facet Books; Philadelphia: Fortress, 1970).

Betori, Giuseppe

Perseguitati a causa del Nome: Strutture dei racconti di persecuzione in Atti 1,12–8,4 (Analecta biblica 97; Rome: Biblical Institute, 1981).

Bieder, Werner

Die Apostelgeschichte in der Historie: Ein Beitrag zur Auslegungsgeschichte des Missionsbuches der Kirche (Theologische Studien 61; Zurich: EVZ-Verlag, 1960).

Bihler, Johannes

"Der Stephanusbericht (Apg 6,8–15 und 7,54–8,2)," *BZ* n.s. 3 (1959) 252–70.

Idem

Der Stephanusgeschichte im Zusammenhang der Apostelgeschichte (MThS 1: Historische Abteilung 16; Munich: Hueber, 1963).

Black, Matthew

An Aramaic Approach to the Gospels and Acts (Oxford: Clarendon, 1946; 2d ed. 1954; 3d ed. 1967).

Idem

"Note on the Longer and Shorter Text of Acts," in *On Language, Culture, and Religion: In Honor of Eugene A. Nida* (ed. M. Black and W. A. Smalley; The Hague/Paris: Mouton, 1974) 119–31.

Bovon, François

Luc le théologien: Vingt-cinq ans de recherches (1950–1975) (Le Monde de la Bible; Neuchâtel/Paris: Delachaux & Niestlé, 1978).

Brown, Schuyler

Apostasy and Perseverance in the Theology of Luke (Analecta biblica 36; Rome: Pontifical Biblical Institute, 1969).

Bruce, Frederick Fyvie

The Speeches in the Acts of the Apostles (Tyndale New Testament Lecture, 1942; London: Tyndale, 1943).

Idem

"The Speeches in Acts—Thirty Years After," in *Reconciliation and Hope: New Testament Essays on Atonement and Eschatology Presented to L. L. Morris on His 60th Birthday* (ed. R. Banks; Grand Rapids: Eerdmans, 1974) 53–68.

Bultmann, Rudolf

"Zur Frage nach den Quellen der Apostelgeschichte," in *New Testament Essays: Studies in Memory of Thomas Walter Manson* (ed. A. J. B. Higgins; Manchester: Manchester University, 1959) 68–80. Reprinted in Bultmann, *Exegetica*, 412–23.

Burchard, Christoph

"Paulus in der Apostelgeschichte," *ThLZ* 100 (1975) 881–95.

Idem

Der dreizehnte Zeuge: Traditions- und kompositionsgeschichtliche Untersuchungen zu Lukas' Darstellung der Frühzeit des Paulus (FRLANT 103; Göttingen: Vandenhoeck & Ruprecht, 1970).

Cadbury, Henry Joel

The Book of Acts in History (New York: Harper, 1955).

Idem

The Making of Luke-Acts (New York: Macmillan, 1927; 2d ed. London: SPCK, 1958).

Idem

The Style and Literary Method of Luke (HTS 6; Cambridge: Harvard University, 1920; reprinted 1969).

Idem

"'We' and 'I' Passages in Luke-Acts," *NTS* 3 (1956–57) 128–32.

Cerfaux, Lucien

"Citations scripturaires et tradition textuelle dans le Livre de Actes," in *Aux sources de la tradition chrétienne: Mélanges offerts à M. Maurice Goguel* (Bibliothèque théologique; Neuchâtel/Paris: Delachaux & Niestlé, 1950) 42–51. Reprinted in *Recueil Cerfaux* 2.93–103.

Idem

"La composition de la première partie du Livre des Actes," *EThL* 13 (1936) 667–91. Reprinted in *Recueil Cerfaux* 2.63–91.

Clark, Albert C.

The Acts of the Apostles: A Critical Edition with Introduction and Notes on Selected Passages (Oxford: Clarendon, 1933; reprinted 1970).

Conzelmann, Hans

"Geschichte, Geschichtsbild und Geschichtsdarstellung bei Lukas," *ThLZ* 85 (1960) 241–50.

Idem

"Luke's Place in the Development of Early Christianity," in *Studies in Luke-Acts*, 298–316.

Idem

"Die Rede des Paulus auf dem Areopag," *Gymnasium Helveticum* 12 (1958) 18–32. Reprinted in his *Theologie als Schriftauslegung: Aufsätze zum Neuen Testament* (BEvTh 65; Munich: Kaiser, 1974) 91–105. Trans.: "The Address of Paul on the Areopagus," in *Studies in Luke-Acts*, 217–30.

Idem

The Theology of St Luke (London: Faber & Faber; New York: Harper, 1960; reprinted Philadelphia: Fortress, 1982).

Idem

"Zur Lukasanalyse," *ZThK* 49 (1952) 16–33. Reprinted in *Das Lukas-Evangelium: Die redaktions- und Kompositionsgeschichtliche Forschung* (Wege der Forschung 280; ed. Georg Braumann; Darmstadt: Wissenschaftliche Buchgesellschaft, 1974) 43–63.

Crehan, Joseph H.

"The Purpose of Luke in Acts," *StEv* 2 (1964) 354–68.

Dahl, Nils Alstrup

"The Purpose of Luke-Acts," in Dahl, *Jesus in the Memory of the Early Church* (Minneapolis: Augsburg, 1976) 87–98.

Dibelius, Martin

"The Text of Acts: An Urgent Critical Task," in *Studies*, 84–92.

Idem

Studies in the Acts of the Apostles (ed. Heinrich Greeven; London: SCM, 1956).

Dietzfelbinger, Christian

Die Berufung des Paulus als Ursprung seiner Theologie (WMANT 58; Neukirchen-Vluyn: Neukirchener, 1985).

Dupont, Jacques

Études sur les Actes des Apôtres (LD 45; Paris: Cerf, 1967).

Idem

"Notes sur les Actes des Apôtres: IV. La famine sous Claude (Actes XI,28)," *RB* 62 (1955). Reprinted in his *Etudes*, 163–71.

Idem

Nouvelles études sur les Actes des Apôtres (LD 118; Paris: Cerf, 1984). 20 essays.

Idem

The Salvation of the Gentiles: Essays on the Acts of the Apostles (trans. J. R. Keating; New York/Ramsey/Toronto: Paulist, 1979). 6 essays.

Idem

The Sources of Acts: The Present Position (London: Darton, Longman & Todd, 1964).

Easton, Burton Scott

Early Christianity: The Purpose of Acts and Other Papers (ed. F. C. Grant; Greenwich, CT: Seabury, 1954; London: SPCK, 1955).

Ehrhardt, Arnold

The Acts of the Apostles: Ten Lectures (Manchester: Manchester University, 1969).

Epp, Eldon Jay

The Theological Tendency of Codex Bezae Cantabrigiensis in Acts (SNTSMS 3; Cambridge/New York: Cambridge University, 1966).

Idem

"The Ascension in the Textual Tradition of Luke-Acts," in *New Testament Textual Criticism: Its Significance for Exegesis: Essays in Honour of Bruce M.*

Metzger (ed. E. J. Epp and G. D. Fee; Oxford: Clarendon, 1981) 131–45.

Feine, Paul

Eine vorkanonische Überlieferung des Lukas in Evangelium und Apostelgeschichte (Gotha: Perthes, 1891).

Filson, Floyd Vivian

Three Crucial Decades: Studies in the Book of Acts (Richmond: John Knox, 1963).

Flender, Helmut

St Luke: Theologian of Redemptive History (Philadelphia: Fortress, 1967).

Franklin, Eric

Christ the Lord: A Study in the Purpose and Theology of Luke-Acts (Philadelphia: Westminster, 1975).

Gärtner, Bertil

The Areopagus Speech and Natural Revelation (ASNU 22; Uppsala: Almqvist & Wiksells, 1955).

Gasque, W. Ward

A History of the Criticism of the Acts of the Apostles (Tübingen: Mohr [Siebeck]; Grand Rapids: Eerdmans, 1975).

Gaventa, Beverly Roberts

From Darkness to Light: Aspects of Conversion in the New Testament (Overtures to Biblical Theology; Philadelphia: Fortress, 1986).

Grässer, Erich

"Die Parusieerwartung in der Apostelgeschichte," in *Les Actes des Apôtres: Traditions, rédaction, théologie* (ed. J. Kremer; BETL 48; Gembloux: Duculot; Louvain: Leuven University, 1979) 99–127.

Idem

Das Problem der Parusieverzögerung in den synoptischen Evangelien und in der Apostelgeschichte (BZNW 22; Berlin: Töpelmann, 1957; 2d ed. 1960; 3d ed. 1977).

Haenchen, Ernst

"The Book of Acts as Source Material for the History of Early Christianity," in *Studies in Luke-Acts*, 258–78.

Idem

"Judentum und Christentum in der Apostelgeschichte," *ZNW* 54 (1963) 155–87. Reprinted in his *Gott und Mensch*, 338–74.

Idem

"Quellenanalyse und Kompositionsanalyse in Act 15," in *Judentum, Urchristentum, Kirche: Festschrift für Joachim Jeremias* (ed. W. Eltester; BZNW 26; Berlin: Töpelmann, 1960) 153–64.

Idem

"Schriftzitate und Textüberlieferung in der Apostelgeschichte," *ZThK* 51 (1954) 153–67. Reprinted in his *Gott und Mensch*, 157–71.

Idem

"Tradition und Komposition in der Apostelgeschichte," *ZThK* 52 (1955) 205–25. Reprinted in his *Gott und Mensch*, 206–26.

Idem

"'We' in Acts and the Itinerary," *Journal for Theology and the Church: 1. The Bultmann School of*

Biblical Interpretation: New Directions? (ed. R. W. Funk; Tübingen: Mohr [Siebeck]; New York: Harper & Row, 1965) 65–99.

Idem

"Zum Text der Apostelgeschichte," *ZThK* 54 (1957) 22–55. Reprinted in his *Gott und Mensch*, 172–205.

Hahn, Ferdinand

Mission in the New Testament (SBT 47; London: SCM, 1965).

Harnack, Adolf

The Acts of the Apostles (New Testament Studies 3; Crown Theological Library 27; New York: Putnam; London: Williams & Norgate, 1909).

Idem

The Date of the Acts and the Synoptic Gospels (New Testament Studies 4; Crown Theological Library 33; New York: Putnam; London: Williams & Norgate, 1911).

Idem

Luke the Physician: The Author of the Third Gospel and the Acts of the Apostles (New Testament Studies 1; Crown Theological Library 20; New York: Putnam; London: Williams & Norgate, 1907).

Hauser, Hermann J.

Abschlusserzählung der Apostelgeschichte (Apg 28,16– 31) (Analecta biblica 86; Rome: Biblical Institute, 1979).

Hengel, Martin

Acts and the History of Earliest Christianity (Philadelphia: Fortress, 1979).

Holtz, Traugott

Untersuchungen über die alttestamentliche Zitate bei Lukas (TU 104; Berlin: Akademie-Verlag, 1968).

Hommel, Hildebrecht

"Neue Forschungen zur Areopagrede Acta 17," *ZNW* 46 (1955) 147–48.

Idem

"Platonisches bei Lukas: Zu Act 17:28a (Leben— Bewegung—Sein)," *ZNW* 48 (1957) 193–200.

Jeremias, Joachim

"Untersuchungen zum Quellenproblem der Apostelgeschichte," *ZNW* 36 (1937) 205–21. Reprinted in his *Abba*, 238–55.

Jervell, Jacob

Luke and the People of God: A New Look at Luke-Acts (Minneapolis: Augsburg, 1972). 7 essays.

Idem

The Unknown Paul: Essays on Luke-Acts and Early Christian History (Minneapolis: Augsburg, 1984). 9 essays.

Jewett, Robert

A Chronology of Paul's Life (Philadelphia: Fortress, 1979).

Johnson, Luke Timothy

The Literary Function of Possessions in Luke-Acts (Society of Biblical Literature Dissertation Series 39; Missoula, MT: Scholars Press, 1977).

Jüngst, Johannes

Die Quellen der Apostelgeschichte (Gotha: Perthes, 1895).

Karris, Robert J.

What Are They Saying about Luke and Acts? (New York: Paulist, 1979).

Keck, Leander E., and J. Louis Martyn, eds.

Studies in Luke-Acts: Essays Presented in Honor of Paul Schubert (Nashville: Abingdon, 1966). 19 essays.

Kilgallen, John J., S.J.

The Stephen Speech: A Literary and Redactional Study of Acts 7,2–53 (Analecta biblica 67; Rome: Biblical Institute, 1976).

Kilpatrick, George Dunbar

"An Eclectic Study of the Text of Acts," in *Biblical and Patristic Studies in Memory of Robert Pierce Casey* (ed. J. N. Birdsall and R. W. Thomson; Freiburg/ Basel/New York: Herder, 1963) 64–77.

Klein, Günther

Die zwölf Apostel: Ursprung und Gehalt einer Idee (FRLANT 77; Göttingen: Vandenhoeck & Ruprecht, 1961).

Klijn, Albertus Frederik Johannes

"In Search of the Original Text of Acts," in *Studies in Luke-Acts*, 103–10.

Knox, Wilfred L.

The Acts of the Apostles (Cambridge: Cambridge University, 1948).

Kremer, Jacob, ed.

Les Actes des Apôtres: Traditions, rédaction, théologie (BETL 48; Gembloux: Duculot; Louvain: Leuven University, 1979). 30 essays.

Linton, Olaf

"The Third Aspect: A Neglected Point of View: A Study in Gal. i–ii and Acts ix and xv," *StTh* 3 (1949) 79–95.

Lohfink, Gerhard

The Conversion of St. Paul: Narrative and History in Acts (Herald Scriptural Library; Chicago: Franciscan Herald, 1976).

Idem

Die Himmelfahrt Jesu: Untersuchungen zu den Himmelfahrts- und Erhohungstexten bei Lukas (SANT 26; Munich: Kösel, 1971).

Idem

Die Sammlung Israels: Eine Untersuchung zur lukanischen Ekklesiologie (SANT 39; Munich: Kösel, 1975).

Löning, Karl

Die Saulustradition in der Apostelgeschichte (NTAbh n.s. 9; Münster: Aschendorff, 1973).

Luedemann, Gerd

Paul, Apostle to the Gentiles: Studies in Chronology (Philadelphia: Fortress, 1984).

Marshall, I. Howard

Luke: Historian and Theologian (Contemporary Evangelical Perspectives; Grand Rapids: Zondervan; Exeter: Paternoster, 1970).

Menoud, Philippe-H.
   "'During Forty Days' (Acts 1. 3)," in *Neotestamentica et Patristica: Eine Freundesgabe, Herrn Professor Dr Oscar Cullmann zu seinem 60. Geburtstag überreicht* (NovTSup 6; Leiden: Brill, 1962) 148–56. Reprinted in his *Jesus Christ and the Faith,* 167–79.

Idem
   Jesus Christ and the Faith: A Collection of Studies (PTMS 18; Pittsburgh: Pickwick, 1978). 10 essays on Luke-Acts.

Morgenthaler, Robert
   Die lukanische Geschichtsschreibung als Zeugnis: Gestalt und Gehalt der Kunst des Lukas (2 vols.; AThANT 14–15; Zurich: Zwingli-Verlag, 1948).

Munck, Johannes
   Paul and the Salvation of Mankind (Richmond: John Knox, 1959).

Maddox, Robert
   The Purpose of Luke-Acts (FRLANT; Göttingen: Vandenhoeck & Ruprecht; Edinburgh: T. & T. Clark, 1982).

Mussner, Franz
   "Die Idee der Apokatastasis in der Apostelgeschichte," in *Lux tua veritas: Festschrift für Hubert Junker* (Trier: Paulinus, 1961) 293–306.

Nock, Arthur Darby
   Review of Dibelius, *Studies,* in *Gnomon* 25 (1953) 497–506. Reprinted as "The Book of Acts" in his *Essays on Religion and the Ancient World* (ed. Zeph Stewart; 2 vols.; Cambridge: Harvard University, 1972) 2.821–32.

O'Neill, J. C.
   The Theology of Acts in Its Historical Setting (London: SPCK, 1961; 2d ed. 1970).

O'Toole, Robert F., S.J.
   Acts 26: The Christological Climax of Paul's Defense (Ac 22:1–26:32) (Analecta biblica 78; Rome: Biblical Institute, 1978).

Idem
   The Unity of Luke's Theology: An Analysis of Luke-Acts (Good News Studies 9; Wilmington: Glazier, 1984).

Pallis, Alex
   Notes on St. Luke and the Acts (London: Oxford University, 1928).

Pesch, Rudolf
   Die Vision des Stephanus: Apg 7,55–56 im Rahmen der Apostelgeschichte (Stuttgarter Bibelstudien 12; Stuttgart: Katholisches Bibelwerk, 1966).

Pereira, Francis, S.J.
   Ephesus: Climax of Universalism in Luke-Acts: A Redaction-Critical Study of Paul's Ephesian Ministry (Acts 18:23–20:1) (Jesuit Theological Forum: Studies 1; Anand, India: Gujarat Sahitya Prakash, 1983).

Plümacher, Eckhard
   Lukas als hellenistischer Schriftsteller: Studien zur Apostelgeschichte (SUNT 9; Göttingen: Vandenhoeck & Ruprecht, 1972).

Quesnel, Michel
   Baptisés dans l'Esprit: Baptême et Esprit Saint dans les Actes des Apôtres (LD 120; Paris: Cerf, 1985).

Radl, Walter
   Paulus und Jesus im lukanischen Doppelwerk: Untersuchungen zu Parallelmotiven im Lukasevangelium und in der Apostelgeschichte (Europäische Hochschulschriften, ser. 23: Theologie 49; Bern: H. Lang; Frankfurt: P. Lang, 1975).

Ramsay, William Mitchell
   St. Paul the Traveler and the Roman Citizen (London: Hodder & Stoughton, 1895; 7th ed. 1898; reprinted Grand Rapids: Eerdmans, 1949).

Rasco, Emilio
   La teología de Lucas: Origen, desarrollo, orientaciones (Analecta Gregoriana 201; Rome: Gregorian University, 1976).

Reicke, Bo
   Glaube und Leben der Urgemeinde: Bemerkungen zu Apg. 1–7 (AThANT 32; Zurich: Zwingli-Verlag, 1957).

Rese, Martin
   Alttestamentliche Motive in der Christologie des Lukas (StNT 1; Gütersloh: Mohn, 1969).

Richard, Earl
   Acts 6:1–8:4: The Author's Method of Composition (Society of Biblical Literature Dissertation Series 41; Missoula, MT: Scholars, 1978).

Schille, Gottfried
   Die urchristliche Kollegialmission (AThANT 48; Zurich/Stuttgart: Zwingli, 1967).

Schmithals, Walter
   Paul and James (SBT 46; London: SCM, 1965).

Schütz, Frieder
   Der leidende Christus: Die angefochtene Gemeinde und das Christuskerygma der lukanischen Schriften (Beiträge zur Wissenschaft vom Alten und Neuen Testament 89; Stuttgart: Kohlhammer, 1969).

Schweizer, Eduard
   "Concerning the Speeches in Acts," in *Studies in Luke-Acts,* 208–16.

Simon, Marcel
   St Stephen and the Hellenists in the Primitive Church (Haskell Lectures, 1956; London/New York: Longmans, Green, 1958).

Sorof, Martin
   Die Entstehung der Apostelgeschichte: Eine kritische Studie (Berlin: Nicolai [Stricker], 1890).

Spitta, Friedrich
   Die Apostelgeschichte, ihre Quellen und deren geschichtlicher Wert (Halle a. S.: Waisenhaus, 1891).

Stolle, Volker
   Der Zeuge als Angeklagter: Untersuchungen zum Paulusbild des Lukas (Beiträge zur Wissenschaft vom Alten und Neuen Testament 102; Stuttgart: Kohlhammer, 1973).

Talbert, Charles H.
   Literary Patterns, Theological Themes, and the Genre of Luke-Acts (Society of Biblical Literature Mono-

graph Series 20; Missoula, MT: Scholars Press, 1975).

Idem, ed.
>   *Luke-Acts: New Perspectives from the Society of Biblical Literature Seminar* (New York: Crossroad, 1984). 12 essays.

Idem
>   *Luke and the Gnostics: An Examination of the Lucan Purpose* (Nashville: Abingdon, 1966).

Idem, ed.
>   *Perspectives on Luke-Acts* (Association of Baptist Professors of Religion: Special Studies Series 5; Danville, VA: Association of Baptist Professors of Religion; Edinburgh: T. & T. Clark, 1978). 15 essays. Reprinted Macon, GA: Mercer University, n.d.

Tiede, David L.
>   *Prophecy and History in Luke-Acts* (Philadelphia: Fortress, 1980).

Torrey, Charles Cutler
>   *The Composition and Date of Acts* (HTS 1; Cambridge: Harvard University, 1916).

Trocmé, Étienne
>   *Le "Livre des Actes" et l'Histoire* (Études d'histoire et de philosophie religieuses 45; Paris: Presses Universitaires de France, 1957).

Tyson, Joseph B.
>   *The Death of Jesus in Luke-Acts* (Columbia: University of South Carolina, 1986).

Vielhauer, Philipp
>   "On the 'Paulinism' of Acts," in *Studies in Luke-Acts*, 33–50.

Vögeli, Alfred
>   "Lukas und Euripides," *ThZ* 9 (1953) 415–38.

Walaskay, Paul W.
>   *'And so we came to Rome': The Political Perspective of St Luke* (SNTSMS 49; Cambridge/New York: Cambridge University, 1983).

Weiss, Johannes
>   *Über die Absicht und den literarischen Charakter der Apostelgeschichte* (Göttingen: Vandenhoeck & Ruprecht, 1897).

Wellhausen, Julius
>   "Noten zur Apostelgeschichte," AGG (1907) 1–21.

Wikenhauser, Alfred
>   *Die Apostelgeschichte und ihr Geschichtswert* (NTAbh 8:3–5; Münster: Aschendorff, 1921).

Wilckens, Ulrich
>   *Die Missionsrede der Apostelgeschichte: Form- und traditionsgeschichtliche Untersuchungen* (WMANT 5; Neukirchen-Vluyn: Neukirchener, 1961; 2d ed. 1963; 3d ed. 1974).

Wilcox, Max
>   *The Semitisms of Acts* (Oxford: Clarendon, 1965).

Williams, Charles Stephen Conway
>   *Alterations to the Text of the Synoptic Gospels and Acts* (Oxford: Blackwell, 1951).

Wilson, Stephen G.
>   *The Gentiles and the Gentile Mission in Luke-Acts*

(SNTSMS 23; Cambridge/New York: Cambridge University, 1973).

Idem
>   *Luke and the Law* (SNTSMS 50; Cambridge/New York: Cambridge University, 1983).

Zehnle, Richard F.
>   *Peter's Pentecost Discourse: Tradition and Lukan Reinterpretation in Peter's Speeches of Acts 2 and 3* (Society of Biblical Literature Monograph Series 15; Nashville: Abingdon, 1971).

Zeller, Edward
>   *The Contents and Origin of the Acts of the Apostles, Critically Investigated, To Which Is Prefixed F. Overbeck's Introduction to the Acts from De Wette's Handbook* (2 vols.; London/Edinburgh: Williams & Norgate, 1875–76).

*Numbers in parentheses following page citations for this volume refer to footnotes.

1.656	97(5)	44.5	71	*Mut. nom.*	
2.122–23	24	46.9	52	126	144
2.162	186	50.5	42	*Op. mundi*	
2.165	192	*Mid.*		2	141
2.174	206	2.3	183	59	143(43)
2.203	216, 223	Philo		*Prob.*	
2.219	93	*Abr.*		1	4
2.238–47	183	62	52	75–87	24
2.243	204	208	199	*Prov.*	
2.247	195	235	23(6)	2.74	143
2.253	204	*Cher.*		2.84	143
2.253–63	198	99—105	56	*Rer. div. her.*	
2.254–57	184	*Decal.*		264	81
2.259–60	184	33	13(3), 15(24)	*Spec. leg.*	
2.261–63	xxxiii, 184			1.32	144
2.271–72	202	46	13, 16(24)	1.36	144
2.308	133	*Det.*		2.56–57	143(43)
2.381	218	55	142	2.61–64	120
2.411	26(8)	*Deus imm.*		2.62	103
2.433	42	121	88	2.189	14
2.441–42	192	*Ebr.*		4.122–23	119
2.559–61	71	2	180	*Vita Mos.*	
2.560	106	145–48	15(18)	1.9	53
3.29	88	*Exsecr.*		1.18	53
3.127	42	165	73	1.20–24	53
3.398	35(9)	*Flacc.*		1.32	53
3.409	81	45–46	14(7)	1.40	53
3.419–20	77	46	15(14)	1.43–44	53
5.70	9(4)	111	93	1.80	53
5.185	28	128–29	228	2.1	53
5.190–206	26(8)	144	189	2.88	56
5.193–94	183	158	53(15)	2.166	54
5.376–98	42	188–91	96	2.291	4
5.377–400	57(60)	*Jos.*		*Pirqe Aboth*	
6.124–25	183	33	218	4.11	43
6.293	94	*Leg. all.*		Ps. -Philo	
7.41–62	88	1.44	145	*Ant.*	
7.368	71	3.4	145	4.3	15(14)
7.451–53	96	3.106	42	*Pss. Sol.*	
C. Apion		*Leg. Gai.*		2.7	21
1.1	3(5)	36	152	8.15	7
1.37	54	134	61	17.15	30
2.1	3(5)	145–47	54(26)	17.22–23	42
2.1–2	4	155	47	18.10	143
2.130	140	203	139	1 QapGen	
2.267	140	212	183	22.27	51
Vita		234–60	203	1QH	
13–14	228	281–83	14(7)	1.10–15	143
15	219, 229	282	99	1.13–14	141
141	203	283	14(14)	1.16–17	144
191	186	350	203	4.26	23
208–9	192	*Migr. Abr.*		1QM	
Jub.		177	52	2.5	56
4.26	42	198–207	52	10.12–13	144
6	16(25)			10.12–16	144

c/New Testament

257

22:3	xxxiii(80), xlvi(119), 42, 53(14), 60(11), 187, 194, 209, 209(4)	23:32	179	26:10	186
		23:33	195	26:11	106
		23:34	xxxvi, 202	26:13	187(10)
		23:35	195	26:14	71, 117(10), 187
22:3–4	210	24	33	26:16	29(19)
22:4	71	24:1	199	26:18	xxviii, 106(35), 174, 211(19)
22:5	192	24:1–23	195		
22:6	68, 81, 88, 210	24:2	199, 203, 209		
		24:3	xxxvi, 209	26:20	xxxvi, 211
22:7	71	24:4	33, 209(1)	26:22	211
22:9	210(12)	24:5–6	180	26:22–23	30(29)
22:10	xxxvi	24:8	200	26:23	5, 28, 29, 32, 134, 210
22:11	72	24:10	198, 209		
22:12	72	24:13–21	180	26:24	206, 211(13)
22:14	29(19), 211	24:14	71	26:26	207, 209
22:14–15	188	24:14–15	210	26:28	89, 212
22:15	211	24:15	146	26:29	xxxvi, 209
22:16	20	24:16	192	26:31	227
22:17	xxxvi, 72, 81	24:17	167, 182	27	221
22:17–21	75, 211	24:20	199	27—28	xl
22:20	57	24:22	xxxvi, 71, 199, 206	27:2	167
22:21	22	24:24	200	27:5	178
22:22	207	24:27	195, 195(7)	27:7	127
22:24–29	183(5)	25	194	27:8	217
22:25	133(33)	25:1	xxxvi, 178	27:9	168, 217, 223(14)
22:29	190(10)	25:2	106, 206, 227		
22:30	183, 192, 194	25:4	xxxvi	27:9–11	217
22:32	183	25:7	207	27:10	xxxvi
23:2	xlviii(134)	25:8	135, 180, 199, 227	27:10–11	218
23:5	187	25:9	207	27:11	217
23:6	111(17), 207	25:9–25	227	27:12	216, 220, 221
23:6–8	32	25:10	xxxvi	27:13	215
23:6–10	42	25:13	xlviii(134), 127(4)	27:15	212
23:6–12	35	25:16	xxxvi	27:18	220
23:9	227	25:18	207	27:20	215, 219
23:11	164, 203	25:19	192(7), 199, 210, 212	27:21	4
23:12–30	202	25:25	212, 227	27:24	164
23:14	42(9)	25:26	135, 183, 206	27:27	218
23:16	187	26	73	27:29	215, 220
23:19	139	26:1	184	27:30	218(39)
23:20	xxxvi	26:2ff	xxxvi	27:33	215
23:22	6	26:3	xxxvi, 210	27:33–36	218
23:23	183	26:4	xxxvi, 186	27:37	xxxvi
23:24	xlviii(132), 106, 199(15), 202(1)	26:5	32, 116, 186	27:38	218
				27:41	219(56)
		26:6–7	227	27:44	52, 129(1)
23:26	120	26:8	211	28:6	82, 110(5)
23:27	211	26:9–18	72, 73(18)	28:8	188
23:29	207, 227			28:11	216, 216(18)

d/Early Christian Literature and the Ancient Church

264 frg. 6	54(34), 83(32), 141(26), 146(73)	3:2.9168	81(9)	27	198(10)
		Isocrates		*Jup. trag.*	
		7.40	186	7	145
323a frg. 1	139(7)	*Itinerarium Antoninianum*		18	142
324 frg. 3	139(7)	32	69	*Lucius*	
458 frg. 5	7(26)	320	134(2)	34	136
Frontinus		331	134(2)	*Merc. cond.*	
Aq.		*Itinerarium Hieros*		1	218
13	153	605	134(2)	*Navig.*	
Heliodorus		Julian		2	183
Aeth.		*Or.*		5	224
6.8	189	8.246b	211	9	216, 219, 224
Heraclitus		Juvenal			
frg. 5	145	*Sat.*		*Pergr. mort.*	
frg. 93	90	6.156–60	206	8	210
Herodotus		Livy		13	24
1.9	152	1.16.1–2	7(26)	22—42	6
2	53(16)	8.11	132	36	60
4.205	97(5)	8.32	132	38—41	6
7.12	127	10.9.4	133	*Philops.*	
Homer		23.3.7	12	2	26(15)
Il.		29.27.1–4	xxxvi	11	223
5.749	94	30.48.6	14(10)	16	163
8.393	94	36.4.9	14(10)	19–20	37
10.157–59	94	39.16.8	164(10)	20	36
20.321	100	40.29	164(10)	22	132(27)
Od.		45.27	138	26	77
9.148–49	221	45.29	130	34	53(16)
9.546	221	Lucian		*Sacr.*	
Horace		*Abdic.*		11	141
Odes		30	212	12	111(10)
1.8	130	*Alex.*		*Salt.*	
Sat.		3	53	83	189
1.5.3	224	13	16	*Scytha*	
Iamblichus		24	77	1	140
Myst.		59	97(5)	*Syr. dea*	
1.1	110	*Bis acc.*		32	14(7)
Vita Pyth.		16	19(2), 198	51	189
30.167	24(9)	16ff	198	*Tox.*	
30.168	24(9)	17	198	19	218
IG		26	198	33	133
5:1.669	149(95)	*Charion*		*Ver. hist.*	
5:1.972	149(95)	12.24	142	1.6	219
5:1.1302	149(95)	*Delucto*		Lucilius	
7.1676	152(12)	11	77	649	33
12.420	110(8)	*Demon.*		Marcellinus	
12.522	110(8)	9	53	*Vita Thuc.*	
14.601	223(11)	13ff	53(18)	1.2	210
14.1072	207(9)	*Dial. deor.*		35	186
IGR		20.7	152	Maximus of Tyre	
3.930	99	*Hermot.*		2	145
4.836.6–7	41(6)	28	218	9 7d–f	71
ILS		*Hist. conscr.*		OGIS	
1.2683	215(2)	16	xl(88)	233.49–50	xxxvi(66)
		24	xl(88)	234.14–15	xxxvi(66)

173d	176
181–82	176
247–48	224
341b	111(11)
378–79	143(43)
379cd	145
477cd	144
507a	218
516b	212
591b	145
777b	212
778c	176
807b	216
957d	145
979d	145
1034b	56(52), 141

Pomp.

36	14(10)

Pollux

5.140	84(38)
8.117	139

Polybius

26.2.13	20

Porphyry
Vita Pyth.

20	24(9)

Procopius
Arc.

10.1	186(5)

Ps.-Callisth.

1.1.1	53(16)
2.4.9	14(7)
2.11.2	14(7)
2.22.3	38
2.22.12	110
3.18ff	68(7)

Ps.-Heraclitus

4th Letter	141

Ps.-Scylax

81ff	14(7)

Ptolemy

3.4.1	219
3.15.1	219
3.17.1	219
3.17.3	217
3.17.11	218

Quintilian
Inst. orat.

10.1.16	145

C. Musonius Rufus

37.3	186

Sallust
Cat.

4.2	3(2)
51.5–6	42

SEG

3.389	153(18)
8.169	183(3)
11.903	149(95)
19.984.34–35	166(34)

Seneca
Ep.

5.7	93
41.1	144
77	224
77.1–2	215(8)
95.47	142

Herc. oet.

1703–4	60
1725–26	60

Nat. quaest.

7.30	56

SIG

1.495.2	45(9)
1.532.7	35(10)
2.547.30	35(10
2.613.25ff	174(20)
2.672.37	166(42)
2.801 D	152(13)
2.810	216(19)
2.850.8	146(79)
2.900.9–10	199(18)
3.1168.110–12	26(15)
3.1174–81	100(26)

Sophocles
Ajax

148–49	140

Ant.

450–60	33(18)

Oed. col.

260	140

Phil.

1418–22	112

Stad.

219	103
318	216
323ff	217
328	217(26), 218
355	216

Strabo

4.179	166
8.378	151
9.396	138
10.471	140
10.472	216
10.475	217(26)
12.564–65	127
12.568	107
12.569	103

12.570–71	103
12.571	127
12.577	103
14.639	171
14.641	157
14.673	75, 184
15.735	14(9)
16.235	145
16.737	14(9)
16.749	88
16.750	88
16.759	68, 77
16.760	88
17.280	68(7)
17.832–34	223
17.835	218

Suetonius
Aug.

31	164(10)

Claud.

18	90(6), 215(8), 216
18—19	217
25	88, 151
28	194

Nero

25	96

Titus

7	206

SVF

1.264–65	56(52)
1.264–67	141(28)
1.537	145(64)
1.548	143(51)
2.1149–50	143(50)

Tacitus
Agr.

	xli(96)

Ann.

2.60	14(8)
4.38	111(11)
12.43	90(6)
12.54	194, 195, 199
14.15	96
15.44	88
16.22	96

Hist.

1.6	206
1.31	224
4.27	132
5.4	145
5.9	194
5.13	94

Thucydides

1.65	218

2. Greek Words

ἄγνοια
28, 104–5, 111, 146–47

ἄγνωστος
xxxi, 140–41, 146

αἷμα
119

αἵρεσις
41, 116, 199, 237

ἀναβαίνω
25, 53, 81, 86

ἀναβλέπω
72(14)

ἀναλάμβανω
xxx, 4

ἀνίστημι
105

ἀποκατάστασις
29

ἀπόστολος
xxx–xxxii, 3, 22, 36, 108, 120

ἀρχισυνάγωγος
103

ἄφεσις ἁμαρτιῶν
106

ἀχλύς
100

βασιλεύς
xxix, 35, 84, 93, 135, 198, 238

γλῶσσα
14, 16, 35

γραφή
xxx, 11, 135

δεισιδαιμονία
140, 206

δεσπότης
34, 235, 238

δῆμος
135, 139, 166, 237

διακονία
11, 45

διαλέγομαι
139

δοῦλος
34

δύναμις
xxx–xxxi, 63, 144, 237

ἐγώ εἰμι
63, 71

ἔθνος
xxviii, xxxi, 14, 16, 30, 82, 84, 86, 116–17, 198, 210

εἰδωλόθυτος
118–19

εἰδωλοποιέω
54

ἐκκλησία
54, 75, 88

ἐπὶ τὸ αὐτό
xxxvi, 10, 24

εὐεργέτης
84

ζηλωτής
132, 186

θεῖος
63, 144–45

θεῖος ἀνήρ
6, 38, 53, 83, 94, 146, 219, 223

θύω
81

ἱερόν
25, 56(51), 140–41,183

Ἰουδαῖος
xxviii, 38, 82, 90, 106, 135, 236

καιρός
29, 142–43, 146, 238

Καῖσαρ
54(26), 83, 135, 199, 240

κατὰ τὸ αὐτό
108

κοιμάω
60

κοινός
xxix, 24, 81, 135–36, 198, 235

κοινωνία
23

κύριος
xxvii–xxix, xxxii, xlvi, 12, 16, 20, 21, 36, 39, 41, 63, 68–69, 83, 132, 141, 164, 199, 207, 238

λαός
81, 84, 117

λόγος
xxviii–xxxi, 3, 35, 45, 53, 62, 83, 88, 106, 110, 120, 140, 154, 174, 238

μάγος
100

μάρτυς
xxxi, 7, 187–88, 211

μετανοέω, μετάνοια
22, 29, 42, 86, 104, 146, 174, 211

νεωποιός
165

νόμος
xxx, 153, 186, 234, 237

ξένος
139–40

ὁδός
71, 111, 158(5), 186, 199

ὄνομα
xxviii, 10, 26, 32–33, 43, 90, 117, 154, 223, 240

ὁρμή
108, 232, 237

ὁροθεσία
143, 147

παῖς
28, 34–35, 63, 140, 169

πάσχω
xxviii, 5, 28, 68, 134, 211

περιτομή
52, 86

πίστις, πιστός
xxxi, 28, 46, 106,

112, 130, 146, 174, 236–37

πνεῦμα
xxvii, xxx–xxxii, 13, 16, 34, 62–63, 69, 116(6), 120, 163, 231–32, 234–35, 239

πνικτός
118–19

πορθέω
74

πορνεία
118–19

πρᾶξις
xxxii, 3, 62, 164

προσευχή
130

προτείνω
189

πρῶτος
3, 28, 30, 63, 105–6, 117, 130, 184, 211, 223, 227–28, 233, 236–37

πύθων
131

πυλών
82, 95, 110

σημαίνω
90, 238

στρατηγός
32, 131

στρέφω
55

συναγωγή
47, 152, 187

συναλίζομαι
6

τόπος
xxvii, 11–12, 48, 52, 95, 206, 215, 220

χειροποίητος
56

χειροτονέω
112

χρηματίζω
88

χριστιανός
88, 212

χριστός
xxviii–xxix, xxxi, xlvi, 21, 28, 62, 68, 74, 83, 88, 211(20), 238–39

χώρα
126, 202, 234–35, 237

ψυχή
xxviii–xxix, 16, 22, 24, 36, 174, 238

3. Subjects

276

4. Modern Authors

Adler, N.
  17(29), 65(1)
Aland, K.
  xxxiv(36), 22(4), 130(13)
Allegro, J. M.
  30(27)
Almqvist, H.
  95(21)
Aly, W.
  145(72)
Anrich, G.
  187(18)
Argyle, A. W.
  19(3)
Aschermann, H.
  173(9)
Avenarius, G.
  4(18)

Ballance, M.
  112(1)
Balmer, H.
  215(7), 217(26), 218(41,
  44), 221(67)
Baltzer, K.
  56(53)
Bammel, E.
  28(14)
Barr, J.
  6(17)
Barrett, C. K.
  60, 60(6), 119(25)
Barth, G.
  148(92)
Bauer, W.
  xxx(13), 7(22), 8(28),
  33(16), 88(8), 93(4),
  158(5), 173(11), 174(22),
  175(29), 212
Bauernfeind, O.
  11(4), 29(20), 39(3), 13(2),
  15(20), 29, 29(18), 64(13,
  14), 66(5), 80(1), 86(7),
  87, 87(4, 5), 136(8),
  158(10)
Baus, K.
  110(10)
Beardslee, W. A.
  12(23)
Begrich, J.
  152(11)
Behm, J.
  216(16)

Bell, H. I.
  61(18), 135(10), 151(5),
  199(16)
Benoit, P.
  xxxvii, xxxviii, xxxviii(77),
  xliii(106, 108), 6(11),
  7(28), 11(12), 91(12), 116,
  116(2), 121(43)
Bergmann, J.
  5(4)
Bertram, G.
  53(17)
Betz, H. D.
  xl(88), 6(9), 16(22),
  26(14), 28(3), 53(13, 16,
  18), 68(9), 77(6, 7), 97(5),
  141(29), 146(82), 164(11),
  198(10), 224(17)
Betz, O.
  17(29), 66(8)
Beyer, H. W.
  xxxvii, xxxvii(72)
Bickermann, E. J.
  88, 88(15), 183(3)
Bidez, J.
  164(10)
Bieler, L.
  39(1, 6), 53(13, 22), 63(9),
  100(22), 219(52), 223(9)
Bihler, J.
  48(7), 58(63), 59, 59(2),
  61(20, 21), 77(4)
Birt, T.
  141(19), 149(94)
Bishop, E. F.
  73(21)
Björck, G.
  xxxv(52), xxxvi(59), 7(24),
  41(8), 192(6)
Black, M.
  xxxv(47), 51, 51(2),
  131(19)
Blake, W. E.
  139(8), 166(32)
Blass, F.
  xxxiv(44), 210, 210(6)
Bleiken, J.
  203(9), 204(10)
Blinzler, J.
  32(9)
Blumenthal, M.
  xli(98), 61(21)
Böhlig, H.
  75(2)

Bolkestein, H.
  25(6), 45(5), 84(38),
  140(16)
Borgen, P.
  xlvi(118)
Bornhäuser, K.
  41(2)
Bornkamm, G.
  xli(95), 15, 16(21), 91(12),
  147(98), 148(92), 160(9)
von Borries, B.
  145(71)
Bousset, W.
  95(18), 117, 117(9)
Bovon, F.
  80(6)
Bowman, T.
  118, 118(21)
Braun, H.
  5(5), 11(6, 7), 12(19),
  20(15), 24(7), 45(5),
  164(10)
Braun, M.
  xli(95)
Breusing, A.
  215(7), 217, 217(28, 36),
  218(39, 40, 46), 219(53,
  55, 59), 220(65, 66)
van den Brink, J. N. B.
  105(21)
Brinkman, J. A.
  15(16)
Broughton, T. R. S.
  126(3), 127(6)
Brown, R.
  30(27)
Brox, N.
  12(17), 187(17), 188,
  188(26)
Bruce, F. F.
  xliii(109)
Brun, L.
  37(1)
Brüne, B.
  xxxv(54)
de Bruyne, D.
  xxvii(1), xxxii
Bultmann, R.
  xxxvii, xxxvii(67, 75), 61,
  61(19), 76(2, 3), 86(8), 87,
  87(3), 90, 90(2), 97, 97(6),
  99, 99(4), 103, 103(1),
  111(16), 117, 117(8), 121,
  121(38, 39), 141(22)

Burchard, C.
  7(20), 60(11), 73, 73(19,
  21), 159(7), 187(21)
Burton, E. D.
  135(9)

Cadbury, H. J.
  xxxv(52), xxxvi(55),
  xxix(84), 36(5), 68(6, 9),
  76(2), 100(25), 110(7),
  127(8), 133(32), 139(7),
  164(13), 165(14, 20), 169,
  169(7), 184(13), 203(8),
  210(7), 220(64)
Cagnat, R.
  41(6), 60
Caird, G. B.
  121(43), 156(6)
Calder, W. M.
  110(6)
Cambier, J.
  75(1)
Cameron, A.
  219(48)
von Campenhausen, H.
  xxxii(26), 84(39), 91(12),
  112(2, 3), 175(23), 180(3)
Casson L.
  178(2), 215(6), 216,
  216(9, 10), 221(71),
  224(20)
Cecchelli, C.
  89(17), 199(14)
Cerfaux, L.
  xxxv(46), xxxvii(74),
  xliii(106, 107), 19(4),
  44(1), 63(8), 96(4), 111,
  111(14), 117(13), 121(43)
Charlesworth, J. H.
  211(16)
Clarke, W. K.
  68(3)
Collart, P.
  129(2), 130(4)
Colson, F. H.
  220(63)
Comblin, J.
  54(27)
Conrad, J. R.
  110(10)
Conzelmann, H.
  xxxiii(34), xxxviii(80),
  xlvi(121), xlvii(125, 127),
  4(20), 5(3), 6(16), 7(25),
  11(3), 20(11, 12), 21(23),

Graefenhain, R.
  3(4)
Graindor, P.
  138(3), 139(9)
Grant, R.
  146(81)
Grass, H.
  84(40)
Grässer, E.
  84(42)
Greeven, H.
  99(6), 180(7)
Gressmann, H.
  152(11)
Groag, E.
  152(13), 153(17, 18)
Grundmann, W.
  17(29)
Günther, E.
  12(17)
Guterman, S. L.
  xlvii(127), 184(12)

Haas, H.
  60(8)
Haefeli, L.
  81(8)
Haenchen, E.
  xxxii(23, 26), xxxiii(35),
  xxxiv(39, 40), xxxv(46,
  48, 50), xxxvi(62, 64),
  xxxvii(67, 68), xxxviii(80),
  xxxix, xxxix(83), xl,
  xl(90), xli(99), xlv(115),
  xlviii, xlviii(130, 137, 138,
  139), 3(14), 5(1), 7, 7(27),
  11(12), 14(12), 19, 19(4),
  20(8), 23(1), 26, 26(13),
  34(3), 38(5), 39(4, 5), 43,
  43(19, 20), 48(7), 55(40),
  60(11), 61(16), 62(2), 63,
  63(10), 64, 64(14, 15),
  68(2), 77(5), 80(1, 2, 5),
  82(26), 85, 85(1), 86(7),
  90(5), 91, 91(8), 93(3), 94,
  94(16), 95(19), 99(13),
  100(17), 104(11), 105(22,
  24), 108(1, 7), 116,
  116(4), 117(13), 119(27),
  120, 120(30), 121,
  121(37, 40), 123(5),
  124(7), 126(1), 127,
  127(5, 11), 132, 132(25),
  135(7), 142(33, 36),
  147(86), 151, 151(4), 152,

152(7), 153(17, 21), 156,
156(5), 158(11), 159,
159(1, 2), 164, 165(15),
167(3), 173(4, 10), 174,
174(13), 176(31), 178(1),
180, 180(8), 182, 183,
183(1, 2, 6), 187, 187(12),
188(25), 192, 192(3, 5),
195(10, 16), 201(1, 3),
206(5), 210(10), 211(13,
17, 18), 212(23, 24),
216(15), 217(24), 218(47),
219(50), 221, 221(70, 71),
224(22), 227(6), 228(15)
Hammond, M.
  184(12)
Hanson, S.
  142(38)
Harnack, A.
  xxvii(1), xxx(16), xxxii,
  xxxvii, xxxvii(67, 71, 76)
  xxxix(81), 35(15), 87,
  87(1), 118(19), 151(5),
  223, 223(13), 228(11)
Harrer, G. A.
  100(25)
Harris, J. R.
  47(4)
Hartman, L.
  104(14)
Hauck, F.
  24(10), 81(17)
Head, B. V.
  166(39)
Heard, R. G.
  xxvii(1), xxxii(24)
Held, H. J.
  148(92)
Helm, R.
  195(9)
Hengel, M.
  9(5), 12(21), 42(16),
  184(9)
Henschel, E.
  152(7)
Hermesdorf, B. H. D.
  221(71)
Hill, I. T.
  138(3)
Hirsh, E.
  72(15)
Hoffmann, O.
  65(2)
Hogarth, D. G.
  166(39)

Holl, K.
  110(5)
Holland, R.
  7(26)
Holmes, B. T.
  99(12)
Hölscher, G.
  88(6)
Holtz, T.
  xlvi(121), 19, 19(4), 52,
  52(6), 58(63), 104(14)
Holzmeister, U.
  5(6)
Hommel, H.
  xlii(104), xliv(110), 138,
  138(2), 140(11, 12, 15),
  141(23), 142(33, 34, 36),
  144, 144(55, 56, 58),
  145(59, 60, 61, 62), 146,
  146(74), 147(90), 149(94)
Howald, E.
  xl(91)
Huck, A.
  xxxii(24)
Huppenbauer, H.
  36(4)

Jacoby, F.
  xl(91), 3(2)
Jaeger, W.
  71(4)
Jaubert, A.
  16(27)
Jentsch, W.
  186(5)
Jeremias, J.
  xxxvii, xxxvii(75),
  xliii(106), 21(18), 23(3, 4),
  28(13), 30(25), 32(2, 3, 7),
  33(11, 12), 41, 41(2),
  45(5), 46(11), 52, 52(9),
  53(22), 55(38), 69(12),
  81(13), 87, 87(2), 90(6),
  94(11), 130(13), 131(20),
  176(31), 186(7), 187(9),
  211(14)
Jervell, J.
  xlvi(118), xlviii(129)
Johnson, S. E.
  24(10)
Jones, A. H. M.
  81(8), 103(7)
Jost, W.
  175(24)

Judeich, W.
  138(3)
Jürgen, R.
  12(16)
Juster, J.
  132(22), 133(32), 190(10)

Kahle, P.
  54(29)
Karst, J.
  195(8)
Kasch, W.
  24(10)
Käsemann, E.
  157(1), 158, 158(6, 7, 9),
  159(3, 8)
Keil, B.
  54(26), 139(9), 165(28)
Keil, J.
  63(7), 110(6), 157(3)
Kenyon, F. G.
  xxxiii(35)
Kerényi, K.
  72(10)
Kilpatrick, G. D.
  xxxiii(35), 19(4), 57(55),
  59(3), 165(23)
Kippenberg, H. G.
  54(30), 63(5)
Kirsten, E.
  130(5), 138(3), 151(2),
  153(19)
Klein, G.
  xxxiii(29), xlv(115),
  xlvi(124), xlviii(130),
  4(17), 9(7), 12(17), 61(17),
  65(3), 73(20, 21), 99(2),
  108(3), 111, 111(14),
  122(43), 159(4), 163,
  163(5), 173(6), 175,
  175(29), 183(2), 187(16),
  188(23)
Kleinknecht, H. M.
  15(18)
Klijn, A. F. J.
  xxxiii(35), xxxiv(40),
  19(4), 58(63), 119(27)
Klostermann, E.
  xxxii(23), 42(17)
Knoll, F.
  110(6)
Knopf, R.
  93(9)
Knox, J.
  xxxiii(29)

Steidle, W.
xli(96)
Stelzenberger, J.
192(2)
van Stempvoort, P. A.
4(17), 8(28)
Stendahl, K.
227(8)
Steve, M. -A.
26(7, 10, 11)
Stonehouse, N.B.
149(94)
Storch, R.
51(1), 52(6), 58(63)
Strathmann, H.
12(19)
Strecker, G.
7(26), 24(12), 52(7),
55(42), 57(60), 90(1),
91(11)
Strobel, A.
xxvii(1), 42(10), 93(6),
131(13)
Strothotte, G.
118, 118(20), 119(24),
122(43), 206(8)
Surkau, H. W.
48(9), 57(58), 59, 59(1),
61(21)
Süss, W.
3(11)
Swoboda, H.
110(6)

Tabachovitz, D.
xxxv(49, 52), xxxvi(62),
3(10), 5(1), 154(25)
Taeger, F.
96(4), 97(5), 111(11)
Talbert, C. H.
xlviii(130)
Teeple, H. M.
30(25)
Theiler, W.
142(30), 144(55)
Thiele,W.
xxxiv(35)
Thiersch, H.
165(18)
Thomsen, P.
69(14), 81(8)
Thyen, H.
58(63)
Tödt, H. E.
60(5, 8)

du Toit, A. B.
24(12)
Tondriau, J.
96(4)
Torrey, C. C.
xxxvi(63), 6(12)
Townsend, J. T.
xliv(109)
Trocmé, E.
xxxvii(67, 68, 74),
xxxix(85), 10(1), 11(4),
17(29), 41(3), 108(3),
116(3), 120, 120(28),
121(43), 125, 125(5),
228(17)
Turner, N.
xxxv(52), 88(9)

van Unnik, W. C.
xlviii(128), 7, 7(21),
53(14), 68(5), 81(13),
131(21), 186(5)

Vielhauer, P.
149(94)
Vincent, L. -H.
26(7, 10, 11), 63(10)
Vögeli, A.
43(23), 94(10), 211(13)
Vogels, H. J.
xxxiv(38)
Vogt, J.
198(7)
Voigt, C.
217(36)
Voss, G.
21(20)

Waitz, H.
118(22)
Walton, F. R.
54(34)
Weigandt, P.
xxxiv(37, 39), 130(13)
Weinreich, O.
94(11, 13, 14), 132(26)
Weinstock, S.
15, 15(15)
Weise, M.
37(4)
Weiss, B.
xxxvii(70)
Weiss, J.
151(2)

Wellhausen, J.
xxxviii, xxxviii(78), 32,
221, 221(68)
Wendland, P.
xxxviii, xxxviii(78),
216(15), 221, 221(68)
Wendt, H. H.
xxxvii, xxxvii(75), 86(6),
100(17), 105(23), 158(8,
10)
Wenger, L.
189(8), 203(7)
Wenschkewitz, H.
56(50)
Werner, A.
xxxv(49), xxxvi(62)
de Wette, W. M. L.
192(4)
Wetter, G. P.
73(21)
Wettstein, J. J.
77(6)
Widengren, G.
63, 63(11)
Wifstrand, A.
xxxv(52), xxxvi(56), 206,
206(2)
Wikenhauser, A.
xxvii(1), xl(91), 3(2, 4),
5(3), 72(9, 17), 97(5),
127(7), 141(20), 223(12)
Wilcken, U.
228(14)
Wilckens, U.
xliv(109), 5(2), 12(18),
19(2), 21(21, 25), 28(9),
74(1, 3), 82(28), 83(34),
84(41), 104(13, 18),
105(24), 106(30), 187(16)
Wilcox, M.
xxxvi(64), 52(4)
Williams, C. S. C.
xxxiv(35, 42)
Wilson, R. McL.
30(25), 63(12)
Wilson, S. G.
8(28)
Windisch, H.
45(7), 72(17), 173(9),
211(14)
Wink, W.
159(4)
Winter, P.
32(9), 42(15), 60(12),
117(11)

Wood, H. G.
73(21)
Wünsch, R.
83(31), 100(26)

Yaure, L.
100(19)

Zahn, T.
xxx(16), xxxii(22),
xxxiv(44), 3(7), 105(23),
153(21), 228(9)
Zimmermann, H.
xliii(106), 23(5)
Zinn, E.
219(58)

In the design of the visual aspects of *Hermeneia*, consideration has been given to relating the form to the content by symbolic means.

The letters of the logotype *Hermeneia* are a fusion of forms alluding simultaneously to Hebrew (dotted vowel markings) and Greek (geometric round shapes) letter forms. In their modern treatment they remind us of the electronic age as well, the vantage point from which this investigation of the past begins.

The Lion of Judah used as visual identification for the series is based on the Seal of Shema. The version for *Hermeneia* is again a fusion of Hebrew calligraphic forms, especially the legs of the lion, and Greek elements characterized by the geometric. In the sequence of arcs, which can be understood as scroll-like images, the first is the lion's mouth. It is reasserted and accelerated in the whorl and returns in the aggressively arched tail: tradition is passed from one age to the next, rediscovered and re-formed.

"Who is worthy to open the scroll and break its
    seals . . ."
Then one of the elders said to me
    "weep not; lo, the Lion of the tribe of David,
    the Root of David, has conquered,
    so that he can open the scroll and
    its seven seals."
Rev. 5:2, 5

To celebrate the signal achievement in biblical scholarship which *Hermeneia* represents, the entire series will by its color constitute a signal on the theologian's bookshelf: the Old Testament will be bound in yellow and the New Testament in red, traceable to a commonly used color coding for synagogue and church in medieval painting; in pure color terms, varying degrees of intensity of the warm segment of the color spectrum. The colors interpenetrate when the binding color for the Old Testament is used to imprint volumes from the New and vice versa.

Wherever possible, a photograph of the oldest extant manuscript, or a historically significant document pertaining to the biblical sources, will be displayed on the end papers of each volume to give a feel for the tangible reality and beauty of the source material.

The title-page motifs are expressive derivations from the *Hermeneia* logotype, repeated seven times to form a matrix and debossed on the cover of each volume. These sifted-out elements will be seen to be in their exact positions within the parent matrix. These motifs and their expressional character are noted on the following page.

Horizontal markings at gradated levels on the spine will assist in grouping the volumes according to these conventional categories.

The type has been set with unjustified right margins so as to preserve the internal consistency of word spacing. This is a major factor in both legibility and aesthetic quality; the resultant uneven line endings are only slight impairments to legibility by comparison. In this respect the type resembles the handwritten manuscripts where the quality of the calligraphic writing is dependent on establishing and holding to integral spacing patterns.

All of the type faces in common use today have been designed between A.D. 1500 and the present. For the biblical text a face was chosen which does not arbitrarily date the text, but rather one which is uncompromisingly modern and unembellished so that its feel is of the universal. The type style is Univers 65 by Adrian Frutiger.

The expository texts and footnotes are set in Baskerville, chosen for its compatibility with the many brief Greek and Hebrew insertions. The double-column format and the shorter line length facilitate speed reading and the wide margins to the left of footnotes provide for the scholar's own notations.

Kenneth Hiebert

Category of biblical writing, key symbolic characteristic, and volumes so identified.

1
Law
(boundaries described)
  Genesis
  Exodus
  Leviticus
  Numbers
  Deuteronomy

2
History
(trek through time and space)
  Joshua
  Judges
  Ruth
  1 Samuel
  2 Samuel
  1 Kings
  2 Kings
  1 Chronicles
  2 Chronicles
  Ezra
  Nehemiah
  Esther

3
Poetry
(lyric emotional expression)
  Job
  Psalms
  Proverbs
  Ecclesiastes
  Song of Songs

4
Prophets
(inspired seers)
  Isaiah
  Jeremiah
  Lamentations
  Ezekiel
  Daniel
  Hosea
  Joel
  Amos
  Obadiah
  Jonah
  Micah
  Nahum
  Habakkuk
  Zephaniah
  Haggai
  Zechariah
  Malachi

5
New Testament Narrative
(focus on One)
  Matthew
  Mark
  Luke
  John
  Acts

6
Epistles
(directed instruction)
  Romans
  1 Corinthians
  2 Corinthians
  Galatians
  Ephesians
  Philippians
  Colossians
  1 Thessalonians
  2 Thessalonians
  1 Timothy
  2 Timothy
  Titus
  Philemon
  Hebrews
  James
  1 Peter
  2 Peter
  1 John
  2 John
  3 John
  Jude

7
Apocalypse
(vision of the future)
  Revelation

8
Extracanonical Writings
(peripheral records)

287